GENERAL LEE

A Biography of Robert E. Lee

BY
FITZHUGH LEE
HIS NEPHEW AND CAVALRY COMMANDER

INTRODUCTION BY
GARY GALLAGHER

MAPS BY
BLAKE MAGNER

Da Capo Press • New York

Library of Congress Cataloging in Publication Data

Lee, Fitzhugh, 1835–1905.
General Lee: a biography of Robert E. Lee / by Fitzhugh Lee; introduction by Gary Gallagher; maps by Blake Magner.—1st Da Capo Press ed.
   p.   cm.
Includes index.
ISBN 0-306-80589-8
1. Lee, Robert E. (Robert Edward), 1807-1870. 2. Generals—United States—Biography. 3. United States. Army—Biography. 4. Confederate States of America. Army—Biography. I. Title.
E467.1.L4L4   1994
973.7′3′092—dc20   94-11564
[B]   CIP

First Da Capo Press edition 1994

This Da Capo Press paperback edition of *General Lee* is an unabridged republication of the edition published in Wilmington, North Carolina in 1989. It is reprinted by arrangement with Broadfoot Publishing Company.

Original copyright © 1894 by D. Appleton and Company
New material copyright © 1989 by Broadfoot Publishing Company

Published by Da Capo Press, Inc.
A Subsidiary of Plenum Publishing Corporation
233 Spring Street, New York, N.Y. 10013

Manufactured in the United States of America

I DEDICATE THIS BOOK

TO THE MEMORY OF THE SOLDIERS

WHO FOUGHT AND FELL

UNDER THE WAVE OF ROBERT E. LEE'S SWORD, AND ARE

"SLEEPING IN UNBROKEN RANKS, WITH THE DEW ON THEIR BROWS

AND THE RUST ON THEIR MAIL."

INTRODUCTION TO THE 1989 EDITION

Fitzhugh Lee crowded a multitude of experiences and accomplishments into sixty-nine years of life. Soldier, politician, and author, he made his most enduring mark as a general in the Confederate army. The blood of several of the first families of Virginia flowed through Lee's veins. His father was Sydney Smith Lee, son of Revolutionary hero "Light-Horse Harry" Lee and Anne Hill Carter and elder brother of Robert E. Lee. Of equally distinguished lineage was his mother, Anna Maria Mason Lee, granddaughter of George Mason of Gunston Hall and sister of Senator James M. Mason. Fitzhugh Lee was born on November 19, 1835, at "Clermont," the home of Anna Lee's father in Alexandria, Virginia.[1] Educated at private schools in Alexandria and Catonsville, Maryland, young Lee developed a love for poetry and drama that would last throughout his life and influence his own prose and oratory.[2] A predilection for having fun also manifested itself early on, and Fitz, as everyone called him, enjoyed both practical jokes and satirical literature.[3]

As a schoolboy in Maryland, Lee looked to the military life as an exciting prospect. Abundant examples from both sides of his family may have influenced him. His father and Uncle Robert were military men. Grandfather John Mason had been a general. Perhaps most influential was the image of his Grandfather Lee, who had won great acclaim under George Washington and Nathanael Greene as a dashing cavalryman during the Revolution. Whatever the reasons behind Lee's interest in the military, his family connections helped bring appointment to the U.S. Military Academy in 1852. Lee arrived at West Point five months shy of his seventeenth birthday in June 1852, and spent the next four years compiling an indifferent record. He cared little for mathematics, engineering, or military science, performing best in French and English and restricting his borrowing from the library to works of fiction. Special favorites included Sir Walter Scott's Waverly novels, Washington Irving's *Knickerbocker Tales*, and the books of James Fenimore Cooper. Among military subjects he performed best in cavalry tactics, finishing thirteenth of fifty in that subject during his first-class (or senior) year.[4]

Lee consistently demonstrated his fun-loving nature while at West Point. Demerits piled up year after year for illegal visits to Benny Havens's tavern, "dancing across the parade ground," "dancing in front of guard tent," "allowing boisterous noise in his tent at one A.M.," and similar offenses.[5] Such behavior contrasted sharply with his Uncle Robert's sparkling record while at West Point—all the more so because Colonel R. E. Lee was superintendent of the Academy during Fitzhugh's tenure as a cadet. A most painful episode for uncle and nephew came in mid-December 1853, when the superintendent received word that Fitzhugh and several other cadets had been away from quarters for several hours. All had admitted their serious violation of the rules, and Colonel Lee promptly called for dismissal or trial before a court martial. Fitz and two classmates escaped with severe punishments; others, their crimes compounded by the possession of liquor, were permitted to resign. Apparently unimpressed with the gravity of his actions, Fitzhugh repeated his escapade in July 1854, when he left camp with another cadet from midnight until 2:30 A.M. R. E. Lee again called for a court martial. Rallying to their popular comrade's side, all the cadets in Lee's class pledged not to duplicate Fitzhugh's behavior during the coming academic year if charges were dropped. There was ample precedent for this type of bargain (the superintendent's son Custis had benefitted from a similar pledge by his classmates in 1851), and Colonel Lee somewhat reluctantly accepted the offer.[6]

Lee captured the essence of his career at West Point in a letter of April 1855. "I entered this Academy a wild, careless and inexperienced youth," he admitted. "I shall leave it a wiser and I hope a better man. Since I have been here I have not studied near as much as I ought to and have got a great many unnecessary demerits, but I begin to see the 'folly of my ways' and shall try and amend."[7]

Surviving his occasionally precarious stay at West Point to graduate, forty-fifth of forty-nine in the class of 1856, Lee received assignment to the Second Cavalry as a brevet second lieutenant. The Second was one of two cavalry regiments formed by Secretary of War Jefferson Davis in 1855; no fewer than nine men who would command armies or corps during the Civil War served among its officers, including Colonel Albert Sidney Johnston, Lieutenant Colonel R. E. Lee, Majors George H. Thomas and William J. Hardee, Captains Earl Van Dorn, E. Kirby Smith, and George Stoneman, and Lieutenants John Bell Hood and Fitz Lee.[8] More than a year's duty as an instructor of cavalry recruits at Carlisle Barracks, Pennsylvania, intervened before Lee, having just been promoted to second lieutenant, joined his regiment on the Texas frontier in January 1858.[9]

The peculiar combination of boredom and danger characteristic of antebellum military service in the West awaited Lee in Texas. First came a year of tedious duty—long, dry, fruitless rides in pursuit of Comanches who "divide up into small parties, & come down into the state, stealing horses and killing sometimes those of the citizens, who have been bold enough to go beyond civilization." In early fall 1858, Lee wrote that he had covered more than 1,200 miles since arriving in Texas. He thanked God that he "had a splendid horse, & a strong constitution, & am none the worse for the trip, except my face a little more tanned perhaps, and my beard more of a mahogany color."[10]

Lee experienced his initial combat against the Comanches in May 1859, when Captain Van Dorn led 500 members of the Second Cavalry north from Camp Radziminski (located on a tributary of the Red River in present-day Oklahoma) toward the Arkansas River. On May 13, a vicious fight broke out between part of Van Dorn's column and about one hundred Indians in a rugged ravine. Thick brush and fallen trees compelled the cavalrymen to wage dozens of isolated fights against warriors masked by the covering growth. As Lee directed a portion of this difficult exercise, a Comanche sprang from behind a log and sent an arrow through his breast. A jarring 200-mile journey back to Camp Radziminski aggravated the wound, but Lee's stout physique carried him through the crisis. "I thought certainly I was going to die," Lee later wrote his family, "I could scarcely breathe, the blood rising in my throat & mouth." "Fortunately for me," he continued, "it was a wet rainy day & the strings of their bows were wet which prevented them in a measure from shooting with force."[11] Three months later Lee reported that he had "entirely recovered, minus a little, very little strength." He mused that Indian warfare offered scant opportunity for glory and subjected the soldiers to wearying rides through hot and dry country, but "I must say I like the life. . . . Apart from the excitement of catching Comanches, there is always fine hunting & fishing. . . ."[12]

The winter of 1859-60 brought another confrontation with the elusive Comanches. Stationed at Camp Colorado in central Texas, Lee took a small patrol into frigid pre-dawn blackness on January 15, 1860. A party of Indians had been sighted driving stolen horses some fifteen miles distant, and Captain E. Kirby Smith ordered Lee to pursue the raiders. Lee's patrol caught up with the Comanches after a day and a half of hard riding and immediately attacked. One warrior fell quickly, another raced his mount toward a woods with Lee and four troopers close behind. A seven-mile game of cat and mouse ensued, at the end of which Lee stalked the Comanche through a thicket of cedar. The drama ended when Lee spotted the man crouching behind a ledge of rocks and "after a short struggle *killed* him."[13] Because few cavalry patrols ever caught marauding Comanches, Lieutenant Lee's modest success stood out. Captain Smith noted that his subordinate showed off the Indian's "shield, head dress and arms with great pride" at Camp Colorado.[14]

Lee left Texas in the summer of 1860 a seasoned professional whom his Uncle Robert could call "a fine young soldier."[15] He passed a pleasant leave before taking up new duty late in 1860 as an instructor of cavalry tactics at West Point. While at the Academy, he kept a close eye on national events. The election of Abraham Lincoln prompted seven states to secede from the Union by February 1861, and Lee anticipated a difficult personal decision. Although promoted to first lieutenant in March 1861, he informed his father that he was "tired of serving a Black Republican administration" and wanted to resign from the army.[16] Virginia's vote for secession on April 17, 1861, settled the question. Lee departed West Point on May 3 and submitted his resignation from the U.S. Army on May 16 (accepted May 21). In the manner of his father, Uncle Robert, and cousin George Washington Custis, Lee did not abandon the old flag lightly. An emotional farewell at West Point produced tears as fellow officers serenaded him and cadets gave expressions of regret. But there was no possibility that he would remain in an army that might be employed to force Virginia back into the Union. Immediately after resigning he offered his expertise to the Confederate government, which made him a lieutenant in its new army.[17]

Lee's Confederate career embraced many of the great campaigns of the Eastern Theater. It began on the hot and confusing field of First Manassas, where he functioned as an acting assistant adjutant general on the staff of Brigadier General Richard S. Ewell. Made lieutenant colonel of the First Virginia Cavalry in August 1861, he received promotion to colonel of that regiment in March 1862.[18] Lee and the First Virginia participated in Jeb Stuart's celebrated "Ride Around McClellan" on June 12-15, 1862. Stuart and Lee would become fast friends in the course of the war, and Stuart spoke highly of his subordinate's part in the expedition. "In my estimation," wrote Stuart on June 17, "no one in the Confederacy possesses more of the elements of what a brigadier of cavalry ought to be than he."[19] Engaged throughout the Seven Days battles, Lee was present on July 3 with Stuart at Evelington Heights, where the cavalry chief ordered Captain John Pelham to fire on the retreating Army of the Potomac. Both Stuart and Lee later defended this precipitate action, which others argued only alerted McClellan to potential danger.[20] The merits of that episode aside, Fitzhugh Lee emerged from the fighting around Richmond with enhanced reputation and, as of July 24, 1862, the wreath and stars of a brigadier general.[21]

The summer and fall campaigning in 1862 resulted in a mixed record for Lee. Briefly considered as a replacement for the fallen Turner Ashby in the Shenandoah Valley, Lee turned in a questionable performance in his first major action as a brigadier. On August 17, Stuart ordered him to march his brigade from a position on the North Anna River to Raccoon Ford on the Rapidan River. Stuart planned to meet Lee on the evening of the 17th at Verdiersville, a village en route to the ford. But Lee, who later explained that he understood his orders to require no haste, chose an alternate route that consumed additional time. Federal cavalry reached Verdiersville ahead of Lee, capturing Stuart's hat and cloak and compelling the embarrassed southern general to flee for his life. Beyond Stuart's discomfiture, Lee's delay frustrated an opportunity to catch the rear elements of John Pope's Federal Army of Virginia in a vulnerable position between the Rapidan and Rappahannock Rivers. Stuart's official report voiced rare criticism of his friend's "failure to comply with instructions."[22]

Lee redeemed himself during the campaigns of Second Manassas and Sharpsburg. In a raid against Pope's headquarters at Catlett's Station on the stormy night of August 22, Lee's troopers seized some of Pope's uniforms and military papers. The next day Lee hailed General Charles W. Field and his staff of A. P. Hill's Light Division. Disappearing behind a large tree as the officers dismounted, Lee reappeared "dressed in the long blue cloak of a Federal general that reached nearly down to his feet, and wearing a Federal general's hat with its big plume." "This masquerade," recalled one of Field's aides, "was accompanied by a burst of jolly laughter that might have been heard for a hundred yards."[23] At Second Manassas Lee functioned efficiently, eliciting from his uncle commendation for "important and valuable service." His troopers fought effectively during the raid into Maryland, especially at South Mountain when Confederate infantry withdrew from the gaps toward Sharpsburg on September 15. "The advance of the enemy was delayed by the brave opposition he encountered from Fitzhugh Lee's cavalry," noted R. E. Lee in alluding to the precious time thus gained for the Army of Northern Virginia to concentrate. Lee's brigade later covered the army's retreat "with boldness and success." Such praise from his uncle, to which Stuart added his own encomium, doubtless took away the sting of criticism from Lee's fiasco at Verdiersville.[24]

Cavalry raids punctuated the fall and winter of 1862-63. Lee missed Stuart's October ride around McClellan but took part in the decidedly less successful operations that winter.[25] The last and largest of the cavalry actions took place under Lee's direction at Kelly's Ford in March 1863. Lee set the stage for this confrontation with a swift strike across the Rappahannock River on February 25 that netted 150 prisoners and much material at a cost of just fourteen casualties. A week after this foray,

R. E. Lee observed to Secretary of War James A. Seddon that "General Fitz. Lee is an excellent cavalry officer. . . . I feel at liberty to call upon him . . . on all occasions."[26] The Federals bested on February 25 belonged to the command of Brigadier General William W. Averell, a friend of Lee's from West Point and the Old Army. Lee's penchant for mischief showed in a note he left for Averell on the Federal side of the Rappahannock: "If you won't go home, return my visit and bring me a sack of coffee." On March 17, Averell accepted the challenge. Nearly three thousand Federals crossed at Kelly's Ford early that morning and soon engaged some eight hundred of Lee's troopers. A classic cavalry battle ensued in which the Federals, for the first time in the Eastern Theater, more than held their own. Southern casualties totaled 133 (among the dead was Stuart's able artillerist John Pelham); Averell lost just seventy-eight. The Federals withdrew in good order, leaving behind a sack of coffee and Averell's taunting rejoinder: "Dear Fitz: Here's your coffee. Here's your visit. How do you like it?"[27]

The campaign of Chancellorsville provided a showcase for Lee's skills at reconnaissance. It was he who determined on May 1 that Joseph Hooker's right flank was vulnerable and thus enabled Lee and Stonewall Jackson to plan the war's most famous turning movement. When the flanking march was underway on May 2, Lee once again stepped forward with vital intelligence. Jackson's original design called for the Confederates to sweep eastward along the Plank Road; however, Lee discovered that the assault would encounter less resistance from O. O. Howard's Federal XI Corps if delivered along the Old Turnpike. After the war, he recalled the critical conversation with Jackson: "General, if you will ride with me . . . I will show you the enemy's right, and you will perceive the great advantage of attacking down the Old turnpike instead of the Plank road. . . ." Conducting Jackson to a knoll along the Plank Road, Lee "watched him closely as he gazed upon Howard's troops." "His eyes burned with a brilliant glow," said Lee, "lighting up a sad face." Yes, decided Jackson after studying the ground, the column should continue to the Old Turnpike. Without a word of praise for Lee, Stonewall rode back down the hill to rejoin his soldiers, "his arms flapping to the motion of his horse, over whose head it seemed, good rider as he was, he would certainly go." "I expected to be told I had made a valuable personal reconnaissance—saving the lives of many soldiers, and that Jackson was indebted to me to that amount at least," Lee remembered. "Perhaps I might have been a little chagrined at Jackson's silence, and hence commented inwardly and adversely upon his horsemanship. Alas! I had looked upon him for the last time."[28] Superb handling of skirmishing near Ely's Ford on May 3 supplied a fitting coda to Lee's performance at Chancellorsville.[29]

Stuart's cavalry expanded to nearly 10,000 sabers in the wake of Chancellorsville. Such a magnificent force deserved to be shown off, thought its commander, and Stuart arranged a review for General Lee near Brandy Station on June 8. Fitz Lee invited John Hood to "come and see the review, and bring any of his people." Lee no doubt meant for his fellow lieutenant in the old Second Cavalry to attend with a party of staff and headquarters personnel. But Hood warmed to the occasion and appeared with his entire division, joking as he shook hands with Lee, "You invited me *and my people*, and you see I have brought them!" "Well, don't let them halloo, 'Here's your mule!' at the review," warned a smiling Lee. "If they do," added Wade Hampton, "we will charge you!"[30]

Lighthearted banter and the pomp of review gave way to strenuous riding and fighting for the remainder of June and into July 1863. Illness forced Lee to miss the great cavalry battle of Brandy Station on June 9, wherein Jeb Stuart just managed to repulse a heavy column of Federal cavalry under Alfred Pleasonton. Although a "sturdy, muscular and lively little giant," as his friend William Averell aptly characterized him,[31] Lee suffered periodic attacks of rheumatism. A tendency toward obesity probably aggravated this condition. One careful student postulates that a bout with this affliction kept Lee out of the battle on June 9.[32] Recovered a few days later, Lee accompanied Stuart on his ill-fated ride around the Army of the Potomac during the Gettysburg campaign. Near the end of that exhausting and fruitless circuit, Lee found himself at Carlisle, Pennsylvania, on July 1. On Stuart's orders, he demanded surrender of the town, then watched as a southern battery conducted a desultory shelling to root out northern defenders. Shortly thereafter the Confederates burned the U.S. Cavalry Barracks. Conflicting emotions must have tugged at Lee's weary mind as he watched smoke rise from the post where he had taught young troopers five years before. Two days later Lee and his brigade participated in the inconclusive cavalry fighting east of Gettysburg. Several days of skirmishing to cover the retreat of the Army of Northern Virginia ended an unhappy experience in Pennsylvania.[33]

Reorganization of the Confederate cavalry after Gettysburg resulted in advancement for Lee. Jeb Stuart asked that his seven brigades be divided between two new divisions commanded by Lee and Wade Hampton, both of whom would become major generals. Stuart believed that in the recent operations Lee's "intelligent appreciation and faithful performance of the duties confided to him, point to one of the first cavalry leaders on the continent, and richly entitle him to promotion." R. E. Lee passed along Stuart's recommendations to Jefferson Davis on August 1, 1863, remarking of Lee, "I do not know any other officer in the cavalry who has done better service."[34] "Dear Fitz," wrote Stuart warmly when he learned that Davis had approved the reorganization, "Accept my hearty congratulations on your long earned promotion."[35] At the tender age of twenty-seven years and three months, Lee led three brigades of cavalry and had achieved rank beyond anything he might have dreamed of as an officer in the prewar army.

The new major general spent the fall and winter of 1863-64 in northern Virginia and the Shenandoah Valley. It was a season of varied experience, including action in the "Buckland Races" in October and a miserable month pursuing Federals and supplies in the cold mountains of northwestern Virginia. In early March 1864, the Ninth Virginia of his command purportedly found incriminating papers on the body of Federal Colonel Ulric Dahlgren, who was killed during a raid on Richmond. "Colonel Dahlgren commanded a force picked to co-operate with Brigadier-General Kilpatrick in his ridiculous and unsoldierly raid," wrote an indignant Lee in transmitting the captured papers to General Samuel Cooper, "and lost his life running off negroes after the failure of his insane attempt to destroy Richmond and kill Jeff Davis."[36] On a lighter note, Lee indulged his taste for theatrics and merrymaking by performing a song-and-dance routine at various Richmond salons. Mary Chesnut wrote of "Fitz Lee's new-found joy—a little negro boy. . . [who] danced Ethiopian minstrel fashion" while Lee sang "corn-shucking tunes." That winter Mrs. Chesnut also noted Varina Davis's high opinion of Lee, whom the Confederate first lady rated "far above Hood—far, as a commander."[37]

U.S. Grant's movement across the Rapidan River in early May 1864 inaugurated another season of campaigning for the Army of Northern Virginia. Fitz Lee's division now numbered two rather than three brigades—one having been assigned to a new division put together for his recently promoted cousin, William Henry Fitzhugh ("Rooney") Lee.[38] During fighting in the Wilderness on May 5-6, Lee's troopers skirmished (often dismounted) with their Federal counterparts in the vicinity of Todd's Tavern and Spotsylvania Court House. On May 7, Grant broke off action in the Wilderness and marched toward the vital crossroads at Spotsylvania. Should he reach that point ahead of the Army of Northern Virginia, he would be astride R. E. Lee's direct line to Richmond. The Federals enjoyed a head start in this race for position, and Jeb Stuart called on Fitz Lee's cavalry to slow the enemy advance.[39]

Lee responded with one of his finest efforts. Cavalrymen from both sides fought throughout May 7 between Todd's Tavern and Spotsylvania. The battle flared again on May 8, with elements of G. K. Warren's Union V Corps joining the action along the Brock Road northwest of the Court House. Lee's men grimly held on while Richard H. Anderson and the Confederate First Corps rushed toward Spotsylvania through the smoking carnage of the Wilderness battlefield. "Lee employed his whole command dismounted," wrote H. B. McClellan of Stuart's staff, in "one of the severest conflicts in which it was ever engaged." Anderson's veterans arrived just as the Federals threatened to overwhelm Lee's tired defenders. Lee subsequently claimed with justifiable pride that his outnumbered troopers had saved the critical crossroads.[40]

As the infantry took over the fighting at Spotsylvania, Philip Sheridan's Union Cavalry Corps mounted a serious threat toward Richmond. Stuart hurried to interpose Lee's troopers between the enemy and the capital. A killing march set the stage for a battle at Yellow Tavern on May 12, where Stuart received a mortal wound. Soon after he was hit, Stuart sent an aide to summon Lee. One eyewitness recalled long after the event—when time might well have clouded memory—that Stuart assured the men around him not to worry, "Fitz will do as well for you as I have done." Presently Lee spurred up to his fallen chief, whose agony prevented more specific direction than, "Go ahead, Fitz, old fellow, I know you will do what is right." That statement from the man he both loved and idolized constituted, Lee said later, "my most precious legacy."[41]

Lee's division saw difficult service in June 1864. On the 7th came word that Sheridan was en route toward Charlottesville and the Shenandoah Valley. Lee and Wade Hampton stopped him on June 11-12 at Trevilian Station, southeast of Gordonsville on the Virginia Central Railroad. Other fighting occurred at Reams's Station on the 22nd and Samaria Church two days later. Although neither Lee nor Hampton had been named successor to Stuart, the South Carolinian exercised overall command at Trevilian Station and in subsequent action. Rivalry certainly existed between the two major generals, but it bore no damaging fruit on the battlefield. "Maj. Gen. Fitzhugh Lee co-operated with me heartily and rendered valuable assistance," read Hampton's generous report of operations in June 1864.[42] Not until August 11, 1864, would R. E. Lee designate Hampton his cavalry commander.[43]

A young man who saw Lee as he passed through Richmond on his way to Chaffin's Bluff late in June 1864 left a detailed and revealing description. The witness was John S. Wise, who paused outside a large home to observe Lee at ease among friends: "In appearance, General Lee was short, thickset, already inclined to stoutness; with a square head and short neck upon broad shoulders, a merry eye, and a joyous voice of great power; ruddy, full-bearded, and overflowing with animal spirits." After a duet with the sister of a member of his staff, Lee's banjo player struck up "Jine the Cavalry." "Fitz and his staff joined in the refrain with mighty zest," observed Wise, "making the house ring with their hilarity." The officers then said their good-byes, which included kisses for all the women present. "Finally, with many fond adieus and waving plumes, they rode away down Cary Street," their banjoist plucking refrains of "Jine the Cavalry."[44] Plumes, pretty women, banjo music—Fitz Lee, it seems, was striving hard to emulate the style of his former chief.

In mid-August 1864, Lee and his division went to the Shenandoah Valley to reinforce Jubal Early's little Army of the Valley. Maneuvering in the Lower Valley for a month, Lee was near Winchester on the morning of September 19. Just past dawn, Philip Sheridan launched a heavy attack across Opequon Creek. Although ill for the previous ten days, Lee mounted Nelly Gray (his favorite horse) and sought to slow the powerful blue columns with his cavalry while Early collected his scattered infantry. Confederate horsemen strained to withstand the pressure of superior Union numbers and firepower at several points along the southern line. One southern veteran wrote afterward that Lee stood out on the battlefield as a "soldierly figure . . . astride his beautiful mare." When Nelly Gray was shot from under him, Lee secured a second mount to carry him back into the fray. But the odds "were too great," Lee later wrote. "I was shot through the thigh & carried from the field." Late in the day Sheridan's troops drove the Confederates from Winchester in disorder.[45]

Lee recuperated in Charlottesville while Sheridan decisively defeated Early at Fisher's Hill on September 22 and in a climactic duel at Cedar Creek on October 19. An abscess prolonged Lee's convalescence into December, but January 1865 found him back in the field. After activity near Gordonsville and in the Upper Valley, Lee returned to the Army of Northern Virginia in February to take charge of all cavalry north of the James River.[46] Sheridan routed a pathetic remnant of Early's Army of the Valley at Waynesboro on March 2 and soon thereafter marched toward the Army of the Potomac. R. E. Lee kept a wary eye to the west, where Sheridan spread destruction in the area around Charlottesville before moving on to White House on the Pamunkey River. Monitoring Sheridan's progress, Fitz Lee informed his uncle on March 25 that Sheridan would reach Grant's left flank on the south side of the James within four days. This development meant that Petersburg would have to be evacuated. To keep Sheridan away from the Southside Railroad and allow time for an orderly withdrawal, Lee ordered his nephew to shift about one thousand of his men to the Confederate right. There he would join his cousin "Rooney," whose 2,500 cavalrymen would pass under Fitz's general authority. George E. Pickett's division of infantry would operate as a mobile reserve in support of the cavalry. Together, these 3,500 cavalry and 5,000 infantry would face 13,000 Union troopers and whatever infantry Sheridan might command.[47]

April 1 ushered in the beginning of the final act of the war in Virginia. Following a successful repulse of Sheridan at Dinwiddie Court House on March 31, Fitz Lee and Pickett believed they could defeat Sheridan's cavalry. Should Union infantry appear, they expected reinforcements from their left. The overconfident generals left their lines around Five Forks near noon on April 1 to join Thomas Rosser for a leisurely meal of fresh shad. They told no one where they were going or when they would return. Lee later explained honestly that he and Pickett "were not expecting any attack that afternoon." Shortly after four o'clock, the officers at Rosser's camp heard musketry to the south. Federals in large numbers soon came into view. The generals scrambled for their horses and hastened to the front, but it was too late. Sheridan had landed a sledgehammer blow at Five Forks. While Lee and Pickett enjoyed conversation and fish, Confederate officers on the scene had searched in vain for their superiors. Disaster was complete; abandonment of the Petersburg and Richmond lines began the next day.[48] Would Fitz Lee's presence at the front have altered the outcome of the battle of April 1? Probably not. By the most generous estimate his overall conduct was lackadaisical, however, and his failure to inform any subordinates of his luncheon engagement must be termed a serious lapse of judgment.

Lee and his cavalry covered both the van and rear of the army on the retreat to Appomattox. On the night of April 8, he joined James Longstreet, John B. Gordon, and William Nelson Pendleton at R. E. Lee's headquarters. "It was the last council of war of the A.N.Va.," Fitz wrote to John Esten Cooke in 1868. "It was a picture for an artist." All the officers agreed that a final attempt to break through encircling Federal lines should be made the next day. Failure would compel surrender. In that case, the younger Lee asked, could he extricate his command for a march to join Joseph Johnston's army in North Carolina? He would do so "provided it could be done without compromising the action of the commanding general." Granted permission, Lee prepared for the next day's effort. When the southern attack gained no ground on April 9, Lee led his men away from Appomattox in the hope of continuing the war. A few days after the capitulation at Appomattox, Lee realized the futility of going on. "I rode into the Federal lines," he wrote in a report dated April 22, "and accepted for myself the terms offered the officers of the Army of Northern Virginia."[49]

As so often with Fitz Lee, humor lightened his sad trip home from the war. Somewhere on the road he met a North Carolinian on his way back to the army from a furlough. "You needn't go back, but can throw your gun away and return home," Lee remembered telling this stalwart man, "for Lee's surrendered." "Lee's surrendered?" came the incredulous reply. "That's what I said," the general answered. "It must have been that damned Fitz Lee, then," said the soldier in disgust, "Rob Lee would never surrender."[50]

Lee faced the aftermath of war as a twenty-nine-year-old soldier with no expertise beyond the profession of arms. For twenty years he led the life of a farmer at "Richland," a 1,200-acre place on the Potomac River in Stafford County, Virginia, given him by his godmother, Mrs. A. M. Fitzhugh.[51] "I had been accustomed all my life to draw corn from the quartermaster," Lee observed of his initial struggles on the land, "and found it rather hard now to draw it from the obstinate soil, *but I did it!*" This agricultural phase of Lee's life pleased his Uncle Robert, whose own yearnings in that direction never found fulfillment. "I am glad to hear that you are about establishing yourself in Stafford," wrote R. E. Lee in September 1865. "I have always heard that Richland was a beautiful & productive farm & I hope will make you a pleasant home." Lee teased his nephew about young women rumored to be after him, prompting Fitz to reply that he wished "one would take me. I know she would soon be miserable and that way I could be partially revenged on the sex." Bachelorhood continued until April 19, 1871, when Lee, at age thirty-six, wed eighteen-year-old Ellen Bernard Fowle of Alexandria, Virginia. The couple eventually had seven children, five of whom survived to adulthood.[52]

After twenty years of farming, Lee turned to politics and the public life in 1885. He had run unsuccessfully for the state senate in 1879 as a conservative Democrat supporting payment of Virginia's debt. In opposition were the "Readjustors," who favored slashing the state debt and appealed strongly to the poorer elements in the electorate. Led by former Confederate General William Mahone, the Readjustors swept the elections in 1879 and controlled the state for several years. In 1885, the conservatives ran Fitz Lee in the gubernatorial race against Republican John S. Wise, who represented the Mahone interests. Possessor of an historic name and widely popular because of his Confederate career, Lee proved to be an excellent speaker with a dramatic flair for campaigning. He shamelessly used "Uncle Robert's" saddle during the canvass and received enthusiastic receptions across the state. A heavy turnout gave Lee a decisive victory that helped restore Democratic control of Virginia. Prevented by the state constitution from succeeding himself, he retired from the governor's mansion after one uneventful four-year term.[53]

The 1890s began badly but ended on a note of triumph for Lee. He accepted the presidency of the Rockbridge Company, which sought to develop real estate in Rockbridge County. The economic depression of 1893 doomed this venture, including the town of Glasgow, founded by the company on the James River thirty miles above Lynchburg.[54] That same year, Lee decided to run for the U.S. Senate. A close friend of newly elected Democratic President Grover Cleveland, he was the popular favorite in the contest. But the General Assembly in Richmond cast its ballots for the largely unknown Thomas S. Martin. It was a stunning setback for Lee, who insisted that the majority of Democrats had been undone by the money of a few prominent businessmen. Though there was substance to this charge, Martin won the seat and began a career that would extend over five terms in Washington.[55] President Cleveland did not forget Lee, however, naming him consul-general to Cuba in April 1896. With Cuban rebels fighting the Spanish and relations strained between the United States and Spain, Lee labored diligently to protect American interests on the chaotic island. So adept was he that Republican President William McKinley retained him in the position until April 1898, when Lee resigned to accept a commission as major general in the U.S. Army. Unlike his Confederate comrade Joseph Wheeler, Lee saw no action in the war with Spain. He did become a national hero, retiring in 1901 as a brigadier general.[56]

Lee spent his final years working on preparations for the Jamestown Tercentennial Exposition of 1907. Though he did not live to see the celebration, his efforts helped to make it a success. "His selection as president of the Exposition Company was an inspiration," noted a speaker at Jamestown. "It could not have been successfully launched without him." Lee died at Providence Hospital in Washington, D.C., on April 29, 1905. His body was taken to Richmond and placed in City Hall, where thousands of people, among them many Confederate veterans, bade farewell to a beloved state hero. From St. Paul's Episcopal Church, Lee's remains made a final journey to Hollywood Cemetery, there to rest in the company of thousands of others who had fought with him in the Army of Northern Virginia.[57]

****

Throughout his postwar years, Fitzhugh Lee displayed keen interest in the history and interpretations of the conflict. He shared views on the background and outcome of the war held by a group of former officers in the Army of Northern Virginia that included Jubal A. Early, J. William Jones, William Nelson Pendleton, and Bradley T. Johnson. Leading architects of the myth of the Lost Cause, these men insisted that an ever-battling South lost its bid for independence because of overwhelming northern numbers and material and identified constitutional rights rather than slavery as the cause of the war. They also sought to canonize R. E. Lee as the South's perfect Christian warrior. Searching for scapegoats to explain Lee's failures at Gettysburg and elsewhere, they concentrated on James Longstreet because of his blunt criticism of some aspects of Lee's record and his conversion to Republicanism after the war. Longstreet became the focus of the celebrated "Gettysburg Controversy," in which Fitz Lee took an active interest from its origins in the early 1870s through the end of the century.[58]

Lee and Jubal Early developed an especially close relationship. Both were involved with the Association of the Army of Northern Virginia, an organization of veterans formed in November 1870—Early as the first president, Lee as a leader of the Virginia Division of the Association. Early also dominated the Southern Historical Society, a principal goal of which was disseminating the Lost Cause interpretation of the war through its published *Papers*. In 1881-82, Lee undertook a speaking tour through the South to raise money for the Society.[59] When Early launched an all-out assault on James Longstreet in the pages of the *Southern Historical Society Papers*, Lee cheerfully pitched in to help. The anti-Longstreet clique charged that Longstreet had cost R. E. Lee a victory at Gettysburg by refusing a direct order to attack at sunrise on July 2. Although based on a bald lie, this view gained wide acceptance across the South. In a letter written prior to publication of his reply to Longstreet in the *Papers*, Fitz Lee assured Early that he would be gentle in his criticism of Richard S. Ewell and Jeb Stuart—whom some blamed for failures during the Gettysburg campaign—in order to keep the spotlight on Longstreet's alleged insubordination. "I am going to clinch your effort," he told Early, "in fixing the responsibility of the 2nd where it properly belongs. . . ."[60] Later refinement of the case against Longstreet at Gettysburg mentioned his failure to attack at eleven o'clock on July 2, his refusal to consider a turning movement at Little Round Top proposed by John Bell Hood, and his use of only a third of his corps in the climactic assault on July 3.

The question of reconciliation with the North divided Lee and Early. Early pledged eternal hatred for the Yankees and called for no cooperation with the South's conquerors. Lee took a more realistic position in support of improved relations. In 1875 he accepted an invitation to speak in Boston at the centennial celebration of the battle of Bunker Hill. Early chided his friend for agreeing to appear on Yankee soil, whereupon Fitz reported that when he read Early's objections aloud to his mother she cried out, "Hurrah for Gen. Early—he & I agree— tell him *great minds* think alike." At the ceremony, Bostonians gave Lee a thunderous ovation when he reminded them that Virginia had fought alongside Massachusetts in the Revolution and that his Grandfather Lee had called the immortal Washington "First in war, first in peace, and first in the hearts of his countrymen."[61] Lee also joined the United Confederate Veterans, an organization founded in 1889 with which Early and Bradley T. Johnson had few ties (Johnson said it harbored too many reconciliationists).[62]

A fresh excuse to explore wartime controversies materialized while Lee struggled to make the Rockbridge Company a profitable venture. The New York publishing house of D. Appleton and Company had inaugurated a "Great Commanders" series under the editorship of James Grant Wilson, and R. E. Lee was among the scheduled subjects. Who better to write a life of the great southern hero than his well-known nephew? At first hesitant, Lee took on the project in 1891. He enjoyed the great advantage of access to unpublished private papers in the possession of R. E. Lee's children. These letters were especially important because Lee hoped to satisfy public demand for "something from Robert E. Lee's pen, by introducing . . . such extracts from his private letters as would be of general interest."[63]   To Colonel Charles Venable of his uncle's staff he mentioned other motivation: "I was eventually induced to do this, because I was anxious to throw more light upon some points of his history than has been hitherto done. I refer more particularly to the West Virginia Campaign and to the Battle of Gettysburg." Lee believed strongly that the published record failed to accord his uncle full credit for his efforts early in the war and in Pennsylvania; he would "make the work attractive, full of facts, and a reference to some extent, for those who come after us."[64]

In preparing his manuscript, Lee undertook a wide correspondence with J. William Jones, Walter H. Taylor, E. Porter Alexander, Evander M. Law, William T. Poague, Charles S. Venable, and other ex-Confederates. Much of his interest centered on Longstreet's culpability for the defeat at Gettysburg. His respondents, for the most part members in good standing of the school of thought represented by Jubal Early and William Nelson Pendleton, urged Lee to paint Longstreet in the darkest hues. But Porter Alexander took issue with Lee's obvious desire to lay blame at Longstreet's feet. "I don't undertake to defend Longstreet because he is Longstreet at all," wrote Alexander of his old corps chief. "I have not hesitated to criticize severely his actions on some occasions. But I have never been able to understand how anyone could maintain that at Gettysburg he acted without Gen. Lee's knowledge & implied approval." Alexander passed along letters from Longstreet bearing on the debate. In one, Longstreet noted that he and R. E. Lee had been together during much of the battle—Lee could have changed his subordinate's dispositions at any time. Quoting Napoleon, Longstreet wrote that "In war men are nothing; a man is everything . . . the commander, in this case, R. E. Lee, was responsible for all the moves on the field." The former commander of the First Corps further insisted that Fitz Lee himself had hurt his uncle's reputation more than any other writer by observing in the *Southern Historical Society Papers* that he "put too much confidence in the fighting qualities of his soldiers."[65]

Plagued by financial difficulty with the Rockbridge Company and failure in his quest for the Senate, Lee nonetheless labored purposefully on his biography. He signed the preface in Glasgow in August 1894, and shortly thereafter D. Appleton and Company published the book under the title *General Lee.* The potent combination of revered subject and famous author inspired brisk sales.[66] In the South, promoters touted *General Lee* as "a history of the Confederacy" that "gives in strong words the story of our hero's life from his cradle to the grave." One advertisement in the *Confederate Veteran* reminded readers that Grant's memoirs sold more than a million copies: "Surely thousands of Confederates and sons and daughters of the Confederates will get this Life of Lee. . . . Can any book be more appropriate for a holiday present?"[67] Reviewers often focussed on Lee's treatment of Gettysburg. The Philadelphia *Times* thought that Lee honestly reflected his uncle's views in placing most of the blame on Longstreet. Porter Alexander, in contrast, wrote Lee that he had "dealt in unequal spirit" with "Old Pete." Alexander questioned not only Lee's handling of Gettysburg, but also his contention that Longstreet's slow marching on July 2, 1862, ruined southern chances of holding

Evelington Heights.[68] Others expressed a wish that Fitz had written his own recollections rather than a life of his uncle.[69]

Modern scholars have rendered varying judgments. Douglas Southall Freeman wrote of the book's "solid narrative, interspersed with letters previously unpublished" but noted as well "many inaccuracies" and "poor proofreading." The standard bibliography on the Civil War termed it "an undistinguished study that includes copious extracts of Lee's private letters." William Garrett Piston, whose careful *Lee's Tarnished Lieutenant* shed considerable light on the squabbling between Longstreet and his postwar opponents, characterized *General Lee* as an influential book that did much to fix a negative image of Longstreet in the southern mind.[70]

General Lee remains a valuable book for students of Lee and his campaigns as well as those interested in southern efforts to write a military history of the Confederacy. Far from perfect, it suffers from errors large and small (business and politics no doubt prevented Lee's employing as much care as he would have liked) and offers a biased perspective on Gettysburg and other aspects of the war in the East. But Lee's passionate indictment of Longstreet is in some ways a strength of the book. Nowhere is the anti-Longstreet case of the Lost Cause more succinctly argued than in *General Lee*. From his contention that Longstreet blocked R. E. Lee's plans on July 2 and 3 at Gettysburg to his insistence that "Old Pete" failed at Evelington Heights and in the Wilderness, Fitz Lee gathered the arguments of more than twenty years into one convenient source. The Lost Cause explanation for southern defeat prominently colors Lee's estimates of Union and Confederate numbers, which consistently give Lee too few and the Federals too many men. In Fitz Lee's account, gallant southerners led by the majestic R. E. Lee perform miracles in holding at bay hordes of Union invaders.[71]

Many telling excerpts from R. E. Lee's letters add significantly to the usefulness of the book. After the battle of Cerro Gordo during the Mexican War, Lee wrote his eldest son, Custis: "I was truly thankful that you were at school, I hope learning to be good and wise. You have no idea what a horrible sight a battlefield is." Another letter from Mexico foreshadowed Lee's reaction to southern defeat nearly two decades later. "It is certain we are the conquerors in a regular war," he observed, "and by the laws of nations are entitled to dictate the terms of peace." Lee took a similar view at Appomattox—southern armies had resisted according to the rules of war, had lost honorably, and must accept terms dictated by the victorious North. Juxtaposition of the splendor of western Virginia and the waste of war highlighted a letter to Mrs. Lee in August 1861: "I enjoyed the mountains as I rode along. The views were magnificent. The valleys so peaceful, the scenery so beautiful! What a glorious world Almighty God has given us! How thankless and ungrateful we are!" Elsewhere, Lee's piety, dislike of war, and familial affection emerge from his letters.[72]

Diligent readers will discover many worthwhile anecdotes and insights in *General Lee*. Some are asides relegated to footnotes, such as the comment regarding Sharpsburg that "General Lee told the writer [Fitz Lee] he fought the battle with 35,000 troops." This indicates that R. E. Lee fully understood the drastic scope of straggling and desertion that bled his army during the 1862 Maryland campaign. Fitz Lee recorded a significantly different version of Lee's oft-quoted—and rather baffling—statement that George B. McClellan was the best of the Union generals: "General Lee said, after the war, that he considered General McClellan the most intellectual of all the Federal generals." It seems far more plausible that Lee would pronounce McClellan the most intellectual rather than the best of the Federals. In a category all its own was Lee's passage on Ambrose Burnside's popularity, which included the amusing fact that

West Point's saloon keeper Benny Havens added Burnside's name to those of St. Paul and Andrew Jackson for "a special toast which he invariably repeated every time he indulged in a stimulant. . . ." Among Lee's literary images, none surpassed his description of the battle of the Wilderness as two hundred thousand soldiers "mixed up in wild, weird struggle, like a hole full of snakes with their tails intertwined."[73]

In sum, Fitzhugh Lee's *General Lee* is a worthy addition to any collection of books on R. E. Lee and the Army of Northern Virginia. Its pages enlighten readers with information on its subject, its author, and the times in which it was written.

Gary W. Gallagher
Penn State University
June 25, 1988

NOTES

[1]Douglas Southall Freeman, "Lee, Fitzhugh," in Allen Johnson and Dumas Malone, eds., *Dictionary of American Biography*, 22 vols. and index (New York, 1928-37), 11: 103-104 (this work cited hereafter as *DAB*). The lack of a biography of Fitzhugh Lee is one of the anomalies of Civil War literature. The fullest studies are James L. Nichols's unpublished "Fitzhugh Lee: A Biography" and Henry Warren Readnour's "General Fitzhugh Lee, 1835-1905: A Biographical Study" (Ph.D. dissertation; University of Virginia, 1971). See also Douglas Southall Freeman, *Lee's Lieutenants: A Study in Command*, 3 vols. (New York, 1942-44), for coverage of Lee's Confederate service, and Robert W. Hunter, "Fitzhugh Lee. An Address Delivered on Fitzhugh Lee Day at the Jamestown Exposition," in *Southern Historical Society Papers*, ed. by J. William Jones et al., 52 vols. and 2 vol. index (1876-1959; reprint ed., New York, 1977-80), 35: 132-45 (this last set is cited hereafter as *SHSP*).

[2]Nichols, "Fitzhugh Lee," pp. 12-13.

[3]*Ibid.*, p. 12; John S. Wise, *The End of An Era* (Boston, 1899), pp. 334-35.

[4]Circulation Records, U.S. Military Academy, 1852-1856, and *Official Register for Officers and Cadets USMA, 1853-1856*, as quoted in Nichols, "Fitzhugh Lee," pp. 14-16.

[5]"Register of Delinquencies" 1853-56, U.S. Military Academy, quoted in *ibid.*

[6]Douglas Southall Freeman, *R. E. Lee: A Biography*, 4 vols. (New York, 1834-36), 1: 332-34.

[7]Fitzhugh Lee to Mrs. A. M. Fitzhugh (his godmother), April 1, 1855, Fitzhugh Lee Papers in the possession of Fitzhugh Lee Opie. Mr. Opie, the general's grandson, kindly granted

permission to publish quotations from these papers (this collection is cited hereafter as FLP-O).

[8]Joseph H. Parks, *General Edmund Kirby Smith, C.S.A.* (Baton Rouge, 1954), p. 87. In a reorganization of August 3, 1861, the First and Second Cavalry became the Fourth and Fifth Cavalry. On the Fifth (Second) Cavalry, see George F. Price, *Across the Continent with the Fifth Cavalry* (New York, 1883).

[9]Freeman, "Lee, Fitzhugh," p. 103. A brief summary of Lee's military career is in Francis B. Heitman, *Historical Register and Dictionary of the United States Army, From It's Organization, September 29, 1789, To March 2, 1903,* 2 vols. (1903; reprint ed., Urbana, Ill., 1965), 1: 623. For anecdotes of Lee's time at Carlisle, see Edward K. Eckert and Nicholas J. Amato, eds., *Ten Years in the Saddle: The Memoir of William Woods Averell 1851-1862* (San Rafael, Calif., 1978), pp. 75-77.

[10]Fitzhugh Lee to Mrs. A. M. Fitzhugh, September 15, 1858, Lee to Maria Wheaton, September [?], 1858, FLP-O.

[11]Fitzhugh Lee to Mama or Papa, June 3, 1859, FLP-O.

[12]Fitzhugh Lee to Mrs. A. M. Fitzhugh, September 1, 1859, FLP-O.

[13]Fitzhugh Lee to Edmund Kirby Smith, January 20, 1860, FLP-O.

[14]Parks, *Kirby Smith*, p. 103.

[15]R. E. Lee to Mrs. A. M. Fitzhugh, June 6, 1860, FLP-O.

[16]Fitzhugh Lee to his mother, April 8, 1861, FLP-O.

[17]Nichols, "Fitzhugh Lee," pp. 38-40; Freeman, "Lee, Fitzhugh," pp. 103-4. Lee's father resigned at about the same time as his son and was commissioned a commander in the Confederate navy on June 11, 1861; George Washington Custis Lee, Fitzhugh's cousin and R. E. Lee's son, resigned on May 2, 1861, and became a captain of Confederate engineers on July 1.

[18]Jedediah Hotchkiss, *Virginia*, being vol. 3 of *Confederate Military History*, ed. by Clement A. Evans, 12 vols. (Atlanta,

1899), p. 623; "General Ewell at First Manassas. Colonel Campbell Brown's Reply to General Beauregard," *SHSP*, 13: 43.

[19]U.S. War Department, *The War of the Rebellion: A Compilation of the Official Records of the Union and Confederate Armies*, 127 vols., index and atlas (Washington, 1880-1901), ser. I, 11, pt. 1: 1040-41 (cited hereafter as *OR*, all citations to ser. I).

[20]For a discussion of the affair at Evelington Heights, see Freeman, *Lee's Lieutenants*, 1: 640-43.

[21]*OR*, 11, pt. 3: 657.

[22]*Ibid.*, 12, pt. 2: 726; Freeman, *Lee's Lieutenants*, 2: 60-61.

[23]W. Roy Mason, "Marching on Manassas," in *Battles and Leaders of the Civil War*, ed. by Robert Underwood Johnson and Clarence Clough Buel, 4 vols. (New York, 1887), 2: 528.

[24]*OR*, 19, pt. 1: 148, 151 (R. E. Lee's report), 819-20 (Stuart's report).

[25]For an overview of these raids, see Freeman, *Lee's Lieutenants*, 2: chapters 18 and 25.

[26]*OR*, 25, pt. 1: 25 (Lee's report of the action on February 25); *ibid.*, pt. 2: 654 (R. E. Lee's response).

[27]Averell, *Ten Years in the Saddle*, pp. 386-87; *OR*, 25, pt. 1: 60-63.

[28]Fitzhugh Lee, "Chancellorsville—Address of General Fitzhugh Lee before the Virginia Division, A.N.V. Association, October 29th, 1879," in *SHSP*, 7: 572-73.

[29]*OR*, 25, pt. 1: 889.

[30]John Esten Cooke, *Wearing of the Gray, Being Personal Portraits, Scenes & Adventures of the War* (1867; reprint ed., Bloomington, Ind., 1959), pp. 226-27, 305-6.

[31]Averell, *Ten Years in the Saddle*, p. 49.

[32]Freeman, *Lee's Lieutenants*, 3:7 (note 21).

[33] *OR*, 27, pt. 2: 696-705.

[34] *OR*, 27, pt. 2: 709; *ibid.*, pt. 3: 1069.

[35] J. E. B. Stuart to Fitzhugh Lee, September 10, 1863, FLP-O.

[36] *OR*, 33: 217. The papers said to be found on Dahlgren's body caused a furor at the time and have remained controversial. George Gordon Meade, commander of the Army of the Potomac, denied any knowledge of a scheme to kill southern leaders and burn Richmond, and many northerners charged that Confederates forged the papers. For Meade's reaction, see George Gordon Meade, ed., *The Life and Letters of George Gordon Meade*, 2 vols. (New York, 1913), 2: 190-91; on the Federal raid in general, see Virgil Carrington Jones, *Eight Hours Before Richmond* (New York, 1957).

[37] C. Vann Woodward, ed., *Mary Chesnut's Civil War* (New Haven, 1981), pp. 504, 590.

[38] *OR*, 36, pt. 1: 1027.

[39] H. B. McClellan, *The Life and Campaigns of Major-General J. E. B. Stuart* (New York, 1885), pp. 406-7.

[40] *Ibid.*, p. 407; Nichols, "Fitzhugh Lee," pp. 115-17.

[41] Fitzhugh Lee, "Speech of General Fitz. Lee, at A.N.V. Banquet, October 28th, 1875," in *SHSP*, 1: 102; J. R. Oliver, "J. E. B. Stuart's Fate at Yellow Tavern," *Confederate Veteran* 19 (November 1911): 531.

[42] *OR*, 36, pt. 1: 1095-97.

[43] For a discussion of the problem of selecting a successor for Stuart, see Freeman, *Lee's Lieutenants*, 3: 436, 517, 523.

[44] Wise, *End of An Era*, pp. 335-37.

[45] Nichols, "Fitzhugh Lee," pp. 144-47; P. J. White, "Recollections of Battle at Winchester," *Confederate Veteran* 15 (December 1907): 566. The bullet that struck Lee passed through his saddle and killed his second horse.

[46]Nichols, "Fitzhugh Lee," pp. 148-49.

[47]Freeman, *R. E. Lee*, 4: 21; Freeman, *Lee's Lieutenants*, 3: 656-57.

[48]*OR*, 46, pt. 1: 1299-1300 (Fitzhugh Lee's report); Freeman, *Lee's Lieutenants*, 3: 664-70.

[49]*OR*, 46, pt. 1: 1303-4; John B. Gordon, *Reminiscences of the Civil War* (New York, 1903), p. 435-36.

[50]"A Story of the Lees," *Confederate Veteran* 4 (January 1896): 23. Lee often recounted this story after the war.

[51]Lee moved to "Richland" immediately after the war and obtained title to the property ten years later under the terms of Mrs. Fitzhugh's will. Between 1881 and 1892 he sold about 160 acres of the land, and in 1893, long after he had moved away from the place, disposed of the remainder. A full discussion of Lee and "Richland" is in chapter six of Nichols, "Fitzhugh Lee."

[52]Freeman, "Lee, Fitzhugh," p. 105 (first quotation); R. E. Lee to Fitzhugh Lee, September 1, 1865; Fitzhugh Lee to R. E. Lee, September 7, 1865, FLP-O. Lee's sons George Mason and Fitzhugh, Jr., attended West Point and became officers in the U.S. Army; two of his daughters married army officers. Obituary for Lee in *Confederate Veteran* 13 (June 1905): 281.

[53]James T. Moore, "Readjustor Movement," in *The Encyclopedia of Southern History*, ed. by David C. Roller and Robert W. Twyman (Baton Rouge, 1979), pp. 1031-32 (this work cited hereafter as *ESH*); Nelson M. Blake, *William Mahone of Virginia: Soldier and Political Insurgent* (Richmond, 1935), pp. 230-31; obituary in *Confederate Veteran*, p. 280.

[54]Chapter nine of Nichols, "Fitzhugh Lee," covers Lee's association with the Rockbridge Company.

[55]Joseph P. Harahan, "Martin, Thomas Staples," in *ESH*, p. 783; Virginius Dabney, "Martin, Thomas Staples," in *DAB*, 12: 346-47.

[56]Freeman, "Lee, Fitzhugh," p. 104; Gaines M. Foster, *Ghosts of the Confederacy: Defeat, the Lost Cause, and the Emergence of the New South* (New York, 1987), pp. 146, 148, 152; obituary in *Confederate Veteran*, p. 281; Hunter, "Fitzhugh Lee," pp. 136-40; Heitman, *Register of U.S. Army*, 1: 623.

[57]Obituary in *Confederate Veteran*, p. 281; Hunter, "Fitzhugh Lee," p. 134.

[58]On the myth of the Lost Cause, the deification of R. E. Lee, and the Gettysburg controversy, see Thomas L. Connelly, *The Marble Man: Robert E. Lee and His Image in American Society* (New York, 1977); Foster, *Ghosts of the Confederacy*; William Garrett Piston, *Lee's Tarnished Lieutenant: James Longstreet and His Place in Southern History* (Athens, Ga., 1987); Douglas Southall Freeman, *The South to Posterity: An Introduction to the Writing of Confederate History* (New York, 1939), chapter 4; and Glenn Tucker, *Lee and Longstreet at Gettysburg* (Indianapolis, 1968).

[59]Foster, *Ghosts of the Confederacy*, pp. 53-56; Connelly, *Marble Man*, p. 82. During his speaking tour, Lee repeatedly delivered a lecture on Chancellorsville that he had given first in 1879 before the Army of Northern Virginia Association.

[60]On the Gettysburg controversy in the *SHSP*, see especially volumes 4-6. Fitzhugh Lee's major contributions were "Letter from General Fitz. Lee," 4: 69-76, and, "A Review of the First Two Days' Operations at Gettysburg and a Reply to General Longstreet by General Fitz. Lee," 5: 162-94. The quotation is from a letter to Early of January 20, 1878, reproduced in Connelly, *Marble Man*, p. 89. See also Piston, *Lee's Tarnished Lieutenant*, pp. 129-31, 133, 135.

[61]Nichols, "Fitzhugh Lee," chapter 6, pp. 41-43.

[62]Foster, *Ghosts of the Confederacy*, pp. 108-9.

[63]This quotation is from Lee's preface to the finished biography.

[64]Fitzhugh Lee to Charles Venable, June 23, 1891, quoted in Nichols, "Fitzhugh Lee," chapter 9, pp. 42-43.

[65]E. Porter Alexander to Fitzhugh Lee, July 26, 1894; James Longstreet to E. Porter Alexander, July 22, 1894, FLP-O.

[66]In addition to the regular first edition of the book published in 1894, D. Appleton and Company issued a Large Paper edition of one thousand copies that same year (the latter included an additional portrait of Lee). Six additional Appleton printings bore imprint dates of 1895, 1897, 1898, 1901, 1907, and 1910. Other publishers also brought out editions: Southwestern Publishing House of Nashville in 1895, J. A. Hill & Company of New York in 1904 as part of the Makers of American History series, and The University Society of New York in 1905. Chapman & Hall of London issued a British edition entitled *General Lee of the Confederate Army* in 1895. Fawcett Publications of Greenwich published a softcover edition in 1961 as one of its Premier Civil War Classics with an introduction by Philip Van Doren Stern. For information on the different printings, see Richard Allen Sauers, *The Gettysburg Campaign, June 3-August 1, 1863: A Comprehensive, Selectively Annotated Bibliography* (Westport, Conn., 1982), p. 166; Tom Broadfoot, et al., *Civil War Books: A Priced Checklist* (second ed.; Wendell, N.C., 1983), p. 102; and C. E. Dornbusch, *Military Bibliography of the Civil War*, 3 vols. (New York, 1961-72), 2: 238.

[67]*Confederate Veteran* 3 (February 1895): [63c].

[68]Philadelphia *Times*, October 28, 1894; E. Porter Alexander to Fitz-hugh Lee, September 24, 1894, FLP-O.

[69]Freeman, *South to Posterity*, pp. 168-69.

[70]Freeman, *R. E. Lee*, 4: 553; Allan Nevins, *et al.*, eds., *Civil War Books: A Critical Bibliography*, 2 vols. (Baton Rouge, 1967, 69), 2: 71; Piston, *Lee's Tarnished Lieutenant*, p. 148.

[71]For examples of Lee's anti-Longstreet prose, see pages 142, 166, 276, 280, 288-89, 299-300, 378, and 422 below; on the power of the North, see, for example, pages 96-97.

[72]The quotations are on pages 40, 43, and 117 below.

[73]The quotations are on pages 209, 220, 221, and 330 below. On Lee's estimate of McClellan, see Warren W. Hassler, Jr., *General George B. McClellan: Shield of the Union* (Baton Rouge, 1957), p. 326.

PREFACE.

THE occasion has been embraced to express the universal regret that General Lee never wrote anything concerning his career and campaigns. His statements would have settled conflicting opinions on all subjects contained therein. We know that it was his intention to record the deeds of his soldiers, but not to write his personal memoirs. He waited for a "convenient season," and waited too long. In this volume the attempt has been made to imperfectly supply the great desire to have something from Robert E. Lee's pen, by introducing, at the periods referred to, such extracts from his private letters as would be of general interest. He is thus made, for the first time, to give his impressions and opinions on most of the great events with which he was so closely connected. Except in a few instances, the scope of the book has not permitted the tactical details of the battlefield, or the mention by name of many of the officers and organizations whose superb courage contributed to their commander's fame.

F. L.

GLASGOW, VA., *August, 1894.*

CONTENTS.

LIST OF ILLUSTRATIONS.

GENERAL LEE.

CHAPTER I.

ANCESTRY.

WESTMORELAND is one of a group of counties in Virginia lying between the Rappahannock and Potomac Rivers. It was originally a portion of Northumberland County, and, though small in geographical extent, its historical record is great. Within a space of thirty miles in length and an average width of fifteen miles were born statesmen, soldiers, and patriots whose lives and characters adorn the pages of American history, and whose courage, genius, and learning are the proud inheritance of those who dwell to-day in the powerful republic of America. Here, from England, in 1665, settled the great-grandfather of the "Father of his Country." Americanized, he became an extensive planter, soldier, magistrate, member of the House of Burgesses, and a gentleman whose virtue and piety were undoubted. In his will he expressed his "sorrow for his sins, and begged forgiveness from Almighty God, Saviour, and Redeemer." Here his son, Lawrence, and his grandson, Augustine, were born. The second wife of Augustine was Mary Ball, and their first child, born February 22, 1732, was named George Washington.

This son was destined to establish, with stainless sword, a free republic, and by great skill, unfaltering faith, and sublime patriotism transfer power from king to people. A grateful country acknowledged his illustrious services, and he was chosen the first President of the United States. This little county was not satisfied with the high honor. On April 28, 1758, James Monroe was born within its limits. He became a distinguished citizen, served as an officer in the Revolutionary War, was a member of the General Assembly of Virginia, of the Congress of Confederation, and the Virginia Convention called in June, 1778, to consider the Federal Constitution, a United States Senator, envoy to France, England, and Spain, twice Governor of his native State, Secretary of State in Mr. Madison's administration, and President of the republic for two terms—from 1817 to 1825—thus adding, by a long and meritorious public career, additional renown to the county of his birth, his State, and his country. James Madison, fourth President of the United States, was born in the adjoining county of King George seven years before Monroe, and but a few miles distant. To this section, from England, came, too, the Lees, who belonged to one of the oldest families in the mother country, its members from a very early date being distinguished for eminent services to sovereign and country. By the side of William the Conqueror, at the battle of Hastings, in 1066, Lancelot Lee fought, and a later descendant, Lionel Lee, followed Richard Cœur de Lion, taking part in the third crusade to Palestine, in 1192, at the head of a company of "gentlemen cavaliers," displaying great bravery at the siege of Acre.

The Lees of Virginia, "a family which has, perhaps, given more statesmen and warriors to their new home than any other of our old colonial progenitors," came of an ancient and distinguished stock in England, and neither country can boast a nobler scion than the subject of these memoirs. General Lee had never the time or inclination to study genealogy, and always said he knew nothing beyond his first American ancestor, Colonel Richard Lee, who migrated to Virginia in the reign of Charles I. He believed, however, from his inherited traditions and the Coat of Arms borne by his progenitors in this country, that his family came originally from Shropshire, England; and when the world rang with his name and fame, and he paid the usual penalty of greatness by being besieged with reiterated queries respecting his pedigree, this was all he would say. Others, however, took more interest in the subject; he was claimed by the Lees of Cheshire, Oxfordshire, Bucks, and Essex, as well as of Shropshire, and much was said and written *pro* and *con* both before and after his death.

In recent years his genealogy has been very persistently and thoroughly investigated by those learned in antiquarian research, and their conclusion is in favor of Shropshire, though in 1663 the first emigrant, Colonel Richard Lee, made a will in which he states that he was "lately of Stafford Langton in the county of Essex." Now, as we have every reason to believe that he was a younger son, the parental nest was probably full; neither was it such a " far cry " from Shropshire to the near vicinity of London, a remove preparatory, possibly, to the still greater one across the Atlantic. He certainly used the arms of the Shropshire Lees.

Colonel Lee's devotion to the House of Stuart was notorious, and had been often proved even by the manner of dating his will—viz., " The 6th of February, in the sixteenth year of the reign of our Sovereign Lord, Charles II, King of Great Britain, etc., and in the year of our Lord 1663.* Being Secretary of State and Member of the Privy Council in Virginia, he had assisted that stanch royalist, Governor Berkeley,in holding the colony to its allegiance, so that after the death of Charles I, Cromwell was forced to send troops and armed vessels of war to reduce it to subjection. Unable to resist, they made a treaty with the " Commonwealth of England," wherein Virginia was described as an "Independent Dominion," this treaty being ratified in the same manner as with a foreign power.

Berkeley was then removed and another governor appointed; but the undaunted Colonel Richard Lee " hired a Dutch vessel, freighted it himself, went to Brussels or Breda, surrendered up Sir William Berkeley's old commission—for the government of that province—and received a new one from his present Majesty, Charles II, " a loyal action and deserving my commendation." † It

---

* The "Restoration," as is well known, only occurred in 1660, so that the Virginian's loyalty utterly ignored the long years of exile, and recognized Charles II as King from the moment of his father's execution.

† Introductis ad Latinum Blasoniam. By John Gibbons, Blue Mantel, London, 1682.

is also said that he offered the exiled monarch an asylum in the New World. It is certain that on the death of Cromwell he aided Governor Berkeley in proclaiming Charles II in Virginia King of England, Scotland, France, Ireland, and Virginia two years before his "restoration" in England. In consequence, the motto to the Virginia Coat of Arms was "En dat Virginia quintam" until after the union of England and Scotland, when it was "En dat Virginia quartam."

The inscription on the tombstone of the second Richard Lee, at Burnt House Fields, Mt. Pleasant, Westmoreland County, describes him as belonging to an "ancient and noble family of Morton Regis in Shropshire." It is clearly established that the three earliest representatives of the family in America, Colonel Richard Lee and his two eldest sons, claimed this Shropshire County descent.

It is our purpose to trace the Lees in America, not in England. The first emigrant, Colonel Richard Lee, is described as a man of good stature, of comely visage, enterprising genius, a sound head, vigorous spirit, and generous nature; and when he reached Virginia, at that time not much cultivated, he was so pleased with the country that he made large settlements with the servants who accompanied him. To his credit it may be added that when he returned to England, some years afterward, he "gave away all the lands he had taken up, and settled at his own expense, to the servants he had fixed on them, some of whose descendants are now possessed of very considerable estates in that colony."

After remaining some time in England he again visited Virginia with a fresh band of followers whom he also established there. He first settled in York County in 1641, where he was burgess and justice in 1647, and when later he removed to the "Northern Neck," between the 'Potomac and Rappahannock Rivers, he filled the offices of Secretary of State and Member of the Privy Council. Of his loyalty to the house of Stuart we have already spoken, and of his various voyages, indicating in themselves his "enterprising genius." When he made his will in London, in 1663, he was returning on what proved to be his last voyage. He had with him his large, young family, his eldest son John not yet being of age; but he was so determined to establish them in Virginia that he ordered an English estate—Stratford—worth eight or nine hundred pounds per annum, to be sold and the money divided between his heirs. He died soon after his return, and as John, the B. A. of Oxford, never married, Richard, the second son, succeeded to the homestead in Westmoreland. He also graduated at Oxford in law, and was distinguished for his learning, spending almost his whole life in study. On October 15, 1667, as " Major Richard Lee, a loyal, discreet person and worthy of the place," he was appointed member of the council. He was born in 1647, married Letitia Corbin, and died in 1714, leaving five sons and one daughter. His eldest son, Richard, the third of the name, married and settled in London, though his children eventually returned to Virginia. Philip removed to Maryland in 1700, and was the progenitor of the Lee family in that State. Francis, the third son, died a bachelor, but Thomas, the fourth, with only a common Virginia education (it could not have been much in those days), had such strong natural parts that he became a good Latin and Greek scholar, long after he was a man, without any assistance but his own genius. Though a younger son, with only a limited patrimony, by his " industry and parts " he acquired a considerable fortune, was a member of the council, and so well known and respected that when his house in Westmoreland burned down Queen Caroline sent him a large sum of money out of her privy purse, with an autograph letter. Stratford was rebuilt on an imposing scale, and, becoming the property of " Light-Horse Harry," on his marriage with Matilda, daughter of Philip Ludwell Lee and granddaughter of Thomas, was eventually the birthplace of General R. E. Lee. On the recall of Sir William Gooch, Thomas became president and commander in chief over the colony, in which station he continued some time, until the King thought proper to appoint him governor, and he is always spoken of as the first native governor, though he died in 1750, before his commission could reach him. He married Hannah Ludwell, of an old and honorable Somersetshire family, originally of German extraction, and left six sons and two daughters.

Stratford is still standing in Westmoreland County, an object of much veneration and respect. Within its walls, in the same chamber, two signers of the Declaration of Independence were born, while the fact that Robert Edward Lee first saw the light there makes it yet more interesting. It is a large, stately mansion, built in the shape of the letter " H," and not far from the banks of the Potomac. Upon the roof were summer houses, with chimneys for columns, where the band played in the evenings, and the ladies and gentlemen promenaded. Thomas Lee was buried at Pope's Creek Church, five miles from Stratford. George Washington was baptized at this church, and in the early days his family, the Lees, Paynes, and other prominent families of the neighborhood worshiped there.

It has been said that as Westmoreland County is distinguished above all other counties in Virginia as the birthplace of genius, so, perhaps, no other Virginian could boast so many distinguished sons as President Thomas Lee. General Washington, in 1771, wrote: "I know of no country that can produce a family all distinguished as clever men, as our Lees." These sons in order of age were: Philip Ludwell, Richard Henry, Thomas, Francis Lightfoot, Henry, and Arthur. Matilda, the first wife of General Henry Lee, the father of General Robert E. Lee, was the daughter of the eldest son, Philip Ludwell Lee. Richard Henry Lee, the second son, is well known to students of American history. He has been generally styled " The Cicero of the American Revolution." He moved on June 10, 1776, that " these colonies are, and of right ought to be, free and independent States "; and with his brother Francis Lightfoot signed the Declaration of Independence. Having moved this declaration, according to parliamentary etiquette, he might have been appointed chairman of the committee to draw up the instrument, but the sickness of his wife called him home ; or he might also have been the author of the Declaration of American Independence in place of Thomas Jefferson. His services to the cause of the colony were great, and their struggle for independence was sustained by his tongue and pen. He was a great orator, an accomplished scholar, a learned debater, and a renowned statesman in that period of our country's history. His father's brother, Henry Lee, the fifth son of the second Richard, married a Miss Bland, a great-aunt of John Randolph, of Roanoke. His only daughter married a Fitzhugh. His son Henry married Miss Grymes, and left a family of six sons and four daughters. Henry, the eldest, was the well-known "Light-Horse Harry" of the Revolutionary War, the father of Robert E. Lee. He and Richard Henry Lee are frequently confounded, and their relationship has often been the subject of inquiry. Richard Henry Lee's father, Thomas, and Henry Lee's grandfather, Henry, were brothers. The former was therefore a first cousin of the latter's father. "Light-Horse Harry" was conspicuous in the military and civil annals of his country as a dashing dragoon in the war between Great Britain and the colonies. His boldness and activity were frequently commended by Washington, and he came out of the war with a brilliant reputation. He possessed the love and confidence of the commander in chief, and it is possible that Washington's interest was first excited because he was once supposed to have had a tender feeling for Lucy Grymes, his mother, a friendship which was continued by reason of the attractive qualities of the son as soldier and statesman. This attachment was deeply appreciated by General Henry Lee, and throughout his career he was steadfast in his devotion to Washington.

"Light-Horse Harry's" father, Henry Lee, of Leesylvania, and Lucy Grymes were married at Green Spring, on James River, December 1, 1753. His mother was the daughter of Lucy Ludwell, who married Colonel Grymes, of the Council of Virginia. Bishop Porteus, of England, was her uncle. Their son Henry was born January 29, 1756, at Leesylvania, some three miles from Dumfries, a village built by Scotch merchants, and then the county town of Prince William. His brother, Charles Lee (not to be confounded with General Charles Lee, an Englishman, and no relation to this family), was subsequently Attorney General in Washington's second Cabinet. The future cavalry leader was educated at Princeton. Dr. William Shippen writes to Richard Henry Lee from Philadelphia, August 25, 1770: "I am persuaded that there is no such school as Princeton on this continent. Your cousin Henry Lee is in college, and will be one of the first fellows in this country. He is more than strict in his morality, has fine genius, and is diligent." The profession of law was thought best for the display of his talents, and he was about to embark for England to study it, under the direction of Bishop Porteus, of London, when stopped by hostilities between the mother country and her American colonies.

Possessing fine descriptive powers, application, great facility for public expression, and with character formed and mind trained by such a distinguished light of the Church of England, a great legal future would seem a safe prediction; but before the smoke cleared away from the first British gun fired in Massachusetts, its report was heard in Virginia. The English volley lighted patriotic fires in the hearts of the colonists with the rapidity electricity flies in this age from the touch of the button. The sword was substituted for the law book in the hands of Henry Lee, and we find him, at the age of nineteen, after the battle of Lexington, a captain of cavalry, being nominated for that position by Patrick Henry, the orator of American liberty. He rose rapidly in his new career. In the Northern Department at Brandywine, Germantown, Springfield, and in the operations in Pennsylvania, New Jersey, and New York, his address, cool courage, great ability, and unceasing activity as an outpost officer speedily drew the attention of his superiors. Congress recognized his services, promoted him, and gave him an independent partisan corps. Ever thereafter his position in the war was near the flashing of the guns. His duties kept him close to the enemy's lines, and his legion was what cavalry should be—the eyes and ears of the army. His communications to Washington were confidential, were sent direct, and he was ordered by the commander in chief to mark them "Private." When Washington was anxious to effect Arnold's capture he consulted the commander of the "Light Horse," who planned the famous desertion of Sergeant Champe. He projected and executed the surprise and capture of Paulus Hook by a brilliant *coup de main,* and for prudence, bravery, and tactical skill was presented by Congress with a gold medal emblematical of his success—a distinction conferred on no other officer below the rank of general during the war. On one side of the medal was a bust of the hero, with the words: "Henry Lee, *Legionis Equit.: Præfecto Comitia Americana,*" and on the reverse is translated: "Nothwithstanding rivers and intrenchments, he, with a small band, conquered the foe by warlike skill and prowess, and firmly bound, by his humanity, those who had been conquered by his arms. In memory of the conflict at Paulus Hook, 19th August, 1779."

In November, 1780, he was promoted to be lieutenant colonel of dragoons, and his corps is spoken of as the "finest that made its appearance in the arena of the Revolutionary War." Washington had it formed expressly for him of equal proportions of cavalry and infantry, both officers and men being picked from the army. Under its victorious guidons rode Peter Johnston, the father of the distinguished soldier, Joseph Eggleston Johnston, who joined the legion when only sixteen years old and led the forlorn hope at the storming of Fort Watson, and was publicly thanked. Afterward he became a judge, and was celebrated for his learning and ability. It is curious that the sons of Judge Johnston and General Henry Lee were afterward classmates at the United States Military Academy, and at the marriage ceremony of Lee, Johnston was a groomsman. These two eminent soldiers were in the front rank of the United States Army, and served with great distinction under the Southern flag, even as their fathers rode boot to boot in the days of the Revolution. When Henry Lee's legion was selected to assist in the defense of the Carolinas and the Virginias in the Southern Department, Washington wrote to Mr. John Matthews, a member of Congress from South Carolina, informing him of its march, saying: "Lee's corps will go to the southward; it is an excellent one, and the officer at the head of it has great reserves of genius." Lafayette held the leader of the legion in high estimation, and bears testimony to his "distinguished services," his "talents as a corps commander," and his "handsome exploits"; while one of the general officers of the army said: "He seemed to have come out of his mother's womb a soldier." General Nathanael Greene, his immediate commander, testified that "few officers, either in America or Europe, were held in so high a point of estimation," in a letter to the President of Congress, February 18, 1782, expressed himself as "more indebted to this officer [Lee] than any other for the advantages gained over the enemy in the operations of the last campaign," and in a letter to Lee himself writes: "No man in the progress of the campaign had equal merit with yourself, nor is there one so reported; everybody knows I have the highest opinion of you as an officer, and you know I love you as a friend." After the British colors were lowered at Yorktown Henry Lee began a civil career which proved to be as great as his military record. In 1778 he was a member of the convention called in Virginia to consider the ratification of the Federal Constitution. In the battle of intellectual giants composing that body, with eloquence and zeal he pleaded for its adoption. By his side, and voting with him on that important question, were such men as James Madison, John Marshall, afterward Chief Justice of the United States, and Edmund Randolph; while in the ranks of the opposition stood Patrick Henry with immense oratorical strength, George Mason, "the wisest man," Mr. Jefferson said, he "ever knew," Benjamin Harrison, William Grayson, and others, who thought the Constitution, as it came from the hands of its framers, conferred too much power on the Federal Government and too little upon its creator, the States. In 1786 he was a delegate to the Continental Congress. From 1792 to 1795 he was Governor of Virginia, and was selected by President Washington to command the fifteen thousand men from Pennsylvania, New Jersey, and Maryland, who were sent into western Pennsylvania to quell what was known as the "Whisky Insurrection," which he successfully accomplished without bloodshed.

This rebellion grew out of a resistance to a tax laid on distilled spirits. Washington accompanied him on the march as far as Bedford, Pa., and in a letter, dated October 20, 1794, to Henry Lee, Esq., commander in chief of the militia army on its march against the insurgents in certain counties of western Pennsylvania, says at its conclusion: "In leaving the army I have less regret, as I know I commit it to an able and faithful direction, and that this direction will be ably and faithfully seconded by all."

While Governor of Virginia, a section lying under the Cumberland Mountains, projecting between Kentucky and Tennessee, was formed into a separate county and named after him. It has since been divided into two, the eastern portion being called after General Winfield Scott. In 1779 General Lee was elected to Congress, and on the death of General Washington was appointed to deliver an address in commemoration of the services of that great man, in which occurs the famous sentence so often quoted: "First in war, first in peace, and first in the hearts of his fellow-citizens."* In 1798–'99, as a representative of the County of Westmoreland in the General Assembly, he took an active part in the debate upon Mr. Madison's famous resolutions of that date. In his opinion, the laws of the United States then under discussion were unconstitutional, and if they were, Virginia had a right to object; "but," he exclaimed, "Virginia is my country; her will I obey, however lamentable the fate to which it may subject me."

When he was Governor of Virginia, six years before, his native State occupied the first place in his heart. In reply to a letter from Mr. Madison, dated Philadelphia, January 21, 1792, asking him if he would relinquish his office and accept command of an army to be organized for the protection of the western frontier, he writes: "Were I called upon by the President to command the next campaign, my respect for him would induce me to disregard every trifling obstruction which might oppose my acceptance of the office, such as my own repose, the

---

* [In this popular quotation the word "countrymen" is almost always substituted for the original words used by its author, Henry Lee.] —EDITOR.

care of my children and the happiness I enjoy in attention to their welfare, and in the execution of the
duties of my present station. As a citizen, I should
hold myself bound to obey the will of my country
in taking any part her interests may demand from me.
Therefore I am, upon this occasion, in favor of obedience to any claim which may be made on me. Yet
I should require some essential stipulations—only to
secure a favorable issue to the campaign." After
speaking of how formidable the enemy was, he adds:
"One objection I should only have (the above conditions being acceded to), and that is, the abandoning of my native county, to whose goodness I am so
much indebted; no consideration on earth could induce
me to act a part, however gratifying to me, which could
be construed into disregard or faithlessness to this
Commonwealth."

His great son therefore inherited this doctrine. It
was branded into his brain and flowed through his
veins; so that later when he had to meet the question of serving under the flag of the United States
or of obeying the will of Virginia, he drew his sword
in defense of his mother Commonwealth. When the
war was declared with England in 1812, Henry Lee
was living in Alexandria, having moved there to facilitate the education of his children; he was offered, and
accepted at once, a major general's commission in the
army. Before entering upon his duties he went to Baltimore on business, and while there visited the house
of Mr. Hanson, the editor of the Federal Republican.
"When he was about to leave he found the house surrounded by an angry mob, who were offended with the
editor for his articles in opposition to the war; as his
friend's life was threatened, he determined to assist him
in resisting the attack of the mob. The results of that
night proved nearly fatal to General Lee, and were disgraceful to party spirit." The injuries he received at
the hands of the excited mob prevented him from entering upon the campaign, obliged him to go to the West
Indies for his health, and ultimately caused his death.
While abroad, amid the fatal march of his disease, his
heart turned ever to his home and family. His letters to

his son, Charles Carter Lee, have been preserved, and are literary models, the object being to impress religion, morality, and learning upon his children, as well as to manifest his great affection for those left behind. "Fame," he writes, "in arms or art, is naught unless betrothed to virtue." And then: "You know I love my children, and how dear Smith* is to me. Give me a true description of his mind, temper, and habits. Tell me of Anne. Has she grown tall? And how is my last, in looks and understanding? Robert was always good, and will be confirmed in his happy turn of mind by his ever-watchful and affectionate mother; does he strengthen his native tendency?" He wanted to know, too, whether his sons rode and shot well, bearing in mind a Virginian's solicitude always that his sons should be taught to ride, shoot, and tell the truth.

In his opinion, Hannibal was a greater soldier than Alexander or Cæsar; for he thought an ardent excitement of the mind in defending menaced rights brings forth the greatest display of genius, of which, forty-four years afterward, his great son was an illustrious example. On June 18, 1817, from Nassau, he writes: "This is the day of the month when your dear mother became my wife, and it is not so hot in this tropical region as it was then at Shirley. Since that happy day, marked only by the union of two humble lovers, it has become conspicuous as the day our war with Great Britain was declared in Washington, and the one that sealed the doom of Bonaparte on the field of Waterloo. The British general, rising *gradatim* from his first blow struck in Portugal, climbed on that day to the summit of fame, and became distinguished by the first of titles, 'Deliverer of the Civilized World.' Alexander, Hannibal, and Cæsar, among the ancients; Marlborough, Eugene, Turenne, and Frederick, among the moderns, opened their arms to receive him as a brother in glory."

Again he tells him "that Thales, Pittacus, and others in Greece taught the doctrine of morality almost in our very words, 'Do unto others as you would they should do unto you,' and directs his son's attention to the fact

---

* Sydney Smith Lee, of the navy.

that the beautiful Arab couplet, written three centuries before Christ, announced the duty of every good man, even in the moment of destruction, not only to forgive, but to benefit the destroyer, as the sandal tree, in the instant of its overthrow, sheds perfume on the axe that fells it." The principles sought to be inculcated in these admirable letters will be found running through their lives, lodged firmly in their characters, and their constant reappearance in the life of one of them is an evidence of the impression made.

At the expiration of nearly five years, finding that there was no hope of his ultimate recovery, he determined to return to his family and friends. In January, 1818, he took passage in a New England schooner bound from Nassau to New Providence and Boston. On nearing the coast of the United States he became so much worse that he requested the captain to direct his course to Cumberland Island, lying off the coast of Georgia. He knew that his former trusted friend, General Nathanael Greene, had an estate there, and that there resided his married daughter, Mrs. James Shaw. Next to dying within the limits of his native State he preferred to furl the flag of a celebrated career under the generous roof and kindly influence of the hospitable daughter of a beloved brother soldier. He was landed at "Dungeness," known as the most beautiful and attractive residence on the Georgia coast, and here he was lovingly received and tenderly cared for. From the window of his sick-room "an extensive view of the Atlantic Ocean, of Cumberland Sound, and the low-lying verdant shores of Georgia could be seen upon the one side, while upon the other lay attractive gardens and groves of oranges and olives, while grand live oaks swayed solemnly to and fro loaded with pendent moss."

General Henry Lee's sufferings, consequent upon the injuries received in Baltimore, were intense. Mrs. Shaw, General Greene's daughter, said that after his arrival at "Dungeness" they still continued, and that a surgical operation was proposed as offering some hope of prolonging his life ; but he replied that an eminent physician, to whose skill and care during his sojourn in the West Indies he was much indebted, had disapproved a resort to the proposed operation. His surgeon in attendance still urging it, he put an end to the discussion by saying: "My dear sir, were the great Washington alive and here, joining you in advocating it, I would still resist." His agony at times was very great, causing irritation to overcome his rarely failing amiability. At times he would lose self-control and order his servants and every one else from the room. At length an old woman who had been Mrs. Greene's favorite maid, and who was then an esteemed and privileged family servant, was selected to wait upon him. The first thing General Lee did as she entered his room was to hurl his boot at her head and order her out. Entirely unused to such treatment, without saying a word she deliberately picked up the boot and threw it back. The effect produced was marked and instantaneous. The features of the stern warrior relaxed, in the midst of his pain and anger a smile passed over his countenance, and from that moment to the day of his death he would permit no one except "Mom Sarah" to do him special service. In the presence of the angel of death he recognized and rewarded pluck and spirit in an old negro nurse, even as he did courage in the breasts of his soldiers.

Not the least among the recollections of "Dungeness" is the fact that the last days of one of the great heroes of the Revolution were passed there; and when the "flowers of spring could no longer charm by their beauty and fragrance, or the soft southern wind bring health and surcease of pain to the suffering and dying, it received into its hospitable bosom and folded in one long and affectionate embrace all that was mortal of the gallant, gifted, and honored dead." Henry Lee and Nathanael Greene now sleep but a short distance apart, where the "recollections of their brave deeds and the grateful songs of the true lovers of liberty are caught up by the billows of a common ocean." Two months after the sick soldier landed he was dead. Every token of respect was shown by the United States Navy vessels in Cumberland Sound; their colors were put at half-mast, as well as the flags at the military headquarters of the army on Amelia Island. Citizens from the adjoining islands united in paying their respects. Commodore

Henley, of the navy, superintended the last details. A full army band was in attendance, and Captains Elton, Finch, and Madison, and Lieutenants Fitzhugh and Ritchie, of the navy, and Mr. Lyman, of the army, acted as pall-bearers. Upon the stone marking his grave is this inscription: "Sacred to the Memory of General Henry Lee, of Virginia. Obiit March 25, 1818, Ætat 63."

Not long before the war of 1861–'65 the Legislature of Virginia passed resolutions for the appointment of a committee who, with the consent of his sons, should remove the remains to the capital city of Virginia, where a suitable monument would be erected to his memory. The commencement of hostilities prevented the accomplishment of this purpose. The sad duty had not been performed before by his sons, because one, Major Henry Lee, was abroad, one was an officer of the army, another of the navy, the fourth a lawyer, and their respective duties kept them widely apart, so that the matter, though frequently referred to in their correspondence, had never been fully arranged. The remains of "Light-Horse Harry," therefore, still rest amid the magnolias, cedars, and myrtles of beautiful "Dungeness."

In many respects this officer was one of the most remarkable men of his day. He was a patriot and soldier, whose personal courage was tested in the fire of battle; an orator, a writer of vigorous and terse English, with a happy facility for expression rarely equaled. His book, called the Memoirs of the War of "76," is the standard work to-day of events in the war in the Southern Department of the United States. Two editions of it had been exhausted, and in 1869 a third was issued by his son, R. E. Lee, who, forgetful of his own great deeds, was desirous only of perpetuating those of his distinguished father.

General Henry Lee was twice married: first to Matilda, the daughter of Philip Ludwell Lee, of Stratford, and afterward to Anne Hill Carter, daughter of Charles Hill Carter, of Shirley. Four children were born from the first marriage. The eldest was named after his beloved commander, General Nathanael Greene, and died in infancy. The second son died when ten years old. The miniature of this child he always thereafter wore, and it is still preserved in the family. The third son,

Henry, was born in 1787, and died in Paris, France, January 30, 1837. He graduated at William and Mary College, and served with credit in the War of 1812. He was appointed by General Jackson Consul to Algiers in 1829. In journeying through Italy he met the mother of the great Napoleon, and, being an admirer of his Italian campaigns, determined to write his life; the book is well written, as are other works of his.

The daughter married Bernard Carter, a brother of her stepmother. The children by General Henry Lee's second marriage were Algernon Sydney, Charles Carter, Sydney Smith, and Robert Edward, and two daughters, Anne and Mildred. The first boy lived only eighteen months. The second, named after his wife's father, was educated at Cambridge. "We have just heard," writes his father from San Domingo, June 26, 1816, "that you are fixed at the University of Cambridge, the seminary of my choice. You will there have not only excellent examples to encourage your love and practice of virtue, but ample scope to pursue learning to its foundation, thereby fitting yourself to be useful to your country." Charles Carter Lee afterward studied law, and was a most intellectual, learned, and entertaining man. His social qualities were of the highest order, his humor inimitable; his classic wit flowed, as clear as the mountain stream, from a well-stored mind. He was a boon companion and the first guest invited to the banquet; around him all clustered, and from his vicinity peals of laughter always resounded. His speeches, songs, and stories are marked traditions in the family to-day. Gifted with a most retentive memory, and being a great reader, especially of history, his recollection of all he had read made him a most instructive and agreeable companion. Every subject received its best treatment from his genius. He was thoroughly conversant with biblical literature, and had been known to maintain the leading part in discussions of the Bible with a roomful of ministers whose duty it was to expound it. In every drawing-room his presence was most warmly welcomed. At every festive board his song or speech was hailed with enthusiastic greeting. He was clever, generous, liberal, and free-hearted. When paying visits

with his brothers—and the three often went together—
should wine happen to be offered, Smith and Robert
with their usual abstemiousness would decline; Carter,
however, would accept, remarking: "I have always told
these boys that I would drink their share of wine, provided they would keep me generously supplied." He
wrote, too, with beauty and fluency of expression, and
once said to his brother Robert :. "The Government em-
ploys you to do its fighting; it should engage me to
write your reports. I admit your superiority in the exercise of the sword and in planning campaigns. I am,
however, as you know, the better writer of the two, and
can make my pen mightier than your sword after the battle is over. We could thus combine and be irresistible."
He died, and was buried at his country seat, Windsor Forest, in Powhatan County. The third son, Sydney Smith,
entered the United States Navy at an early age, and
served with marked distinction in that service for thirty-
four years. When Virginia withdrew from the Union of
States he accepted service in the Southern navy.

A daughter of General R. E. Lee writes of him: "No
one who ever saw him can forget his beautiful face,
charming personality, and grace of manner, which, joined
to a nobility of character and goodness of heart, attracted all who came in contact with him, and made him
the most generally beloved and popular of men. This
was especially so with regard to women, to whom his
conduct was that of a *preux chevalier*, the most chivalric
and courteous; and, having no daughters of his own,
he turned with the tenderest affection to the daughters
of his brother Robert. His public service of more than
thirty years in the navy of the United States is well
known. He entered it as a boy of fifteen, and faithfully
served his country by land and sea in many climes and on
many oceans. He was in Japan with Commodore Perry,
commanding his flagship, when that inaccessible country was practically opened to the commerce of the
world. He was Commandant of the Naval Academy at
Annapolis, and afterward in command of the navy yard
at Philadelphia. When the war of secession began he
was stationed in Washington, but when Virginia seceded
he did not hesitate to abandon the comforts and security

of the present and ambitions of the future and cast his lot with his native State in a war which, from the very nature of things, there could be but little hope for a naval officer. Uninfluenced then by hope of either fame or fortune, he sadly parted with the friends and comrades of a lifetime, including General Scott, who had been likewise devoted to him as he was to his brother, and for four years served the Southern Confederacy with the same ardor and energy and unselfishness that he had previously given to the whole country. When the end came he accepted the situation with characteristic resignation and fortitude."

The eldest daughter married Mr. William Marshall, and lived in Baltimore. When the war cloud overshadowed the land, Judge Marshall was ardently devoted to the cause of the Union; their only son was educated at West Point, and remained in the army of the United States during the war which followed. It was natural, therefore, that the wife's sympathies in the pending struggle should be with husband and child. For many years she was a great invalid and rarely left her couch. Sick and tortured with conflicting emotions, her days were days of trial. It is said she would smilingly agree with her husband in the hope that the armies of the United States would gain victories over the troops of the South, and then into a thousand pieces dash all former arguments by shaking her head and saying: "But, after all, they can't whip Robert." It was the triumph of ties of consanguinity over all other bonds. Mildred, the youngest daughter, married Mr. Edward Vernon Childe, of Massachusetts, who removed to and lived in Paris, where she died, where her children were brought up and educated. The eldest son, Edward Lee Childe, possessing an excellent education, fine literary ability, and a love for the memory of his great uncle, wrote a life of him in French, which has been well received by the people of that country, and was translated into English, in 1875, by Mr. George Litting, of London.

CHAPTER II.

SEVENTY-FIVE years after the birth of Washington,
Robert Edward, the fourth son of General Henry Lee
and Anne Hill Carter, was born at Stratford, Westmoreland County, Virginia, on the 19th of January, 1807. If
he inherited much from a long and illustrious line of
paternal ancestors, he no less fell heir to the strong
characteristics of his mother's family, one of the oldest
and best in Virginia. The unselfishness, generosity,
purity, and faithfulness of the Virginia Carters are widely known, and they have always been "true to all occasions true." In his mother was personified all the gentle
and sweet traits of a noble woman. Her whole life was
admirable, and her love for her children beyond all other
thoughts. To her watchful care they were early confided by the long absence and death of her distinguished
husband.

Robert was four years old when his father removed
the family to Alexandria, six when he visited the West
Indies for his health, and eleven when he died. If he
was early trained in the way he should go, his mother
trained him. If he was "always good," as his father
wrote, she labored to keep him so. If his principles
were sound and his life a success, to her, more than
to any other, should the praise be given. This lovely
woman, as stated, was the daughter of Charles Carter,
of Shirley, who resided in his grand old mansion on the
banks of the James River, some twenty miles below
Richmond, then, as now, the seat of an open, profuse,
and refined hospitality, and still in the possession of the
Carters. Mrs. Henry Lee's mother was Anne Moore,

and her grandmother a daughter of Alexander Spotts-
wood, the soldier who fought with Marlborough at Blen-
heim, and was afterward sent to Virginia as governor
in 1710, and whose descent can be traced in a direct
line from King Robert the Bruce, of Scotland.

Robert Edward Lee could look back on long lines
of paternal and maternal ancestors, but it is doubtful
whether he ever exercised the privilege; in a letter to
his wife, written in front of Petersburg, February, 1865,
he says: " I have received your note. I am very much
obliged to Mr. —— for the trouble he has taken in
relation to the Lee genealogy. I have no desire to
have it published, and do not think it would afford
sufficient interest beyond the immediate family to compensate for the expense. I think the money had better
be applied to relieving the poor. . . ."

He felt a natural pride in their achievements, but
no one knew better than he that in a republic, and in
a great war, a man's ancestry could not help him, but
that place and promotion depended upon individual
merit. His lineage has been traced because the descent of a celebrated man excites attention, just as it
is interesting to discover the source of a noble river
whose blessings to commerce can not be measured. In
consequence of the absence of the elder brothers, the
ill health of one sister, and the youth of another, to
Robert's care, in a measure, his mother was committed.
After his father's departure to the tropics she watched
over his daily life with tender solicitude, and he was,
she said, both a daughter and a son to her. With filial
devotion to her comfort his hours out of school were
given. He waited on her, nursed her when sick, drove
with her, obeyed her every wish, and this reciprocal love
was a goodly picture in old Alexandria to those who
saw mother and son in those days. As Robert grew in
years he grew in grace; he was like the young tree
whose roots, firmly imbedded in the earth, hold it
straight from the hour it was first planted till it de-
velops into majestic proportions. With the fostering
care of such a mother the son must go straight, for she
had planted him in the soil of truth, morality, and religion, so that his boyhood was marked by everything

that produces nobility of character in manhood. The handsome boy was studious and sedate, was popular with other boys, stood high in the estimation of his teachers, and his early inspiration was good, for his first thoughts were directed upon lofty subjects by an excellent mother.

His birthplace and that of Washington were not only in the same county but only a short distance apart. The landscape of that section of Virginia was the first that greeted the eyes of each. The Potomac River, in all its grandeur and beauty, flowed past Stratford as well as Pope's Creek. Alexandria afterward became his town, as it had before been the town of Washington. The married life of the two was respectively passed at Mount Vernon and Arlington, the same river rolling at their feet, while the old town stood dignified and historic between the mansions proudly connecting the name and fame of their occupants.

Robert went first to the Alexandria Academy, being under the tuition of Mr. Leary, who was ever after his firm friend. Later he attended the famous school of Mr. Benjamin Hallowell, in Alexandria, whose house, still standing, is yet conducted as a popular school. Ben. Hallowell was a Quaker of the Quakers. His school stood high; so did he as a teacher. "Brimstone Castle" the boys called it, on account of its color. Mr. Hallowell says that young Lee was an exemplary student, perfectly observant and respectful, and those who knew him, either in the charm of the domestic circle or amid the roar of battle, knew that good old Mr. Hallowell's opinion must have been correct.

The time had now arrived to select a profession, and to the army his inclination pointed—a direction which probably resulted from a son's desire to follow in his father's footsteps, especially when that father had been so distinguished in the profession. He was now a modest, manly youth, in his eighteenth year, who resolved to take care of himself and relieve his mother to that extent. His father's career had reflected credit upon his country; could he not hope to do the same? Sydney Smith Lee, his next oldest brother, had already entered the navy, and was supporting himself; so he decided to go in the army. The application for an appointment to the United States Military Academy was successful, and in 1825 his name was entered upon the rolls of that celebrated institution. He had now four years of hard study, vigorous drill, and was absorbing strategy and tactics to be useful to him in after-years. His excellent habits and close attention to all duties did not desert him; he received no demerits; was a cadet officer in his class, and during his last year held the post of honor in the aspirations of cadet life—the adjutancy of the corps. He graduated second in a class of forty-six, and was commissioned second lieutenant in the Corps of Engineers. It is interesting to notice that his eldest son, George Washington Custis Lee, also entered the Military Academy twenty-five years after his father, was also the cadet adjutant, graduated first in his class, and was assigned to the Engineer Corps. During his whole course at West Point Robert was a model cadet, his clothes looked nice and new, his crossbelts, collar, and summer trousers were as white as the driven snow mounting guard upon the mountain top, and his brass breast and waist plates were mirrors to reflect the image of the inspector. He conscientiously performed his tours of guard duty, whether the non-commissioned officer of the guard was approaching his post or sleeping in his quarters. He never "ran the sentinel post," did not go off the limits to the "Benny Havens" of his day, or put "dummies" in his bed, to deceive the officer in charge as he made his inspection after taps, and at the parades stood steady in line. It was a pleasure for the inspecting officer to look down the barrel of his gun, it was bright and clean, and its stock was rubbed so as to almost resemble polished mahogany.

Cadet Lee in 1829 became Lieutenant Lee of the Engineer Corps of the United States Army. The cadets who graduate in each class with first honors are assigned to it, and its ranks are kept full of first-class material; its members are composed of students who obey the regulations, are proficient in their studies, and receive few demerits. From this scientific corps distinguished men and great soldiers have issued, and to be an officer of the United States Engineer Corps is a passport everywhere.

A short time previous to the late war a number of officers of the different arms of service were assembled in one of the rooms at West Point. The conversation turned, as it often did, upon the relative merits of the different arms of services, each officer contending for his own branch; finally an officer of infantry, who afterward became a distinguished major general in the army of the United States, said: "You gentlemen who graduate at the head of your respective classes are of opinion that you are the most talented, and possibly will make the best soldiers and most intelligent officers of the army; you will find, however, that should war actually take place between the Northern and Southern States, and you get in a tight place on the field of battle, you can not work yourself out *with equations.*" All of which is very true. A courier has been known to tell his superior officer how to extricate his troops in a perilous position under fire, because he had more military perception, though less education and engineering skill.

Great soldiers, like poets, are born, not made. Military training, discipline, the study of strategy, and grand tactics are powerful re-enforcements to natural genius. All the army commanders from 1861 to 1865, on either side, were West Point graduates; but many West Pointers were indifferent officers; on the other hand, others climbed high on Fame's military ladder who never attended a military school. Generals Logan and Terry on the Northern, and Generals Forrest and Gordon on the Southern side, were distinguished examples; but if to their soldierly qualifications a military education had been added, their ascent to distinction would have been greatly facilitated.

Lieutenant Lee entered upon the usual life of a young officer of engineers; his chosen profession had his earnest attention, and every effort was made to acquire information. He knew his studies at West Point were only the foundation upon which to build the life edifice. Without continued application to the principles of engineering and study he could not hope to rise above the ordinary level of the military graduate. So his army career began with the fixed determination to put aside daily pleasures of life where they conflicted with daily hours of duty. Officers in this branch of the service had pleasant stations, necessarily near or in the cities. Fortifications for the defense of harbors, forts for the protection of seaports, streams whose currents made bars at wrong places, and other similar works must receive the attention of the engineer. His location was therefore near the centers of civilization. Cavalry and infantry graduates of West Point were ordered to posts where the sun goes down behind the western hills; guarding long lines of frontier, scouting, and fighting hostile tribes of Indians were their particular duties. The temptations incident to city life did not lie so much in their course as in the path of the engineer. The pleasures and fascinations of social life everywhere surrounded him. As soon as he unbuckled sword belt there was but a step to take to get into the gay world. It is not to be wondered at, therefore, that sometimes the engineer drank wine when it was red, and did not seek his quarters till the sun had gilded with its first glance the spires of the neighboring church. The artillery officer enjoyed with his comrades his mess table; the infantry officer occasionally had moistened lips from a canteen of frontier fire water; while the "bold dragoon who scorned all care" rode far and sometimes drank deep.

Lee was naturally exposed to an engineer's temptations, but was careful and abstemious. He went much in the society of ladies—always most congenial to him. His conversation was bright, his wit refined and pleasant. Cement, mortar, lime, curves, tangents, and straight professional lines disappeared then. He enjoyed a dress parade of this kind, was happy in the drawing-room in the evening, and happy in his work on the parapet next day. He was in love from boyhood. Fate brought him to the feet of one who, by birth, education, position, and family tradition, was best suited to be his life companion. Mary Custis, the daughter of George Washington Parke Custis, of Arlington, and Robert E. Lee, were married on the 30th of June, 1831, only two years after he had

emerged from his Alma Mater. They had known
each other when she was a child at Arlington and he
a young boy in Alexandria, some eight miles away.
It is said she met him to admire when he came back
to Alexandria on furlough from the Military Academy. It was the first time any one in that vicinity had ever seen him in his cadet uniform. He
was handsomer than ever; straight, erect, symmet-
rical in form, with a finely shaped head on a pair of
broad shoulders. He was then twenty years old
and a fine specimen of a West Point cadet on leave
of absence. The impressions produced were of an
enduring nature, and the officer, upon graduation,
followed up the advantage gained by the attractive
cadet.

G. W. P. Custis was the adopted son of Washington and the grandson of Mrs. Washington. Lee was
therefore to marry a great granddaughter of Mrs.
Washington, and was a fortunate man, not so much,
perhaps, from these ties, but because of the great qualities of head and heart possessed by Mary Custis, his
affianced bride. It is difficult to say whether she was
more lovely on that memorable June evening when the
Rev. Mr. Keith asked her, "Wilt thou have this man to
be thy wedded husband?" or after many years had
passed, and she was seated in her large armchair in
Richmond, almost unable to move from chronic rheumatism, but busily engaged in knitting socks for sockless
Southern soldiers. The public notice of the marriage
was short:

"Married, June 30, 1831, at Arlington House, by
the Rev. Mr. Keith, Lieutenant Robert E. Lee, of the
United States Corps of Engineers, to Miss Mary A.
R. Custis, only daughter of G. W. P. Custis, Esq."
The modesty of the newly married couple was spared
the modern newspaper notice of what the bride
wore at her wedding and what she had packed in
her trunks, and her presents and trousseau are in
happy oblivion. Beautiful old Arlington was in all
her glory that night. The stately mansion never held
a happier assemblage. "Its broad portico and wide-

spread wings held out open arms, as it were, to welcome the coming guest. Its simple Doric columns
graced domestic comfort with a classic air. Its halls
and chambers were adorned with the patriots and
heroes and with illustrations and relics of the great
Revolution and of the 'Father of his Country,' and
without and within, history and tradition seemed to
breathe their legends upon a canvas as soft as a dream
of peace."

At the expiration of the usual leave of absence
granted officers who marry, Lieutenant Lee returned
to his duties as assistant engineer at Hampton Roads.
For four years he labored to make the harbor defensible, and to construct there strong works, little dreaming that it would be his fate to study how to demolish
them twenty-seven years afterward. While stationed
there the negro insurrection in Southampton took place,
and the young lieutenant writes to his mother-in-law
about it, telling her that it is at an end, and adding that
the troops returned to Fort Monroe last night "from
Jerusalem, where they did not arrive until the whole
affair was concluded. Colonel Worth says that, from
all he can learn, he is satisfied the plot was widely extended, and that the negroes, anticipating the time of
rising by one week, mistaking the third Sunday for the
last in the month, defeated the whole scheme and prevented much mischief. It is ascertained that they used
their religious assemblies, which ought to have been devoted to better purposes, for forming and maturing their
plans, and that their preachers were the leading men. A
man belonging to a Mrs. Whitehead, and one of their
preachers, was the chief, under the title of Major Nelson,
and his first act was to kill his mistress, five children, and
one grandchild. However, there are many instances of
their defending their masters, and one poor fellow, from
the inconsiderate and almost unwarrantable haste of the
whites, was sadly rewarded. He belonged to a Mr. Blunt,
and himself and two others, assisted by his master and his
son, nobly fought with them against twenty of the blacks;
after beating them off and running in great haste after
horses for them to escape on, a party of whites suddenly
came up and, thinking the horses were for other pur-

poses, shot him dead.   The whole number of blacks
taken and killed did not amount to the number of whites
murdered by them."

From that point he was ordered to Washington and
made assistant to the chief engineer, an agreeable change,
for it brought him near the home of his wife.   A fine
horse carried him every morning from Arlington to his
Washington office and back every evening.   He loved
his chosen profession, and was rising rapidly in it.   Now
he could combine equestrianism with engineering, and he
was happy, and must have been sometimes merry, for his
late lamented military secretary, General Long, narrates
an incident of his inviting Captain Macomb, a brother
officer, to get behind him on horseback one evening on
his return to Arlington.   Macomb accepted the invitation, and the two gayly rode along the great public
avenue in Washington, passing by the President's house,
bowing to Cabinet officers, and behaving in rather a
hilarious way generally.   It is difficult for a soldier of
the Army of Northern Virginia to picture his commanding general in a scene such as has been described.

Five years after leaving his Alma Mater he was promoted from second to first lieutenant of engineers, and
in two years more reached a captaincy.   In 1835 he was
made assistant astronomer of the commission appointed
to lay the boundary line between Ohio and Michigan.
Two years afterward he bade adieu to Arlington to obey
an order to proceed to St. Louis to make estimates, prepare plans, and devise means to prevent the "Great
Father of Waters" from leaving his legitimate channel
and overrunning property upon which he had no claims,
for the Mississippi had threatened to leave the St. Louis
side and become a flowing citizen of Illinois.   In the
performance of this duty he came prominently into
notice again; he was so active, so indefatigable, and
worked so intelligently and successfully, that the system of river improvements first introduced there is to
this day followed.   Some of the citizens of that section
did not understand his methods, and threatened to drive
him and his working parties away, and at one time actually brought cannon to accomplish their purpose.   They
did not comprehend the labors of this quiet, methodical

engineer, or understand the reason why piles were driven and cofferdams made at acute angles to the shore; nor did they understand that the flow of the waters being retarded in these angles, sediment was deposited, land made, and the river, in consequence, forced back and confined to its channels on the St. Louis side.

While thus professionally engaged it occurred to him that he would like to possess a seal with the family's Coat of Arms, and he writes to an Alexandria cousin about it:

ST. LOUIS, *August* 20, 1838.

MY DEAR CASSIUS AND COUSIN: I believe I once spoke to you on the subject of getting for me the Crest, Coat of Arms, etc., of the Lee family, and which, sure enough, you never did. My object in making the request is for the purpose of having a seal cut with the impression of said Coat, which I think is due from a man of my large family to his posterity, and which I have thought, perhaps foolishly enough, might as well be right as wrong. If, therefore, you can assist me in this laudable enterprise I shall be much obliged, and by enveloping it securely, directed to me at this place, and sending it either by mail or some safe hand to the Engineer Office, Washington City, without any word or further direction, it will come safely to hand. I once saw in the hands of Cousin Edmund, for the only time in my life, our family tree, and as I begin in my old age to feel a little curiosity relative to my forefathers, their origin, whereabouts, etc., any information you can give me will increase the obligation.

So sit down one of these hot evenings and write it off for me, or at any rate the substance, and tell my Cousin Phillippa not to let you forget it. I wish you would at the same time undeceive her on a certain point, for, as I understand, she is laboring under a grievous error.

Tell her that it is the farthest from my wish to detract from any of the little Lees, but as to her little boy being equal to Mr. Rooney,* it is a thing not even to be supposed, much less believed, although we live in a credulous country, where people stick at nothing from a coon story to a sea serpent. You must remember us particularly to her, to Uncle Edmund, Cousins Sally, Hannah, and all the Lloyds.

I believe I can tell you nothing here that would interest you, except that we are all well, although my dame has been a little complaining for a day or two. The elections are all over, the "Van-ites" have carried the day in the State, although the Whigs in this district carried their entire ticket, and you will have the

---

* A pet name for his son, William H. F. Lee.—EDITOR.

pleasure of hearing the great expunger again thunder from his place in the Senate against banks, bribery, and corruption. While on the river I can not help being on the lookout for that stream of gold that was to ascend the Mississippi, tied up in silk-net purses! It would be a pretty sight, but the tide has not yet made up here. Let me know whether you can enlighten me on the point in question. And believe me,

Yours very truly, R. E. LEE.

C. F. LEE, ESQ., Alexandria, Virginia.

And to Mrs. Lee he writes:

ST. LOUIS, *September* 4, 1840.

A few evenings since, feeling lonesome, as the saying is, and out of sorts, I got on a horse and took a ride. On returning through the lower part of the town, I saw a number of little girls all dressed up in their white frocks and pantalets, their hair plaited and tied up with ribbons, running and chasing each other in all directions. I counted twenty-three nearly the same size. As I drew up my horse to admire the spectacle a man appeared at the door with the twenty-fourth in his arms. "My friend," said I, "are all these your children?" "Yes," he said, "and there are nine more in the house, and this is the youngest." Upon further inquiry, however, I found that they were only temporarily his, and that they were invited to a party at his house. He said, however, he had been admiring them before I came up, and just wished that he had a million of dollars and that they were all his in reality. I do not think the eldest exceeded seven or eight years old. It was the prettiest sight I have seen in the West, and perhaps in my life. . . .

On the completion of his great services here he was sent to New York and stationed at Fort Hamilton to perfect the defenses of the splendid harbor of that great city. A letter to his wife from that point gives a glimpse of the humor which constantly found vent in his private life. He writes:

FORT HAMILTON, NEW YORK, *January* 14, 1846.

This week I have been closely occupied here. I have kept "Jim" and "*Miss* Leary" (his servants) constantly moving, cleaning up, and fear I will wear them down. I do not know whether it was your departure or my somber phiz which brought Miss Leary out Sunday in a full suit of mourning. A black alpaca trimmed with crape and a thick row of jet buttons on each sleeve, from the shoulder to the wrist, and three rows on the skirt, diverging from the waist to the hem; it was, however, surmounted by a dashing cap with gay ribbons.

He was now a captain of engineers, and his mettle was soon to be tried in the fiery furnace of war, for his country and the Republic of Mexico were daily growing more angry with each other. Mexico, from 1519, when Hernando Cortez marched through the causeway leading into its Capital City to the present period, has been an object of much interest to other countries. Commencing with the Indian Emperor Montezuma's costly presents to Cortez, the land has been associated with inexhaustible supplies of gold and silver. The Spanish commander, from his quarters near the temple of the Aztec god of war, dreamed of infinite wealth for himself, his soldiers, and his country.

A fascinating interest in Mexico has always kept pace with the progress and growth of the contiguous American Republic. Upon the final overthrow of the Mexicans by the Spaniards, the adjoining sections were settled by the latter, and a permanent location was made in Texas, at San Antonio de Bexar, in 1692. France, in selling to the United States Louisiana, claimed the boundary line to be the River Rio Grande del Norte, and assigned this boundary claim to the United States. It was, however, relinquished by the American Republic to Spain, in a treaty made with that country in 1812. When Mexico, in 1820, threw off the Spanish yoke, she obtained at the same time the domain of Texas. Afterward Stephen F. Austin obtained from the Mexican Government large tracts of land in Texas and established colonies on them. Citizens of the United States were naturally attracted there, and as they grew in numbers wanted a government similar in form to the one they had left. Stephen Austin was sent to Santa Anna, then Emperor of Mexico, with petitions praying for a separate state organization, and to be no longer united with Cohahuila, the neighboring Mexican province. Austin's petition, it seems, was more than Santa Anna could stand, and he threw him into prison and kept him there over a year. The American Texans, some ten thousand in number, were indignant, and determined to resist the Mexican Emperor's authority. A war ensued, and the redoubtable Santa Anna was finally overthrown and captured at the battle of San Jacinto, April 21, 1836.

Texas was later an applicant for membership to the union of American States. Her independence had been acknowledged by Great Britain, the United States, and other Powers; but Bustamente, who succeeded Santa Anna, repealed the treaty Mexico had with Texas and declared war. In the United States opinion was divided between annexation and war. President Van Buren, a citizen of New York, would not entertain annexation, while a successor—John Tyler, of Virginia—favored it. A treaty made to carry out the provisions of annexation was rejected by the Senate. In 1844 it became a party question, and by the election of James K. Polk, of Tennessee, who was in favor of it, over Henry Clay, of Kentucky, whose adherents were opposed to it, the people of the United States practically decided in favor of annexation. It was then natural and proper that the United States Government should look closely after the interests of her new possessions, and to General Zachary Taylor they were confided. A Virginian by birth, he was appointed a lieutenant in the Seventh Infantry, United States Army, in 1808, being one of the new regiments authorized by Congress, upon the recommendation of President Thomas Jefferson. He became conspicuous in the Indian contests, and was especially famous after winning the battle of Okeechobee in the Seminole War. Promoted to be a brigadier general in 1837, three years thereafter he was assigned to the command of the Southern Division of the Western Department. He was in place, therefore, to defend Texas against the Mexicans, to insist on the Rio Grande boundary line, and to prevent Mexican authority from being extended to the River Nueces, which was claimed as the proper line. He was the right man in the right place, and when Arista, the Mexican general, crossed the Rio Grande with six thousand men, near Fort Brown, Taylor, being in the vicinity, promptly attacked with two thousand men and defeated him, assumed the offensive, crossed the Rio Grande, and war with Mexico became an accomplished fact. Palo Alto, Resaca de la Palma, Matamoras, Monterey, and Buena Vista are the stars in the military crown on the brow of " Old Rough and Ready," as he was called. Calm, silent. stern, possessed of military genius, this soldier at once became a favorite with the American people, and for his services was afterward elected to be the twelfth President of the United States. When Mexico's capital was decided to be the objective point of the campaign, Taylor's base of operations was too distant and his line of communication too long. It was thought advisable to select as the base of future operations Vera Cruz. General Winfield Scott, then commander in chief of the United States Army, was assigned to the command of the army to be concentrated for its reduction. The new army commander, Scott, was born near Petersburg, Va., in June, 1786, and was sixty-one years old when he began the siege of Vera Cruz on the 19th of March, 1847. He was an alumnus of William and Mary College, Williamsburg, Va., and a lawyer for two years before he was appointed to a lieutenancy in the artillery of the United States Army. His services in the war of 1812, and especially in the battles of Chippewa and Lundy's Lane, had made him famous. With a grand physique and imposing presence in full uniform, he was a splendid specimen of the American soldier. Being in command of the whole army, and in active charge of the army of invasion, his requests for the best officers, as well as ordnance, quartermasters' and commissaries' supplies, were promptly acceded to. A war with a foreign country was highly exciting and new to most of the army and navy officers, so that applications for service in Mexico rapidly rained upon the War Department, and the Secretary of War had no difficulty in sending to Mexico the most capable officers.

Engineers are as necessary to an army as sails are to a ship; they locate lines of battle, select positions for the artillery, make reconnoissances, and upon their reports the movements of the army are based. They draw topographical maps, construct roads and bridges, and guide troops in battle to positions they had previously reconnoitred. Scott soon drew to him from this branch of the service Totten, J. L. Smith, R. E. Lee, Beauregard, McClellan, Foster, Tower, Stevens, G. W. Smith, and others, and at once placed Captain Lee on his personal staff. This officer, when Scott was assembling the army at Tampico, for the purpose of investing and capturing Vera Cruz, was with General Wool, who had been assigned the duty of invading Mexico from the north, while Taylor advanced from Matamoras, and General Kearny from New Mexico.

In a letter to Mrs. Lee, dated Rio Grande, October 11, 1846, Captain Lee says: "We have met with no resistance yet. The Mexicans who were guarding the passage retired on our approach. There has been a great whetting of knives, grinding of swords, and sharpening of bayonets ever since we reached the river."

It seems on the eve of active operations Captain Lee's thoughts were ever returning to his family and home. In a letter to his two eldest sons (one thirteen and the other nine years of age), written from Camp near Saltillo, December 24, 1846, he says: "I hope good Santa Claus will fill my Rob's stocking to-night; that Mildred's, Agnes's, and Anna's may break down with good things. I do not know what he may have for you and Mary (his daughter), but if he only leaves for you one half of what I wish, you will want for nothing. I have frequently thought if I had one of you on each side of me riding on ponies, such as I could get you, I would be comparatively happy."

The little fellows had been writing to their father asking about his horses and the ponies in Mexico, etc. In reply he tells them "the Mexicans raise a large quantity of ponies, donkeys, and mules, and most of their corn, etc., is carried on the backs of these animals. These little donkeys will carry two hundred pounds on their backs, and the mules will carry three hundred on long journeys over the mountains. The ponies are used for riding and cost from ten to fifty dollars, according to their size and quality. I have three horses. Creole is my pet; she is a golden dun, active as a deer, and carries me over all the ditches and gullies that I have met with; nor has she ever yet hesitated at anything I have put her at; she is full-blooded and considered the prettiest thing in the army; though young, she has so far stood the campaign as well as any horses of the division." He then tells them about his other two—a dark bay, deep-chested, sturdy, and strong, that his servant Jim rides, and says that Jim has named him after himself; he goes on to say that he has ridden them all very hard, sometimes fifty or sixty miles a day.

He was still at Saltillo the next day: it was Christmas, and he had arranged a campaign in his own heart, which would result in his taking advantage of the holiday to write a letter to his wife. He tells Mrs. Lee that he had put aside that Christmas day to write to her, but just after breakfast orders were received to prepare for battle, intelligence having reached General Wool that the Mexican army was coming. " The troops stood to their arms and I lay on the grass with my sorrel mare saddled by my side and telescope directed to the pass of the mountain through which the road approached. The Mexicans, however, did not make their appearance. Many regrets were expressed at Santa Anna's having spoiled our Christmas dinner for which ample preparation had been made. The little roasters remained tied to the tent pins wondering at their deferred fate, and the headless turkeys retained their plumage unscathed. Finding the enemy did not come, preparations were again made for dinner. We have had many happy Christmases together. It is the first time we have been entirely separated at this holy time since our marriage. I hope it does not interfere with your happiness, surrounded as you are by father, mother, children, and dear friends. I therefore trust you are well and happy, and that this is the last time I shall be absent from you during my life. May God preserve and bless you till then and forever after is my constant prayer."

The American commander promptly availed himself of the talents of the engineer and summoned Lee to his side, and in the memorable campaign which followed, Lee was his military adviser and possessed his entire confidence. The high estimation and cordial friendship which the army commander ever thereafter displayed for his subordinate was born at Vera Cruz.

The city of Vera Cruz was surrounded by a wall and strengthened by forts, the castle of San Juan de Ulloa, its fortress, was defended by four hundred guns and five thousand men under General Morales. The soldierly genius of Scott at once told him there were but two ways to capture the city—either by storming or by the scientific principles of regular siege approaches.   In his " Little Cabinet," as he called it (it appears he was even then thinking of a future presidency)—consisting of Colonel Totten, Chief Engineer; Lieutenant-Colonel Hitchcock, Acting Inspector General; Captain R. E. Lee, Engineer; First-Lieutenant Henry L. Scott, Acting Adjutant General—these questions were taken up.   A deathbed discussion could hardly have been more solemn, the army commander tells us.   To his Cabinet he said : " We, of course, gentlemen, must take the city and castle before the return of the vomito, and then escape by pushing the contest into the healthy interior."   He was " strongly inclined to attempt to capture the place by laying siege to it, not by storming it."   The first method, in his opinion, " could be accomplished with moderate loss on his side.   The second method would, no doubt," said Scott, " be equally successful, but at the cost of immense slaughter on both sides, including non-combatants, Mexicans, and children, because the assault would have to be made in the dark, and the assailants dare not lose time in taking or guarding prisoners without incurring the certainty of becoming captives themselves, until all the strongholds of the place had been captured." The council determined upon a siege.   In two weeks the army and navy were ready to open fire, and one week's bombardment resulted in the capitulation of Vera Cruz, and the adjacent forts on the 29th of March, 1847.   In the preparatory two weeks Lee spent nights and days in incessant labor, and his enterprise, endurance, energy, and intelligent arrangement of all the necessary details of the siege were most conspicuous, and to him has been ascribed much credit for the victory.

At Vera Cruz Captain Lee met his brother, Lieutenant Sydney Smith Lee, of the United States Navy, and the soldier and sailor fought together.   In a letter written from Vera Cruz at the time, after describing a battery which had been placed in position by him, Captain Lee adds: " The first day this battery opened, Smith served one of the guns.   I had constructed the battery, and was there to direct its fire.   No matter where I turned, my eyes reverted to him, and I stood by his gun whenever I was not wanted elsewhere. Oh! I felt awfully, and am at a loss what I should have done had he been cut down before me. I thank God that he was saved. He preserved his usual cheerfulness, and I could see his white teeth through all the smoke and din of the fire. I had placed three 32- and three 68-pound guns in position. . . . Their fire was terrific, and the shells thrown from our battery were constant and regular discharges, so beautiful in their flight and so destructive in their fall. It was awful! My heart bled for the inhabitants. The soldiers I did not care so much for, but it was terrible to think of the women and children. . . . I heard from Smith to-day; he is quite well, and recovered from his fatigue."

And to his naval brother he writes on March 27, 1847, when it seems he wanted some liquors, in all probability for his guests, as his own abstemiousness was well known:

My DEAR SMITH: I tried to see you the night you went on board, but failed. I was too thankful you were saved through that hot fire. I felt awful at the thought of your being shot down before me. I can't get time to see you, nor have I time to attend to anything for myself. There is a French bark anchored by your fleet, and detained at Anton Lizardo—or was—from Bordeaux. She has some wines, etc. Can you, through any of your comrades, get me a box or two of claret, one of brandy, and four colored shirts. The latter are seventy-five cents each (I have two of them), and the brandy thirty-seven and a half cents per bottle. God bless and preserve you. Your battery (naval) has smashed that side of the town. I have been around the walls to examine. The Quartet Battery has been silenced. I grieve for the fine fellows that were killed there.

Very affectionately your brother,   R. E. LEE.

P. S.—Can you buy me a good telescope from the fleet? I have lost mine and am woefully at a loss.

Before leaving for the interior with the army, Captain Lee sought his brother to say good-by. In one of his letters he writes: "Went on board the Mississippi, and passed the night with Smith. I had scarcely been able to see him before, and wished, ere commencing work, to have one night with him. He was very well, but what a place is a ship to enjoy the company of one's brother!"

When Scott set out, on the 12th of April, from Vera
Cruz, to join his advanced divisions under Patterson
and Twiggs, in front of the heights of Cerro Gordo, Lee
accompanied him. It was the reconnoissance of this
officer at the head of the pioneers which found a possible
route for the troops and their light batteries, by which
the Mexican left could be turned. Santa Anna, who
commanded the Mexican army, said he did not believe
a goat could have come from that direction. In his
final report Scott thus speaks: "The reconnoissance,
begun by Lieutenant Beauregard, was continued by
Captain Lee, of the engineers, and a road made along
one of the slopes over chasms—out of the enemy's view
though reached by his fire—was discovered, till, arriving
at the Mexican lines, further reconnoissance became impossible without an action. I am compelled to make
special mention of Captain R. E. Lee, Engineer. This
officer greatly distinguished himself at the siege of Vera
Cruz; was indefatigable during these operations in reconnoissances, as daring as laborious, and of the utmost
value. Nor was he less conspicuous in planning batteries and in conducting columns from stations under
the heavy fire of the enemy." General Lee thus describes
the battle of Cerro Gordo:

"*Perote, April 25, 1847.*—The advance of the American troops, under Generals Patterson and Twiggs, were
encamped at the Plano del Rio, and three miles to their
front Santa Anna and his army were intrenched in the
pass of Cerro Gordo, which was remarkably strong.
The right of the Mexican line rested on the river at a
perpendicular rock, unscalable by man or beast, and
their left on impassable ravines; the main road was defended by field works containing thirty-five cannon; in
their rear was the mountain of Cerro Gordo, surrounded
by intrenchments in which were cannon and crowned by
a tower overlooking all—it was around this army that
it was intended to lead our troops. I reconnoitered the
ground in the direction of the ravines on their left, and
passed around the enemy's rear. On the 16th a party
was set to work in cutting out the road, on the 17th I
led General Twiggs's division in the rear of a hill in
front of Cerro Gordo, and in the afternoon, when it be-

came necessary to drive them from the hill where we intended to construct a battery at night, the first intimation of our presence or intentions were known. During all that night we were at work in constructing the battery, getting up the guns, ammunition, etc., and they in strengthening their defenses on Cerro Gordo. Soon after sunrise our batteries opened, and I started with a column to turn their left and to get on the Jalapa road. Notwithstanding their efforts to prevent us in this, we were perfectly successful, and the working party, following our footsteps, cut out the road for the artillery. In the mean time our storming party had reached the crest of Cerro Gordo, and, seeing their whole left turned and the position of our soldiers on the Jalapa road, they broke and fled. Those in the pass laid down their arms. General Pillow's attack on their right failed. All their cannon, arms, ammunition, and most of their men fell into our hands. The papers can not tell you what a horrible sight a field of battle is, nor will I, owing to my accompanying General Twiggs's division in the pursuit, and being since constantly in the advance. I believe all our friends are safe. I think I wrote you that my friend Joe Johnston * was wounded the day before I arrived at the Plano del Rio while reconnoitering. He was wounded in the arm and about the groin; both balls are out, and he was doing well and was quite comfortable when I left; the latter wound was alone troublesome. Captain Mason, of the rifles, was badly wounded in the leg, and General Shields was wounded in the chest; I have heard contradictory reports that he was doing well and that he was dead. I hope the former. Jalapa is the most beautiful country I have seen in Mexico, and will compare with any I have seen elsewhere. I wish it was in the United States, and that I was located with you and the children around me in one of its rich, bright valleys. I can conceive nothing more beautiful in the way of landscape or mountain scenery. We ascended upward of four thousand feet that morning, and whenever we looked back the rich valley below was glittering in the morning sun and the light morning clouds flitting around us. On

---

* Afterward the distinguished commander.

reaching the top, the valley appeared at intervals between the clouds which were below us, and high over
all towered Orizaba, with its silver cap of snow.   The
castle or fort of Perote is one of the best finished that
I have ever seen—very strong, with high, thick walls,
bastioned fronts, and deep, wide ditch.   It is defective
in construction and is very spacious, covers twenty-five
acres, and although there is within its walls nearly three
thousand troops, it is not yet full.   Within the fort is a
beautiful chapel, in one corner of which is the tomb of
Guadalupe Victoria.   There are various skulls, images,
etc., in the sanctuaries.   This morning I attended the
Episcopal service within the fort.   It was held on the
parade.   The minister was a Mr. McCarty, the chaplain
of the Second Brigade, First Division.   Many officers
and soldiers were grouped around.   I endeavored to
give thanks to our heavenly Father for all his mercies to
me, for his preservation of me through all the dangers I
have passed, and all the blessings which he has bestowed
upon me, for I know I fall far short of my obligations.
We move out to-morrow toward Pueblo.   The First
Brigade—Duncan's battery, light infantry and cavalry—
form the advance.   I accompany the advance.   General
Worth will remain a day or two with the remainder of
his division till the Second Division, under General
Twiggs, shall arrive.   General Scott is still at Jalapa,
Major Smith with him.   I have with me Lieutenants
Mason, Tower, and the Engineer Company.   In advance,
all is uncertain and the accounts contradictory.   We
must trust to an overruling Providence, by whom we
will be governed for the best, and to our own resources.''

And in another letter to his eldest son, dated same
day and place, he writes: "I thought of you, my dear
Custis, on the 18th in the battle, and wondered, when
the musket balls and grape were whistling over my head
in a perfect shower, where I could put you if with me to
be safe.   I was truly thankful that you were at school,
I hope learning to be good and wise.   You have no
idea what a horrible sight a battlefield is."   The writer
then describes to him the battle of Cerro Gordo, and
tells him about the dead and dying Mexicans; how he

had them carried to a house by the roadside, where they were attended by Mexican surgeons; of his finding by the side of a hut a little Mexican boy who had been a bugler or drummer, with his arm terribly shattered, and how a large Mexican soldier, in the last agonies of death, had fallen on him; how he was attracted to the scene by the grief of a little girl; how he had the dying Mexican taken off the boy, and how grateful the little girl was. "Her large black eyes," he said, "were streaming with tears, her hands crossed over her breast; her hair in one long plait behind reached her waist, her shoulders and arms bare, and without stockings or shoes. Her plaintive tone of ' *Mille gracias, Signor,*' as I had the dying man lifted off the boy and both carried to the hospital, still lingers in my ear. After I had broken a way through the chaparral and turned toward Cerro Gordo I mounted Creole, who stepped over the dead men with such care as if she feared to hurt them, but when I started with the dragoons in the pursuit, she was as fierce as possible, and I could hardly hold her."

From Cerro Gordo to the capital of Mexico, Captain Lee at every point increased the reputation he was acquiring. At Contreras, Churubusco, Molino del Rey, and Chapultepec he was constantly in the saddle, performing with alacrity and courage the duties of a trusted staff officer. "Before the battle of Contreras," wrote one of the most distinguished soldiers of that war, "General Scott's troops had become separated in the field of Pedrigal, and it was necessary to communicate instruction to those on the other side of this barrier of rocks and lava. General Scott says in his report that he had sent seven officers since about sundown to communicate instructions; they had all returned without getting through, but the gallant and indefatigable Captain Lee, of the engineers, who has been constantly with the operating forces, is just in from Shields, Smith, Cadwalader, etc. . . ."

Subsequently Scott, while giving testimony before a court of inquiry, said: "Captain Lee, of the engineers, came to me from Contreras with a message from Brigadier-General Smith. I think about the same time (midnight) he, having passed over the difficult ground by daylight, found it just possible to return on foot and alone to St. Augustine in the dark, the greatest feat of physical and moral courage performed by any individual to my knowledge, pending the campaign."

His deeds of personal daring, his scientific counsels, his *coup d'œil* of the battlefield, his close personal reconnoissances under the scorching rays of a tropical sun, amid the lightning's flash or thunder's roar, did much to mold the key which unlocked the gates of the Golden City. The reports of his commander are filled with commendations of his bravery: " That he was as famous for felicitous execution as for science and daring "; that at " Chapultepec Captain Lee was constantly conspicuous, bearing important orders " from him, " till he fainted from a wound and the loss of two nights' sleep at the batteries." This veteran general, in referring afterward to this campaign, was heard to say that his " success in Mexico was largely due to the skill, valor, and undaunted courage of Robert E. Lee," and that he was " the greatest military genius in America, the best soldier that he ever saw in the field, and that if opportunity offered, he would show himself the foremost captain of his time."

It is certain that Captain Lee came from this Mexican campaign crowned with honors and covered with brevets for gallant and meritorious conduct. In a brief six months' campaign he had demonstrated in a wonderful manner his qualities as a soldier. He was then forty years old. Brevet major, brevet lieutenant colonel, and brevet colonel followed each other in rapid succession. An examination of his career in Mexico will show that the flanks of the hostile army were his favorite points of reconnoissance. If they could be successfully turned, victory would save human life; a reference to his campaigns, when he afterward became an army commander, will show that the flanks of his enemy were still objects of his greatest attention.

The Mexican campaign was finished, and the Peace Treaty occupied the front rank of importance. In a letter to his wife, dated City of Mexico, February 8, 1848, Captain Lee says: " You will doubtless hear many speculations about peace. The boundary is said to be the Rio Grande, giving us Texas, New Mexico, California, for which we pay twenty million dollars—five millions to be reserved for liquidation of claims of her citizens. These are certainly not hard terms for Mexico, considering how the fortune of war has been against her. For myself, I would not exact now more than I would have taken before the commencement of hostilities, as I should wish nothing but what was just, and that I would have sooner or later. I can readily see that the terms said to be offered on the part of Mexico may not prove satisfactory to a large part of our country, who would think it right to exact everything that power and might could require. Some would sacrifice everything under the hope that the proposition of Messrs. Clay, Calhoun, etc., would be acted upon, and save what they term the national honor. Believing that peace would be for the advantage of both countries, I hope that some terms, just to one and not dishonorable to the other, may be agreed on, and that speedily."

And again, five days later : " If any early session of the Mexican Congress can be obtained, I have still hopes that the treaty will be ratified, though I think the speeches and resolutions of some of our leading men, and probably by this time some action of Congress, may so confuse the Mexican mind in reference to her future course as to encourage the recusant members to absent themselves so as to defeat it. I think it is late on our part to stop now to demonstrate who are the first aggressors. It is certain we are the conquerors in a regular war, and by the laws of nations are entitled to dictate the terms of peace. We have fought well and fought fairly. We hold and can continue to hold their country, and have a right to exact compensation for the expenses of a war continued, if not provoked, by ignorance and vanity on the part of Mexico. It is true we bullied her. For that I am ashamed, for she was the weaker party, but we have since, by way of set-off, drubbed her handsomely and in a manner no man might be ashamed of. They begin to be aware how entirely they are beaten, and are willing to acknowledge it. The treaty gives us all the land we want; the amount we pay is a trifle, and is the cheapest way of ending the

war. How it will all end I can not say, but will trust to
a kind Providence, who will, I believe, order all things
for the best."

The brighter the deeds of the soldier and statesman,
the greater the opportunity for the shaft of the critic.
General Scott's behavior to a subordinate drew upon him
a court of inquiry. In a letter to his wife, dated City of
Mexico, March 15, 1848, he says: "The members of the
court to sit on General Scott have arrived, and begin
proceedings to-day. I fear nothing for General Scott,
if the whole truth be known, though the whole country
will have suffered by his suspension. The prospects of
peace seem to be brightening, and all may yet be well."

Naturally, when the objective point in a campaign has
been reached, and the swords go to the scabbards and
the guns are stacked, the distribution of the rewards for
meritorious services are of much interest to the friends
of those who perform them. Mr. Custis, of Arlington,
was properly concerned about the claims to honorable
official mention of his son-in-law, and wrote to him on
the subject, and the reply he received was eminently
characteristic of that modest officer:

CITY OF MEXICO, *April* 8, 1848.

I hope my friends will give themselves no annoyance on my
account, or any concern about the distribution of favors. I know
how those things are awarded at Washington, and how the
President will be besieged by clamorous claimants. I do not
wish to be numbered among them. Such as he can conscientiously bestow, I shall gratefully receive, and have no doubt that
those will exceed my deserts. It is a singular coincidence that in
1836 Santa Anna, as he passed through Fredericktown, Md.,
should have found General Scott before the court of inquiry
clapped upon him by General Jackson. Our present President
thought perhaps he ought to afford the gratification to the same
individual to see Scott before another court in presence of the
troops he commanded. I hope, however, all will terminate in
good. The discontent in the army at this state of things is great.

Captain Lee was a great observer of Nature: he
loved the country, the bright foliage of trees, the running waters, and flowery grasses. His beautiful mare
carried him to all points outside of the city. To Mrs.
Lee he writes:

CITY OF MEXICO, *April* 12, 1848.

I rode out a few days since for the first time to the "Church of Our Lady of Remedies." It is situated on a hill at the termination of the mountains west of the city, and is said to be the spot to which Cortez retreated after being driven from the city on the memorable "noche triste." I saw the cedar tree at Popotla, some miles nearer the city, in which it is said he passed a portion of that night. The trees of the "noche triste"—so called from their blooming about the period of that event—were in full bloom. The flower is a round ellipsoid, and of the most magnificent scarlet color. The Holy Image was standing on a large silver maguey plant, with a rich crown on her head. There were no votaries at her shrine, which was truly magnificent, but near the entrance of the church, on either side, were the offerings of those whom she had relieved. They consisted of representations in wax of those parts of the human body that she cured of the diseases with which they had been afflicted.

The inactive life was growing burdensome. The strains of "Home, sweet home" were falling on the ears of the Americans, and their hearts were beating in anticipation of meeting once more relatives and friends. In a letter, dated City of Mexico, May 21, 1848, he writes to his naval brother, Sydney Smith Lee:

MY DEAR ROSE (he calls him by a pet name): I have a little good news to tell you this evening and as little time to tell it in. The mail from Quereton last night brought letters from reliable persons, one of whom I saw, stating that on the evening of the 15th inst. a vote was taken in the Chamber of Deputies on the general passage of the Treaty of Peace and carried in the affirmative by forty-eight votes to thirty-six. That it would come up on the 19th on its final passage, and, after being passed, be sent to the Senate, where it would undoubtedly pass by an unusual majority and probably by the 24th. So certain was its passage through the Senate considered, that the President, Pena y Pena, had determined, as soon as it had finally passed the Deputies, to write our Commissioners to Quereton to be ready to make the interchange, etc. This morning at 10 A. M. a special express arrived from Quereton with the intelligence of the final passage by the Chamber of Deputies of the Treaty, with all the modifications of our Senate, by a vote of fifty-one to thirty-five. It therefore only wants the confirmation of the Senate, of which those who ought to know, say there is no doubt. We all feel quite exhilarated at the prospect of getting home, when I shall again see you and my dear Sis Nannie. Where will you be this summer? I have heard that the Commissioners start for Quereton to-morrow. I know not whether it is true. General Smith will probably leave here for Vera Cruz on the 24th or 25th to make arrangements for the embarkation of troops. As soon as it is certain that we march out, and I make the necessary arrangements for the engineer transportation, etc., I shall endeavor to be off. I shall therefore leave everything till I see you. Several of your naval boys are here who will be obliged to "cut out." Love to Sis Nannie and the boys. Rhett Buchanan and all friends are well.

Very truly and affectionately, R. E. LEE.

Again: "Mr. Gardner and Mr. Trist depart to-morrow. I had hoped that after the President had adopted Mr. Trist's treaty, and the Senate confirmed it, they would have paid him the poor compliment of allowing him to finish it, as some compensation for all the abuse they had heaped upon him; but, I presume, it is perfectly fair, having made use of his labors and taken from him all he had earned, that he should be kicked off as General Scott has been, whose skill and science, having crushed the enemy and conquered a peace, can now be dismissed and turned out as an old horse to die."

In Scott's army in Mexico at that time were many subordinate officers fighting under a common flag, who were destined to become familiar to the public fourteen years afterward by the skill and courage with which they fought each other. Their swords, then drawn for victory against a common foe, were to be pointed against each other's breasts, and those who had slept beneath the same blanket, drank from the same canteen, and formed those ties of steel which are strongest when pledged amid common dangers around a common mess table, were to be marshaled under the banners of opposing armies. Ulysses S. Grant was then twenty-five years old, a lieutenant of the Fourth Infantry, self-reliant, brave, and fertile in resources. He fought with old "Zach" at Palo Alto, Resaca de la Palma, and at Monterey; was at Vera Cruz, and in all the battles which followed until the Mexican capital was entered. George Gordon Meade was an officer of topographical engineers, first on the staff of General Taylor and afterward on the staff of General Patterson at Vera Cruz. There too was George B. McClellan, twenty-one years old, as an engineer officer, who received brevets as first lieutenant and captain for his bravery in battle. Irvin McDowell, who afterward became first commander of the Army of the Potomac, was aid-de-camp to General John E. Wool. George H. Thomas was second lieutenant, Third Artillery, and was brevetted three times for gallantry; Joseph Hooker was assistant adjutant general on the staff of General Persifor F. Smith; Gideon J. Pillow was brevetted three times. Ambrose E. Burnside joined the army on its march, with some recruits. Winfield Scott Hancock was there as second lieutenant, Sixth Infantry, twenty-three years of age, and was brevetted for his conduct at Contreras and Churubusco. There too was Albert Sidney Johnston of the First (Texas) Rifles and afterward inspector general of Butler's division; so also Joseph E. Johnston, lieutenant colonel of voltigeurs, wounded twice and brevetted three times. Braxton Bragg was present as a captain of a light battery in the Third Artillery, the first man to plant the regimental colors on the rampart of Chapultepec; and there too was Thomas Jonathan Jackson, twenty-three years old, second lieutenant of Magruder's light battery of artillery. Young in years and rank, he gave early evidence of those qualities of a soldier for which he became distinguished under the name of Stonewall Jackson. Magruder, his captain, commended him highly in his report, writing that " if devotion, industry, talent, and gallantry are the highest qualities of a soldier, then Lieutenant Jackson is entitled to the distinction which their possession confers." In the army also was Longstreet, lieutenant of infantry, twenty-six years old, brevetted twice and wounded at Chapultepec; and Magruder, known among his comrades as " Prince John," from courtly manners, distinguished appearance, and fine conversational powers, who commanded a light battery in Pillow's division, was twice brevetted and wounded at Chapultepec. John Sedgwick was with the army, first lieutenant of artillery, a classmate of Bragg and Early and Hooker, twice brevetted; and so was Richard S. Ewell, a typical dragoon; Ambrose P. Hill, only twenty-one years old, second lieutenant of the First Artillery; and Daniel H. Hill, Jubal Early, and many others who afterward became famous.

Little did these young fellows, who marched, bivouacked, fought, and bled side by side on the burning
sands of old Mexico, imagine that in less than two decades McDowell would be training his guns on Johnston and Beauregard at first Manassas, while McClellan,
Pope, Burnside, Hooker, Meade, and Grant would each
in turn test the prowess of Lee; nor did their old commander, Scott, dream he was training these young men
in practical strategy, grand tactics, and the science of
war, in order that they might direct the information thus
acquired against each other.

The memory of Winfield Scott has not been securely
embalmed in the hearts of the people of the Southern
States, because he was a Virginian who did not resign
his commission in the United States Army and tender
his sword to his native State in 1861. It should be remembered, however, that for over half a century he had
fought for the flag and worn the uniform of the army
of the United States, and had been permanently partially
disabled by wounds. Before his Mexican campaign he
had served with distinction from where the Northern
lakes are bound in icy fetters, to Florida, the land of
sun and flowers, in a great degree losing touch with the
citizens of States. In fifty-three years of continuous
army service he had developed into a sort of national
military machine, and when war began between the States
of the North and those of the South he was seventy-
five years old. Neither the Indian "Black Hawk," with
his Sacs and Foxes, the Seminoles, the Mexicans, nor the
unhappy condition of his own land, greatly disturbed
him, for already his vision was fixed "across the river,"
and his tent was being erected upon the eternal camp-
ing ground. Naturally, he wanted to go to his grave
wrapped in the folds of the starry flag he had so long
defended. In the North his decision was highly ap-
plauded; in the South opinion was divided. In the
estimation of some, he should have returned to his
mother Commonwealth, for, under their construction of
our forms of Government, his first allegiance was due to
her. Others, however, heartily concurred in his decision
to remain in the North, because "he might have been in
the way." The solemn game of war can only be played

by active participants, and when a soldier becomes inactive his place is in the rear rank. The aged warrior
was consigned to a back seat by the Federal War Department, and quietly waited the summons of the trumpet
of the Angel of Death. It is true Scott was pompous
and vain of a splendid physical appearance, and had a
full appreciation of the high and distinguished position he had attained, but he was a soldier of undoubted
military capacity. The people nicknamed him "Fuss
and Feathers," because, in gaudy uniform, he sometimes
made the atmosphere blue around him and imparted to
it a smell of sulphur when things did not go exactly to
suit him. He was a disciple of the doctrine of Epicurus
so far as it related to the organ of taste. When he indulged in "a hasty plate of soup" it was unavoidable,
and he has been known to raise a storm because the
guest at his table would cut lettuce instead of rolling
the leaf around his fork so as not to bruise it. The
old soldier is resting quietly now where the "Hudson's
silvery sands roll 'mid the hills afar," and if he lacked
to some degree personal popularity, was without mag-
netic influence, and did not possess that power which
Carnot calls the "Glory of the soldier and the strength
of armies," he is remembered by the whole country as a
courteous and chivalric gentleman and as a great commander of true military genius.

His unswerving friendship for Robert E. Lee and
his never-failing belief in his military ability was demonstrated by his recommendation that he should be
his successor, and which doubtless prompted the United
States Government to offer to Brevet-Colonel Lee the
position of commander in chief of their armies in 1861.

"Peace hath her victories no less than war." A treaty
was ratified between the United States and Mexico which
was received with joy by the inhabitants of both countries, and was most heartily welcomed by the Americans
in Mexico. Captain Lee was once more at home, bearing with him the plaudits of the army and the high appreciation of its commander. He wrote from Arlington,
June 30, 1848, to his brother of the navy:

Here I am once again, my dear Smith, perfectly surrounded
by Mary and her precious children, who seem to devote them-

selves to staring at the furrows in my face and the white hairs in my head. It is not surprising that I am hardly recognizable to some of the young eyes around me and perfectly unknown to the youngest, but some of the older ones gaze with astonishment and wonder at me, and seem at a loss to reconcile what they see and what was pictured in their imaginations. I find them too much grown, and all well, and I have much cause for thankfulness and gratitude to that good God who has once more united us. I was greeted on my arrival by your kind letter, which was the next thing to seeing you in person. I wish I could say when I shall be able to visit you, but I as yet know nothing of the intention of the Department concerning me, and can not now tell what my movements will be. Mary has recently returned from a visit to poor Anne,* and gives a pitiable account of her distress. You may have heard of her having hurt her left hand; she is now consequently without the use of either, and can not even feed herself. She has suffered so much that it is not wonderful her spirits should be depressed. She sent many injunctions that I must come to her before even unpacking my trunk, and I think of running over there for a day after the Fourth of July, if practicable. You say I must let you know when I am ready to receive visits. Now! Have you any desire to see the celebration, etc., of the Fourth of July? Bring Sis Nannie and the little ones; I long to see you all; I only arrived yesterday, after a long journey up the Mississippi, which route I was induced to take for the better accommodation of my horse, as I wished to spare her as much annoyance and fatigue as possible, she already having undergone so much suffering in my service. I landed her at Wheeling and left her to come over with Jim. I have seen but few of our friends as yet, but hear they are all well. Cousin Anna is at Ravensworth. I met Mrs. John Mason yesterday as I passed through W. All her people are well. I hear that that pretty Rhett, hearing of my arrival, ran off yesterday evening to take refuge with you. Never mind, there is another person coming from Mexico from whom she can not hide herself. Tell her with my regrets that I brought *muchas cosas* from her young rifleman, who is as bright and handsome as ever. No, Sis Nannie, your sister was not here when I arrived. Are you satisfied? She had gone to Alexandria to learn the news and do a little shopping, but I have laid violent hands on her now. An opportunity has just offered to the Post-office and I have scribbled off this to assure you of my love and remembrance. With much love to Sis Nannie and the children, and kind regards to Mrs. R. and Misses V. and C., I remain,

Affectionately your brother,

R. E. LEE.

---

* His sister, Mrs. Marshall.

After the Treaty of Peace with Mexico, Lee was assigned to the important duty of constructing works for the defense of the harbor of Baltimore, and was so occupied until 1852, when he was made Superintendent of the United States Military Academy, from whose walls he had emerged as a cadet twenty-three years before. At West Point he was employed for three years in watching over the drill, discipline, and studies of cadets, who were one day to become officers of the army. The detail was a complimentary one, and the office of superintendent at that time, by law, could only be filled by engineer officers. His accustomed ability was displayed in these new duties, and the Academy received great benefit from a sagacious administration of its affairs. While so engaged, Mrs. Lee's mother—Mrs. Custis—died. She was a perfect type of the Christian woman: soft in manner, kind in heart, affectionate in nature, and refined and ladylike in everything. From West Point, April 27, 1853, Captain Lee writes to his wife: "May God give you strength to enable you to bear and say, 'His will be done.' She has gone from all trouble, care, and sorrow, to a holy immortality, there to rejoice and praise forever the God and Saviour she so long and truly served. Let that be our comfort and that our consolation. May our death be like hers, and may we meet in happiness in heaven." And later, on the 10th of May, he says: "She was to me all that a mother could be, and I yield to none in admiration for her character, love for her virtues, and veneration for her memory."

CHAPTER III.

A CAVALRY OFFICER OF THE ARMY OF THE UNITED STATES.

HIS term of office at West Point terminated by his assignment to cavalry. The great civilizing arms of the United States had been extended so as to embrace large extents of territory, and more cavalry was required. An expenditure of one hundred and sixty millions of dollars, thirty victories in Mexico, and the capture of ten fortified places, including the capital city of the enemy, resulted in adding to the Republic New Mexico, Arizona, Utah, Nevada, and California. The increase in population made it necessary to increase the army in order to give full protection to all citizens within the new boundary lines. After the United States had secured independence, cavalry was not at first recognized as a component part of the regular army. The first mounted regiment, called the First Dragoons, was not organized until 1833. Then followed the Second Dragoons in 1836, and in 1846 another regiment was added, designated as " Mounted Riflemen." With a vast extent of territory and a population of whites numbering about twenty millions in 1855, the cavalry arm of the service consisted of but three regiments. General Scott, in his report of the operations of the army for 1853, first urged that the army be increased by two regiments of dragoons and two regiments of infantry. The following year Hon. Jefferson Davis, then Secretary of War, renewed the commander in chief's recommendation, and President Pierce asked its favorable consideration by Congress, stating that the army was of " inestimable importance as the nucleus around which the volunteer force of the nation can promptly gather in the hour of danger." And that he thought it "wise to maintain a military peace establishment." Mr. R. M. T. Hunter, at that time a distinguished senator in Congress from the State of Virginia, offered an amendment to the Army Appropriation Bill which had passed the House in 1854, authorizing the increase of the army by two regiments of cavalry and five hundred mounted volunteers, who were to serve for twelve months. James Shields, an Irishman by birth, who had served conspicuously in the Mexican War as a brigadier general, and who was then a senator from the State of Illinois, offered a substitute to Hunter's amendment, embodying the views of his former commander in chief, Scott. A protracted debate resulted. Sam Houston, of Texas, and Thomas H. Benton, of Missouri, led the opposition to the measure, the former saying that in the Texas Republic, before its annexation to the United States, the expenses of the Indian War had not exceeded ten thousand dollars a year, and that the settlers had better protection against hostile tribes of Indians than they had received from regiments of the regular army, while the latter indulged in a tirade of abuse against the army generally, calling them "schoolhouse officers and pothouse soldiers"; that he did not believe the aim of the Administration was to relieve the frontier settlements, but to furnish places for graduates of West Point and the friends of the Secretary of War, stating that the object of Mr. Pierce and Jefferson Davis was the ultimate conquest of the island of Cuba.

These views seem to have made an impression upon some sections of the country. The Comte de Paris adopted them in his History of the Civil War in America. He says: "In 1855 Congress passed a law authorizing the formation of two new regiments of cavalry, and Mr. Jefferson Davis, then Secretary of War, took advantage of the fact that they had not been designated by the title of dragoons to treat them as a different arm, and to fill them with his creatures, to the exclusion of regular officers, whom he disliked." It is hardly necessary to say that the comte was writing with limited knowledge. His epithet was applied to such officers as Sumner, Sedgwick, McClellan, Emory, Thomas,

Stoneman, Stanley, Carr, etc., who served with much distinction on the Union side of the war from 1861 to 1865; as well as to Albert Sidney Johnston, Joseph E. Johnston, Lee, Hardee, Kirby Smith, Field, Hood, J. E. B. Stuart, and a number of others who espoused the cause of the South in the late war—"names the world will not willingly let die." Edwin Sumner was promoted by Mr. Davis from major of Second Dragoons to colonel of First Cavalry, and Joseph E. Johnston, a captain in the Topographical Engineers, was made its lieutenant colonel. The colonelcy of the Second Cavalry was tendered to Albert Sidney Johnston, then a major in the Paymaster's Department of the army. This officer, who afterward became so distinguished, graduated at West Point in 1826, and was assigned as a lieutenant to the Second Infantry. His subsequent career in Texas and in the Mexican campaign is well known to the whole country. Zachary Taylor said of him that " he was the best soldier he had ever commanded," while Scott remarked that his appointment as colonel of the Second Cavalry " was a Godsend to the army and country."

Captain and Brevet-Colonel R. E. Lee, of the engineers, was promoted to be lieutenant colonel of this regiment, and William J. Hardee and William H. Emory to be its majors. The latter was soon transferred to the First Cavalry, and the vacancy offered to Braxton Bragg, of the artillery, who declined it because he did not want to remain in the service, and recommended George H. Thomas, of the Third Artillery, who was appointed. Van Dorn, Kirby Smith, James Oakes, Innis Palmer, Stoneman, O'Hara, Bradfute, Travis, Brackett, and Whiting were its captains, and Nathan G. Evans, Richard W. Johnson, Charles Field, and John B. Hood were among its first lieutenants.

Secretary of War Davis graduated at West Point in 1828, two years after Albert Sidney Johnston and one year before Robert E. Lee. He possessed an accurate knowledge of the individual merits of army officers, and time and history have indorsed his selection of officers for these new regiments ; for on their respective sides in the late war nearly every one became celebrated. Mr. Davis said to the writer that when he carried the list to the President, the latter remarked that he thought too many of the officers were from the Southern States, and that for the first time his attention was directed to the section from which many of these officers came. In their appointment he had only considered that past services richly entitled them to promotion. At the date of the organization of the two new cavalry regiments seventy officers were appointed by Secretary Davis, but only twenty-nine of them came from States which seceded from the Union in 1861. It is, however, a " historical fact that the officers thus selected were superb soldiers, and that they were from the best to be found in the army and in civil life."

Brevet-Colonel Lee left the Engineer Corps with great regret ; he had thoroughly mastered its scientific details, and, with a national reputation, stood in the front rank of military engineers. At West Point he had been instructed in cavalry, artillery, and infantry tactics, and, like all cadets at the date of graduation, was supposed to be equally well informed as to the drill and duties of each arm of service ; but twenty-six years had rolled around since graduation, during which his attention had been entirely absorbed in the profession of engineer, and it was necessary that he should again study cavalry tactics. Promotion was slow in the United States Army, and in a long official life he had only reached the lineal rank of captain. By sudden transition, in a single bound he had been promoted to a lieutenant colonelcy, a position he possibly would not have reached in the ordinary course of promotion for many years ; his duty to all concerned demanded that he should accept the position. It was an unwritten law in the army that if promotion was offered and declined, the reputation of the officer suffered ; it was regarded as a confession on his part that he had not capacity to perform the duties of a higher grade.

Next to the engineer, the cavalry service was the most agreeable to Lee. He was fond of horses, and liked to see them cleaned, fed, and well taken care of ; he had a firm seat in the saddle, and rode gracefully and well. He might never become, in the language of the cavalry song,

A bold dragoon, who scorns all care
As he stalks around with his uncropped hair.

And indeed it is difficult to picture him in short jacket, long boots coming above his knees, jingling spurs, clanking saber, and slouched hat, upon whose looped-up side gay feathers danced. Or can we imagine him with the devil-may-care look and jaunty bearing generally ascribed as attributes of the " rough rider "? We can not fancy him charging the French columns with the fury of a Ponsonby at Waterloo ; or riding boot to boot with dashing Cardigan and his " death or glory " squadrons " into the jaws of death, into the mouth of hell " at Balaklava ; or side by side with fearless Murat and his twelve thousand cavalry at Jena ; or as fast and furious as Stuart, or Sheridan, Forrest, or Custer. And yet it is safe to say, had the opportunity offered, this new cavalry officer would have been found equal to the emergency. The cavalry genius of Cromwell is readily admitted, in spite of the fact that he was forty-four years of age when he first drew his sword, and Lee was now forty-six. General Foy, in his history of the Peninsular War, writes : " *Après les qualités nécessaire* [s] *? au commandant en chef, le talent de guerre plus sublime est celui du général de cavalrie.*" Lee was endowed with youth, health, strength, and "talent for war"; he had been shaken well into the saddle by his Mexican campaign, and was buoyant and brave. A fearless and graceful rider, he could have manœuvred squadrons, and when the bugle sounded the charge, reins loosened, and sabers flashed in the air, lead them to victory.

The headquarters of the Second Cavalry were established at Louisville, Ky., where Lieutenant-Colonel Lee assumed command on the 20th of April, 1855. Afterward he was transferred to Jefferson Barracks, Missouri, where the companies were to be organized and instructed, and which was then the temporary regimental headquarters. He writes Mrs. Lee from that post, July 1, 1855 : " The chaplain of the post, a Mr. Fish, is now absent ; he is an Episcopal clergyman and well spoken of ; we have therefore not had service since I have been here. The church stands out in the trees, grotesque in its form and ancient in its appearance. I have not been in it, but am content to read the Bible and prayers alone, and draw much comfort from their holy precepts and merciful promises. Though feeling unable to follow the one, and truly unworthy of the other, I must still pray to that glorious God without whom there is no help, and with whom there is no danger. That he may guard and protect you all, and more than supply to you my absence, is my daily and constant prayer. I have been busy all the week superintending and drilling recruits. Not a stitch of clothing has as yet arrived for them, though I made the necessary requisition for it to be sent here more than two months ago in Louisville. .Yesterday, at muster, I found one of the late arrivals in a dirty, tattered shirt and pants, with a white hat and shoes, with other garments to match. I asked him why he did not .put on clean clothes. He said he had none. I asked him if he could not wash and mend those. He said he had nothing else to put on. I then told him immediately after muster to go down to the river, wash his clothes, and sit on the bank and watch the passing steamboats till they dried, and then mend them. This morning at inspection he looked as proud as possible, stood in the position of a soldier with his little fingers on the seams of his pants, his beaver cocked back, and his toes sticking through his shoes, but his skin and solitary two garments clean. He grinned very happily at my compliments. I have got a ·fine puss, which was left me by Colonel Sumner. He was educated by his daughter, Mrs. Jenkins, but is too fond of getting up on my lap and on my bed; he follows me all about the house and stands at the door in an attitude of defiance at all passing dogs."

In the November following he was in Kansas, having been temporarily detached from his regiment and detailed to serve as a member of a court-martial ordered to convene to try an assistant surgeon of the army for leaving his station in the midst of a fatal epidemic, and wrote Mrs. Lee, from Fort Riley, November 5, 1855: "The court progresses slowly. A good deal was told in the evidence of Saturday; Mrs. Woods, wife of Brevet-Major Woods, Sixth Infantry, whose husband had left on the

Sioux expedition, was taken ill at 9 P. M. on the 2d of August. Her youngest child, a boy of three years, was taken that night at twelve, and about six next morning her eldest, a girl of five years. The mother, when told that her end was approaching, asked her only attendant, a niece of the chaplain, to take down the last request to her children and absent husband. The sickness of her children had kindly been concealed from her by this young lady, who managed, by the aid of a soldier, to attend to them all. They all died that morning, the 3d of August. The boy preceded, and the girl followed the mother by about an hour. Their bodies rest in the same grave. I pray their spirits may be united in heaven. The husband, stripped of all he loved, is still absent; and the same day Major Ogden, Mrs. Woods's nurse, a soldier and his wife, died—making seven corpses in the house in one day. Major Ogden was a valuable soldier and much beloved by his men. They have erected to his memory, on an adjacent hill overlooking the fort and the beautiful valley of the Kansas and its branches, a stone monument, their own design and workmanship. The epitaph on it relates in touching simplicity his services and death. He died as he had lived—a soldier and a Christian, and repeated the Lord's Prayer with his last breath. There were fifty-nine deaths during the epidemic. Mrs. Armistead, wife of Major Armistead (General Lewis Armistead, killed at Gettysburg), died in six hours after she was taken. Her husband had marched with his company, but only proceeded thirty miles when overtaken by an express. He returned in the night, found his wife dead, and after her funeral in the morning—this same fatal 3d of August—started for his camp, carrying his two little children with him. A soldier has a hard life and but little consideration."

The Second Cavalry, under the command of Colonel Johnston, on the 27th of October following began its long march from Jefferson Barracks to western Texas. It numbered seven hundred and fifty men and eight hundred horses. It marched under the command of its colonel, Major Hardee being the only other field officer who accompanied it, Lee and Thomas being on court-martial detail. The regiment was destined for the next few years to be stationed at the various posts of western Texas, and its duty was to protect the scalp of the settler from the tomahawk of the savage. Texas has an area of two hundred and seventy-four thousand square miles, or one hundred and fifty million acres of land, and is two and a half times the area of Great Britain and Ireland. In order to watch over such a stretch of frontier it was necessary to divide the regiment up so that only a few companies occupied the same post.

Lieutenant-Colonel Lee arrived in Texas in March, 1856: To Mrs. Lee he writes from San Antonio on March 20, 1856: "To-morrow I leave for Fort Mason, where Colonel Johnston and six companies of the regiment are stationed. Major Hardee and four companies are in camp on the Clear Fork of the Brazos, about forty miles from Belknap. I presume I shall go there. I have left it with Mr. Radiminski (a native of Poland and a lieutenant in the Second Cavalry) to make provision for the journey, and have merely indicated that I should be content with a boiled ham, hard bread, a bottle of molasses, and one of extract of coffee—all of which have been provided." Lee was afterward stationed at Camp Cooper, on the Clear Fork of the Brazos, so named in honor of Samuel Cooper, then adjutant general of the army; and from that point in June, 1856, he was dispatched with four companies of his regiment on an expedition against the Comanches, but was unsuccessful in finding them. It is mentioned because it was his first service of this nature, and the largest command he had ever exercised in the field up to that period. The Indians of western Texas in those days roved over the prairies in small bodies, and would descend suddenly upon the frontier settlements, scalping and killing the settlers and driving off their horses and cattle. They were fine specimens of irregular cavalry, were splendid riders, and when compelled to fight, used the open or individual method of warfare, after the manner of the Cossacks.

From Camp Cooper, Texas, August 4, 1856, remembering that Mr. Custis always celebrated his country's birth by a patriotic speech of welcome to the many who visited him on such occasions, he says to Mrs. Lee: "I hope your father continued well and enjoyed his usual celebration of the Fourth of July; mine was spent, after a march of thirty miles on one of the branches of the Brazos, under my blanket, elevated on four sticks driven in the ground, as a sunshade. The sun was fiery hot, the atmosphere like the blast from a hot-air furnace, the water salt, still my feelings for my country were as ardent, my faith in her future as true, and my hopes for her advancement as unabated as they would have been under better circumstances."

A week later, having received intelligence of the death of his youngest sister, Mildred, who, having married a Mr. Childe, had removed to and was a resident of Paris, France, he writes: " The news came to me very unexpectedly, and in the course of nature I might never have anticipated it, as indeed I had never realized that she could have preceded me on the unexplored journey upon which we are all hastening. Though parted from her for years, with little expectation but of a transient reunion in this life, this terrible and sudden separation has not been the less distressing because it was distant and unlooked for. It has put an end to all hope of our meeting in this world. It has cut short my early wishes and daily yearnings, and so vividly does she live in my imagination and affection that I can not realize she only exists in my memory. I pray that her life has but just begun, and I trust that our merciful God only so suddenly and early snatched her away because he then saw that it was the fittest moment to take her to himself. May a pure and eternal life now be hers, and may we all live so that when we die it may be open to us." On the 25th of the same month he tells Mrs. Lee: "I shall leave here on the 1st proximo for the Rio Grande, and shall be absent from two and a half to three months; will go from here to Fort Mason and pick up Major Thomas * and take him on with me, and thus have him as a traveling companion all the way, which will be a great comfort to me." And then mentioning the Comanche raids on the settlers of Texas, he says: "These people give a world of trouble to man and horse, and, poor creatures, they are not worth it."

---

* General George H. Thomas.

Whenever a vacancy occurred in the army in a grade above lieutenant colonel, his chances for promotion were always discussed. His reply to a letter from his wife, informing him that his name was frequently mentioned for a brigadier generalcy, was written the day he set out for Ringgold Barracks to serve as a member of the court-martial ordered to try Major Giles Porter, of the rifles, and is very characteristic:

CAMP COOPER, TEXAS, *September 1,* 1856.

We are all in the hands of a kind God, who will do for us what is best, and more than we deserve, and we have only to endeavor to deserve more, and to do our duty to him and ourselves. May we all deserve his mercy, his care, and protection. Do not give yourself any anxiety about the appointment of the brigadier. If it is on my account that you feel an interest in it, I beg you will discard it from your thoughts. You will be sure to be disappointed; nor is it right to indulge improper and useless hopes. It besides looks like presumption to expect it.

The journey to the Rio Grande is best told in his own words:

RINGGOLD BARRACKS, TEXAS, *October 3,* 1856.

I arrived here on the 28th, after twenty-seven consecutive days of travel. The distance was greater than I had anticipated, being seven hundred and thirty miles. I was detained one day on the road by high water—had to swim my mules and get the wagon over by hand. My mare took me very comfortably, but all my wardrobe, from my socks up to my plume, was immersed in the muddy water—epaulets, sash, etc. They are, however, all dry now. Major Thomas traveled with me from Fort Mason. We are in camp together. Captain Bradford, whom we knew at Old Point, is on the court. Colonel Chapman, of the infantry, from Georgetown, Captain Marsey, Colonels Bainbridge, Bumford, Ruggles, and Seawell, and Captain Sibley, an old classmate of mine. Colonel Waite is president of the court and Captain Samuel Jones, of the artillery, judge advocate. The latter brought his wife and child with him in a six-mule road wagon from Sinda, about one hundred and twenty miles up the river. All the court are present and yesterday we commenced the trial of our old friend, Giles Porter. I hope he will clear himself of the charges against him. I am writing with much inconvenience from a stiff finger, caused by a puncture from a Spanish bayonet, while pitching my tent on the road, which struck the joint. Every branch and leaf in this country nearly are armed with a point, and some seem to poison the flesh. What a blessed thing the children are not here! They would be ruined.

The discomforts of army travel and army life were very great in those days. Officers would scarcely get within their assigned quarters at one post before they would be ordered to another, and as transportation was limited to a few Government wagons, the transfer would always result in loss to the officers. Lieutenant-Colonel Lee gives as a glimpse of this in a letter to Mrs. Lee, dated :

RINGGOLD BARRACKS, TEXAS, *October* 24, 1856.

Major Porter had for his counsel two Texan lawyers, a Judge Bigelow and a Colonel Bowers, very shrewd men, accustomed to the tricks and stratagems of special pleadings, which, of no other avail, absorb time and stave off the question. The movement of troops to Florida will not take place, I presume, until the beginning of November. They are packing up and getting ready. The officers are selling their surplus beds and chairs, cows, goats, and chickens. I am sorry to see their little comforts going, for it is difficult on the frontier to collect them again. Mrs. Sibley told me her chairs and cow had gone, and Mrs. Waite her goats. The pigeons and chickens are disposed of on the table. General Vidaun, in his attack on Camargo, seems to progress *pari passu* with the court. I am more interested in the state of health of my man Johnson, who has fever. I hope it will prove a slight case for his sake and my own, for, though he is a poor cook, he is all I have, and neither the major [George H. Thomas] nor I can stand these long and interesting sessions of the court without eating. I have read in a stray number of the New York Times, that reached here somehow, a violent attack upon Secretary Davis [Jefferson Davis, then Secretary of War] for the removal of Professor Sprole [West Point]. It makes out a severe charge against the Secretary, the merits of which, though I am sorry for the professor, I am too dull to see. The Secretary and President have surely the right to appoint whom they think best to fill the station. I sincerely hope he will not suffer on account of his losing his place. He has some strong friends in the city of New York. At any rate you had better write to Miss Becky [his daughter] to stay with you till her father is located. In the same paper there are ill-natured strictures upon our regiment. The writer is opposed to the new regiments, particularly the First and Second Cavalry and the Ninth and Tenth Infantry, and calls for their early disbandment. They may suit themselves in everything relating to my services, and whenever they tell me they are no longer required they will not be obtruded on them.

Two months later Lieutenant-Colonel Lee was at Fort Brown, Texas, with thoughts filled with the approaching Christmas and his family's happiness. He writes in December, 1856: "The time is approaching when I trust many of you will be assembled around the family hearth at dear Arlington another Christmas. Though absent, my heart will be in the midst of you, and I shall enjoy in imagination and memory all that is going on. May nothing occur to mar or cloud the family fireside, and may each be able to look back with pride and pleasure at their deeds of the past year, and with confidence and hope to that in prospect. I can do nothing but hope and pray for you all. Last Saturday I visited Matamoras, Mexico, for the first time. The town looked neat, though much out at the elbow, and nothing apparently going on of interest. The plaza or square was inclosed and the trees and grass flourishing, for which I am told the city is indebted to Major William Chapman, of the Quartermaster's Department, who made the improvement while it was in the occupation of the American army. The most attractive thing to me in town were the orange trees loaded with unripe fruit. The oleander was in full bloom, and there were some large date, fig, and palm trees."

Two days after the great festival the following letter to Mrs. Lee, giving in graphic words his views on slavery, a sly slap at the Pilgrim Fathers, and his personal Christmas doings, was written:

FORT BROWN, TEXAS, *December* 27, 1856.

The steamer has arrived from New Orleans, bringing full files of papers and general intelligence from the "States." I have enjoyed the former very much, and, in the absence of particular intelligence, have perused with much interest the series of the Alexandria Gazette from the 20th of November to the 8th of December inclusive. Besides the usual good reading matter, I was interested in the relation of local affairs, and inferred, from the quiet and ordinary course of events, that all in the neighborhood was going on well. I trust it may be so, and that you and particularly all at Arlington and our friends elsewhere are well. The steamer brought the President's message to Congress, and the reports of the various heads of the departments, so that we are now assured that the Government is in operation and the Union in existence. Not that I had any fears to the contrary, but it is satisfactory always to have facts to go on; they restrain supposition and conjecture, confirm faith, and bring contentment. I was much pleased

with the President's message and the report of the Secretary of
War.   The views of the President on the domestic institutions of
the South are truthfully and faithfully expressed.   In this en-
lightened age there are few, I believe, but will acknowledge that
slavery as an institution is a moral and political evil in any country.   It is useless to expatiate on its disadvantages.   I think it,
however, a greater evil to the white than to the black race, and
while my feelings are strongly interested in behalf of the latter,
my sympathies are stronger for the former.   The blacks are im-
measurably better off here than in Africa, morally, socially, and
physically.   The painful discipline they are undergoing is necessary for their instruction as a race, and, I hope, will prepare and
lead them to better things.   How long their subjection may be
necessary is known and ordered by a wise and merciful Providence.   Their emancipation will sooner result from a mild and
melting influence than the storms and contests of fiery controversy.   This influence, though slow, is sure.   The doctrines and
miracles of our Saviour have required nearly two thousand years
to convert but a small part of the human race, and even among
Christian nations what gross errors still exist !   While we see the
course of the final abolition of slavery is onward, and we give it
the aid of our prayers and all justifiable means in our power, we
must leave the progress as well as the result in his hands, who
sees the end and who chooses to work by slow things, and with
whom a thousand years are but as a single day ; although the
abolitionist must know this, and must see that he has neither the
right nor the power of operating except by moral means and sua-
sion ; and if he means well to the slave, he must not create angry
feelings in the master.   That although he may not approve the
mode by which it pleases Providence to accomplish its purposes,
the result will never be the same ; that the reasons he gives for
interference in what he has no concern holds good for every kind
of interference with our neighbors when we disapprove their conduct.   Is it not strange that the descendants of those Pilgrim
Fathers who crossed the Atlantic to preserve the freedom of their
opinion have always proved themselves intolerant of the spiritual
liberty of others?   I hope you had a joyous Christmas at Arlington, and that it may be long and often repeated.   I thought of
you all and wished to be with you.   Mine was gratefully but
silently passed.   I endeavored to find some little presents for the
children in the garrison to add to their amusement, and succeeded
better than I had anticipated.   The stores are very barren of such
things here, but by taking the week beforehand in my daily walks
I picked up little by little something for all.   Tell Mildred I got
a beautiful Dutch doll for little Emma Jones—one of those crying babies that can open and shut their eyes, turn their head, etc.
For the two other little girls, Puss Shirley and Mary Sewell, I
found handsome French teapots to match cups given to them by

Mrs. Waite ; then by means of knives and books I satisfied the boys. After dispensing my presents I went to church ; the discourse was on the birth of our Saviour. It was not as simply or touchingly told as it is in the Bible. By previous invitation I dined with Major Thomas at 2 P. M. on roast turkey and plum pudding. He and his wife were alone. I had provided a pretty singing bird for the little girl, and passed the afternoon in my room. God bless you all.

From the same place—Fort Brown, Texas, January 7, 1857—writing to Mrs. Lee, whom he hears has been sick, he says: "Systematically pursue the best course to recover your lost health. I pray and trust your efforts and the prayers of those who love you may be favorably answered. Do not worry yourself about things you can not help, but be content to do what you can for the well-being of what belongs properly to you. Commit the rest to those who are responsible, and though it is the part of benevolence to aid all we can and sympathize with all who are in need, it is the part of wisdom to attend to our own affairs. Lay nothing too much to heart. Desire nothing too eagerly, nor think that all things can be perfectly accomplished according to our own notions."

Mr. Custis, of Arlington, was very fond of cats, and his large yellow "Tom" was his constant attendant. Some of his household naturally grew fond of these animals, his son-in-law being among them. Lieutenant-Colonel Lee would not cut the skirt of his robe, as did Mohammed, to prevent disturbing his cat, which was sleeping on it, nor, like Cardinal Wolsey, give audience with a cat seated beside him, nor let his cat rest among his papers and books, as did Richelieu, nor wish a statue with his right hand resting on his cat, as did Whittington, the famous Lord Mayor of London, but he liked to see a well-fed puss, such as Gray described in his ode "On the Death of a Favorite Cat":

> Her conscious tail her joy disclosed,
> The fair round face, the snowy beard,
> The relish of her paws ;
> Her coat that with the tortoise vies,
> Her ears of jet and emerald eyes,
> She saw and purr'd applause.

From Fort Brown, Texas, February 16, 1857, he tells
Mrs. Lee: "Tell your father Mrs. Colonel Waite has a
fine large cat which she takes with her everywhere. He
is her companion by day, and sleeps on her bed at night.
In public conveyances she leads him in the leash, and
carries along a bottle of milk for his use. In her own
carriage he sits on her lap. I have been trying to persuade her to let me take him up to Camp Cooper, but
she says she can't part from him. He must go to Florida. I have seen some fine cats in Brownsville in the
stores kept by Frenchmen, but no yellow ones; the dark
brindle is the favorite color on the frontier. In my
walk the other evening I met a Mexican with a wild
kitten in his arms enveloped in his blanket; it was a
noble specimen of the Rio Grande wildcat, spotted all
over with large spots like the leopard. I tried very
hard to buy him, but he said he was already sold. I
should prefer one of those at Camp Cooper. I fear,
though, I should have to keep him chained, for they are
very wild and savage."

And again from Indianola, Texas, March 27, 1857,
he writes to his youngest daughter: "It has been said
that our letters are good representatives of our minds.
They certainly present a good criterion for judging of
the character of the individual. You must be careful
that yours make as favorable an impression of you as I
hope you will deserve. I am truly sorry for the destruction of the Long Bridge. [Spans the Potomac between
Arlington and Washington.] It will be an injury to the
business of many and an inconvenience to you in taking
your music lessons. You must be a great personage
now—sixty pounds! I wish I had you here in all your
ponderosity. I want to see you so much. Can you not
pack up and come to the Comanche country? I would
get you such a fine cat you would never look at 'Tom'
again. Did I tell you Jim Nooks, Mrs. Waite's cat, was
dead? He died of apoplexy. I foretold his end. Coffee and cream for breakfast, pound cake for lunch, tur-
tle and oysters for dinner, buttered toast for tea, and
Mexican rats, taken raw, for supper. He grew enor-
mously and ended in a spasm. His beauty could not
save him. I saw in San Antonio a cat dressed up for

company: He had two holes bored in each ear, and in each were two bows of pink and blue ribbon. His round face, set in pink and blue, looked like a big owl in a full blooming ivy bush. He was snow white, and wore the golden fetters of his inamorata around his neck in the form of a collar. His tail and feet were tipped with black, and his eyes of green were truly catlike. But I 'saw cats as is cats' in Sarassa, while the stage was changing mules. I stepped around to see Mr. and Mrs. Monod, a French couple with whom I had passed the night when I landed in Texas, in 1846, to join General Wool's army. Mr. Monod received me with all the shrugs of his nation, and the entrance of madame was foreshadowed by the coming in of her stately cats, with visages grave and tails erect, who preceded, surrounded, and followed her. Her present favorite, Sodoiska, a large mottled gray, was a magnificent creature, and in her train she pointed out Aglai, her favorite eleven years ago when I first visited her. They are of French breed and education, and when the claret and water was poured out for my refreshment they jumped on the table for a sit-to. If I can persuade the mail stage to give a place to one of that distinguished family, I will take it to Camp Cooper, provided madame can trust her pet into such a barbarous country and Indian society. I left the wildcat on the Rio Grande; he was too savage; had grown as large as a small-sized dog, had to be caged, and would strike at anything that came within his reach. His cage had to be strong, and consequently heavy, so I could not bring it. He would pounce upon a kid as Tom Tita [the cat at Arlington] would on a mouse, and would whistle like a tiger when you approached him. Be a good child and think always of your devoted father."

From the same place on the next day he lets his wife know how difficult it was for army officers to retain their servants:

INDIANOLA, TEXAS, *March* 28, 1857.

Major Thomas, anticipating a long sojourn, brought down Mrs. Thomas with him, who told me last evening of her troubles in relation to her womenkind. She brought two sisters from New Orleans under obligation to remain in her service two years. One of them has become enamored of a soldier at Fort Mason, and has engaged herself to marry him. Colonel Taylor informs me that his two women servants married soldiers at Fort Brown without his knowledge about a fortnight after his arrival. It seems we have our troubles wherever we are and can not escape them.

The court-martials being over, Colonel Lee started for his post, and at Fort Mason, *en route*, on the 4th of April, 1857, writes: " I write to inform you of my progress thus far on my journey. I arrived here yesterday in a cold norther, and though I pitched my tent in the most sheltered place I could find, I was surprised to see this morning, when getting up, my bucket of water, which was sitting close by my bed, so hard frozen that I had to break the ice before I could pour the water into the basin. On visiting the horses in the night they seemed to suffer much with cold, notwithstanding I had stretched their picket line under the lee of a dense thicket to protect them from the wind. This post has the advantage of Camp Cooper in providing habitable though homely quarters for officers and men. This is Easter Sunday. I hope you have been able to attend the services at Church. My own have been performed alone in my tent, I hope with a humble, grateful, and penitent heart, and will be acceptable to our Heavenly Father. May he continue his mercies to us both and all our children, relatives and friends, and in his own good time unite us in his worship, if not on earth, forever in heaven."
And on his arrival writes:

CAMP COOPER, TEXAS, *April* 19, 1857.
After an absence of over seven months I have returned to my Texas home. I heard of Indians on the way but met none. I feel always as safe in the wilderness as in the crowded city. I know in whose powerful hands I am, and on Him I rely and feel that in all our life we are upheld and sustained by Divine Providence, and that Providence requires us to use the means he has put under our control. He designs no blessing to idle and inactive wishes, and the only miracle he now exhibits to us is the power he gives to Truth and Justice to work their way in this wicked world. After so long an absence I found my valuables in a better condition than I had anticipated. My tent had frequently been prostrated by storms but always rose again. It was, of course, attended by a natural crash not worth considering, could you re-place your crockery, buckets, etc., which is impossible.

The change of the weather in Texas is the subject of a letter dated April 26, 1857 : " The changes of the weather here are very rapid. Yesterday, for instance, I was in my white linen coat and shirt all the afternoon, and the thermometer in my tent, with the walls raised and a fine breeze blowing through it, stood at eighty-nine degrees. I could not bear the blanket at night, but about twelve o'clock a 'norther' came roaring down the valley of the Clear Fork and made all my blankets necessary. This morning fires and overcoats are in fashion again. A general court-martial has been convened here for the trial of Lieutenant Eagle, Second Cavalry. I am president of the court, I am sorry to say. Colonel Bainbridge, Major Thomas, Major Van Horn, Major Paul, Captain King, and others are members. I have pitched a couple of tents by the side of mine for the Major and Mrs. Thomas, for she has accompanied him again, and they are to take their meals with me. The major can fare as I do, but I fear she will fare badly, for my man Kumer is both awkward and unskilled. I can, however, give them plenty of bread and beef, but, with the exception of preserved vegetables, fruits, etc., I can give very little else. I sent yesterday to the settlements below and got a few eggs, some butter, and one old hen. I shall not *reflect* upon *her*. The game is poor now and out of season, and we are getting none of it. In my next I shall be better able to tell you how I got on with my entertainments."

In a letter dated Camp Cooper, June 9, 1857, he mentions the sickness of the troops : " The great heat has produced much sickness among the men. The little children, too, have suffered. A bright little boy died a few days since from it. He was the only child, and his parents were much affected by his loss. They expressed a great desire to have him buried with Christian rites, and asked me to perform the ceremony ; so for the first time in my life I read the beautiful funeral service of our Church over the grave to a large and attentive audience of soldiers."

And on the 25th of June, 1857, Lieutenant-Colonel Lee, in advising his wife and one of his daughters to go

to the Springs, suggested that they be escorted by his
youngest son, saying: "A young gentleman who has
read Virgil must surely be competent to take care of
two ladies, for before I had advanced that far I was my
mother's outdoor agent and confidential messenger.
Your father [G. W. P. Custis] must have a pleasant
time at Jamestown, judging from the newspaper report
of the celebration. Tell him I at last have a prospect
of getting a puss. I have heard of a batch of kittens
at a settler's town on the river, and have the promise
of one. I have stipulated if not entirely yellow, it must
at least have some yellow in the composition of the
color of its coat; but how I shall place it—when I get
it—and my mouse on amicable terms I do not know."

In a letter dated Camp Cooper, June 22, 1857, he
tells his wife again of the sickness of the troops and
of the death of a little boy, the son of a sergeant, about
one year old. "His father came to me," he writes,
"with the tears flowing down his cheeks, and asked me
to read the funeral services over his body, which I did
at the grave for the second time in my life. I hope I
will not be asked again; for, though I must believe it
is far better for the child to be called by its heavenly
Creator into his presence in its purity and innocence,
unpolluted by sin and uncontaminated by the vices of
the world, still, it so wrings a parent's heart with anguish
that it is painful to see. Yet I know it was done in
mercy to both. The child has been saved from all
misery and sin here. The father has been given a
touching appeal and powerful inducement to prepare
for hereafter."

In the summer of 1857, Colonel Johnston being ordered to report to Washington for the purpose of taking
charge of the Utah expedition, Lieutenant-Colonel Lee
assumed command of his regiment. The death of his
father-in-law, Mr. Custis, recalled him to Arlington in
the fall of that year; but he returned as soon as possible to his regimental headquarters in Texas. The
death of the "adopted son of Washington," October 10,
1857, in his seventy-sixth year, was greatly deplored.
His unbounded hospitality was as broad as his acres,
and his vivid recollections of the Father of his Country,

though only eighteen when he died, and whose memory he venerated, were most charmingly narrated. His father, John Parke Custis, the son of Mrs. Washington by her first husband, was Washington's aid-de-camp at the siege of Yorktown, and died at the early age of twenty-eight.

G. W. P. Custis, the grandson of Mrs. Washington, was educated at Princeton. His early life was passed at Mount Vernon, but after the death of his grandmother, in 1802, he built Arlington House, opposite the city of Washington, on an estate left him by his father. In his will he decreed that all of his slaves should be set free after the expiration of five years. The time of manumission came in 1863, when the flames of war were fiercely raging; but amid the exacting duties incident to the position of army commander, Robert E. Lee, his executor, summoned them together within his lines and gave them their free papers, as well as passes through the Confederate lines to go whither they would.

Mr. Custis in his will says: " I give and bequeath to my dearly beloved daughter, Mary Custis Lee, my Arlington House estate, containing seven hundred acres, more or less, and my mill on Four Mile Run, in the County of Alexandria, and the lands of mine adjacent to said mill in the counties of Alexandria and Fairfax, in the State of Virginia, the use and benefit of all just mentioned during the term of her natural life. . . . My daughter, Mary Custis Lee, has the privilege by this will of dividing my family plate among my grandchildren; but the Mount Vernon plate, together with every article I possess relating to Washington, and that came from Mount Vernon, is to remain with my daughter at Arlington House during said daughter's life, and at her death to go to my eldest grandson, George Washington Custis Lee, and to descend from him entire and unchanged to my latest posterity." These articles were taken from Arlington, General McClellan writes, and put into the Patent Office in Washington for safe-keeping until such times as they should be restored to their rightful owner, and that he [McClellan] would be willing to testify to that fact in a court of justice, if it were necessary. They were removed afterward from the

Patent Office and placed in the National Museum, where they are now, and all applications for their restoration have been refused. A decision of the Supreme Court restored to General Custis Lee Arlington, and Congress should return these articles of Washington, which had been taken from his grandfather's house during the war.

Petty frontier war with savages was not congenial to the tastes or in accord with the genius of such a soldier as Lee. Army life there was not pleasant to officers of his rank; the forts were surrounded on all sides by long strips of dreary, uninhabited territory, and in order to better protect this vast section of western Texas, the ten companies constituting his regiment of cavalry were divided up into garrisons of one or two companies to each post. Prairie scouting was done principally by subalterns with small detachments, a lieutenant and twenty troopers being frequently detailed for that purpose. The duties of a department or regimental commander were for the most part supervisory.

No great continental lines of railroad bound in those days ocean to ocean with bands of steel. No telegraphs bore on electric wings communication from fort to fort; the United States mail was carried by armed soldiers on small mules, whose habitual gait was the gallop, while officers and their families were transported in ambulances drawn by mules, and accompanied by armed escorts. At the end of each day's journey the night was spent in tents. Sibley, of the Second Dragoons, when traveling in this way with his wife and daughter over Texas prairies, first conceived the idea of the famous tent called after him; he was caught in a "norther," and made a fire in his wall tent during the night, hoping the smoke would go out of the opening in front; it did not do so, and the next day he worked at the model of the tent, in shape similar to the Indian tepee; the present army Sibley tent is the result. Officers stationed at frontier posts in those days could not communicate with the headquarters of the Department at San Antonio for many days, or hear from their homes in the States for many weeks.

The Indians, too, were not foemen worthy of Lee's steel; the Comanches were then the largest and fiercest tribe in Texas. Attached to Lee's first station, Camp Cooper, was an "Indian reserve." The Government was making its first experiment toward civilizing the savage. The Indians were induced to come to such reservation, where they were fed and taken care of at Government expense; the great majority of them did not deign to associate so familiarly with the pale faces; some, however, came, especially in the winter months; but when the grass grew high in the spring, and the game fat, they resumed their wandering life, and with bent bow and a quiver full of arrows, lay in ambush to kill those who had fed them. Catumseh, one of the Co-manche chiefs, was at the reserve when Lee was at Camp Cooper. With true official courtesy the lieutenant colonel, as the commandant of the fort and the representative of the Great Father at Washington, decided to visit him, and told the interpreter to say to the chief that he would treat him as a friend so long as his conduct and that of the tribe deserved it, but would meet him as an enemy the moment he failed to keep his word. Catumseh was not much pleased with Lee's views, receiving them with an emphatic grunt, relying principally upon producing a profound impression upon his visitor by the information that he was a "big Indian" and had six wives, and would have more respect for Lee if he had followed his example. The visit was not productive of results, and failed to establish the desired *entente cordiale* between the two chiefs. They separated, mutually convinced that the other was a cunning specimen who had to be watched. During the interview Catumseh was in all probability taking the measure of Lee's scalp, while Lee was in turn disgusted with the paint and ornaments of the In-dian, for we find him writing word that he "was ren-dered more hideous than Nature made him." These Indians were treacherous in disposition and filthy in habit; a nomadic life made them active, vigilant, and a foe not to be despised. Their strength, however, was in-ferior to that of the soldier, because their food, clothing, and exposure were not conducive to its development. For breakfast, dinner, and supper, they had the raw meat of the antelope, deer, and buffalo. It was their habit to cut it into long strips, put it over the backs of their ponies,

ride on it to keep it in place, and whenever hungry on
the march, cut off a piece and eat it. They were matchless horsemen, and could crawl under or over the side
of a horse with the ease a squirrel could circumscribe a
tree. The bow and arrow was their principal weapon,
and the precision of their aim was wonderful. They
would draw rings a few feet in diameter on the ground,
and shooting an arrow to a surprising height in the air,
cause it to return and stick in a previously designated
circle. The green turf was the couch of the red man,
the blue sky his coverlet; stoicism and courage were
the characteristics of the race, but combined with murder,
theft, and perfidy. Colonel Lee was doubtless glad to
get away from them. On that Sunday afternoon, October 16, 1859, when John Brown with a small force
marched into Harper's Ferry with the avowed purpose
of liberating slaves and inaugurating war between the
whites and blacks, Colonel Lee was enjoying the hospitality of his Arlington home; having asked for the second furlough, in a long career, to settle up the estate of
Mr. Custis, being his sole executor, he was within range
of the Secretary of War when that officer decided to
take prompt measures to regain the United States Arsenal which Brown had captured. No one then knew
the limits of this aggressive action of Brown. An officer well equipped by experience, courage, and bal-
anced judgment was required to represent the Government. The needle in the Secretary of War's office
turned by mere force of instinct to Lee, and he promptly responded to the summons. A battalion of marines
from the navy yard at Washington was ordered to be
put at his service, and the troops of the regular army,
at Fort Monroe. The "John Brown raid," as it was
termed, was the natural outgrowth of the agitation by
the abolitionists of the slavery question on the mind of
a wild fanatic. The mad actor in the Harper's Ferry
tragedy was born in the State of Kentucky, and for the
greater part of fifty-nine years had been a monomaniac
on the subject of freedom for the negro. His mind had
become overexcited, and in his frenzy he had already
performed deeds which placed him close to the dangling
rope. At Springfield, Mass., where he once resided, he

formed an order called the "League of Gileadites," pledged to rescue fugitive slaves. To this order he delivered addresses in manuscript, saying in one of them: "Stand by one another and by your friends while a drop of blood remains and by hanging, if you must." Nine years afterward in Virginia the rope was placed in uncomfortable proximity to his own neck.

Kansas when a Territory, and an applicant for admission to the American Union, was made the abolition battlefield; John Brown went there, of course, for agitation was the business of his life. Acts of violence were frequent. Excitement in the Territory grew, and finally culminated in the Pottawattamie massacre, where five unoffending citizens were called from their beds and assassinated by Brown and his companions. The commotion created by the carnage increased the notoriety of the butcher, and he was an abolition hero. Eastern agitators placed on his head the crown of heroism, and offers of arms and money were freely tendered. His fanaticism grew, and his zeal knew no proper bounds. Virginia was selected as the best point to carry out his plans. There he would incite the negroes to rebellion and furnish them with arms from the United States Arsenal. In his madness he pictured a great and growing army of black recruits from all portions of the Southern States.

War for the extermination of slavery should begin in the State where the Dutch first landed the negro. The choice was approved by New England supporters who lost their money while Brown lost his life. Lee went to Harper's Ferry. The marines, under their gallant officers, battered down the door of the engine-house into which he had fled with a portion of his men for refuge from the aroused citizens. Brown was captured, tried, convicted, and hung on the 2d of December, 1859.

Lieutenant-Colonel Lee, from Harper's Ferry, December 1, 1859, says in a letter to his wife: "I arrived here yesterday, about noon, with four companies from Fort Monroe, and was busy all the evening getting accommodations for the men and posting pickets to insure timely notice of the approach of the enemy. The feelings of the community seem to have calmed down, and

I have been received with every kindness. I presume
we are fixed here until after the 16th. To-morrow will
probably see the last of Captain Brown (Old John
Brown). There will be less interest for the others, but
still I think the troops will not be withdrawn till they
are similarly disposed of. This morning I was introduced to Mrs. Brown, who with a Mr. Tyndale and Mrs.
McKim, all from Philadelphia, has come on to have a
last interview with her husband. As it is a matter over
which I have no control, and wish to take none, I referred them to General William B. Taliaferro.* Tell
Smith [his brother in the navy] that no charming women
have insisted on taking charge of me, as they are always
doing of him. I am left to my own resources."

A committee of Congress was appointed to investi-
gate the matter, who reported that the invasion was an
act of lawless ruffians under the sanction of no public
or political authority, distinguished from ordinary violence only by the ulterior ends in contemplation by them
and by the fact that the money to maintain the expedition, and the large amounts they had brought with them,
had been contributed by other States of the Union.

Virginia, not knowing the extent of the insurrection, was preparing for war. Henry A. Wise, then
Governor, promptly took active measures to preserve
the peace of his State, and everywhere volunteers tendered their service. When Colonel Lee was ordered to
Harper's Ferry, J. E. B. Stuart, a young lieutenant of the
First Cavalry, was in Washington on leave of absence,
and happened to be at Arlington on that day. Fond of
enterprise and indifferent to danger, he at once volunteered as aid-de-camp to Lee, asked and received permission to accompany him, and was the first to recognize
Brown, having seen him in Kansas. Afterward he became the great cavalry chieftain of the army Lee commanded. The prisoners at Harper's Ferry were at once
turned over to the United States District Attorney, Mr.
Robert Ould, and Lee returned to Washington and Arlington, and in a short time was again on his way to
resume his official duties in Texas. We find him writing

---

* Commanding the Virginia troops.

from San Antonio, Texas, June 25, 1860, to Mrs. Lee, his impressions of one of the holidays there: "Yesterday," he says, "was St. John's Day, and the principal, or at least visible, means of adoration or worship seemed to consist in riding horses. So every Mexican, and indeed others, who could procure a quadruped were cavorting through the streets, with the thermometer over a hundred degrees in the shade, a scorching sun, and dust several inches thick. You can imagine the state of the atmosphere and suffering of the horses, if not the pleasure of the riders. As everything of the horse tribe had to be brought into requisition to accommodate the bipeds, unbroken colts and worn-out hacks were saddled for the occasion. The plunging and kicking of the former procured excitement for, and the distress of the latter merriment to the crowd. I did not know before that St. John set so high a value upon equitation."

There he remained until summoned to Washington in February, 1861, reaching that city on the 1st of March. Once more, and for the last time, he was with his family under the roof of stately old Arlington.

CHAPTER IV.

WAR.

ROBERT E. LEE was now fifty-four years old, and the wheel of time had recorded thirty-two years of honorable service in the army of the United States. During that time his country had grown in population and increased in wealth and territory far exceeding the expectations and hopes of her people. His profession had absorbed his attention to such an extent that he had scarcely noticed a gathering war cloud destined to discharge death and destruction upon the American Republic, as well as mark a most important epoch in his own life and career. The Constitution adopted by the Convention at Philadelphia in 1787 was the result of a compromise of the opinions of its members. The scope and extent of the powers to be conferred on a government to be created by the representatives of the States, the line marking those powers, and the rights reserved by the States, was a most difficult problem to solve. On the one hand, if too little power were conferred on the legislative, executive, and judicial departments of the Federal Government, its organization might at any moment be broken to pieces, because not strong enough to enforce its legal decrees. On the other hand, should too much power be delegated, a strong central government might result, and the creators—the States—might be crushed out of existence by an instrument of their own creation. The people would in that case be returned to a form of government they abhorred, and from whose tyrannical methods their forefathers had breasted the waves of the Atlantic, and incurred all dangers in settling a newly discovered country. The safety of the States was the safety of the people, and only limited and defined powers must be conferred upon the Government of the United States. The Constitution, the supreme law of the land, must state in writing exactly the rights delegated by the States for their common government. The powers not so delegated were reserved by the States to themselves. They possessed them because they had never parted with them. An attempt in the Philadelphia Convention to insert a clause in the Constitution prohibiting a State's withdrawal from the Union then being formed could not have succeeded, while an express provision authorizing such secession would have been regarded as unwise and suggestive of disunion of States which were then trying to form "a more perfect union." If the framers of the Constitution, when at work in the Quaker City, said nothing upon this very important point, the States to be bound, if they ratified it, said much. They did not purpose to be blindly gagged and bound to the wheels of the Federal chariot, for they possessed sovereign power.

In the Declaration of Independence the colonies were not declared independent of Great Britain in a collective capacity, but each separate colony was transformed thereby into an independent State; and so his Britannic Majesty treats them by name in a provisional agreement in 1782. When George III withdrew the scepter of his power from the Virginia colony it was an empire in territory, and became absolutely a free, independent, and sovereign State. The allegiance of her citizens to her was undisputed and admitted. Before the life-blood could circulate in the veins of the new Government it must be stamped with the approbation of the States; it had no power to act unless ratified by nine of these States. If the other four did not ratify the Constitution, the government so formed was not binding on them. The State conventions called for this purpose were for the most part cautious and exceedingly slow of action.

To the State of Lee's nativity the independence of the colonies and their union afterward as States was largely due. One of her sons held the sword and another the pen that accomplished this great work. The superb oratory of another kept the camp fires of the Revolution burning brightly, while in ringing tones still another of her citizens moved " That these united colonies are, and of right ought to be, free and independent States, and that all political connection between these States and the State of Great Britain is, and ought to be, totally dissolved."   Nine States, a requisite number, had approved the Constitution before Virginia acted.   The debates in her convention on this subject have no equal in intellectual vigor.   Mental giants, full-armed with wisdom, fought on either side.   In one rank—opposed to the adoption of the Constitution as it came from the hands of its framers—was Patrick Henry, George Mason, Richard Henry Lee, James Monroe, Benjamin Harrison, and William Grayson.   In the other were James Madison, John Marshall, Edmund Randolph, Edmund Pendleton, and General Henry Lee, and behind them, as a powerful reserve, was the great influence of Washington.   On the final vote friends of the measure secured a majority of only ten votes.   The next State to adopt it after Virginia was New York, and she did so by only three votes.   North Carolina did not join the Union immediately, and Rhode Island for fifteen months, after the new Constitution had gone into operation.   The delay in the action of these States, and the close votes in so many others, was the result of an undefined fear in the public mind that as years rolled on the government they were then creating might in turn destroy the autonomy of the various States.

Massachusetts, South Carolina, and New York had made, as the price of their ratifying the Constitution, amendments to guard as far as possible against consolidated powers.   Robert Lee knew all this; he knew also that his own State had been remarkably careful upon this important point, for she had declared, upon consenting to go into the Union then formed by the action of nine States, "that the powers granted under the Constitution, being truly derived from the people of the United States, may be resumed by them whenever the same shall be perverted to their injury or oppression."   Without any act of his, face to face he was confronted with the great question—loyalty to the General Government or loyalty to Virginia.   Would it be treason to substitute for the *E Pluribus Unum* written upon the scroll of the beak of the eagle Virginia's *Sic Semper Tyrannis?* He had been taught when a boy that his first duty was to his mother Commonwealth. How, then, could he be a traitor if he placed his hand in hers and knelt at her feet when she called him lovingly to her side? His elevated character and conscientiousness of purpose appealed to him to decide in an honorable way this question. During those anxious moments how his thoughts must have marched and countermarched upon constitutional questions! At that very time he might have heard a distinguished senator, who afterward became Vice-President and President of the United States, declare from his seat that the Federal Government possessed no sovereign power; that it could not coerce a State; that under the Constitution you can not apprehend any of the States as a party; and that all the powers of the General Government were derived, and that it had no single primitive power. The study of the early history of his country convinced Lee that while the secession of a State from the Union might not be a remedy, it was not a violation of the Constitution so far as the original thirteen States were concerned. He probably found also, in the anxious study he was then making to arrive at a proper solution of the question, that this theory of constitutional government was recognized by most of the States when the Union was formed.

For instance, Massachusetts had declared in 1809, when the Embargo Act was passed by Congress, that it was not binding upon her citizens; and in December, 1810, one of her members of Congress declared that if Louisiana were admitted into the Union it would lead to its dissolution; the New England States would secede, "amicably if they might, forcibly if they must." And he found similar instances in the history of Pennsylvania and Kentucky. In Pennsylvania he found that that State had placed herself on record by an act of her Legislature, as well as by her Governor, to prevent a decree of a United States judge from being executed, boldly asserting that it was her duty to protect her citizens, and to her their allegiance must first be given. In his examination of this perplexing subject he might have noticed that the Constitution of the United States at that time made it mandatory on the Governor of a State to give up a fugitive from justice to the Governor of the State he had fled from, in order that he might be tried by the laws of that State; but that, notwithstanding the Constitution, governors of sovereign States did not give up offenders unless they chose to do so. Indeed, in a rendition contest between the States of Ohio and Kentucky, Mr. Taney, then Chief Justice of the United States, delivering a decision of the Court, said: "While admitting that the Constitution was mandatory on the governors, there was not a line in it which gave power to the General Government to compel a State to do anything."

Lee had probably read, too, that a convention composed of the representatives of the New England States had assembled in Hartford, Conn., in 1814, to protest against the war with England because of the great damage it was inflicting on the shipping interests of that section. He might have seen that secession was advocated as the remedy, while the declaration was made that "if the Union be destined to dissolution," some new form of confederacy should be substituted among those States which shall not need to maintain a federal relation with each other. Fortunately, peace was declared with Great Britain, or at that time there might have been a secession of the New England States. It was an interesting question to this lieutenant colonel of cavalry, that if this action had been taken by the New England States, and the States remaining in the Union had invaded their territory for the purpose of coercion, upon what side would the large majority of the citizens of the New England States have been found fighting?

The more Robert E. Lee thought upon the subject the more he became convinced, first, that Virginia in seceding from the Union was exercising the right she had reserved when she entered it. Second, that if war must follow, his sword should be drawn in her defense, and not be pointed against her. In the soil of old Virginia were buried those nearest and dearest to him. His ancestors had first settled within her limits. She was to be invaded because she exercised a right not denied her

by the Constitution, and her course had been determined
by a convention of the representatives of her people duly
called to consider the question; and a convention voiced
the highest authority of a State. He may have deplored
her action, but he could not oppose his judgment to the
collective wisdom of her representatives whose action
had been solemnly indorsed by her people at the polls.
The irrepressible conflict had to be met in his own person. He had seen, but could not prevent the sections
from drifting apart. If the interests of the manufactur-
ing and shipping States of the North and the agricultural States of the South were not in entire harmony, he
had hoped that a possible remedy might be found. Mr.
Lincoln received only 1,857,000 of the popular vote,
while Breckinridge, Douglas, and Bell received 2,800,-
000; but that was not a sufficient reason in his opinion
to declare war. If he had much to do with John
Brown's body lying moldering in the ground, the fact
that his spirit was marching on down the abolition ranks
did not disturb him. His State when a colony was opposed to slavery. The first speech his eloquent relative, Richard Henry Lee, ever made was in favor of the
motion to lay so heavy a duty on the importation of
slaves as effectually to put an end to the iniquitous and
disgraceful traffic in the colony of Virginia.

Lee had read, too, Jefferson's indictment of Great
Britain for allowing the slave trade when he penned the
Declaration of Independence. He knew that slavery existed in the Northern States so long as it was profitable,
and was abolished when it was not, and that the May-
flower which landed the Pilgrim Fathers on Plymouth
Rock sailed on its very next voyage with a cargo of
slaves. He had found the negroes shucking corn and
hoeing potatoes. They had always been kindly treated
by him; and no more happy, contented, well-clothed
and well-fed negroes ever existed than those at Arlington. He would not have fought to preserve slavery; he
disapproved of it and had years before freed his own,
and Mr. Custis had freed by will all of his. He regretted war, but did not regret as one of its results the
probable freedom of the slave, although he knew that
slavery had called a race of savages from superstition

and idolatry and imparted to them a general knowledge
of the precepts of religion. Indeed, he is recorded as
saying at that time that if he owned all the negroes of
the South he would gladly yield them up for the preservation of the Union. In 1861 Lee hoped and prayed
that the Temple of American Liberty might still stand
in the majesty of its vast proportions, complete in all of
its parts, each pillar representing with equal strength an
American State. He sincerely hoped each State would
pursue the path designated for it by the Constitution,
as the planets revolve in well-defined orbits around the
great central sun. He wrote from Texas in 1861 that
he could not anticipate a greater calamity for the country than the dissolution of the Union, and that he was
willing to sacrifice anything but honor for its preservation. And in another letter from Fort Mason, Texas,
January, 1861, to Mrs. Lee, he says: "You see by a former letter that I received from Major Nicholl, Everett's
Life of Washington you sent me, and enjoyed its peru-
sal very much. How his spirit would be grieved could
he see the wreck of his mighty labors! I will not, however, permit myself to believe, till all ground for hope is
gone, that the work of his noble deeds will be destroyed,
and that his precious advice and virtuous example will
soon be forgotten by his countrymen. As far as I can
judge from the papers, we are between a state of anarchy
and civil war. May God avert from us both. I fear
mankind for years will not be sufficiently Christianized
to bear the absence of restraint and force. I see that
four States have declared themselves out of the Union.
Four more apparently will follow their example. Then
if the border States are dragged into the gulf of revolution, one half of the country will be arrayed against
the other, and I must try and be patient and wait the
end, for I can do nothing to hasten or retard it."

It was hard for Lee to give up his position in the
army and separate himself from his army comrades and
associations. He wrote in 1849, from Mobile, Ala.:
"I have met many officers of the garrison who were
with me in Mexico. You have often heard me say
the cordiality and friendship in the army was the great
attraction of the service. It is that, I believe, that has

kept me in it so long, and it is that which now makes me fear to leave it. I do not know where I should meet with so much friendship out of it."

While he was wrestling with this disturbing question at Arlington his old commander, Scott, just across the river, was pleading for him to remain in the service of the United States. The veteran general had impressed the President with the distinguished services of Colonel Lee, and urged that every effort should be made to keep him on the side of the Union, going so far as to say that he would be worth fifty thousand men to their cause. Probably it was due to Scott that Mr. Lincoln requested Mr. Francis Preston Blair to have an interview with Lee, and secure him by the tempting offer of the command of the active army of the United States. Neither the President nor his officers knew the man. Three years after the war, in a letter to the Honorable Reverdy Johnson, of Maryland, dated February 25, 1868, is found for the first time his account of this interview: "After listening to Blair's remarks," writes Lee, "I declined the offer he made me to take command of the army that was to be brought into the field, stating, as candidly and courteously as I could, that, though opposed to secession and deprecating war, I could take no part in an invasion of the Southern States.

"I went directly from the interview with Mr. Blair to the office of General Scott, told him of the proposition that had been made me, and my decision. After reflection upon returning home, I concluded that I ought no longer to retain any commission I held in the United States Army, and on the second morning thereafter I forwarded my resignation to General Scott. At the time I hoped that peace would have been preserved; that some way would be found to save the country from the calamities of war; and I then had no other intention than to pass the remainder of my life as a private citizen. Two days afterward, on the invitation of the Governor of Virginia, I repaired to Richmond, found that the convention then in session had passed an ordinance withdrawing the State from the Union, and accepted the commission of commander of its forces, which was tendered me."

"Since the Son of Man stood on the mount," said an

orator, "and saw all the kingdoms of the earth and the glory thereof stretching before him, and turned away from them to the agony and bloody sweat of Gethsemane, and to the Cross of Calvary beyond, no follower of the meek and lowly Saviour can have undergone a more trying ordeal, or met it with a more heroic spirit of sacrifice."

Two and a half months before Colonel Lee's resignation the conventions of South Carolina, Mississippi, Florida, Alabama, Georgia, Louisiana, and Texas had respectively passed ordinances taking these States out of the Union; and their delegates had assembled at Montgomery, Ala., and formed a new government, under the name of the Confederate States of America. On February 4th, the date of the birth of the new government, at Virginia's request, a peace conference, composed of delegates from twenty-one States, met in Washington. The Congress of the United States rejected all terms of settlement proposed by it, and the rising tide of sectional strife passed the high-water mark.

If the seven Southern States which first formed the Confederacy were terribly in earnest, so equally were the Northern and Eastern States in opposition to the new government. The border States, upon whose breast the storm of war must break, were still hoping for a peaceable solution of the trouble; the problem was soon solved for them. In Charleston Harbor, South Carolina, out of the waters rises a fortress of the United States called Sumter. It is situated in the middle of the harbor, and was erected on an artificial island built on the shoals. Its walls were eight feet thick and forty feet high. It was five-sided, inclosing a space of about three hundred and fifty feet. On its ramparts and in its casements one hundred and forty guns could be mounted, and its full garrison was six hundred men. This fort was originally occupied only by an engineer, who was employing some workmen in its repairs; but at Fort Moultrie, on a narrow neck of land extending into the harbor, was a garrison of sixty-nine soldiers and nine officers under the command of Major Robert Anderson. This officer, having every reason to apprehend an attack upon his position, decided to abandon Moultrie and take possession of Sumter, which he did on the night of December 26th. Robert Anderson was a Kentuckian, and a West Point graduate of the class of 1827, whose sympathies at the beginning of the war were rather on the side of the South. He continued to occupy with his little force this island fort, while Beauregard, who had resigned from the United States Army and was already commissioned by the seceding States, was building hostile batteries on every side. A crisis in this harbor was fast approaching. The Government of the United States decided to make an attempt to throw men and provisions into the fort, and when this became known, orders were issued from Montgomery for Beauregard to open his batteries. In the gray of the morning at half-past four on a certain Friday, April 12, 1861, a single shot fired from the Confederate batteries at Fort Johnson announced that the bombardment of a fort over whose grim walls floated the Stars and Stripes was about to begin. The report of the bursting of this shell startled the country from center to circumference. The Angel of Peace which for months had been hovering over the republic plumed his wings for flight and the Demon of War reigned supreme. President Lincoln followed this act of war by issuing a proclamation calling for seventy-five thousand troops. A prompt response was given to him by the governors of the Northern States; but those of Arkansas, Tennessee, Kentucky, North Carolina, Virginia, and Missouri declined in terms more or less emphatic. The secession of all these States from the Union followed, except Kentucky and Missouri, whose sympathies were divided, and their union with the Government formed at Montgomery, Ala., was speedily made. On April 17, 1861, the Ordinance of Secession was passed by the Virginia Convention, and the day following, Lee had a long interview with his old commander, General Scott. On the 20th the die was cast; his Rubicon was crossed, for the resignation * of his commission in the

---

* ARLINGTON, WASHINGTON CITY P. O., *April* 20, 1861.
Honorable Simon Cameron, Secretary of War.
    SIR : I have the honor to tender the resignation of my commission as colonel of the first regiment of cavalry.
    Very respectfully your obedient servant,
                R. E. LEE, *Colonel, First Cavalry.*

army of the United States was respectfully tendered to the War Department. His letter explanatory of his position at that time, though familiar to the public, is given here as the best expression of his feelings upon so momentous a subject :

ARLINGTON, VA., *April* 20, 1861.

GENERAL : Since my interview with you on the 18th inst. I have felt that I ought no longer to retain my commission in the army. I therefore tender my resignation, which I request you will recommend for acceptance. It would have been presented at once but for the struggle it has cost me to separate myself from a service to which I have devoted the best years of my life and all the ability I possessed. During the whole of that time— more than a quarter of a century—I have experienced nothing but kindness from my superiors and a most cordial friendship from my comrades. To no one, General, have I been as much indebted as to yourself for uniform kindness and consideration, and it has always been my ardent desire to merit your approbation. I shall carry to the grave the most grateful recollections of your kind consideration, and your name and fame shall always be dear to me. Save in the defense of my native State I never desire again to draw my sword. Be pleased to accept my most earnest wishes for the continuance of your happiness and prosperity, and believe me, most truly yours,

(Signed) R. E. LEE.

To his sister in Baltimore, whose husband was a strong Union man, Colonel Lee wrote the same day, telling her that he had resigned ; that he had decided the question whether he should take part for or against his native State, saying: " With all my devotion to the Union and the feeling of loyalty and duty of an American citizen, I have not been able to make up my mind to raise my hand against my relatives, my children, my home. I know you will blame me, but you must think as kindly of me as you can, and believe I have endeavored to do what I thought right. May God guard and protect you and yours, and pour upon you every blessing, is the prayer of your devoted brother."

He wrote still a third letter, upon this eventful day, to his brother, Sydney Smith Lee, at that time a commander in the United States Navy :

ARLINGTON, VA., *April* 20, 1861.

MY DEAR BROTHER SMITH : The question which was the subject of my earnest consultation with you on the 18th inst. has in my own mind been decided. After the most anxious inquiry as to the correct course for me to pursue, I concluded to resign, and sent in my resignation this morning. I wished to wait till the Ordinance of Secession should be acted on by the people of Virginia; but war seems to have commenced, and I am liable at any time to be ordered on duty, which I could not conscientiously perform. To save me from such a position, and to prevent the necessity of resigning under orders, I had to act at once, and before I could see you again on the subject, as I had wished. I am now a private citizen, and have no other ambition than to remain at home. Save in the defense of my native State, I have no desire ever again to draw my sword. I send you my warmest love.

Your affectionate brother,

(Signed)   R. E. LEE.

It was necessary now to bid farewell to old Arlington, where so many happy memories of the past had clustered. He must say good-by to his army comrades, and his sword must soon be crossed with many of them on the bloody field of battle. With conflicting emotions he departed from what had been the capital of his country so long, and went immediately to Richmond, the capital of his State. His coming had been anxiously looked for, and his mother Commonwealth opened wide her arms to embrace her distinguished son. He was at once nominated by the Governor to the Virginia Convention still in session there, to be a major general and commander in chief of the Virginia forces. When the question of his nomination was put to that body, there was an immediate and ardent response, which attested the cordial and unbounded confidence in the man to whom Virginia committed her fortunes. The next day Major-General Lee was invited to appear before the convention. The invitation greatly disturbed him; he was so modest, so opposed to display, so little accustomed to be gazed at by the public, and certainly never before had been placed in such a trying position. But what could he do? The ceremony had been prepared; he had accepted the command of the troops of Virginia after having declined the command of the United States Army. Virginia, through her convention, wanted to see him. A committee had been appointed to transmit its invitation and conduct him to its presence. " The hall was crowded," said the historian, "with an eager audience." All the members of the convention stood as a mark of respect. On the right of the presiding officer were Governor Letcher, of Virginia, and Mr. Stevens, the Vice-President of the Confederacy, and on the left members of the Advisory Council of Virginia. Leaning on the arm of Mr. Marmaduke Johnson, of Richmond, chairman of the committee, General Lee entered the hall. Every spectator admired the personal appearance of the man, his dignified figure, his air of self-composure, his strength of feature, in which shone the steady animation of a consciousness of power, purpose, and decision. He was in the full and hardy flush of ripe years and vigorous health. His form was tall, its constituents well knit together; his head, well shaped and squarely built, gave indication of a powerful intellect. The face, not yet interlined by age, still remarkable for its personal beauty, was lighted up by eyes black in the shade, but brown in the full light, clear, benignant, but with a deep recess of light, a curtained fire in them that blazed in moments of excitement; the countenance and natural expression were gentle and benevolent, yet striking the beholder as masking an iron will. His manners were at once grave and kindly without gayety or abandon. He was also without any affectation of dignity. Such is the man whose stately figure in the capital at Richmond brought to mind the old race of Virginians, and who was thereafter to win a reputation not only as the first commander, but also as a perfect and beautiful model of manhood.

When about half-way up the main aisle Mr. Johnson stopped, and in ponderous tones said : " Mr. President, I have the honor to present to you and to the convention Major-General Lee." The general's retreat was cut off by the crowd of people who pressed up the hall in his rear. The president of the convention, Mr. Janney, of the County of Loudoun, was to voice the sentiments of the body over which he had ably presided, and Lee must face the music of Janney's eloquence, so he stood calmly while the president of the convention said :

" Major-General Lee, in the name of the people of our native State here represented, I bid you a cordial and heartfelt welcome to this hall in which we may yet almost hear the echo of the voices of the statesmen and soldiers and sages of bygone days who have borne your name, whose blood now flows in your veins. When the necessity became apparent of having a leader for our forces, all hearts and all eyes, with an instinct which is a surer guide than reason itself, turned to the old county of Westmoreland. We know how prolific she had been in other days of heroes and statesmen. We know she had given birth to the Father of his Country, to Richard Henry Lee, to Monroe, and last, though not least, to your own gallant father; and we knew well by your deeds that her productive power was not yet exhausted. We watched with the most profound and intense interest the triumphal march of the army led by General Scott, to which you were attached, from Vera Cruz to the capital of Mexico. We read of the sanguinary conflicts and blood-stained fields, in all of which victory perched upon our banners. We know of the unfading luster that was shed on the American armies by that campaign, and we know also what your modesty has always disclaimed—that no small share of the glory of these achievements was due to your valor and military genius. Sir, we have by this unanimous vote expressed our convictions that you are at this time among the living citizens of Virginia, '*first in war.*' We pray to God most fervently that you may conduct the operations committed to your charge, that it will soon be said of you that you are the '*first in peace,*' and when that time comes you will have earned the still prouder distinction of being '*first in the hearts of your countrymen.*' When the Father of his Country made his last will and testament he gave his swords to his favorite nephews with the injunction that they should never be drawn from their scabbards except in self-defense, or in defense of the rights and principles of their country, and that if drawn for the latter purpose, they should fall with them in their hands rather than relinquish them. Yesterday your mother Virginia placed her sword in your hand upon the implied condition that in all things you will keep it to the letter and spirit, that you will draw it only in defense, and that you will fall with it in your hand rather than that the object for which it is placed there should fail."

The reply of General Lee was simple and short,

Washington-like in modesty and touching in language. His heart was filled with emotion as he heard the very language his father had used in reference to the great Washington, applied so many years afterward to himself. The scene was solemn as well as new to the soldier.

" Mr. President and Gentlemen of the Convention," said he in reply, " profoundly impressed with the solemnity of the occasion, for which I must say I was not prepared, I accept the position assigned me by your partiality. I would have much preferred had the choice fallen upon an abler man. Trusting in Almighty God, an approving conscience, and the aid of my fellow-citizens, I devote myself to the service of my native State, in whose behalf alone will I ever again draw my sword." It was his first and last speech, and under all the circumstances he could safely rest his oratorical reputation upon this single effort. It is possible, had he selected a public profession after the war, we could have said of him as Pope said of Argyll :

> The State's thunder born to wield,
> And shake at once the Senate and the field.

He had now entered upon the discharge of new duties and assumed new responsibilities. The bridge over which he had crossed from Colonel Lee, of the United States Army, to Major-General Lee, of the Virginia forces, had been burned behind him. He was enlisted for the war. In the prime of manhood and physical vigor he held what he considered the greatest honor—his State's highest commission. He had sacrificed exalted rank, home, and fortune, and had followed only the conscientious voice of duty. The words of his own father were ringing in his ears as he once exclaimed, " No consideration on earth could induce me to act a part, however gratifying, which could be construed into a disregard or forgetfulness of this Commonwealth." Therefore he would not join the confederacy of States, but was waiting for the endorsation by the people of Virginia of the action of her representatives duly assembled in convention. One hundred and twenty thousand votes were cast for the ratification of the Ordinance ot Secession, some twenty thousand against it. Before this popular decision was reached, the convention gave to the Confederate Government the control of the military operations within her border, and the Secretary of War, Mr. L. P. Walker, had, by an order dated Montgomery, Ala., in May, 1861, placed under General Lee's command all troops of the Confederate States as soon as they arrived in Virginia. Previous to this, his command was limited to the Virginia forces. Virginia having united her fortune with her Southern sister States, the Confederate Congress in session at Montgomery ten days afterward adjourned to meet in Richmond, Va. A letter from General Lee to his wife, who was still at Arlington, April 30, 1861, tells her that he is "glad to hear all is well and as yet peaceful. I fear the latter state will not continue long. I think, therefore, you had better prepare all things for removal from Arlington — that is, plate, pictures, etc., and be prepared at any moment. Where to go is the difficulty. When the war commences no place will be exempt; in my opinion, indeed, all the avenues into the State will be the scene of military operations. I wrote to Robert [his son] that I could not consent to take boys from their schools and young men from their colleges and put them in the ranks at the beginning of the war when they are not needed. The war may last ten years. Where are our ranks to be filled from then?"

And again he writes: "I am very anxious about you. You have to move, and make arrangements to go to some point of safety which you must select. The Mount Vernon plate and pictures ought to be secured. War is inevitable, and there is no telling when it will burst around you. Virginia yesterday, I understand, joined the Confederate States. What policy they may adopt I can not conjecture." And Mrs. Lee, from Arlington, May 5, 1861, sent the following note to General Scott in Washington:

MY DEAR GENERAL: Hearing that you desire to see the account of my husband's reception in Richmond, I have sent it to you. No honors can reconcile us to this fratricidal war which we would have laid down our lives freely to avert. Whatever may happen, I feel that I may expect from your kindness all the protection you can in honor afford. Nothing can ever make me forget your kind appreciation of Mr. Lee. If you knew all you

would not think so hardly of me. Were it not that I would not
add one feather to his load of care, nothing would induce me to
abandon my home. Oh, that you could command peace to our
distracted country !   Yours in sadness and sorrow,
                                        M. C. LEE.

Occasionally this wife and mother's heart would beat
with happiness at the stories of successful compromise
between the sections and then sink in despair at the
continued prospects of war. From Richmond, May
13, 1861, her husband wrote her : " Do not put faith in
rumors of adjustment. I see no prospect for it. It can
not be while passions on both sides are so infuriated.
Make your plans for several years of war. If Virginia
is invaded, which appears to be designed, the main
routes through the country will, in all probability, be
infested and passage interrupted. I agree with you in
thinking that the inflammatory articles in the papers do
us much harm. I object particularly to those in the
Southern papers, as I wish them to take a firm, dignified
course, free from bravado and boasting. The times
are indeed calamitous. The brightness of God's countenance seems turned from us, and its mercy stopped in
its blissful current. It may not always be so dark, and
he may in time pardon our sins and take us under his
protection. Tell Custis * he must consult his own judgment, reason, and conscience as to the course he may
take. I do not wish him to be guided by my wishes or
example. If I have done wrong, let him do better.
The present is a momentous question which every man
must settle for himself and upon principle. Our good
Bishop Meade has just come in to see me. He opens
the convention to morrow, and, I understood him to
say, would preach his fiftieth anniversary sermon.
God bless and guard you." A few days before he had
written :

                              RICHMOND, *May* 8, 1861.
     I received yesterday your letter of the 5th. I grieve at the
anxiety that drives you from your home. I can appreciate your
feelings on the occasion, and pray that you may receive comfort
and strength in the difficulties that surround you. When I re-

---

* His son, then a lieutenant in the Engineer Corps, U. S. Army.

flect upon the calamity pending over the country my own sorrows sink into insignificance.

On the 2d of the same month he told her: "I have just received Custis's letter of the 30th, inclosing the acceptance of my resignation. It is stated it will take effect on the 25th of April. I resigned on the 20th, and wished it to take effect on that day. I can not consent to its running on further, and he must receive no pay if they tender it beyond that day, but return the whole if need be." And again, in a letter May 16, 1861, he writes: "I witnessed the opening of the convention yesterday, and heard the good bishop's sermon for the fiftieth anniversary of his ministry. It was most impressive, and more than once I felt the tears coursing down my cheeks. It was from the text: 'And Pharaoh said unto Jacob, How old art thou?' It was full of humility and self-reproach."

Mr. Jefferson Davis, the provisional President of the new Government, reached Richmond on the 29th of May. Virginia's capital then became the capital of the Confederacy. The journey from Alabama by the Southern President was a triumphal march. At every station crowds of people met and cheered him, and on his arrival in Richmond he received an ovation. He had graduated at West Point the year before General Lee, but was one year and a half his junior in age. He had served in the infantry, and later in the dragoons in the United States Army, and then resigned his commission. When the Mexican War broke out his soldierly instincts could not be repressed. His services were greatly demanded, and he entered Mexico as the colonel of a Mississippi regiment. He had also held the highest positions in civil life, as a member of the United States House of Representatives, as a Senator of the United States, and Secretary of War in Mr. Pierce's Cabinet. Distinguished in war and in peace, a statesman and a soldier, he combined in his person the qualities necessary for the head of a new government born amid the throes of war, whose cradle had been lighted by the rifle's flash. No stain had ever been found on the polished armor of his career during a long term of public service. His courage could not be assailed, his honor questioned, or his ability denied. He had been made on the secession of Mississippi commander in chief of her forces, just as General Lee had been commissioned in the Virginia forces. Had he consulted his own wishes he would have respectfully declined the position of President, and upon the pages of history, from 1861 to 1865, might have been found the record of his deeds as an army commander.

The *rôle* assigned to him in the tragedy of war was a most difficult one to discharge, and in the eyes of his opponents he was "the villain of the play." When the red curtain of war rolled up from the American stage, to the world were revealed two presidential chairs. In one was seated Mr. Abraham Lincoln, in the other Mr. Jefferson Davis. These two chief magistrates were both born in Kentucky. One, when a small child, was carried by his parents to Mississippi; the other, when about eight years old, was taken to Indiana, and afterward to Illinois. Each absorbed the political theories of their respective States. Had Davis been carried to Illinois and Lincoln to Mississippi, in the war between the States Lincoln might have been carrying a Mississippi rifle, while Davis held aloft the star-spangled banner. Each represented, as powerful exponents, the constructions of the Constitution, referred to the sword for decision, there being no common arbiter in such case. Mr. Davis's office had none of the elements of popularity. Upon it was showered the criticisms of the South, while at the North every finger, every pen, every gun was pointed at its occupant. Davis used every possible effort to make two republics grow on this continent where only one grew before; and so likewise did Lee.

The former, as President, could not have written success on the standards of the Confederacy; it was not so ordained—the contest was too unequal in men, money, and means of war. The people of the whole South, who stood behind their guns, or were left at their hearthstones, numbered only six million whites, while the population in the Northern States amounted to eighteen million. The former were animated by the tie which binds the heart to home, and which it is said "stretches from the cradle to the grave, spans the heavens, and is riveted through eternity to the throne of God on high." On the other hand, the Northern people desired to see the great republic stretch from the waves of the Atlantic to the golden sands of the Pacific, and from the Northern lakes to where the Father of Waters rolls his tribute to the Gulf as an undivided country. The North was thickly populated, and the whole machinery of its Government was in running order. It had its regular army around which the volunteer regiments could rally. Its navy rode undisputed the adjoining seas; its arsenals and forts were crammed with weapons, and its Treasury filled with precious metals, out of which could be manufactured all the sinews of war. In a long struggle, under these circumstances, victory was to the strong. The deeds of a brave soldier, even if unsuccessful, excite the admiration of mankind. The civil ruler of the vanquished is not so fortunate when the power to sustain his government departs. Mr. Davis was not the demon of hate his enemies have painted. He did not thirst for the blood of his countrymen. His whole character has been misunderstood by the mass of the people who opposed his public views. His heart was tender as a woman's; he was brave as a lion, and true as the needle to the pole to his convictions; in disposition generous, in character courteous and chivalric.

When his voice was heard for the last time in the Senate Chamber of the United States it did not breathe hatred to sections of the country other than his own, but he spoke in affectionate terms of those with whom he had to conscientiously differ upon great questions. "I am sure," said he, "that I feel no hostility to you Senators from the North. I am sure there is not one of you, whatever sharp discussion there may have been between us, to whom I can not say in the presence of my God, I wish you well, and such is the feeling, I am sure, of the people whom I represent and those whom you represent. For whatever offense I have given, I have, Senators, in this hour of our parting, to offer you my apology."

General Lee found himself surrounded on all sides by war. From Richmond, June 9, 1861, he wrote his wife: "You may be aware that the Confederate Government is established here. Yesterday I turned over to it the command of the military and naval forces of the State, in accordance with the proclamation of the Governor, under an agreement between the State and the Confederate States. I do not know what my position will be. I should like to retire to private life, so that I could be with you and the children, but if I can be of service to the State or her cause, I must continue. Mr. Davis and all his Cabinet are here." And two days afterward he tells her: "I am sorry to learn that you are anxious and uneasy about passing events. We can not change or hinder them, and it is not the part of wisdom to be annoyed by them. In this time of great suffering to the State and country, our private distresses we must bear with resignation, and not aggravate them by repining, trusting to a kind and merciful God to overrule them for our good."

Preparations were now being rapidly made for war, which could be no longer prevented or postponed. The firing upon and capture of Fort Sumter, the hostile reception given the Massachusetts troops in Baltimore on April 19th, the great excitement all through the country, caused every one to speedily join the side he desired to unite with. In the North every arsenal was put to work on the manufacture of arms for their troops. It was the first duty of the Federal Government to make Washington, the capital, secure. Then an army of invasion must be organized and a plan of campaign mapped out, whose objective point was the capture of Richmond, the capital of the Southern Confederacy.

CHAPTER V.

INVASION OF VIRGINIA.

ON the 24th of May the advance guard of the Federal army occupied the heights of Washington, with Arlington, the former home of General Lee, as headquarters, as well as all the country stretching down the Potomac eight miles below to Alexandria. Only a few persons understood the magnitude of the impending contest. The "Rebellion" many thought was to be crushed in ninety days, and most of the volunteer troops were enlisted by the North for that period.

One hundred and fifteen miles away, at Richmond, great activity prevailed also. The sagacity, skill, and experience of Lee were taxed to the uttermost equipping and sending to threatened points the troops rapidly arriving from the South. There was no regular army to serve as a nucleus, or navy, commissary, quartermaster's, or ordnance departments. Everything had to be provided. General Gorgas, the Chief of Ordnance of the Confederate States, reported that he found in all the arsenals of the Confederate States but fifteen thousand rifles and one hundred and twenty thousand inferior muskets. In addition there were a few old flint muskets at Richmond, and some Hall's rifles and carbines at Baton Rouge. There was no powder, except some which had been left over from the Mexican War and had been stored at Baton Rouge Arsenal and at Mount Vernon, Ala. There was but little artillery, and no cavalry, arms, or equipments. Raw recruits had to be drilled and disciplined, companies assigned to regiments, regiments to brigades, brigades to divisions. With the map of Virginia before him, Lee studied to make a successful defensive campaign. He knew that the object

of the greatest importance to his enemy was the capture
of Richmond, and that the fall of that city early in the
contest might terminate the war.   His genius for grand
tactics and strategy taught him at once that the most
natural advance to Richmond from Washington would
be along the Orange and Alexandria Railroad, as it was
called then.   It was the only railway running into the
State at that time from Washington, and troops moving
along its line could be so directed as not to uncover
their capital, while prompt facilities could be obtained
for transportation of supplies from the base established
at Alexandria or Washington.   Another route lay up
the peninsula lying between the James and York Rivers,
with Fort Monroe and its vicinity as a base for operations.   Another way to enter the State was by crossing
the upper Potomac at Harper's Ferry and Williamsport,
and then on through the great valley of Virginia between the Blue Ridge and Shenandoah Mountains; and
still another entrance might be effected through the
mountain ranges of West Virginia.   Norfolk, too, by
the sea, had to be watched and protected.   Troops,
therefore, as fast as they arrived in Richmond and
could be prepared for the campaign, were sent principally to these points.   It was necessary that organized
forces should be in such position as to check any forward movements by any of these routes.   General Lee
early had predicted the march of the Army of the Potomac, as the Washington army was called, and pointed out
what would in all probability be the battlefield.   He
ordered the largest number of troops to Manassas Junction, that being the point of union of the railroad coming into Virginia from Washington with a branch road
leading into the Valley of Virginia.   It was a strategic
point, because an army in position there would be able
to resist the further progress of the opposing hosts,
and could, if necessary, re-enforce the troops in the
valley.   Competent and experienced officers were at
an early date placed in command of the important
stations.   For Manassas, General P. G. T. Beauregard
was selected.   This officer, having been the first employed in active operations, and having compelled the
surrender of Fort Sumter, was the military hero of the

hour. He was a graduate of West Point, and had served in the Engineer Corps with marked distinction. His skill in that branch of the service was admirably displayed in the selection of positions for the batteries erected to defend Charleston Harbor, and his vigilance, activity, and military knowledge were rewarded by the prompt reduction of the fort. He assumed command of the troops at and in the vicinity of Manassas about the 1st of June, and possessed the entire confidence of his army.

Harper's Ferry received also the prompt attention of the Confederate authorities. To this important post General Joseph E. Johnston was ordered, superseding in the command there Colonel T. J. Jackson. General Johnston assumed command of the Army of the Shenandoah on May 23, 1861. He was a classmate of Lee's at West Point. On being graduated he was assigned to the artillery, and then to the topographical engineers. He became distinguished before his beard grew. In the Indian wars in Florida and in Mexico his coolness, address, soldierly bearing, daring deeds, and his many wounds made him famous. General Scott is reported to have said " Johnston is a great soldier, but was unfortunate enough to get shot in nearly every engagement." In 1861 he was at the head of the Quartermaster's Department of the United States Army, with the rank of brigadier general. Upon the resignation of his commission he was commissioned a general officer in the Virginia service by Governor Letcher. Later he was given a brigadier general's commission in the Confederate service in the regular army, then the highest grade in it. The resignation of his commission and his decision to fight under the flag of the South was hailed with delight by the Southern people, who felt they were securing the services of an army commander of undoubted merit. General Benjamin Huger, another distinguished officer of the army of the United States, who had also resigned, was charged with watching over Norfolk. General John Bankhead Magruder, who had acquired distinction in the Federal army but had joined his fortunes to the South, was ordered to Yorktown to defend the peninsular route. General Holmes,

who had rendered conspicuous service in the army of
the United States, was sent to command at Acquia
Creek, some twelve miles east of Fredericksburg. Robert Garnett, also an officer of the United States Army,
of tested ability, was ordered to West Virginia to take
charge of the department and of the forces assembling
in that region. All of these officers had been selected
with great care, and had been more or less distinguished
in the army, but not one of them had ever before been
in command of large numbers of men.

The regular army of the United States previous to
1861 was a small organization of fifteen thousand soldiers. Including the quartermaster general, there were
only five general officers in it—Scott, Wool, Harney,
Twiggs, and Joe Johnston. A few only of the officers,
to whom was assigned on either side the command of
armies, corps, and divisions, had ever previous to the
war commanded a regiment, the great majority of them
not more than one company.

In these operations of defense General Lee's whole
time was employed. The larger number of troops were
sent to Beauregard and Johnston, it being evident that
one or both of the points occupied by their armies would
be the scene of the earliest conflicts. His services were
great and indispensable, but it can be readily seen that
after supplying the threatened points with troops, and
after providing commanding officers for the different
armies when the battles of the war began, there would
be no place for him in the field, but that the active operations there would be intrusted to others at first.

To Mrs. Lee, from Richmond, June 24, 1861, he
wrote : " My movements are very uncertain, and I wish
to take the field as soon as certain arrangements can be
made. I may go at any moment to any point where it
may be necessary. Custis is engaged on the works
around this city, and many of our old friends are dropping in. E. P. Alexander is here. Jimmy Hill, Alston,
Jenifer, etc., and I hear that my old colonel, A. S. Johnston, is crossing the plains from California."

Preparations for the advance of the Federal army
of the Potomac on Manassas were rapidly nearing completion. Everything needed was bountifully provided

from an overflowing Treasury. General Scott was still Commander in Chief of the United States Army, and still the possessor of the entire confidence of his country. Mr. Simon Cameron, Mr. Lincoln's Secretary of War, wrote to Mr. John Sherman, then in the field as a volunteer aid-de-camp to General Patterson, that the whole administration has but one safe course in this emergency, and that is to be guided by the counsels of the general in chief in all that relates to the plans, movements, and commands of the campaign. He has superior knowledge, wisdom, and patriotism over any other member of the administration, said Cameron, and enjoys the unlimited confidence of the people, as well as that of the President and his advisers.

The day after General Scott's last interview with General Lee he published General Order No. 3, which created the Department of Washington, embracing Pennsylvania, Delaware, Maryland, and the District of Columbia, and Major-General Robert Patterson, of Pennsylvania, was placed in command. On June 3, 1861, the headquarters of this officer were at Chambersburg, Pa., where he was busy organizing and equipping the army whose objective point was Harper's Ferry, at that time occupied by a small number of the Southern troops. It was General Scott's original plan to make Patterson fight the first great battle in the war, giving him all the troops he could possibly spare from the defense of Washington. It was his first purpose to make a feint on Beauregard at Manassas, while making a real attack upon Joe Johnston in the Valley of Virginia. With the defeat of Johnston the victorious army could march on Beauregard at Manassas, re-enforced by the troops around the Federal capital. Soldiers of high reputation and great merit were ordered to report to Patterson. Fitz John Porter was his adjutant general, Amos Beckwith commissary of subsistence, Crosman quartermaster, Sampson topographical engineer, Newton engineer; while such men as A. E. Burnside, George H. Thomas, Miles, Abercrombie, Cadwalader, Stone, and Negley commanded troops; and then, the laws being silent in the midst of arms, Senator John Sherman, of Ohio, was his aid-de-camp. From Patter-

son's position two routes led to the Valley of Virginia,
one *via* Frederick, Md., across the Potomac at Harper's Ferry, the other by Hagerstown, Md., crossing
at Williamsport and thence to Martinsburg. Patterson
wisely selected the latter route, because it was a flank
movement on his enemy at Harper's Ferry, who could
present no obstacle to a successful passage to the Potomac. He therefore marched his army to Hagerstown,
where, on the 15th of June, he had ten thousand men.
On that day General Johnston evacuated Harper's Ferry,
and two days later, with a force of sixty-five hundred
men, was at Bunker Hill, a point twelve miles from
Winchester and between that city and Martinsburg.

This was wise on the part of Johnston. His intention to do so was accelerated from a well-authen-
ticated rumor that had reached him of the advance
of the Federal forces in the direction of Winchester
from Romney, some forty-three miles west of that
place. Indeed, he had detached two regiments under
Colonels A. P. Hill and Gibbons, and sent them to
Winchester with orders to proceed out on the road
toward Romney for the purpose of checking any
march of hostile troops from that direction. These
troops were thought to be the advance of a force under
General McClellan, which had been organized in that
section of western Virginia. When Patterson crossed
the Potomac Johnston very properly moved to Bunker
Hill, so as to be in position to prevent the junction of
McClellan and Patterson, by fighting a battle with Patterson before McClellan could reach Winchester, if indeed the force reported to be advancing from the direction of Romney were McClellan's troops. He soon
became convinced that no considerable body of United
States troops was approaching Winchester from the
direction of Romney, and so the two regiments sent
there were recalled to Winchester. If the action of
Johnston had not been guided by the reports received,
he would have evacuated Harper's Ferry at once upon
the passage of the Potomac by Patterson. Harper's
Ferry was not a defensible point. It was a *cul-de-sac*
commanded thoroughly by Maryland Heights. Later
in the war a large force of Federal troops was easily

forced to capitulate by a' portion of the Confederate army approaching from the direction of Maryland.

Patterson commenced to cross the Potomac with the avowed purpose of fighting a battle with the army under Johnston, but when about two thirds of his troops had crossed he received a telegram from General Scott ordering him to send to Washington at once all the regular troops he had, horse and foot, as well as the Rhode Island regiment under Burnside, which was a very fine one. If this telegram had not been received, and Patterson had continued the march of his troops into Virginia, he would have reached Martinsburg on the 17th of June, and on the 18th could have attacked the Confederate troops then in line of battle awaiting him at Bunker Hill, eleven miles distant, and there might have been on the pages of American history a second battle of that name. The explanation of General Scott's telegram is to be found in the fact that he had changed his plan of offensive operations. He had reversed his former purposes and now proposed to fight the first battle with the army around Washington, while the army of Patterson should make the feint, to prevent a junction of Johnston's army with that of Beauregard's at Manassas. General Sanford, who commanded the State troops of New York, was the senior officer at that time on duty in Washington; and at two o'clock on the morning of May 21, 1861, with eleven thousand men first invaded Virginia and took possession of Arlington Heights and the adjacent section as far as Alexandria. The Department of Virginia was created, and General Irvin McDowell was selected by the Washington Cabinet to command it.

Up to that time it is said General Scott did not want anything done on the Virginia side of the Potomac except to fortify Arlington Heights. He was "piqued and irritated" that the Cabinet should have sent McDowell into Virginia, and sent him two messages by his aid-de-camp asking him to make a personal request not to be sent on the other side of the river, and took occasion to say to the Cabinet that he was never in favor of going over into Virginia. He did not believe in a little war by piecemeal, but he believed in a

war of large bodies. He was in favor of moving down
the Mississippi River with eighty thousand men, fight all
the battles that were necessary, take all the positions
he could find and garrison them, fight a battle at New
Orleans, win it, and thus end the war. His marvelous
plan met with serious objections from the powers at
Washington. Could it have been submitted to those in
Richmond it would have been unanimously adopted.

Irvin McDowell, the commander selected to lead the
Federal army against its opponent at Manassas, was a
native of Ohio, and graduated at the Military Academy
at West Point in 1838. He was assigned to the First
Artillery, served in the Mexican War, and was brevetted
major for gallant and meritorious conduct at Buena
Vista. He was afterward transferred to the Adjutant
General's Department, and served there till he was
promoted brigadier general in 1861. At this period
McDowell was about forty-three years of age, a capable
soldier, and a gallant and courteous gentleman. He
was kind-hearted, considerate, and tender of the feelings of others. His letter to Mrs. Lee, in reply to one
received from her, addressed to the commander of the
Federal forces at Arlington, has the ring of the pure
metal, and is as follows:

HEADQUARTERS, DEPARTMENTS NORTHEASTERN VIRGINIA,
ARLINGTON, *May* 30, 1861.

Mrs. R. E. Lee.

MADAM: Having been ordered by the Government to relieve
Major-General Sanford in command of this Department, I had
the honor to receive this morning your letter of to-day addressed
to him at this place. With respect to the occupation of Arlington
by the United States troops I beg to say it has been done by my
predecessor with every regard for the preservation of the place.
I am here temporarily in camp on the grounds, preferring this to
sleeping in the house under the circumstances which the painful
state of the country places me with respect to these properties.
I assure you it will be my earnest endeavor to have all things so
ordered that on your return you will find things as little disturbed as possible. In this I have the hearty concurrence of the
courteous, kind-hearted gentleman in the immediate command
of the troops quartered here, and who lives in the lower part
of the house to insure its being respected. Everything has been
done as you desire with respect to your servants, and your wishes,
so far as they have been known or could have been understood,

have been complied with. When you desire to return every facility will be given you for doing so. I trust, Madam, you will not consider it an intrusion when I say I have the most sincere sympathy for your distress, and, so far as compatible with my duty, I shall always be ready to do whatever may alleviate it. I have the honor to be, very respectfully,

Your most obedient servant, I. McDOWELL.

P. S.—I am informed it was the order of the general in chief if the troops on coming here should have found the family in the house, that no one should enter it, but that a guard should be placed for its protection.

Generals Scott and Lee were organizing their respective armies with the same celerity apparently, for on the 24th of June McDowell had twenty regiments of infantry, aggregating less than fourteen thousand men, two hundred and fifty cavalry, two batteries of light artillery, and three other batteries in the earthworks. His field return, dated June 26th, makes his aggregate forces sixteen thousand six hundred and eleven. At that time the Confederate army, under Beauregard, had nineteen regiments of infantry. The Federal commander estimated Beauregard's force at twenty thousand, and a statement upon which he said he relied, told him that the South Carolina regiments were the best armed and equipped, had negroes with them as servants, were in high spirits, and though the month was June, were *freezing* for a fight.

It was fully determined now that the Federal army should move against Manassas, and General McDowell was requested to submit a plan of operations and an estimate of the force necessary to carry it out. He did so, and the plan was approved by General Scott, the Cabinet, and Generals Sanford, Tyler, Mansfield, and Meigs, who were present. It was then given to the engineer officers to discuss, and finally was fully adopted. The Federal army was to move out from the vicinity of Washington and Alexandria in four columns and give battle to the enemy by turning their right flank. McDowell exacted two conditions: One that he should be provided with thirty thousand troops; the other that he should not be required to fight any of the Confederate forces then opposed to General Patterson in the Valley of Virginia. The first condition was pledged, and he was told by General Scott that if Johnston joined Beauregard he should have Patterson at his heels.

General Lee had worked incessantly, leaving no stone unturned to give Beauregard a sufficient force to cope successfully with McDowell. He put away personal ambition, and had no thought except to do all in his power to enable others to win victories. From Richmond, July 12, 1861, he wrote Mrs. Lee: "You know that Rob has been made captain of Company A of the University. He has written for a sword and sash, which I have not yet been able to get for him. I shall send him a sword of mine, but can not procure him a sash. I am very anxious to get into the field, but am detained by matters beyond my control. I have never heard of the assignment to which you allude—of commander in chief of the Southern army—nor have I any expectation or wish for it. President Davis holds that position. I have been laboring to prepare and get into the field the Virginia troops to strengthen those from other States, and the threatened commands of Johnston, Beauregard, Huger, Garnett, etc. Where I shall go I do not know, as that will depend upon President Davis."

The press on both sides, North and South alike, excited by the probability of a battle, began to severely criticise the delay in decisive movements. They did not understand that armies composed almost exclusively of citizen soldiers had to be organized with great care. Regiments had to be placed in brigades, and they in turn formed into divisions; ammunition, the means of subsistence, and the requisite amount of transportation had to be provided. General Lee resisted public clamor in his usual calm and dignified way. McDowell too, like a seasoned soldier, stood the pressure against him as long as he could, but at last it became so great he could wait no longer. So he issued General Order No. 17, dated Arlington Heights, July 16th, which started from camp and put on the march thousands of armed men, as a vast engine is put in motion by pressure on a button. Some thirty miles away, behind a small stream called Bull Run, Beauregard waited the arrival of McDowell. The two army commanders were classmates at West Point, and had studied and marched side by side for four years. It was a strange sight to see them now manœuvring hostile armies.

The capture of Washington should have been the legitimate military result of the Southern victory at Manassas. A great part of Beauregard's army had not fired a gun on the 21st; the brigades of Ewell, D. R. Jones, Longstreet, Bonham, and Holmes had been quietly resting all day, if we except a small skirmish by Jones. Ewell moved to the battlefield in the afternoon, but was not engaged. If these fresh troops had been led direct on Centreville by the roads crossing the fords they were guarding, they could easily have reached that point, four or five miles distant, before the fugitives of the Federal army, who for the most part were returning by the circuitous route over which they marched in the morning, and which was the only road they knew. The six thousand Federal reserve at Centreville, under Miles, certainly, in view of the demoralization of the rest of the army, could not have made a successful resistance. Bonham and Longstreet crossed Bull Run in pursuit, but were stopped by three regiments of General Blenker's brigade. Three hours and a half of daylight still remained.

The Confederates had nineteen companies of cavalry, McDowell seventeen. In neither army at that time was the employment of cavalry understood. It was not massed, but distributed around among the various infantry brigades where the troopers were principally used for couriers. If the whole of the Southern cavalry had been ordered forward under an enterprising soldier like Stuart, supported by the troops that had not been engaged, Centreville might have easily been reached that night. The next day, while Stuart was moving in the direction of Alexandria and Washington, with some of the freshest infantry as supports, the head of the Confederate army might have been turned toward White's Ford, on the upper Potomac, some twenty-five or thirty miles away. Patterson's army was disintegrating by the expiration of enlistments; Banks, his successor, had at Harper's Ferry about six thousand men and was fearing an attack. Dix, at Fort McHenry and

Baltimore, with a small force, was uncomfortable ; and Butler, at Fort Monroe, was protesting against Scott's order to send to Washington his Illinois volunteers. All conditions were favorable to a march through Maryland by the Southern army, and either capture the Federal capital or occupy the strategic point at the junction of the Baltimore and Ohio Railroad with the Washington and Baltimore Railroad at the Relay House. Thousands of Marylanders whose sympathies were with the South would have increased the numbers of the Confederate army. Fairfax and Loudoun counties in Virginia, and Howard and Montgomery counties in Maryland, were teeming with food for men and horses. Half a million rounds of ammunition for small arms had been captured. Gorgas, chief of ordnance, had many rounds also in Richmond, for on July 14th General Lee ordered him to send a full supply to General Wise in West Virginia. Besides ammunition, large quantities of muskets, pistols, knapsacks, swords, cannons, blankets, wagons, ambulances, hospital and subsistence stores, and camp and garrison equipment were captured.

On July 22, 1861, there were no troops in Baltimore with which any defense of that city could have been made. There were a few regiments for provost duty, but no available fighting force. Banks was ninety-five miles from Baltimore by the nearest road. White's Ford, on the Potomac, where Johnston and Beauregard could have crossed, is about forty-five miles from Baltimore. The occupation of the Relay House might have produced the immediate evacuation of Washington by the Federals, the transfer of the seat of war to Pennsylvania, the accession of Maryland to the Confederacy, and fifty thousand more men as recruits as fast as they could have been armed, for Baltimore would have clothed and equipped them. Next year, when the second battle of Manassas was fought, General Lee crossed the Potomac and entered Maryland without difficulty under much less favorable conditions. His inferiority of numbers to those of his antagonists were greater, and his ammunition, supplies, and transportation less in proportion to the strength of his army.

The extent of the Southern victory was not known

on that hot afternoon of July 21, 1861, because the pursuit had been feeble.   Later in the evening, when the Federals were in full retreat, the report reached the Confederate commanders that a strong body of Union troops was advancing *via* Union Mills on Manassas, and orders were issued in consequence for the rapid march of some troops back to this position, infantry being mounted behind cavalry in order to get there at the earliest possible moment, and Beauregard started in that direction in person with the understanding that Johnston should send him re-enforcements.

The defeat of McDowell's army not being fully utilized by the Confederates caused the victory to be regarded by some at the South as unfortunate, for it was followed by a period of fancied security, while the opposite effect was produced at the North.   So great was the confidence in the power to establish another republic on this continent that politicians at the South already began to plot for the Presidential succession.   Beauregard was one of those named for office, and he wrote a letter to the public press, dated " within the hearing of the enemy's guns," declaring that he was not a candidate. On the other hand, the day that Washington was crowded with fugitives from the Federal army the House of Representatives passed a resolution pledging to the country and to the world " the employment of every resource, national and individual, for the suppression and punishment of armed rebels."   While the South rested on the laurels of Manassas the North went vigorously to work to repair its fortunes.   Congress authorized an army of half a million of men to be enlisted for three years, an increase of the navy, and a large loan.

CHAPTER VI.

THE CAMPAIGN IN WEST VIRGINIA.

GENERAL LEE was in Richmond during the operations at Manassas, and contributed his humble part by
the organization and equipment of the army, as well as
in the selection of the battlefields. He was not dazzled
by the blaze of victory which glistened from the tips
of the Southern bayonets, or filled with undue elation.
He was one among the very few in the South who
always felt the contest would be obstinate and prolonged. No one knew better than he the great resources of one of the combatants, as well as the determination and courage of both. Six days after the
battle he writes Mrs. Lee from Richmond, July 27, 1861:
" That, indeed, was a glorious victory, and has lightened the pressure upon us amazingly. Do not grieve
for the brave dead, but sorrow for those they left behind—friends, relatives, and families. The former are
at rest; the latter must suffer. The battle will be repeated there in greater force. I hope God will again
smile on us and strengthen our hearts and arms. I
wished to partake in the former struggle, and am mortified at my absence. But the President thought it more
important that I should be here. I could not have done
as well as has been done, but I could have helped and
taken part in a struggle for my home and neighborhood.
So the work is done, I care not by whom it is done. I
leave to-morrow for the army in western Virginia."

As no immediate hostile advance now threatened
the Federal or Confederate capitals, other sections began to receive attention. Northwest Virginia lies between the Alleghany Mountains and the Ohio River. It
is a rough, mountainous district, with only a few passable

roads connecting it with the remainder of the State. The iron horse had never penetrated its soil or watered in its mountain streams. There was not that touch and feeling of interest that is derived from personal contact between the citizens of northwest Virginia and other portions of the Old Dominion. On the question of secession the majority of them differed widely from the great mass of Virginians. It was doubtful territory, and both the Governments at Washington and at Richmond recognized the importance at an early date of sending troops there, the one to protect and nourish the Union sentiment, the other to aid and encourage those who sympathized with the South. Henry A. Wise, once their governor, was made a brigadier general and assembled a force with which he advanced to Charleston, on the Kanawha River, but afterward returned to Lewisburg, on the Greenbrier. It was thought by his presence and eloquence that the resident population might be made confederate in feeling and his army largely recruited. General John B. Floyd, who had been President Buchanan's Secretary of War, had been commissioned at Richmond as brigadier general, and had recruited and organized a brigade in southwest Virginia, and in July led it over to the region of the Kanawha. This was the first field assigned to George B. McClellan by the Federal War Department, an officer of great promise, who, graduating at West Point in 1846, had for his classmates, among others, Burnside and Stonewall Jackson. He served first in the Engineer Corps, and in 1855 was appointed a captain in the First Cavalry. His previous military experience had been much the same as Lee's. In 1857 he resigned, to take up railroad work, and when war commenced he was made a major general of Ohio volunteers. He crossed into northwest Virginia on the 26th of May, he says, of his own volition and without orders. A portion of his command was under General Cox on the Kanawha. In McClellan's immediate front was a Confederate force under General Robert S. Garnett, who had been ordered to defend that portion of northwest Virginia.

Garnett was a Virginian, who had graduated at the Military Academy five years before McClellan. He had won his laurels in the Mexican campaign and afterward against the Indians. Upon resigning from the United States Army his first service in the South was as adjutant general of the Virginia forces. He was considered an excellent officer, a rigid disciplinarian, and, in consequence of many soldierly traits, had at one time been appointed commandant of the Cadet Corps at West Point. In June this officer occupied, with a force of about five thousand men, Laurel Hill, thirteen miles south of Philippi, on the turnpike leading to Beverly, in Randolph County. McClellan reached Grafton on the 23d of the same month, and on the same day issued a proclamation to the inhabitants of West Virginia, and on the following day another to the "soldiers of the Army of the West," both in the bombastic, inflated style followed by officers on each side in the early days of the war. He called his enemies hard names and charged them with grave offenses, and in many ways differed from the same McClellan who afterward commanded the Army of the Potomac. "Soldiers," said he, "I have heard there was danger here. I have come to place myself at your head and share it with you. I fear now but one thing—that you will not find foemen worthy of your steel." He had evidently been reading some of the proclamations of a "great master of war," and attempted to follow his style. The attention of the public was drawn to this Napoleonic imitation, for about that time he received the appellation of the "Young Napoleon," and was so called after he had been brought from West Virginia to the command of the Army of the Potomac. The headquarters of the Department of the Ohio were established at Buckhannon, and from this point McClellan determined to attack the force on Rich Mountain, and advanced and deployed in front of the opposing army, which he found strongly intrenched. He promptly resorted to the only method left in military operations in the mountains, and decided to turn their flank and rear, which General Rosecrans successfully did with four regiments. The troops at this point were a portion of Garnett's force under Lieutenant-Colonel John Pegram. Beverly was occupied by the Federal troops the next day, and General Garnett with the remainder of his army, finding that retreat had been cut off in that direction, abandoned his intrenchments on Laurel Hill and made a hasty retreat in the night over a rough country road in the direction of St. George, in Tucker County. He was rapidly followed and his rear overtaken at Carrick's Ford, on the Shafer Fork of the main branch of Cheat River. In the engagement which followed Garnett was killed.

Lieutenant-Colonel Pegram, who had escaped with a force of some five hundred men from Laurel Hill, not being able to join General Garnett in consequence of the latter's retreat, determined to surrender his little force, which had been without food for two days, as prisoners of war, and on July 12th surrendered to General McClellan five hundred and sixty men and thirty-three commissioned officers. Four days afterward McClellan issued another address to his troops: "Soldiers of the Army of the West," said he, "I am more than satisfied with you; you have annihilated two armies commanded by educated and experienced soldiers." The two armies here referred to were the four thousand men under Garnett, and Pegram's small force. In his dispatch of July 12th to the adjutant general at Washington he estimated Garnett's force at ten thousand, beginning at this time a habit of multiplying the number of his enemy by two, which he never afterward abandoned. The success of the campaign, however, had a marked effect upon his future. General Scott telegraphed: "The General in Chief, the Cabinet, the President, are charmed with your activity and valor. We do not doubt that you will in due time sweep the rebels from western Virginia, but we do not mean to precipitate you, as you are fast enough." After McDowell's defeat at Manassas, McClellan was selected to command the defenses at Washington, and the day after that battle, while at Beverly, was informed by Adjutant-General Thomas, at Washington, that his presence there without delay was necessary. General William S. Rosecrans succeeded him.

On July 28th McClellan assumed command of the Department of Northeastern Virginia and of Washington. Being necessary to select another commanding officer for the Southern troops in Northwest Virginia, General Lee designated Brigadier-General Loring, who had been a distinguished officer in the United States service, to be Garnett's successor. Loring left Richmond July 22d and proceeded at once to Monterey, in Highland County, and thence to Huntersville, where a force was being organized for the purpose of securing the Cheat Mountain pass, a strategic point of great value over which the Staunton and Parkersburg turnpike crossed. The Confederate authorities—having been informed of the advance of the Federal General Cox in the Kanawha Valley and that there would probably be two armies operating in northwest Virginia, and also being disappointed in what had been accomplished in that section—determined to send out there an officer of high rank and reputation. Mr. Davis offered the command of that department, therefore, to General Joseph E. Johnston first, as there was no necessity for Johnston and Beauregard both to remain at Manassas. General Johnston declined the offer, because he thought the most important battles would be fought between Washington and Richmond. It was then determined that General Lee should assume command in person of that department, for his duties of organizing and assigning troops to the different sections had nearly terminated. The Secretary of War and the adjutant general, under the direction of the President, were the proper persons to direct army movements now. General Lee proceeded at once to West Virginia, and for the first time assumed active command of the troops in the field. He went at first to Huntersville, where he found Loring, then to Valley Mountain, where Colonel Gilliam had been stationed. From the former point he wrote to his wife, August 4, 1861:

" I reached here yesterday to visit this portion of the army. The points from which we can be attacked are numerous, and the enemy's means unlimited, so we must always be on the alert ; it is so difficult to get our people, unaccustomed to the necessities of war, to comprehend and promptly execute the measures required for the occasion. General Johnson, of Georgia, commands on the Monterey line, General Loring on this line, and

General Wise, supported by General Floyd, on the Kanawha line. The soldiers everywhere are sick. The measles are prevalent throughout the whole army. You know that disease leaves unpleasant results and attacks the lungs, etc., especially in camp, where the accommodations for the sick are poor. I traveled from Staunton on horseback. A part of the road I traveled over in the summer of 1840 on my return to St. Louis after bringing you home. If any one had told me that the next time I traveled that road would have been my present errand, I should have supposed him insane. I enjoyed the mountains as I rode along. The views were magnificent. The valleys so peaceful, the scenery so beautiful! What a glorious world Almighty God has given us! How thankless and ungrateful we are!"

And from Valley Mountain, August 9, 1861, he writes: "I have been three days coming from Monterey to Huntersville. The mountains are beautiful, fertile to the tops, covered with the richest sward and blue grass and white clover. The inclosed fields wave with a natural growth of timothy. This is a magnificent grazing country, and all it wants is labor to clear the mountainsides of timber. It has rained, I believe, some portion of every day since I left Staunton. Now it is pouring. Colonel Washington, Captain Taliaferro, and myself are in one tent, which as yet protects us. I have enjoyed the company of our son while I have been here. He is very well and very active, and as yet the war has not reduced him much. He dined with me yesterday and preserves his fine appetite. To-day he is out reconnoitering, and has the full benefit of this fine rain. I fear he is without his overcoat, as I do not recollect seeing it on his saddle. I told you he had been promoted to a major in the cavalry, and he is the commanding cavalry officer on this line at present. He is sanguine, cheerful, and hearty as ever. I sent him some corn meal this morning, and he sent me some butter—a mutual exchange of good things. The men are suffering from measles and so on, as elsewhere, but are cheerful and light-hearted. The nights are cool and the water delicious. Send word to Miss Lou Washington that her father* is sitting on his blanket sewing a strap on his haversack. I think she ought to be here to do it."

And on September 1st, from the same place, he tells her: "We have had a great deal of sickness among the soldiers, and those now on the sick list would form an army. The measles is still among them, but I hope is dying out. The constant cold rains, mud, etc., with no shelter or tents, have aggravated it. All these drawbacks, with impassable roads, have paralyzed our efforts."

It was Loring's purpose to attempt a movement on Reynolds's rear. This officer occupied, with two thousand men, Cheat Mountain pass, through which the Staunton and Parkersburg pike passed, and had three thousand men in Tygart's Valley on the road to Huttonsville, with a reserve at Huttonsville, so he could re-enforce his troops on the Staunton road, or on the Valley Mountain road, as necessary. Loring, with thirty-five hundred effective troops, was in front of him on the latter, while General H. R. Jackson, with twenty-five hundred men, opposed him on the Staunton road. The natural topographical features, supplemented by artificial means, rendered his position very strong on both. General Lee promptly took the offensive by threatening his front, while a column should proceed, if possible, around one of his flanks and assault his rear—a plan similar to that adopted by McClellan at Rich Mountain.

The greatest difficulty in a campaign of this description is to discover suitable routes or paths over the rocks and precipitous mountain sides for the troops of the turning column. General Lee's experience as an engineer in Mexico had taught him the duties of a reconnoitering officer. He therefore not only availed himself of the information derived from others, but would personally proceed daily long distances for that purpose.

At this time Rosecrans was in the Kanawha Valley with Cox's column, and was opposed by the troops of the Confederate Generals Floyd and Wise, and was not with the force in General Lee's front. He and Lee commanded the whole department on their respective sides. The army whose movements General Lee was about to

---

* His aid-de-camp, Colonel John Augustine Washington.

superintend in person consisted, as stated, of about six thousand men, including a few companies of cavalry, as well as a fine battalion of the same arm under General Lee's son, Major W. H. F. Lee. Reynolds's force was estimated at about ten thousand.

After Floyd's clever defeat of Tyler at Cross Lane, on the 26th of August, he and General Wise seem to have kept on different sides of the Gauley River, and there did not seem to be that concert of action between them necessary to win success. General Rosecrans, an able and sagacious officer, was not slow to recognize the detached positions of these commands, and determined to re-enforce Cox and attempt the defeat of one or both of them. He advanced rapidly and assaulted Floyd's position, but was repulsed. Floyd then crossed the Gauley, followed by Rosecrans, and with Wise fell back to Sewell Mountain, the latter remaining on its eastern front, while the former fell still farther back to Meadow Bluff, eighteen miles west of Lewisburg.

Leaving the operations in this section for the present to the immediate commanders of the troops, General Lee proposed first to win a victory, if possible, over Reynolds. He was combative, anxious to strike, but many difficulties confronted him. He fully realized he had been sent to West Virginia to retrieve Confederate disasters, and that he had a most difficult task to perform. The Federal commander held the center summit of Cheat Mountain pass, the mountain having three well-defined summits. The center one was selected by the Federals as the best one to defend, and there a block fort was constructed with flanking outworks consisting of intrenchments of earth and logs, the whole line of defense being protected by dense abatis. The position chosen was inaccessible in many directions by the steep, rugged walls of the mountain. It was necessary first to carry this well-selected position of the Federal troops. A citizen surveyor, in sympathy with the South and familiar with the mountain paths, had made a trip to an elevated point where he could clearly see the Federal position, and reported his observations to General Lee. Afterward he made a second reconnoissance, accompanied by Colonel Albert Rust, of the Third

Arkansas Regiment, who was anxious to see the nature of the ground and the strength of the position for himself. They reported to General Lee that in their opinion the enemy's position could be assailed with success with troops which could be guided to the point they had reached. General Lee decided to make the attack, and gave to Rust a column of twelve hundred infantry, with such capable officers as Taliaferro and Fulkerson. General Jackson was to advance *via* the turnpike to confront the enemy from that direction, while another column, under Brigadier-General Anderson, was to advance to the third or west top of Cheat Mountain, where they could secure possession of the turnpike and be in the rear of the enemy. The rest of the army was to move down the Tygart's River valley upon the forces of the enemy stationed there. The attack on these troops, however, was to depend on the successful assault of the fortified position on Cheat Mountain. It was an admirably conceived plan. The key point was first to be carried; the report of the guns of the troops engaged there was the signal for an assault in front, while a force was thrown in the rear of both positions to cut off retreat. General Loring issued his order of attack on September 8, 1861. General Lee issued an order approving it on the same date, telling his troops that the safety of their lives and the lives of all they held dear depended upon their courage and exertions. "Let each man," said he, "resolve to be victorious, and that the right of self-government, liberty, and peace shall in him find a defender." The movement was to begin at night, which happened to be a very rainy one. All the troops, however, got in the positions assigned to them without the knowledge of the enemy, where they waited, every moment expecting to hear the rattle of Rust's muskets, who had been charged with the capture of the pass on Cheat Mountain; but hour after hour passed, and no sounds were heard. After a delay of many hours, and the enemy had divined the nature of the attack, the troops were ordered back to their former position. There had been only a small conflict between cavalry, in which Colonel John A. Washington, General Lee's aid-de-camp, who had been sent with Major W.

H. F. Lee to reconnoiter the enemy, was killed from an ambuscade. Colonel Rust did not report to General Lee until the next day—September 13, 1861; he admits that he got to the designated place at the appointed time, notwithstanding the rain; that he seized a number of pickets and scouts, and learned from them that the enemy in front of him was between four and five thousand strong and was strongly fortified. He made a reconnoissance and found these representations were fully corroborated. Rust claims in his reports that spies had communicated the movements of the Confederate troops to the enemy. This officer evidently did not attack, because he found, on getting close to the Federal position, that it was much stronger than he thought it was from the preliminary reconnoissances he had made. As the attack of the whole depended on the assault of this force, the failure to attack caused a corresponding failure of the whole movement. The plan of operations was well devised, and, under ordinary circumstances, might have proved successful.

Military operations are often like a vast piece of machinery: with one part out of gear, the successful operation of the whole machine is not possible. In a letter to Mrs. Lee, dated Valley Mountain, September 17, 1861, the general writes: "I had hoped to have surprised the enemy's works on the morning of the 12th, both at Cheat Mountain and on Valley River. All the attacking parties with great labor had reached their destination over mountains considered impassable to bodies of troops, notwithstanding the heavy storm that had set in the day before and raged all night, in which they had to stand till daylight; their arms were then unserviceable, and they in poor condition for a fierce assault. After waiting till ten o'clock for the assault on Cheat Mountain, which did not take place, and which was to be the signal for the rest, they were withdrawn, and after waiting three days in front of the enemy, hoping he would come out of his trenches, we returned to our position at this place. I can not tell you my regret and mortification at the untoward events that caused the failure of the plan. I had taken every precaution to insure success, and counted on it; but the Ruler of

the Universe willed otherwise, and sent a storm to dis-
concert the well-laid plan. We are no worse off now
than before, except the disclosure of our plan, against
which they will guard. We met with one heavy loss
which grieves me deeply: Colonel Washington, accompanied Fitzhugh [his son] on a reconnoitering expedition. I fear they were carried away by their zeal and
approached within the enemy's pickets. The first they
knew there was a volley from a concealed party within
a few yards of them. Three balls passed through the
colonel's body, three struck his horse, and the horse of
one of the men was killed. Fitzhugh mounted the colonel's horse and brought him off. I am much grieved.
He was always anxious to go on these expeditions.
This was the first day I assented. Since I had been
thrown in such immediate relations with him, I had
learned to appreciate him very highly. Morning and
evening have I seen him on his knees praying to his
Maker. 'The righteous perisheth, and no man layeth
it to heart; the merciful men are taken away, none considering that the righteous are taken away from the evil
to come.' May God have mercy on us all!"

And on the 26th of the same month he writes from
his camp on Sewell Mountain: "I told you of the
death of Colonel Washington. I grieve for his loss,
though I trust him to the mercy of our heavenly Father.
It is raining heavily. The men are all exposed on the
mountains, with the enemy opposite to us. We are
without tents, and for two nights I have lain buttoned
up in my overcoat. To-day my tent came up and I am
in it, yet I fear I shall not sleep for thinking of the poor
men. I have no doubt the socks you mentioned will be
very acceptable to the men here and elsewhere. If you
can send them here I will distribute to the most needy."

This movement having failed, and knowing that
the enemy would be prepared for any second attempt
which, from the nature of the country, would have to
be similar to the one already tried, General Lee decided to turn his attention to the commands of Wise
and Floyd in front of Rosecrans, leaving General H. R.
Jackson in Reynolds's front. He proceeded at once
to Floyd's command, which he reached on September

20th, and then to Wise's camp, closely inspecting both.
He at once perceived that Wise's position was the strongest and offered the best means for successful defense,
and promptly concentrated his forces at that point.

General Lee expressed regret at not finding the
commands of Floyd and Wise united, and said it would
be the height of imprudence to submit them separately
to the attack of Rosecrans.   He desired the troops to
be massed at once, so that "We conquer or die together," a most extravagant and unusual form of speech
for him to adopt. "You have spoken," said he to Wise,
"of want of consultation and concert.   Let that pass
till the enemy is driven back.   I expect this of your
magnanimity.   Consult that and the interest of your
cause, and all will go well."   "Just say, then," replied
Wise, "where we are to 'unite and conquer or die together,' and I will delight to obey you."

Rosecrans had advanced to the top of Big Sewell
Mountain and had placed his army in a strong position.
General Lee, with the troops of Wise, Floyd, and Loring
—about eight thousand men—occupied a position on a
parallel range.   The two armies were now in close proximity to each other, both occupying strong defensive
positions.   Lee and Rosecrans, having been officers of
the engineers, were fully aware of the great disadvantage an attacking army would have, and each waited,
hoping the other would attack.   After occupying these
positions for twelve days, Rosecrans, on the night of
October 6th, retreated.   The condition of the roads, the
mud, the swollen streams, the large numbers of men
with typhoid fever and measles, the condition of the
horses, of the artillery, and transportation, were such
that Lee decided not to pursue.   It is possible that had
he known Rosecrans would not attack he would have
given battle himself, notwithstanding the great advantage Rosecrans would have possessed by accepting it in
his strong defensive position.   The rapid approach of
winter and the rainy season terminated the campaign
in this section.

In a letter dated Sewell Mountain, October 7, 1861,
General Lee tells Mrs. Lee that at the time of the reception of her letter "the enemy was threatening an at-

tack, which was continued till Saturday night, when, under cover of darkness and our usual mountain mist, he suddenly withdrew. Your letter, with the socks, was handed to me when I was preparing to follow. I could not at the time attend to either, but I have since; and as I found Perry [his colored servant from Arlington] in desperate need, I bestowed a couple of pairs on him as a present from you; the others I have put in my trunk, and suppose they will fall to the lot of Meredith [a colored servant from the White House], into the state of whose hose I have not yet inquired. Should any sick man require them first he shall have them, but Meredith will have no one near to supply him but me, and will naturally expect that attention. The water is almost as bad here as in the mountains I left. There was a drenching rain yesterday, and as I left my overcoat in camp, I was thoroughly wet from head to foot. It has been raining ever since, and is now coming down with a will; but I have my clothes out on the bushes, and they will be well washed. The force of the enemy, estimated by prisoners captured, is put down at from seventeen to twenty thousand—General Floyd thinks eighteen thousand. I do not think it exceeds nine or ten thousand, but it exceeds ours. I wish he had attacked, as I believe he would have been repulsed with great loss. The rumbling of his wheels, etc., were heard by our pickets; but as that was customary at night in moving and placing his cannon, the officer of the day, to whom it was reported, paid no particular attention to it, supposing it to be a preparation for an attack in the morning. When day appeared the bird had flown, and the misfortune was that the reduced condition of our horses for want of provender, exposure to cold rains in these mountains, and want of provisions for the men, prevented the vigorous pursuit of following up that had been prepared. We can only get up provisions from day to day, which paralyzes our operations. I am sorry, as you say, that the movements of the armies can not keep pace with the expectations of the editors of papers. I know they can regulate matters satisfactory to themselves on paper. I wish they could do so in the field. No one wishes them more success than I do, and would be happy to see them have full swing. General Floyd has three editors on his staff. I hope something will be done to please them."

It is true West Virginia, as it is called, would have been a desirable accession to either side. Both Governments were actuated in its occupation by a desire to protect the citizens who adhered respectively to their cause. The country abounded in vast forests, coal, and iron, presenting fields of wealth and enterprise. The advantage, however, in a campaign there was in favor of the Federals. The proximity of their railroads on the one side made it easier for them to concentrate troops rapidly and furnish them with supplies, while on the other hand the Southern lines of communication from Staunton and other portions of eastern Virginia were necessarily long and difficult.

At the termination of this campaign of General Lee's the Confederate Government did not bestow much attention upon this section. The majority of the people seemed inclined to support the Federal side; indeed, most of the counties sent representatives to a convention which passed an ordinance creating them into a new State, which the Government at Washington recognized as the State of Virginia.

It must be admitted that General Lee retired from West Virginia with diminished military reputation. Great results had been expected from his presence there. Garnett's defeat and death were to be avenged, and the whole of that portion of Virginia speedily wrested from the Federal arms. The public did not understand the difficulties of the situation, or comprehend why he did not defeat Reynolds, or the failure to attack Rosecrans. The news of the expected great victories did not reach Richmond. Men apparently wise shook their heads and said he had been overrated as a soldier; that he relied upon a "showy presence" and a "historic name," and that he was "too tender of blood" and leaned too much to the engineer side of a military question, preferring rather to dig intrenchments than to fight. There were two men, however, who stood by him faithfully in this doubtful period of his career. One of them was the President of the Confederate States, the other the Governor of Virginia.

They knew him well, and that the failure of the West Virginia campaign could not be fairly attributed to him. General Lee remained quiet under the occasional attacks of the public press. He knew that his duty had been discharged conscientiously. He was not aware that he had a "showy presence." On the contrary, he was modest, unassuming and simple. He conducted the campaign in the most unostentatious manner. He had only two aid-de-camps, Colonels Washington and Taylor. The former was killed; the remaining aid-de-camp shared the same tent with him. The mess furniture was of the plainest kind—tin cups, tin plates, tin dishes, which Colonel Taylor says were carried all through the war. In the full zenith of his fame as a great army commander, any one who accepted his hospitality would be obliged to eat from this same old tinware with which he commenced the war in West Virginia. It is not known that General Lee ever attempted in any way to make explanation or defense of these attacks. In a private letter to Governor Letcher, dated September 17, 1861, he simply states that "he was sanguine of success in attacking the enemy's works on Rich Mountain"; that "the troops intended for the surprise had reached their destination, having traversed twenty miles of steep and rugged mountain paths, and the last day through a terrible storm, which had lasted all night, in which they had to stand, drenched to the skin, in a cold rain"; that he "waited for an attack on Cheat Mountain, which was to be the signal, till 10 A. M., but the signal did not come. The chance for surprise was gone. The provisions of the men had been destroyed the preceding day by the storm. They had nothing to eat that morning and could not hold out another day, and were obliged to be withdrawn. This, Governor," he writes, "is for your own eye. Please do not speak of it; we must try again. Our greatest loss is the death of my dear friend, Colonel Washington. He and my son were reconnoitering the front of the enemy. They came afterward upon a concealed party who fired upon them within twenty yards, and the colonel fell, pierced by three balls. My son's horse received three shots, but he escaped on the colonel's horse. His zeal for the cause to which he had devoted himself carried him too far."

General Lee, in obedience to instructions, returned to Richmond, but not amid the shouts of the populace. The bands did not play, "See the Conquering Hero Come"; the chaplet of victory was missing from his brow, the scalps of Rosecrans and Reynolds from his belt. The public looked at the cold facts, and were interested in actual results. The difference between war in the mountains and war amid the hills and valleys and green fields was never for a moment considered. Four hundred and eighty-four years before the birth of our Saviour, history tells us that Xerxes marched with over one million men and twelve hundred war ships to invade Greece. And that Leonidas, with three hundred Spartans and about four thousand men from the other parts of Greece, defied the King of Persia and for two days held the defile in the mountains known as the Pass of Thermopylæ.

In 1861 there were still passes among the mountains, and a few men could hold them against an army, and could only be dislodged by flank and rear attacks over long, steep, circuitous paths. Lee made the attempt when in front of Reynolds. Had his well-laid plans been carried out, possibly he might have defeated the Federal general. In an offensive movement against Rosecrans the elements of success were against him. The naturally strong, elevated position on Sewell Mountain, made still stronger by the methods of an engineer of such great ability as Rosecrans, could not have been easily carried. When it was abandoned, the Federal rear guard, every few miles, could have found other strong positions where Lee's army could have been detained for days had the condition of his troops and the roads permitted pursuit. On General Lee's return to Richmond his duties as military adviser at the side of the chief executive officer of the Confederacy were resumed. No response was ever made to public criticisms. His vision swept the future, his vindication would come if opportunity offered.

CHAPTER VII.

ATLANTIC COAST DEFENSES.—ASSIGNED TO DUTY IN
RICHMOND AS COMMANDER IN CHIEF UNDER THE
DIRECTION OF THE SOUTHERN PRESIDENT.

THE defenseless condition of the States south of
Virginia bordering on the Atlantic coast was an object of solicitude to the Confederate War Department.
Important seaports and the sections adjoining them
were at the mercy of combined Federal fleets and
armies. Their proper defense was most difficult, the
means most inadequate. It was a good field for a
capable engineer. Lee was available, and the emergency demanded his services. Reluctantly he was ordered from Richmond, cheerfully he obeyed, and on
November 6th proceeded to South Carolina, where he
at once commenced to erect a line of defense along the
Atlantic coasts of that State, Georgia, and Florida.

His four months' labors in this department brought
prominently into view his skill. Exposed points were no
longer in danger. Well-conceived defensive works rose
rapidly. Public confidence in that department was permanently restored, and with it came to Lee a new accession of popularity and esteem. His headquarters was
wisely established at Coosawhatchie on the railroad, a
point midway between Charleston, S. C., and Savannah,
Ga., and from which he could give close supervision to
the defenses of these important cities. From this point,
referring to the union of his family on Christmas day,
he writes:

COOSAWHATCHIE, S. C., *December 22,* 1861.

I shall think of you on that holy day more intensely than
usual, and shall pray to the great God of heaven to shower his
blessings upon you in this world and to unite you all in his

(128)

courts in the world to come. With a grateful heart I thank him for his preservation of you thus far, and trust to his mercy and kindness for the future. Oh, that I were more worthy and more thankful for all that he has done and continues to do for me!

And again on Christmas day he wrote:

I can not let this day of grateful rejoicing pass without some communion with you. I am thankful for the many among the past that I have passed with you, and the remembrance of them fills me with pleasure. As to our old home, if not destroyed it will be difficult ever to be recognized. Even if the enemy had wished to preserve it, it would almost have been impossible. With the number of troops encamped around it, the change of officers, the want of fuel, shelter, etc., and all the dire necessities of war, it is vain to think of its being in a habitable condition. I fear, too, the books, furniture, and relics of Mount Vernon will be gone. It is better to make up our minds to a general loss. They can not take away the remembrances of the spot, and the memories of those that to us rendered it sacred. That will remain to us as long as life will last and that we can preserve. In the absence of a home I wish I could purchase Stratford. It is the only other place I could go to now acceptable to us, that would inspire me with pleasure and local love. You and the girls could remain there in quiet. It is a poor place, but we could make enough corn-bread and bacon for our support, and the girls could weave us clothes. You must not build your hopes on peace on account of the United States going to war with England. Our rulers are not entirely mad, and if they find England is in earnest, and that war or a restitution of the captives* must be the consequence, they will adopt the latter. We must make up our minds to fight our battles and win our independence alone. No one will help us.

In still another letter from the same place the general writes Mrs. Lee:

I am truly grateful for all the mercies we enjoy, notwithstanding the miseries of war, and join heartily in the wish that the next year may find us in peace with all the world. I am delighted to hear that our little grandson is improving so fast and is becoming such a perfect gentleman. May his path be strewn with flowers and his life with happiness. I am very glad to hear also that his dear papa is promoted. It will be gratifying to him, I hope, and increase his means of usefulness. While at Fernandina I went over to Cumberland Island and walked up to Dungeness, the former residence of General Greene. It was my first visit to

---

* Mason and Slidell.

the house, and I had the gratification at length of visiting my father's grave. He died there, you may recollect, on his way from the West Indies, and was interred in one corner of the family cemetery. The spot is marked by a plain marble slab, with his name, age, and date of his death. Mrs. Greene is also buried there, and her daughter, Mrs. Shaw, and her husband. The place is at present owned by Mr. Nightingale, nephew of Mrs. Shaw, who married a daughter of Mrs. James King. The family have moved into the interior of Georgia, leaving only a few servants and a white gardener on the place. The garden was beautifully inclosed by the finest hedge of wild olive I have ever seen.

The harbor of Charleston, S. C., was now greatly strengthened. Floating batteries were constructed and earthworks at proper places erected. At Savannah forts were built opposite Hilton Head, and at the best points to cover the river approaches. Lee watched every detail, and his eye, with a soldier's glance, overlooked the whole Department. His lines were admirably located, and his dispositions for the general defense of the department were so skillfully planned that it was not until near the close of the four years' war that his enemy could surmount the difficulties they presented. These cities were the cherished objective points of the administration at Washington, and large numbers of soldiers and sailors were at various times during the war employed to secure their capture. Their safety for so long a period from impending dangers upon every side was due to the military skill of Lee, as well as to the efforts of the accomplished officers who were in immediate command—General Ripley at Charleston and General Lawton at Savannah. Well might a prophetic tongue utter at this period that the "time would come when Lee's superior abilities would be vindicated, both to his own renown and the glory of his country."

On February 8, 1862, he writes his wife from Savannah: "I wrote you the day I left Coosawhatchie. I have been here ever since endeavoring to push forward the works for the defense of the city. Guns are scarce as well as ammunition. I shall have to bring up batteries from the coast, I fear, to provide for this city. Our enemies are trying to work their way through the creeks and soft marshes along the interior of the coast, which communicate with the sounds and sea, through which the Savannah flows, and thus avoid the entrance to the river, commanded by Fort Pulaski. Their boats require only seven feet of water to float them, and the tide rises seven feet, so that at high water they can work their way and rest on the mud at low. I hope, however, we shall be able to stop them, and my daily prayer to the Giver of all victory is to enable us to do so. We must make up our minds to meet with reverses and overcome them. But the contest must be long, and the whole country has to go through much suffering. It is necessary we should be humble and taught to be less boastful, less selfish, and more devoted to right and justice to all the world."

And again from the same place, he says on February 23d: " The news from Tennessee and North Carolina is not at all cheering. Disasters seem to be thickening around us. It calls for renewed energies and redoubled strength on our part. I fear our soldiers have not realized the necessity of endurance and labor, and that it is better to sacrifice themselves for our cause. God, I hope, will shield us and give us success. I hear the enemy is progressing slowly in his designs. His gunboats are pushing up all the creeks and marshes to the Savannah, and have obtained a position so near the river as to shell the steamers navigating it. I am engaged in constructing a line of defense at Fort Jackson, which, if time permits and guns can be obtained, I hope will keep them out."

Spring was now rapidly approaching, and active military operations would soon be resumed in many quarters. Richmond, the dual capital city, was menaced by an army from the North large in numbers and splendidly equipped. Forts Henry and Donelson had fallen in February before the combined attacks by land and water of the Federals, opening the Cumberland and Tennessee Rivers, and resulting in the capitulation of Nashville, the capital of Tennessee. The outlook was a serious one from a Southern standpoint, and demanded the counsel of the wisest, coolest, and most courageous leaders. The great interests at stake induced the President to summon General Lee from the

Southern Department to Richmond, and on March 13th he was assigned to the position of commander of the armies of the Confederacy and charged with the duty of conducting all the military operations of the Southern armies under the direction of the President. A few months previous to this his name had been mentioned in connection with the position of Secretary of War. The appointment, however, was not made, possibly because it was considered unwise to confine such great military talent within the bureau of a cabinet officer.

General Lee's youngest son, Robert, eighteen years old at this time, made up his mind to leave the University of Virginia and go into the army. His father gave him permission, saying in a letter to his wife:

RICHMOND, *March* 16, 1862.

I went with him to get his overcoat, blankets, etc. There is great difficulty in getting what is good. They have all to be made, and he has gone to the adjutant general's office of Virginia to engage in the service. God grant it may be for his good. I told him of the exemption granted by the Secretary of War to the professors and students of the University, but he expressed no desire to take advantage of it. As I have done all in the matter that seems proper, I must now leave the rest in the hands of our merciful God. I hope our son will make a good soldier.

During that month the Federal commanders displayed great activity. McClellan's large and well-organized army was being transferred to the Peninsula. General Lee wrote to his wife from Richmond, March 22, 1862: "Our enemies are pressing us everywhere and our army is in the fermentation of reorganization. I pray that the great God may aid us, and am endeavoring by every means in my power to bring out the troops and hasten them to their destination."

Much had happened during his absence from Virginia. The campaign was subjected to new conditions, and the location of the two principal armies in that State had been changed. The next battlefield was to be much closer to Richmond. Johnston and Beauregard after the battle of Manassas continued to occupy that section, extending their outposts, however, closer to Washington, while partially blockading the Potomac River by some heavy guns at a point near the mouth of Quantico Creek, where the channel runs on the Virginia side.

The inactivity of this army during the remainder of the summer and the fall months convinced the Federal authorities that no offensive campaign would be undertaken by it. About the latter part of September the Southern President visited the army and held a conference with Generals Johnston, Beauregard, and G. W. Smith in reference to active operations. These officers proposed, General Johnston states, a plan to cross the upper Potomac and place their army in the rear of Washington and fight the battle there. They demanded that the army should be increased for that purpose by troops drawn from all parts of the Confederacy, so as to number sixty thousand effectives. These conditions the President was unable to comply with, so all hope of any advance was abandoned, and the army prepared to go into winter quarters. Mr. Davis frankly told them that the whole country was applying for arms and troops, and that he could do no more to increase the strength of the army at that point than to send it as many recruits as there were arms in the ordnance stores at Richmond—namely, twenty-five hundred. Many advantageous changes were now made in the organization of the army. Brigades were put into divisions and placed under such commanding officers as Van Dorn, G. W. Smith, Longstreet, T. J. Jackson, and Holmes. The northern frontier of Virginia was formed into a new military department, and General Johnston's command was extended to the Alleghany Mountains on one side, Chesapeake Bay on the other, and divided into three districts: the Valley, to be commanded by T. J. Jackson; the District of the Potomac, under the immediate charge of Beauregard; and that section lying around the mouth of Acquia Creek was placed under the immediate charge of Major-General Holmes. On August 31st the President nominated to the Senate five persons to be generals in the Confederate army: First, Samuel Cooper, from May 15, 1861; second, A. S. Johnston, May 28th; third, R. E. Lee, June 14th; fourth, J. E. Johnston, July 4th; fifth, G. T. Beauregard, July 21st. Officers who resigned from the United States Army had been

promised by the Confederate Government when it was
first established at Montgomery, Ala., that they should
hold the same relative rank to each other when commissioned in the army of the Confederate States. Cooper,
who had been the adjutant general of the United States
Army, was the senior colonel. Albert Sidney Johnston
resigned a colonelcy, General Lee a colonelcy, which he
had only held a short time, and Beauregard a captaincy.
General Joseph E. Johnston but a short time previous
to the outbreak of the war had been a lieutenant colonel
of the First Cavalry, United States Army, and was ranked
in that army by all the officers named except Beauregard.
Upon the death of General Jesup, the quartermaster general shortly before the war, General Scott was asked to
recommend an officer to fill the vacancy, and he is reported to have said that if the Secretary of War would
put into a hat the names of A. S. Johnston, R. E. Lee,
and J. E. Johnston, and one of said names be taken out,
a good quartermaster general would be secured. Mr.
John B. Floyd, who was the Secretary of War at the
time, naturally threw his influence in favor of J. E.
Johnston, as he came from his section of Virginia and
was a relative, and he received the appointment. In
those days the quartermaster general had the rank of
brigadier general. When the writer once asked Mr.
Davis if J. E. Johnston was not entitled to be the rank-
ing senior general in the Southern army, he replied, "No,
because the quartermaster general was not considered
in the line of promotion or eligible to active work in the
field. It was a staff position, and by law he could not
command troops except by special assignment, and that
therefore I went back to General Johnston's old rank
in determining the relative rank of the five generals."

As the Confederate army showed no disposition to
enter upon an offensive campaign, it soon became an
interesting problem to the Washington authorities how
to defeat Johnston's army and capture Richmond. This
indisposition to attack gave McClellan ample time to
arrange his plans, and he took it. His deliberate methods were very provoking to his own Government, and
a matter of much suspense to the one opposed to him.
He leisurely organized and equipped his army. The

North liberally and rapidly responded to the demand for more men. For the three months succeeding the battle of Manassas troops were poured into the Department at Washington at the rate of 40,000 per month, so that at the end of that period McClellan officially reported that he had 147,695 men present for duty. In December following, his report shows 175,854 present for duty, and in March, 1862, 171,602, while the army of his opponent in February had only 47,306 present for duty, including the force under Jackson in the valley and a small number under Holmes at Acquia Creek, and in March about 50,000.

It is difficult to conceive why, with these immense odds in his favor, McClellan did not advance in the early spring against Johnston's position. This plan was discussed as well as two or three others. McClellan at last, it seems, told the Federal President in positive language that he did not approve the movement on Johnston's position at Centreville, but preferred to take his army down the Potomac River into Chesapeake Bay, up the Rappahannock River, and form a base of operations at a place called Urbana; or, better still, continue down Chesapeake Bay and around to Fort Monroe, using that formidable fort as a base, and advance on Richmond from that direction up the Peninsula formed by the James and York Rivers, upon whose surfaces the gunboats of his navy could be floated, and thus a thorough protection be given to his flanks. A solemn conclave of twelve general officers of the Federal army considered these various propositions, and, by a vote of eight to four, agreed to approve McClellan's plan of the peninsular route as opposed to Mr. Lincoln's proposition for a movement similar to the one made by McDowell. The difficulties in the way at the time for a change of base to the lower Peninsula were the fact that the proximity of Johnston's army to Washington seriously threatened the safety of that city. In March, however, General Johnston solved the problem by a retrograde movement to the line of the Rappahannock, trebling his distance from the Federal capital. While this retreat gave up a great deal of valuable country and raised the blockade of the Potomac, its strategic ad-

vantages were great. His army could then be in a
position to better receive a direct advance from the
Federal troops, or could by a rapid march prevent any
army which should be transported by water and landed
at points closer to Richmond from reaching that city
before he could.

As soon as Johnston had retreated McClellan advanced his troops to the position Johnston had occupied
during the winter. They were then countermarched
and brought back to Alexandria, a Virginia city a few
miles below Washington, where arrangements were made
as rapidly as possible to transport them to the Peninsula, Mr. Lincoln stipulating that at least fifty thousand
men should be left in and around Washington for its
immediate defense. He did not propose to "exchange
queens," because the capture of Washington by Johnston would be attended with much greater results than
the capture of Richmond by McClellan.

At that time the Southern forces on the Peninsula
were under the command of Major-General J. Bankhead
Magruder, an accomplished and well-known officer, who
had formerly distinguished himself in the service of the
United States. "Prince John," as he was called, occupied a strong position from river to river. The embarkation of McClellan's troops began on March 17th,
and he left in person on April 1st, reaching Fortress
Monroe on the afternoon of the 2d. When he arrived fifty-eight thousand men and one hundred guns
had preceded him. Magruder was a short distance in
his front with eleven thousand men. His left was at
Yorktown, on York River, and his line of battle extended along the Warwick River to Mulberry Island, on
the James, where his right rested. Gloucester Point,
opposite Yorktown, projects well out into the river.
Fortifications had been constructed there, and it was
expected that the guns at that point as well as those at
Yorktown by crossfire could prevent the passage of the
Federals up York River in any attempt to reach the
Confederate rear.

It will be remembered that when the British held
Yorktown over a century ago they also fortified and
held Gloucester Point, and to it, at one time, Corn-

wallis attempted to retreat when the troops of Washington were closing around him. Magruder's front was twelve miles long and in many respects strong. In a portion of it the ground was swampy, while dams had been constructed by which the water could be backed up, rendering the passage of the stream impracticable for artillery and infantry nearly three fourths of its distance. McClellan stopped in front of this line on April 5th, having left Fort Monroe the day before. Until he reached it he was ignorant of its existence. In addition to the large army which McClellan proposed should accompany him up the Peninsula, was a separate or detached corps under McDowell, over forty thousand strong, which was intended to operate upon either bank of York River in order to turn the Confederate position, should much resistance be offered to McClellan's advance on Richmond. After McClellan left Washington, the military governor, General Wadsworth, reported to President Lincoln that he had left only twenty thousand troops for its defense. This report, and General Jackson's movements in the Valley of Virginia, alarmed the Federal authorities, and they immediately ordered McDowell's corps to return to Washington. With the corps of McDowell's added to McClellan's great army the fall of Richmond might have been accomplished.

These movements of the Federal troops were of course speedily communicated to General Johnston on the Rappahannock, and D. H. Hill's, D. R. Jones's, and Early's divisions were put in march to re-enforce Magruder. General Beauregard had been detached from Johnston and sent to Kentucky. When later it was evident the Peninsula would be the route selected for the Federal advance, Johnston at once proceeded to that point with the remainder of his army, except General Ewell's division, which with a regiment of cavalry was left on the line of the Rappahannock, and Jackson's division, in the Valley of Virginia. Had McClellan assailed Magruder's lines at once his largely superior numbers would have won a victory in all probability, though the defensive line was a strong one. General Johnston arrived in person April 14th, and assumed command on the 17th. His advance did not arrive at Yorktown till the 10th, the other divisions following a few days later. For six days McClellan was in front of Magruder before Johnston's arrival, but instead of assaulting, he commenced arrangements for a dilatory siege. Johnston, upon the arrival of all of his troops, had, together with Magruder's forces, fifty-three thousand men; McClellan one hundred and thirty-three thousand, including twelve thousand of Franklin's division on board of transports in readiness to move up York River. He sat down in front of Magruder's position to await the arrival of his siege trains, and began the construction of scaling ladders, which might be useful to assault permanent works, and the erection of batteries for his heavy guns, much to the annoyance of the Washington authorities, for the falling back of his opponents to new intrenched lines in rear would render useless his great guns and his great labor in getting them in position.

On Johnston's arrival in the Peninsula he closely examined the defensive lines of Magruder, but did not like them, and returned at once to Richmond to lay his views before his President. "McClellan's army," said he, "should be encountered in front of Richmond by uniting there all the available forces of the Confederacy; the grand army thus formed, surprising that of the United States by an attack, when it was expecting to besiege Richmond, would be almost certain to win." Mr. Davis declined to decide so important a question hastily, and asked General Johnston to call upon him at a stated hour, when he would have Randolph, his Secretary of War, and General Lee both present. Johnston suggested that he invite Generals G. W. Smith and Longstreet also, and the conference was duly held. The Secretary of War objected to Johnston's plan because it involved the evacuation of Norfolk and the destruction of the famous Merrimac, or Virginia, as she was last named. General Lee could not vote in favor of General Johnston's proposition because the withdrawal of troops from South Carolina and Georgia would expose the important seaports of Charleston and Savannah to danger and capture. He thought that the Peninsula had excellent battlefields for a small army contending with a great one, and for that reason argued that the contest with McClellan's army should be made there. General G. W. Smith agreed with General Johnston's views, while Longstreet took but little part, which Johnston attributed to his deafness. Mr. Davis announced his decision in favor of the opinion of General Lee, and ordered Johnston to concentrate his army on the Peninsula as soon as possible, giving him in addition the command of the Department of Norfolk. McClellan threw up an immense amount of earth in front of the Confederate position. Batteries were erected for one hundred of the heaviest Parrott guns and thirty mortars, the range of some of the former being over four miles. His big gun batteries were out of the reach of any guns in Johnston's army, and therefore would be unmolested while delivering their fire. Ascertaining that these batteries would be ready for action in a few days, General Johnston gave orders to General Huger, in command at Norfolk, and to General Lee's brother, Captain Sydney Smith Lee, of the navy, who was in command of the Gosport navy yard, to evacuate these places and to remove to a safe place as much of the valuable public property as possible.

On May 3d General Johnston issued his orders for the withdrawal of his army from the Yorktown lines. He had delayed McClellan's advance for a month, which gave time to greatly strengthen the works around Richmond, as well as to advance the preparations for the great battle which now was inevitable. The Confederate army marched out of its lines at midnight. The rear guard of cavalry followed at daylight.

This retreat of Johnston's was a surprise to McClellan. He did not anticipate a retrograde movement on the part of the Confederates till they should have been hammered out of their lines by his big guns. His pursuit was not commenced for six hours after the departure of the Southern rear guard. At noon on the 4th Johnston's army had only reached Williamsburg and its vicinity. At this point the Federal advance encountered his rear guard. Some fighting took place in the afternoon, and on the next day a heavy conflict ensued between portions of the two armies, resulting in the loss to the Federals of twenty-two hundred and twenty-eight men, and to the Confederates of twelve hundred.   Johnston then leisurely continued his retreat. A force under Franklin was sent up York River by Mc-Clellan to make an attempt to get on his flank and rear. When they landed they were attacked and driven back to their boats, and held in that position till the whole of Johnston's force had passed the threatened point.   His army was now composed of four divisions under G. W. Smith, Magruder, D. H. Hill, and Longstreet.   Jackson was in the Shenandoah Valley, while Ewell, who had been left on the Rappahannock, had retired to Gordons-ville.   He could not depend, therefore, upon these two commands for immediate re-enforcement.

It can not be denied that a battle fought at Rich-mond would liberate troops from other points and thus give additional re-enforcements to Johnston; but the evacuation of Norfolk and the destruction of the Vir-ginia—which had been such a protection to James River—as well as the moral effect of a retreat which allowed a vast hostile army to knock at the very gates of Richmond, were undesirable.

McClellan, with his five corps under Sumner, Frank-lin, Porter, Heintzelman, and Keyes, slowly followed the Confederate army as it fell back on Richmond.   As he arrived in its immediate vicinity he began to deploy his legions, taking care to extend well his right so that it might reach out for McDowell's junction.   This offi-cer, with an army nearly equal to Johnston's whole force, was directly charged with the protection of Washington, and was specially instructed in any manœuvres he should attempt, that the safety of the Federal capital must be steadily kept in view.   From the vicinity of Washington he moved out on the line of railroad beyond Manassas to Culpeper Court House.   Ewell, who had been on the Rappahannock with his division, was then at Gordons-ville, and later went over into the Shenandoah Valley to join Jackson.   There being no enemy directly threat-ening Washington then, McDowell wisely marched to Fredericksburg.   He was well located there, being about fifty miles from his capital and about the same distance from McClellan's right flank.   He could therefore easily return to Washington, if necessary, or re-enforce McClellan in his attack on Richmond.

In order to watch this movement of McDowell's, General Joseph R. Anderson, with nine thousand men, had taken up a position between Fredericksburg and Richmond, with the object of holding McDowell in check as well as he could with such an inferior force, while General Johnston attacked McClellan's army. Both commanders knew well that if these forty-one thousand men could be added to the Federal army, the capture of Richmond would follow. McClellan at last succeeded in getting orders issued from Washington for McDowell to advance to his support. General Johnston promptly decided, upon this information reaching him, to try at once the fortunes of battle; but was greatly relieved, when he received word from Stuart's cavalry that McDowell, after starting from Fredericksburg, had countermarched and was proceeding in the direction of Washington. A Confederate commander in the Valley of Virginia was responsible for McDowell's change of direction.

Thomas Jonathan Jackson was born at Clarksburg, Harrison County, then in Virginia, now West Virginia. Thirty-seven years afterward he was born again on the field of Manassas, and, amid the rifle's flash and cannon's roar, christened "Stonewall." Neither of the two Governments lost sight of the great importance of the "Valley District"—one, because Washington could be easily reached by hostile troops from that section; the other, because the force there was a part of General Johnston's army, and might enter into future military combinations as an important factor. It was most fortunate for the South that Stonewall Jackson was selected to command this department. He was combative; his facial characteristics, "including a massive iron-bound jaw," have been compared to those of Julius Cæsar and William of Normandy. Activity, vigilance, and restlessness were marked traits of his character. His thoughts were with God and his cause. In camp he organized prayer meetings among his soldiers, and when the meeting began, the hymn raised, and the proceedings evidently a success, he often went to sleep.

"If silence be golden, he was a bonanza." It was said of him at that time that he sucked lemons, ate hard-tack and drank water—and praying and fighting appeared to him to be the whole duty of man. General Ewell, it is related, once said he admired Jackson's genius, but he never "saw one of his couriers approach him without expecting an order to assault the North Pole."

From a humble professor in the Virginia Military Institute he rapidly grew into a giant of war. He believed in a short, sharp, decisive contest. When first appointed a professor he occupied a room on one of the upper floors of barracks. Some of the cadets, in a mischievous spirit, took away a portion of the steps below his room during the night. The next morning, having an appointment to fill, he came out at an early hour, and, seeing what had been done, without a moment's hesitation seized one of the supporting posts and lowered himself hand over hand. "In civil war," said he, in 1860, "when the swords are drawn the scabbards should be thrown away"; and he would have fought under the "black flag" with as pleasant a smile as his countenance could assume. Earnestly and conscientiously believing the South was right, in the spring of 1861 he was strongly inclined to war.

In some respects he resembled Blucher; like him he was bold, bluff, and energetic, and, as with Blucher, his loyalty to the cause he adopted was a passion. The grim old soldier whom Wellington welcomed at Waterloo smoked, swore, and drank at seventy, and just there the resemblance ceased. Above others, on either side, Jackson understood the great value of celerity in military movements, and his infantry was termed "foot cavalry." To be under heavy fire, he said, filled him with a "delicious excitement." His death afterward, at Chancellorsville, lost the South Gettysburg; for General Lee has said, "Had I Stonewall Jackson at Gettysburg I would have won a great victory."

He was a blazing meteor of battle; his enterprising and aggressive spirit sought relief in motion—always motion. To such a commander the defense of the beautiful Valley of Virginia was intrusted.

After his return from Romney he was at Winchester,

then Woodstock, some forty miles below, then following Shields from Strasburg, and on March 23d attacked him at Kernstown and was repulsed; Banks, who was on his way from the Valley to Manassas, was ordered back to destroy this bold soldier; and Blenker, with ten thousand men on his way to Fremont, was instructed to report to him as he followed Jackson up the Valley, where later the latter took up position at Swift Run Gap in the Blue Ridge Mountains, the Shenandoah River being in his front, his flanks protected by the mountain sides, while Ewell was not far away across the mountains in his rear at Gordonsville. "Stonewall" did not like to be cooped up in the mountains, and wrote General Lee at Richmond, asking him to re-enforce him with five thousand men, intimating that he would then be glad to get reports from him. On April 29th Lee replied that his request could not be complied with, but suggested his union with General Edward Johnson, who had some thirty-five hundred men near Staunton. Lee was anxious to gain success in the Valley, because it would retard the offensive campaign against Richmond, and informed Jackson that if he was strong enough to hold Banks in check, Ewell might, by uniting with Anderson's force between Fredericksburg and Richmond, attack and possibly destroy McDowell, then at Fredericksburg. Banks had some twenty thousand men at Harrisonburg watching General Edward Johnson, and six thousand men, under Milroy and Schenck, had moved west of the mountains, and were in front of Johnson, while Fremont was marching with ten thousand men to join them.

Evading Banks at Harrisonburg, Jackson moved to Staunton, joined his force with Johnson's, and defeated Milroy and Schenck; Ewell marched then from Gordonsville to the Valley, and Banks fell back to Strasburg. Jackson, having disposed of the two Federal commanders, returned with great swiftness, united with Ewell, defeated the Federal forces at Front Royal, and then pushed on with great rapidity to attack Banks, who, hearing of his approach, fell back to Winchester, where he was defeated and followed to the Potomac River. The defeat of the Federal troops in the Valley, and Jackson's presence on the Potomac, produced consternation at the Federal capital. General McDowell, who had commenced his march from Fredericksburg to join McClellan, was turned back toward Washington, being directed to send twenty thousand men of his command at once to the Shenandoah Valley to reinforce Fremont, who had moved down the Valley to get in Jackson's rear and capture him. McClellan wanted McDowell badly, and McDowell desired to go to his support, and both generals practically intimated to the Washington authorities that they were scared; that they did not think Washington was in danger of capture by Jackson, and that moving a part of McDowell's troops to the Shenandoah Valley would not succeed in destroying Jackson's forces.

Jackson in the mean time, having disposed of Banks, determined to prevent the union of Shields (who had arrived from McDowell's army) with Fremont, and by a series of brilliant manœuvres fought the battles of Cross Keys and Port Republic, holding one commander at arm's length while he hammered the other. By this admirable campaign, in which his great military genius was displayed, McClellan was deprived of the co-operation of McDowell's army, while Jackson contributed largely to the success of the battles around Richmond.

His splendid work in the Valley is summed up by one of his biographers: "In three months he had marched six hundred miles, fought four pitched battles, seven minor engagements, daily skirmishes, defeated four armies, captured seven pieces of artillery, ten thousand stand of arms, four thousand prisoners, and a very great amount of stores." His movements produced a panic at the Federal capital. The Secretary of War issued a call to the governors of the loyal States for militia to defend the city. On May 25th, to the Governor of Massachusetts he declared that "intelligence from various quarters leaves no doubt that the enemy in great force are marching on Washington. You will please organize and forward immediately all the militia and volunteer forces in your State." John A. Andrew, the Governor of Massachusetts, issued a proclamation: "Men of Massachusetts, the wily and barbarous horde of traitors menaces again the national capital." Todd,

Ohio's Governor, following suit, said: "To the gallant men of Ohio: I have the astounding intelligence that the city of our beloved Government is threatened with invasion, and am called upon by the Secretary of War for troops to repel the overwhelming and ruthless invaders."

Richmond was probably saved at that period by Jackson. McClellan determined to clear the way for McDowell's march by attacking a brigade of North Carolinians under Branch, which was then at Hanover Court House, some fourteen miles from Richmond, guarding and watching the country in front of Johnston's left. To make this attack certain, General Fitz John Porter was given twelve thousand men, and partially accomplished the object of the expedition by defeating Branch and destroying the bridges and railroads in the vicinity of Ashland. Slowly but surely McClellan was diminishing the distance between the lines of his army and the Southern capital, and his big Parrott guns were now nearly in a position to throw shot within the walls of the city. On May 23d the Fourth Corps, under Keyes, crossed the Chickahominy at Bottom's Bridge and took position at a place called Seven Pines, some five miles from the city; the Third Corps, under Heintzelman, followed. The Chickahominy now divided McClellan's army into two parts. Two of his corps were on the south, and three—Sumner's, Franklin's, and Porter's—on the north side, McClellan's headquarters being at Gaines Mill. The Chickahominy River rises some twelve miles northwest of Richmond, flows in an easterly direction at first, and then takes a southeasterly course, till it empties into the James, some thirty miles below Richmond. It was directly interposed between McClellan and Richmond, being in some places not more than four or five miles from the city, and the numerous roads leading out from Richmond to the Peninsula and adjacent sections of country cross it on bridges. North of Richmond was Meadow Bridge; a little farther down, and opposite to Gaines Mill, New Bridge; still farther down, where the Williamsburg road crosses the Chickahominy, Bottom's Bridge; while lower down still is Long Bridge.

McClellan spent two weeks in traversing the forty miles from Williamsburg to the Chickahominy at Bottom's and New Bridges. His base of supplies was established at West Point; his stores could be safely transported by water, and from West Point the railroad running to Richmond had been put in good order in his rear, so that his supplies could be easily brought within reach for distribution. The Chickahominy proper afforded no greater obstacle to the advance of an army than an ordinary small river, the obstruction being the swamps and bottom lands. The stream flowed through a belt of heavy timbered swamp, which averaged three hundred or four hundred yards wide, sometimes in a single channel and sometimes in two or three, and the water when high overflowed the land.

The Federal army having large pontoon trains, as well as facilities for making trestle bridges, surmounted these difficulties. After two of McClellan's corps crossed this stream and took position nearer to Richmond, it was evident the battle could be no longer postponed. General Johnston therefore decided to attack these advance corps, and if possible overwhelm them before they could be re-enforced by any portion of the three corps upon the other side of the Chickahominy. The heavy rains had swept away the communicating bridges between the two wings of McClellan's army, but the railroad bridge, which had been repaired, was not affected by the swollen condition of the stream. On it planks were laid, and in that way the left wing supplied.

The battle of Seven Pines, or Fair Oaks, was well planned, and had the Southern attack been made in the forenoon instead of the afternoon, Johnston would have had greater success. " It can never be too often repeated that war, however adorned by splendid strokes of skill, is commonly a series of errors and accidents." Sumner succeeded in crossing his corps over the bridges trembling with the current's rush, and over causeways on each side covered with mud and water. His guns had to be unlimbered and prolonges used, while the men who were tugging at the ropes were nearly waist deep in some places in the water. It can not be said that this battle was a complete success for the Southern arms. Sumner's arrival enabled the other two Federal corps to maintain their ground until the curtain of night lowered on the scene. Ten pieces of artillery, sixty-seven hundred rifles and muskets, and quantities of stores and tents were, however, secured by the Confederates. The two corps of the Federals numbered thirty-eight thousand, and after Sumner's re-enforcements arrived, fifty-six thousand. The former lost some six thousand men, the latter fifty-seven hundred and thirty-nine; and McClellan had received a check to his "On to Richmond!"

Johnston, after giving orders to his troops to sleep on the ground they occupied when the contest for the night ceased, and to renew the battle at dawn the next morning, was wounded, at first slightly in the shoulder by a musket ball, and a few moments afterward was struck on the breast by a heavy fragment of shell, knocked from his horse, and had to be carried from the field in an ambulance. General Gustavus W. Smith, the next officer in rank, immediately assumed command of the army. He determined to carry out Johnston's plans and continue the attack on the next day, and so informed General Lee, asking for all the assistance he could give him. In a note dated Richmond, June 1st, 5 A. M., General Lee replies:

Ripley will be ordered, and such forces from General Holmes as can be got up will be sent; your determination to strike the enemy is right. Try and ascertain his position and how best he can be hit. It will be a glorious thing if you can gain a complete victory. Our success on the whole, yesterday, was good, but not complete.

Truly,   R. E. LEE, General.

To General G. W. SMITH, *Commander of the Army of Northern Virginia.*

When that note was penned, General Lee knew he had been directed to take command of the army on that day; he did not reach Smith's headquarters until 2 P. M., and was magnanimous enough to wish that Smith should gain and get the credit for a great victory.

The attack on June 1st was not made as contemplated by General Johnston first and Smith afterward, because it was apparent that the destruction of a portion of McClellan's army before it could be succored was no longer a possibility. There was no demoralization in the Confederate ranks anywhere, and the assertion that the Federal army could have gone into Richmond on the second day—June 1st—can not be maintained. General G. W. Smith, commanding, sums up the fighting on that day by saying: "The Federals, in position, were attacked on the first day of June by but two Confederate brigades. That attack was repulsed. Four Federal regiments then advanced and attacked the position held by one Confederate brigade. These four regiments were withdrawn from the front of that brigade." Only small portions of either army were engaged on the first of June.

The battle on the Williamsburg road on the day before was fought by D. H. Hill with four of his brigades and one of General Longstreet's. The other five of Longstreet's and the whole of Huger's division, which General Longstreet was expected to employ, were not put into the fight, while the troops charged with the duty of attacking the Federal right were advanced too late to be of service. Napier has well said that "he who wars walks in a mist through which the keenest eye can not always discern the right path." If the incomplete battle of Seven Pines or Fair Oaks did not add to the military fame of the Union commander or to that of the officer charged with the details of the attack on the Confederate side, it was nevertheless of benefit to the Southern commander, for it kept McClellan quiet for a month, and enabled him to complete his preparations to beat him.

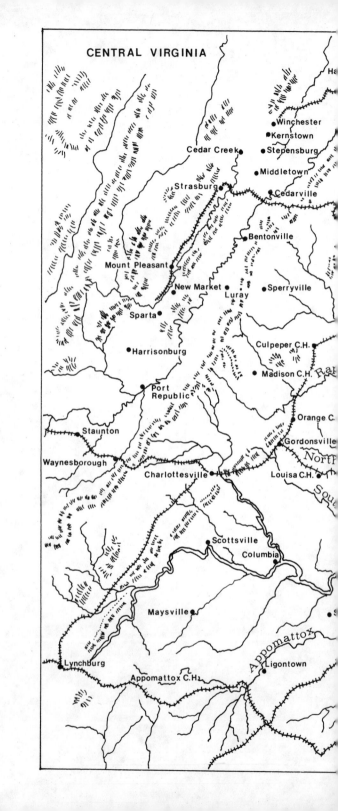

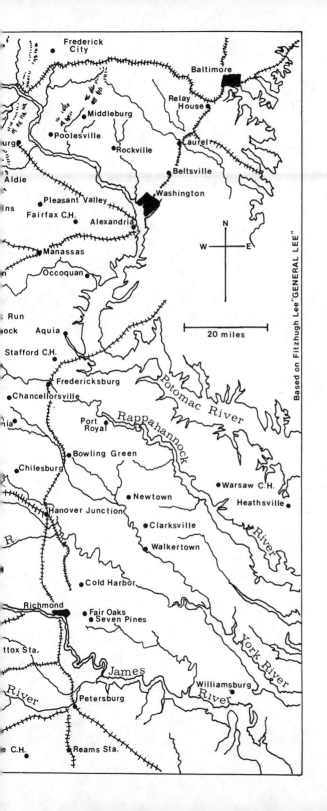

CHAPTER VIII.

COMMANDS THE ARMY DEFENDING RICHMOND, AND SEVEN DAYS BATTLES.

GENERAL LEE and Mr. Davis were on the field on May 31st, and the latter was at once informed of General Johnston's being wounded. Riding back with General Lee to Richmond that night, Mr. Davis told him he proposed to assign him at once to the command of the Confederate army defending Richmond, and would make out the order as soon as he reached the city. Accordingly, very early the next morning General Lee received the following:

RICHMOND, VA., *June* 1, 1862.

General R. E. Lee.

SIR: The unfortunate casualty which has deprived the army in front of Richmond of its immediate commander, General Johnston, renders it necessary to interfere temporarily with the duties to which you were assigned in connection with the general service, but only so far as to make you available for command in the field of a particular army. You will assume command of the army in eastern Virginia and in North Carolina, and give such orders as may be needful and proper.

Very respectfully,　　JEFFERSON DAVIS.

On the reception of this note, General Lee published

Special Orders No. 22.

HEADQUARTERS, RICHMOND, VA., *June* 1, 1862.

In pursuance of the orders of the President, General R. E. Lee assumes command of the armies of eastern Virginia and North Carolina. The unfortunate casualty that has deprived the army in front of Richmond of the valuable services of its able general is not more deeply deplored by any member of the command than by its present commander. He hopes his absence will be but temporary, and while he will endeavor to the best of his ability to perform his duties, he feels he will be totally inadequate to the task unless he shall receive the cordial support of every officer and man.

By order of General Lee.

W. H. TAYLOR, *Assistant Adjutant General.*

On June 2d Special Orders No. 126 were issued from the Adjutant and Inspector General's office.

Special Orders No. 126.

RICHMOND, VA., *June* 2, 1862.

By direction of the President, General Robert E. Lee, Confederate States army, will assume the immediate command of the armies in eastern Virginia and North Carolina.

By command of the Secretary of War.

JOHN WITHERS, *Assistant Adjutant General.*

At an early hour on June 1st the Southern President rode to the front to direct, in person, General Smith to transfer the command of the army to General Lee, in order to relieve the latter from the embarrassment of first announcing this change. Later General Lee rode out, reaching the field about two o'clock, and formally assumed command of the Army of Northern Virginia, which he was thereafter destined to lead against the Army of the Potomac on many hard-fought fields. Eighteen hours afterward General G. W. Smith, whose health had not been strong, was taken ill, and had to be relieved of all military duty.

At last, one year after the commencement of the war, Robert E. Lee was in active command of a large army in the field. His task was difficult, his responsibility great. The opposing hosts were thundering at the city's gates. Inch by inch they had crept so close that spectators on the housetops could see their fire-fringed lines and hear the angry roar of their cannon. Upon his shoulders rested the safety of his capital. With quiet dignity he assumed his duties. The troops were immediately ordered back to their former stations, and the battle of Seven Pines was confided to the Muse of History. The next move on the military chessboard absorbed his immediate attention. The strongly constructed battle lines of his powerful enemy were uncomfortably close. McClellan had already commenced to strengthen his front at Seven Pines. Franklin's corps was brought from the north to the south side of the Chickahominy and posted on the right of that portion of his line. On the left was Sumner, and to his left Heintzelman extended as far as the White Oak swamp. In their rear Keyes was in reserve. On the north or left bank of the Chickahominy Fitz John Porter's corps was still stationed, near Gaines Mill, with McCall's division of Pennsylvania reserves at Mechanicsville and on Beaver Dam Creek—eleven divisions in all. Richmond, McClellan's coveted prize, was but five miles away. To reach it he had to pass over the lines of the Army of Northern Virginia. These lines were held by five divisions—A. P. Hill's on the left at Meadow Bridge, Huger's and Magruder's next, supported by Longstreet's and D. H. Hill's. Lee at once considered the best manner to attack. The intrenchments in his front were too strong for a direct assault, so the only alternative left was to turn one or both of his enemy's flanks. The Federal left was "defended by a line of strong works, access to which, except by a few narrow roads, was obstructed by felling the dense forests in front." These roads were commanded to a great distance by heavy guns in the fortifications. The difficulties here were as great as would be encountered in a direct attack. The only way to get at McClellan was by assaulting his right, and the Confederate commander was not long in finding it out. In order to do this successfully he must fortify his lines, particularly his center and right, so that they could successfully resist any attack made upon them, while his left wing was withdrawn to be thrown on the Federal right and rear.

In Lee, as with McClellan, the military engineer was combined with the army commander. Earthworks were rapidly constructed. The topographical features of the country were scientifically made available; and ere many days had passed the Southern troops were everywhere behind strong intrenchments, while between them and the city was a line of more permanent works, which had been constructed some time before as a precautionary measure, and behind which the troops could be rallied if the first lines were successfully assailed. Almost every day now a soldierly looking man, clad in a neat but simple gray uniform, conspicuous by the absence of the wreath, gold braids and stars usually found on the uniforms of general officers, sitting his horse like a dragoon, might be seen riding along the lines. No long column of staff or couriers followed him, no display, no ostentation, none of the pomp of war. His enemy's right was the place to attack, but where was it located and how was it defended? Were the roads leading to it obstructed, and were the woods "slashed," or would the attacking column have to assault lunettes, redans, irregular pentagons, and inclosed redoubts? How was he to ascertain all this? Fortunately he had the very officer in his army who could obtain replies to these important questions, and he was the commander of his cavalry, James Ewell Brown Stuart, commonly called Jeb Stuart from the three first initial letters of his name. This distinguished cavalryman was a native of Patrick County, Va., a graduate at West Point of the class of 1854, and a soldier from the feathers in his hat to the rowels of his spurs. He was twenty-nine years old when Lee ordered him to locate McClellan's right flank and in the full vigor of a robust manhood. His brilliant courage, great activity, immense endurance, and devotion to his profession had already marked him as a cavalry commander of unquestioned merit. He had the fire, zeal, and capacity of Prince Rupert, but, like him, lacked caution; the dash of Murat, but was sometimes rash and imprudent; was as skillful and vigorous as Frederick the Great's celebrated cavalry leader, and, like Seidlitz, was willing to break the necks of some of his men by charging over rough ground if he made bold horsemen of the rest and gained his object. He would have gone as far as Cardigan, with "cannon to right of him, cannon to left of him, cannon in front of him." He was a Christian dragoon—an unusual combination. His Bible and tactics were his text-books. He never drank liquor, having given a promise to his mother to that effect when a small boy, but when wet from the storm and wearied from the march he would drink, without cream or sugar, the contents of a tin quart cup of strong coffee. Duty was his guiding star. Once when on the eve of an expected battle he was telegraphed that his child was dying and urged to go to her, he replied: "I shall have to leave my child in the hands of God; my duty requires me here." Lee knew him well. He had been a classmate at the United States Military Academy of his eldest son, and was his aid-de-camp when John Brown was captured. Such was the man who stood before his commander on June 11, 1862, to receive his instructions. The next morning, at an early hour, Stuart was in the saddle, and, with twelve hundred cavalry and a section of artillery, started to blaze the way for Stonewall Jackson's descent on the right rear of the Federal army, and for an assault on the Federal right by the left wing of the Confederate army. That night he went into camp twenty-two miles north of Richmond. His line of march conveyed the impression that he had been sent to re-enforce Jackson in the Valley, but the next day the head of his column was turned eastward toward Hanover Court House, which he reached about nine o'clock, driving out a body of the enemy's cavalry. Between that point and Old Church his advance squadron, under Captain Latané, met and charged a squadron of regular cavalry under Captain Royall. Latané was killed, and Royall severely wounded by a saber cut and his squadron put to flight. The Southern cavalry now followed rapidly to Old Church, where the Federal cavalry made another stand, but was soon driven from its position. Stuart was now far enough on the right flank of the Federal army to get all the information he desired. He could return only by the way he had marched, which would be attended with much danger, as the troops on that flank were thoroughly roused, or make the entire circuit of the Federal army. He determined upon the latter course, and, in defiance of many dangers and difficulties, succeeded in moving his whole command not only around the right of McClellan's line of battle, but along his rear and around his left, bringing it in safety to the Richmond lines. It was hazardous, because any prolongation of McClellan's left from White Oak swamp to James River would have cut him off from his own army.

This celebrated raid brought the Southern cavalry leader prominently before the public, and his rapid and successful march received favorable comment. From the left of his own army he had marched for Hanover Court House, Old Church, Tunstall's Station, on the York River Railroad, and Talleysville, to the lower Chickahominy, where the road from Providence Forge to Charles City Court House crosses it thirty-five miles from Richmond. Finding that the bridge had been carried away by the swollen stream, he tore down an old barn in the vicinity, and, as rapidly as his men could work, threw over another bridge, upon which he crossed men and guns, returning to his quarters near Richmond, having been continuously in the saddle for thirty-six hours. The whole distance was traversed in forty-eight hours, with but a single halt after reaching the south bank of the Chickahominy. He was enjoined by Lee to "remember that one of the chief objects of the expedition is to gain intelligence for the guidance of future movements."

The news of this expedition amazed the North. It did not understand how twelve hundred troopers could ride so close to the right, rear, and left of one hundred and fifteen thousand men in line of battle without being killed or captured. In his march he had crossed all roads leading to McClellan's right, and located his lines of communication. General Lee's General Orders No. 74 in part read:

HEADQUARTERS, ARMY OF NORTHERN VIRGINIA.

The commanding general announces with great satisfaction to the army the brilliant exploit of Brigadier-General J. E. B. Stuart with part of the troops under his command. This gallant officer, with portions of the First, Fourth, and Ninth Virginia Cavalry, and part of the Jeff Davis Legion, with the Boykin Rangers and a section of the Stuart Horse Artillery, on June 13th, 14th, and 15th, made a reconnoissance between the Pamunkey and Chickahominy Rivers and succeeded in passing around the rear of the whole of the Union army, routing the enemy in a series of skirmishes, taking a number of prisoners, destroying and capturing stores to a large amount. Having most successfully accomplished its object, the expedition recrossed the Chickahominy, almost in the presence of the enemy, with the same coolness and address that marked every step of his progress, and with the loss of but one man, the lamented Captain Latané, of the Ninth Virginia Cavalry, who fell bravely leading a successful charge against a force of the enemy. In announcing the signal success to the army, the general commanding takes great pleasure in expressing his admiration of the courage and skill so conspicuously exhibited throughout by the general and the officers and men under his command.

General Lee had secured, by this brilliant exploit of Stuart's, the information he desired. As early as June 8th he had suggested to the Secretary of War that "Jackson be prepared to unite with the army near Richmond, if called on." The next day he announced to the Secretary of War "a glorious victory by the gallant Jackson and his troops," and writes to him that reenforcements should be sent to Jackson to enable him to take the offensive again. The 11th of June was a busy day. Lee first prepared the instructions to start Stuart on his expedition, and then wrote Jackson as follows:

HEADQUARTERS NEAR RICHMOND, *June* 11, 1862.

Brigadier-General THOMAS J. JACKSON, *Commanding the Valley District.*

GENERAL : Your recent successes have been the cause of the liveliest joy to this army, as well as to the country. The admiration caused by your skill and boldness has been constantly mingled with solicitude for your situation. The practicability of reenforcing you has been the subject of earnest consideration. It has been determined to do so at the expense of weakening this army. Brigadier-General Lawton, with six regiments from Georgia, is on the way to you, and Brigadier-General Whiting, with eight veteran regiments, leaves here to-day. The object is to enable you to crush the forces opposed to you, then leave your unavailable troops to watch the country and guard the passes covered by your cavalry and artillery and with your main body, including Ewell's division and Lawton's and Whiting's command, move rapidly to Ashland by rail or otherwise, as you may find most advantageous, and sweep down between the Chickahominy and Pamunkey, cutting up the enemy's communications, while this army attacks General McClellan in front. He will thus, I think, be forced to come out of his intrenchments, where he is strongly posted on the Chickahominy, and apparently prepared to move by gradual approaches on Richmond. Keep me advised of your movements, and, if practicable, precede your troops, that we may confer and arrange for simultaneous attack. I am, with great respect, your obedient servant,

(Signed)   R. E. LEE, *General.*

On the same day, Lee writes to Randolph, the Secretary of War at Richmond:

HEADQUARTERS, DOBB'S HOUSE, *June* 11, 1862.

Honorable GEORGE W. RANDOLPH, *Secretary of War, Richmond, Va.*

SIR: It is very desirable and important that the acquisition of troops to the command of Major-General T. J. Jackson should be kept secret. With this view I have the honor to request that you will use your influence with the Richmond newspapers to prevent any mention of the same in the public prints. I am, most respectfully, your obedient servant,

(Signed) R. E. LEE.

The Southern commander desired to give Jackson a sufficient force to enable him to fight a decisive battle in the Valley, and then, before his enemy could recover, watch him with a picket line while he reported at Richmond with the greater part of his effective forces. Lee wished the first information of the arrival of Whiting and Lawton to Jackson to be given to his enemy by a victory in the Valley. On this day, too, he published Special Orders No. 130, Headquarters, Northern Virginia, June 11, 1862, directing Brigadier-General W. H. C. Whiting, with two brigades of Smith's division to be selected by himself, to report to General T. J. Jackson, commanding the Army of the Valley. He directed that this command be detached for temporary special service, and that it should move in light marching order. Three days after these various instructions were issued, General Lee decided that it would not do to wait for Jackson to fight before he should bring him to the army in front of Richmond, and told him to form a junction at once, and "to be efficacious, the movement must be secret." This detachment of troops from Lee's army, then in front of his powerful antagonist, did not produce in the Southern mind a feeling of uneasiness; so great was the confidence in the Southern leader that the movement, without knowing for what intended, was considered proper, timely, and judicious! Lee's object was to render the diversion of McDowell from McClellan's army more decided by re-enforcing the commander whose victories had already directed the attention of the Federal authorities from the capture of Richmond to their own security at Washington. Mr. Lincoln telegraphed McClellan on June 20th that Jackson is being heavily re-enforced from Richmond, and that he did not think he could send him more troops. Two days previous McClellan had informed Lincoln that some ten thousand troops from Lee's army had been sent to Jackson, to which the Union President replied that if the report were true, it would be as good as a re-enforcement to him of an equal force, and that he would be glad to be informed what day he would attack Richmond. While these telegrams were being exchanged Jackson was rapidly moving to the support of Lee. The main portion of his army left the Valley on June 18th, marching by Charlottesville and Gordonsville, which latter place was reached on the 21st. Jackson, leaving his army to follow, took an express car accompanied only by his chief of staff, who, strange to say, was not a military man, but a Presbyterian minister and a professor in a theological seminary. When Sunday morning, June 22d, dawned, Jackson, with his ministerial aid, had reached Frederickshall, a point on the Central Railroad, now called the Chesapeake and Ohio, some fifty-two miles from Richmond. Being the Sabbath, and against his religious convictions to travel on Sunday, he left his car and went to a gentleman's house and remained quiet that day, except that he attended camp services of some of the troops stationed near there in the afternoon. Not desiring to be transported to Richmond in a car, as he might be recognized, he determined to proceed the rest of his journey on horseback; and accordingly at one o'clock Monday morning he mounted a horse and started with a single borrowed courier for General Lee's headquarters near Richmond, fifty-two miles away. He had requested Major Dabney to get from the senior officer an order to impress horses on the way, and also a pass, in case he should get into the pickets of General Lee's army. At 3 P. M. on Monday, the 23d, he had covered the whole distance, and, travel-stained, dusty, and weary from riding all night, he participated in a conference called that afternoon by General Lee, of the commanding officers of the divisions he proposed should attack McClellan's right and rear, namely, Longstreet, D. H. Hill, and A. P. Hill. These officers, with Jackson, having received the instructions of the army commander, rejoined their respective commands. Perhaps if "Old Stonewall" had traveled to Richmond on his car, and been spared the loss of sleep and the all-night ride on the eve of a great battle, he would have swept around on A. P. Hill's left in time to have saved the lives of many brave men at Mechanicsville and Beaver Dam Creek.

Jackson's troops had been rapidly approaching Richmond since his departure. The night of the 25th his command was encamped in the vicinity of Ashland, on the Richmond and Fredericksburg Railroad, some sixteen miles from Richmond. Early on the morning of the 26th he moved easterly, crossing the Central Railroad below Hanover Court House about ten o'clock, and, taking the Mechanicsville road, camped for the night south of the Totopatomoy Creek at a place called Hundley's Corner, some seven or eight miles northeast of Mechanicsville. He was thus getting well in the rear of the right of the Federal army. Lee's preparations for assault had been completed. His battle order was as follows:

HEADQUARTERS, ARMY OF NORTHERN VIRGINIA, *June* 24, 1862.
General Orders No. 75.

1. General Jackson's command will proceed to-morrow from Ashland toward the Slash Church and encamp at some convenient point west of the Central Railroad. Branch's brigade, of A. P. Hill's division, will also to-morrow evening take position on the Chickahominy near Half-Sink. At three o'clock Thursday morning, 26th inst., General Jackson will advance on the road leading to Pole Green Church, communicating his march to General Branch, who will immediately cross the Chickahominy and take the road leading to Mechanicsville. As soon as the movements of these columns are discovered, General A. P. Hill, with the rest of his division, will cross the Chickahominy near Meadow Bridge and move direct upon Mechanicsville. To aid his advance the heavy batteries on the Chickahominy will at the proper time open upon the batteries at Mechanicsville. The enemy being driven from Mechanicsville and the passage across the bridge opened, General Longstreet, with his division and that of General D. H. Hill, will cross the Chickahominy at or near that point, General D. H. Hill moving to the support of Jackson, and General Longstreet supporting General A. P. Hill. The four divisions—keeping in communication with each other and moving

en echelon on separate roads, if practicable, the left division in advance, with skirmishers and sharpshooters extending their front—will sweep down the Chickahominy and endeavor to drive the enemy from his position above New Bridge, General Jackson bearing well to his left, turning Beaver Dam Creek and taking the direction toward Cold Harbor. They will then press forward toward the York River Railroad, closing upon the enemy's rear and forcing him down the Chickahominy. Any advance of the enemy toward Richmond will be prevented by vigorously following his rear and crippling and arresting his progress.

2. The divisions under Generals Huger and Magruder will hold their positions in front of the enemy against attack, and make such demonstrations on Thursday as to discover his operations. Should opportunity offer, the feint will be converted into a real attack, and should an abandonment of his intrenchments by the enemy be discovered, he will be closely pursued.

3. The Third Virginia Cavalry will observe the Charles City road. The Fifth Virginia, the First North Carolina, and the Hampton Legion (cavalry) will observe the Darbytown, Varina, and Osborne roads. Should a movement of the enemy down the Chickahominy be discovered, they will close upon his flank and endeavor to arrest his march.

4. General Stuart with the First, Fourth, and Ninth Virginia Cavalry, the cavalry of Cobb's Legion and the Jeff Davis Legion, will cross the Chickahominy to-morrow and take position to the left of General Jackson's line of march. The main body will be held in reserve, with scouts well extended to the front and left. General Stuart will keep General Jackson informed of the movements of the enemy on his left and will co-operate with him in his advance. The Tenth Virginia Cavalry, Colonel Davis, will remain on the Nine-mile road.

5. General Ransom's brigade, of General Holmes's command, will be placed in reserve on the Williamsburg road by General Huger, to whom he will report for orders.

6. Commanders of divisions will cause their commands to be provided with three days' cooked rations. The necessary ambulances and ordnance trains will be ready to accompany the divisions and receive orders from their respective commanders. Officers in charge of all trains will invariably remain with them. Batteries and wagons will keep on the right of the road. The Chief Engineer, Major Stevens, will assign engineer officers to each division, whose duty it will be to make provision for overcoming all difficulties to the progress of the troops. The staff departments will give the necessary instructions to facilitate the movements herein directed.

By command of General Lee.

(Signed)   R. H. CHILTON,
Assistant Adjutant General.

Lee designed that Jackson should progress sufficiently far on the 26th to relieve A. P. Hill from any difficulty in capturing Mechanicsville. This being done, it would unmask the bridge at that point, and Longstreet and D. H. Hill could cross. The four commands, being thus united, with Jackson in advance and on the left, would flank the very strong position of the Federals on the left bank of Beaver Dam Creek, which emptied into the Chickahominy about one mile below Mechanicsville. But Jackson was one day behind time. He did not proceed from Ashland on the 25th, as ordered, because he arrived there only that night, and did not leave till the next morning. A. P. Hill, after waiting the greater part of the 26th for Jackson, grew impatient, and, fearing there might be a failure of the offensive plan, crossed the Chickahominy at Meadow Bridge at 3 P. M. and moved direct on Mechanicsville, hoping that as soon as he became engaged at that point Jackson would appear on his left and they would open the way for a union with D. H. Hill and Longstreet; and then these troops could all, as directed in General Lee's order, "sweep down the north side of the Chickahominy." They were to advance in two lines: Jackson on the left and A. P. Hill on the right of the first line, the former being supported by D. H. Hill and the latter by Longstreet. This movement rapidly and successfully executed would unmask the "new bridge" on the Chickahominy below, by means of which General Lee could reunite the left wing of his army with Huger's and Magruder's divisions on its right bank. The strategy was a repetition of that adopted by McDowell at the first Manassas, and afterward by Lee at Chancellorsville. After A. P. Hill drove the Federals out of Mechanicsville he found himself in front of the strongly intrenched lines on Beaver Dam, and the remainder of the afternoon of the 26th was occupied in attempting to carry them, assisted by Ripley's brigade, of D. H. Hill's division. The approach to the Federal position being over an open plain and exposed to a murderous fire of all arms, was not successful that night. Had Jackson been up he would have crossed the Beaver Dam Creek above the right of the Federal line that evening, as he did the next day, and thus prevented a great loss of life.

It has been said we were lavish of blood in those days, and it was thought to be a great thing to charge a battery of artillery or line of earthworks with infantry. On the morning of the 27th the attack was renewed at dawn. While it was in progress Jackson crossed the creek above, and the enemy at once abandoned his intrenchments, retiring rapidly down the river, destroying a great deal of property and leaving much in his deserted camps. As soon as the bridges could be repaired across the Beaver Dam, Lee's left wing resumed its march. About noon the Federal troops were found in position behind Powhite Creek. This second line taken by Fitz John Porter was a strong one, and made more so by breastworks of trees and rifle trenches, while the crests of the position were crowned with artillery. General Lee says the approach to this position was over an open plain about a quarter of a mile wide commanded by a triple line of fire and swept by the heavy batteries south of the Chickahominy. Hill, still in advance, first encountered the enemy, was soon hotly engaged, and met the large force with the "impetuous courage for which that officer and his troops are distinguished." The battle raged fiercely and with varying fortune for more than two hours. The attack on the Federal right being delayed by the length of Jackson's march and the obstacles he encountered, Longstreet was directed to make a feint on the enemy's left, which he soon converted into a real attack. Jackson arrived about this time, and, after a short and bloody conflict, his troops forced their way through the morass and obstructions and drove the Federals from the woods on the opposite side. Lee now ordered a general advance from right to left. The enemy's breastworks were quickly stormed, and he was forced back with great slaughter toward the banks of the Chickahominy till night put an end to the pursuit. On the morning of the 28th there were no Federal troops in Lee's front north of the Chickahominy. McClellan had united what was left of Porter's corps with the rest of his army on the south side of that stream.

What would McClellan do now? Would he attempt
to open communication with his base of supplies at the
White House, or would he retreat down the Peninsula
in the direction of Fort Monroe, skirting the James
River, where he could be in communication with the
Federal gunboats on that stream, or would he seek
shelter at the nearest point on James River? If he attempted to go down the Peninsula or to fight for his line
of communication on York River, Lee was on the proper
side of the Chickahominy to meet such movements.
Should he retreat in a direct line across the White Oak
Swamp for James River it would be necessary for the
Southern troops to get on the south bank of the Chickahominy as soon as possible in order to pursue. The
seizure of the York River Railroad by Ewell's division
and a portion of the cavalry under Stuart convinced the
Southern commander that McClellan had abandoned his
York River base, and shortly afterward it was ascertained that there were no indications of a retreat down
the James River. Lee then knew McClellan had determined to get to the James by the nearest practicable
route. The Federal right had been so pounded to
pieces that Lee did not fear an advance on Huger and
Magruder, because in that case the victorious Southern
legions would have been in his rear, and such an attempt
would have resulted in the sacrifice of his army. The
battle of Gaines Mill having been won and the future
purpose of his enemy discovered, early on the 29th
Longstreet and A. P. Hill were directed to recross the
Chickahominy at New Bridge, while Jackson and D. H.
Hill crossed at Grape Vine Bridge.

General Lee had now united his whole army south of
the Chickahominy. That afternoon Magruder attacked
the enemy near Savage Station, being the rear guard of
a retreating army. The lateness of the hour and the
small force employed did not produce a decisive result.
On the next day, the 30th, at 4 P. M., the Union troops
were again overtaken, and the battle of Frazier's Farm,
sometimes called Glendale, or Nelson's, Farm, was fought
by Longstreet and A. P. Hill. Huger did not get up,
and Jackson was unable to force a passage through the
White Oak Swamp. The battle raged from 4 till 9 P. M.

By that time, General Lee says, his enemy had been driven with great slaughter from every position but one, which he maintained till he was enabled to withdraw under cover of darkness. Jackson reached the battlefield on July 1st, having succeeded in crossing the swamp, and was directed to continue the pursuit down the Willis Church road, and soon came upon the enemy, who occupied the high range extending obliquely across the road in front of Malvern Hill, a position of great natural strength. There McClellan had concentrated his artillery, supported by large masses of infantry, protected by earthworks. Immediately in the Federal front the ground was open, varying in width from a quarter to a half mile, sloping gradually from the crest, and completely swept by the fire of his infantry and artillery. General Lee in his report says: "To reach this open ground our troops had to advance through a broken and thickly wooded country, traversed nearly throughout its whole extent by a swamp passable at but few places, difficult at those. The whole was in range of the batteries on the heights and the gunboats on the river, under whose incessant fire our movements had to be executed." Here the Federals were assaulted by portions of Jackson's, D. H. Hill's, Magruder's, and Huger's divisions, but from want of concert among the attacking columns, General Lee reports, their assaults were too weak to break the Federal line, and, after struggling gallantly and inflicting great loss, they were compelled successively to retire. Night was approaching when the attack began, and it soon became difficult to distinguish friend from foe. "The firing continued," General Lee reports, "till after 9 P.M., but no decided result was gained. The lateness of the hour at which the attack necessarily began gave the enemy the full advantage of his superior position and augmented the natural difficulties of our own." In these offensive movements the Southern cavalry under Stuart were directed to move to the left of Jackson, breaking the Federal lines of communication and giving notice of any attempt to get down the Peninsula. The greater part of McClellan's cavalry, under Stoneman, which had been picketing on Porter's right flank, was cut off from his army by the march of

Jackson and Stuart, and, not being able to reach their troops, proceeded rapidly down the Peninsula. Stuart reached McClellan's base at the White House on the 29th, to find it abandoned. On Stuart's approach the greater part of the enemy's stores were destroyed, but a large amount of property was rescued, including ten thousand stand of small arms, partially burned. Stuart took up his march to again place himself on Jackson's left, reaching the rear of the Federals at Malvern Hill at the close of the engagement on the night of July 1st. The next day the Federals, having again retreated, were pursued by Lee, with his cavalry in front, in the midst of a violent storm, which somewhat retarded their progress. The Union troops, having retired during the night, succeeded in reaching the protection of their gunboats. At Westover on the James River, the approach to their front was commanded by the heavy guns of the shipping in addition to those mounted in intrenchments. In view of these facts General Lee deemed it inexpedient to attack him. His troops had been marching and fighting for seven days, and after remaining in close vicinity to McClellan's army, on July 8th they were returned to their former position. In concluding his report of these engagements, General Lee says that "under ordinary circumstances the Federal army should have been destroyed. Its escape was due to the causes already stated. Prominent among these is the want of correct and timely information. This fact, attributable chiefly to the nature of the country, enabled General McClellan skillfully to conceal his retreat and to add much to the obstructions with which Nature had beset the way of our pursuing columns, but regret that more was not accomplished gives way to gratitude to the Sovereign Ruler of the Universe for the results achieved. The siege of Richmond was raised, and the object of a campaign which had been prosecuted after months of preparation at an enormous expenditure of men and money completely frustrated. More than ten thousand prisoners (including officers of rank), fifty-two pieces of artillery, and upward of thirty-five thousand stand of small arms were captured. The stores and supplies of every description which fell into our hands were great in amount and value, but small in comparison with those destroyed by the enemy."

When McClellan's army, worn with conflict and broken by defeat, reached, on July 2d, the plains of the James River, above Westover, had the Southern infantry moved along the route taken by the cavalry of Stuart, he might have been attacked again with every element of decisive success. During the night of the 1st Stuart's celebrated horse artillery commander, Pelham, informed his chief that the Federal troops, after leaving Malvern Hill, had reached this position in a disorderly state, and that their position on the James River flats was completely commanded by a ridge parallel to the river called Evelington Heights. These heights commanded the enemy's encampment, and, crowned with artillery and taken possession of by infantry, would have compelled, in all probability, McClellan's surrender. Stuart forwarded Pelham's report at once to the commanding general, and proceeded to gain these heights. A squadron of the Federal cavalry vacated them without much hesitation on his approach. Upon getting in sight of the enemy Stuart determined to send back for one of his howitzers to fire upon their camp below. It was ascertained that the main body of the enemy were there much reduced and demoralized. These facts were promptly furnished to the commanding general, who in turn informed him that Longstreet and Jackson were *en route* to his support. Stuart held this ground from 9 A. M. till 2 P. M., when he was finally driven off by bodies of the enemy's infantry, after the exhaustion of his howitzer ammunition. He held the heights as long as it was possible, till he learned that Longstreet had taken the wrong road, and was then at Nance Shop, six or seven miles off, and could not possibly reach him in time to secure them. It was suggested to Stuart by one of his officers not to occupy the heights in force, nor to fire cannon from them, because it would call the attention of McClellan to the great importance of securing and fortifying them (before Lee's army could arrive), as necessary to his own protection. The cavalry commander disregarded this suggestion, and was driven from them. It seems absolutely certain that had Longstreet followed Stuart's march, Jackson Longstreet's, and the remainder of the army followed them, on July 2d, these heights could have been occupied by Lee's army and McClellan's command attacked and destroyed. The guns of the gunboats had to be so greatly elevated to fire over the banks of the river that the projectiles passed over the heights, so that the Southern army would not be much exposed to that fire, while a plunging fire from Lee's batteries on the Federal troops in the plains below must have resulted most disastrously.*

McClellan, in a dispatch to Mr. Lincoln on the 4th, two days afterward, says: "We now occupy Evelington Heights, about two miles from the James, a plain extending from there to the river. Our front is about three miles long; these heights command our whole position, and must be maintained."

The total losses to the Army of the Potomac in these seven days of conflict are put down at fifteen thousand eight hundred and forty-nine, and the list of casualties in the Army of Northern Virginia in the fights before Richmond, commencing June 22d and ending July 1, 1862, is placed at sixteen thousand seven hundred and eighty-two. The Southern losses were the greater because during the battles they invariably formed the attacking column, while the Federal troops fought more or less behind intrenchments.

It can not be denied that the retreat of McClellan from his position in front of Richmond to the James River was cleverly executed. After his right was rolled up the various positions selected to keep the Southern troops from destroying his army were well selected and ably defended. The Federal commander got unduly excited over what he supposed was the great preponderance of the Southerners in numbers, as well as over the re-enforcements which they were supposed to be receiving. On the night Stonewall Jackson encamped at Ashland McClellan told the Secretary of War by telegraph that

---

* The only reference known to the loss of this great opportunity by the Southern army is to be found in the valuable work entitled Four Years with General Lee, by Colonel Walter Taylor, his distinguished adjutant general.

he had received information from various sources that Beauregard and his troops had arrived in Richmond; and a half hour later he telegraphed Casey in command of his depot supplies at the White House that "it was said Jackson is coming from Fredericksburg with the intention of attacking the right flank soon." Six and a half hours later, on the morning of the 26th, at three o'clock, he informed Mr. Stanton that his "impression was confirmed that Jackson would soon attack our right rear," and added if he "had another good division he would laugh at Jackson." At 9 A. M. on the morning of the 26th a negro servant who had been in the employ of some of the officers of the Twentieth Georgia was brought before him, and, after questioning him, he telegraphed Stanton, "There is no doubt that Jackson is coming upon us." At midnight on June 24th he had informed Stanton that a "peculiar case of desertion had just occurred from the enemy." The deserter stated that he had left Jackson, Whiting, and Ewell, and fifteen brigades at Gordonsville on the 21st, and that it was intended to attack his [McClellan's] rear on the 28th, and asked for the latest information about Jackson. Mr. Stanton replied to him on June 25th, Jackson then being at Ashland, that he had no definite information as to the number or position of Jackson's forces; that it was reported as numbering forty thousand men. He had also heard that "Jackson was at Gordonsville with ten thousand rebels. Other reports placed Jackson at Port Republic, Harrisonburg, and Luray, and that neither McDowell, who was at Manassas, nor Banks and Fremont, who were at Middletown, appear to have any knowledge of Jackson's whereabouts." On the day Jackson arrived at Ashland McClellan was engaged in pushing Heintzelman's corps closer to the Richmond lines in prosecution of his general plan of advance. The night of the 25th, when Jackson was sleeping at Ashland, McClellan again telegraphed to the Secretary of War that he was inclined to think that Jackson would attack his right and rear, and that the rebel force was at least two hundred thousand; that he regretted his inferiority of numbers, but felt he was not responsible for it, and that if his army was destroyed by overwhelming numbers he could at least die with it and share its fate; that he felt there was no use in his again asking for re-enforcements. It seems that McClellan was deceived to some extent by the report of his chief of Secret-Service Corps. This was a corps one of whose objects was to question prisoners and deserters and ascertain in every other possible way the numbers of Lee's army. He was fully convinced he had to fight two hundred thousand troops. Lee's army numbered at the beginning of these combats eighty-one thousand. It was composed of thirty-nine brigades of infantry (twelve more, including those under Jackson, than General Johnston had when he relinquished the command at Seven Pines), six regiments and three battalions of cavalry, and sixteen batteries of reserve artillery (exclusive of those with the various infantry divisions). Fifty-three thousand Southern troops were massed on McClellan's right, and constituted the force which attacked Porter's command, numbering of all arms of service about thirty-six thousand men; while twenty-eight thousand Confederate troops stood between some seventy thousand of McClellan's army on the south bank of the Chickahominy and Richmond. The certified morning reports of the Federal Army of the Potomac, dated June 20, 1862, gives 115,102 as the aggregate present for duty. Six days later, when the battles commenced, the force probably did not exceed one hundred and five thousand. If in round numbers we put it at one hundred thousand, Lee was outnumbered nineteen thousand. When McClellan discovered that his opponent had on the left bank of the Chickahominy two thirds of his army, but three courses were left to him: One, to re-enforce the three divisions of Porter. Another, to strengthen and fortify the position along Beaver Dam Creek, and, relying on Porter to hold at bay as long as possible Jackson, Longstreet, and the two Hills, boldly set in motion his four corps on the right bank of the Chickahominy for the coveted prize, his enemy's capital. By destroying Huger and Magruder or crippling them, a portion of his troops could have kept them quiet, and then, facing about with the remainder, he might have marched to Porter's assistance and possibly defeated Lee. It was hazardous, however.

Richmond was not Austerlitz, nor McClellan Napoleon. Third, to rescue Porter from his enemy, get him safely across to the south side of the Chickahominy, and unite him with the rest of his army.

This plan, if it had been adopted before the Confederate attack, might have forced the Southern commander to attack his united army on the right bank. He decided to receive the attack in the position then occupied by Porter, and only withdrew him to the Richmond side of the Chickahominy after he had been badly hammered and had lost some six thousand men.

Perhaps if McClellan had known that he was fighting eighty-one thousand men, and not two hundred thousand, he might have acted with more confidence. Mr. Lincoln telegraphed June 26th that his suggestion of the probability of his being overwhelmed by two hundred thousand men, and talking about where the responsibility would belong, pained him very much. On June 27th McClellan began to realize that he was going to have some very serious work, and begged the Secretary that he would put some one general in command of the Shenandoah Valley and of all troops in front of Washington for the sake of the country. On the same day he complimented Porter for his fine efforts at Gaines Mill, says he looks upon the day as decisive of the war, and tells him to "try and drive the rascals, and take some prisoners and guns." This was an hour or two before Porter's defeat. General Hooker did not seem to be so confident, for about the same time he reported that he had just returned from the front, where "we have nothing but a stampede, owing to the behavior of the troops occupying the picket line. The first shot from a rebel was sufficient to start regiments." Later that day Admiral Goldsborough, the flag officer of the Federal squadron on the James, was notified by McClellan that he had met with a severe repulse, and asked him to send gunboats up the James River to cover the left flank of his army.

The Washington War Secretary was confident of Federal success as late as the evening of June 29th, for he telegraphed Hon. William H. Seward, at New York, that his inference is, from what has taken place around

Richmond, that McClellan will be in the city within two days; and the day after, to General Wool, at Fort Monroe, that McClellan had a favorable position near Richmond, and that it looked more like occupying that city than any time before. At 11.30 on the night of June 30th the Union army commander had begun to realize that his "change of base," as he termed it, would not be attended with favorable results, and telegraphed Mr. Stanton that he feared he would be forced to abandon his material in order to save his men, under cover of the gunboats, and that if none of them escaped, they would at least have done honor to the country.

On July 1st his army was at Haxall's plantation, on the James, and McClellan says he dreaded the result if he was attacked; that if possible he would retire that night to Harrison's Bar, where the gunboats could aid in covering his position. "I now pray for time. We have failed to win only because overpowered by superior numbers." On July 2d McClellan's army had succeeded in reaching Harrison's Landing. He told Mr. Lincoln that if he were not attacked during that day his men would be ready to repulse the enemy on the morrow. On the same day he received a dispatch from President Lincoln in that vein of humor for which he was remarkable. "If you think you are not strong enough to take Richmond just now, I do not ask you to. Try just now to save the army material and *personnel*, and I will strengthen it for the offensive again as fast as I can. The governments of eighteen States offered me a new levy of three hundred thousand, which I accepted." And in a letter of the same date, in reference to sending him re-enforcements, Mr. Lincoln adds a postscript: "If at any time you feel able to take the offensive, you are not restrained from doing so."

The respective commanders of the two armies decided to rest and recruit their forces. McClellan resumed the habit he contracted in West Virginia of issuing proclamations. On July 4th the following was read to his army from the headquarters of the Army of the Potomac, camped near Harrison's Landing.

SOLDIERS OF THE ARMY OF THE POTOMAC: Your achievements of the last ten days have illustrated the ability and endurance of the American soldier. Attacked by vastly superior forces, and without hope of re-enforcements, you have succeeded in changing your base of operations by a flank movement, regarded as the most hazardous of military expedients. You have saved all your material, all your trains, and all your guns, except a few lost in battle. Upon your march you have been assailed day after day with desperate fury by men of the same race and nation, skillfully massed and led, and under every disadvantage of numbers, and necessarily of position also. You have in every conflict beaten back your foes with enormous slaughter.

.   .   .   .

(Signed)   GEO. B. McCLELLAN,
                  Major General Commanding.

By a series of brilliant movements General Lee had driven an army superior to him in numbers from the gates of his capital, and had fully restored himself in the confidence of his people by the exercise of military genius and by his personal conduct and supervision of the troops on the battlefield. It might be said of him, as Addison wrote of the great Marlborough, that

"His mighty soul inspired repulsed battalions to engage,
And taught a doubtful battle where to rage."

Or, as was written of Wellington, "no responsibility proved too heavy for his calm, assured, and fertile intellect. If he made a mistake, he repaired it before the enemy could profit by it. If his adversaries made one, he took advantage of it with immediate decision. Always cool, sagacious, resolute, reliant, he was never at a loss for expedients, never disturbed by any unforeseen accidents, never without a clear conception of the object to be achieved, and the best way of achieving it."

The character of Lee is most apparent from his own words, only written for the eyes of the members of his family. When by his skill his brave soldiers had removed from the front of his capital McClellan's army, in a letter to his wife he disposes of the matter in a few lines by saying, on July 9, 1862, from Dobb's Farm, on the Nine Mile Road: "I have returned to my old quarters, and am filled with gratitude to our Heavenly Father for all the mercies he has extended to us. Our success has not been as great or complete as we could have desired, but God knows what is best for us. Our enemy has met with a heavy loss, from which it must take him some time to recover before he can recommence his operations."

General Henry Clitz had been wounded and was a prisoner in Richmond. General Lee answered a letter in reference to him and other wounded prisoners:

HEADQUARTERS, *July* 15, 1862.

MY DEAR FITZ: I have just received your letter of the 13th. I am very sorry to hear of the sufferings of the wounded prisoners, and wish I could relieve them. I proposed to General McClellan on Tuesday, before the battle of that day, to parole and send to him all his wounded if he would receive them. Since that the arrangement has been made, and the sick and wounded are now being conveyed to him. This will relieve them very much, and enable us to devote our attention to those retained. In addition, the enemy has at last agreed to a general exchange of all prisoners of war, and Generals Dix and D. H. Hill are to meet to-morrow to commence the negotiations. I hope in this way much relief will be afforded; at first the hospitals were overtaxed, men could not be had to bury the dead, and the sufferings of all were increased. Friend Clitz ought to recollect that this is a matter of his own seeking, and he has only to blame himself. I will still be happy to do for him all I can, and will refer your letter to the director of the hospital if I can find him.

Your loving uncle, R. E. LEE.

General FITZ LEE.

The offensive tactics of the Confederate commander raised the siege of Richmond and the hopes of the South. From the various churches prayers ascended to the throne of the God of Battles, and humble supplications were offered for the cessation of hostilities.

The removal of McClellan's army from the walls of Richmond brought great relief to its inhabitants; the blood of the bravest had been poured at their feet, the moans of the wounded had fallen upon their ears, and the dead lay silent and cold before their eyes. The war had been brought to their hearthstones.

General Lee now proposed to transfer its horrors to fields at a greater distance from the Southern capital, for the proximity of a large hostile army still menaced its safety. McClellan had been driven from its gates, but Richmond was still his objective point. But two marches away there were encamped on James River ninety thousand men; twenty days after the battle of Malvern Hill it numbered 101,697—a grand army, well equipped with all the sinews of war, whose principal officers were men of undoubted courage and military ability.

Lee had three alternatives: First, to attack; second, to await an attack; third, manœuvre so as to threaten Washington and draw McClellan's army from the vicinity of Richmond. The Army of the Potomac was now behind too much dirt, and had too many big guns in position on land and water to admit of an attack with reasonable hopes of success; and time was too precious to wait for it to get in condition to assume the offensive again, so Lee promptly decided to move it to a safe distance. Mr. Lincoln was naturally solicitous about the security of the Federal capital. After McClellan's defeat he determined to do two things: One, to concentrate the commands which Jackson had scattered and put them under one officer, who should be charged with the guardianship of Washington; the other, to buckle to his side by day and night a military adviser in whose abilities he had confidence, and who should be commander in chief of all the Federal armies.

He was singularly unfortunate in the selection of the officers to fill these two important places. The forces of Fremont, Banks, and McDowell were united into what was termed the Army of Virginia, and its command was assigned to Major-General John Pope. This officer, a Kentuckian by birth and a West Point graduate, was then forty years old. When a captain of engineers in the United States Army he had been detailed as one of the army officers to escort Mr. Lincoln to Washington where he was to assume the duties of the presidency, and, it is presumed, did not fail to impress upon the President his qualifications for command. Pope had met with some success in the campaigns in the West, and was looked upon as a rising officer whose military capacity would be productive of great results, and ultimately seat him in McClellan's saddle. On assuming his new command, it must be confessed he made a bad beginning, which was not attended with the usual good ending. He was evidently deeply impressed with the idea that the war in Virginia had not been conducted properly, and that he had been brought from the West—where, as he said, he had only seen the backs of his enemies—to destroy the human race at the South generally, whether they were armed soldiers or unarmed citizens.   There was a striking contrast between McClellan and Pope.   The former had announced that private property and unarmed citizens should be protected, and that neither confiscation of property, political execution of persons, nor forcible abolition of slavery should be contemplated for a moment; the latter had ordered the arrest of all disloyal male citizens, and their banishment from their homes unless they took the oaths of allegiance, threatening them if they should ever return that they would be visited with the extreme rigor of military law, and should their oaths be violated, the offenders would be shot and their property confiscated.   He also directed that prominent citizens, however inoffensive they might be, should be seized on every side and held as hostages for Union soldiers captured by "roving bands."   The intimation to his soldiers that they were free to enter upon a campaign of robbery and murder against unarmed citizens and peaceful tillers of the soil produced a sensation in the army of Lee, which had been accustomed to encounter troops under leaders of a different type, and also a desire to get at Pope at the earliest moment. The North was not prepared at that date for such extreme measures.   Men who at home would have shuddered at the suggestion of taking another's property now appropriated remorselessly whatever came within their reach.   The Southern President directed General Lee to say to the authorities at Washington that a cartel for the exchange of prisoners between the belligerents had just been signed by Generals Dix and D. H. Hill, representing their respective governments, stipulating that all prisoners hereafter taken will be discharged on parole till exchanged, and that Pope had violated it, because his orders contemplated the murder of peaceful inhabitants as spies; that innocent people had been seized, to be murdered in cold blood if any of his soldiers should be killed by unknown persons; and that, in consequence, neither Pope nor his commissioned officers, if captured, should be considered as prisoners of war. To this communication President Lincoln's new military adviser replied that the communication of Mr. Davis, inclosed to him by General Lee, was couched in language exceedingly insulting to the Government of the United States, and that he [Halleck] must respectfully decline to receive it. Later it was stated that the Government disavowed these measures of the commander of the Army of Virginia. Pope was more or less ridiculed by soldiers on both sides for his bombastic declamations. He did not want to hear, he told his troops, of taking strong positions and holding them, of lines of retreat and bases of supply. His "headquarters" were reported "in the saddle," and his army was to be launched upon a sea of strife without a compass. The safety of Washington, with which he was particularly charged, was to be secured by marvelous methods. He proposed to keep his army on the flank of any hostile force that approached it, because he thought that no commander would have the temerity to pass him, in the first place; and, in the second, if he should seek to attack him, he could lead him off in another direction, and was satisfied that if he had McClellan's numbers he could march to New Orleans and dictate the terms of peace in the Crescent City.

General Lee early measured Pope, and when it became necessary to transact military business with him paralyzed him with movements as brilliant as they were bold, but which it is safe to say he would never have attempted against an army commander for whose military genius he had profound respect. In a letter from near Richmond, July 28, 1862, after telling Mrs. Lee: "In the prospect before me I can not see a single ray of pleasure during this war; but so long as I can perform any service to the country I am content," he could not resist giving Pope a slight slap, and adds: "When you write to Rob again" (his youngest son, who was a private in the Rockbridge Battery) "tell him to catch Pope for me, and also to bring in his cousin Louis Marshall, who, I am told, is on his staff. I could forgive the latter fighting against us, but not his joining Pope."

Out in the West, too, President Lincoln found his

commander in chief, and on July 11th ordered that Major-General Henry W. Halleck be assigned to command the whole land force of the United States as general in chief, and that he repair to the capital. The Confederates were re-enforced by these appointments of Halleck and Pope. If the latter was, as Swinton, the historian of the Army of the Potomac, puts it, "the most disbelieved man in the army," the former was a perpetual stumbling-stone in the path of the field commanders of the Federal army. His position was a most difficult one to fill. Mr. Lincoln's attention was drawn to him by his past record. Halleck graduated at the United States Military Academy in the class of 1849, and was forty-seven years old when summoned to Washington. Like Lee, McClellan, and Pope, he was an engineer officer, but resigned in 1854 to practice law, and was so engaged in San Francisco, Cal., when the war began. General Scott had a high opinion of his ability. A lawyer, a soldier, and an author, he had written on both military and legal topics. He had many of the qualifications necessary for his trying office. This appointment was made by Mr. Lincoln immediately after a personal inspection of McClellan's army on the James River. On that visit, July 8th, the Northern President ascertained that the Army of the Potomac numbered 86,500 men present and 73,500 absent to be accounted for. The tri-monthly return for July 10th fixed the number of men present equipped for duty at 98,631. "To make this army march to Richmond with any hope of success it must be re-enforced by at least 100,000 good troops; any officer here whose opinion is worth one penny will not recommend a less number," wrote one of his corps commanders on the day of this return, and strongly advised the removal of the army to Washington. Whether to re-enforce McClellan or Pope was the question. The former could not well be attacked in his fortified camp, nor could he assault with much prospect of success Lee's lines, as they were much stronger now than when he was last in front of them. Burnside, who had been ordered from the South to re-enforce McClellan, was halted at Newport News, ready, as Mr. Lincoln informed McClellan on July 14th, " to move on short notice one way or the other when ordered." By which he meant up the Potomac to Washington, or up the James to McClellan, and a week afterward he wrote McClellan that he would decide what he should do with Burnside in the next two or three days.

General Lee decided the question for him. With watchful eye he had noticed the concentration of Pope's army and its gradual extension into Virginia. He saw that it had passed McDowell's battlefield, crossed the Rappahannock, and was getting too near to the important town of Gordonsville, where the railroad from Richmond met the one from Washington. He resolved to stop Pope, and, if possible, overwhelm him before he could be largely re-enforced by McClellan, for a victory over him would remove McClellan's army to Washington. On July 10th Lee had 65,419 men, exclusive of the Department of North Carolina, which was under his command, or some 23,000 less than the army opposed to him. This fact did not deter him three days afterward from making the disparity of numbers still greater by sending a detachment of 8,000 men to Pope's front. For the commander of this force Lee wisely selected Jackson, who was so aggressive and so swift in his movements that he would create a disturbance in the guardian army of Washington before his departure from Richmond would be known. Stonewall Jackson left Lee on July 13th with his old division and that of Ewell's, both having been much weakened by hard marches and severe fighting. One week afterward Mr. Lincoln was informed by McClellan that he had heard Jackson had left Richmond by rail, going either toward Gordonsville or Fredericksburg, that the movement continued three days, and that he might be going against Buell in the West *via* Gordonsville, so as to leave the Petersburg and Danville roads free for the transportation to Lee of recruits and supplies. On the same day Pope reported to Lincoln that Ewell was at Gordonsville with six thousand men, and Jackson at Louisa Court House, but a few miles distant, with twenty-five thousand, and that his [Pope's] advanced posts were at Culpeper and Madison Court

House. Jackson, the *bête noir* of the Federal capital, was on the war path, and again produced consternation. Halleck hurried to McClellan, and had a personal interview on July 25th, urging upon him to attack Richmond at once, or he would have to withdraw him to re-enforce Pope. McClellan finally agreed to attack if Halleck would send him twenty thousand more troops, all that Halleck could promise. McClellan would not say, says Halleck, that " the probabilities of success were in his favor, but there was a chance, and he was willing to try it; that the force of the enemy was two hundred thousand; and that in this estimate most of his officers agreed." His own effective force was ninety thousand, which, with twenty thousand re-enforcements, would make one hundred and ten thousand; and his officers were about equally divided in opinion in regard to the policy of withdrawing or risking an attack on Richmond.

Five days before Halleck's visit General Lee's army numbered 57,328. Estimating it at 60,000 when McClellan and Halleck were in conference, it is seen the former overestimated Lee's strength only about 140,000. The interview between these two officers highest in rank in the Federal army was productive of temporary respect, confidence, and friendship. Halleck writes McClellan a few days afterward that " there was no one in the army under whom I could serve with greater pleasure." McClellan replies: " Had I been consulted as to who was to take my place, I would have advised your appointment; and that if we are permitted to do so, I believe that together we can save this unhappy country and bring this war to a comparatively easy termination. The doubt in my mind is whether the selfish politicians will allow us to do so." The next few days saw changes not only in the relations between these two officers, but in the plans and purposes of the contending forces. Jackson arrived at Gordonsville on July 19th, and at once began to consider the best way to strike Pope. Finding that his antagonist had practically concentrated the corps of Sigel (formerly Fremont's), Banks's, and McDowell's, and had nearly six times his numbers, he wisely decided to apply to General Lee for more troops

before he assumed the offensive. On July 27th Lee
sent A. P. Hill's division, which gave him an army of
18,623. While he could not hope to beat the whole of
Pope's army, numbering on July 31st, according to
Pope, 40,358, or, if we accept the reports of the various
corp commanders, 47,000 men, the disposition of these
forces gave him an opportunity to strike a part of it.
Banks was in advance at Culpeper Court House, with
his cavalry picketing the line of the Rapidan. Jackson always availed himself of such opportunities, and
promptly moved forward and crossed the Rapidan on
August 8th. Pope, on learning of Jackson's advance,
ordered Banks to move in his direction from Culpeper
Court House; so Jackson encountered him on the 9th
about eight miles in front of that place, a short distance
west and north of Slaughter Mountain near Cedar Run.
A well-tested battle was fought, resulting in a victory
for the Southern troops, their pursuit being stopped
by night. Banks fell back to his old position north
of Cedar Run, while Jackson remained in the field
next day, and then, hearing that Banks had been heavily re-enforced, returned to the vicinity of Gordonsville. The Confederates sustained a loss of thirteen
hundred officers and men, including General Charles
Winder, of Maryland, one of the most promising and
gallant soldiers of the South. Jackson mourned him as
one of his most accomplished officers. " Richly endowed," he wrote, " with those qualities of mind and
person which fit an officer for commanding, and which
attract the admiration and excite the enthusiasm of the
troops, he was rapidly rising to the front rank of his
profession. His loss has been severely felt." By this
movement Jackson, as usual, had rendered great service. The question whether to re-enforce Pope or Mc-
Clellan was decided. Stonewall Jackson was in front
of the army covering Washington. Halleck's orders for
the evacuation of the Peninsula by McClellan's army
must be carried out. Burnside, hanging for so long a
time between McClellan and Pope, must go to Pope.

The anticipations of General Lee had been realized;
it was now a race who should get to Pope first—the
Army of Northern Virginia or the Army of the Po-

tomac. The movements of the Southern general had been delayed because he did not desire to risk the detachment of too many troops from Richmond lines until he had a reasonable confidence that McClellan's offensive operations were at an end. Four days after Jackson's fight he determined to transfer the theater of action to Pope's front, and accordingly ordered Major-General Longstreet, with ten brigades, commanded by Kemper, Jenkins, Wilcox, Pryor, Featherstone, D. R. Jones, Toombs, Drayton, and Evans, to Gordonsville, and on the same day Hood, with his own and Whiting's brigades, was sent to the same place. Two days afterward—namely, August 15th—General Lee proceeded in person to join Longstreet and Jackson. He was distressed at being deprived of the services of Richmond, his *cheval de bataille*, in the approaching campaign. His favorite riding mare was a sorrel called Grace Darling. When the war began he had her sent down from Arlington to the White House. He writes that he heard of Grace. She was seen bestridden by some of the Federal soldiers, with her colt by her side, and adds that he could have been better resigned to many things than that. " I have also lost my horse Richmond." (Presented to him by some citizens of Richmond.) " He died Thursday. I had ridden him the day before. He seemed in the morning as well as ever; but I discovered in the evening he was not well. I thought he was merely distressed by the heat, and brought him along very slowly. Finding at bedtime he had not recovered, I had him bled, which seemed to relieve him. In the morning he was pronounced better; at noon he was reported dead. His labors are over and he is at rest. He carried me very faithfully, and I shall never have so beautiful an animal again. His fate is different from Grace's, and to his loss I can easily be resigned. I shall want but few horses more, and have as many as I require."

Three days after Longstreet, and one day after Lee left, McClellan telegraphed (August 16th) Halleck: " Movement has commenced by land and water. All sick will be away to-morrow night. Everything being done to carry out your orders. I do not like Jackson's movements. He will suddenly appear when least expected." It is apparent that General Lee was confident of McClellan's withdrawal, or he would hardly have left in person or detached Longstreet from Richmond. On Lee's departure, General G. W. Smith, who had returned to duty, was left in command with his own division and that of D. H. Hill (at Petersburg commanding the Department of North Carolina), as well as McLaw's and R. H. Anderson's divisions and Hampton's cavalry brigade; but on the 15th Lee telegraphed to Mr. Davis requesting him to order R. H. Anderson's division to him, and on the 17th General G. W. Smith was ordered to join him also. The great value of time was appreciated by the Southern leader. It was his plain duty to force Pope to accept battle before he was joined by the whole of McClellan's army. When Pope discovered that Lee was marching to fight him he fell back behind the line of the Rappahannock, though he thought that river was too far to the front, because, he said, " the movements of Lee were too rapid and those of McClellan too slow to make it possible with his force to hold that line, or to keep communication with Fredericksburg without being turned on my right flank by Lee's whole army and cut off altogether from Washington." He was told that in two days more he would be largely re-enforced by the Army of the Potomac, and would not only be secure, but strong enough to assume the offensive. He was instructed, he reports, to hold on there, " and fight like the devil." Lee therefore found Pope on the Rappahannock, with his right at the Waterloo Bridge and his left at Kelly's Ford. He had stretched down the river as far as he well could so as to keep his communication open with Fredericksburg, from which point Burnside and Fitz John Porter's corps of the Army of the Potomac were coming. Lee was anxious to get at Pope at once, but there was a river rolling between them. From " Camp near Orange Court House," August 17, 1862, he wrote: " Here I am in a tent instead of my comfortable quarters at Dobbs's " (his headquarters in front of Richmond). " The tent, however, is very comfortable, and of that I have nothing to complain. General Pope says he is very strong, and seems to feel so, for he is moving apparently up to the Rapidan. I hope he will not prove stronger than we are. I learn since I have left that General McClellan has moved down the James River with his whole army. I suppose he is coming here, too, so we shall have a busy time. Burnside and King from Fredericksburg have joined Pope, which, from their own report, has swelled Pope to ninety-two thousand. I do not believe it, though I believe he is very big. Johnny Lee saw Louis Marshall after Jackson's last battle, who asked him kindly after his old uncle, and said his mother was well. Johnny said Louis looked wretchedly himself. I am sorry he is in such bad company, but I suppose he could not help it." *

Lee promptly decided to destroy the railroad in Pope's rear so as to capture re-enforcements and supplies from the direction of Washington and Alexandria, for he knew that the portion of McClellan's army which should be transferred by water would take that route to join Pope. This duty he intrusted to his chief of cavalry, J. E. B. Stuart, who had been commissioned as a major general on July 25th. Three days thereafter his cavalry was organized into a division consisting of two brigades under Wade Hampton and Fitz Lee: Hampton's, the First North Carolina Cavalry, Cobb Legion Cavalry, Jeff Davis Legion, Hampton Legion, and the Tenth Virginia, while Fitz Lee's brigade consisted of the First, Third, Fourth, Fifth, and Ninth Virginia Cavalry. When these new operations commenced, Stuart, leaving Hampton on the Richmond lines, moved Fitz Lee's brigade to the Rapidan, while he went by rail to join General Lee at Orange Court House for consultation. After his consultation with General Lee, Stuart proceeded to Verdierville, on the road from Orange Court House to Fredericksburg, where he had expected to find Lee's brigade on the evening of the 17th, a proceeding which came very near resulting in the capture of himself and staff. Not finding the brigade as contemplated, he sent one of his staff officers in the direction he expected to meet it to conduct it to his headquarters. A body of the enemy's

---

* Louis Marshall, son of his sister, who remained on the Federal side, and was a member of General Pope's staff; Johnny Lee was General Lee's nephew, and met Marshall under a flag of truce after the fight at Cedar Mountain.

cavalry, which had started on a reconnoissance the day before, was marching in that direction, and into their ranks in the darkness of the night Major Fitzhugh, of his staff, rode, and was captured. On his person was found an autograph letter from General Lee to Stuart, disclosing the design of turning his left flank. Stuart and his staff proceeded to pass the night on the porch of an old house. He was awakened at dawn by the sounds of approaching horsemen; sent two of his aids off in that direction to find out who was coming, and walked out to the front gate, bareheaded, to greet, as he supposed, his brigade commander; but in another instant he heard pistol shots and saw Mosby * and Gibson rapidly returning, pursued by a party of the enemy. He and the rest of his staff then rushed back, jumped over the fence, and made across the fields to the nearest woods. They were pursued only a short distance. When the pursuit stopped, Stuart returned to a point where he could observe the house, and saw the enemy departing with his cloak and hat, which he had been compelled to leave on the porch where he had slept. Stuart's hat was generally a conspicuous one, having a broad brim looped up on one side, over which always floated large black feathers, and for many days thereafter he was subject to the constant inquiry of "Where's your hat?" The brigade commander he had expected did not understand from any instructions he received that it was necessary to be at this point on that particular afternoon, and had marched a little out of his direct road in order to reach his wagons and get from them a full supply of rations and ammunition. After Stuart reached the army, to the brigade he brought from Richmond was added another which had previously served in the Valley, and was commanded by General Beverley Robertson, which consisted of the Second, Sixth, Seventh, Twelfth, and Seventeenth Battalions of Virginia cavalry. Having detached a regiment under Munford to operate on the left of the army, Stuart crossed the Rapidan on the 20th with Fitz Lee's brigade and the remainder of Robertson's, and

---

* John S. Mosby, afterward the famous partisan officer.

proceeded at once to drive the Federal cavalry from out of the section between the Rapidan and Rappahannock Rivers, across the latter stream. Lee now began to extend his left, and on the 22d and 23d Jackson moved up the Rappahannock River to the Warrenton Springs ford. Stuart started on his mission, crossing at Waterloo Bridge, a point above Warrenton Springs, and, moving by way of Warrenton, reached the vicinity of Catlett's Station, twelve miles in Pope's rear, after dark. The rain fell in such torrents and the night was so dark that it was not possible for him to damage the road to any great extent. At that point was encamped the whole reserve, baggage, and ammunition train of Pope's army as well as his headquarters tent and personal effects. Stuart captured a number of officers and men, a large sum of money in a safe in one of the tents, dispatches and other papers of Pope's office, and his personal baggage. Had it not been raining so hard the destruction of the railroad bridges and of the track itself, as well as an immense number of wagons, would have seriously crippled Pope, and the object of the expedition would have been accomplished. He was obliged to withdraw before daylight, and returned to his army at Warrenton Springs the next day, bringing back with him over three hundred prisoners. Pope now ascertaining that Lee was turning his attention to a flank movement on his right, began extending his lines up the river. The Southern commander was not content with what had been done by Stuart, and determined to execute the same movement on a larger scale, which would have the effect of severing Pope's communications with his base of supplies and compel him to leave the lines of the Rappahannock.

CHAPTER IX.

SECOND BATTLE OF MANASSAS.

THE strategy of Lee was daring and dangerous, the conception brilliant and bold. Self-reliant, he decided to separate his army into two parts. On August 24, 1862, he had fifty thousand troops, while Pope, including his own army, had, with Reno's corps of Burnside's army and Reynolds's division of Pennsylvania reserves, about the same number, which two days later was increased to seventy thousand by the arrival of the corps of Fitz John Porter and Heintzelman. Lee proposed to hold the line of the Rappahannock and occupy Pope's attention with thirty thousand troops under the immediate command of Longstreet, while he rapidly transferred Jackson by a circuitous march of fifty-six miles to a point twenty-four miles exactly in rear of Pope's line of battle. On August 25th Jackson, with three divisions of infantry, under Ewell, A. P. Hill, and W. B. Taliaferro, preceded by Munford's Second Virginia Cavalry, crossed the upper Rappahannock, there called the Hedgman River, at Hinson Mills, four miles above Waterloo Bridge, where the left and right of the two opposing armies respectively rested. The "Foot Cavalry" were in light marching order, and were accompanied only by a limited ordnance train and a few ambulances. Three days' cooked rations were issued and duly deposited in haversacks, much of which was thrown away in the first few hours' march, the men preferring green corn, seasoned by rubbing the meat rations upon the ears, and the turnips and apples found contiguous to their route. After the sun sank to rest on that hot August day, Jackson went into bivouac at Salem, a small village on the Manassas Gap Railroad, having

marched in the heat and dust twenty-six miles. But one
man among twenty thousand knew where they were going. The troops knew an important movement was on
hand, which involved contact with the enemy, and possibly a reissue of supplies. At early dawn the next day
the march was resumed at right angles to the course of
the day before, following the Manassas Gap Railroad
and passing through Bull Run Mountains at Thoroughfare Gap. At Gainesville, Stuart, with Robertson and
Fitz Lee's brigades of cavalry, overtook Jackson, whose
subsequent movements were "greatly aided and influenced by the admirable manner in which the cavalry
was employed and managed by Stuart." On reaching
the vicinity of Manassas Junction, his objective point,
Jackson inclined to the right and intersected the main
railroad in Pope's rear at Bristoe Station, four miles
closer to Pope, where he halted for the night, having
marched nearly thirty miles. That night he sent General
Trimble, who had volunteered for the occasion, with five
hundred men, and Stuart, with his cavalry, to capture
Manassas, which was handsomely done. Pope claims
that Jackson's movement was known, and that he reported it to Halleck, but on the day Jackson marched
Pope was disposing his army along the Rappahannock
from Waterloo to Kelly's Ford. On the night of the
26th, when Jackson began to tear up the railroad at
Bristoe, the nearest hostile troops were the corps of
Heintzelman and Reno at Warrenton Junction, ten miles
away. The next day, leaving General Ewell's division
at Bristoe to watch and retard Pope's march to open his
communications, Jackson, with the remainder of his
troops, proceeded to Manassas. He found that Stuart
and Trimble had captured eight guns, three hundred
prisoners, and an immense quantity of stores. The vast-
ness and variety of the supplies was a most refreshing
sight to his tired and hungry veterans. All of the 27th
his troops, transformed from poverty to affluence, reveled
in these enormous stores, consisting of car loads of provisions, boxes of clothing, sutler's stores containing
everything from French mustard to cavalry boots.
Early that morning Taylor's New Jersey brigade, of
Slocum's division of Franklin's corps, which had been

transported by rail from Alexandria to Bull Run for the purpose of attacking what was presumed to be a small cavalry raid, got off the cars and marched in line of battle across the open plain to Manassas. Fitz Lee, who with his cavalry brigade had crossed Bull Run to make a reconnoissance in the direction of Alexandria, ascertained that Taylor was not supported by other troops and sent information of this fact to Jackson, suggesting that Taylor be allowed to march to Manassas, where he and his whole command would be most certainly captured. The artillery, however, opened on the brigade, giving them notice that a large force was present, which resulted in the killing of many men, including the gallant brigade commander, and capturing many others. The remainder beat a hasty retreat. That afternoon Ewell was attacked by Hooker's division of Heintzelman's corps, who had been ordered to re-open the Federal communications, and retired, as he had been directed, to join Jackson. This enterprising officer, having executed General Lee's instructions and having torn up the railroad and burned the bridges in that vicinity, now determined to move in such a manner as to avoid disaster to his own troops, while he united them at the earliest possible moment with those under Longstreet *en route* to his assistance. He had successfully thrown his fourteen brigades of infantry, two of cavalry, and eighteen light batteries in Pope's rear; but his position was perilous.

Two plans were open to Pope after he had ascertained that Jackson was on the line of his communication and between him and his capital—one to throw his whole force on Longstreet and, if possible, destroy him, and then move with his victorious legions on Jackson; the other to hold Longstreet apart from Jackson with a portion of his force, in which he would be greatly assisted by the topographical features of the country, while moving with the remainder of his command on the Confederate forces in his rear. He decided to adopt the latter, and might have succeeded had he so manœuvred as to prevent the junction of the two wings of Lee's army. There can be no fault found with the skillful directions issued for the movements of Pope's army on

Jackson on the 27th. At sunset of that day Jackson's command was still eating, sleeping, and resting at Manassas. McDowell, with his own, Sigel's corps, and Reynolds's division of Pope's army, was at Gainesville, fifteen miles from Manassas and five from Thoroughfare Gap, through which Lee's route to Jackson lay, being directly between Jackson and Lee, while Reno's corps and Kearny's division of Heintzelman's corps were at Greenwich, in easy supporting distance. Hooker at Bristoe Station was four miles from Manassas, and Banks and Fitz John Porter at Warrenton Junction ten miles. On the night of the 27th everything was favorable to Pope, and it seemed his various corps would only have to be put in motion on the morning of the 28th to crush Jackson. McDowell was told by Pope if he would move early with his forty thousand on Manassas he would, as Pope expressed it, with the assistance of troops coming in other directions, " bag Jackson and his whole crowd."

But Pope made two great mistakes—one in not holding, with a large force, at all hazards, Thoroughfare Gap, five miles from McDowell's position at Gainesville, and thus shut the door of the battlefield in Longstreet's face. The other, in supposing Jackson was going to remain at Manassas in order that he might carry out his plans to beat him; for while Pope was arranging that night to his own satisfaction his tactical bagging details for the next day, the three divisions of that wide-awake officer were marching away from Manassas: A. P. Hill to Centreville, Ewell to the crossing of Bull Run at Blackburn Ford, and up the left bank of that stream to Stone Bridge, where the Warrenton turnpike crosses, and Taliaferro, whose march Jackson in person accompanied, to the vicinity of Sudley Mills, north of Warrenton turnpike and west of Bull Run, at which point Jackson designed to concentrate his command. The movements of the two divisions across Bull Run were made to mislead Pope, and did so. When he reached Manassas the next day Jackson was not there. He thought from the passage of Bull Run he had gone to Centreville, and so the march of his converging troops was directed upon that point. Jackson had exercised his usual skill in the

selection of his position. He could attack any of Pope's
troops marching down the Warrenton turnpike in the
direction of Centreville, where they hoped to find him,
and at the same time by prolonging his right he would
be in a position to communicate at the earliest possible
moment with General Lee as he came through Thoroughfare Gap with Longstreet. After Jackson had arrived
at his new position a courier of the enemy was captured
by the cavalry, who was conveying a dispatch from Mc-
Dowell to Sigel and Reynolds, which disclosed Pope's
intention to concentrate on Manassas. One of Jackson's division commanders writes that the messenger
bearing the captured orders " found the Confederate
headquarters established on the shady side of an old-
fashioned fence, in the corners of which General Jackson and the commanders of his divisions were profoundly
sleeping after the fatigue of the preceding night, and
there was not as much as an ambulance at his headquarters. The headquarters train was back beyond the Rappahannock, with servants, camp equipage, and all the
arrangements for cooking and serving food. The property of the general, of the staff, and of the headquarters
bureau was strapped to the pommels and cantles of the
saddles, which formed pillows for their weary owners.
The captured dispatch roused Jackson like an electric
shock ; he was essentially a man of action, and never
asked advice or called council. " Move your division
to attack the enemy," said he to Taliaferro ; and to
Ewell, " Support the attack." The slumbering soldiers
sprang from the earth. They were sleeping almost in
ranks, and by the time the horses of the officers were
saddled, lines of infantry were moving to the anticipated
battlefield. It was Stonewall's intention to attack the
Federals who were on the Warrenton road moving on
his supposed position, but after marching some distance
north of the turnpike in the direction of Thoroughfare
Gap no enemy was found. McDowell, after sending
Rickett's division to the gap to retard the advance of
Longstreet, moved it direct to Manassas and not down
the Warrenton pike ; so finding this pike clear of his
enemy, he halted, and, keeping his flanks guarded by
cavalry, watched it, while ever and anon he turned a

wistful eye in the direction of the gap in the mountain to his right.

Pope now seemed to have lost his military head. It did not occur to him that his success lay wholly in keeping Longstreet and Jackson apart. Jackson alone was a subject of concern to him. He reached in person Manassas about midday on the 28th, and found that Jackson had left the night before after burning five thousand pounds of bacon, a thousand barrels of corned beef, two thousand barrels of salt pork, two thousand barrels of flour, together with large supplies of every sort. While Pope was following his supposed route to Centreville, Jackson in his war paint was in line beyond the Warrenton turnpike waiting for Longstreet. He had evidently determined to attack any and every one who dared to occupy the pike he was keeping open for Longstreet. It so happened that King's division of McDowell's corps, which on the night of the 27th was near Buckland, in getting the order to march to Centreville had to pass without knowing it in front of Jackson, by whom he was promptly and furiously attacked, and a most stubborn contest followed. King's troops fought with determined courage, and his artillery was admirably served. In addition to the four brigades of his division, he had two regiments of Doubleday's, and fought two of Ewell's and three of Taliaferro's brigades of Jackson's command. A. P. Hill's division was not engaged. It was an exhibition of superb courage and excellent discipline on both sides, and a fight face to face. "Out in the sunlight, in the dying daylight, and under the stars they stood," neither side yielding an inch, while brave men in blue and gray fell dead almost in each other's arms. Jackson's loss was heavy. Ewell and Taliaferro were both wounded, the former losing a leg, while King lost over a third of his command. The Federal commander held his ground till 1 A. M., when, being without support or orders, he marched to Manassas Junction. Jackson, who was not at Manassas or Centreville on the days Pope desired him to be, informed that officer by this fight exactly where he was; so on the 29th Pope once more changed the march of his columns, still hoping he would be able to defeat him before being re-enforced by General Lee. General Lee, with Longstreet's command, left the Rapidan on the 26th and followed Jackson's route. A little before dark on the 28th he reached and occupied the western side of Thoroughfare Gap with one brigade. At the same time Ricketts came up from Gainesville with his division and occupied the eastern side of the same pass. Longstreet describes this pass as rough and at some points not more than one hundred yards wide. A turbid stream rushes over its rugged bottom, on both sides of which the mountain rises several hundred feet. On the north the face of the gap is almost perpendicular. The south face is less precipitous, but is covered with tangled mountain ivy and projecting bowlders, forming a position unassailable when occupied by a small infantry and artillery force. This gap and the Hopewell Gap, three miles north, if seriously disputed by the Federals would have embarrassed Lee. Prompt measures were taken to prevent it. Hopewell was occupied, and through it three brigades under Wilcox were passed during the night, while Hood climbed over the mountain near Thoroughfare Gap by a trail. At dawn on the 29th, much to General Lee's relief, Ricketts had marched away to join McDowell. At 9 A. M. the head of Longstreet's column reached Gainesville on the Warrenton pike. The troops passed through the town and down the turnpike and were deployed on Jackson's right, and ready for battle at twelve o'clock on the 29th. At daylight on that day, to Sigel, supported by Reynolds, was delegated the duty of attacking Jackson and bringing him to a stand, as Pope expressed it, until he could get up Heintzelman and Reno from Centreville, and Porter, with King's division, from Bristoe and Manassas. Pope reached in person the battlefield about noon, and found nearly his whole army in Jackson's front. Longstreet had connected with Jackson's right, which Pope did not know, but rode along his lines and encouraged his men by stating that McDowell and Fitz John Porter were marching so as to get in Jackson's right and rear. The Federal attack had been principally made with the center and right against Jackson. The left, under Fitz John Porter—some ten thousand men—was stationary, McDowell hav-

ing gone to the support of the rest of the army. Lee's
line had been advanced in the fierce contests of the day,
but during the night was retired to its first position.

Porter's inaction in front of Longstreet has been the
subject of much comment, and did not please either
Longstreet or Pope. Both wanted him to attack—Pope,
because he was under the impression it would be a flank
and rear attack on Jackson's position; Longstreet, because, having nearly three men to Porter's one, he could
easily defeat him. It is certain that when Pope ordered
Porter at half past four o'clock in the afternoon to attack, Longstreet's whole force had been in front of him
for four hours and a half. Porter reported the enemy
were in great force in front of him. " They had gathered
artillery, cavalry, and infantry, and the advancing masses
of dust showed the enemy coming in great force," said
he. The "indefatigable Stuart " had ridden out in the
direction of Thoroughfare Gap to meet General Lee and
inform him of the exact position of Jackson and the
general disposition of the troops on both sides. He then
passed the cavalry he had on that flank through Longstreet's column so as to get on his right, and directed
Rosser to have brush dragged up and down the road by
the cavalry from the direction of Gainesville so as to
deceive the enemy, and, according to Porter's dispatch,
it had the desired effect. Stuart found an elevated ridge
in front of Porter, and sent back and got three brigades
of infantry and some artillery, which, in addition to his
cavalry and the effect produced by dragging the brush
and making a great dust, gave the impression that he
had a large force in Fitz John Porter's front. The next
day—the 30th—Pope, desiring to delay as long as possible
General Lee's further advance on Washington, renewed
the engagement. He advanced Porter, whom he had
called to him during the night, supported by King's gallant division, to attack the Confederates along the Warrenton pike, while he assaulted with his right wing Jackson's left. His first impression in the morning was that
General Lee was retreating, and he so telegraphed to
Washington, having derived the impression from the retirement of Lee the night before to his original lines.
Jackson was still Pope's objective point. It was evident

Lee must re-enforce Jackson or attack with Longstreet. He did the latter after first pounding the flanks of Pope's assaulting columns with artillery, under Stephen D. Lee, splendidly massed and served. Pope and Lee were of the same mind that day from their respective stand-points, for as the former was moving on Lee's center and left, the latter was marching to attack the Federal left. A bloody and hard-fought battle resulted, in which the Federal troops were everywhere driven back, and when night put an end to the contest, Pope's line of communication was threatened by the Southern troops occupying the Sudley Springs road close to the stone bridge on Bull Run. He could stay in Lee's front no longer, for he had been badly defeated, and that night withdrew to Centreville, having lost, since he left the Rappahannock, in killed, wounded, and missing, nearly fifteen thousand men. On the 31st his army was posted on the heights of Centreville. Halleck telegraphed him on that day from Washington: "You have done nobly. All reserves are being sent forward. Do not yield another inch if you can avoid it. I am doing all I can for you and your noble army."

Pope now occupied a strong and commanding position along the Centreville heights. He had been re-enforced by the corps of Franklin, which arrived on the 30th, and Sumner on the 31st, and the divisions of Cox and Sturgis. These two latter amounted to seventeen thousand men, and the infantry of Sumner's and Franklin's corps to twenty-five thousand. The march of these troops and their junction with Pope had been reported to General Lee by the cavalry, under Fitz Lee, which, having left Manassas the day of Jackson's arrival there, had penetrated the country as far as Fairfax Court House. Near that point the cavalry commander captured a squadron of the Second Regular Cavalry, which was sent out reconnoitering by General Sumner, having surrounded it while halting to feed their horses. The officers were captured in the house just as they were going to dinner. The cavalry commander did not know whether they would be considered as belonging to McClellan's or Pope's army; and as orders had been received not to parole any of Pope's officers, he kept the Federal

officers with him, having simply exacted from them
their pledged word that they would not attempt to
escape. These officers rode with his staff during the
battle of the 30th, and one of them bore a dispatch for
the Confederate commander, who had sent off all his staff
officers on the ground that he had been kindly and
courteously treated. After the battles were over they
were duly paroled and permitted to ride their horses to
the Federal lines near Washington. McClellan reports
this capture in a dispatch to Halleck on December 31st,
and adds that he had no confidence in the dispositions
made by Pope; that there appeared to be a total absence
of brains, and he feared the total destruction of the
army; while Halleck, in a dispatch from Washington on
August 29th, telegraphs McClellan, then in Alexandria,
that he had been told on good authority that Fitzhugh
Lee had been in that town the Sunday preceding for
three hours.

The great strength of the Federal position with the
large re-enforcements Pope had received decided General Lee to turn Centreville by moving to Pope's right
and striking his rear in the vicinity of Fairfax Court
House. Jackson was again employed for this purpose.
He crossed Bull Run at Sudley, and marched to the Little River turnpike, pursuing that road in the direction
of Fairfax Court House. As soon as this movement was
perceived Pope abandoned Centreville. Hooker was
immediately ordered to Fairfax Court House to take up a
line on the Little River pike to prevent Lee's troops
getting in his rear at the point where it joins the Warrenton pike, the movement to be supported by the rest
of his army. As his troops reached the vicinity of Fairfax Court House, Jackson determined to attack them, and
moved at once upon the force which had been posted
on a ridge near Germantown for the purpose of driving
them before him, so he could be in a position to command the pike from Centreville to Alexandria, down
which Pope's troops must pass on their retreat. A sanguinary battle ensued just before sunset, terminated by
darkness. The battle of Oxhill, as it was called, was
fought in the midst of a thunderstorm. Longstreet's
troops came on the field toward its conclusion. The

loss on both sides was heavy, the Federals losing two of their best generals, Kearny and Stevens. The former was a dashing officer of undoubted courage and great merit. Had he lived he might have been an army commander. He rode into the Confederate lines, thinking they were occupied by a portion of his troops. It was nearly dark and raining. Seeing his mistake, he whirled his horse around, threw himself forward in the saddle, Indian fashion, and attempted to escape. A few men close to him fired, and he fell from his horse. General Lee had his body returned to the Federal lines the next day, accompanied with a courteous note to Pope.

On September 2d Pope's army, by Halleck's direction, was withdrawn to the intrenchments around Washington. While Pope was undoubtedly overmatched in generalship, an analysis of his tactics on the battlefield will show that they are of a higher order of merit than he is credited with, and many of his troops fought with stubbornness and courage. It is true he did not at times seem to appreciate his situation, and his orders were the subject of rapid and radical change. He telegraphed after the battle of the 30th: "We have fought a terrific battle here which lasted with continuous effort from daylight till dark, by which time the enemy was driven from the field, which we now occupy." Whereas the facts of the case were that the Confederate lines were advanced and were only retired after the fighting was over, during the night, to their former positions. The very next day, however, at Centreville, he wires Halleck that his troops were in position there, "though much used up and worn out," but that he could rely upon his giving his enemy as desperate a fight as he could force his men to stand up to, and adds that he should "like to know if you feel secure about Washington should this army be destroyed." He had still an army much greater than Lee's, but there was more or less demoralization in the ranks.

General Franklin, who arrived at Centreville on the 30th with his corps, threw out Slocum's division across the road between that point and Bull Run at Cub Run, to stop, as he says, "an indiscriminate mass of men, horses, guns, and wagons all going pellmell to the rear.

Officers of all grades, from brigadier general down, were in the throng." McClellan estimated the number of stragglers he saw two days later at twenty thousand; and Assistant-Adjutant-General Kelton, who had been sent out by Halleck, puts the number at thirty thousand. Much uneasiness prevailed in the Federal capital, disorder reigned, and confusion was everywhere. As a precautionary measure, it was said, the money in the Treasury and in the banks was shipped to New York, and a gunboat with steam up lay in the river off the White House, and yet there was in and around Washington one hundred and twenty thousand men. On the 1st of September McClellan was again assigned to the command of the defenses around Washington. He had been much mortified in listening to the distant sound of the firing of his men, and asked General Halleck on the night of the 30th of August for permission to go to the scene of battle, telling him his men would fight none the worse for his presence; and that if it was deemed best not to intrust him with the command of even his own army, he simply desired permission to share their fate on the field of battle. Kelton had reported that General Pope was entirely defeated and was falling back to Washington in confusion, and McClellan reports that Mr. Lincoln told him he regarded Washington as lost, and asked him to consent to accept command of all the forces, to which McClellan replied that he would stake his life to save the city, but that Halleck and the President said it would, in their judgment, be impossible to do that.

General McClellan having accepted command, on September 2d rode out in the direction of Upton's Hill to meet Pope's army and direct them to their respective positions in the line of the Washington defenses. He met Pope and McDowell riding toward Washington, escorted by cavalry, when the former asked if he had any objection to McDowell and himself going to Washington; to which McClellan replied: "No, but I am going in the direction of the firing."

Lee's military plans had been wisely conceived, and the tactical details splendidly executed by his officers and men. Only three months had elapsed since he had been in command of the army, and in that brief period he had transferred a hostile army superior in numbers from the lines in front of his capital to the redoubts of the capital of his enemy. Richmond had been relieved; Washington was threatened. He could not hope with prospect of success to attack the combined armies of Pope and McClellan in their intrenchments on the Virginia side of the Potomac, for behind them they could fight two soldiers where he could bring only one in front of them. Apart from these difficulties a wide and unfordable river rolled between Virginia and Washington. His residence at Arlington had made him familiar with the topography of that section. He had but two alternatives: One, to withdraw his army and take up a line farther back in Virginia, rest and recruit his army, and patiently wait, as was done after the first battle of Manassas, till his antagonist should again assume the offensive. The other, to continue the active prosecution of the campaign and fight another battle while he had the prestige of victory and his enemy the discomfiture of defeat. He determined to adopt the latter method, and decided to cross the Potomac at the fords near Leesburg, some forty miles above Washington, and march into western Maryland.

Having received the approval of the Southern President to this plan, he immediately proceeded to put it into execution. First, because he believed if he could win a decisive victory the fall of Washington and Baltimore would follow, with far-reaching results. Second, because it would relieve Virginia and the Confederate quartermasters and commissary departments at Richmond of the support of his army for a time. Third, because it was hoped that large accessions to his decimated ranks would be obtained from those who sympathized with his cause in Maryland. Accordingly, the heads of his columns were turned toward the Potomac, and on September 5th successfully crossed that river and advanced to Frederick, where he established himself behind the Monocacy. He had been joined by the divisions of McLaws and D. H. Hill, which had been left at Richmond, but many of his men were obliged to be left on the Virginia side on account of their condition—long marches in bare feet had incapacitated them for further service. His army had been so constantly engaged in marching and fighting during the past few months that its condition was not favorable to further active work. The soldier was still there with his gun and his ammunition, but his clothes—from the hat on his head to his shoeless feet—were tattered and torn. The army was not presentable to the inhabitants of a State who had been accustomed to the sight of Federal troops well clothed and well fed. It was with difficulty they could understand that these troops had gained fame. The Southern feeling had been overawed and kept down in Maryland for so long a time by Federal occupation that recruits from that State did not care to join the Southern army till it was demonstrated that it could seize and hold their territory. They were not prepared to leave their homes and accompany the army back to Virginia.

Near Frederick, on September 8th, General Lee issued a proclamation to the people of Maryland in accordance with the suggestion of President Davis, who wrote him that it was usual on the occupation by an army of another's territory. General Lee told them that the people of the Confederate States had seen with profound indignation their sister State deprived of every right and reduced to the condition of a conquered province. That his army was there to enable them again to enjoy the inalienable rights of freemen, and restore independence and sovereignty to their State. That no constraint upon their free-will was intended, and no intimidation would be allowed. That it was for them to decide their destiny freely and without restraint, and that his army would respect their choice, whatever it might be; for, "while the Southern people will rejoice to welcome you to your natural position among them, they will only welcome you when you come of your own free-will."

Lee's crossing the Potomac and marching to Frederick relieved the Federal authorities from their immediate anxiety about the safety of their capital. As he had supposed, they determined to send an army after him, marching in such a way as not to uncover the capital, because it was feared that, after drawing their troops away from Washington, Lee might suddenly cross the Potomac and, with the rapidity of march for which he was noted, seize Washington, which attempt would be facilitated by its lines being weakened by troops taking the field. The time had arrived for the Federal army to advance, but no commander had been assigned to take the field with it. Halleck had intimated that McClellan would not be allowed to have it. The latter has stated that he was expressly told that no commander had been selected, but that he determined to solve the question for himself, so left his "cards at the White House and War Department with 'P. P. C.' written upon them, and then went to the field." That he "fought the battles of Antietam and South Mountain with a halter around his neck." If he had been defeated and had survived, he "would have been tried for assuming authority without orders, and probably been condemned to death." There is no doubt that at that time much dissatisfaction existed in the Federal councils with McClellan. His great personal popularity with his troops, the threatened safety of Washington, and the difficulty of finding a suitable successor, all combined to produce a negative acquiescence in his assuming command of the army for offensive operations. McClellan pushed slowly and cautiously his march in Lee's direction; for he said he knew Lee well, had served with him in Mexico, and had the "highest respect for his ability as a commander, and knew that he was a general not to be trifled with or carelessly tendered an opportunity of striking a fatal blow." General McClellan was deceived, too, as usual, in reference to his opponent's numbers, which he estimated to be one hundred and twenty thousand men—about three times the actual strength of Lee's army.

The determination of the boundary line between Maryland and Virginia has been attended with much expense and discussion. It never has been satisfactorily ascertained, because, as a talented son of Maryland put it, "there is no real division between them." The acquisition of Maryland would have added a bright star to the Southern constellation; but for many reasons there was no rushing to arms or many recruits added

to Lee's army.   The sons of Maryland in the Confederate army were splendid soldiers, enthusiastic in the
cause, and brave in battle; and they knew, as the
Southern commander did, that a battle fought and
won in western Maryland, followed by a rapid march
in the direction of Baltimore and Washington, would be
attended with immense results, and that nothing would
be accomplished, so far as Maryland was concerned, till
then.   Much curiosity existed in that State to see the
victors of the first Manassas, the Seven Days' Battles
around Richmond, and the three days' combats on the
plains of the second Manassas.   Inquisitive crowds
hung around the commanding officers.   Jackson was
especially an object of much interest.   The magic name
of "Stonewall" had been heard at the hearthstones of
the people, and they wanted to see him.   He was described by one of them as wearing a coarse homespun,
over which flapped an old soft hat that any Northern
beggar would have considered an insult to have offered
him.   It was reported that he was continually praying,
and that angelic spirits were his companions and coun-
selors, and a desire was expressed to see him at his
"incantations."   His dress and deportment disappointed many who expected to see a great display of gold
lace and feathers; and when he ordered his guards,
said a writer, to clear his headquarters of idle crowds,
many went away muttering, "Oh, he's no great shakes
after all!"

Lee did not move on Washington after crossing the
Potomac, because his numbers were too small to encounter the fortifications and large force assembled for
their defense.   His line of march was so directed as
to draw a portion of the force at Washington after him
and then defeat it.   Frederick, in Maryland, was his first
objective point, and then, it was said, Harrisburg, Pa.
The Monocacy River, flowing from north to south, empties into the Potomac about twenty miles below Harper's Ferry.   Behind the line of that river he determined to halt and be governed by the movements of his
enemy.   From that point he could open his communications with the Valley of Virginia by Shepherdstown and
Martinsburg; resupply his ammunition; gather in de-

tachments of his men left behind in Virginia, from bare feet and other causes, and fill up his supply trains.   He knew his enemy occupied Harper's Ferry in large force, and Martinsburg in his rear, and that his proposed line of communication could not be opened so long as these places were garrisoned, and that sound military principles required that they should be evacuated when his army passed beyond them.   So did McClellan, and urged it more than once.   Halleck, the strategist of the Federal administration, differed from both Generals Lee and McClellan.   Harper's Ferry was in his opinion the key to the upper door of the Federal capital, and should be held till the wings of the Peace Angel were spread over the republic.   General Lee promptly planned to show that McClellan was right and Halleck wrong, though it involved a change of his original designs. His cavalry, under the vigilant Stuart, was at Urbana and Hyattstown, and well advanced on the road from Frederick to Washington, and every mile of McClellan's march was duly recorded and reported.   The progress of this officer was so slow, his movements so cautious, that Lee determined to detach sufficient troops from his army to capture Harper's Ferry and Martinsburg, and bring them back in time to present a united front to McClellan.   Daring, skill, celerity, and confidence were the qualifications of an officer to execute the movement. In Jackson they were all combined.   He moved on September 10th from Frederick with three divisions; crossed the Potomac into Virginia; marched on Martinsburg, which was evacuated on his approach; and then to Harper's Ferry, which he reached on the 13th. McLaws, with his own and Anderson's division, was directed to seize the Maryland heights overlooking Harper's Ferry, while Brigadier-General Walker was instructed to cross the Potomac below Harper's Ferry and seize the Loudoun heights in Virginia.   These movements were successfully accomplished, and on the 14th Harper's Ferry was closely invested.   The heights were crowned with artillery ready to open at command on the doomed garrison.   The little village of Harper's Ferry lies in an angle formed by the Shenandoah and Potomac where their united waters break through the

Blue Ridge Mountains. It is a troop trap unless defended by the adjacent heights. Colonel Miles had strongly fortified the ridge in Virginia called Bolivar Heights, lying between the rivers; but Maryland heights, the key to the situation, was only feebly garrisoned. At dawn on the 15th, in response to Jackson's order, a line of fire leaped from the mountain-crowned heights and told Colonel Miles, the Federal commander, in no uncertain tones, that his surrender was demanded. For two hours this plunging fire was maintained, and at the moment A. P. Hill advanced to storm the town from the Virginia side a white flag was displayed. The firing ceased, and Hill entered the village to receive the surrender of its garrison. Jackson's work was well done. Twelve thousand men stacked their arms. Seventy-three pieces of artillery, thirteen thousand stand of small arms, large numbers of horses and wagons, and immense supplies were the results of his expedition. The cavalry, skillfully conducted by Colonel B. F. Davis, alone escaped on the Sharpsburg road.

When Jackson left Lee, five days before, McClellan was less than five marches from him. It was necessary that he should return as soon as possible, so leaving A. P. Hill to manage the details of surrender with his other two divisions, he marched day and night, recrossing the Potomac and reaching Sharpsburg on the 16th, followed by Walker. For the purpose of facilitating this reunion, Lee had retraced his steps from Frederick, directing the only two divisions Longstreet had left under Hood and Jones to move to Hagerstown, west of the mountains, while D. H. Hill with his division should halt at Boonsboro', where were parked most of his wagons, and where he would be only three miles west of Turner's Pass on the Frederick road. Two days after Lee left Frederick, McClellan occupied it, and at eleven o'clock on the night of the 13th informed Halleck that an order of General Lee's, addressed to D. H. Hill, had accidentally fallen into his hands, the authenticity of which he thought was unquestionable. "It discloses," said he, "some of the plans of the enemy, and shows most conclusively that the main rebel army is now before us. It may therefore be regarded as certain that this rebel army, which I have good reason for believing amounts to one hundred and twenty thousand men or more, and known to be commanded by Lee in person, intended to penetrate Pennsylvania." Lee was fortunate in having the Federal commander overestimate his strength by eighty-five thousand; for confidence, a great attribute in war, is much more easily instilled into troops attacking an army of thirty-five thousand than one of one hundred and twenty thousand. But he was unfortunate in having a confidential order to one of his commanders find its way to the headquarters of the enemy. General D. H. Hill was under Jackson's command. When the latter received Special Orders No. 191 he had a copy of it made and sent to Hill before starting for Harper's Ferry, which Hill produced after the termination of the war, and his adjutant general made affidavit that no other order was received at his office from General Lee. As Hill was to remain with Lee and not march with Jackson, another copy of this order was addressed to him, but how transmitted from Lee's headquarters to Hill's camp, and who was guilty of gross carelessness in losing it, has never been ascertained. The Twelfth Federal Army Corps stacked arms when they arrived at Frederick on the 13th, on the ground that had been previously occupied by General D. H. Hill's division; and Private B. W. Mitchell, of Company F, Twenty-seventh Indiana Volunteers, Third Brigade, First Division, found it on the ground wrapped around three cigars. Little did he think how his discovery would affect a great campaign! The knowledge of its contents had a marvelous effect upon McClellan. Lee had been informed by his cavalry of McClellan's reaching Frederick. He did not know that his designs had been disclosed to him, and therefore did not understand the sudden life infused into the legs of the Federal soldiers; but learning at Hagerstown that McClellan was advancing more rapidly than he had anticipated, he determined to return with Longstreet's command to the Blue Ridge, to strengthen D. H. Hill's and Stuart's divisions, engaged in holding the passes of the mountains, lest the enemy should fall upon McLaws's rear, drive him from Maryland Heights, and thus relieve

the garrison at Harper's Ferry.   Stuart, who had occupied Turner's Gap with Hampton's brigade of cavalry—
this gallant officer having rejoined his army—moved to
Crampton's Gap, five miles south of Turner's, to re-
enforce his cavalry under Munford there, thinking, as
General Lee did, that should have been the object of
McClellan's main attack, as it was on the direct route
to Maryland Heights and Harper's Ferry.   When D. H.
Hill, at dawn on the 14th, re-enforced his two advance
brigades in Turner's Gap, Stuart had gone, leaving one
regiment of cavalry and some artillery under Rosser to
guard Fox's Gap, a small one to the south of Turner's.
As Hill reached the top of the mountain on that September morning a magnificent spectacle was presented.
Far as the eye could reach flashed the bayonets of
the advancing columns of McClellan's army.   It was
a sight not often vouchsafed to any one, and was both
grand and sublime.   Hill must have felt helpless with
his five small brigades numbering less than five thousand men, and must have been impressed vividly with
"how terrible was an army with banners!"   It was
his duty to retard the march of this immense host,
to give Lee time to get his trains at Boonsboro' out of
the way, to bring Longstreet from Hagerstown to his
support, and to give Jackson time for his work at Harper's Ferry.   The resistance of Hill's troops—from nine
in the morning till half-past three in the afternoon—to
the attack of Reno's corps reflected great credit upon
the capacity of the commander and the courage of his
men.   The combat later in the afternoon between Longstreet and Hill on the one side, and Burnside with the
two corps of Reno and Hooker on the other, was marked
by great gallantry on the part of both.   Of the nine
brigades Longstreet had with him, whose strength he
estimated at thirteen thousand men (three of his brigades were with Jackson), Hill says only four were
seriously engaged.   So the struggle on the part of the
Confederates was made with nine thousand men, one
third less in numbers than their antagonists.   The Southern lines were generally held, but when night put an
end to the contest the advantage of the position was
with the Federals.

In a consultation that night between Generals Lee, Longstreet, and Hill, it was decided to withdraw the troops from that point, and form a line of battle at Sharpsburg, where he would be in a position to unite with Jackson, when he should recross the Potomac at Shepherdstown. Fitz Lee, who had been with his cavalry brigade in the rear of the Federal army at Frederick, arrived at Boonsboro' during the night, and was directed by General Lee to remain there and retard as much as possible the Federal advance the next day. On the morning of the 15th, when the Federal army debouched from the mountains, the cavalry brigade was alone between the Federals and Lee at Sharpsburg to dispute with their advance every foot of ground between the base of the mountains and Boonsboro'. This was done with artillery, dismounted cavalry, and charges of mounted squadrons. The object having been accomplished, the brigade was slowly withdrawn and placed on the left of the line of battle at Sharpsburg.

While McClellan was attempting the passage of Turner's Gap with his main army, Franklin with the Sixth Corps, supported by Couch's division, was struggling to get through Crampton's Gap, where McLaws had left a brigade and regiment of his division, and a brigade of Anderson's, to prevent the enemy from passing through the mountains at that point, and threatening his rear at Maryland Heights. The work of these brigades and a portion of Stuart's cavalry was well performed; and when the fighting, which had been going on from twelve o'clock, ceased at night, Franklin had made such progress that they were withdrawn also. On the morning of the 15th, as McClellan was passing through the mountains near Boonsboro', Franklin was marching through Crampton Pass at about the same time, and occupying Pleasant Valley. Both were too late to relieve Miles at Harper's Ferry, who surrendered about half-past seven that morning. Franklin declined to attack McLaws after reaching Pleasant Valley, remained there (the 16th) without receiving any orders, and on the morning of the 17th marched for the battlefield at Sharpsburg, arriving at ten o'clock.

McClellan did not anticipate Lee would offer battle

on that side of the Potomac. When the head of his columns arrived west of the mountains he informed Halleck that his enemy was making for Shepherdstown in a perfect panic, and that General Lee had stated publicly the night before that he must admit he had been shockingly whipped, and that Lee was reported wounded. Mr. Lincoln was well pleased with this statement, and replied to McClellan: "God bless you and all with you. Destroy the rebel army if possible." A little later, when the Federal commander discovered Lee's army in line of battle waiting an attack, he declined to make it, stating that his troops had arrived in Lee's front in sufficient force too late in the day to attack. He remained quiet all the next day, because he said the fog had prevented him from developing the situation of the enemy. Both sides had lost heavily in the mountain passes, and the deaths of such capable officers as Reno on the Federal and Garland on the Confederate side were greatly deplored by their respective armies.

CHAPTER X.

THE small town of Sharpsburg, lying amid surrounding hills, formed an attractive center to the beautiful landscape stretching away on every side. Here, in the embrace of the Potomac on the west and the Antietam Creek on the east, with rolling fields well cultivated and fenced, and fringed here and there with picturesque patches of woodland, it presented an inviting field for battle; but the rich fields were destined to be plowed by cannon balls and fertilized with blood; while against such desecration the peaks above the passes in the mountains loomed up in the distance, as if pointing to heaven in solemn protest.

The position was well selected by Lee to deliver a defensive battle; and while a big, though fordable, river a few miles in the rear was objectionable, its concave curve allowed each of his flanks to rest on the river, though the center of his line of battle was some three miles to the front. There could be no overlapping his flanks by the superior numbers of his opponent, who had to meet a line of battle at whatever point he might select for the attack. It is true the scattered Southern troops could have been more easily concentrated in Virginia and, if necessary, a battle avoided; but Lee had entered Maryland with the intention of fighting, and did not care to change his plans until he had appealed to the God of War.

The troops under Longstreet and D. H. Hill were leisurely marched the four or five miles from Boonsboro' to Sharpsburg. After crossing the Antietam Creek on the morning of September 15th, Lee formed his line of battle along the hills—Longstreet on the right and D.

H. Hill on the left of the road facing the creek, which runs north and south. General Lee reported that the advance of the enemy was delayed by the brave opposition encountered from his cavalry, and did not appear on the opposite side of the Antietam until about 2 P. M., when the battalions began filing to the right and left of the road, taking up their position in his front and exchanging artillery salutations. The sluggish creek flowing between the two armies was spanned by four bridges at the various road crossings converging at Sharpsburg, and was fordable at other points.

McClellan, always deliberate, consumed the whole of the 16th in making his arrangements for approaching battle, much to General Lee's relief. At 4 P. M. in the afternoon Hooker from the Northern right crossed the Antietam with instructions to take position in front of the Southern left, and during the night Mansfield's Twelfth Corps also crossed. In anticipation of such a movement Lee had ordered Longstreet to send Hood with two brigades to prolong D. H. Hill's left, so that when Hooker, with three divisions under Meade, Ricketts, and Doubleday (an officer that Jackson in one of the few jokes of his life called " Forty-eight Hours "), proceeded to execute his orders, he found General Hood across his path with a command equal in efficiency and courage to the best troops of either army, and each claimed the advantage in the engagement which followed.

Jackson reached Sharpsburg that morning from Harper's Ferry, and Walker later. At night Hood was relieved by Lawton's and Trimble's brigades of Ewell's division. Jackson's division, under General J. R. Jones, was placed on Lawton's left, supported by the remaining brigades of Ewell, while General Walker with his two brigades was placed on Longstreet's right. The cavalry were located on either flank.

These are all the troops McClellan would have encountered if he had attacked on the 16th. Anderson's six brigades, McLaws's four, and A. P. Hill's five—making fifteen brigades—did not reach Lee until the 17th. After they had arrived the total infantry amounted to 27,255 men, which, with eight thousand cavalry and artillery, would make Lee's army at Sharpsburg 35,255.* Mc-Clellan reports he had in action, on the 17th, 87,164 troops of all arms. He had therefore present fifty-two thousand more men than Lee. When the inequality in numbers and the difference in quality of cannon, small arms and ammunition, food and raiment is considered, Sharpsburg, as it is called at the South, Antietam at the North, is a superb monument to the valor of the Con-federate soldier and the tactical genius of a great com-mander.

The picture of the private soldier of Lee's army at Sharpsburg, as he stood in the iron hail with the old torn slouch hat, the bright eye glistening with excite-ment, powder-stained face, rent jacket and torn trousers, blanket in shreds, and the prints of his shoeless feet in the dust of the battle, should be framed in the hearts of all who love true courage wherever found. He was a veritable tatterdemalion, loading and firing his rifle with no hope of reward, no promise of promotion, no pay, and scanty rations. If he stopped one of the ene-my's bullets he would be buried where the battle raged, in an unknown grave, and be forgotten, except by com-rades, and possibly a poor old mother who was praying in her Southern home for the safe return of her soldier boy.

Six corps of Federal troops, under Hooker, Sumner, Burnside, Franklin, Mansfield, and Fitz John Porter, stood in battle array, while Pleasonton had forty-three hundred and twenty cavalry. McClellan's plan of battle was to envelop the Confederate flanks—first the left, and then the right—and could he have succeeded in break-ing through either of them and gaining the Williams-port road in Lee's rear and cutting him off from the Potomac, his victory would have been decisive. Had General Lee not divined the main struggle would be on his left, McClellan informed him when he ordered Hooker over the Antietam the evening before?

The fighting at Sharpsburg on the Federal side was done by four corps, numbering fifty-seven thousand six hundred and fourteen men, with a loss of twenty per cent of their numbers. Porter's and Franklin's corps

* General Lee told the writer he fought the battle with 35,000 troops.

and the cavalry, numbering twenty-nine thousand five hundred and fifty troops, were not engaged. As all of General Lee's army fought except a portion of his cavalry, the actual difference between the active combatants was some twenty-six thousand.

On that memorable autumn morning, about the center of his long, slim, gray battle line, Lee stood on a large rock to the right of the Boonsboro' road, east of the town, calm, dignified, and confident, as his glance swept the country in front. "His fine form was sharply outlined against the sky," says a Confederate general, "and I thought I had never seen a nobler figure. He seemed quite unconscious that the enemy's shells were exploding around and beyond him."

Most of the time he was on foot, having both arms and hands injured before leaving Virginia from being thrown violently to the ground, his horse making a sudden jump when he was standing by his side with the bridle reins over his arm. Some of the bones in one hand were broken, and the other arm injured. He was obliged to ride in an ambulance or let a courier lead his horse. In the tumult of battle he could ride but little along his lines on his famous war horse Traveler. So McClellan on that day had the advantage of him as he galloped about on his black charger Daniel Webster.

Jackson, too, had been stunned by the rearing and falling back of a large gray mare which had been presented to him a few days before by an enthusiastic admirer, and was obliged to ride in an ambulance, but fortunately recovered in time for the battle. His horse at Sharpsburg seemed to be gentle enough, for during a lull in the firing Jackson was found under an apple tree, with one leg over the pommel of the saddle, eating apples. The fate of a battle with Generals Lee and Jackson both in ambulances would have been uncertain.

At dawn on the 17th the Federal artillery opened on Hood's front, being directed against the Confederate left, to mask and assist the advancing columns of attack on Jackson. "For several hours the conflict raged," says General Lee, "with great fury and alternate success." The troops advanced with great spirit and the enemy's lines were repeatedly broken and forced to retire. Fresh troops, however, replaced those that were beaten, and Jackson's men were in turn compelled to fall back. General J. R. Jones was obliged to leave the field, and "the brave General Starke" (as General Lee called him), who succeeded him, was killed. General Lawton was wounded, and was succeeded by Early, who had been supporting the cavalry and horse artillery in defending a most important hill, which if occupied by the enemy would have commanded and enfiladed Jackson's position, and who "got in" with his brigade, as he usually did, at the proper moment. Hood and Early, re-enforced by the brigades of Ripley, Colquitt, and Garland, under Colonel McRae, of Hill's division, and D. R. Jones, under Colonel G. T. Anderson, now took up the fighting; the Federals were again driven back, and again brought up fresh troops. General McLaws arrived just in time to meet them; General Walker brought from the right, together with Early's division, drove the Federals back in confusion, beyond the position occupied at the beginning of the engagement.

The long lines of blue which first recoiled from the walls of gray on the Southern left were Hooker's corps, fourteen thousand eight hundred and fifty-six men, which was to have formed, with the Ninth Corps, the left of McClellan's battle line, both to be commanded by Burnside. But Hooker was ambitious and enterprising and secured permission to lead the assault on Lee's left against Jackson, around the well-known Dunker Church, a mile to the north of Sharpsburg on the Hagerstown road, and over the historic cornfields and the "east and west woods," where raged all the morning, with varying fortunes, the bloody combat.

As early as 7 A. M. Hooker had given up the task assigned him, and Mansfield's corps, ten thousand one hundred and twenty-six in numbers, with flags flying, advanced to his support; but in the midst of deploying his columns this veteran general was killed, and in two hours "the corps seems to have about lost all aggressive force," said a Federal historian. Sumner's corps marched next into the battle—Sedgwick's division in advance. The Federal troops previously fighting had melted away, and the march of Sedgwick in close

column of three brigades in the direction of the Dunker
Church was unsupported, and it appeared as if he had
been assigned to fight the remainder of the battle alone.
The First Corps had been disposed of and Hooker
wounded and carried to the rear, the Twelfth broken
into fragments and Mansfield killed. Sedgwick was annihilated by the Confederate fire in front and on both
flanks. The ground was strewn with the bodies of the
dead and wounded, while the unwounded men moved
rapidly away. " Nearly two thousand men were disabled in a moment."

The other divisions of the Second Corps under
Richardson—who was mortally wounded—and French
were ordered up to support Sedgwick, but too late, for
R. H. Anderson's division, just from Harper's Ferry, had
re-enforced D. H. Hill in his position on the famous
Sunken road, which enabled the Confederates to vigorously assume the offensive, and the assaults of the remainder of Sumner's corps were repulsed.

The terrible carnage had progressed six hours.
Franklin, with his Sixth Corps from Pleasant Valley,
arrived about 10 A. M.—having sent Couch's division of
the Fourth Corps to guard Maryland Heights. His
leading division under Smith, whose advance brigade
was commanded by Hancock, went to the support of
Sumner; a forward movement of this division and that
of Slocum, which had arrived about noon, was stopped
by McClellan, who feared a counter attack on his vanquished right. The attack on the Confederate left being foiled, McClellan next threw a heavy force on the
Southern center, which was repulsed by a part of Walker's division and the brigade of General G. B. Anderson, and Rodes of D. H. Hill's, assisted by a few pieces
of artillery. R. H. Anderson came to the support of
this line too, and formed in rear. The Fifth Alabama,
on Rodes's right, was being enfiladed by battery fire,
and Rodes gave directions to retire it, when the whole
brigade, through a misapprehension of orders, moved
back, making a gap which was immediately occupied
by the Federals. G. B. Anderson's brigade was broken,
its commander being mortally wounded, and Major-
General R. H. Anderson and Brigadier-General Wright

were also borne from the field wounded.   General Lee
says that "heavy masses of the enemy again moved
forward, being opposed by only four pieces of artillery, supported by a few hundreds of men rallied by
General D. H. Hill, being parts of Walker's and R. H.
Anderson's commands.   Colonel John R. Cook, with the
Twenty-seventh North Carolina, stood boldly in line
without a cartridge.   The firm front presented by this
small force, and the well-directed fire of the artillery
under Captain Miller of the Washington Artillery, and
Captain Boyce's South Carolina Battery, checked the
progress of the enemy, and in about an hour and a half
he retired."   Longstreet states that the only troops
there were Cook's regiment, and that as he rode along
he saw two pieces of Washington Artillery, but that
there were not enough men to man them, and that he
put his staff officers to work the guns, while he held
their horses.

During the battle McClellan held Fitz John Porter's
corps, twelve thousand nine hundred and thirty men,
with his cavalry, in reserve in the rear of his center.   The
"Little Napoleon," as he was then sometimes called,
was reserving it to be used as the Great Napoleon employed the "Old Guard," to win a battle at the opportune moment, or save an army from destruction should
defeat ensue.   Had they supported Burnside even as
late as his attack was made, McClellan might still have
gained a great victory.

"In the afternoon," General Lee says, "the enemy
began to extend his line as if to cross the Antietam
below, and at 4 P. M. Toombs retired from the position he had so bravely held.   The enemy immediately
crossed the bridge in large numbers, and advanced
against General D. R. Jones, who held the crest with
less than two thousand men.   After a determined and
brave resistance he was forced to give way and the
enemy gained the summit.   General A. P. Hill had now
arrived from Harper's Ferry, having left that place at
7 A. M., and immediately attacked, while his batteries and
those of D. R. Jones and D. H. Hill opened an enfilade
fire north of the Boonsboro' road, and the Federal progress was arrested, seeing which, General Jones ordered

Toombs to charge the flank, while Archer, supported by Branch and Gregg, moved upon the front of the Federal line. The enemy made a brave resistance, and then broke and retired in confusion toward the Antietam, pursued by the troops of Hill and Jones until he reached the protection of the batteries on the opposite side. In this attack the brave and lamented General L. O. B. Branch was killed, gallantly leading his brigade."

While this attack was going on, Lee ordered Jackson to turn the enemy's right, but found it extended nearly to the Potomac, and was so strongly defended with artillery that the attempt had to be abandoned. J. E. B. Stuart had been selected to command the advance in this movement. The Union attack on the Confederate right was made by Burnside's Ninth Corps of four divisions. It was on the eastern side or left bank of the Antietam Creek in front of a bridge, and he was ordered early in the morning to hold his men in readiness to assault.

At eight o'clock McClellan says he sent Burnside orders to cross the creek and take the heights beyond, and move so as to gain possession of them and cut Lee off from the Williamsport or Shepherdstown road, and Burnside immediately prepared to execute them. Toombs had only some four hundred Georgians at this bridge, but his defense of the passage was well executed. Burnside's thirteen thousand troops took three hours to cross, and lost five hundred men. It was now one o'clock, and two hours more were consumed in preparations to assault the ridge held by Jones. The opportune arrival of A. P. Hill, with his thirty-four hundred men, saved Lee's right. Had McClellan placed a portion of his large cavalry force on that flank, Hill's approach might have been retarded and the battle won before his arrival. It is difficult to explain, too, why Couch was not recalled from the vicinity of Maryland Heights after Harper's Ferry was abandoned by Hill.

The bloody battle of Sharpsburg, or Antietam, has passed into impartial history as a drawn combat. The next day neither side would renew the fighting—Lee says because he was too weak to renew the offensive; but that he awaited without apprehension the renewal of the attack. He had received reports that McClellan was expecting the arrival of re-enforcements, and as he could not look for a material increase of his strength, it was not thought prudent to wait until his adversary should be ready to again fight a battle.   During the night of the 18th his army was passed to the south of the Potomac, near Shepherdstown.   The enemy advanced next morning, but was held in check by cavalry, who covered his movements with success.

The Southern loss in the Maryland campaign was ten thousand two hundred and ninety-one—eight thousand at Sharpsburg.   McClellan's loss in the battle was twelve thousand four hundred and ninety-six.   He did not claim a victory until Lee had recrossed the Potomac.   At 1.20 P. M., during the battle, he telegraphed Halleck : " We are in the midst of the most terrible battle of the war—perhaps of history.   Thus far it looks well, but I have great odds against me."   And at 8 A. M. on the 18th he telegraphed : " The battle of yesterday continued for fourteen hours, and until after dark.   We hold all we gained, except a portion of the extreme left.   Our loss was very heavy, especially in general officers.   The battle will probably be renewed to-day."   But it was only on the 19th—thirty-six hours after the fighting was over—that he informed Halleck that " we may safely claim a complete victory."

General Lee's Maryland campaign was a failure. He added but few recruits to his army, lost ten thousand men, and fought a drawn battle, which for an invading army is not a success.   It was preferable, in his opinion, to consuming the substance of the Confederacy in Virginia after the second Manassas, and the result of a victory in Maryland was worth the attempt.   McClellan threw two divisions of infantry across the river, but was driven back, the Confederates losing four guns—a part of their reserve artillery.

The Confederate army then moved back to the Opequan, near Martinsburg, and after a few days' rest to the vicinity of Bunker Hill and Winchester.   McClellan occupied Harper's Ferry and the surrounding heights with two corps under Sumner, and encamped the remainder near the scenes of its late exploits, amid the picturesque hills and vales of southwestern Maryland.

Rest with regular rations at regular times was most grateful to both armies, for both were more or less exhausted. General Lee's two weeks' campaign in Maryland had demonstrated that his army, without re-enforcements, was too small for offensive operations.

His son Robert was at that time a private in the Rockbridge Battery, and was in the thickest of the fight. Just after the battle the general wrote to Mrs. Lee: "I have not laid eyes on Rob since I saw him in the battle of Sharpsburg going in with a single gun of his battery for the second time after his company had been withdrawn in consequence of three of its guns having been disabled. Custis has seen him, and says he is very well and apparently happy and content. My hands are improving slowly, and with my left hand I am able to dress and undress myself, which is a great comfort. My right is becoming of some assistance, too, though it is still swollen, and sometimes painful. The bandages have been removed. I am now able to sign my name. It has been six weeks to-day since I was injured, and I have at last discarded the sling."

In his tent near Winchester he heard of the death of his daughter Annie, who had always been the greatest favorite with her father, and on October 26, 1862, in a letter to Mrs. Lee, he said: "I can not express the anguish I feel at the death of our sweet Annie. To know that I shall never see her again on earth, that her place in our circle, which I always hoped one day to enjoy, is forever vacant, is agonizing in the extreme. But God in this, as in all things, has mingled mercy with the blow in selecting that one best prepared to leave us. May you be able to join me in saying, 'His will be done!' When I reflect on all she will escape in life, brief and painful at the best, and all we may hope she will enjoy with her sainted grandmother, I can not wish her back. I know how much you will grieve, and how much she will be mourned. I wish I could give you any comfort, but beyond our hope in the great mercy of God, and the belief that he takes her at the time and place when it is best for her to go, there is none. May that same mercy be extended to us all, and may we be prepared for his summons."

It was now McClellan's turn to assume the offensive. To cross the Potomac, having that river at his back, and to fight Lee, was too hazardous for a man of his prudence; but by crossing below Harper's Ferry and marching into Virginia he could keep interposed between his capital and the Confederate army, and at the same time move on interior lines toward Lee's capital, which would bring Lee from the Valley of Virginia to offer battle at a point where, if he could be defeated, Richmond might fall. Both armies had increased in numbers. Three days after the battle Lee had 40,000 men, and McClellan—notwithstanding his loss in the two battles, had 80,930, exclusive of the two divisions of Couch and Humphreys, which reached him the day after the battle. The morning report, dated September 20th, sent by McClellan—which included the troops at Washington under Banks and 3,500 men at Williamsport, Frederick, and Boonsboro'—showed an aggregate present for duty of 164,359, and an aggregate absent of 105,124, making a total present and absent of 293,798.

"General McClellan was never in a hurry, but wanted to reach the ideal of preparation before action." He was deliberate, his Government impatient. The chasm between the two was widening. The blood on the field of Sharpsburg was not dry before the Federal army commander was expressing his regret that every dispatch from his general in chief, Halleck, was fault-finding; he asked him to say something in commendation of his army; that it had been lately "badly cut up and scattered by the overwhelming numbers brought against them in the battle of the 17th, and it was only by very hard fighting that we gained the advantage we did. As it was, the result was at one period very doubtful, and we had all we could do to win the day." On the other side Halleck was, with Mr. Lincoln's assistance, putting hot coals on his back. "The country is becoming very impatient at the want of activity in your army, and we must push it on," the former writes, October 7, 1862. And again: "There is a decided want of celerity in our troops. They lie still in camp too long."

Three days after the withdrawal of the Southern

army from Maryland the President of the United States issued his proclamation proclaiming freedom to the slaves. It was admitted to be a war measure, whose purpose, if necessary, was to kindle insurrectionary fires in the Southern States, which should assist the Federal arms in crushing the "Rebellion," as it was termed; but to McClellan and a large part of his army it was objectionable. In his General Order No. 163, of October 7th, in reference to it, he deprecated in the army heated political discussions, and reminded them that the remedy for political errors is at the polls, thus widening the growing gulf between him and his administration, which President Lincoln's visit to him on October 1st, and charging him with being overcautious, did not diminish.

As soon as Lincoln returned to Washington he directed Halleck to order McClellan to "cross the Potomac and give battle to the enemy and drive him South." But many suns were destined to rise and set before that order was executed. General Lee, as well as the Union President, was growing impatient, and wondering why McClellan did not promptly obey orders. So he directed his chief of cavalry, Stuart, on October 8th, to cross the Potomac above Williamsport with his cavalry and ascertain McClellan's positions and designs; to enter Pennsylvania, and to do all in his power to impede and embarrass the military operations of his enemy.

Stuart left the army next morning with detachments of six hundred men from each of the brigades of Hampton, Fitz Lee, and W. E. Jones, and four guns. He was considerate in his orders to his own troops, directing them to give receipts for everything that they were obliged to take in the way of subsistence for man and horse, and also that whenever his column met ladies in Maryland and Pennsylvania, it should turn out of the road to let them pass with their conveyances without molestation. He marched to Chambersburg, in Pennsylvania, passing the right flank of the Federal army, and made a complete circuit, returning by the left flank. He rode eighty miles in twenty-seven hours, and by his swiftness and boldness deceived and evaded every effort to intercept him. "His orders were executed," says General Lee, "with skill, address, and courage." He had destroyed a large amount of public property, reported McClellan's exact position to General Lee, and recrossed the Potomac without loss. "Not a man should be permitted to return to Virginia," telegraphed Halleck to McClellan in informing him that Stuart was at Chambersburg, Pa., and was answered that, in spite of all precautions, Stuart "went entirely around this army"; and calls attention to his deficiency in cavalry, and complained that "the horses of the army were fatigued and had sore tongues," which called forth an inquiry from Mr. Lincoln: "Will you pardon me for asking what the horses of your army have done since Antietam that fatigues anything?" And that "Stuart's cavalry had outmarched ours, having certainly done more marked service in the Peninsula and everywhere since." And yet McClellan had received seventeen thousand nine hundred and eighteen fresh horses since the Sharpsburg battle.

At last on October 26th, three weeks after he had received orders, he began crossing his army over the Potomac into Loudoun County, Va., at Berlin, below Harper's Ferry. This occupied nine days. A slow concentration of his army in the direction of Warrenton followed. Lee met this movement, and later, on November 3d, marched Longstreet's corps to Culpeper Court House to McClellan's front, and brought the corps of Jackson to the east side of the mountain. He had crossed swords, however, for the last time with his courteous adversary. The axe had fallen, and with it McClellan's official head into the basket already containing Pope's. General Order No. 182 from the War Department, dated November 5, 1862, announced, by direction of President Lincoln, that General McClellan be relieved from the command of the Army of the Potomac, and that Major-General Burnside take command of that army.

"Late at night," says McClellan, "I was sitting alone in my tent writing to my wife. All seemed to be asleep. Suddenly some one knocked upon the tent pole, and upon my invitation to enter, there appeared

Generals Burnside and Buckingham, both looking very solemn. After a few moments Buckingham said to Burnside: 'Well, General, I think we had better tell General McClellan the object of our visit'; whereupon Buckingham handed me the order of which he was the bearer. I read the papers with a smile, and immediately turned to Burnside and said: 'Well, Burnside, I turn the command over to you.'" When General Lee heard of it he said he was sorry to part with McClellan; * not that he anticipated his army would be defeated by a change of commanders, but it was a satisfaction to know that as long as McClellan was in command everything would be conducted by the rules of civilized warfare. The soldiers parted with McClellan with great grief, and tears stood in many an eye that had learned to look on war without a tremor.

Many circumstances directed Mr. Lincoln's course. The *entente cordiale* between his Secretary of War, Commander in Chief, and McClellan had been broken. The little value the latter placed upon time as an important element in military operations had been exasperating to them. It had been charged, too, that his different political faith from the party in power, his popularity with his troops, and the probability of his becoming the presidential candidate of his party in opposition to Mr. Lincoln, united to effect his removal. It is not thought that this last condition weighed with the Federal President, or tipped the scales, but rather McClellan's procrastination and his overcautiousness, added to an absurd overestimation of his opponent's strength, and the impatience of the Northern people for more battles. McClellan was always and everywhere a gentleman, who believed in conducting war in a Christian and humane manner. He had strategic, but no tactical ability. Risks have to be taken when battle is joined, but he never took them. Broken, wavering lines were not restored beneath the wave of his sword, and his personal presence was rarely felt when it might have been beneficial. He had none of the inspiration of war.

---

* General Lee said, after the war, that he considered General McClellan the most intellectual of all the Federal generals.

Lee had a great respect for him as a soldier, though he counted on his being slow when manœuvring in his front. The Federal general could organize with great ability and inspire confidence in his troops, and would have been a great commander had he been more rapid in his movements and adventurous in his plans.

His unwilling successor, Ambrose E. Burnside, was the soul of good-fellowship, an amiable officer, and a kind-hearted gentleman. He possessed these qualities as a cadet. The celebrated Benny Havens, who kept a saloon in the old days outside of West Point limits, had a special toast which he invariably repeated every time he indulged in a stimulant—and the repetition of the toast was very frequent during the day. He drank to the health of the two greatest men, in his opinion, who had ever lived—St. Paul and Andrew Jackson; but he took such a fancy to Burnside, when he was a cadet, that he added his name to his toast, and ever thereafter, to the day of his death, he drank to St. Paul, Andrew Jackson, and A. E. Burnside.

This officer conceived the idea of concentrating his army on the Rappahannock River opposite Fredericksburg. The position there would be about sixty miles from Richmond, and by a short railroad to his rear he could reach the Potomac near Acquia Creek, and then, by water some fifty miles, his Washington base. He divided his six corps into three grand divisions—the right, composed of the Second and Ninth, under Sumner; the Third and Fifth Corps, the center, under Hooker; and the left, under Franklin, consisting of the First and Sixth. Sumner, in advance, arrived opposite Fredericksburg on November 17th. Franklin was in supporting distance on the 18th, and Hooker on the 19th, but their pontoons did not arrive for eight days afterward. The vigilance of Stuart informed Lee of this movement on the 15th, and he ordered at once two divisions of infantry and a brigade of cavalry and a battery to proceed to Fredericksburg. A forced reconnoissance of Stuart to Warrenton told him that the whole of Burnside's army had gone to the Rappahannock opposite Fredericksburg. On the 19th Longstreet was ordered to Fredericksburg with the remainder of his corps, and Jackson, who had been moved to Orange Court House, was, about the 26th, ordered to Fredericksburg also. There was much deliberation in Lee's movements. His army was stretched out from the mountains to the river, and it was only after he was satisfied that the Federal army had gone to the Rappahannock that he moved Longstreet, and not for nine days afterward did he direct Jackson to unite with him. He knew a large army changing its line of communication with its base of supplies required time to assume the offensive.

When Sumner arrived at Falmouth, a little village on the left bank of the river a mile above Fredericksburg, with his thirty-three thousand men, across the river was only a regiment of cavalry, a battery, and four companies of infantry. Four days afterward Longstreet arrived, and his attempt to cross then would have been resisted. The surrender of the town had been demanded by Sumner just before the arrival of Longstreet. If not granted, the women, children, aged and infirm, could have sixteen hours to leave their homes, and then "I shall proceed," said Sumner, "to shell the town."

Fredericksburg, a typical Virginia town, is built on a plain every foot of which is commanded by the heights opposite in Stafford County. A plunging fire would destroy it, and Sumner's threat was a serious one to the inhabitants. The man of the house was in the Southern army, and it was a heart-rending experience for the women and children to have their homes and their household goods battered to pieces with cannon. Before the expiration of the time arranged, Longstreet arrived and told the authorities he would not occupy the town for military purposes, and that there was no reason why it should be shelled, and this being communicated to Sumner, he decided not to execute his threat.

It was not wholly Burnside's fault that he was sluggish in his preparations. The railroad to the Potomac had to be prepared, his pontoons were late getting up, and many unexpected matters had to be considered. The twenty-four days which elapsed before he delivered battle were greatly appreciated by Lee. It gave him time to concentrate his army and deploy and strengthen his line of battle on a most defensible position. He would have preferred fighting the battle at North Anna, a defensive point in his rear, because it would draw Burnside farther from his base, and if in the fortunes of battle he could assume the offensive, decisive results would follow, and so thought Jackson; but an unwillingness to give up more of the country, and a desire to draw supplies from the Rappahannock Valley, decided him to fight at Fredericksburg.

Picture a river about two hundred yards wide running east the short distance you see it, and then southeast, the little village of Falmouth, in Stafford County, being on its left, and the town of Fredericksburg, in Spottsylvania, a mile below on its right bank. Imagine a high line of hills from Falmouth down the river whose western slopes touch the water. These are Stafford Heights. On the Fredericksburg side a level plateau stretches out to a range of hills which, beginning at a point above the town, runs parallel to the river for a mile or two, then extends back in a curve for four miles, until at its southern extremity at Hamilton's Crossing they gradually sink to the level of the surrounding country. Along Stafford Heights was posted the army of Burnside—104,903 infantry, 5,884 cavalry; and 5,896 artillery, making, by the report of December 10th, 116,-683 men present for duty equipped. On the Spottsylvania hills, a cannon-shot away, lay Lee's legions 78,-513 of all arms, which included the cavalry brigades of Hampton and W. E. Jones, both of whom were absent.

A river and a plain lay between the hostile forces, and the Northern troops had to cross both to reach the Southern position. The Federal batteries commanded the town of Fredericksburg and the contiguous plain, while the Confederate batteries everywhere swept the open plain nearest to the Southern lines. Burnside's army had to cross this open plain in full view of Lee, and he knew that it would be plowed by shot and shell, and any assault would have to be made amid the iron hail of small arms. Lee's position was strong by nature and made stronger by art. No troops could successfully assail it, and no commanding general should have ordered it to be done. Burnside's order for battle was fathomless; he could not carry Lee's position by surprise, as he told Franklin he expected to, or hope for success least of all by the tactics adopted and made known to his right and left grand division commanders on the morning of battle. Three weeks after Burnside arrived on the Rappahannock, public pressure pushed him across it. He did not cross some miles below Fredericksburg, as first contemplated, because he said Lee had divined his intention and prepared for it, but would cross directly in his front, because General Lee was not expecting it, and attack him before re-enforced by the troops detached to prevent his crossing at the lower point.

The night of December 10, 1862, was a long one for Burnside. One hundred and forty-seven rifled cannon, 20-pound Parrotts, and 4-inch siege guns were distributed along Stafford Heights by Hunt, Burnside's able chief of artillery. The pontoons were placed in position, and at three o'clock on the morning of the 11th the task of constructing four or five bridges opposite the town and two miles below began.

Scarcely had the work commenced before Lee's signal gun announced the news to his sleeping troops. He had never contemplated making a serious resistance at the river banks. To use his own words: "The plain of Fredericksburg is so completely commanded by the Stafford Heights that no effectual opposition could be made to the construction of bridges or the passage of the river. Our position was therefore selected with a view to resisting the enemy's advance after crossing, and the river was guarded only by a force sufficient to impede his movements until the army could be concentrated."

The Thirteenth, Seventeenth, Eighteenth, and Twenty-first Mississippi, of Barksdale's brigade of McLaws's division, and the Third Georgia and Eighth Florida of Anderson's division, guarded the points where pontoons were to be laid, and displayed such skill as marksmen and such courage as men, sheltered behind the houses at the river banks, that the Federal army was delayed at the river bank for sixteen hours, giving the Confederate commander ample time to prepare for battle. During the night of the 11th and succeeding day Sumner's two corps, with one hundred and four cannon, crossed at the upper, and Franklin's two corps, with one hundred and sixteen guns, crossed at the lower bridge, and by the night of the 12th Burnside's army was in readiness for the attack. His plans for the next day were ambiguous. A Federal general reports him as riding about on the evening of the 12th as if he had arrived at the conclusion to attempt to do something with his left, and, if successful, to do something with his right. The tremendous responsibility of having one hundred thousand men on the wrong side of the Rappahannock was having its full effect. He seemed to expect Franklin to get in somewhere on Lee's right and Sumner on his left, and these lodgments being made, the Confederate line between would have to retire or be crushed. He increased Sumner's troops to about sixty thousand, and added Butterfield's corps and Whipple's division to Franklin's command, giving him about forty thousand. At 5.55 A. M. on the 13th, the day of battle, he sent orders to Franklin—which he received two hours and a half afterward (it was said, because the staff officer who carried them stopped to get his breakfast)—to keep his command in readiness to move down the old Richmond road, and send out at once a division at least to seize the heights at Hamilton's Crossing, where Lee's right rested, taking care to keep it well supported. In an order dated 6 A. M., the same morning, he directs Sumner to " push a division or more along the streets and roads on the line from the town to Lee's left, with a view to seizing the heights in the rear of the town," but not to attack until he got additional orders.

Lee was quietly awaiting him. Earthworks had been constructed at points on the crests of the hills, skillfully designed by General Pendleton, chief of artillery, and the engineer officers. His army was divided into two corps, under Longstreet and Jackson, Longstreet being on the left. Anderson's division rested on the river, and then McLaws, Pickett, and Hood extended to the right in the order named. Ransom's division supported the batteries on Marye's and neighboring hills, at the foot of which Cobb's brigade, of McLaws's division, and the Twenty-fourth North Carolina, were stationed, protected by a stone wall. The Washington Artillery, under Colonel Walton, occupied the redoubts on the crest of Marye's Hill, and those on the heights to the right and left were held by a part of the reserve artillery. Colonel E. P. Alexander was in charge of the division batteries of Anderson, Ransom, and McLaws. A. P. Hill, of Jackson's corps, was posted between Hood's right and Hamilton's Crossing. Early's and Taliaferro's divisions composed Jackson's second line, while D. H. Hill's division was formed in reserve. Stuart, with two brigades of cavalry, under General Lee's son and nephew, was on Jackson's right. A dense fog overhung the plain and river until after 9 A. M., obscuring from view the movements of the Federals. Then, as the struggling rays of the sun lifted the mist, it unmasked to Lee and his army a picture unparalleled in surpassing splendor, unequaled in terrible sublimity.

From his lofty position on Telegraph Hill, in the center of his line, Lee saw the mass of Federals deploying in A. P. Hill's front. Franklin was about to assault with "one division at least," as ordered. As a matter of fact, his attack was afterward made with Reynolds's First Corps of three divisions, under Meade, Gibbon, and Doubleday. Meade, an excellent soldier, was sent in first; Gibbon to support him, and Doubleday to follow. Meade selected for his point of attack the place where the ridge on Lee's right terminated and where it gradually reached the level of the plain. It was a salient point, and at its southern end devoid of fortification. Stuart had placed his cavalry and horse artillery far out on the plain, and his guns enfiladed the march of this attacking column. The fire of his horse artillery, under his celebrated boy chief, Pelham, was very effective. The second ball from a Whitworth gun tore through the knapsack of a Federal infantryman, distributed his clothing to the winds, threw a pack of playing cards twenty feet in the air, and created consternation and death as it flew a long distance down the line. Doubleday's division was halted by Pelham's fire and the presence of cavalry on its flank, and Reynolds was deprived of its support, and with only two divisions and two regiments of Stoneman's Third

Corps was attempting to overthrow Jackson, who lay in his front with thirty thousand men in a sheltered, and for a portion of the line, fortified position. Why Reynolds was not supported by Smith's Sixth Corps of twenty-four thousand men, which was a short distance behind him, is one of the mysteries of war. Franklin would still have had fourteen thousand men—namely, two divisions of the Third Corps and one of the Ninth —exclusive of thirty-five hundred cavalry, under the gallant Bayard, as a reserve. The Federal advance marched to destruction. Meade broke through a gap in Jackson's line between Thomas's and Archer's brigade, but fresh troops came up under Taliaferro and Early, amid cries of "Here comes Old Jubal!" "Let Jubal straighten that fence!" and it was securely rebuilt.

The Union troops were broken and driven back with great slaughter. Meade lost in killed, wounded, and missing, 1,853, and Gibbon 1,266 men, in a short, fierce, furious and useless combat. Meade told Franklin he "found it quite hot," taking off his slouch hat and showing two bullet holes between which and the top of his head there must have been little space. To Lee—calm, self-contained and self-reliant as Wellington at Waterloo—from his position on Telegraph (since called Lee's) Hill, the movement appeared like an armed reconnoissance, and was only considered a precursor to something more serious. Jackson was much pleased at the result on his front. He appeared that day for the first and last time in a bright new uniform which replaced his former dingy suit, having actually exchanged his faded old cap for another which was resplendent in gold lace, a present from J. E. B. Stuart. It was a most remarkable metamorphosis of his former self, and his men did not like it, fearing, as some of them said, that "Old Jack would be afraid of his clothes and would not get down to his work."

Burnside's plans seem to have been to attack simultaneously on both of Lee's flanks, like Napoleon when he had the river and three bridges behind him at Dresden, and he may have reasoned, as did that great French soldier, that an assault on both flanks would demoralize the center, which he would overwhelm by concentrated

attack. Sumner's right grand division held the town.
Couch's Second Corps occupied it, and Wilcox's Ninth
Corps stretched out from Couch's left toward Franklin's
right. At 8.15 A. M. Couch received an order from Sumner, who was across the river at the Lacy House, "to
form a column of a division for the purpose of seizing
the heights in the rear of the town"; to advance in
three lines, and be supported by another division to be
formed in the same manner as the leading division; but
the movement should not begin until further orders.
French's division in column of three brigades, at two
hundred yards' interval, was selected to lead, Hancock's
in similar formation to follow. About eleven o'clock, the
fog lifting, Couch signaled to Sumner that he was ready,
and received orders to move. The troops debouched
from the town, crossed with difficulty the bed of an old
canal at right angles to their course, and deployed along
the bank bordering the plain over which they were to
charge. At this time Burnside, the army commander,
was two miles away, across the river at his headquarters, the Phillips House. Sumner, the right grand commander, was at his headquarters also, on the other side
of the Rappahannock. Couch, in command of the corps,
and Howard, his remaining division commander, climbed
the steeple of the courthouse in the town, and the battle began. It was not long before Couch exclaimed
to Howard: "Oh, great God! See how our men,
our brave fellows, are falling!" And so they were.
They "could not make reply" or protest, and nothing
was left but "to do and die." "I remember," said
Couch, "that the whole plain was covered with men
prostrate and dropping, the live men running here and
there, and in front, closing upon each other, and the
wounded coming back. The commands seemed to be
mixed up. I had never before seen fighting like that, or
anything approaching it in terrible uproar and destruction. There was no cheering on the part of the men,
but a stubborn determination to obey orders and do
their duty. As they charged, the artillery fire would
break their formation and they would get mixed. Then
they would close up together, everywhere receiving the
withering infantry fire, and those who were able would

run to the lines and fight as best they could; and then
the next brigade coming up in succession would do its
duty and melt like snow coming down on a warm morning." Hancock and French sent promptly for assistance.
Two brigades of Wilcox's corps were sent to the slaughter pen, and one of Howard's, and then a division of
Stoneman's, of Hooker's center grand division, as well
as Gifford's division of Butterfield's corps. The other
divisions of the same corps were also put in supporting
distance, and it now began to look like a genuine attempt to crush Lee's left.   At 3 P. M. Couch was told by
a dispatch from Sumner that Hooker had been ordered
to put in everything.   "His coming to me," said Couch,
"was like the breaking out of the sun in the storm."   It
had been demonstrated the storm was there, but what
became of the sun? Hooker consulted Hancock, who
had been in the leaden hail and had lost two thousand
out of five thousand men composing his division in a
very brief interval of time, after which, without obeying
orders, he rode back at 2 P. M. across the river to Burnside, and did not return for two hours.

The battery of artillery on Marye's Hill was relieved
in the meantime by fresh batteries, under Wolfolk and
Moody, which produced the impression that the hill
was being abandoned, so Couch directed Humphreys
to attack with his two brigades and Getty's division of
the Ninth Corps. This was bravely done, but with the
same result. Humphreys lost seventeen hundred out
of three thousand men. It was hardly possible for
Hooker's whole army to have carried Marye's Hill by
direct assault as long as Confederate ammunition lasted.
It resisted the successive charges of the Federals as
Gibraltar withstands the surging seas. It was defended
by the famous battalion of Washington Artillery from
New Orleans. The men and officers were full of fight,
enthusiastic, vigilant, enterprising, and brave. No mistake had been made in committing this important post
to that organization. Around and stretching on either
side was the left wing of the army. Marye's Hill met
the streets leading from the town, and offered the most
inviting point of attack. The front sloped to a sunken
road, on the town side of which was a stone wall some

four feet high; the exacavated dirt had been thrown on the other side of the wall, so that no part of the wall showed on the side of the Federal advance, and their troops were in ignorance of its existence. Behind this wall, four files deep, was the Georgia brigade of General Thomas R. Cobb, which was afterward re-enforced by portions of Kershaw's and Cook's brigades. To reach this wall the Union troops were obliged to march over a plain swept by artillery. General E. P. Alexander, Longstreet's accomplished artilleryman, remarked before the battle: "We cover that ground now so well that we will comb it as with a fine-toothed comb. A chicken could not live on that field when we open on it."

The dauntless courage displayed by the Federal officers and men availed nothing against the rapid plunging fire of well-served 12-pound howitzers, Napoleons, and rifle guns. The three-inch rifle balls of the Federals that fell near these batteries were hurled back at them out of Confederate guns. "On they came in beautiful array," wrote a Washington Artillery participant, "more determined to hold the plain than ever; but our fire was murderous, and no troops on earth could stand the *feu a'enfer* we were giving them. In the foremost line we distinguished the green flag with the golden harp of old Ireland, and we knew it to be Meagher's Irish brigade."

It was a picturesque field, the blue, the red breeches of the Zouaves, and the green of old Ireland were mingled in Death's cold embrace. Imagine troops, as soon as deployed, stormed at with shot and shell, and those who escaped, treated next to canister, and the brave survivors exposed to the severe fire of concealed infantry which scorched the ground beneath their feet! The battle on Lee's left was fought principally by the artillery and the few thousand infantry in the sunken road—troops whose courage, steadiness, and endurance has been honorably mentioned. Were it possible to have scaled Marye's Hill no hostile force could have lived there, for a concentrated, converging fire from the heights in the rear which commanded it, and of which it was simply an outpost, would have swept it from its face.

The battle of Fredericksburg was a grand sight as

Lee witnessed it from Lee's Hill in the center of his lines, and Burnside through his field glass from a more secure position, two miles in the rear of the battlefield, with the river flowing between himself and his troops. The roar of over three hundred cannon—the Federals alone had three hundred and seventy-five in their army —formed an orchestra which had the city of Fredericksburg for audience, as well as both armies.

> Earth shook, red meteors flashed along the sky,
> And conscious Nature shuddered at the cry.

A hundred thousand men in line of battle, both flanks being visible, from whose bristling bayonets were reflected the rays of the morning sun as they penetrated the rising mists, was a gorgeous pageant viewed from the Confederate lines.

The battle of Fredericksburg was a farce which one could laugh at, except for the sacrifice of human life. A grand army seeks offensive battle, makes isolated attacks by fractional forces, remains in position two days, and secretly, in the midst of a violent storm, recrosses the river during the night, with a loss of twelve thousand six hundred and fifty-three. If Burnside had held fast with a small force in Fredericksburg, protected by the reserve artillery on Stafford Heights, while re-enforcing Franklin with the bulk of Sumner's and Hooker's forces so as to have threatened the Confederate line of communication, he would have drawn Lee from Marye's Hill and forced him to deliver battle on more equal terms.

The popular notion that General Jackson wanted to move on the Federals after their repulse and drive them into the river is disposed of by his own report, in which he says: "The enemy making no forward movement, I determined, if prudent, to do so myself; but the first gun had hardly moved from the woods a hundred yards when the enemy's artillery reopened and so completely swept our front as to satisfy me that the projected movement should be abandoned."

Lee had really fought a defensive battle to a finish without knowing it. Only one third of his army had been engaged, and in killed, wounded, and missing his losses were only five thousand three hundred and seventy-seven. The Washington Artillery, which for four hours and a half mowed down the charging columns until their canister, case, and solid shot had been exhausted, lost three killed and twenty-four wounded. Naturally the Southern commander waited in his advantageous position for the big battle, but he waited in vain. It would have been a mistake to have done otherwise; and " in war the crown of laurel is reserved for him who makes the fewest mistakes himself and most promptly profits by the mistakes of others."

Lee greatly regretted the loss of his brave men, the wounding of the gallant Cook and the death of such splendid soldiers as Cobb, and Maxey Gregg. Cobb fell mortally wounded at the foot of the stone wall he had so bravely defended, at the door of the house of Mrs. Martha Stevens, who must have been a sort of " Molly Pitcher," for it is related that she was very active all day in the Confederate cause, and after using all her materials for bandages for the wounded, actually tore from her person most of her garments, on that cold December morning, in her anxiety to minister to their necessities.

After one or two abortive attempts to assume the offensive were made later by Burnside, the two armies looked quietly at each other from their respective positions on either side of the Rappahannock for four months. A few wall and common tents, pitched half way between Fredericksburg and Hamilton's Crossing on the border of an old pine field, marked the headquarters of the Confederate commander, and here Lee labored to promote the efficiency of his troops and prepare them for the active operations which he knew must commence when spring succeeded winter.

It was at this time, Long tells us, that among a number of fowls presented to the general was a sprightly hen, who went into the egg business before her turn came to lose her head, and thus persuaded Bryan, General Lee's well-known steward, that her egg, which she each morning deposited in the general's tent, was better for the general's breakfast than herself. Lee, fond of domestic animals, appreciated her selection of his quarters, and would leave the tent door open for her and wait elsewhere until her cackle informed him that he could return to his canvas home. She roosted and rode in his wagon, was an eye-witness of the battle of Chancellorsville, and there it is said she refused to lay until victory perched upon her general's plume, when she at once recommenced. Many months she soldiered —participated, in her way, in the battle of Gettysburg, but when the orders were given to fall back, and the head-quarters wagons had been loaded, the hen could not be found. General Lee joined others in a search for her, and finally she was found perched on top of the wagon seemingly anxious to return to her native State.

In the fall of 1864, when Lee's headquarters were near Orange Court House, the hen had become fat and lazy, and on one occasion when the general had a distinguished visitor to dine with him, Bryan, finding it difficult to procure suitable material, unknown to every one, killed the hen. At dinner the general was surprised to see so fine a fowl, and all enjoyed it, not dreaming of the great sacrifice made upon the altar of hospitality.

Lee's forced inactivity brought homesickness. He longed to be reunited to his family. In his letters he tells them of the noble spirit displayed by the people of Fredericksburg; that the faces of the old and young were wreathed with smiles and glowed with happiness at their sacrifices for the good of their country. "Many have lost everything. What the fire and swords of the enemy spared, their pillagers destroyed; but God will shield them I know." That the only place he "can be found is in camp, and there I will have to be taken with the three stools, the sun, the rain and mud." That "Hooker, Burnside's successor, is obliged to do something, but what, I do not know." That "he plays the Chinese game, runs out his guns, starts his wagons and troops up and down the river, and creates an excitement generally. Our men look on in wonder, give a cheer, and immediately again subside." That "God is kind and gives me plenty to do in good weather and bad, and that I owe Mr. J. Hooker no thanks for keeping me here, for he ought to have made up his mind long ago what to do." Later he writes: "The cars have arrived from Richmond and brought me a young

French officer, full of vivacity and ardor, for service with me. I think the appearance of things will cool him. If they do not the night will, for he brought no blankets."

In a letter to his daughter Mary, previous to Burnside's attack, dated Camp near Fredericksburg, November 24, 1862, he says: "I have just received your letter of the 17th, which has afforded me great gratification. I regretted not finding you in Richmond, and grieve over every opportunity at not seeing you that is lost, for I fear they will become less and less frequent. The death of my dear Annie was, indeed, to me a bitter pang, but ' the Lord gave and the Lord has taken away, blessed be the name of the Lord.' In the quiet hours of the night, when there is nothing to lighten the full weight of my grief, I feel as if I should be overwhelmed. I have always counted, if God should spare me a few days of peace, after this cruel war was ended, that I should have her with me, but year after year my hopes go out, and I must be resigned. General Burnside's whole army is apparently opposite Fredericksburg, and stretches from the Rappahannock to the Potomac. What his intentions are he has not yet disclosed. I am sorry he is in position to oppress our friends and citizens of the Northern Neck. He threatens to bombard Fredericksburg, and the noble spirit displayed by its citizens, particularly the women and children, has elicited my highest admiration. They have been abandoning their homes night and day during all this inclement weather cheerfully and uncomplainingly, with only such assistance as our wagons and ambulances could afford—women, girls, children, trudging through the mud and bivouacking in the open fields."

Again, in a letter to his wife from the same camp, on December 2, 1862, he writes: "I am glad you had the opportunity of visiting New Kent; but the sight of the White House must have brought particularly sad thoughts. It will all come right in the end, though we may not live to see it. That is Lieutenant Spangler who addressed me so familiarly. He was orderly sergeant of Captain Evans's company, Second Cavalry, United States Army, and was a good soldier. I tremble for my country when I hear of confidence expressed in me.   I know too well my weakness, and that our only hope is in God."

On December 11th, at the commencement of the Federal operations, General Lee writes Mrs. Lee: "I return a bit sent up by Custis.   It is not the one I wished, but I do not want the one I wrote for now, as I have one that will answer as well.   The enemy, after bombarding the town of Fredericksburg, setting fire to many houses, and knocking down nearly all those along the river, crossed over a large force about dark, and now occupy the town.   We hold the hills commanding it, and hope we shall be able to damage him yet.   His positions and heavy guns command the town entirely."

On December 16th he thus writes of the recrossing of the Federals, and also of the liberation of the Arlington slaves: "I had supposed they were just preparing for battle, and was saving our men for the conflict.   Their hosts crown the hill and plain beyond the river, and their numbers to me are unknown.   Still, I felt a confidence we could stand the shock, and was anxious for the blow that is to fall on some point, and was prepared to meet it here.   Yesterday evening I had my suspicions that they might return during the night, but could not believe they would relinquish their hopes after all their boasting and preparation, and when I say that the latter is equal to the former, you will have some idea of the magnitude.   This morning they were all safe on the north side of the Rappahannock.   They went as they came—in the night.   They suffered heavily as far as the battle went, but it did not go far enough to satisfy me.   Our loss was comparatively slight, and I think will not exceed two thousand.   The contest will have now to be renewed, but on what field I can not say.   As regards the liberation of the people [slaves] I wish to progress in it as far as I can.   Those hired in Richmond can still find employment there if they choose. Those in the country can do the same or remain on the farms.   I hope they will all do well and behave themselves.   I should like if I could to attend to their wants, and see them placed to the best advantage.   But that is impossible.   All that choose can leave the State before the war closes.   The quartermaster informs me he has received the things you sent. The mitts will be very serviceable. Make as many as you can obtain good material for. I have everything I want." General Lee was the executor, and the date of the emancipation of the slaves under Mr. Custis's will had arrived.

From the same camp on Christmas day he writes Mrs. Lee : " I will commence this holy day by writing to you. My heart is filled with gratitude to Almighty God for the unspeakable mercies with which he has blessed us in this day, for those he has granted us from the beginning of life, and particularly for those he has vouchsafed us during the past year. What should have become of us without his crowning help and protection ? Oh, if our people would only recognize it and cease from vain self-boasting and adulation, how strong would be my belief in final success and happiness to our country ! But what a cruel thing is war; to separate and destroy families and friends, and mar the purest joys and happiness God has granted us in this world; to fill our hearts with hatred instead of love for our neighbors, and to devastate the fair face of this beautiful world ! I pray that on this day, when only peace and good-will are preached to mankind, better thoughts may fill the hearts of our enemies and turn them to peace. Our army was never in such good health and condition since I have been attached to it. I believe they share with me my disappointment that the enemy did not renew the combat on the 13th. I was holding back all that day and husbanding our strength and ammunition for the great struggle for which I thought I was preparing. Had I divined what was to have been his only effort he would have had more of it. My heart bleeds at the death of every one of our gallant men." Again, from the same place he tells her : " We had quite a snow day before yesterday, and last night was very cold. It is thawing a little this morning, though the water was freezing as I washed. I fear it will bring much discomfort to those of our men who are barefooted and poorly clad. I can take but little pleasure in my comforts for thinking of them. A kind lady—Mrs. Sallie Braxton Slaughter—of Fredericksburg, sent me a mattress, some catsup, and preserves during the snowstorm. You must thank Miss Norvell [Caskie] for her nice cake, which I enjoyed very much.   I had it set out under the pines the day after its arrival, and assembled all the young gentlemen [of his staff] around it; and though I told them it was a present from a beautiful young lady, they did not leave a crumb.   I want a good servant badly.   Perry [an old Arlington servant] is very willing, and I believe does as well as he can.   You know he is very slow and inefficient, and moves very like his father Lawrence.   He is also very fond of his blankets in the morning—the time I most require him.   I hope he will do well when he leaves me, and get in the service of some good person who will take care of him."

On the 8th of January he again makes reference to the Arlington servants, and says: "I executed the deed of manumission sent me by Mr. Caskie, and returned it to him.   I perceived that John Sawyer and James's names among the Arlington people had been omitted, and inserted them.   I fear there are others among the White House lot which I did not discover.   As to the attacks of the Northern papers, I do not mind them, and do not think it wise to make the publication you suggest.   If all the names of the people at Arlington and on the Pamunkey are not embraced in the deed I have executed, I should like a supplementary deed to be drawn up containing all those omitted.   They are all entitled to their freedom, and I wish to give it to them. Those that have been carried away I hope are free and happy.   I can not get their papers to them, and they do not require them.   I will give them if they ever call for them.   It would be useless to ask their restitution to manumit them.   The enemy is still in large force opposite to us.   There is no indication of his future movements." And on the 29th of January he writes: "The storm has culminated here in a deep snow, which does not improve our comfort.   It came particularly hard on some of our troops whom I was obliged to send some eleven miles up the Rappahannock to meet a recent move of General Burnside.   Their bivouac in the rain and snow was less comfortable than at their former stations, where they had constructed some shelter.   General Burnside's designs have apparently been frustrated, either by the storm or by other causes, and on last Saturday he took a special steamer to Washington, to consult the military oracles at the Federal seat of Government. Sunday I heard of his being closeted with President Lincoln, Secretary Stanton, and General Halleck. I suppose we shall have a new programme next week. You had better finish all the gloves you intend making at once, and send them to the army. Next month they will be much needed. After that no use for this winter. Tell Mr. Haskins I am delighted the turkey was so good. I was that day up at United States Mine Ford, on the Rappahannock. Did not get back till late at night. After our nocturnal repast was over, having been on horseback from early breakfast, you can imagine how I would have enjoyed it. I was, however, thinking so much of General Burnside's playing us such a shabby trick, running off to Washington when we were waiting for him, that I did not then miss my dinner."

General Lee was surrounded by embarrassments during the winter—the troops were scantily clothed, rations for men and animals meager. The shelters were poor, and through them broke the sun, rains, and winds. He could not strike his enemy, but must watch and be patient, for he remembered the favorite maxim of Marlborough, "Patience will overcome all things, and the gods smile on those who can wait." He was obliged to send Longstreet with two of his four divisions to the section south of James River, nearly one hundred miles away, to relieve his commissary department and to collect supplies, and was thus deprived of their support when the campaign opened. Across the river his better sheltered, fed, and clothed opponent had his troubles too. Burnside had lost the confidence of many of his principal officers, and after a harmless attempt to reach Lee by Banks's Ford, six miles above Fredericksburg, further winter operations were suspended.

Then Burnside prepared a sweeping order, dismissing from the army Generals Hooker, Brooks, Cochrane, and Newton, and relieving from their commands Generals Franklin, W. F. Smith, Sturgis, Ferrero, and Colonel Joseph Taylor, Sumner's adjutant general. To approve the order, or accept his resignation, was the alternative presented to the President. Mr. Lincoln accepted his resignation, and immediately placed the baton of the army commander in the hands of Joseph Hooker, the head and front of the caballed officers. Mr. Lincoln's letter of January 26, 1863, to Hooker, is characteristic. He tells him he has thwarted Burnside as much as he could, doing a great wrong to his country and to a most meritorious brother officer; that he had heard of his saying that both the army and country needed a dictator. "What I ask," he adds, "is military success. In that event I will risk the dictatorship"; and concludes by begging him to "Beware of rashness!"

Hooker, or "Fighting Joe," as he was sometimes called, had managed a corps well, possessed personal magnetism and a fine presence, but had not the ability to conduct great operations; and yet it must be admitted his preliminary steps toward reorganization and the promotion of the battle power of his army were well taken. He found his army amid the Stafford hills, on the left bank of the Rappahannock, and stretching back to the Potomac some twelve miles, which river gave him a splendid line of communication with his capital, secure from an enemy who had no boats. Much discontent prevailed in the ranks, and his men were deserting at the rate of two hundred per day. A majority of the officers, too, were hostile to the policy of the Government, and the number of absentees without leave amounted to 2,922 officers and 81,964 non-commissioned officers and privates, while the express trains to the army were filled with citizens' clothing, sent to assist soldiers to desert. Hooker, by judicious furloughs, stopped this in a measure, filled up his ranks, instilled discipline, gave leaves to the officers, consolidated his cavalry into a corps, and replaced the Corps d'armée or Grand Divisions by an army organization of seven corps, commanded by, First, Reynolds; Second, Couch; Third, Sickles; Fifth, Meade; Sixth, Sedgwick; Eleventh, Howard; and Twelfth, Slocum. Then he began to study strategy, for Mr. Lincoln had said, "Go forward and give us victories." Lee's army, his objective point, must be reached— but how? The more the problem was considered the more he was convinced its solution involved reaching General Lee's left rear.

CHAPTER XI.

CHANCELLORSVILLE.

CHANCELLORSVILLE was the most wonderful of Lee's battles, and demanded the highest exercise of his military ability. The Army of Northern Virginia amounted to 53,303 present for duty at Chancellorsville, with one hundred and seventy pieces of artillery.*

The Federals numbered, according to the return of April 30th, an aggregate of officers and men present of 138,378, and, under the head of "present for duty equipped," which embraces those actually available for the line of battle at the date of the report, the army numbered 133,708. Hooker had by these returns, therefore, a numerical superiority on the field of 80,000.

The Southern commander, penetrating the Federal plan of operations, placed one of the only two cavalry brigades with his army in the vicinity of Culpeper Court House, and had the Rappahannock picketed for twenty-five miles above the left of his infantry. Hooker determined to break up this observation cavalry, for they would be too near his flanking route, and on the 16th dispatched three thousand cavalry under Averell to attack them. The Southern brigade was small at the time. The cavalrymen owned their horses, and many of them had been detailed to go home to get fresh horses for the spring campaign. Owing to that fact, and the absence of many squadrons on detached service, only eight hundred men could be placed in the saddle. Butterfield, Hooker's chief of staff, reported the combat

---

* The returns make the numbers 57,112. This included Hampton's and Jones's cavalry brigades, which, though included in the returns, were absent, making the cavalry at Chancellorsville 2,700 instead of 6,500, as in the returns.

that followed as the best cavalry fight of the war, lasting five hours, charging and recharging on both sides,
and that the Confederate cavalry were driven back
three miles into cover of earthworks and heavy guns.
Stanton, the Federal Secretary of War, congratulated
Hooker on the success of the expedition. "You have
drawn the first blood, and I hope now to see the boys
up and at them." It was Sir Walter Raleigh who said
that human testimony was so unreliable that no two
men could see the same occurrence and give the same
report of it. The Confederate official reports state that
Averell was defeated and driven back across the river.
Major John Pelham, who was accidentally present, being
summoned to Culpeper Court House as a witness in a
court-martial, borrowed a horse and rode out on the
field, where he acted temporarily as aid-de-camp, and
was killed. He was Stuart's chief of horse artillery,
and a graduate of West Point of the class of 1861. The
death of this blue-eyed Alabama boy was a great loss.
His superb courage and dash had been immortalized by
Jackson's expression, after seeing him handle his guns
at Sharpsburg, that "an army should have a Pelham on
each flank," while General Lee called him, at Fredericksburg, "the gallant Pelham"; and Stuart in General Orders wrote: "The memory of the gallant Pelham, his
many virtues, his noble nature, his purity of character,
is enshrined as a sacred legacy in the hearts of all who
knew him."

On the arrival of spring the two armies were still in
sight of each other occupying the old lines. Hooker
must now assume the offensive. In addition to his
twelve corps of infantry—three divisions to a corps, except Slocum's, who had two—he had a large, finely appointed cavalry corps under Stoneman, numbering thirteen thousand three hundred and ninety-eight sabers,
and three hundred and seventy-five cannon. The Confederate force consisted of McLaws and Anderson's divisions of Longstreet's corps (Hood and Pickett's divisions of that corps being absent in the vicinity of
Suffolk, south of James River), and Jackson's corps,
composed of the divisions of A. P. Hill, Early, and D. H.
Hill under Rodes, and Trimble under Colston.

The Federal general's designs were well conceived. He proposed to march three of his corps up the Rappahannock twenty-seven miles, cross them at Kelly's Ford, add to them one corps which should cross below at United States Ford, and with these four corps make a great turning column, which should move down on Lee's left rear, while the remaining three corps, constituting his left wing, should cross *à la* Burnside in Lee's front at Fredericksburg, hold him steady by the menace of a direct attack, and when he was manœuvred out of his intrenchments, pursue him. In order to make the blow more effective, Stoneman was directed to make a wide detour well around the Southern left and rear, throw ten thousand sabers between Lee and Richmond, breaking up his communications, stopping his supplies, and be in a position to obstruct the Confederate retreat until Hooker could deliver a final blow.

The Union cavalry were put in motion as early as the 13th of April to cross the upper fords of the Rappahannock. Mr. Lincoln, who was alive to all that was going on, telegraphed Hooker: " The rain and mud were, of course, to be calculated upon. General Stoneman is not moving rapidly enough to make the expedition come to anything. He has now been out three days, two of which were unusually fair weather, and all free from hindrance by his enemy, and yet he is not twenty-five miles from where he started. To reach his point he has still sixty to go. By arithmetic how many days will it take him to do it ?" The general impatience for a move was prevalent everywhere. Even the Union General Peck, at Suffolk, hoping to be relieved from Longstreet's presence, wired urging it, to which Hooker replied on April 21st: " You must be patient with me. I must play with these devils before I can spring."

On the 27th Hooker's turning column of the Eleventh, Twelfth, and Fifth Corps began its march, while two divisions of Couch's Second Corps were sent to United States Ford, between Kelly's and Fredericksburg. On the night of the 28th and the morning of the 29th the right wing crossed the Rappahannock River, marched under Hooker's immediate command in two columns for the Rapidan, crossing that stream at Germania and

Ely's Fords. Having brought Couch to him, Hooker was concentrated on the night of the 30th at Chancellorsville, ten miles west of Fredericksburg, but had consumed four days in getting this far on Lee's left.

The day before Hooker moved, Sedgwick, proceeding to carry out his part of the plan, crossed the Rappahannock below Fredericksburg with the First, Third, and Sixth Corps, numbering fifty-two thousand four hundred and one. This imposing demonstration on Lee's front, it was expected, would make him arrange for another defensive battle, and while doing so, Hooker's right wing would overwhelm his left and attack in reverse his fortified lines. The next day Sickles's Third Corps, having assisted Sedgwick to demonstrate, went to Hooker at Chancellorsville to join in the contemplated crushing; but Sedgwick still had for his feint thirty-seven thousand six hundred and seventy-three troops.

Hooker was greatly elated at the situation on the night of the 30th. The next day he would advance with "the finest army on the planet," as he called it, uncover Banks's Ford six miles below, and thus have direct communication by a short route with Sedgwick. He congratulated in General Orders the right wing at the great success attending their operations, telling them that his enemy "must ingloriously fly, or come out from behind his defenses and give us battle on our own ground, where certain destruction awaits him." On May 1st Hooker started for Fredericksburg. The four corps with him, less Gibbon's division of the Second at Falmouth, and exclusive of a cavalry brigade, amounted to seventy-three thousand one hundred and twenty-four. What a grand army to hurl on an enemy's flank!

If the Union general's tactics had kept pace with his strategy, his numbers might have given him a great victory. His well-devised plans were divined by his alert antagonist. Stuart's cavalry pickets, which were driven away from Kelly's Ford on the 28th, reported infantry crossing there that night; their line of march was quickly ascertained next day and reported to General Lee by telegraph from Culpeper Court House. Stuart made a detour with one of his two brigades of cavalry, after throwing a regiment in front of the Federal advance, and reaching Todd's Tavern on the 30th, placed his cavalry across the routes leading to Lee's lines of communication. Jackson, whose right stretched fourteen miles below Fredericksburg, was brought up to Hamilton's Crossing the same day Hooker's right wing was crossing the river at Kelly's, and then Lee waited for his enemy's plans to be more fully developed, believing the war maxim, "When your enemy is making a mistake he must not be interrupted." He readily perceived that with Hooker at Chancellorsville and Sedgwick three miles below Fredericksburg, the two wings were thirteen miles apart, and that his army was directly between them. He understood the military problem— drive the wedge in and keep them separate, hold one still by a feint or retard his march by fighting, concentrate on and overwhelm the other. Sedgwick lay quiet while Hooker was massing at Chancellorsville.

"Jackson at first," says Lee, "preferred to attack Sedgwick's force in the plain of Fredericksburg, but I told him I feared it was as impracticable as it was at the first battle of Fredericksburg. It was hard to get at the enemy, and harder to get away, if we drove him into the river, but if he thought it could be done, I would give orders for it." Jackson asked to be allowed to examine the ground, and did so during the afternoon, and at night came to Lee and said he thought he [Lee] was right. It would be inexpedient to attack there. "Move, then," said Lee, "up to Anderson," who had been previously ordered to proceed to Chancellorsville. "And the next time I saw Jackson," says General Lee, "was the next day—May 1st—when he was on our skirmish line, driving in the enemy's skirmishers around Chancellorsville."

McLaws reached Anderson's position before sunrise on the 1st, and Jackson at 8 A. M. It was determined to hammer Hooker while Sedgwick was held at arm's length. Lee wisely selected Early to keep, if possible, Sedgwick out of the difficulty he proposed to have with Hooker, and, in addition to his own division, gave him Barksdale's brigade of McLaws's division and the reserve artillery under General Pendleton. Jackson found Anderson some six miles from Chancellorsville, intrenching. He ordered the work discontinued, for, as usual, he wanted at once to find his enemy. At 11 A. M. the Confederates, in two columns under Anderson and McLaws, with Jackson closely following, moved on Chancellorsville.

The same morning Hooker put his troops in motion in three columns on the roads Lee was marching, thinking the latter was held at Fredericksburg by his demonstration there, and ordered his headquarters to be established at Tabernacle Church, half-way between Chancellorsville and Fredericksburg, at 2 P. M.; but the church was not destined to be so marked. As the head of his columns debouched from the forest a few miles from Chancellorsville, they encountered the Army of Northern Virginia advancing in line of battle, which so surprised Hooker that he lost for the first time his self-confidence. He had not dreamed that Lee would assume the offensive. It embarrassed him so much that he decided on defensive tactics—a decision fatal to him. Fearing he could not throw his troops through the forest fast enough, and apprehensive of being whipped in detail, he ordered his army to retire to their lines around Chancellorsville. Lee, with brilliant daring worthy of the hero of Malakoff, followed him and established a line of battle in front of him, at some points within a mile of Chancellorsville. "Here," says he, "the enemy had assumed a position of great natural strength, surrounded on all sides by a dense forest filled with tangled undergrowth, in the midst of which breastworks of logs had been constructed with trees felled in front so as to form an almost impenetrable abatis. His artillery swept the few narrow roads by which his position could be approached from the front, and commanded the adjacent works." The left of Hooker's line extended from Chancellorsville to the Rappahannock River, covering the United States Ford, while on the other side it reached west as far as Wilderness Church. His left flank was unassailable, as Lee found from a personal reconnoissance that afternoon, and his front impregnable. Of the five miles of battle line, his right alone could be considered. That night Stuart brought the Rev. Dr. B. T. Lacy to Lee, who told him a circuit could be made around by Wilderness Tavern, and General Lee directed Jackson to make his arrangements to move early next day around the Federal right flank.

The sun rose on this eventful 2d of May unclouded and brilliant, gilding the hill tops and penetrating the vapors of the valley—as gorgeous as was the sun of Austerlitz, which produced such an impression upon the imagination of Napoleon. Its rays fell upon the last meeting in this world of Lee and Jackson. The Duke of Wellington is reported to have said: " A man of fine Christian sensibilities is totally unfit for the position of a soldier "; but here were two great soldiers who faithfully performed all their duties as Christians.

Lee, erect and soldierly, emerged from the little pine thicket where he had bivouacked during the night, and stood on its edge at sunrise to see Jackson's troops file by. When Jackson came along he stopped and the two conversed for a few moments, after which Jackson speedily rejoined his troops, now making their famous flank march. Bold, but dangerous, was Lee's strategy. He had decided to keep some 14,000 men, under Anderson and McLaws, in front of Hooker's 73,000, while Jackson marched by a wide circuit with less than 30,000, to gain the Union right rear. Reynolds's First Corps on that day was marching from Sedgwick to Hooker. It numbered 19,595, and reached Hooker at daylight on the 3d. General Hooker then had around Chancellorsville 92,719 men.

At Austerlitz, when the Russians made the flank movement around the French right, Napoleon moved at once upon the weakened line of the allies in his front and burst through it. Leaving some battalions to hold the right wing, he wheeled the remainder upon the left and destroyed it, and then, turning toward the right wing, he directed upon it a terrible onset, and it too was no more. In some places the men in Lee's thin gray line in front of Hooker were six feet apart. Jackson marched rapidly diagonally across the front of Hooker's line of battle, screened from view by the forest and by three regiments of cavalry which had been ordered to mask the movement as well as to precede it.

As early as 8 A. M. Birney, of Sickles's corps, reported a

continuous column of infantry trains and ambulances passing his front. His division was on Howard's left, whose corps formed the right of the Union army. Sickles sent a battery forward to a commanding position on his front and fired at the moving column, and at 12 M. moved with two of his divisions and Barlow's brigade of Howard's corps and gained the road Jackson was moving on, capturing a few hundred of his men. Howard did not fear an attack on his right, for his brigade, in reserve at that point, was selected to assist in Sickles's pursuit.

At 9.30 A. M. Hooker notified Slocum and Howard that the right of their line did not appear to be strong enough. "We have good reason to suppose the enemy is moving to our right." Howard does not admit that he ever received the notification—Slocum says he read it; but at 10.50 A. M. Hooker received a dispatch from Howard that a column of infantry had been observed moving west, and that he had taken measures to resist an attack from the west. Later he became convinced it was a retreat, not an attack. At 2 P. M. Couch, next in command, was told by Hooker that Lee was in full retreat toward Gordonsville, and that he had sent out Sickles to capture his artillery; and at 4.10 P. M., the hour Jackson was forming his column of attack behind his right, Hooker sent a dispatch to Sedgwick: "We know the enemy is flying, trying to save his trains. Two of Sickles's divisions are among them."

About 3 P. M. Jackson's van reached the plank road, three miles west of Chancellorsville. The commander of the cavalry accompanying him had made a personal reconnoissance while waiting for Jackson to come up, and had located the exact position of the Union right. When Jackson arrived, at his request, he accompanied him through a concealed wooded road to a hill overlooking the rear of the Federal right. Below and but a few hundred yards' distant ran their line of battle, with abatis in front and long lines of stacked arms in the rear. Cannon in position were visible, and the soldiers were in groups, chatting, smoking, and playing cards, while others in the rear were driving up and butchering beeves. Stonewall's face bore an expression of intense interest during the five minutes he was on the hill, and the Federal position was pointed out to him. His eyes had a brilliant glow. The paint of approaching battle was coloring his cheeks, and he was radiant to find no preparation had been made to guard against a flank attack. He made no remarks to the officer with him; his lips were, however, moving, for, sitting on his horse in sight of and close to Howard's troops, he was engaged in an appeal to the God of Battles. He quickly perceived what had been suggested—that by moving to the old turnpike, a little farther to the rear, and not turning down the plank road as proposed, he would take Howard's line in reverse and not in front. "Tell General Rodes," said he, suddenly wheeling his horse to a courier, "to move across the plank road and halt when he gets to the old turnpike. I will join him there." And then he rode rapidly back.

The cavalry, supported by Paxton's brigade of infantry, was placed a short distance down the plank road to mask the march of the remaining troops across it. Jackson's troops reached the old turnpike at 4 P. M. Two hours were consumed in getting the command up and organizing for the attack. At this point Jackson wrote his last note to General Lee:

Near 3 P. M., *May* 2, 1863.

GENERAL: The enemy has made a stand at Chancellors,* which is about two miles from Chancellorsville. I hope as soon as practicable to attack. I trust that an ever-kind Providence will bless us with great success. Respectfully,

T. J. JACKSON, *Lieutenant General.*

The leading division is up, and the next two appear to be well closed. T. J. J.

General R. E. LEE.

As the different divisions arrived they were formed at right angles to the road, Rodes's in front, Trimble's division, under Colston, in the second line two hundred yards in the rear, and A. P. Hill's in supporting distance in column. At 6 P. M., all being ready, Jackson ordered the advance. His men burst with a cheer upon the startled enemy, and, like a disciplined thunderbolt, swept down the line and captured cannon before they could be re-

---

* Also known as Dowdall's Tavern.

versed to fire on them.   Howard had two regiments and
two guns, under Von Gilsen, at right angles to his main
line.   The Confederate rush first struck him, and he
called for re-enforcements.   Howard told him he must
"hold his post with the men he had and trust to God!"
His command of fourteen hundred did not hold on long,
as they only lost one hundred and thirty-three killed,
wounded, and missing.   Rabbits and squirrels ran and
flocks of birds flew in front of the advance of these
twenty-six thousand men who had dropped so suddenly
into their forest haunts, giving in some instances the
first notice of an unusual disturbance there.

The Union commander, whose surprised troops were
about to be overwhelmed, was recalled to the period
when, as a youth, he says, he watched the appearance of
contending winds, when the clouds, black and blacker,
swift and swifter, rose high and higher as they pushed
forward their angry front.   He heard the low rumbling
from afar, and, as the storm came nearer, the woods bent
forward and shook furiously their thick branches.   The
lightning zigzagged in flashes.   The deep-bassed thunder echoed more loudly, till there was scarcely an interval between its ominous crashing discharges.

One half of the eleven thousand five hundred of Howard's corps were Germans, and occupied the exposed
flank.   Devens's, Steinwehrs's, Schurz's, Schimmelfen-
nig's, and Kryzancerski's troops were rolled over and
under by this rapid "rolling reconnoissance."   Quickly
there was a blind panic and great confusion.   Sickles,
who had moved to the front from his place in line to
attack Jackson's marching flank, and to whom Howard
had sent re-enforcements "to make a grand attack with
brilliant results," was near the furnace, and came near
being severed from his army.   The air was filled with
noise and smoke; the mighty current of panic-stricken
men grew momentarily deeper and wider.   Dickinson,
one of Hooker's staff, implored Howard to fire on his
own men to stop their flight.   The surging, seething sea
swept away all barriers.   Many of the officers attempted
to turn back the human tide, but as well might Pharaoh
have tried to resist the walls of the Red Sea.   Riderless horses and men without arms were everywhere,

and guns, caissons, forges, ambulances, battery wagons rolled and tumbled like runaway wagons in a thronged city. Mules tied in couples (a device of Hooker's to carry ammunition) added unearthly brays to the uproar and scattered the ammunition. One pair of them entangled around a tree, was struck by a shell which exploded their load and blew them to pieces. Into all Jackson's ranks blazed a ceaseless fire. Lee's brilliant tactics had succeeded, and Hooker's right had been fairly turned and rolled in a sheet of flame upon his center.

Rodes, who led with so much spirit, says: "The enemy, taken in flank and rear, did not wait for an attack." Colston's division followed so rapidly that it went over the enemy's works at Dowdall's with Rodes's troops, and both divisions fought with mixed ranks until dark. In a piece of woods the line was then halted to reform. There was no apparent line of battle between them and Chancellorsville, and Crutchfield's guns were turned on Chancellorsville. They were immediately responded to by a terrific fire from twenty-two guns on the plank road, loaded with double canister. Jackson was most impatient to work to Hooker's rear and cut him off from the United States Ford, his line of retreat, and drive him on the lines of McLaws and Anderson, where Lee was. These lines, from the nature of the country, had been greatly strengthened with axe and spade. To "huddle" in confusion Hooker's army in the tangled wilderness and surround it seemed possible.

A. P. Hill was now ordered to the front to take charge of the pursuit. While he was engaged in forming his lines, Jackson, who was a little in advance, sent a staff officer to order Hill to move forward as soon as possible, and then, accompanied by Captain Wilbourn, of the Signal Corps, Captain Boswell, and some of his signal men and couriers, rode slowly along the road toward the enemy to reconnoiter for Hill's advance, thinking perhaps a skirmish line was in his front. He had not proceeded far before he came upon a line of Federal infantry lying on their arms. Fired at, he turned his horse, but unfortunately rode a little outside of the route toward the front of some of his own troops, who, ignorant that Jackson had passed out of the lines and mistaking his party for a squad of Union cavalry, fired upon it, killing his engineer officer, Captain Boswell, and Sergeant Cunliff, of the Signal Corps. Jackson immediately crossed the road to avoid the fire and enter his lines at another point, when, again mistaken by his troops, he received at a few paces another volley from the right company of Pender's North Carolina Brigade. Three balls penetrated him at the same time. A round ball from a smooth-bore Springfield musket passed through his right hand, and was cut out that night under the skin. Another entered the outside of his left forearm near the elbow, coming out near the wrist, while still another struck him three inches below the left shoulder joint, divided the artery, and fractured the bone. Reeling in his saddle and losing hold of his bridle rein, he was caught by Captain Wilbourn and placed on the ground. A. P. Hill was soon at his side, as well as his two aids, Smith and Morrison. The two latter placed him in a litter, and then in an ambulance he was carried from the field amid the shrieks of the shells, the whistling of the bullets, and the groans of the wounded and dying. His last order, after being so fearfully wounded, was to tell General Pender to hold his ground. "You must hold your ground, sir," said he.

The ambulance which carried to the field hospital at Wilderness Tavern this great soldier contained his chief of artillery, Crutchfield, also dangerously wounded, and each seemed more concerned about the other's injuries than his own. Here Jackson's left arm was amputated two inches below the shoulder, and three days afterward he was taken to the Chandler House, near Guinea Station, on the railroad from Fredericksburg to Richmond, where he died on the following Sunday. "Order A. P. Hill to prepare for action," he cried in the delirium just before death. "Pass the infantry to the front rapidly. Tell Major Hawkes——" He stopped, and then with a feeling of relief he said: "Let us cross over the river and rest under the shade of the trees." The sword which carved his name upon the shield of fame had returned forever to its scabbard. His wish was fulfilled. "I have always desired to die on Sunday,"

he had said.   When Lee received a notification of his
being wounded he wrote to Jackson that, could he have
directed the course of events, he would have chosen for
the good of his country to have been disabled in his
stead.   "I congratulate you," he added, "upon the victory which is due to your skill and energy."   Howard
thought his death was providential, "for in bold planning, in energy of execution, in indefatigable activity
and moral ascendency, he was head and shoulders above
his *confrères.*"

During the flank march of his great lieutenant, Lee
reminded the troops in his front of his position by frequent taps on different points of their lines, and when
the sound of cannon gave notice of Jackson's attack,
Lee ordered that Hooker's left be strongly pressed to
prevent his sending re-enforcements to the point assailed.   Sunday, May 3d, was an eventful day.   Jackson's corps must complete its work; but who should
lead it?   A. P. Hill, the next in rank, had been disabled
shortly after Jackson was struck down.   Rodes, as
modest as he was daring, was next in rank to Hill, but
in a conference with Major Pendleton, Jackson's chief
of staff, and some of the general officers, quickly acquiesced in a suggestion that General J. E. B. Stuart be
sent for, because he was satisfied the good of the service
demanded it.   Stuart was at Ely's Ford with the cavalry
and Sixteenth North Carolina Infantry, having gone
there to watch Averell, who, having returned from his
raid, was reported to be at that point.   At 10.30 P. M.
Captain Adams, of Hill's staff, summoned him to the
command of Jackson's corps.   Upon Stuart's arrival
upon the battlefield, Jackson had been taken to the rear,
but A. P. Hill, still there, turned over the command to him.
With the assistance of Colonel E. P. Alexander, of the
artillery, he was engaged all night in preparations for
the morrow.   At early dawn on the 3d Stuart pressed
the corps forward—Hill's division in the first line, Trimble's in the second, and Rodes's in the rear.

As the sun lifted the mist, the hill to the right was
found to be a commanding position for artillery.   Quickly thirty pieces, under Colonels T. H. Carter and Hillary
P. Jones, were firing from it, and their fire was very

effective. Hooker was standing on the steps of the portico of the Chancellor House, giving directions about the battle, which was now raging with great fury, when a solid shot struck the pillar near him, splitting it in two, and throwing one half longitudinally against him. He says for a few moments he was senseless, and the report spread that he had been killed. To correct the impression, as soon as he revived he insisted on mounting his horse and riding back toward a white house, which subsequently became the center of his new position. Just before reaching it the pain from the wound became so intense that he was obliged to dismount, and was laid upon a blanket spread out upon the ground. He was revived by brandy and assisted to remount. He had hardly risen from the blanket when a solid shot struck in the very center of it, where a moment before he had been lying, and tore up the earth in a savage way. Pleasonton says, when he saw him, about 10 A. M., he was lying on the ground, usually in a doze, except when awakened to attend to some important dispatch. General Couch was temporarily called to the command of the army.

In the meanwhile Stuart was pressing the attack. At one time his left was so strongly resisted that his three lines were merged into one. To a notice sent him that the men were out of ammunition, he replied that they must hold their ground with the bayonet. About this time Stuart's right connected with Anderson's left, uniting thus the detached portions of General Lee's army. He then massed infantry on his left and stormed the Federal works. Twice he was repulsed, but the third time Stuart placed himself on horseback at the head of the troops, ordered the charge, carried the intrenchments, and held them, singing with ringing voice, "Old Joe Hooker, won't you come out of the wilderness?" An eye-witness says he could not get rid of the impression that Harry of Navarre led the charge, except that Stuart's plume was black, for everywhere the men followed his feather. Anderson at the same time moved rapidly upon Chancellorsville, while McLaws made a strong demonstration in his front. At 10 A. M. the position at Chancellorsville was won, and Hooker had

withdrawn to another line nearer the Rappahannock.
Preparations were at once made by Lee to attack again,
when further operations were arrested by intelligence
received from Fredericksburg.

Sedgwick, after the departure of the First and Third
Corps from his position below Fredericksburg, was still
left with twenty-nine thousand three hundred and forty-
two troops, which included Gibbon's division of five
thousand, but excluded his reserve artillery. On May
2d, at 9.55 A. M., Hooker telegraphed him : "You are all
right. You have but Early's division in your front—
balance all up here." To oppose Sedgwick, Early had
his division of seventy-five hundred officers and men,
and Barksdale's brigade of fifteen hundred, making nine
thousand. In addition, Early had Andrew's battalion
of artillery of sixteen guns, Graham's four guns, a Whitworth gun posted below the Massaponax, and portions
of Walton's, Cabell's, and Cutts's battalions of artillery,
under General Pendleton, making in all some forty-five
or fifty guns. At 9 P. M. on the 2d Hooker telegraphed
Sedgwick to cross the Rappahannock at Fredericksburg
and move toward Chancellorsville until he connected with
him, destroying Early in his front. He tells him that
he "will probably fall upon the rear of the troops commanded by General Lee, and between us Lee must be
used up." This order was issued under the impression
that Sedgwick was on the north side of the river, but it
found him below Fredericksburg on the south side. He
moved up during the night, and on the morning of the
3d, after three assaults, carried Marye's Hill, capturing
eight pieces of artillery upon that and the adjacent
heights. Wilcox, who was at Banks's Ford, threw himself in front of Sedgwick's advance up the plank road
and gallantly disputed it, falling slowly back until he
reached Salem Church, five miles from Fredericksburg.
When Lee heard that Sedgwick, with thirty thousand
men, was marching on his rear, he stopped his projected
attack on Hooker and dispatched McLaws with his
division and one of Anderson's brigades to re-enforce
Wilcox, that Sedgwick might be kept back. McLaws
arrived in time to assist Wilcox to repulse Sedgwick's
further advance. On the morning of the 4th Early ad-

vanced along the telegraph road and regained Marye's
and the adjacent hills.

General Lee now determined to crush Sedgwick if
possible; so leaving Stuart with Jackson's corps in
Hooker's front, he marched to McLaws and Early's assistance with Anderson's division. Anderson reached
Salem Church about noon, but the attack did not begin
until about six, owing, General Lee says, to the difficulty
of getting the troops in position. When the signal was
given, Anderson and Early moved forward at once in
gallant style, driving Sedgwick across the plank road
in the direction of the Rappahannock. The approaching darkness, we are told by General Lee, prevented
McLaws from perceiving the success of the attack, until
the enemy began to cross the river below Banks's Ford.
When the morning of the 5th dawned, Sedgwick had
made good his escape and removed his bridges. Fredericksburg was also evacuated. Early was left to hold
the lines as before, while Anderson and McLaws returned
to Chancellorsville, which place they reached on the
afternoon of the 5th in a violent thunderstorm. At daylight on the 6th these two divisions were ordered to assail the enemy's works in conjunction with Jackson's
corps, but during the storm of the night before, Hooker
retired over the river. One can hardly conceive a
greater risk than that taken by General Lee in these
operations. For two days Hooker's immense army was
kept in place by Jackson's corps, while General Lee assaulted Sedgwick.

The Confederate cavalry operations, from smallness
of numbers, were much circumscribed. Stuart only had
five regiments at Chancellorsville, three of them being on
Lee's left and two on his right, while two more had been
left to contend as best they could with Stoneman's ten
thousand troopers. Stoneman accomplished nothing.
Hooker's official report says that no officer ever made
a greater mistake in construing his orders, and no one
ever accomplished less in so doing. He returned to the
army on the 4th, the day Sedgwick was disposed of.
General Lee's official report said that " the conduct
of the troops can not be too highly praised. Attacking
largely superior numbers in strongly intrenched posi-

tions, their heroic courage overcame every obstacle of Nature and of art, and achieved a triumph most honorable to our arms."

Hooker's General Order No. 49, of May 6th, congratulates his army on its achievements, saying that, in withdrawing from the south bank of the Rappahannock before delivering a general battle, the army has given renewed evidence of its confidence in itself and its fidelity to the principles it represents. That the Army of the Potomac was profoundly loyal, and confident of its strength, and would give or decline battle when its interests or its honor might demand. "The events of last week," said he, "might well swell with pride the heart of every officer and soldier of this army." And then in a letter to Mr. Lincoln, dated May 13th, 1863, Hooker says: "Is it asking too much to inquire your opinion of my Order No. 49? If so, do not answer me. Jackson is dead, and Lee beats McClellan with his untruthful bulletins." It is not known whether Mr. Lincoln ever answered this question. The truth is, the Army of the Potomac was woefully mismanaged. Its commander guided it into the mazes of the Wilderness and got it so mixed and tangled that no chance was afforded for a display of its mettle. General Paxton was killed while leading his brigade with conspicuous courage in the assault of the 3d. Generals A. P. Hill, Nichols, McGowan, Heth, Hoke, and Pender were wounded.

Chancellorsville is inseparably connected in its glory and gloom with Stonewall Jackson. General Lee officially writes: "I do not propose to speak here of the character of this illustrious man, since removed from the scene of his eminent usefulness by the hand of an inscrutable but all-wise Providence. I nevertheless desire to pay the tribute of my admiration to the matchless energy and skill that marked this last act of his life, forming, as it did, a worthy conclusion of that long series of splendid achievements which won for him the lasting gratitude and love of his country."

Jackson's purely military genius resembled Cæsar's and Napoleon's. Like the latter, his success must be attributed to the rapid audacity of his movements and to his masterly control of the confidence and will of his men. He had the daring temper and fiery spirit of Cæsar in battle. Cæsar fell at the base of Pompey's statue, which had been restored by his magnanimity, pierced by twenty-three wounds at the hands of those he had done most for. Jackson fell at the hands of those who would have cheerfully joined their comrades in the dismal, silent bivouacks, if his life could have been spared. With Wolfe, Nelson, and Havelock he takes his place in the hearts of English-speaking people.

General Lee wrote Mrs. Lee from camp near Fredericksburg, May 11, 1863: "In addition to the death of friends and officers consequent upon the late battle, you will see we have to mourn the loss of the good and great Jackson. Any victory would be dear at such a price. His remains go to Richmond to-day. I know not how to replace him, but God's will be done. I trust He will raise some one in his place."

The battle of Chancellorsville increased immensely General Lee's fame. The difference in the numbers of the contestants was very marked. The three corps originally crossed to Lee's front at Fredericksburg were about equal in numbers to the whole of his army, so that Hooker's right flanking wing of four corps represented his numerical superiority.

The tactical and strategical operations of Chancellorsville is a remarkably interesting military study. Two armies seek, like the knight La Mancha, a foe to combat. One is much stronger than the other, and in quartermaster, commissary, and ordnance supplies is vastly superior. The larger army assumes the offensive, and plans to hold the smaller in place with one of its wings, while making a three or four days' detour with the other and greater portion to attack it in reverse. The flanking movement is arrested, while the identical tactics proposed are adopted by the other army, which in turn successfully assails their flank and rear, and holds them in the close embrace of a portion of the assailing troops, while two divisions which had been in their original front are countermarched and added to the division left at Fredericksburg. The three then attack and drive over the river the troops which were attempting to get in their rear at Chancellorsville, after which they are marched back to join in the expected battle around Chancellorsville next day, which did not take place because their opponents retreated across the river during the night. The bold conception of Lee was faultlessly executed by officers and men. It is true the wretched terrene assisted him in holding the lines in front of Hooker, for his axes could quickly make it defensible; that the forest concealed Jackson's march, and that an unpardonable negligence permitted twenty-five or thirty thousand troops to pass near a line of battle for many hours and mass for attack a short distance behind one of its flanks.

Had Hooker kept the ten thousand sabers of Stoneman, which he sent away on a fruitless mission, and placed them on the right or in front of his flank, his infantry would not have been surprised; or had he continued his advance on Fredericksburg when first moving out of Chancellorsville, and, pushed his cavalry along the route toward Todd's Tavern and Spottsylvania Court House, the chances of success would have been in his favor. General Lee fought the battle in the only way it could have been won, but the risks assumed were very great. To say that he committed faults is only to say that he made war. Once more the armies surveyed each other from their old camps; twice had one of them attempted the offensive. It was but fair that the Confederates should make the next move.

Lee devoted the few weeks of rest and recuperation which now followed in placing his army in better condition and reorganizing it. He now divided it into three corps instead of two—three divisions to the corps—commanded respectively by Longstreet, Ewell, and A. P. Hill. Ewell had been next in command to Jackson, participating in the glories of his Valley campaign, and maintaining his reputation as an excellent assistant to his great chief. He graduated at West Point in 1840, and served twenty-one years in the United States Army; was in Mexico, and brevetted for gallantry at Contreras and Churubusco; served on the frontier in the dragoons; was forty-three years old; had lost a leg at second Manassas, and was just able to rejoin the army. He

succeeded to much of Jackson's spirit and the quick-
ness and ardor of his strokes in battle, was kind-hearted,
eccentric, and absent-minded.   It has been said this
last trait came very near being fatal to him, for, forget-
ting he had lost his leg, he suddenly started one day to
walk and came down on the stump, imperfectly healed,
which produced a violent hæmorrhage.   " Virginia never
had a truer gentleman, a braver soldier, nor an odder,
more lovable fellow."

A. P. Hill's promotion to a corps commander was
bestowed on account of meritorious service.   He had
graduated at West Point seven years later than Ewell,
and was an artillery officer in the United States Army.
His bravery at the first Manassas, around Richmond—
where he drew the first blood—at second Manassas,
Harper's Ferry, and at Sharpsburg, had been conspicuous, and drew to him the attention of his commanding
general.*

The artillery arm consisted of fifteen battalions of
four batteries each, besides the batteries of horse artillery, and to each infantry corps was assigned its own
battalions of artillery, commanded by its own chief,
while the reserve artillery of the whole army was in
charge of General Pendleton, Lee's chief of artillery.
This arm of the service was well commanded, and was
rapidly asserting its claim to the front rank of the artillery armament of an army.   Parrott, Napoleon, Whitworth, and Armstrong guns, acquired by capture and
foreign purchase, were replacing the 6- and 12-pound
howitzers.   Longstreet's two absent divisions had returned under their distinguished commander.   The
cavalry had again been brought together, and was more
numerous and effective than ever.   At the end of May,

---

* In October, 1862, eight months before the army was reorganized,
General Lee wrote Mr. Davis, recommending that Generals Longstreet and Jackson be made corps commanders, and saying : " Next to
these two officers I consider A. P. Hill the best commander with me ;
he fights his troops well and takes good care of them, but two corps
are enough for the present."   In a published article since the war,
General Longstreet has stated that General Lee would not recommend General D. H. Hill or McLaws, both of whom ranked A. P.
Hill for the Third Corps, because they were not Virginians, which is
not true, and does General Lee very great injustice.

Lee commanded a splendid army, numbering present for duty, by the returns of May 31, 1863, 54,356 infantry, 9,536 cavalry, and 4,460 artillery, or a total of 68,352, with over two hundred guns. Its efficiency, confidence, and *morale* made it worthy of being led by a great chief.

The time for active operations to be resumed had arrived. Lee would have preferred that Hooker should assume the offensive, but as he showed no disposition to do it, the financial condition of the South and the scarcity of supplies made time too precious to wait longer for such action on his part.

Moltke, with his impassive student face, his bent figure, and his periodic pinches of snuff, directing operations as if they were certain calculations, was not more diligent than Lee, as under his canvas shelter he planned the Pennsylvania campaign, and designated, it is said, Gettysburg or its vicinity as the place of battle. It is certain that at that time he foretold his enemy's movements, knew his own, and predicted a meeting in Pennsylvania east of the mountains. Among the results to be reached by a march to Pennsylvania was the relief of the Confederate commissariat. Indeed, when making requisition for a supply of rations, the commissary general is reported to have said, "If General Lee wants rations let him seek them in Pennsylvania." Among other results of a decisive successful battle on Northern soil, might be a recognition of the Confederacy by foreign powers and a lasting peace.

General Lee had been accustomed to expose himself unnecessarily on the field of battle, and about this time his son W. H. F. Lee wrote to him: "I hear from every one of your exposing yourself. You must recollect, if anything should happen to you the cause would be very much jeopardized. I want very much to see you. May God preserve you, my dear father, is the earnest prayer of your devoted son." Lee remarked upon one occasion, when remonstrated with about endangering his life: "I wish some one would tell me my proper place in battle. I am always told I should not be where I am." On May 20, 1863, from camp near Fredericksburg, the general writes to Mrs. Lee in Richmond: "I learn that

our poor wounded are doing very well. General Hooker
is airing himself north of the Rappahannock and again
threatening us with a crossing. It was reported last
night that he had brought his pontoons to the river, but
I hear nothing of him this morning. I think he will
consider it a few days. He has published a gratu-
latory order to his troops, telling them they have covered themselves with new laurels, have destroyed our
stores, communications, thousands of our choice troops,
captured prisoners in their fortifications, filling the country with fear and consternation. 'Profoundly loyal and
conscious of its own strength, the Army of the Potomac
will give or decline battle whenever its interests or
honor may demand. It will also be the guardian of its
own history and its own honor.' All of which is signed
by our old friend S. Williams, A. A. G. It shows at
least he is so far unhurt, and is so far good, but as to
the truth of history I will not speak. May the great
God have you all in his holy keeping and soon unite us
again!" On the 31st of May, two days before he began
his campaign, he writes: " Camp Fredericksburg, May 31,
1863.—General Hooker has been very daring the past
week, and quite active. He has not said what he intends
to do, but is giving out by his movements that he designs
crossing the Rappahannock. I hope we may be able to
frustrate his plans in part if not in whole. He has General
Heintzelman's corps now, on whom the Northern papers
seem to place great reliance. I pray that our merciful
Father in Heaven may protect and direct us! In that
case I fear no odds and no numbers."

Three days before, Hooker had dispatched to Secretary Stanton that he was certain important movements
were being made, and that he was in doubt as to the direction Lee would take, " but probably the one of last year,
however desperate it may appear." As Hooker could
not be attacked except at a disadvantage, General Lee
determined to draw him from his position and transfer
the scene of hostilities beyond the Potomac.

This embraced the expulsion from the Valley of Virginia of the Federal force under General Milroy. On the
2d of June Ewell's Corps marched for Culpeper Court
House, and a day or two afterward Lee followed with

Longstreet's Corps. Hill's Corps was left to watch Hooker and follow as soon as he should retire. A daring commencement of a campaign! Hill, with less than twenty thousand troops, was between Hooker and Richmond, sixty miles away, while Lee, with the other two corps, was at Culpeper Court House, some thirty miles distant in another direction.

Mr. Lincoln and Halleck would not let Hooker attack Hill, as General Lee supposed, because it was "perilous to allow Lee to move on the Potomac while your army is attacking an intrenched position on the other side of the Rappahannock," wrote Halleck. "If left to me," said Mr. Lincoln, "I would not go south of the Rappahannock upon Lee's moving north of it. Lee's army, not Richmond, is your true objective point. Fight him when opportunity offers; if he stays where he is, fret him and fret him."

Hill would have retarded Hooker's progress, falling back toward the defenses of Richmond, while Lee would have taken Washington before Hooker could have countermarched and interposed; or he could have placed his troops in Richmond from Culpeper by railroad in time to support Hill. "No," reiterated the Union President to Hooker, "I would not take any risk of being entangled upon the river like an ox jumped half over the fence and liable to be torn by dogs front and rear without a fair chance to gore one way or kick the other."

Lee's two infantry and his cavalry corps were concentrated around Culpeper by the 7th of June. Hooker knew Stuart was at Culpeper and thought he meant mischief, so determined to break him up, if possible, by sending all of his cavalry against him, stiffened by three thousand infantry.

General Lee reports that on the 9th of June the cavalry under General Stuart was attacked by a large force of Federal cavalry, supported by infantry, which crossed the Rappahannock at Beverly's and Kelly's Fords. After a severe engagement from early in the morning until late in the afternoon, "the enemy was compelled to recross the river with heavy loss, leaving about five hundred prisoners, three pieces of artillery, and several colors in our hands." On the other hand, Hooker dispatched that "Pleasonton pressed Stuart three miles, capturing two hundred prisoners and a battle flag. Our cavalry made many hand-to-hand combats, always driving the enemy before them."

General Lee wrote Mrs. Lee the day of the battle at Culpeper, June 9, 1863: "I reviewed the cavalry in this section yesterday. It was a splendid sight. The men and horses looked well. They had recuperated since last fall. Stuart was in all his glory. Your sons and nephews are well and flourishing. The country here looks very green and pretty, notwithstanding the ravages of war. What a beautiful world God in his loving kindness to his creatures has given us! What a shame that men endowed with reason and knowledge of right should mar his gifts!"

And again on the 11th of the month, from the same place, he wrote: "My supplications continue to ascend for you, my children, and my country. When I last wrote I did not suppose that Fitzhugh (his son) would so soon be sent to the rear disabled, and I hope it will be but for a short time. I saw him the night after the battle—indeed, met him on the field as they were bringing him from the front. He is young and healthy, and I trust will soon be up again. He seemed to be more concerned about his brave men and officers who had fallen in the battle than himself."

The day after the conflict between Pleasonton and Stuart, Ewell left Culpeper, and crossed the Shenandoah near Front Royal, where Jenkins's cavalry brigade joined him, while at the same time Imboden's cavalry was moved to Romney to keep the troops guarding the Baltimore and Ohio Railroad from re-enforcing Milroy. On the 13th Ewell was in line of battle in front of Winchester, and next day he stormed and carried the works there, Milroy, the Union commander, and a few of his men alone escaping. Four thousand prisoners, twenty-eight pieces of superior artillery, wagons, horses, small arms, ordnance, commissary and quartermaster stores were captured. Ewell then entered Maryland. How very daring these movements were! On June 12th, when Ewell was at Winchester, Longstreet was at Culpeper and Hill at Fredericksburg, while Hooker was still, with the larger part of his army, in front of Hill.

Hooker, having at last found that General Lee had left, determined to move too, and issued orders on the 13th for four corps to rendezvous at Manassas Junction. At five o'clock next afternoon Hooker was at Dumfries, some twenty miles north of Fredericksburg, on the road to Washington, and Mr. Lincoln asked him by telegraph if he thought it " possible that fifteen thousand of Ewell's men can now be at Winchester?" and later tells him that the enemy have Milroy surrounded at Winchester, and Tyler at Martinsburg, and asks him if he could help them if they could hold out a few days, and then with habitual humor said: " If the head of Lee's army is at Martinsburg, and the tail of it on the plank road between Fredericksburg and Chancellorsville, the animal must be very slim somewhere. Could you not break him?"

There was nothing now for the Union commander to do except to keep interposed between his enemy and Washington, and Hooker therefore concentrated his troops along the Orange and Alexandria Railroad. The movement of the Army of the Potomac depended on that of the Army of Northern Virginia. As Lee proceeded north, so did Hooker, on parallel lines. Five days after Ewell's departure from Culpeper Court House Longstreet left. His route was east of the Blue Ridge with Stuart's cavalry in his front and on his right flank to mask his position. Hill, who had joined Lee again, was then passed into the Valley behind Longstreet's lines. Hooker was mystified, and pushed his cavalry on Stuart to see what was going on. He thought Stuart was preparing for a raid, "which may be a cover to Lee's re-enforcing Bragg or moving troops to the west." Stuart and Pleasonton had frequent encounters for three days, but the cavalry mask was not torn away, and no information gained by Hooker.

General Lee wrote Stuart, June 22d, that he thought Pleasonton's efforts were made to arrest the progress of his army and ascertain its location, and that " perhaps he is satisfied " that he was afraid the Federals would " get across the Potomac before we are aware "; and that if he found Hooker moving northward, and "two brigades can guard the Blue Ridge and take care of your rear, you can move with the other three into Maryland and take position on General Ewell's right." The same day Ewell was ordered toward the Susquehanna and told " if Harrisburg comes within your means, capture it."   Stuart was to go to Ewell's right flank on the Susquehanna, provided (Lee wrote Longstreet) he could be spared from his front, and that he could move across the Potomac if Longstreet thought he could do so without disclosing Lee's plans. He was then guarding Longstreet's front and flank, which brought him under that officer's command. General Lee suggested that Stuart move through Hopewell Gap in the Bull Run Mountains, pass in rear of Hooker, and then cross the Potomac. Longstreet wrote Stuart that if he " crossed by our rear at Shepherdstown it would in a measure disclose our plans," and that he " had better not leave us unless you can take the proposed route in rear of the enemy."   The next day Stuart received from Lee an order to cross the Potomac with three brigades, either at Shepherdstown or " east of the mountains in rear of the enemy," and that he must " move on and feel the right of Ewell's troops," then marching toward the Susquehanna. Stuart marched through Hopewell Gap, as suggested by General Lee, and took the route in rear of the enemy as directed by Longstreet.   He crossed the Potomac at Seneca, thirteen miles above Washington, the day Lee was at Chambersburg and Ewell at Carlisle. This officer has been unjustly criticised for not being in front of Lee's army at Gettysburg, but Lee and Longstreet must be held responsible for his route. Lee crossed the Potomac west of the Blue Ridge, Hooker east of it, and Stuart between him and Washington.

General Lee continued to march his columns over the river into Maryland and Pennsylvania. Ewell, the first of the invaders, with Jenkins's cavalry brigade and White's battalion under its fine commander, was in advance. His march was directed by Hagerstown to Chambersburg, Pa., and Carlisle, where he arrived on June 27th with two of his divisions. His remaining division, under Early, was sent to York to break the railroad between Harrisburg, Pa., and Baltimore, and seize the bridge over the Susquehanna at Wrightsville. Longstreet and Hill encamped near Chambersburg the day Ewell reached Carlisle. Lee was spreading over Northern territory in order to collect as large an amount of supplies as possible, as well as to draw the Army of the Potomac away from Washington before delivering battle. Under the supposition that the Union army was still in Virginia guarding the approaches to Washington, Lee had issued orders to move upon Harrisburg. Stuart captured a wagon train at Rockville, on the direct road from Washington to Hooker's army, the nearest wagon being taken four miles from Washington city, burned a large number, and marched away with two hundred wagons and their teams, burned the railroad bridge at Sykesville, cut the telegraph wires, drove the Delaware cavalry in confusion out of Westminster, fought Kilpatrick's cavalry at Hanover, Pa., prevented two infantry corps from reaching Meade until the second day at Gettysburg, and drew in pursuit of his three cavalry brigades two Federal cavalry divisions, and after ceaseless combats and night marches reached Dover, Pa., on July 1st. Whole regiments slept in their saddles, their faithful animals keeping the road unguided. Without rations for men, and with horses exhausted, Stuart arrived at Carlisle the day Hill and Ewell were engaged at Gettysburg. He wanted to levy a contribution for rations on Carlisle, but the Federal General "Baldy" Smith, with his Pennsylvania reserves, would not surrender the place. Its probable capture the next day was prevented by news received for the first time of General Lee's position and intentions. Stuart did not know until he received a dispatch from General Lee on the night of July 1st where he was, for the Union army had been between his march and his own army. Leaving Carlisle, he marched at once for Gettysburg, prevented a movement of the enemy's cavalry on Lee's rear by way of Hunterstown, and took his position on the York and Heidelburg roads on the left of his army late on the evening of July 2d.

Cavalry raids are dazzling, but do not generally accomplish enough to compensate for the number of broken-down horses and men. The cavalry chief could not tell Lee when and where Hooker's army crossed the Potomac, because, when it was crossing, he was in its rear, moving to cross the day afterward lower down the same stream, and after that he had no opportunity. It was left to an adventurous scout to report to General Lee, on the night of June 28th, that Hooker had crossed the Potomac and was approaching the south mountains. The information obliged him to draw in his advance and concentrate his army east of the mountain, to prevent his communications from being intercepted. Had Lee had all of his cavalry in Pennsylvania, the irrepressible conflict would not have taken place at Gettysburg, but possibly on Pipe Creek; and had Hooker not detached his cavalry out of his reach, the battle fought at Chancellorsville would possibly have taken place on the confines of Fredericksburg.

On the 29th Hill's corps was directed to move toward Cashtown and Longstreet to follow next day, leaving Pickett's division at Greenwood as a rear guard until Imboden should get up with his cavalry brigade, while Ewell was recalled from Carlisle to Cashtown or Gettysburg, as circumstances might require. As the Army of Northern Virginia was ordered to concentrate in a southerly direction, while Hooker slowly advanced his columns north, it was manifest the two armies must meet. Topographically, Gettysburg was a strategic point, available for concentration by both armies. Roads from Washington, Baltimore, and all points in the section south of it, where the Union army lay in its fan-shaped position, entered it, as well as the roads from Chambersburg, twenty miles off, *via* Cashtown, and from Carlisle and York.

Lee was coming south to guard his communications and fight if opportunity presented. Hooker was going north to prevent the occupation of so much territory by the detached parts of Lee's army and to deliver battle when opportunity offered. Each army was manœuvring for defensive combat, but each was prepared to assume the offensive if occasion required, and neither intended to decline an encounter. There was a cry too for blood from noncombatants everywhere—as strong as once resounded in the Roman Coliseum.

The night that Lee heard of the Federal advance crossing the Potomac, a new commander was in the saddle. "Fighting Joe Hooker" had fought his last battle as an army commander. Halleck, after the battle of Chancellorsville, did not want to trust Hooker with the management of another battle, and had been sustained in his opinion by Mr. Lincoln and Secretary Stanton at a council held between them. It was even said that politics was dragged into the subject, and that the friends of Mr. Chase, a prospective presidential candidate, were bound up in the fortunes of Hooker, and that they interposed to prevent his removal, for "the general who should conquer the rebellion would have the disposal of the next presidency." The friends of presidential aspirants were on the lookout for the right military alliance, and it was stated that if it should be Hooker's fortune to bring the war to a successful close nothing would induce him to accept other than military honors in recognition of his services. At any rate, it is certain Hooker naturally resented interference in the field from a general safely shut up in his office in Washington, and properly contended that one man should command all the troops whose operations could be combined against Lee. Halleck not consenting, the difficulty culminated when Hooker requested that Maryland Heights, the gate to Harper's Ferry, be evacuated, that he might mobilize the ten thousand troops there. Halleck refused, and Hooker, now at Frederick, Maryland, finding he was not allowed to manœuvre his army in the presence of the enemy, asked to be relieved from command, which, being in accordance with the views of the Washington authorities, was promptly done.

CHAPTER XII.

GETTYSBURG.

THE fifth commander of the Army of the Potomac was Major-General George Gordon Meade, then in command of the Fifth Corps. This officer was born in Cadiz, Spain, in December, 1815, and was consequently forty-six years old. He graduated at West Point in 1835, and was assigned to the artillery arm of the service. A year afterward he resigned from the army, but after six years was reappointed second lieutenant of the Topographical Engineers, and was in Mexico on General Patterson's staff. Meade's father served as a private soldier in the Pennsylvania troops to suppress the "Whisky Insurrection" in western Pennsylvania, and therefore was under General Lee's father, who commanded the forces raised for that purpose. He was afterward a merchant, a shipowner, and a navy agent in Cadiz, but shortly after his son's birth returned to the United States.

In justice to this officer, it may be said that he protested against being placed in command of an army that had been looking toward Reynolds as Hooker's successor, but, loyal to authority, he assumed the command in obedience to orders. His position was environed with difficulties, for he was ignorant of Hooker's plans. Awakened from sleep by General Hardee, the War Department messenger, he had not much time to get any knowledge of them from Hooker, while a battle in the next few days could not be avoided. He determined to continue the move northward through Maryland into Pennsylvania, and force Lee to give battle before he could cross the Susquehanna.

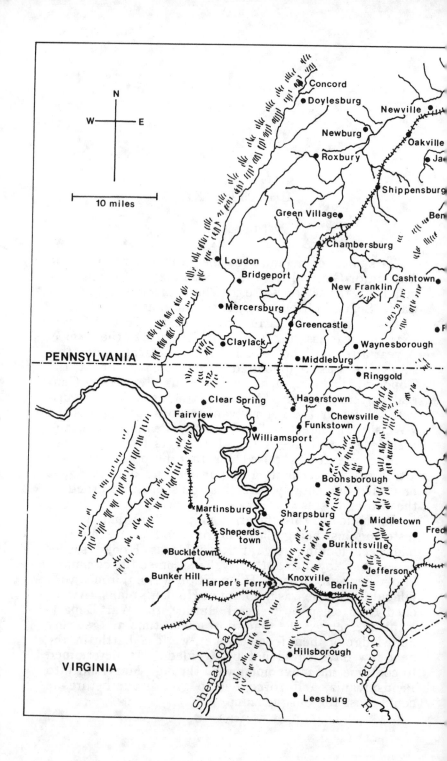

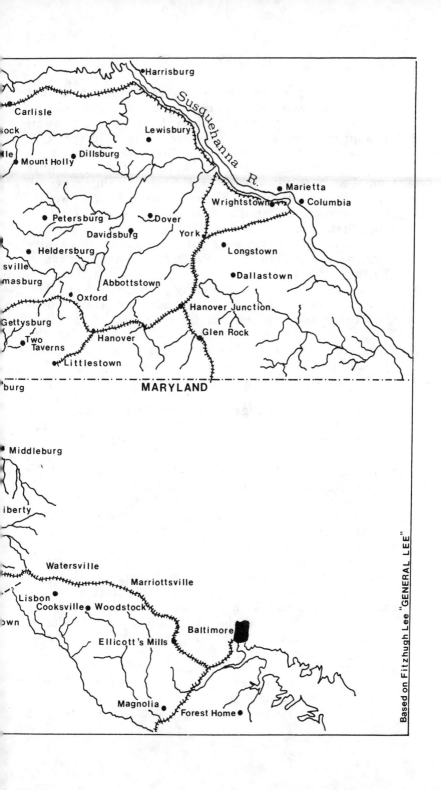

Based on Fitzhugh Lee "GENERAL LEE"

After two days' march, he received information that Lee was concentrating and coming toward him, and he at once began to prepare the line of Pipe Creek to await his approach and fight a defensive battle. On the night of June 30th his headquarters and reserve artillery were at Taneytown; the First Corps, at Marsh Creek, six miles from Longstreet and Hill at Cashtown; the Eleventh Corps, at Emmittsburg; Third, at Bridgeport; Twelfth, at Littletown; Second, at Uniontown; Fifth, at Union Mill; Sixth, at Winchester, Md., with Gregg's cavalry, that being his extreme right. Kilpatrick's cavalry division was at Hanover, Pa., while Buford's cavalry guarded his left.

Lee was rapidly concentrating. Longstreet and Hill were then near Cashtown, Hill's advance (Heth's division) being seven miles from Gettysburg, and Ewell at Heidelburg, nine miles away. Had Lee known of the defensive position at Gettysburg, he could have easily massed his whole army on July 1st there; but he was in no hurry to precipitate a battle, and would have preferred to fight at some point not so far from his base.

On the 30th Pettigrew, commanding a brigade of Heth's division, Hill's corps, was directed to march to Gettysburg to get shoes for the barefooted men of the division, but returned the same evening without them and reported that Gettysburg was occupied by the Federal cavalry, and that drums were heard beating on the other side of the town. So Heth told Hill if he had no objection, he would take his whole division there the next day, July 1st, and "get the shoes," to which Hill replied, " None in the world."

Buford, with his cavalry division, reached Gettysburg on the day Pettigrew made his visit, and threw out his pickets toward Cashtown and Hunterstown. In an order of march for July 1st, Meade, not knowing Lee was so near, directed the First and Eleventh Corps, under that excellent officer Reynolds, to Gettysburg; Third, to Emmittsburg; Second, Taneytown; Fifth, Hanover; Twelfth to Two Taverns; while the Sixth was to remain at Manchester, thirty-four miles from Gettysburg, and await orders.

Heth, after his coveted shoes, reached McPherson's

Heights, one mile west of Gettysburg, at 9 A. M. on July
1st, deployed two brigades on either side of the road,
and advanced on the town.   Promptly the few sputtering shots which first announced the skirmish line's opening told him that Buford's dismounted cavalry were
blocking the way ; and the great struggle which was to
determine, like Waterloo, the fate of a continent, and
whether there should be one or two republics on this
continent, had commenced.   Precipitance was neither
desired by Meade nor Lee, but "shoes" took command
that day, and opened a contest which drew in its bloody
embrace one hundred and seventy thousand men.   For
Reynolds, hearing Buford's guns, hastened to him with
the First Corps, Wadsworth's division leading.   Hill,
who had followed Heth with Pender's division, sent it
rapidly to his support, while the Eleventh Corps hastened to the First Corps's assistance.   Ewell, with his
leading division (Rodes's), at 2.30 P. M. came to Heth's
and Pender's support, while Early's division, at about
3.30 P. M., moved in such a way as to attack the Federal
flank, and at 4 P. M. the Federal force was in full retreat
through the town of Gettysburg, toward the heights to
the south of it, where a brigade of Howard's had been
posted as a reserve and rallying point in case of disaster
when his corps marched to the battlefield.   A well-con-
tested combat had occured between two infantry corps,
a cavalry division, and the artillery on one side, and
four divisions of infantry, with the artillery, on the
other.

Fifty thousand men fought (after all were up), about
equally divided in numbers between the contestants.*
For six hours the battle raged.   General Lee reached
McPherson Heights about 2.30 P. M., and, getting off
his horse, swept with his field glasses the country in his
front; he saw the Union troops retreating over the hills
south of the town, and ordered Walter Taylor, of his
staff, to ride to Ewell and tell him to move on and occupy them, but that he did not want to bring on a gen-

---

* Federals—First Corps, 10,089 ; Eleventh, 9,893 ; Buford's cavalry, 3,000.   Total, 22,982.   Confederates—Two thirds of Ewell's corps,
two thirds of Hill's—four divisions—26,000.

eral engagement until Longstreet arrived. A false report, however, caused Ewell to send out first one, then
another brigade to guard his flank, and while waiting
for them and his remaining division under Johnson to
get up, the shades of coming night covered his proposed
field of operations. Lee had made a good beginning;
his troops had captured more than five thousand prisoners, including two general officers, exclusive of a large
number of the wounded, and three pieces of artillery.
Heth had been slightly, General Scales seriously, wounded, and General Archer captured; his enemy had been
driven through Gettysburg with great loss, and General
Reynolds, their commander, killed.

The death of this splendid officer was regretted by
friend and foe. Able, brave, with military talents of
the highest order, his place could not well be filled. His
Government recognized his merit, and he was next on
the list for the command of the army. Napier's eulogy
on Ridge has been happily applied to him: "No man
died on that field with more glory than he, yet many
died, and there was much glory!"

The Confederate success was not followed up. Lee
wanted Longstreet's troops to be present before delivering a general battle, and, perhaps, did not make his order
for pursuit positive. He says Ewell was directed to pursue "if practicable." Had Ewell decided to go forward
on the 1st of July, the Southern troops would have been
in line of battle on Cemetery Heights that afternoon,
and Meade would have been occupied during the night
in forming defensive lines on Pipe Creek, ten or twelve
miles distant, or elsewhere. Heth lost on the 1st twenty-
five hundred killed, wounded, and missing, which left him
forty-three hundred. The losses in the other division
were not so heavy. Allowing them forty-five hundred
effectives at the close of the action, would give the four
divisions seventeen thousand eight hundred to pursue.

A letter of Hancock's, the officer dispatched by
Meade, on hearing of Reynolds's death, to supersede
Howard, his senior in command at Gettysburg, says:
"When I arrived upon the field, about 3 P. M. or between
that and 3.30 P. M., I found the fighting about over; the
rear of our troops were hurrying through the town, pur-

sued by the Confederates. There had been an attempt
to reform some of the Eleventh Corps as they passed
over Cemetery Hill, but it had not been very successful.
I presume there may have been one thousand or twelve
hundred organized troops of that corps in position on
the hill." Twenty-four hundred and fifty men, the shattered remains of the First Corps, were there too, and Buford's cavalry were drawn up upon the plain, making a
total of six thousand troops, which could not have
offered much resistance against the victorious seventeen
thousand of Ewell and Hill, and two hours must elapse
before they could receive re-enforcements, and then only
at 6 P. M., of two divisions of the Twelfth Corps; but
Johnson's division of Ewell's corps reached the town at
six, and Anderson's, of Hill's, could have been there too
if necessary, which would have maintained the original
status.

At sunset two brigades of Sickles's Third Corps arrived; Sickles in person reached the field an hour earlier. They would have been too late, and would have
been recalled to Pipe Creek, with all other troops then
in motion toward Gettysburg. Two brigades of Pender's and one of Early's division had scarcely fired a
shot. Dole's, Hoke's, and Hays's brigades were in good
condition. "The artillery was up, and had an admirable position to cover an assault, which could have been
pushed under cover of the houses to within a few rods
of the Union position." The impartial military critic
will admit Confederate camp fires would have blazed at
night and Confederate banners waved in the afternoon
from the high places south of Gettysburg had Ewell
and Hill marched again on the broken and vanquished
Federal battalions.

Gettysburg is a small town near the Pennsylvania
and Maryland boundary line, ten miles east of the south
range of mountains—"the eastern wall of the Cumberland Valley"—and through whose passes Lee's army debouched. The intervening section is described as full
of long ridges running north and south, as the mountains
do. On Lee's route from Cashtown to Gettysburg one
of these ridges is crossed at right angles one and a half
mile west of Gettysburg, and a little farther on an-

other; Willoughby Run flows between them, and here the combat of July 1st opened. Closer to the town and about half a mile west of it is the now famous Seminary Ridge, so called from a Lutheran theological seminary on it, upon which were located the battle lines of portions of two of Lee's corps on the 2d and 3d of July.

Directly south of Gettysburg is the beginning of another series of heights, hills, and depressions which, running in a southerly direction for three miles, terminate in "a lofty, wooded, rocky peak" called Round Top. Adjoining this peak on its north side is Weed's Hill, better known as Little Round Top—a spur to Round Top—"rough and bald." Round Top is at the southern extremity of this ridge. A cemetery at the northern point gives to the ridge its name. Upon this ridge the Federal line of battle was formed. An undulating valley stretches up to Seminary Ridge, a mile distant, and on the elevated tableland between the two runs the Emmittsburg road.

Gettysburg lies at the base of Cemetery Hill, where the ridge bends in a curve, east, and then southeast, to an elevation called Culp's Hill. On Culp's Hill and around this curve, and then south to Round Top for three miles, was the Union battle line. Its shape has been not inaptly compared to a fish hook, with long side and curve. The formation was convex, allowing the Union commander to operate tactically on interior lines, so that he could rapidly re-enforce along his rear the threatened points. The ground in rear of this splendid battle line fell in gradual slope to Rock Creek, affording capital shelter for reserves and trains.

Five hundred yards west of Little Round Top, and one hundred feet lower, is Devil's Den, "a bold, rocky height, steep on its eastern face, but prolonged as a ridge to the west." It lies between two streams in the angle where they meet. The northern extremity is covered with huge bowlders and rocks, forming crevices and holes, the largest of which gives the name to the ridge. Gettysburg is the hub of the wheel, and the Baltimore, York, Harrisburg, Carlisle, Mummasburg, Chambersburg, Millerstown, Emmittsburg, and Taneytown roads the spokes. Lee's troops were distributed over a larger "fishhook," surrounding the smaller or inner one; his extreme left was in front of Meade's refused right at Culp's Hill. Johnson's, Early's, and Rodes's divisions, in order named, were located on the curve and through the town to Seminary Ridge from left to right; then came Hill's corps, stretching south, and later, Longstreet's was formed on its right.

The army smallest in numbers had the longest or outside line, while the largest force occupied in its front a superb defensive position. Lee's army was practically concentrated on the night of the 1st, except his cavalry and Pickett's infantry division, Ewell and Hill in front of the enemy, and Longstreet in camp only four miles in the rear. Meade and his Second Corps were at Taneytown, in Maryland, when the sun went down on the 1st, thirteen miles distant; the Fifth Corps, at Union Mills, twenty-three miles distant and the Sixth Corps, sixteen thousand men, thought to be the largest and finest in the army, was at Manchester, thirty-four miles away. Both Meade and Lee would have preferred to postpone the battle a few days, but were face to face sooner than contemplated.

Meade received Hancock's report on the evening of the 1st, and determined in consequence to fight the battle at Gettysburg, and issued orders for the movement of his troops at 7.30 P. M. that evening. In two hours he left Taneytown, and arrived on Cemetery Ridge at 1 A. M. There is testimony that he did not like his position, and his chief of staff says he was directed to prepare an order to withdraw the army from it.

The Union commander was uncertain whether he could bring his two fine corps, the Fifth and Sixth, on the field in time, and was solicitous about his depot of supplies at Westminster.

As late as 3 P. M. on the 2d, and before he was attacked, he telegraphed in cipher to Halleck that if his enemy did not attack, and he "finds it hazardous to do so, or is satisfied the enemy is endeavoring to move to my rear and interpose between me and Washington, I shall fall back to my supplies at Westminster."

Lee, impressed with the idea of whipping his opponent in detail, on the other hand, was practically ready and

eager for the contest next day, and so was his confident
army. He was under no obligation, as has been affirmed,
to any one to fight a defensive battle; he sought the
enemy's soil to gain a victory, whether by offensive or
defensive tactics, and his objective point was the Army
of the Potomac. He knew the Union army had not yet
concentrated, and was anxious to attack before it could.
He had already talked with Longstreet, who, following
Hill's corps, joined him, at 5 P. M., the afternoon of July
1st, on Seminary Ridge, where both made a careful survey with glasses of the hostile heights opposite, and, it
is presumed, attempted to impress him with the importance of· an early attack next day, and later that night
saw him again. On the same evening he rode into the
town of Gettysburg, and met, in an arbor attached to a
small house on the Carlisle road north of the town, Ewell,
Early, and Rodes.

The Confederate commander was anxious at first
that Ewell and Hill should commence the battle, and
seemed apprehensive that Longstreet might not get into
position as soon as the conditions demanded, but finally
yielded to the opinion expressed, that Longstreet should
commence the battle by a forward movement on Hill's
right, seize the commanding positions on the enemy's
left, and envelop and enfilade the flank of the troops in
front of the other two corps. Lee left the conference,
Early states, with the "distinct understanding that
Longstreet would be ordered to make the attack early
next morning."   General W. N. Pendleton, his chief of
artillery and his honored and trusted friend, has put on
record that General Lee told him that night, after he
[Pendleton] returned from a reconnoissance on the right
flank, that he "had ordered General Longstreet to attack
on the flank at sunrise next morning."

Hill, in his official report, says, "General Longstreet
was to attack the flank of the enemy and sweep down
his line." And General Long, of Lee's staff, writes, in
his opinion orders were issued for the movement to
begin on the enemy's left as early as practicable.

Lee's plan of battle was simple. His purpose was to
turn the enemy's left flank with his First Corps, and
after the work began there, to demonstrate against his

lines with the other two in order to prevent the threatened flank from being re-enforced, these demonstrations to be converted into a real attack as the flanking wave of battle rolled over the troops in their front.

Lee did not like Ewell's bent line—his left was too far around the curve of the fishhook—and decided to draw him more to his right. But that fine old soldier had seen that Culp's Hill was the key to the Federal right, and was told that it was unoccupied at dark, by two staff officers who said they were on its top at that time. At his request he was allowed to remain to secure the hill at daybreak. Hancock, however, reports that he ordered Wadsworth's division with a battery of artillery to take post there in the afternoon. The Federal right was very strong. The woods on Culp's Hill enabled its defenders, with a multitude of axes and spades, to convert it promptly into a fort.

When Lee went to sleep that night he was convinced that his dispositions for battle next day were understood by the corps commanders, for he had imparted them to each one in person. On the morning of July 2d Lee was up before light, breakfasted, and was "ready for the fray," but his chariot of war had hardly started before he found his corps team were not pulling together; the wheel horse selected to start it was balky and stubborn, and, after stretching his traces, did not draw his share of the load with rapidity enough to be effective.

We hear from General Longstreet that on the evening of the 1st he was trying to induce Lee not to attack, but manœuvre, and on the 2d he "went to General Lee's headquarters at daylight and renewed my views against making an attack; he seemed resolved, however, and we discussed results."

In consequence of the reluctance of the officer next in command to fire the opening gun, Lee was induced to send Colonel Venable, of his staff, to Ewell at sunrise to see whether, after viewing the position in his front by daylight, he could not attack from his flank, but the work of thousands of men during the night made the hills too strong to assault; indeed, Meade was then massing there to attack Ewell. Later, Lee rode there

himself, not wishing to drive his right corps commander
into battle when he did not want to go, but saw nothing
could be done, so at eleven o'clock gave a positive
order to Longstreet to move to his right and attack.

It was clearly the duty of Longstreet to carry out
his commander's views and not lapse into refractori-
ness. Lee might possibly have moved toward Frederick on the 2d, and thus forced Meade to fall back to
Westminster, but he could not hope to reach Baltimore
or Washington, or a point between these cities before
Meade. From Westminster cars could have conveyed
the Union troops more rapidly than his could have
marched, and if Meade had followed him toward Washington he would have been caught between the powerful works then defended by thirty or forty thousand
troops and General Meade's army, while the change of
base would have greatly endangered his lines of communication.

The closer the two armies approached Westminster
the larger the numbers of the Unionists would grow.
Lee could not move around now and manœuvre, or scat-
ter his legions to gather supplies as he had done, because
his opponent was uncomfortably near. He could not
march *en masse*, with a host subsisting by pillage, and to
concentrate was to starve. There was no alternative—
he must fight.

He was obliged to adopt the tactics of William the
Conqueror when he invaded England, who, similarly situated, assumed the offensive and defeated Harold at Hastings. Napoleon waited at Waterloo for the ground to
dry and lost hours, during which he might have defeated
Wellington before the arrival of re-enforcements. Why
should Lee lose the advantages of his more rapid concentration? His "superb equipoise" was not threatened by "subdued excitement." His unerring sagacity
told him he would catch General Meade partially in
position, but he was disturbed because one of his principal officers had not the faith and confidence necessary
to win success.

Longstreet's troops not long after daybreak stacked
arms near the battlefield. Hood reports he was in front
of the heights of Gettysburg shortly after daybreak.

General Lee was there walking up and down under the large trees near him, and seemed full of hope, but at times buried in deep thought. He seemed anxious that Longstreet should attack, says Hood. "The enemy is here," Lee said, "and if we don't whip him he will whip us." Hood states that Longstreet afterward said, seating himself near the trunk of a tree by his side: "The general is a little nervous this morning. He wishes me to attack. I do not want to do so without Pickett. I never like to go into battle with one boot off."

McLaws says that his orders were to leave his camp at 4 A. M., but were afterward changed to sunrise; that he reached Gettysburg at a very early hour, and halted the head of his column within a hundred yards of where General Lee was sitting on a fallen tree with a map beside him; that he went to Lee, who pointed out to him on the map the road to his right as the one he wanted him to place his division across, and that he wished him to get there, if possible, without being seen by the enemy; that the line pointed out was perpendicular to the Emmittsburg road, about the position he afterward occupied, and that "Longstreet was then walking back and forth some little distance from General Lee, but came up and, pointing to the map, showed him how he wanted his division located, to which General Lee replied: 'No, general, I wish it placed just the opposite,'" and "that Longstreet appeared as if he were irritated and annoyed, but the cause I did not ask."

McLaws, while waiting, reconnoitered in his front, and was soon convinced that by crossing the ridge where he was then his "command could reach the point indicated by General Lee in half an hour without being seen." McLaws then went back to the head of his column and sat on his horse, he says, and "saw in the distance the enemy coming, hour after hour, on to the battle ground." Wilcox's brigade of Anderson's division, Hill's corps, which had been left on picket on Marsh Creek, east of which stream Longstreet's corps bivouacked the night of the 1st, left its post after sunrise, passed through Hood's and McLaws's divisions, whose arms were stacked, and went into line of battle on Anderson's right at 9 A. M. Wilcox's right rested in a piece of woods, and seven hours afterward, at 4 P. M., McLaws formed in these same woods.

Longstreet admits that he was ordered at eleven to move to the right to attack with the portion of the command then up, but delayed, on his own responsibility, to await General Laws's brigade, which had been detached on picket. His disobedience of orders in failing to march at once with his command then present, many believe, lost to Lee the battle of Gettysburg. With a corps commander who knew the value of time, obeyed orders with promptness and without argument, Lee's movement on Meade's left could have commenced at seven or eight o'clock A. M., with all the chances for success, and there would probably have been no combat on the 3d. The Third Federal Corps was not all up at the hour the attack should have been made, or a division of the Fifth, or the reserve artillery, or the Sixth Corps.

When McLaws and Hood advanced, eight or nine hours afterward, the conditions had changed; Meade, having relinquished his design to attack from his right, had been steadily strengthening his left, and his whole army was concentrated on a splendid defensive line, for Lee had waited, as if he did not purpose to take advantage of his being first prepared to fight. The fine Federal position would have been useless to Meade had Longstreet attacked only a few hours earlier, as he might have done, for in that case he would have secured Round Top, six hundred and sixty-four feet high, and one hundred and sixteen feet higher than Little Round Top, one thousand yards north of it, and crowned it with artillery. "Little Round Top would have been untenable, and Little Round Top was the key point of my whole position," said Meade; "and if they" (his opponents) "had succeeded in occupying that, it would have prevented me from holding any of the ground I subsequently held to the last."

Lee to the strong courage of the man united the loving heart of the woman. His "nature was too epicene," said an English critic, "to be purely a military man." He had a reluctance to oppose the wishes of others, or to order them to do anything that would be disagreeable and to which they would not consent.

" Had I Stonewall Jackson at Gettysburg, I would have won a great victory," he said to Professor White, of the Washington and Lee University, after the war, because he knew it would have been sufficient for Jackson to have known his general views without transmitting positive orders, and that Stonewall, quick and impatient, would have been driving in the enemy's flank ere the rays of the morning sun lifted the mists from the Round Tops. If Lee had issued by his chief of staff his battle order for the 2d in writing, as is customary, Longstreet would have carried it out probably in good faith, and not have wasted most valuable time in attempting to convince his commander it was faulty.

The attack on the right, commencing five or six hours after the positive order had been given, even then had some elements of success. Sickles, with the Third Corps, had become dissatisfied with his location, and had moved out about twelve o'clock nearly a mile in his front and taken a new alignment, which became a salient to the main line. Lee was deceived by it, and gave general orders to " attack up the Emmittsburg road, partially enveloping the enemy's left," which Longstreet " was to drive in." There was much behind Sickles, and Longstreet was attacking the Marye Hill of the position only. " Sickles's right was three fourths of a mile in front of Hancock's left," says Meade, " and his left one quarter of a mile in front of the base of the Little Round Top, leaving that key point unoccupied," which should have been seized by Longstreet before Meade did so with the Fifth Corps.

Sickles's right rested on the Emmittsburg road, and then his line was refused in the direction of the Round Top, making an angle at that point, his corps facing westerly and southerly. Lee wanted to get possession of this point to assail and carry the more elevated ground beyond, but the Fifth Corps had then been placed on the ground referred to, and the Sixth Corps, under sturdy old Sedgwick, had arrived, having marched thirty-four miles since 9 P. M. the previous night, and was in position before the two divisions of Lee's First Corps, which were in bivouac only four miles in rear of the field. The tired troops of the Sixth Corps were

massed on the Taneytown road, in the rear of Little
Round Top. When that gallant officer, Hood, was informed by his Texas scouts, that instead of attacking
Sickles's left he could turn Round Top, he sent three
officers, at different intervals of time, to Longstreet,
asking to do it, but in every case was answered, "General Lee's orders are to attack up the Emmittsburg
road." As he was going into battle Longstreet rode up,
and Hood again asked permission to make the move,
but was told, "We must obey General Lee's orders."
A strange acknowledgment from one who a few hours
before had disregarded them.

In twenty minutes Hood was borne from the field
badly wounded. The immense bowlders of stone so
massed as to form narrow openings offered great obstruction to the advance of Hood's right, and he was
exposed to a heavy fire from the crest of the high range
adjoining Little Round Top. Had Lee known the situation Hood would have been thrown more to his right.
He would not have succeeded in getting around the
Union left rear, for the Sixth Corps would have blocked
his way, but he would have secured and held Round
Top, and in all probability Little Round Top too, for
a plunging fire from big Round Top would have cleared
its crest and sides of Federal troops.

The Fifteenth Alabama, under the brave Colonel
Oates, was on the extreme right of Hood's line, and advanced up the southern slope of the Round Top in the
face of an incessant fire from behind rocks and crags
that covered the mountain side "thicker than grave-
stones in a city cemetery." Oates pushed forward until
he reached the top of Round Top; the Forty-seventh,
Alabama, on his left, also reached the top, where both
regiments rested a short time, and were then ordered
forward, and went down the north side of the mountain.
Oates saw at a glance the great value of the position,
but was obliged to obey orders and move on.

With the whole division there, some higher officer
with authority to act would have quickly placed artillery
on its summit, and the next day from that point Lee
would have been master of the situation.

The Alabamians, after reaching the level ground, came

upon a second line behind excellent fortifications of irregular rocks, from which was poured a murderous fire
into their very faces. After a prolonged and most courageous contest, these brave men were forced back and
retreated to the top of the mountain, losing out of six
hundred and forty-two men and forty-two officers in
the Fifteenth Alabama, three hundred and forty-three
men and nineteen officers, killed and wounded. When
nearly dark they fell back to the point from which they
advanced. This is ample proof that big Round Top was
not occupied by Northern troops at dark on the evening of the 2d. Buford's cavalry from that flank had been
sent away early in the day to guard supplies at Westminster. Over the splendid scene of human courage
and human sacrifice at Gettysburg there arises in the
South an apparition, like Banquo's ghost at Macbeth's
banquet, which says the battle was lost to the Confederates because "some one had blundered."

Longstreet's two divisions made a superb record, if
late when they began to fight. The attack on Sickles's
corps was bravely made and bravely resisted; Sickles's
left was turned, and had it not been that Warren sent a
brigade of the Fifth Corps and battery on Little Round
Top, that most important point might have been seized,
and, if held, decided the battle. For its possession there
was furious fighting. Sickles first, and then Warren,
Meade's chief engineer, called Meade's attention to
Little Round Top, and Sykes's column, then in motion, was hurried forward to save it. Sykes, Meade reports, was fortunately able "to throw a strong force on
Little Round Top, where a most desperate and bloody
struggle ensued to drive the enemy from it and secure
our foothold upon that important position." Longstreet
did not engage Sickles alone, for the Fifth Corps, part
of the Second, two regiments of the Twelfth, and a
brigade of the First Corps re-enforced him, while he received assistance from Anderson's division of Hill's
corps, which went into action with the left of McLaws's
division. Lee intended Ewell to make a diversion in
his front when he heard the guns of Longstreet, to be
converted into a genuine attack if opportunity offered;
but Ewell's infantry were under fire as soon as the

bugles blew the advance, so a demonstration could only be made by artillery, which was done.

If an early attack on the Union right had been successful, and Ewell, in consequence, had discovered confusion in his front, or that his enemy had weakened his line in his front, then his orders required him to attack because the "opportunity offered"; but Longstreet had not enveloped the enemy's left, and the Federal main line behind Sickles's outlying corps was intact. After the partial success there, Lee directed Ewell to assault with his whole corps. Johnson on the slopes of Culp's Hill to start first, then Early up Cemetery Hill, and Rodes to advance on Early's right.

Johnson had in front a rugged and rocky mountain difficult of ascent—"a natural fortification, rendered more formidable by deep intrenchments and thick abatis." His left brigade carried a line of breastworks of the Twelfth Corps, which (with the exception of Greene's brigade) had gone to support Sickles against Longstreet's attack, and captured prisoners and colors. The firing continued until late at night.

Early had only two of his brigades in the attack, and they made a brilliant charge. His Louisianians and North Carolinians continued to ascend the hill in the face of a blaze of fire, reached and entered the Union works, and while fighting for the battery were attacked by Carroll's brigade and three regiments of fresh troops, and forced to retire, but not in disorder. Had Rodes, as expected, been on his right, with Hill's troops co-operating, permanent possession of the line might have resulted, for Hancock would have been kept busy in his own front, and could not have sent troops to help Howard to hold Culp's Hill.

Rodes reports: "He had commenced to make the necessary preparations, but he had to draw his troops out of town by the flank, change the direction of the line of battle, and traverse a distance of twelve or fourteen hundred yards, while Early had to move only half that distance, without change of front, and before he drove in the enemy's skirmishers General Early had been compelled to withdraw." Gregg, with a division of Federal cavalry and horse artillery, was in position east of Slocum, and with dismounted cavalry and artillery made Johnson detach Walker's brigade to meet him.

When night stopped Johnson he was but a short distance from Meade's headquarters and the Union reserve artillery. A strong night attack then in conjunction with Stuart, who had at last reached the battlefield, would have secured the Baltimore pike in Meade's rear, and perhaps been productive of great results, all of which is easy to see now, but was difficult to know then.

The sentinel stars set their watch over a ghastly field of dead, dying, and wounded soldiers, lying in blue and gray heaps everywhere. Both contestants sought rest, but battlefields are not pleasant couches when dyed in the blood of numerous brave men, who, sleeping their last sleep, lie cold and quiet, while the piteous moans of the wounded pierce the ear and reach the heart. The armies rested without pleasant anticipations of the morrow, knowing well that at the roll call next evening many would not respond. The pickets alone were on duty, the surgeons alone at work.

When Lee summed up his day's work he found on his right that he had gained possession of Devil's Den and its woods, the ridge on the Emmittsburg road with its fine positions for artillery, and made lodgments on the bases of the Round Tops. On his left he had occupied a portion of the Federal works, which gave him an outlet on the Baltimore pike, and was partially successful against the Federal center by penetrating it with Anderson's division of Hill's corps, though ultimately expelled. His cavalry was all up except Jones's and Robertson's brigades; and J. E. B. Stuart was again in the saddle near him. The result of the day's operations, Lee reported, "induced the belief that with proper concert of action, and with the increased support that the positions gained on the right would enable the artillery to render the assaulting columns, we should ultimately succeed, and it was accordingly determined to continue the attack."

His opponent was doubtful what he should do next day; his efforts to prevent an entrance into his lines had been, on the whole, successful, but there had been moments when an unwelcome intrusion seemed inevitable. So he called another council of war at night, having called one before the fighting began. In a little front room not twelve feet square in the Liester House his commanders assembled. "Should the army attack or wait the attack of the enemy?" was the written question they were required to answer; and they voted—as they should have done, being in superior position, with interior lines—to wait, as Lee had done at Fredericksburg, for another attack, and found him more accommodating than Burnside.

General Lee had a difficult task: the lines of his enemy had grown stronger during the night; Slocum, Howard, Newton (in Reynolds's place), Hancock, Sickles, Sykes, and Sedgwick's troops were all before him, and on his right and left flank was a division of cavalry under Gregg and Kilpatrick respectively. The Union flanks, five miles apart on Culp's Hill and the Round Tops, were almost impregnable and difficult to turn. Lee's strategy at Chancellorsville was bold, but his determination to assault the left center of the Union army with his right corps and its supports was consummate daring. "Longstreet, re-enforced by Pickett's three brigades, which arrived near the battlefield during the afternoon of the 2d, was ordered to attack next morning," said Lee, "and General Ewell was directed to assail the enemy's right at the same time." During the night General Johnson was re-enforced by two brigades from Rodes and one from Early.

"General Longstreet's dispositions were not completed as early as was expected," continues Lee, and before he could notify Ewell the enemy attacked Johnson, was repulsed, and Johnson, thinking the fighting was going on elsewhere, attacked in his turn and forced the Union troops to abandon part of their intrenchments, but "after a gallant and prolonged struggle" was not able to carry the strongly fortified crest of the hill. "The projected attack on the enemy's left not having been made," Lee states, "he was enabled to hold his right with a force largely superior to that of General Johnson, and finally to threaten his flank and rear, rendering it necessary for him to retire to his original position about 1 P. M." The delay to attack on the right was but a repetition of the preceding day's tactics. It was impossible to move from different flanks a slow officer and a prompt one "at the same time." Longstreet was delayed, General Lee's report tells us, by a force occupying the high rocky hills * on the enemy's extreme left from which his troops could be attacked in reverse as they advanced, and he deemed it necessary to defend his flank and rear with the divisions of Hood and McLaws. " He was therefore re-enforced by Heth's division and two brigades of Pender's (Hill's corps), to the command of which Major-General Trimble was assigned, and General Hill was ordered to afford General Longstreet further assistance if requested, and avail himself of any success that might be gained."

Meade had sent Kilpatrick's division of cavalry—two brigades—under Merritt and Farnsworth, to his left; they arrived there about 12 M., and may have looked, mounted and dismounted, formidable on Longstreet's flank, but were not. Nothing could be gained by charging Longstreet's infantry in the position they held, and later the same day, when it was attempted, the cavalry were easily driven off and held at bay by two or three regiments of Law's brigade on the extreme right. Cavalry charges against infantry can not be made as formerly, because the improved range and rapidity of fire of cannon and small arms mow them down before they get to close quarters.

The Federal cavalry rendered the greatest assistance, however, to Meade, and his thanks are due to them for keeping out of the fight the fine infantry divisions of Hood and McLaws. The assaulting column was at last formed: Pickett's division of three brigades, five thousand men, was formed in two lines, Kemper on the right, Garnett on his left, and Armistead in the rear. Hill's troops—six small brigades—having passed through the fiery furnace of two days' battles, did not number seven thousand men; they were sent to support Longstreet's corps, but, curiously, were placed in an attacking column that had no support.

Four brigades—Pettigrew's, Davis's (a nephew of the

---

* There were none except on the Federal main line.

Southern President), Brockenbrough's, and Archer's (of Heth's division, under that fine officer Pettigrew, Heth having been wounded the day before)—were placed on Pickett's left, and two, Lane's and Scales's, about twenty-five hundred men of Pender's division, under Trimble, in a second line, while Wilcox's was to march on the extreme right to protect their flank. Thirteen thousand five hundred, or at most fourteen thousand troops, had been massed to attack an army, but with no more hope of success than had the Spartans at Thermopylæ, the English cavalry at Balaklava, or the "Old Guard" of the French at Waterloo.

Pickett's division formed at 10.30 A. M. in line nearly parallel and in rear of the rise upon which runs the Emmittsburg road, but rather diagonally to the Union position at the contemplated point of attack. Kemper's right was one thousand eight hundred and sixty yards distant from it, while Pettigrew prolonged the line somewhat *en echelon*. Pickett's first formation was in one line, Armistead, Garnett, and Kemper from left to right. Garnett's troops were twenty yards only in rear of Wilcox's brigade of Anderson's division, which had been sent out to the front between daylight and sunrise to protect guns then being put in position by Colonel E. P. Alexander, of the artillery. Wilcox states that the four brigade commanders were together nearly all the time before the artillery opened "in the yard near the Spangler House," and that there was no officer present in that open field at any time higher in rank than a brigade general, which differs with an account by the right corps commander, who has said that Lee rode with him "twice over the line to see that everything was arranged according to his wishes, and that there was no room for a misconstruction of his orders." Lee's object was to cut the Federal army at its left center as Marlborough split that of Vendôme in the same month one hundred and fifty-five years before, thinking perhaps its right wing could be destroyed first, or driven so far out of the way that he could turn in whole or part against the left wing before it could disentangle itself from the rocks and woods of the Round Tops.

It is fortunate three of General Lee's trusted staff

officers—Taylor, Venable, and Long—have recorded that the plan of assault involved an attack by Longstreet's whole corps, supported by one half of Hill's, or all of it if he called for it, or upon the bright shield of the Southern chieftain there might have been a lasting blot. Taylor, the adjutant general of the army, says it was originally intended to make the attack with Hood and McLaws, re-enforced by Pickett, and it was only because of the apprehensions of General Longstreet that his corps was not strong enough that General Hill was called on to support him; and Hill, in an official report, states that his troops were sent to Longstreet "as a support to his corps." Lee "rode along a portion of the line held by A. P. Hill's corps, and finally took a position about the Confederate center on an elevated point, from which he could survey the field and watch the result of the movement." Long says the order for the assault by the whole corps was given verbally by General Lee in his presence and that of Major Venable and other officers of the army.* Venable states that he heard the orders given to support Pickett's attack by McLaws and Hood, and that when he called General Lee's attention to it afterward he said: "I know it, I know it."

A consummate master of war such as Lee would not drive *en masse* a column of fourteen thousand men across an open terrene thirteen or fourteen hundred yards, nearly every foot of it under a concentrated and converging fire of artillery, to attack an army, on fortified heights, of one hundred thousand, less its two days' losses, and give his entering wedge no support! Why, if every man in that assault had been bullet proof, and if the whole of those fourteen thousand splendid troops had arrived unharmed on Cemetery Ridge, what could have been accomplished? Not being able to kill them, there would have been time for the Federals to have seized, tied, and taken them off in wagons, before their supports could have reached them. Amid the fire and smoke of this false move these troops did not know "some one had blundered," but had a right to feel that

---

* Memoirs of Robert E. Lee, by Long, p. 294.

the movement had been well considered, and ordered because it had elements of success. But there was no chance to write victory upon their fluttering flags. The pages of history which record the magnificent exhibition of human courage drip with the useless sacrifice of blood.

At 1 P. M. on July 3, 1863, two signal guns were fired by the Washington Artillery, and instantly the brazen throats of nearly one hundred and fifty cannon barked defiance at the grim, blue battle line in the distance. Two hours before, Colonel E. P. Alexander, of Longstreet's artillery, reported he was ready to open fire. Seventy-five guns were in position from the peach orchard on the right to the woods on the left, where the Third Corps rested, and near by, the other corps had as many more, under R. L. Walker. Salvos by battery were practiced, to secure greater deliberation and power. The Union batteries, under the alert and able chief of artillery, Hunt, were ready to return the greeting with seventy-seven guns [Meade had two hundred and twelve guns with his seven infantry corps, fifty with the cavalry, and one hundred and eight in reserve—three hundred and seventy in all], which were placed on the Second Corps line within the space of a mile. It was a grand spectacle, never before witnessed on this continent. Hunt reported he could see "from Cemetery Hill the Southern guns stretched, apparently in one unbroken mass, from opposite the town to the peach orchard, the ridges of which were planted thick with cannon. It was a cannonade to crush our batteries and shake our infantry previous to an assault." Most of the projectiles, he states, passed overhead and swept the ground in his rear. The Union batteries along the Second Corps front suffered heavily, however; wounded soldiers, dead and dying horses, and exploded caissons were on every side. Meade's headquarters, a little to the rear, had been plowed up by the swift-flying missiles, and had been abandoned, forcing Meade to go over to Powers Hill and seek shelter at Slocum's headquarters. The horses of many of his staff were killed. This sublime exhibition, with its great roar, throwing out huge black smoke clouds, was protracted for nearly two hours.

For waste of ammunition on both sides without compensating results it stands unequaled, and towers in unrivaled superiority above all similar displays. One hundred and fifty Southern guns raining metallic tons on the Northern infantry for two hours ought to have made a desert of their lines wide and broad enough to admit an army, but three days' work on a strong, natural, and defensive ridge had placed the infantry under cover, and resting securely, they were not "shaken," as those who participated in the charging column can testify. Hunt, with a soldier's instinct, knew so much noise meant a fight with other arms. Anticipating Meade's orders, he gave instructions to cease firing, to let his guns cool, ran up fresh batteries, replenished his limber chests and caissons, and "cleared decks" for the real work to follow. Amid the clamor produced by fiery flashes from nearly three hundred guns, the gray heroes selected to destroy an army lay close under the cover of a friendly ridge.

Longstreet was disappointed when he received the order to make this attack, and wanted to move to the Federal left, but Lee knew his relations with Meade had been too intimate during the last two days and the relative hosts too close for such tactical folly. His right corps chief says he took Pickett, who was to command the charge, to the crest of Seminary Ridge, pointed out the direction to be taken and the point to be assaulted, that he "could see the desperate and hopeless nature of the charge and the cruel slaughter it would cause," and that his "heart was heavy" when he left Pickett; that his objections to Pickett's battle had been overruled, and that the day was one of the saddest of his life, for he foresaw what his men would meet, and would gladly have given up his position rather than share in the responsibilities of that day. Lee, *au contraire*, was impatiently waiting to see Longstreet's corps and one half of Hill's, or, if necessary, all of it, break, with the force of the tempest which strands navies, through the hostile lines, if the testimony of his staff officers is worthy of credence.

The details of the attack were properly left to the officer who was to make it. Lee did not care whether Hood and McLaws attacked, re-enforced by Pickett and

Hill's troops, as at first intended, or whether Pickett
led and the remainder followed; but he wanted the
muskets numerous enough to plant the victory upon *his*
standards.   To fight to a finish a protracted struggle
was a bold conception; to give in audacious form a *coup
de grace* to his enemy was the acme of daring.   But Lee,
calm, quiet, conservative, and self-controlled, was fearless when occasion demanded, as a study of his campaigns will demonstrate.

Colonel E. P. Alexander, the commander of a battalion of artillery of a division of the First Corps, but
whose functions had been enlarged that day, a well-
equipped, intelligent, and active officer, was directed by
Longstreet to station himself at a point where he could
observe the effect of the great cannonade; and when he
discovered the Federal batteries crippled or silenced to
send word to Pickett, who, upon receipt of such notice, was
to move forward.   At twelve o'clock Alexander, with a
courier of Pickett's, stood on a favorable spot on the
left side of his guns, and was loaded, like them, with a
terrible responsibility.   In a short time a note from
Longstreet told him if the artillery fire did not drive off
the enemy or greatly demoralize them, he would "prefer he should not advise Pickett to make the charge,"
that he relied a great deal on his good judgment to determine the matter, and expected him to• let Pickett
know when the moment arrived.   That the responsibility and fate of a great battle should be passed over to
a lieutenant colonel of artillery, however meritorious he
might be, is, and always will be, a subject of grave comment.

Alexander replied that he could only judge of the
effect of the enemy's fire by the return fire, that his infantry was but little exposed to view, and that if there
was any alteration to this attack it should be carefully
considered before opening fire, for it would take all the
artillery ammunition left to test this one, and leave
none for another effort.   To this Longstreet responded
in another note that "the intention is to advance the
infantry if the artillery has the desired effect of driving
the enemy off, or the effect is such as to warrant us in
making the attack; when the moment arrives, advise

General Pickett, and of course advance such artillery as you can use in aiding the attack."

With Alexander at the time was General Wright, of Georgia, commanding a brigade in Anderson's division of Hill's corps, who practically told him to "brace up," that "it is not so hard to go there as it looks. I was nearly there with my brigade yesterday. The trouble is to stay. The whole Yankee army is there in a bunch." He was further stiffened by hearing "a camp rumor that General Lee had said he was going to send every man he had upon that hill." Afterward it occurred to him that he would ride over and see Pickett and feel his pulse, as it were, and how he felt about the charge. He ascertained that Pickett "seemed very sanguine, and thought himself in luck to have the chance."

By this time Alexander had risen to the height of the great occasion, and felt that he could not let the attack suffer through indecision on his part. "General," he then wrote to Longstreet, "when our artillery fire is at its best I shall order Pickett to charge." It was a fearful order for a subaltern to give, but what could he do? Pendleton, the chief of artillery of the army, offered him nine howitzers from Hill's corps, and Alexander put them in a safe place, to wait until he sent for them, intending to take these guns in advance of Pickett's infantry, nearly to musket range; but they could not be found when he wanted them.

General Pendleton had sent for a part of them, thinking Alexander would not need them; and those remaining had moved to another place, and his courier did not find them. At first Alexander thought he would turn the infantry loose in twenty minutes after the firing began; but when he looked at the enemy's batteries and knew his infantry was protected from the artillery by stone walls and swells of ground, "it seemed madness to launch men into that fire with three quarters of a mile to go at midday under a July sun," and he "could not bring himself to give the word." Then he wrote Pickett, who was in view and in rear of his observation point: "If you are coming at all you must come at once, or I can not give you proper support; but the enemy's fire has not slackened."

Two minutes afterward the Federal fire ceased, and some of his guns limbered up and vacated their positions. Then he wrote to Pickett, "For God's sake, come quick." Pickett had taken his first note to Longstreet and asked him if the time for his advance had come, and Longstreet bowed his assent; he could not speak, because he says he was convinced that Pickett was going to lead his troops to useless slaughter. Longstreet then rode to Alexander's position, and, upon being told the artillery ammunition might not hold out, directed Alexander to stop Pickett and replenish it; but was told there "was very little to replenish with," and that the enemy would recover from the effect of the fire if there was further delay, and just then, says he, Pickett swept out and showed the full length of the gray ranks and shining bayonets—as grand a sight as ever man looked on—and that on the left Pettigrew stretched farther than he could see. General Garnett, just out of the sick ambulance and buttoned up in an old blue overcoat, riding at the head of his brigade, passed just then, and saluted Longstreet. Alexander had served with him on the Plains before the war, and they "wished each other luck and a good-by"—a last farewell for Garnett. Alexander followed Pickett with eighteen of his guns which had most ammunition, whose fire was very effective against Stanard's Vermont troops. The small thunderbolt had been discharged, and the red-crested wave of assault rolled forward, destined to break into fragments on the murderous rocks athwart its path.

At the word of command, in compact form, with flying banners and brave hearts, the Southern column sprang to the attack. It was a magnificent and thrilling spectacle. "It is well war is so terrible," said Lee at Fredericksburg; "we should grow too fond of it." No such inspiring sight was ever witnessed in this country. Two long lines of angry men, who for two days had been trying to destroy each other, lay within cannon range. Their mutual roar of defiance had ceased when suddenly there swept into the intermediate space nine small brigades of infantry, whose "tattered uniforms and bright muskets," as the smoke of the battle lifted, were plainly in view of both.

The divisions of Hood and McLaws, one half of Hill's corps, and the whole of Ewell's stood like the fixed stars in the heavens as their comrades marched into the " jaws of death." Over the ridge, then a slight wheel to the left, and down the slope with confident step they advanced. The Codori farm building had been passed, and the guides instructed to take a directing point for the Union left center held by the Second Corps, exposing by the move their right flank to an enfilade fire from the batteries near and on little Round Top.

In an instant the masses in their front were preparing for the shock of battle. " Here they come ! Here they come ! Here comes the infantry ! " was heard on every side. At an average of eleven hundred yards the Union batteries began to open, and solid shot first tore through their ranks, but with no more effect than firing a pistol at the rock of Gibraltar. The skirmish lines, composed of the Sixteenth Vermont and One Hundred and Sixty-sixth Pennsylvania, and parts of Hall's brigade, were next encountered and brushed from their front, as the hurricane sweeps the breast of the mountain.

Screaming shells broke in front, rear, on both sides, and among them ; but the devoted band, with their objective point steadily in view, kept step to their music. The space between them and the Federal lines grew rapidly less, and soon they were in the " mouth of hell " within range of the well-protected infantry, and then there came a storm of bullets on every side, before which men dropped in their ranks as ripe fruit from a shaken tree. Still they closed the gaps and pressed forward, though canister was now raining on flanks and front with a terrible destructive fire. Brave men along the Union line could scarcely refrain from cheering at the perfect order and splendid courage exhibited by the Southern soldiers as they staggered on amid death and destruction, like a great pugilist, whose fast-failing strength denotes the loss of the contest, but resolves to stand in front of his antagonist to the last. What was left of the right of the assaulting troops struck the portion of the Federal lines held by Webb's brigade, Second Corps, and from the stone wall drove two Pennsyl-

vania regiments, capturing the three guns in charge of
Lieutenant A. H. Cushing and mortally wounding this
brave young officer, who had been fighting for an hour
and a half after being wounded in both thighs by the
cannonade.

The Confederate advance had been thrust into the
Federal works, and from the top of the stone wall their
battle flags were victoriously flying; the wedge had entered, but the power to drive it through was nearly a
mile distant and motionless. What could this handful
of heroes accomplish? A second line and a second
stone wall was in front of them, while from every side
hostile regiments rushed to overwhelm them. Their
three brigade commanders had fallen as the brave fall,
every field officer, except one, killed or wounded, while
their route was red with the blood of their dead and
dying. Kemper had been shot down, Garnett killed within twenty-five yards of the stone wall, while Armistead
and Lieutenant-Colonel Martin, of the Fifty-third Virginia, fell thirty-three yards beyond Webb's line, moving on with a few courageous followers to attack the
second line, which had been hurriedly formed. Brave
old Armistead's behavior deserves more than a passing
word. When the troops halted at the captured line, seeing still another force in his front, he drew his sword
for the first time and placed his hat on its point, so that
his men could see it through the dense smoke of the unequal combat, and sprang over the wall, crying: "Boys,
we must use the cold steel. Who will follow me?" It
is said that when the head of what had been so grand
an attack got within a few yards of the second defensive
line it consisted of Armistead, his lieutenant, Colonel
Martin, and five men; with the destruction of the head
the body perished, and one half of those who crossed
the road and followed Armistead were killed. To the
left of Pickett the four brigades under Pettigrew and
the two under Trimble charged. Archer's brigade, under Colonel B. D. Fry, of the Thirteenth Alabama, was
on the right and was the directing brigade of the whole
force. They made their assault in front of Hays's and
Gibbon's division, Second Corps, in the vicinity of
Ziegler's Grove. "Stormed at with shot and shell," this

column moved steadily on, closing up the gaps made and preserving the alignment.

"They moved up splendidly," wrote a Northern officer, " deploying as they crossed the long sloping interval. The front of the column was nearly up the slope and within a few yards of the Second Corps's front and its batteries, when suddenly a terrific fire from every available gun on Cemetery Ridge burst upon them. Their graceful lines underwent an instantaneous transformation in a dense cloud of smoke and dust; arms, heads, blankets, guns, and knapsacks were tossed in the air, and the moan from the battlefield was heard amid the storm of battle." Sheets of missiles flew through what seemed a moving mass of smoke, human valor was powerless, and the death-dealing guns were everywhere throwing blazing projectiles in their very faces. No troops could advance and live. The fiery onslaught was repulsed as Pickett's division had been, and then the survivors of both came back to their former positions, but not one half of the fourteen thousand. The famous charge was over.

Pickett's column had gone to the front four hundred yards, when Wilcox, whose brigade had not formed part of the attacking column, was ordered by Longstreet to advance in rear of Pickett's right. His twelve hundred Alabamans moved promptly, but were soon subjected to a concentrated fire from the artillery of the Federals; the distance between his left and the smoke-enveloped force which had preceded them increased; his own flank was threatened; he could not see, he reports, what had become of Pickett, so halted and returned, losing two hundred and four killed, wounded, and missing of his five regiments.

Lee was bitterly disappointed at the day's results. He had confidently expected to hurl at least one half of his army on his enemy, cut him in two, and then with a portion of it wheel to the left, annihilate Meade's right, and before troops of his left could recover and unite with the remainder of the army he proposed to give support to that portion of the attacking column holding them at bay. He was playing for big stakes and a decisive victory, which would bring in its train peace to his people and success to his cause. Reasoning, doubtless, that the tendency of separated wings of an army is to seek a reunion in the rear, he had thrown J. E. B. Stuart, with four brigades of cavalry and three batteries of horse artillery, around the Union right rear, so as to be in position to reach his opponent's lines of communication when driven from Cemetery Heights. Between Stuart and the Baltimore pike, two and a half miles off, directly in the rear of General Meade's center were three brigades of Union cavalry, some five or six thousand troops, with horse batteries, under General Gregg, both commands being between the York and Hanover roads.

Stuart had hardly reached the point where he proposed to rest and await developments before he saw, advancing to his front, a heavy line of dismounted sharpshooters, and a cavalry combat followed, creditable to the courage and skill of the contestants. Charges and countercharges were made on both sides, and in the resulting *mêlée* there was hand-to-hand fighting, during which the brave and distinguished General Wade Hampton was seriously wounded twice. Both sides claim a victory, but neither were driven beyond the positions originally occupied, to which they mutually retired from a midway charging ground — Stuart to watch his opportunity if Pickett was successful, as first contemplated; Gregg to watch Stuart. One of Stuart's brigades, under Jenkins, had only ten rounds of ammunition, and was therefore ineffective. The great battle of Gettysburg should be an object lesson to students of military science—first, as illustrating the difficulty of carrying strong positions behind which sheltered troops shoot with the latest improved guns; second, the great advantage of celerity of execution after carefully considered plans have matured—a qualification so conspicuous in the careers of Napoleon and Stonewall Jackson.

"This has been a sad day to us," said Lee, "but we can not always expect to win victories." It was a sad day for the South, for at that time it was "within a stone's throw of peace." Fate was against Lee; the high-water mark of Southern independence had been reached, and from that hour it began to ebb from the

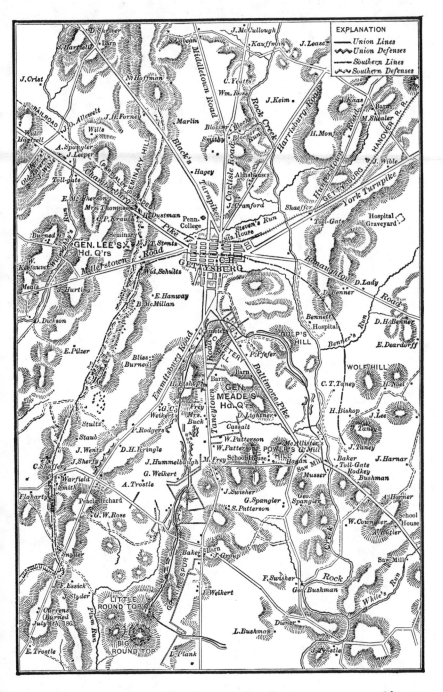

THE BATTLEFIELD OF GETTYSBURG, PA., JULY 1, 2, AND 3, 1863.

mountains of Pennsylvania until lost in the hills of Appomattox. "It is all my fault," Lee exclaimed, and proceeded in person to rally and reform his shattered troops. "There was much less noise, fuss, or confusion of orders than at any ordinary field day; the men were brought up in detachments, quietly and coolly," said an English colonel who rode by his side.

With that wonderful magnanimity which Lee so fully possessed he took all the responsibility on his own broad shoulders, and some of it must be put there. First, the discretion allowed, which separated him from his cavalry; second, the omission of positive orders to Ewell to advance on the evening of the 1st,* and the failure to replace an officer who opposed his plans with one who would have entered into them heartily, and readily cooperated with him to " whip the enemy in detail."

In justice to Stuart, it may be said that he did not foresee that a marching, intervening, hostile army would keep him away from Lee so long, or that he would be required before he could get to the Susquehanna, and it is fair to Ewell to recall his instructions about not bringing on a general battle, the absence of a division of his corps, and the false alarm of an advance on his left, after the battle of the 1st was over; but it will be difficult to comprehend how two thirds of his right corps, which lay four miles behind a battlefield the night before, did not get into action until 4 P. M. on the succeeding day, in spite of the "subdued excitement," the earnest aggressiveness, and the reported utterances of the commanding general; and hard to palliate the conduct of a corps commander, who acknowledged the reception of a direct order at 11 A. M. to attack with his troops then up, and did not get into action for five hours thereafter, because he took the responsibility of waiting for one of his brigades to arrive—a delay which

---

* General Meade told General Ewell, after the war, had he occupied Culp's Hill at 4 P. M., July 1st, it would have produced the withdrawal of the Federal troops by the Baltimore pike, Taneytown, and Emmittsburg roads. See letter to Colonel G. G. Benedict, Burlington, Vt., March 16, 1876.

allowed the remaining Union troops to reach the battle-field before he did.

The delay in getting two or three miles to the right, after the early hour Longstreet's command got near Lee's headquarters, can not be wholly laid at the door of his guide—Lee's engineer officer, Colonel S. P. Johnston. That officer states he called attention to the fact that the road they were following would pass over a hill in view of the Federal line, and pointed out a shorter route across a field screened from observation; but the corps commander preferred the road, and followed it to the top of the hill, then halted, and changed the position of his divisions in column. At that time the distance to the place Hood occupied was only a mile and a half, and could have been reached, Johnston says, in less than an hour. And, finally, if the positive assertions of Lee's staff officers can be believed—and they must be, from their well-known high characters—he disobeyed orders when he attacked with one third and not with his whole corps. Lee knew all the facts, for, in addition to what was said to Ewell, Early, and Pendleton, he told Governor Carroll, of Maryland, "that the battle would have been gained if General Longstreet had obeyed the order given him and attacked early instead of late; that Longstreet was a brilliant soldier when once engaged, but the hardest man to move in my army."

At 1 A. M. on the 4th General Imboden was sent for by Lee to get orders about the movements of the trains and ambulances which his command was to escort to the Potomac, and says that Lee, after expressing his admiration for the splendid behavior of the troops in "the grand charge," added, "and if they had been supported as they were to have been, but, for some reason not yet fully explained to me, were not, we would have held the position and the day would have been ours." Military critics are not able to understand why the official head of the officer did not "drop in the basket." They do not know Lee or his great heart, or that self-denying for himself, self-suffering for others, which made him live in a tent for fear of incommoding the occupants of houses, eat the most frugal food, or sit in the most uncomfortable chair, lest some other person might get it.

He could not harden himself to hew to the strict military line in whatever directions the chips might fall, but tried to believe that the reasons given for noncompliance with implied or direct instructions might possibly have some force, that the delays on the 2d could not be foreseen, and that the right flank of the assaulting column on the 3d might have suffered if not protected by two fine divisions of infantry. Captain Mangold, a German officer, Instructor of Artillery and Engineer in the Royal Academy, Berlin, and a distinguished and active military student, says the defect in General Lee's military character was a too kindly consideration for incompetent officers, resulting from an excess of good-nature.

The intelligent and impartial critic must admit the offensive dispositions of Lee skillful; the Union left on the 2d to a late hour was most vulnerable, and upon it the attack was designed; while the assault on the 3d, if not surrounded with as many chances of success as on the former day, was made at a point where, if successful, he would have secured the great roads to Baltimore and Washington. It was not unlike Napoleon's tactics at Waterloo; the artillery fire was opened there on the allied right, and Reille directed to carry Hougoumont, but the real plan of the great soldier was to break through Wellington's left center, which he ordered to be assaulted with D'Erlon's whole corps supported by Loban's, to drive back the allies on their own right, and secure the great road to Brussels before the helmets of the Prussian squadrons could be seen on the heights of St. Lambert. Lee, too, was infused with the confidence of the fighting power of an army "trembling with eagerness to rush upon the enemy," though occupying very strong positions and with a numerical superiority of at least thirty thousand.

The numbers on each side in this great contest have been variously given. Colonel Walter Taylor, Lee's adjutant general, among whose duties was the consolidation of the corps returns into the army returns, and who, after the war, examined the Federal archives

with much care, puts Meade's army at one hundred and
five thousand and Lee's at sixty-two thousand, and in his
Four Years with General Lee gives his reasons. The difference in these numbers is forty-three thousand, so the
statement that the Army of the Potomac had thirty
thousand more than the Army of Northern Virginia at
the battle of Gettysburg, seems conservative. Meade
did not use them all. His largest corps—the Sixth,
some sixteen thousand men—was in reserve and remained intact, only losing two hundred and forty-two
in killed, wounded, and missing. Lee had no reserve.

The loss in each army was about the same, Meade's
killed being 3,072; wounded, 14,477; missing, 5,434.
Lee's report claims nearly 7,000 prisoners, which makes
a total of 23,003. In Lee's, killed, 2,592; wounded,
12,709; missing, 5,150; total, 20,451. It will thus be
seen that not only is the aggregate loss nearly equal,
but that the killed, wounded, and missing respectively
does not vary much. Lee's loss was the greatest on the
two last days of the combat, Meade's the first day. In
the great struggle thirty thousand men were killed and
wounded in both armies. The killed, wounded, and
missing of the French at Waterloo have been reported
at twenty-five thousand, the Anglo-Belgians at fifteen
thousand, Napoleon having seventy-two thousand men,
and Wellington sixty-eight thousand, a total of one hundred and forty thousand, while the total of the Army of
the Potomac and the Army of Northern Virginia was
about one hundred and sixty thousand.

Both armies mourned the death of brave men and
competent officers. In the Army of the Potomac four
general officers were killed—Reynolds, Vincent, Weed,
and Zook—and thirteen wounded, viz., Hancock, Sickles,
Gibbon, Warren, Butterfield, Barlow, Doubleday, Paul,
Brook, Barnes, Webb, Stanard, and Graham. In the Army
of Northern Virginia five general officers were killed—
Pender, Garnett, Armistead, Barksdale, and Semmes—
and nine wounded, viz., Hood, Hampton, Heth, J. M.
Jones, G. T. Anderson, Kemper, Scales, and Jenkins.

Meade showed no disposition to assume the offensive
after Pickett's repulse. Like Lee at Fredericksburg, he
did not want to lose the advantages of position, and was

not certain the battle was over. The relative numbers in each army were still about the same, for their losses did not vary much, and the greater part of Lee's army was ready to receive him; he might have been repulsed in turn, producing perhaps other combinations and other results. Lee's ammunition was short, it is true—a fact which was unknown to him when the assault was made, but there was sufficient to still make "many tongues of flame." The natal day of American liberty broke upon both armies occupying nearly the same position, except that Lee had drawn in his left and retired it to a new line out of the town covering his lines of communication, and at the same time strengthened his right by defensive works at right angles to his main line to guard against any flank attack there.

The Southern leader knew on the night of the 3d that he could no longer resume the offensive, and there was nothing to be done except to withdraw from Meade's front. While not declining but rather inviting an attack on the 4th, he had started his long trains, his prisoners and such of his wounded as could bear transportation, back to the Potomac at Williamsport under a cavalry escort, and was busy in burying his dead and gathering up the badly wounded for treatment. At dark, in the midst of a heavy rain storm, the army was put in motion by the Fairfield road which crossed the South Mountain range seven miles south of Cashtown, being the direct road to Williamsport; but the rain and mud so impeded progress that the rear corps—Ewell's—did not leave Gettysburg until late in the forenoon of the 5th. With the exception of the loss of some wagons and ambulances by cavalry attacks, there was no interruption to the retrograde movement.

Lee reached Hagerstown, Md., on the 6th, the same day his trains arrived at Williamsport, a few miles distant. On account of the swollen condition of the Potomac from recent rains, and the destruction of the pontoon bridge at Falling Waters, a short distance below, by a roving detachment sent by French at Harper's Ferry, Lee could not cross his impedimenta or his army over the river, but sent the wounded and prisoners over in boats. Calm and quiet as usual, he had a line of de-

fense skillfully traced to cover the river from Williamsport to Falling Waters, and confidently awaited the sub-
sidence of the angry flood and the approach of his
opponent.　His cavalry had guarded his flanks in the
retreat and had saved his trains at Williamsport from
an attack of the Union cavalry before his army reached
there, and had a creditable affair at Hagerstown.

Six days after his arrival, Meade, marching from
Gettysburg by a different route from that pursued by
Lee, began to deploy his legions in his front.　Lee's
position was not altogether agreeable, a rapid, rolling, impassable river sweeping by his rear and a
powerful army going into line of battle in his front.
Meade was very deliberate and circumspect at Gettysburg, for he did not forget the bullet holes through his
hat when he attacked on his left at Fredericksburg, or
the knowledge gained of the unfavorable conditions
always surrounding an attacking force.　He was still
waiting further demonstrations from Lee, and when
night appeared without a movement he called a council of his corps commanders, and in writing asked:
First, "Shall the army remain here?"　Second, "If we
remain here shall we assume the offensive?"　And
then wanted to know if they deemed it expedient to
move toward Williamsport through Emmittsburg, or if
his enemy was retreating, should he pursue on the direct
line of his retreat.　The majority of the responses to
his first question were in favor of remaining at Gettysburg, but all voted against assuming the offensive, for
councils of war rarely, if ever, decide to fight.　Pleasonton, his cavalry commander, was very clamorous the day
before, for he says he rode up to Meade after the repulse of Pickett and said: "General, I will give you an
hour and a half to show yourself a great general; order
the army to advance while I take the cavalry, get in
Lee's rear, and we will finish the campaign in a week."

While this advice, if followed, might have been of
great benefit to Lee, its most remarkable feature was its
presumption.　Thirty-six hours after Lee abandoned the
field of Gettysburg, Meade, recalling Sedgwick, who had
gone toward Fairfield, marched from Gettysburg south
to Frederick, Md., thence slowly around by Middletown

and the old Sharpsburg battlefield to Lee's position. While he was moving around the horseshoe, General Lee, with a good start, had gone across from heel to heel, and, had it not been for high water, would have been in Virginia before the last of the Army of the Potomac left the battlefield of Gettysburg.

Meade telegraphed Halleck on the 6th that if he could get the Army of the Potomac in hand he would attack Lee if he had not crossed the river, but hoped if misfortune overtook him that a sufficient number of his force would reach Washington and, with what was already there, make it secure. Halleck, from his office in Washington, urged him to "Push forward and fight Lee before he can cross the Potomac." And Mr. Lincoln was cramming him with the comforting information that Vicksburg, on the Mississippi, had surrendered to Grant on July 4th, and that if "Lee's army could be destroyed, the rebellion would be over."

While waiting at Williamsport General Lee received the news of the capture (by raiding Federal cavalry) of his son, General W. H. F. Lee, who was wounded at Brandy Station on June 10th, and had been taken to Hickory Hill, the residence of the Wickhams, near Hanover Court House. He wrote Mrs. Lee: "I have heard with great grief that Fitzhugh has been captured by the enemy. Had not expected that he would have been taken from his bed and carried off; but we must bear this additional affliction with fortitude and resignation, and not repine at the will of God. It will eventuate in some good that we know not of now. We must all bear our labors and hardships manfully. Our noble men are cheerful and confident. I constantly remember you in my thoughts and prayers."

On July 12th, in camp near Hagerstown, Lee heard his son had been carried to Fort Monroe, and wrote: "The consequences of war are horrid enough at best surrounded by all the amelioration of civilization and Christianity. I am very sorry for the injuries done the family at Hickory Hill, and particularly that our dear old Uncle Williams in his eightieth year should be subjected to such treatment. But we can not help it and must endure it. You will, however, learn before this reaches you that our success at Gettysburg was not so great as reported. In fact, that we failed to drive the enemy from his position, and that our army withdrew to the Potomac. Had the river not unexpectedly risen all would have been well with us; but God in his all-wise providence willed otherwise, and our communications have been interrupted and almost cut off. The waters have subsided to about four feet, and if they continue, by to-morrow I hope our communications will be open. I trust that a merciful God, our only hope and refuge, will not desert us in this hour of need, and will deliver us by his almighty hand, that the whole world may recognize his power, and all hearts be lifted up in adoration and praise of his unbounded loving-kindness. We must, however, submit to his almighty will whatever that may be. May God guide and protect us all is my constant prayer."

The Federal commander could not decide to attack Lee, though he had been heavily re-enforced, and called another council of war on the 13th. All his corps commanders opposed attacking except two. Later that day Halleck telegraphed him to "call no council of war. It is proverbial that councils of war never fight. Don't let the enemy escape." The Washington assaults had been so continuous that the Union commander, in spite of the council's decision, advanced his army on the 14th with a view of attacking, if justified by a closer examination; but on the night of the 13th the Army of Northern Virginia recrossed the river at Williamsport, and on the pontoon bridge at Falling Water, which had been repaired. "The escape of Lee's army without another battle has created great dissatisfaction in the mind of the President," said Halleck, "and it will require an energetic pursuit on your part to remove the impression that it has not been sufficiently active heretofore." To a high-minded, meritorious, conscientious officer like Meade this censure was irritating. His request to be immediately relieved was declined on the ground that the dispatch was intended as a "stimulus."

The river was still deep though fordable. Ewell crossed by 8 A. M. on the 14th, but the passage of Longstreet and Hill was not completed until 1 P. M.

Had Meade made a vigorous attack in the forenoon he might have defeated and captured the portion of Lee's army which had not yet crossed. About 11 A. M. his cavalry, supported by artillery, appeared in front of Heth's division, which, acting as rear guard, was first encountered, and Brigadier-General Pettigrew, "an officer of great promise and merit," was killed. As soon as the bridge was clear Hill began to cross. The advance of the Federals cut off some of Hill's troops, who fell into their hands, as well as men from various commands, who, Lee reported, "lingered behind overcome by previous labors and hardships and the fatigues of a most trying night march, supposed to amount in all to about five hundred men, together with a few broken-down wagons and two pieces of artillery which the horses were not able to draw through the mud."

The Union commander made no effort to follow the Army of Northern Virginia across the river, except with Gregg's cavalry, which was attacked by two of Stuart's brigades and driven back with loss. Lee proceeded to Bunker Hill and its vicinity, intending to cross the Shenandoah and move into Loudoun County, Va.; but that river was past fording, and when it subsided, Meade, who had crossed the Potomac east of the Blue Ridge, seized the passes Lee designed to use and moved along the eastern slope of the mountains, as if to cut off Lee's communications with his capital. To prevent this, Lee crossed Chester Gap and went into Culpeper, his advance reaching Culpeper Court House July 24th. Afterward, with a view of placing his force in a position to move readily to oppose the enemy, should he proceed south, and to better protect Richmond, he made the Rapidan his defensive line. While at Bunker Hill he wrote Mrs. Lee on July 15th: " The army has returned to Virginia. Its return is rather sooner than I had originally contemplated, but, having accomplished much of what I proposed on leaving the Rappahannock—namely, relieving the Valley of the presence of the enemy, and drawing his army north of the Potomac—I determined to recross the latter river. The enemy, after centering his forces in our front, began to fortify himself in his position and bring up his troops, militia, etc., and those around Washington and Alexandria. This gave him enormous odds. It also circumscribed our limits for procuring subsistence for men and animals, which, with the uncertain state of the river, rendered it hazardous for us to continue on the north side. It has been raining a great deal since we first crossed the Potomac, making the roads horrid and embarrassing our operations. The night we recrossed it rained terribly ; yet we got all over safe, save such vehicles as broke down on the road from the mud, rocks, etc. We are all well. I hope we will yet be able to damage our adversaries when they meet us, and that all will go right with us. That it should be so we must implore the forgiveness of God for our sins and the continuance of his blessings. There is nothing but his almighty power that can sustain us. God bless you all."

And from Camp Culpeper, July 26, 1863 : "After crossing the Potomac, finding that the Shenandoah was six feet above fording stage, and having waited a week for it to fall so that I might cross into Loudoun, fearing that the enemy might take advantage of our position and move upon Richmond, I determined to ascend the Valley and cross into Culpeper. Two corps are here with me. The third passed Thornton's Gap, and, I hope, will be in striking distance to-morrow. The army has labored hard, endured much, and behaved nobly. It has accomplished all that could be reasonably expected. It ought not to have been expected to perform impossibilities, or to have fulfilled the anticipations of the thoughtless and unreasonable." Meade crossed the Potomac at Harper's Ferry and Berlin on pontoon bridges, moved through Loudoun and Fauquier, forcing Lee to conform to his movements, so that when he eventually took up the line of the Rappahannock, Lee occupied a parallel line on the Rapidan. From his tent in Culpeper he wrote Mrs. Lee on August 2d : "I have heard of some doctor having reached Richmond who had seen our son at Fort Monroe. He said that his wound was improving, and that he himself was well and walking about on crutches. The exchange of prisoners that had been going on has for some cause been suspended, owing to some crotchet or other, but I hope will soon be resumed, and that we shall have him back soon. The armies are in such close proximity that frequent collisions are common along the outposts. Yesterday the enemy laid down two or three pontoon bridges across the Rappahannock and crossed his cavalry and a large force of his infantry. It looked at first as if it were the advance of his army, and, as I had not intended to deliver battle, I directed our cavalry to retire slowly before them and to check their too rapid pursuit. Finding later in the day that their army was not following, I ordered out the infantry and drove them back to the river. I suppose they intended to push on toward Richmond by this or some other route. I trust, however, they will never reach there."

The Army of the Potomac seeming reluctant to advance, General Lee, having made his campaign, did not then propose to do so. In the rest following, his thoughts turned to the operations at Gettysburg, and the difficulties and dangers of the campaign. He grew sensitive under press criticisms, it being charged that nothing had been accomplished, and began to depreciate himself and rate too low his high military abilities. He had voluntarily assumed the faults of his subordinates. " The twin disasters of Gettysburg and Vicksburg," with a surrender of thirty thousand men at Vicksburg, were dispiriting, and the thought that he was held in some degree responsible for one of them seized him.

Gradually the conclusion was reached that perhaps he was occupying a position which might be filled by one who could render greater service with the means at command. On August 8th, from his camp in Orange, General Lee wrote the Southern President "that the general remedy for the want of success in a military commander is his removal," and that his reflections had prompted him " to propose to your Excellency the propriety of selecting another commander for this army "; that he did not know how far the expressions of discontent in the public journals extended in the army; his brother officers had been too kind to report it, and so far the troops too generous to exhibit it. He begged Mr. Davis to take measures to supply his place, because he could not accomplish what he himself desired; how, then, could he fulfill the expectations of others? He confessed his sight was not good, and that he was so dull that in making use of the eyes of others he was frequently misled.

"Everything, therefore," he wrote, "points to the advantages to be derived from a new commander, and I the more anxiously urge the matter upon your Excellency from my belief that a younger and abler man than myself can readily be obtained. I know that he will have as gallant and brave an army as ever existed to second his efforts, and it would be the happiest day of my life to see at its head a worthy leader—one that would accomplish more than I can perform and all that I have wished. I hope your Excellency will attribute my request to the true reason—the desire to serve my country and to do all in my power to insure the success of her righteous cause.

"I have no complaints to make of any one but myself. I have received nothing but kindness from those above me, and the most considerate attention from my comrades and companions in arms. To your Excellency I am specially indebted for uniform kindness and consideration. You have done everything in your power to aid me in the work committed to my charge without omitting anything to promote the general welfare. I pray that your efforts may at length be crowned with success, and that you may long live to enjoy the thanks of a grateful people."

The reply of Mr. Davis is refined in sentiment and tender in phrase: "I admit the propriety of your conclusions that an officer who loses the confidence of his troops should have his position changed, whatever may be his ability; but when I read the sentence I was not at all prepared for the application you were about to make. Expressions of discontent in the public journals furnish but little evidence of the sentiment of the army. I wish it were otherwise, even though all the abuse of myself should be accepted as the results of honest observation. Were you capable of stooping to it, you could easily surround yourself with those who would fill the press with your laudations, and seek to exalt you for what you had not done, rather than detract from the achievements which will make you and your army the subject of history and the object of the world's admiration for generations to come. But suppose, my dear friend, that I were to admit, with all their implications, the points which you present, where am I to find the new commander who is to possess the greater ability which you believe to be required? I do not doubt the readiness with which you would give way to one who could accomplish all that you have wished, and you will do me the justice to believe that if Providence should kindly offer such a person for our use I would not hesitate to avail myself of his services.

"My sight is not sufficiently penetrating to discover such hidden merit, if it exists, and I have but used to you the language of sober earnestness when I have impressed upon you the propriety of avoiding all unnecessary exposure to danger, because I felt our country could not bear to lose you. To ask me to substitute you for some one, in my judgment, more fit to command, or who would possess more of the confidence of the army or of the reflecting men of the country, is to demand an impossibility. It only remains for me to hope that you will take all possible care of yourself, that your health and strength will be entirely restored, and that the Lord will preserve you for the important duties devolved upon you in the struggle of our suffering country for the independence which we have engaged in war to maintain."

The commanding generals of both armies, upright in character and scrupulous in the performance of their respective duties, were naturally sensitive to criticism, and the curious spectacle was presented that, after a gigantic and fierce contest against each other, both should ask to be relieved from their commands. Fancy the grim veterans of the Army of Northern Virginia paraded in their camp grounds in that month of August, 1863, to hear the announcement that Mr. Davis had accepted General Lee's resignation. There would have resounded from flank to flank "*Le roi est mort!*" but when the "younger and abler man" assumed command, the mummies of the Nile, or the bones beneath the ruins of Pompeii, could not be more silent than the refusal of these heroes to shout to Robert E. Lee's successor, "*Vive le roi !*"

The Angel of Peace would have appeared in the hour General Lee bid farewell to the Army of Northern Virginia and mounted Traveler to ride away, for the rapid termination of the war would have simplified the duties of "the younger and abler man." Traveler, the most distinguished of the general's war horses, was born near the Blue Sulphur Springs, in West Virginia, and was purchased by General Lee from Major Thomas L. Broun, who bought him from Captain James W. Johnston, the son of the gentleman who reared him. General Lee saw him first in West Virginia and afterward in South Carolina, and was greatly pleased with his appearance. As soon as Major Broun ascertained that fact the horse was offered the general as a gift, but he declined, and Major Broun then sold him. He was four years old in the spring of 1861, and therefore only eight when the war closed. He was "greatly admired for his rapid, springy walk, high spirit, bold carriage, and muscular strength." When a colt he took the first premium at the Greenbrier Fair, under the name of Jeff Davis.* The general changed his name to Traveler. He often rode him in Lexington after the war, and at his funeral Traveler followed the hearse. He was appraised by a board in August, 1864, at $4,600 in Confederate currency.

Though Lee was ready to cover his face with his mantle and die like the Athenian, it would have broken his heart to have separated himself from troops who, with empty haversacks, shoeless feet, tattered uniforms, but full cartridge boxes and bright bayonets, had with such undaunted courage nobly supported him at all times. And where would the Southern President have found an officer who was superior in vigorous strategy, fertility of resource, power of self-command, influence over others, patient endurance, or one more composed in victory or dignified in defeat ?

An English officer described him in the Pennsylvania campaign as having courtly manners and being full of

---

* General Grant also had a horse called Jeff Davis.

dignity; that he had none of the small vices—such as smoking, drinking, chewing—and his bitterest enemy never accused him of any of the greater ones; that Lee was the handsomest man of his age that he ever saw—"broad shoulders, well made, well set up, a thorough soldier in appearance." He generally wore a long gray jacket with three stars on the collar, blue pants tucked into his Wellington boots, and a high felt hat. He never carried arms,* was always neat in dress and person, and on the most arduous marches looked smart and clean, and, "what is very pleasing to an Englishman, he rides a handsome horse, which is extremely well groomed." The removal from the command of the Union army of such an excellent officer as Meade would have been an act of kindness to the Confederates, the appreciation of which would have been increased if Halleck had been appointed his successor.

The season of repose which now followed was much enjoyed by both sides. Lee was employed in looking after the welfare of his troops, for their rations and clothing were both getting scarce. He took great interest in the religious progress of his soldiers, and did everything in his power to promote sacred exercises in his camps. The relative location of the hostile forces made partial reduction of their numbers comparatively safe. If the Army of the Potomac did not want a battle, it could fall back on the defenses of Washington. If the Army of Northern Virginia declined the encounter, it could withdraw to the Richmond line.

At this period it was determined to re-enforce General Bragg in the West with two divisions of Longstreet's corps, to enable him to defeat the Federal General Rosecrans, which he did at Chickamauga, while the third division—Pickett's—should be detached for duty south of the James River.

Meade then crossed over the Rappahannock and occupied Culpeper and the country between the two

---

* He always carried a pistol in the holster on the left of his saddle, because more convenient to reach when dismounted, and ammunition in the right holster. This pistol always hung over his bedpost in Lexington after the war and was discharged after his death—not a barrel missing fire.

rivers, so as to be closer to Lee should he decide to re-sume offensive operations, but his plans were set aside by troops being detached from him also. The Eleventh and Twelfth Corps under Hooker were sent West, and a considerable number to South Carolina and New York —to this latter place to prevent riots resulting from an enforcement of the recruiting draft. Meade and Lee for some weeks, with reduced forces, simply observed each other. From his camp near Orange Court House, August 23, 1863, General Lee wrote Mrs. Lee that he hears his son is "doing well, is walking about, and has everything he wants except his liberty. You may see that a distinguished arrival at Washington is chronicled in the papers of that city—Miss Catherine Burke. She is reported to have given interesting accounts of the Lee family. (This was one of the colored servants from Arlington.) My camp is near Mr. Erasmus Taylor's house, who has been very kind in contributing to our comfort. His wife sends us every day buttermilk, loaf bread, ice, and such vegetables as she has. I can not get her to desist, though I have made two special visits to that effect. All the brides have come on a visit to the army—Mrs. Ewell, Mrs. Walker, Mrs. Heth, etc. General Meade's army is north of the Rappahannock, along the Orange and Alexandria Railroad. He is very quiet." And again, September 4, 1863: "You see I am still here. When I last wrote, the indications were that the enemy would move against us any day; but this past week he has been very quiet, and seems at present to continue so. I was out looking at him yesterday from Clark's mountain. He has spread himself over a large surface, and looks immense, but I hope will not prove as formidable as he looks. He has, I believe, been sending off some of his troops to re-enforce Rosecrans, and has been getting up others; among them several negro regiments are reported. I can discover no diminu-tion." And on September 18, 1863, from the same camp he tells her: "The enemy state that they have heard of a great reduction in our forces here, and are now going to drive us back to Richmond. I trust they will not succeed. But our hope and refuge is in our merciful Father in heaven."

CHAPTER XIII.

CAMPAIGN IN VIRGINIA.—BRISTOL STATION.—MINE RUN.—WILDERNESS.

For three weeks Lee waited, hoping to be attacked, and then suddenly, on October 9th, put his own army in motion with a design of making a wide circuit around his antagonist's right, to manœuvre him out of Culpeper to his rear, and force him to deliver battle by intercepting his march toward Washington. He left a small force of infantry and cavalry to hold his old line on the Rapidan, which the Union cavalry attacked the next day, and was repulsed and pursued rapidly toward Culpeper Court House, where Stuart was driving Meade's rear guard under Kilpatrick.

The Army of Northern Virginia, numbering, without Longstreet's corps, forty-four thousand, was placed by a wide swing, *via* Madison Court House, around Meade's right, and in forty-one miles reached Culpeper Court House to find the Army of the Potomac had been promptly withdrawn to the north bank of the Rappahannock. Lee then essayed another swing around the circle, and forced a passage over the Rappahannock at the White Sulphur Springs on the 12th, roughly handling Gregg's cavalry division, which guarded Meade's right, marching eighteen miles that day; but while Lee was moving north, Meade, not hearing from him, recrossed the river and moved south to Culpeper again, leaving one corps on the river. As soon as Gregg reported Lee's position, the Union troops were countermarched in haste, and on the morning of the 13th, after a night march, were again north of the Rappahannock. That morning Lee only went to Warrenton—seven miles. He was still the nearer to Washington, and ahead. A five-mile march from Warrenton to Auburn, or nine miles to Warrenton Junction, or fourteen to Bristoe, would have placed him in position to strike as Meade's columns marched South. The 13th, after a march of a few miles, was passed at Warrenton by Lee, while Meade's rear, under Warren, bivouacked five miles away at Auburn. That delay, which General Lee says was due to being out of rations, allowed Meade to pass beyond him.

The next morning, the 14th, Ewell was sent *via* Auburn to Bristoe, and A. P. Hill by New Baltimore to the same place. The former struck Warren's rear, the latter the head of his column at Bristoe, and attacked it with only two brigades, which were repulsed by the masterly management of Warren, who seized with Hays's division a cut on the railroad. So skillfully was this done that Warren captured from Hill four hundred and fifty prisoners, five pieces of artillery, and two stand of colors, and passed his whole corps across the broad run, following Meade's rear without further molestation, though one half of Lee's army might have been hammering his head and the other half his tail.

The adventurous Stuart got caught near Auburn on the night of the 13th between two marching parallel columns of Federal infantry, and, with a portion of his cavalry and some guns, lay *perdue* during the night within a mile or two of Meade's headquarters and some four hundred yards from General Warren's rear division, but dexterously extricated his whole command next morning.

While Lee lay at Warrenton on the 13th, Meade was twenty miles south of Bristoe, but, in spite of his night march on the 12th, succeeded in placing his whole army beyond Lee on the 13th, except Warren, who stopped opposite him and only a few miles away. Meade fell back to Centreville and its vicinity, where he prepared to offer battle. The position might have been turned, as in the case of Pope, but the immense works around Washington held out hospitable arms in case Meade again declined the contest. Nothing was accomplished except to demonstrate that the army which first left Gettysburg first assumed the offensive in Virginia.

When General Lee retired, Meade followed, and his advance cavalry, under Kilpatrick, was routed by Stuart wheeling about and attacking it in front, while another portion of his horsemen assailed their flank at Buckland on the Warrenton road in an affair christened "Buckland races."

"I have returned to the Rappahannock," wrote General Lee to his wife, October 19, 1863; "I did not pursue with the main army beyond Bristoe or Broad Run. Our advance went as far as Bull Run, where the enemy was intrenched, extending his right as far as Chantilly, in the yard of which he was building a redoubt. I could have thrown him farther back, but I saw no chance of bringing him to battle, and it would have only served to fatigue our troops by advancing farther. If they had been properly provided with clothes I would certainly have endeavored to have thrown them north of the Potomac; but thousands were barefooted, thousands with fragments of shoes, and all without overcoats, blankets, or warm clothing. I could not bear to expose them to certain suffering on an uncertain issue." The Union troops around Warrenton waited for the railroad which the Confederates had torn up to be repaired.

From Camp Rappahannock, October 28, 1863, the General said to Mrs. Lee: "I moved yesterday into a nice pine thicket, and Perry is to-day engaged in constructing a chimney in front of my tent which will make it warm and comfortable. I have no idea when F. [his son, W. H. F. Lee] will be exchanged. The Federal authorities still resist all exchanges, because they think it is to our interest to make them. Any desire expressed on our part for the exchange of any individual magnifies the difficulty, as they at once think some great benefit is to result to us from it. His detention is very grievous to me, and, besides, I want his services. I am glad you have some socks for the army. Send them to me. They will come safely. Tell the girls to send all they can. I wish they could make some shoes, too. We have thousands of barefooted men. There is no news. General Meade, I believe, is repairing the railroad, and I presume will come on again. If I could only get

some shoes and clothes for the men I would save him
the trouble."

On November 1st Lee reviewed his cavalry corps,
much to the delight of J. E. B. Stuart, who, like Murat,
was not averse to the pomp of war. The cavalry chief
was in all his glory with his "fighting jacket" and dancing plume. The cavalry corps numbered—by the returns of the day before—seven thousand nine hundred
and seventeen. Many squadrons were absent on picket
and other detached duty, but at least five thousand sabers
passed his front. It was an inspiring sight. The privates, who were graceful riders, owned the horses, which
were generally good.

From Camp Rappahannock, November 1, 1863, he
wrote Mrs. Lee: "I have just had a visit from my nephews, Fitz, John, and Henry. They looked very well. The
former is going on a little expedition. As soon as I was
left alone I committed them in a fervent prayer to the
care and guidance of our heavenly Father. I think my
rheumatism is better to-day. I have been through a
great deal with comparatively little suffering. I have
been wanting to review the cavalry for some time, and
appointed to-day with fear and trembling. I had not
been on horseback for five days previously and feared I
would not get through, but, to my surprise, I got along
very well. The Governor was here and told me Mrs.
Letcher had seen you recently."

Meade now decided to get closer to Lee so as to be
in a position where he in turn could take the offensive,
and began to advance on November 7th. His left wing of
three corps, under French, was directed to cross the Rappahannock at Kelly's Ford; his right, under Sedgwick,
at Rappahannock Station. French progressed without
much opposition, but Sedgwick found a *tête-de-pont* with
lines of rifle trenches on the north side of his crossing
point. This was a fort or redoubt, being in part some
old intrenchments, but without a ditch and open to the
south, with which it was connected by a pontoon bridge.
It was occupied by two of Early's brigades under Colonels Penn and Godwin, with four pieces of artillery.
Daylight was fast disappearing; Russell's division of
the Sixth Corps was in line of battle in its front, with

Upton's brigade deployed as skirmishers. Russell thought he could carry the work, so Sedgwick gave the order. The conditions were favorable to success; the wind blowing strong from south to north, the firing could not be heard by the supporting batteries on the south side, so Russell stormed the redoubt with so much dash that it was captured before the Southern force on the south side knew it.

It was a brilliant *coup de main*, reflecting credit on those engaged, particularly the Maine and Wisconsin regiments. The troops assailed by a division amounted to one thousand six hundred and seventy-four, and so rapid was the Federal rush that only six were killed and thirty-nine wounded; eight captured flags were carried to Meade's headquarters by Russell and Upton, preceded by a band, and then sent in charge of Russell to the War Department at Washington, after the manner Napoleon's trophies went sometimes to Paris, but the Secretary sent the gallant officer word he was too busy to see him, so the concluding ceremony was not as ostentatious as planned. Lee withdrew on the night of the 8th to his lines behind the Rapidan, while Meade reoccupied his camp between the rivers. Both sides wanted a battle, but on ground of their own selection.

About this time the city of Richmond presented General Lee with a house. In consequence, the President of the City Council received the following letter, dated November 12, 1863: "I assure you, sir, that no want of the appreciation of the honor conferred upon me by this resolution, or insensibility of the kind feeling that prompted it, induces me to ask, as I most respectfully do, that no further proceedings be taken with reference to the subject. The house is not necessary for the use of my family, and my own duties will prevent my residence in Richmond. I shall therefore be compelled to decline the generous offer, and trust that whatever means the City Council may have to spare for this purpose may be devoted to the relief of the families of our soldiers in the field who are now in need of assistance, and more deserving of it than myself."

The general was still worried about his imprisoned son, who was an affectionate, lovable fellow, as well as a fine officer, and wrote: "Camp, November 21, 1863.—I see by the papers that our son has been sent to Fort Lafayette. Any place would be better than Fort Monroe with Butler in command. His long confinement is very grievous to me, yet it may all turn out for the best."

The people of Richmond, not being able to do anything for General Lee, doubled their acts of kindness to his wife. She was deeply grateful for their love and friendship, and so informed her husband, who replied from camp, November 25, 1863: "The kindness exhibited toward you as well as myself by our people, in addition to exciting my gratitude, causes me to reflect how little I have done to merit it, and humbles me in my own eyes to a painful degree. I am very sorry the weather was so bad that I could not give the President a review. I wanted him to see the troops, and wanted them to see him."

Over two weeks elapsed, after the Army of the Potomac and the Army of Northern Virginia were face to face along the Rapidan, before Meade executed a well-considered plan to turn Lee's right and either throw him nearer to his capital or beat him before he could concentrate his force, which was much scattered, in order to secure supplies more easily. At dawn on November 26th his columns were put in motion to cross the Rapidan at its lower fords, reach the country south of the river and east of Orange Court House, and there be directed to Orange Court House on the roads leading from Fredericksburg to that point. He was in light marching order, well supplied with ten days' rations, and his wagons were left north of the Rapidan; but around his Culpeper camp hovered Southern cavalry scouts, and Lee early knew Meade's preparations and movements.

Flowing northerly into the Rapidan and almost at right angles was Mine Run, on whose western banks Lee rapidly deployed a line of battle, his great engineering talent assisting him in locating his troops, and with great rapidity breastworks were constructed too strong to be assailed. When Meade reached the line of Mine Run *en route* to Orange Court House, Lee's army confidently blocked his way. He could not make a direct assault, so the Union commander resolved to attack both wings, by Sedgwick on Lee's left, by Warren on his right; but the latter, formerly an engineer officer, who was to begin, reported that closer reconnoissance disclosed his enemy's lines too were well defended. There was no alternative left Meade except to withdraw, which he did during the night.

To Mrs. Lee the general gave his account of the affair from Camp Rapidan, December 4, 1863: "You will probably have seen that General Meade has retired to his old positions on the Rappahannock without giving us battle. I had expected, from his movements and all that I had heard, that it was his intention to do so, and after the first day, when I thought it necessary to skirmish pretty sharply with him on both flanks to ascertain his views, I waited patiently his attack. On Tuesday, however, I thought he had changed his mind, and that night made preparations to move around his left next morning and attack him. But when day dawned he was nowhere to be seen. He had commenced to withdraw at dark Tuesday evening. We pursued to the Rapidan, but he was over. Owing to the nature of the ground, it was to our advantage to receive rather than to make the attack, and as he about doubled us in numbers, I wished to have that advantage. I am greatly disappointed at his getting off with so little damage, but we do not know what is best for us. I believe a kind God has ordered all things for our good."

In the latter part of December General W. H. F. Lee, still in prison, was overtaken by a great calamity. His wife and his two children died. When General Lee was informed of their death he wrote:

Sunday Morning, December 27, 1863.

Custis's dispatch which I received last night demolished all the hopes in which I had been indulging during the day of dear Charlotte's recovery. It has pleased God to take from us one exceedingly dear to us, and we must be resigned to his holy will. She, I trust, will enjoy peace and happiness forever, while we must patiently struggle on under all the ills that may be in store for us. What a glorious thought it is that she has joined her little cherubs and our angel Annie [his daughter] in heaven! Thus is link by link of the strong chain broken that binds us to earth, and smoothes our passage to another world. Oh, that we may be at last united in that haven of rest, where trouble and sorrow never enter, to join in an everlasting chorus of praise and glory to our Lord and Saviour! I grieve for our lost darling as a father only can grieve for a daughter, and my sorrow is heightened by the thought of the anguish her death will cause our dear son, and the poignancy it will give to the bars of his prison. May God in his mercy enable him to bear the blow he has so suddenly dealt and sanctify it to his everlasting happiness!

Rations and clothing for his men and forage for his animals were sources of great anxiety to him. In the midst of winter many of his brave men were without blankets and barefooted. From camp, January 24, 1864, he wrote: "I have had to disperse the cavalry as much as possible to obtain forage for their horses, and it is that which causes trouble. Provisions for the men, too, are very scarce, and with very light diet and light clothing I fear they suffer; but still they are cheerful and uncomplaining. I received a report from one division the other day in which it was stated that over four hundred men were barefooted and over a thousand without blankets."

Difficulties surrounded him on every side! From camp, February 6, 1864, he wrote Mrs. Lee: "I received your letter some days ago, and last night your note accompanying a bag of gloves and socks and a box of coffee. Mrs. Devereux sent the coffee to you, not to me, and I shall have to send it back. It is so long since we have had the foreign bean that we no longer desire it. We have a domestic article, which we procure by the bushel, that answers very well. You must keep the good things for yourself. We have had to reduce our allowance of meat one half, and some days we have none. The gloves and socks are very acceptable, and I shall give them out this morning. The socks of Mrs. Shepherd are very nice, but I think it is better to give them to the soldiers than to dispose of them as you suggest. The soldiers are much in need. We have received some shoes lately, and the socks will be a great addition. Tell 'Life' [his youngest daughter] I think I hear her needles rattle as they fly through the meshes."

The very day after this letter was written these destitute men joyfully sprang to arms. General Butler, at Fort Monroe, but commanding the Department of

Virginia and North Carolina, thought, from what he had heard, he could capture Richmond with cavalry from the Peninsula—the general ability of Butler was great, his military qualifications small. Brigadier-General Wister marched from New Kent Court House to the Chickahominy and marched back again. A portion of the Army of the Potomac, in pursuance of Butler's plan, were to cross the Rapidan and threaten Lee, to prevent him from dispatching troops to Richmond by rail. This Army-of-the-Potomac diversion was under gallant old Sedgwick, who was commanding the army during Meade's temporary absence.

General Lee gives his account of the diversion in a letter dated Camp, Orange County, February 14, 1864: " This day last week we were prepared for battle, but I believe the advance of the enemy was only intended to see where we were and whether they could injure us. They place their entire loss in killed, wounded, and missing at twelve hundred, but I think that is exaggerated. Our old friend Sedgwick was in command. In reference to Rob " (his youngest son, who was a private in the Rockbridge artillery battery, and who Mrs. Lee desired to be with his father), " his company would be a great pleasure and comfort to me, and he would be extremely useful in various ways, but I am opposed to officers surrounding themselves with their sons and relatives. It is wrong in principle, and in that case selections would be made from private and social relations rather than for the public good. There is the same objection to going with Fitz Lee. I should prefer Rob's being in the line in an independent position, where he could rise by his own merit and not through the recommendation of his relatives. I expect him here soon, when I can better see what he himself thinks. The young men have no fondness for the society of the old general. He is too heavy and sombre for them."

Again Lee's rest was disturbed by a diversion on his left flank by infantry and cavalry, in order to allow Kilpatrick, with some four thousand horsemen, to ride past his right, make a dash for Richmond, release the Union prisoners, and disturb the peace generally. It accomplished nothing. The idea originated in Wash-

ington, it is said, for Meade disapproved it. Upon one
of Kilpatrick's officers—Colonel Ulric Dahlgren, who
was killed—some remarkable papers were found, including a sort of an address to the soldiers to burn
Richmond, "kill Jeff Davis and Cabinet," and do many
other horrible things. The United States Government
promptly disclaimed any knowledge of such orders, and
so did Meade. Dahlgren was a daring, dashing young
fellow, but was too enthusiastic. It is certain the
papers published at the time were taken from his person. The Southern President laughed as he read over
the originals in his office, and turning to Mr. Benjamin, his Secretary of State, who was with him, said,
when he reached the word Cabinet, "That is intended
for you, Mr. Benjamin."

Lee was now making every effort to promote the
efficiency of his army for the great struggle he knew
must come in the spring. On March 18, 1864, he
wrote: "I arrived safely yesterday." (He had been
on a short visit to Richmond.) "There were sixty-
seven pairs of socks in the bag I brought up instead
of sixty-four, as you supposed, and I found here three
dozen pairs of beautiful white-yarn socks, sent over
by our kind cousin Julia and sweet little Carrie, making one hundred and three pairs, all of which I sent
to the Stonewall brigade. One dozen of the Stuart
socks had double heels. Can you not teach Mildred
[his daughter] that stitch? They sent me also some
hams, which I had rather they had eaten. I pray that
you may be preserved and relieved from all your troubles, and that we may all be again united here on earth
and forever in heaven." His wife and daughter and
other friends of the cause were knitting socks for the
soldiers, and the commanding general had brought some
of them back to the army *himself!*

The cavalry, for the better subsistence of men and
horses, had been moved back to Charlottesville for the
winter, and, not having much to do, some of the officers
proposed to dance. General Lee wrote his son Robert,
then belonging to that arm of service, from Camp Orange
Court House, January 17, 1864: "I inclose a letter
for you which has been sent to my care. I hope you

are well and all around you. Tell Fitz I grieve over the hardships and sufferings of his men in their late expedition. I would have preferred his waiting for more favorable weather. He accomplished much under the circumstances, but would have done more in better weather. I am afraid he was anxious to get back to the ball. This is a bad time for such things. We have too grave subjects on hand to engage in such trivial amusements. I would rather his officers should entertain themselves in fattening their horses, healing their men, and recruiting their regiments. There are too many Lees on the committee. I like them all to be present at battles, but can excuse them at balls. But the saying is, 'Children will be children.' I think he had better move his camp farther from Charlottesville, and perhaps he will get more work and less play. He and I are too old for such assemblies. I want him to write me how his men are, his horses, and what I can do to fill up his ranks."

From camp, April 2, 1864, he wrote Mrs. Lee: " Your note with the socks arrived last evening. I have sent them to the Stonewall brigade; the number all right—thirty pairs. Including this last parcel of thirty pairs, I have sent to that brigade two hundred and sixty-three pairs. Still, there are about one hundred and forty whose homes are within the enemy's lines and who are without socks. I shall continue to furnish them till all are supplied. Tell the young women to work hard for the brave Stonewallers." And once more, from Orange County, April 21, 1864: " Your note with bag of socks reached me last evening. The number was correct—thirty-one pairs. I sent them to the Stonewall brigade, which is not yet supplied. Sixty-one pairs from the ladies in Fauquier have reached Charlottesville, and I hope will be distributed soon. Now that Miss Bettie Brander has come to the aid of my daughters, the supply will soon be increased."

The preparations of the Government of the United States for prosecuting the war in 1864 were on a vast scale. Stupendous efforts were made to crush armed resistance everywhere. An irresistible invasion was designed to destroy " rebellion " from center to circumference. The principal objective points were the two principal armies of the Confederacy—the one then at Dalton, Ga., under J. E. Johnston, and the other in Virginia under Robert E. Lee. The Washington authorities decided that there should be only *one* head to direct these immense plans of campaign, and it determined the head should be on the shoulders of General U. S. Grant. This officer was commissioned lieutenant general on March 9, 1864, and placed in the command of all the armies of the United States. His success in the West had brought him prominently to the notice of Mr. Lincoln. In the exercise of supreme command his especial attention was to be bestowed upon General Lee, and his headquarters were to be established with Meade's army. Hiram Ulysses, as christened, or Ulysses S. Grant, as he was registered at West Point, was a native of Ohio, who graduated at the United States Military Academy in 1843; was assigned to the Fourth Infantry and became regimental quartermaster; served with distinction in Mexico, and was bold and adventurous—for instance, at Molino del Rey he climbed to the roof of a house and demanded the surrender of Mexicans occupying it; and at another point placed howitzers in the belfry of a church to drive his enemy out of a defensive position near the City of Mexico. After eleven years in the United States Army he resigned, was afterward on a small farm near St. Louis, and then became a clerk in 1860 in the hardware and leather store of his father in Galena, Ill. When the war broke out he offered his services to his Government in writing, but received no reply, and was afterward made colonel of the Twenty-first Illinois Regiment by the Governor of that State. He was thirty-nine years old when he confronted Lee, and was not to be despised as a commander. He was fortunate in being placed in command at a time when the resources of men and means of the Confederacy were smaller than ever before, and his peculiar direct tactics could be employed in consequence of superiority in numbers, for he admitted to Meade he never manœuvred. With two hostile armies of approximate strength commanded by Lee and Grant in a campaign demanding a high order of military sagacity and a familiarity with strategic science, the chances of success would be with Lee.

The Union chief had, however, many excellent qualities for a soldier. He was taciturn, sturdy, plucky, not afraid of public responsibility or affected by public opinion. There was no ostentation in his position, and to an outsider he was not as showy as a corporal of the guard. Meade had a Solferino flag with a golden eagle in a silver wreath for his headquarters. When General Grant first saw it unfurled, as they broke camp for the Wilderness campaign, he is reported to have exclaimed, "What's this? Is imperial Cæsar anywhere about here?"

Lee, who had campaigned against McClellan, Pope, Burnside, Hooker, and Meade, had now to measure swords with Grant. Sheridan, too, made his first bow in Virginia at this time. He had served with distinction under Halleck in the West, and when Grant asked for the best officer that could be found to be his chief of cavalry, Halleck suggested Sheridan, and his suggestion was instantly adopted. This officer graduated in 1853 at West Point, was a classmate of McPherson, Schofield, and Hood, had served in the Fourth Infantry—Grant's old regiment—and was thirty years of age when he first drew his sabre in Virginia in 1864.

The Federal Government laid at the feet of Grant its unbounded treasures. His Virginia army was increased to one hundred and eighteen thousand men of all arms and three hundred and eighteen cannon, as some authorities have it; but the report of the Union Secretary of War to the first session of the Thirty-ninth Congress gave one hundred and forty-nine thousand one hundred and sixty men. Some idea of its vast proportions may be had by the statement that one hundred and eighteen thousand men, disposed for battle two ranks deep, would cover a front of thirty miles, while sixty-two thousand men, similarly disposed, would cover only sixteen miles. Grant says, in his Memoirs, his wagon train would have reached on a single road from the Rapidan to Richmond, sixty-five miles. To meet this grand "On to Richmond!" Lee had sixty-two thousand men and two hundred and twenty-four field guns.

At midnight on May 3d Grant began to cross the Rapidan at Ely's and Germanna fords, some distance below Lee's right, but at the very points Lee had predicted, a few days before, in a conference with his officers. The Army of the Potomac was now consolidated into four corps—Second, Fifth, and Sixth—commanded by Hancock, Warren, and Sedgwick, and the Ninth under Burnside. (Under the consolidation the First and Third Corps disappeared.) When the sun sank to rest on the 4th, Grant had crossed his whole army, and on the morning of the 5th confidently started across the Wilderness in a southerly direction to force Lee to accept battle.

Crossing the river without opposition relieved his mind from serious apprehensions; but it was no part of Lee's plan to resist him there. Indeed, he generally gave plenty of room on his side of a stream for his opponent to form, hoping to make it as difficult for him to get back as it was easy for him to get over. It is safe to say he would never have formed his troops at the water edge of the Bull Run fords as Beauregard did at the first Manassas, but upon commanding positions back, with only sufficient force to delay and give notice of the crossing. Had Beauregard done this, he would not have had his left turned, for the opportune arrival of Johnston alone gave him the battle. Grant's move did not, as he expected, compel Lee to fall back toward Richmond and fight a defensive battle; but hardly had he filled the Wilderness with men as thick as "raging locusts" than Lee marched to meet and attack him.

Early on the morning of May 4th he bade adieu to the three or four tents near Orange Court House which had been the winter home of himself and personal staff, and with Ewell's corps, two detached brigades, and two divisions of Hill's corps, with artillery and cavalry, marched by the most direct course for Grant's army. Longstreet, who was near Gordonsville then with two divisions (Pickett's was south of James River), was directed to follow, as well as Anderson's division of Hill's corps which was on Rapidan Heights. On the 5th, in two columns, Lee advanced by the old turnpike and plank roads, which, leading east from Orange Court

House *via* Chancellorsville to Fredericksburg, were being crossed by Grant at right angles, who was marching south. Ewell was on the former and Hill moved on the latter road, and by Hill's side at the head of the column rode Lee, while his cavalry marched still farther to the right. Grant did not know of the proximity of the Confederates, though Ewell's advance had bivouacked on the night of the 4th three miles from Warren's corps, which was at the intersection of the Germanna road with the old turnpike, called Wilderness Tavern. So on the 5th Grant gave orders for his army to move in two columns—Fifth and Sixth Corps from Wilderness Tavern to Parker's Store, where their route intersected the plank road, and Hancock from Chancellorsville to Shady Grove Church. Warren, as a military precaution, threw Griffin's division up the old turnpike toward Orange Court House to protect his moving column, and Ewell, coming down the pike about this time, met and engaged Griffin, and the battle of the Wilderness began, for shortly thereafter Hill became engaged with a force at Parker's Store.

Hancock, whose troops formed Grant's left advance, was stopped, and the heads of his columns turned toward Parker's Store to meet Hill. Grant discovered that he had Lee's army on his right marching flank and would have to fight in the Wilderness.

As Ewell and Warren became more engaged, lines of battle were formed—Warren in the center and Sedgwick on his right, and afterward Hancock on his left. On the plank road Hill's left did not connect with Ewell's right. Getty's division, Sixth Union Corps, was sent first to retard Hill's progress, and then Hancock's corps arrived. Ewell and Warren had their encounter, and then Hancock and Hill took up the fighting. Warren gained ground at first against Ewell, but was in turn driven back with the loss of three thousand men, while Hancock's vigorous assaults on Hill's two divisions on the plank road were successfully resisted.

Night came and both sides prepared for the morrow's desperate battle, when Lee and Grant each proposed to assume the offensive. It was a terrible region to receive or deliver battle: thousands of acres of tangled forest, interlaced undergrowth, scrub oaks, dwarf pine and cedar, were on every side, with here and there a few narrow roads. Grant did not manœuvre, so it suited him in that respect; but his preponderance of numbers could not be made effective, and his men were in each other's way, just as Hooker's had been in this same Wilderness nearer to Chancellorsville. Artillery was of but little service, mounted cavalry none; no man could command the battle, because no man saw but a few yards around him. Two hundred thousand men were mixed up in a wild, weird struggle, like a hole full of snakes with their tails intertwined. On the morning of the 6th, Sedgwick, Warren, Burnside (now up), and Hancock faced Ewell and Hill, while Longstreet was rapidly marching to Hill's position.

Lee's plan was to feign attack on Grant's right and assail his left flank, Grant's to attack along his whole line. Sedgwick was attacked before his orders required him to attack; but Longstreet was not yet up, nor was Anderson's division of Hill's corps. So Lee had to wait on his right; but Hancock * with nearly forty thousand men did not wait, but rushed on Heth and Wilcox's division of Hill's corps, and finally carried their whole front and drove their right back in some confusion. Lee's right wing was threatened with disaster; neither Longstreet's corps nor Anderson's division of Hill's had arrived. The former left his camp near Gordonsville at 4 P. M. on the 4th, and marched that afternoon sixteen miles. The next day, when Hill and Ewell were fighting, he resumed his march, lost his way, had to retrace his steps, and finally went into camp on the night of the 5th near Verdiersville, some ten miles in the rear of where Hill and Ewell had been fighting, broke camp at 12.30 A. M. on the 6th, and reached Hill, whose two divisions had been assailed by six Federal divisions under Hancock, just in time to save Lee's right.

Lee has stated since the war † that he sent an officer to Longstreet to stay with him and show him the roads,

---

* His own corps and Getty's division of the Sixth, and Wadsworth's of the Second Corps; afterward he was re-enforced by a division of the Ninth Corps.

† Told his son, General G. W. Custis Lee.

anticipating he would move him when Grant crossed the Rapidan, but Longstreet discharged him, and, by taking the wrong road, did not get up to his position until May 6th, when he might have joined him on the 5th. Gordonsville was only ten miles from Orange Court House and the court house thirteen from Verdiersville, where Longstreet bivouacked the night of the 5th. By the route he should have marched he could have reached Verdiersville in twenty miles. He consumed one day and a half of precious time in getting there. Though late in his arrival, no one could have made dispositions to assume the offensive with more celerity, or have attacked with more promptness. Hancock was now in turn assailed. Holding his front with three brigades under Gregg, Benning, and Law, Longstreet threw four—viz., Mahone's, G. T. Anderson's, Wofford's, and Davis's—around Hancock's left flank. Attacked in flank and front, Hancock's troops were routed and driven rapidly back three quarters of a mile to his line of works.

It was a well-planned, well-executed movement. As Longstreet rode down the plank road at the head of his column he came opposite to his brigades, which had made the flank movement, and were drawn up parallel to the plank road and some sixty feet from it. He was mistaken in the thick woods for the Federals, and a volley was fired at him by his own men, which severely wounded him and killed General Jenkins by his side. It was most unfortunate. Jackson at Chancellorsville had been shot down by his troops at the moment of victory, and here in the Wilderness in the midst of a deserved success, and when Longstreet had given orders for the advance of his whole force, he, too, fell by the fire of his own men. His fall arrested the movement. R. H. Anderson was taken from Hill's corps and put in command of Longstreet's, and Mahone given Anderson's division; but the change required time.

Lee had in person been in the midst of Hill's troops, restoring confidence and order, and his presence, as he rode along the lines on his gray horse, was most inspiring. In splendid style the troops of Longstreet went into battle. As the Texans swept by with enthusiastic cheers Lee rode with them in the charge until those brave fellows insisted he should go back. A sergeant actually seized his horse, and just then Colonel Venable, of his staff, called his attention to Longstreet sitting on his horse on a little knoll not far away, and he rode off and joined him. The Texas soldiers were, like "Scipio's veterans, ready to die for him if he would only spare himself." General Lee had served in Texas when in the United States Army, and was familiar with the State and her people; he had the highest admiration for the Texas troops, as the whole army had. They were descendants of the adventurous spirits who first settled Texas, were good marksmen, and their eyes could look down a gun barrel without a tremor of the lid. He asked Senator Wigfall, of Texas, to get him more Texans, and said after Sharpsburg if he had more of them he would feel more certain of results.

Hancock's troops were driven behind their log breastworks, upon which a later attack failed. The same afternoon Gordon, with three brigades of Ewell's corps, made a successful assault on Sedgwick's line, Wright's division; but night stopped the contest. During the day severe combats had taken place between the cavalry of the two armies on the Furnace and Brock roads and at Todd's Tavern, with no decisive results. Both armies were locked in their temporary breastworks. Lee could no longer hope to successfully assail the immense masses of Grant, and on Grant, imperturbable and calm, the impression had been made that to again "attack along the whole line" would be hopeless. It was a terrible field for a battle—a region of tangled underbrush, ragged foliage, and knotted trunks. "You hear the saturnalia, gloomy, hideous, desperate, raging unconfined. You see nothing, and the very mystery augments the horror; nothing was visible, and from out the depths came the ruin that had been wrought in bleeding shapes borne in blankets or on stretchers." The Wilderness was a tract of gloom, and over all was the shadow of death. Grant had lost * seventeen thousand six hundred and sixty-six men, his opponent one half that number. Science had little to do with such a struggle. "Two wild

---

* Fifteen thousand three hundred and eighty-seven.—Humphreys.

animals were hunting for each other; when they heard each other's footsteps they sprang and grappled." It was like a huge Indian fight, and different from any other battle. The two days' contest on this unique ground can be compared to nothing in military records, ancient or modern. "Charges were made and repulsed, the men in the lines scarcely seeing each other. Soldiers fell, writhed, and died unseen, their bodies lost in the bushes, their death groans drowned in the steady, continuous, never-ceasing crash."

To add to the horrors, the woods caught fire and many wounded men perished in the flames. Lee's army was Grant's objective point, but the objective point sought Grant, and the latter, after remaining in its front all of the 7th, deliberately marched away during the night and attempted to interpose between it and Richmond at the strategic point of Spottsylvania Court House, fifteen miles southeast of the battlefield. His infantry did not begin to march until 9 P. M.; but during the afternoon a portion of his wagon train was first moved toward Chancellorsville, and the watchful Stuart, who had cavalry on all sides, at once reported the fact. Lee divined Grant's plans, and promptly ordered Anderson, commanding Longstreet's corps, to move around General Hancock's left to the same point.

Warren, the Union van, was much delayed during the night. Meade's large escort was first in his way, and then Merritt's cavalry, which was preceding his march, failed to drive the Confederate cavalry in his front, but finally gave the right of way to Warren; it was then daylight. Indeed, so effectual was the resistance of a dismounted division of Confederate cavalry that Warren's leading division, Robinson's, did not get in sight of Spottsylvania Court House until after 8 A. M., and then found Anderson's troops in his front, which, marching by a parallel road, had replaced the cavalry and received Robinson with a savage musketry fire, severely wounding him and driving back his line. As the Union troops came up they formed on Warren, while Anderson formed the nucleus for Lee's lines. The race had been finished, and Lee, between Grant and Richmond, cried Check!

Both armies intrenched, and two formidable lines of earthworks sprang into existence. For twelve days Grant repeatedly and vainly assaulted at different points his opponent's position. The small army in gray stood as immovable as the mountains. Twice Grant assailed on the 8th of May, five times on the 10th, and on the 12th, when he succeeded in carrying a salient. On the 18th and 19th he attacked again. Grant lost eighteen thousand three hundred and ninety-nine men, making forty thousand * in the two weeks of overland travel, or in numbers equal to two thirds of Lee's whole army. The "hammering" process was costly, but might ultimately succeed as long as General Lee lost one man to his three, because the Federal reservoir of human supply was so much greater.

Here the Union commander lost one of his best and bravest corps commanders—John Sedgwick, of the Sixth Corps. On the 11th, while walking along a portion of his line, a ball from the gun of a Confederate sharpshooter pierced his cheek under the left eye. A soldier in front of him a moment before dodged to the ground as he heard the shrill whistle of a bullet. Sedgwick touched him gently with his foot, telling him to get up, he was ashamed of him, and remarked, "They could not hit an elephant at this distance." The man rose, saluted, and said, "General, I dodged a shell once, and if I hadn't it would have taken my head off." Sedgwick laughed and told him to go to his place in line, and was immediately afterward killed. He had two mourners—his friend and his foe. With Lee and others who had served with him before the war he was a great favorite; he was so true, so faithful in all of life's relations. In his death the Army of the Potomac lost an arm. General Horatio G. Wright succeeded to the command of his corps.

The Union assault of the 12th was partially successful. There was a salient on Ewell's works, and its V-shape was enwrapped by the Federals. Hancock's corps was brought from Grant's right during the stormy night before and massed twelve hundred yards from the

---

* Thirty-seven thousand three hundred and thirty-five.—Humphreys.

work, and at half-past four in the morning, with Barlow's and Birney's divisions in advance, successfully and gallantly stormed the position, capturing General Edward Johnson, one of Ewell's division commanders, between three and four thousand prisoners, and twenty pieces of artillery.

Lee had detected the weak point, and had already commenced a line across the base of the triangle. It was well conceived, as his right center would have been pierced and his army divided. This second line received the victorious rush of the Federals, who were in turn driven back with great slaughter to the salient, where the fiercest and most deadly fighting in the war took place. Lee concentrated his efforts to retake the salient, Grant to hold it. The musketry fire with its terrific leaden hail was, beyond comparison, the heaviest of the four years of war. In the bitter struggle, trees large and small fell, cut down by bullets. Grant re-enforced Hancock by the Sixth Corps and by two of Warren's divisions, after failing to get Warren and Burnside in at other points. He then had over half of his army—over fifty thousand men—holding on to the advantage gained, while Lee, equally as determined, purposed to retake the position. Rodes's, Ramseur's, and Gordon's troops, three brigades under McGowan, Perrin, and Harris, and two battalions of artillery were "put in," and all day the savage contest raged.

Late in the night Lee drew back his troops on the new line. On the 11th he thought Grant was preparing for another move, and that night ordered most of the cannon out of the salient so as to be ready for a counter move, all of which a deserter from Johnson's line reported, and which may account for the assault which, though favored by a climatic condition, was courageously executed. Johnson during the night, becoming suspicious of ominous sounds in his front, ordered them back, but was attacked before getting them in position. The famous salient has been called the "bloody angle." Some trenches almost ran with blood, while others had to be cleared of dead bodies. The lips of the dead were incrusted with powder from biting cartridges. It was a horrible scene. Two days before

Upton's brigade of the Sixth Corps broke through the Confederate lines. General Lee was very sensitive about his lines being broken. It made him more than ever personally pugnacious, and ready and desirous to lead in their recapture.

On this occasion the general rode to the head of the column forming for the charge, took off his hat, and pointed to the captured line; but General John B. Gordon proposed to lead his own men, and no one in the army could do it better, for he was in dash and daring inferior to none. "These are Virginians and Georgians who have never failed," said Gordon. "Go to the rear, General Lee." And appealing to his men, he cried: "Is it necessary for General Lee to lead this charge?" "No, no," they exclaimed; "we will drive them back if General Lee will go to the rear." The Union troops were hurled back in the charge that followed and the line re-established. Grant again had no alternative but to flank—or fall back. He had written Halleck, addressing him as "Chief of the Staff of the Army," that he was sending back his wagons for a fresh supply of provisions and ammunition, and proposed "to fight it out on this line if it takes all the summer," and asking that "re-enforcements be sent as fast as possible, and in as great numbers." Grant, who said he never manœuvred, states in his official report that from the 12th to the 18th "was consumed in manœuvring and awaiting the arrival of re-enforcements," which to the number of some thirty-five thousand were sent to him from the Middle and Washington Departments.

When Grant reached Spottsylvania Court House he determined to throw Sheridan's cavalry corps between Lee and Richmond, tear up his communication, and be in position to dispatch what was left of Lee after he had crushed him in Spottsylvania, just as Hooker had proposed to use Stoneman at Chancellorsville. So on the 9th of May, at 6 A. M., Sheridan, clearing widely Lee's right, turned toward Richmond. Ten thousand horsemen riding on a single road in columns of fours made a column thirteen miles in length, and with flashing sabres and fluttering guidons were an imposing array. Stuart was not long in ascertaining and following the movement, but had only three brigades available for that purpose, one of which, a small North Carolina brigade, was directed to follow Sheridan's rear, while the other two, riding over the chord of the arc traveled by Sheridan, reached Yellow Tavern, six miles from Richmond, on the 11th, before Sheridan, and were thrown directly across his route. Here a fierce though most unequal cavalry combat ensued, the numbers of the contestants being as ten thousand to three thousand. Nearly all day these two cavalry brigades held their ground in Sheridan's front, while General James B. Gordon's small force attacked his rear, losing their gallant commander, giving General Bragg, commanding the Richmond defenses, ample time to get some troops from below Richmond, so that when Sheridan finally broke through them and arrived in front of the defenses his valor was replaced by prudence, and he marched around them, making a long circuit, and rejoined his army after an absence of over two weeks. It would have been the usual record of nothing accomplished and a broken-down command, except that at Yellow Tavern the Confederate cavalry chieftain was mortally wounded, and died the following day in Richmond. This sad occurrence was more valuable to the Union cause than anything that could have happened, and his loss to Lee irreparable. Stuart was the "best cavalry officer," said General Sedgwick, the late Sixth Corps commander, who had been an officer in that arm of service, "ever foaled in America." He was the army's eyes and ears—vigilant always, bold to a fault; of great vigor and ceaseless activity, he was the best type of a *beau sabreur*. He had a heart ever loyal to his superiors, and "duty" was "the sublimest word in the language" to him.

In a letter from Spottsylvania Court House, May 16, 1864, General Lee said to his wife: "As I write I am expecting the sound of the guns every moment. I grieve the loss of our gallant officers and men, and miss their aid and sympathy. A more zealous, ardent, brave, and devoted soldier than Stuart the Confederacy can not have. Praise be to God for having sustained us so far. I have thought of you very often in these eventful days. God bless and preserve you." And in his order, May

20th, announcing the death of Stuart to the army, he said: "Among the gallant soldiers who have fallen in this war, General Stuart was second to none in valor, in zeal, and in unflinching devotion to his country. His achievements form a conspicuous part of the history of this army, with which his name and services will be forever associated. To military capacity of a high order and to the nobler virtues of the soldier he added the brighter graces of a pure life, guided and sustained by the Christian's faith and hope. The mysterious hand of an all-wise God has removed him from the scene of his usefulness and fame. His grateful countrymen will mourn his loss and cherish his memory. To his comrades in arms he has left the proud recollections of his deeds and the inspiring influence of his example."

Lee was much attached to Stuart and greatly lamented his death; he had been a classmate and friend at West Point of his son Custis, and his whole family were fond of him. In his tent in the hours of the night, when he knew not what the morrow would bring forth, his thoughts constantly turned to the great cavalryman whose saber had been sheathed forever. Stuart's superb personal gallantry was conspicuous to the last. His death wound was received while from the back of his horse he was steadying dismounted men by words of encouragement, and firing his pistol over their heads at the Federal cavalry in close proximity.

Once more General Grant, "deeming it impracticable," he said, to make any further attack upon the enemy at Spottsylvania Court House, drew his troops from Lee's front on the night of the 20th and started on another flank march, this time for the North Anna; but when his leading corps, the Fifth, reached that stream on the afternoon of the 23d Lee was there too, still between his capital and his enemy, where he again exclaimed, Check! To Mrs. Lee, from Hanover Junction, May 23, 1864, the general wrote: "General Grant, having apparently become tired of forcing his passage through, began on the night of the 20th to move around our right toward Bowling Green, placing the Mattapony River between us. Fearing he might unite with Sheridan and make a sudden and rapid move upon Richmond, I determined to march to this point so as to be in striking distance of Richmond, and be able to intercept him.   The army is now south of the North Anna.   We have the advantage of being nearer our supplies and less liable to have our communication trains, etc., cut by his cavalry, and he is getting farther from his base.   Still, I begrudge every step he takes toward Richmond."   Lee's position south of the North Anna River was an admirable one, and his defensive lines showed the skill of the engineer.   Grant crossed his army at two points some miles apart.   Lee kept his center on the river, but retired his wings so that the Union forces in front of them were separated from each other, and could only hold communication by crossing the river twice or by breaking through his army.   It was his intention to assume the offensive here, and to strike Grant a stunning blow; but, unfortunately, he was taken ill.   Colonel Venable, of his staff, writes that as he lay in his tent he would say in his impatience: "We must strike them.   We must never let them pass us again."   He wanted to seize the advantage of his position.   Warren, on the right of Grant's army and Hancock on the left, supposed, after crossing the river, they could unite, but were totally unprepared to find Lee's lines of battle between them.   The Confederate army was posted upon two long lines of an obtuse-angle, whose strong apex rested on the river.   It had received its first re-enforcements in the force under Breckinridge and Pickett's division, and Hoke's brigade of Early's division—in all seventy-five hundred men.   And the whole army was in good condition; but its commanding general was ill, and so was one of his corps commanders, while another had been disabled by wounds.   Lee's sickness made it "manifest he was the head and front, the very life and soul of his army."

Grant did not like his North Anna situation.   He said he found Lee's position stronger than either of the two previous ones, so he withdrew "during the night of the 26th and moved *via* Hanovertown to turn the enemy's position by his right."   Hanovertown is on the Pamunkey River, which is formed by the North Anna and South Anna; the Mattapony is formed by the junction of the Mat, Ta, Po, and Ny, and the two make the York.   When

Grant crossed the Pamunkey and marched south he was
on the Peninsula, and when his advance reached Cold
Harbor on May 31st he was on McClellan's former
grounds. Across his path, and once more between him
and Richmond, was the Army of Northern Virginia. Its
commander was again in the saddle, and again he heard
Check! The duty of keeping from his capital an army
nearly three times as great in number as his own was
an occupation sufficient to employ all the military skill
of Lee; but so great were the resources of the United
States Government that it was able to converge several
armies on the one objective—Richmond. Butler was
to concentrate the troops of his department, largely re-
enforced from detachments hitherto operating in the
South, and march on Petersburg, twenty miles south
of Richmond, destroy the railroads running south, and
invest the Confederate capital from his side of the
James, so as to be in position to co-operate with Grant
when his conquering banners should wave from the other
side. The columns of Crook and Averell were to debouch
from West Virginia, and Sigel to advance up the great
Valley of Virginia, capture Staunton, Charlottesville, and
Lynchburg, and then be guided by future instructions.

But the co-operating armies did not co-operate;
Butler, with an army of over thirty thousand men,
"marched up the hill and then marched down again."
On transports he conveyed his troops up the James
River, landed them at City Point, and above, at Bermuda Hundred, in the angle between the junction of
the Appomattox River flowing from Petersburg and the
James from Richmond, and intrenched across the narrow neck of land on a line some three miles only from
the Richmond and Petersburg Railroad, less than ten
from Petersburg and twenty from Richmond. Here he
established his *entrepôt* of supplies, and from this base
proceeded to play his part in the campaign drama. He
was too slow, for after some preliminary success, just as
he was about to achieve fame, he was attacked by
Beauregard on the morning of the 16th, and driven
within his fortified lines, in front of which Beauregard
threw up works stretching from river to river. He was
caged, so far as any further advance from that point

could be made, for Beauregard had locked him up and put the key in his pocket, or, as General Barnard, Grant's chief engineer, expressed it—and General Grant adopted the phrase in his report—he was in a bottle which Beauregard had corked, and with a small force could hold the cork in place. Beauregard had been brought from the Southern Department, and his command consisted of detachments from South Carolina, Georgia, and other points. His plans to defeat Butler were most skillfully arranged, and would have been crowned with great success but for the unpardonable and admitted nonaction of one of his division generals, to whom had been confided the duty of cutting off General Butler's retreat.

Sigel, the Valley co-operator, with sixty-five hundred men, was defeated by Breckinridge with five thousand troops on May 15th at New Market, the day before Beauregard beat Butler, in which he was greatly assisted by a battalion of cadets from the Virginia Military Institute at Lexington, Va. The boys were transformed by the crash of arms, roar of cannon, and shouts of combatants, into young heroes, and displayed marked heroism. The cadets of the Virginia Military Institute are responsible for the fact that many soldiers fought for the last time "mit Sigel." Breckinridge was then called to Lee, and General David Hunter replaced Sigel in command in the Valley, with whom Crook and Averell later united.

When General Lee faced Grant at Cold Harbor, Butler was still "bottled up"; but twelve thousand five hundred of his force under General "Baldy" Smith, as he was called, had been taken out from the bottom of the bottle, placed on transports, carried down the James and up the York, landed, and marched to Grant. Lee was also re-enforced by a division of North Carolinians. On June 1st, at 5 P. M., Smith's command and the Sixth Corps attacked, the other corps being held by Grant in readiness to advance on receipt of orders. The Confederate thick skirmish or preliminary line was carried, but the main position was immovable, of which, after the loss of two thousand men, Smith and Wright became convinced. "The 2d of June," says Grant, "was spent in getting troops into position for attack on the 3d; on the 3d of June we again assaulted the enemy's work in the hope of driving him from his position. In this attempt our loss was heavy while that of the enemy, I have reason to believe, was comparatively light."

This remarkable assault deserves more attention than the brief statement in which Grant disposes of it. Its isolation on the pages of history as the most extraordinary blunder in military annals will alone make it famous. Nearly all of the one hundred and thirteen thousand troops then at Cold Harbor, in double lines of battle six miles long, sprang to arms at half-past four on the morning of the 3d, and, in obedience to the customary order "to attack along the whole line," assailed the army of Lee and were terribly slaughtered at every point. There has been no instance of such destructive firing attended with such small loss to the men who were shooting from stationary lines. The troops went forward, said Hancock, "as far as the example of their officers could carry them"; but that was not far, for eight or ten minutes was the time of actual advance— sixty minutes of battle from first to last. Grant seemed willing to submit everything to the "nice hazard of a doubtful hour." Death and destruction everywhere enveloped charging columns, and direct and cross fires tore them to pieces. Lee's men were hungry and mad: three hard biscuits and one piece of fat pork were all the rations many had obtained since leaving the North Anna, and the pork was eaten raw because cooking involved waste. One cracker to a man, with no meat, became a luxury, and the lament of a poor fellow who had his shot out of his hand before he could eat it was ludicrous: "The next time I'll put my cracker in a safe place down by the breastworks where it won't get wounded, poor thing!" said he.

In front of the Confederate defenses the scene was heartrending. The ground was strewn with the dead, dying, and wounded Federals, and yet at 8 A. M. an order came from the chief of staff of the Army of the Potomac for the corps to assault again, each without reference to the other's advance. It is known that "Baldy" Smith positively refused to obey it, while some of the other

corps commanders went through the form of opening
fire, but there was no advance. Again the order was
given for a general assault. It was transmitted to corps
commanders, from them to the division chiefs, down
through brigades to regiments; but immobile ranks
entered a solemn protest against human butchery, and
men who had charged to the cannon's mouth when there
was a chance for victory lay in long lines as still as their
dead comrades. The rank and file knew the hopelessness of another attack upon Lee's lines; they had been
there, and did not propose to make another useless,
bloody experiment. In an incredibly short time twelve
thousand seven hundred and thirty-seven of their number had dropped from their ranks. Who knew how
many would fail to answer roll call after another attack?
"Cold Harbor," said General Grant after the war, "is
the only battle I ever fought that I would not fight over
again under the circumstances." Wellington, victorious
at Waterloo, said to Lord Fitzroy: "I have never
fought such a battle, and I trust I shall never fight
such another." Lee proudly stood at the gate of his
capital. If Grant was going to fight it out on that
line, he must enter there. Another flank move would
carry him farther from his objective, so he determined
to lay siege to Lee's position and dig up to it, and began
the construction of parallels united by zigzag trenches,
the work on which had to be done at night; but he soon
gave up the substitution of spades and picks for guns
and determined to move his army south of James River,
and on the night of June 12th began the movement.

Five days before, he sent Sheridan on an expedition
against the railroad which runs from Richmond to
Charlottesville and Staunton, as well as to meet Hunter,
who was expected from the Valley, and conduct him to
the Army of the Potomac. Sheridan started on the 7th
with the divisions of Gregg and Torbert, ten thousand
strong, in light marching order; two days' "short forage," three days' rations, and one hundred rounds of
ammunition were carried by each trooper. On the evening of the 10th Sheridan bivouacked three miles from
Trevilian's Station in Louisa County. Hampton, with
a division of cavalry, moved at once after him, while

another division speedily followed; with these two divisions Hampton intercepted Sheridan at Trevilian's, and interposed between him and Charlottesville. Here he was attacked on the 12th by Sheridan, all of whose assaults—principally apon General Butler's command—were handsomely repulsed, and that night Sheridan started back to his army, having accomplished nothing. Hampton, with half of his numbers, was not strong enough to seriously interrupt his retrograde movement.

After the battle of Cold Harbor, Lee had such great confidence in his ability to keep Grant from getting closer to Richmond that he detached Breckinridge to meet Hunter, who, having defeated the small Confederate force in the Valley, under W. E. Jones, was advancing *via* Staunton and Lexington to Lynchburg. On the 13th he sent Early with the Second Corps (Ewell's), eight thousand muskets and twenty-four pieces of artillery, to join him. Lee then crossed the James, and on that night his tent was pitched near Drewry's Bluff. Grant had sent Smith's troops around by water, down the York and up the James to City Point, with orders to try and capture Petersburg, and on the morning of the 15th Smith was in front of the lines there. He was slow and cautious. That afternoon Lee's army began to arrive, any opportunity to capture the city by a *coup de main* was gone, and the siege of Petersburg, destined to last ten long, weary months, began. The campaign from the Wilderness to Petersburg was brilliantly conducted on Lee's part. It was a magnificent exhibition of defensive warfare.

For one month his gigantic opponent fought him over nearly every mile between the Rapidan and the James. Practically every soldier in Lee's army placed *hors de combat* a soldier in Grant's, for the latter's losses equaled in numbers the strength of the former's command. Colonel Taylor, General Lee's able adjutant general, places the number of re-enforcements Lee received in the thirty days' campaign at fourteen thousand four hundred men, which, added to his original strength, gives seventy-eight thousand four hundred as the aggregate of all troops under his command from the Wilderness to Cold Harbor. And to Grant, Taylor assigns fifty-one thousand during the same period, giving him an aggregate under his command from the Wilderness to Cold Harbor of one hundred and ninety-two thousand one hundred and sixty men. This is a marvelous monument to the skill of Lee and the courage of his troops. Grant's hammering process was expensive in time and men. It took him thirty days to march seventy-five miles, at a loss of sixty odd thousand men, and then he was only on ground reached by McClellan without firing a gun, if we except the affair at Williamsburg.

CHAPTER XIV.

SIEGE OF PETERSBURG.

RICHMOND, on the left bank of the James, and Petersburg, on the right bank of the Appomattox, were strategic twin cities twenty-one miles apart. The capture of one embraced the fall of the other. Richmond proper, from a point on the river below to a position on the river above, was easily defended. Its investment would still leave the Weldon, Lynchburg, or Southside, and Danville Railroad open for supplies. Circumvallating lines around Petersburg would ultimately close all of them; this done, Richmond must be evacuated. But were it possible to capture Richmond first, to Burkeville, the junction of the Southside and Danville roads, the Southern army must retreat, not to Petersburg.

Grant, though not remarkable as a strategist, promptly saw the way to reach the Confederate capital. To reach Richmond it was necessary to batter down the gates of Petersburg. Butler made several attempts to capture the city before Grant took him under his charge, but failed. Grant, having decided to cross the Army of the Potomac to the south side of the James, determined to essay the capture of Petersburg before Lee—who had drawn most of Beauregard's force to him on the north side—could prevent it, and would have been successful if he had not lost a day in getting his pontoons ready; and even then it could have been done if General Smith, of the Eighteenth Corps, to whom the duty was confided, had attacked when he arrived before it. Beauregard was in peril. He had re-enforced Lee, but Lee had not yet returned the compliment, and when "Baldy" Smith began to deploy on his front, about ten o'clock on the morning of June 15th, with eighteen

thousand men, he had but twenty-two hundred soldiers to return his greetings, and had to station them so as to allow one man for every four yards and a half of his works. At 7 P. M. Smith carried with a "cloud of *tirailleurs*" the lines on a portion of his front, in spite of the heroic resistance of General Henry A. Wise, and held on to them during the night. Had Hancock, who was on the morning of the 15th on the south side of the James, been ordered to Petersburg, he could have been there by twelve or one o'clock, and Petersburg would have certainly fallen. Meade knew nothing of Smith's proposed *coup de main*, nor did Hancock, until he received orders at half-past five that afternoon to join General Smith, reaching his position about dark, after he had made a lodgment.

About the same time Hoke's division, from Drewry's Bluff, re-enforced Beauregard. On the morning of the 16th Hancock was in command of the operating troops, but was instructed by Meade not to attack until Burnside arrived with his corps. He reached the field at 10 A. M., but Hancock did not attack until after 5 P. M. In the meantime Beauregard drew to him Bushrod Johnson's division, who had been playing the cork to the Butler bottle in front of the Bermuda lines. But the inequality in numbers was still very great—Beauregard then having ten thousand, and Hancock fifty-three thousand. For three hours the battle raged, and at night the result was a serious loss on the Southern right, but Beauregard gained some advantage on the left. Warren had now arrived, but too late for the attack, making the Federal army in front of Petersburg sixty-seven thousand. All day on the 17th the contest was maintained with no decisive results. About dusk a portion of the Confederate lines was wholly broken, which might have ended in irreparable disaster; but at the opportune moment a fine brigade, under General Gracie, an excellent officer, reached the scene from Chaffin's Bluff, leaped the breastworks captured by Burnside, and drove out his troops, capturing two thousand prisoners.

Petersburg was still in danger. Fortunately, Beauregard's engineering skill, as well as that of his chief of engineers, Colonel D. B. Harris, was brought into requisition, and during the day selected the site of another and shorter line of defense, near Taylor's Creek, to his rear, and at midnight successfully made a retrograde movement, occupied and began fortifying his new line. On the 18th a general assault on the Southern lines was ordered at an early hour, but finding the old line had been abandoned, it was not made until noon—then only partially; but about 6 P. M. the "predetermined great attack," as Beauregard called it, was made by the Second Corps and everywhere repulsed, as were like attempts later by the Fifth and Ninth. Hancock's, Burnside's, and Warren's corps, Martindale's division of Smith's, and Neill's division from the Sixth Corps— or ninety thousand effectives—were present, while on that day Beauregard had been re-enforced by Kershaw's and Field's division of Longstreet's corps, making his total twenty thousand.

At half-past eleven General Lee rode up and was warmly welcomed by Beauregard, who had been anxiously hoping to see him for three days. He had been very slow in giving credence to Beauregard's telegrams about Grant's movements, and even as late as the night of the 17th dispatched, "Am not yet satisfied as to General Grant's movements, but upon your representations will move at once on Petersburg." And it was well he did, for the remarkable resistance of Beauregard's troops alone saved the city from capture on the 15th, 16th, and 17th. It was very difficult for Lee to ascertain on the north side of the James what troops Grant was crossing to its southern side, because his crossing was masked by the presence of troops interposed between the point of crossing and Lee's position; and he had to be most careful lest, in his anxiety to save Petersburg, he would lose Richmond. He could not afford to take the risk of denuding the Richmond lines until it had been demonstrated beyond doubt that the real battle was to be delivered at Petersburg. The admirably selected new line of Beauregard was strengthened, and maintained until the end of the war.

The next day the main portion of the Army of Northern Virginia arrived, and Beauregard wanted to throw the entire disposable force on the Union left and rear before they began to fortify; but General Lee pronounced against the plan. Grant and Meade, satisfied that nothing more could be gained by direct assaults —ten thousand men had been lost in three days—decided to play another game for the prize in which spades should be trumps, and the siege of Petersburg began. In an incredibly short time high, impregnable, bastioned works began to erect their crests. It was designed to make the Union defensive lines so formidable as to be unassailable. A system of redans chained together by powerful parapets, whose approaches were to be obstructed by abatis, were constructed. Behind these gigantic earthworks a small force could safely remain, and thus the "loyal legions" could be drawn out at any time for other work. The Federal plan, wisely adopted, was to extend their ramparts south, then west, to seize and retain the Weldon Railroad and cut off Lee's communication with the coast States, then gradually work westerly toward the Lynchburg Railroad, which once in Grant's possession, would have confined Lee to the Danville and Richmond Railroads to supply his army. The short road from Petersburg to Richmond connected him with it and the Staunton road, running north from Richmond. It was intended to throw a huge steel cordon around Petersburg, which would force Lee with his limited numbers to so extend his lines that they would snap or be weak enough to break under blows.

Grant had now established his troops in the best location for the achievement of his purpose. With bloody hands he had reached the confines of the object of his campaign; but he was there and most excellently situated; his water line of communication down the James and up the Potomac with Washington and the North was absolutely free from hostile interruption. His headquarters—City Point, at the junction of the Appomattox and the James—was connected with his army by rail, and from a point on that road a field railroad, moving in the rear of his lines, made the transportation of supplies from his water base easy in sunshine or storm. Field telegraph connected army headquarters with those of subordinate commanders; so with plenty of commissary, quartermaster, and medical supplies, and plenty of men, he anticipated with confidence future success. At Deep Bottom, on the James, he had thrown a pontoon bridge and protected it by strongly fortified works on the north side, manned by a sufficient force to defend them, thus always securing a debouch on the Richmond side of the river. He could thus make a mock assault on Richmond and a real attack at Petersburg, or the reverse.

General Lee was uneasy; he was defending two cities and a line of intrenchments enveloping both thirty-five miles long, and could not know with certainty at what point on them the real blow would be delivered. Grant's troops withdrawn from one portion of his front at night, could appear at another before the sun lifted the mists of morning. Lee too had communication with the Richmond defenses by a pontoon bridge above Grant's at Drewry's Bluff, but in any movement of troops across the river Grant, if the aggressor, would move first and thereby gain a start. Then, too, Lee's days were full of other troubles: the question of supplies, always a serious one, was growing daily more so. The subjugation of productive portions of the South and the devastation of other sections made the collection of food for men and forage for animals more difficult than ever. The supply of men was exhausted. Conscription in 1862 first placed on the rolls all men between eighteen and thirty-five, and later between thirty-five and forty. After Gettysburg and Vicksburg, a call was made for men between forty and forty-five, and in February, 1864, the Conscript Act was more stringent, and the population between seventeen and fifty were made subject to call—"a robbery," designated at the time, "of the cradle and the grave." The end of conscription had been reached. The currency in the Confederate Treasury was in value as sixty to one of coin. A deficiency in supply of arms and ammunition was imminent. The Ordnance Department contained only twenty-five thousand stand of small arms for the whole Confederacy; the foreign market supplied one half of the arms used, but that market was nearly cut off; many workshops had been destroyed, and the usefulness of others much impaired by the withdrawal of details of men.

Then General Lee was distressed at the condition of his army. It had been exposed in a violent campaign against overwhelming numbers, was badly fed—a pound of flour and a quarter of a pound of meat to the man— badly paid and cared for in camp and hospital, and every letter brought news of the families of the troops suffering at home. As his resources diminished, those of his opponent seemed to increase. He was too weak to assume the offensive against fortification, and yet something must be attempted. In the midst of the gathering gloom, Lee once more attempted to diminish the troops in his front by threatening the Federal capital.

Ewell, suffering from the loss of his leg, had relinquished the command of his corps to Early, and with eight thousand muskets this officer had been sent, as already stated, to Lynchburg, to re-enforce Breckinridge in Hunter's front. Hunter had retreated from Lynchburg to the mountains of West Virginia before Early could strike him. Then General Lee submitted to Early the question whether the condition of his troops would permit him to threaten Washington as originally contemplated ; if not, to return to his army. Early determined to take the responsibility of carrying out the original plan, so he turned the head of his column toward the Potomac. On June 26th he was at Staunton, July 2d at Winchester, crossing the Potomac on the 6th, fought and defeated six thousand troops under General Lew Wallace on the Monocacy on the 9th, and arrived in front of the works at Washington at noon on July 11th with about ten thousand men and forty pieces of artillery. That afternoon his army was placed in position with orders to assail the works at daylight next morning ; but learning during the night that the Sixth Corps from the Army of the Potomac and the Nineteenth, under Emory, from New Orleans, had arrived, he countermanded the order, remained in front of Washington during the 12th, and that night withdrew and began his march back to Virginia, reaching Strasburg, in the Valley of Virginia, on the 22d. General Early could not have held Washington if he had entered its gates with his small force. No re-enforcements were nearer to him than Richmond, and from the North and

General Grant's army a large force could have been speedily assembled.

Grant, in consequence of the opportune arrival of Emory, only detached the Sixth Corps from his lines, which did not materially reduce his great numbers in Lee's front, and hence Lee did not dare to weaken his lines by re-enforcing Early. Early's presence in the lower valley was menacing to Washington, preserved a threatening attitude toward Pennsylvania and Maryland, prevented the use of the Baltimore and Ohio Railroad and the Chesapeake and Ohio Canal, and kept a large force from Grant's army to defend the Federal capital.

The greater part of this force was moved south of the Potomac, organized into the Army of the Shenandoah, and the command of it given, on August 7th, to General Sheridan. With the Sixth and Nineteenth Corps, and the Army of West Virginia, as General George Crook's force was called, Sheridan had a total present for duty on September 10th, including Averill's cavalry, of forty-eight thousand men and officers. He was abundantly able to assume the offensive, for he had in addition garrisons of seven thousand men at Harper's Ferry, Martinsburg, and other points, making his whole force about fifty-five thousand. General Lee was very anxious to win a battle in the lower valley—it was the only way he could relieve Petersburg—and so re-enforced Early by a division of cavalry and one of infantry, both under General Anderson, the commander of Longstreet's corps. This officer was selected to produce the impression, the remaining divisions of his corps were to follow, in order to induce Grant to send troops to Sheridan equivalent to Longstreet's whole corps. In that case Lee would again re-enforce Early and transfer the principal scene of hostilities to the Potomac, just as he had successfully drawn McClellan from the James and Hooker from the Rappahannock at Fredericksburg by similar movements; but Grant refused to follow the precedent. Sheridan had already an army numerically equal to the one Lee commanded on the Petersburg lines, and was strong enough to stand alone. Lee could not detach more troops, but instead was obliged to recall Anderson and his infantry. The failure to transfer the seat of war from in front of Petersburg was due to the decreasing Confederate strength and the increase of that of their opponents.

Lee could only wait, watch, and frustrate Grant's plans as far as possible. After Anderson's departure from the Valley Sheridan assumed the offensive, and on September 19th, with nearly fifty thousand troops, fought and defeated, at Winchester, fourteen thousand under Early, the Confederate loss being about four thousand, the Federal five thousand, of which nearly forty-four hundred were killed or wounded. On the 22d Early was again defeated at Fisher's Hill, but, being reenforced near Port Republic by Kershaw's division of infantry and Cutshaw's battalion of artillery, and later by Rosser's brigade of cavalry, he assumed the offensive and again moved down the Valley to Fisher's Hill, Sheridan retiring in his front to Cedar Creek. Here he was attacked by Early on the 19th of October before daybreak and defeated, but afterward, rallying his troops, he in turn attacked and routed Early, who lost twenty-three pieces of artillery, eighteen hundred and sixty in killed and wounded, and over one thousand prisoners.

Major-General Ramseur, one of Early's best and bravest officers, was mortally wounded. The operations here were practically over, and both Grant and Lee called to them the greater part of their respective troops. The beautiful Valley of Virginia was a barren waste, and from the breasts of its mountains was reflected the light of two thousand burning barns, seventy mills filled with wheat and farming utensils, while in front of the victorious army were driven thousands of head of stock. In the expressive language of the Federal commander—"A crow flying across the Valley would have to carry its rations."

General Lee's duties were very exacting, and he was constantly called upon to meet some movement of his enemy. He was closer to his family in Richmond than he had been, and the citizens around him were very kind, considerate, and generous. In a note to Mrs. Lee, dated Petersburg, June 19th, he says: "I am much obliged to the kind people for the clothes; but if they are not gray they are of no use to me in the field. I hope to go to church this blessed day, and shall remember you all in my poor prayers." The ladies were always contributing to his comfort. He writes from Camp Petersburg, July 24, 1864: "The ladies of Petersburg have sent me a nice set of shirts. They were given to me by Mrs. James R. Branch, and her mother, Mrs. Thomas Branch. In fact, they have given everything—which I fear they can not spare—vegetables, bread, milk, ice cream. To-day one of them sent me a nice peach—the first one I think I have seen for two years. I sent it to Mrs. Shippen. Mr. Platt held services again to-day under the trees near my camp. We had quite a large congregation of citizens, ladies and gentlemen, and our usual number of soldiers. During the services I constantly heard the shells crashing among the houses of Petersburg. Tell Life [his youngest daughter] I send her a song composed by a French soldier. As she is so learned in that language I want her to send me a reply in verse." And from Camp Petersburg, June 26, 1864: "I hope it is not as hot in Richmond as here. The men suffer a great deal in the trenches; and this condition of things, with the heat of the sun, nearly puts an end to military operations."

And again: "Camp Petersburg, June 30, 1864.—I was very glad to receive your letter yesterday, and to hear that you were better. I trust you will continue to improve and soon be as well as usual. God grant that you may be entirely restored in his own good time! Do you recollect what a happy day thirty-three years ago this was? How many hopes and pleasures it gave birth to! God has been very merciful and kind to us, and how thankless and sinful I have been! I pray that he may continue his mercies and blessings to us and give us a little peace and rest together in this world, and finally gather us and all he has given us around his throne in the world to come. The President has just arrived, and I must bring my letter to a close. God bless you all."

And on July 10, 1864: "I was pleased, on the arrival of my little courier this morning, to hear that you were better, and that Custis Morgan (a pet squirrel) was still among the missing. I think the farther he gets from you the better you will be. The shells have scattered the poor inhabitants in Petersburg, so that many of the churches are closed. Indeed, they have been visited by the enemy's shells. Mr. Platt, pastor of the principal Episcopal Church, had services at my headquarters today. The services were under the trees, and the discourse on the subject of salvation."

Lee and Grant, dissimilar in many characteristics, were similar in others : both were quiet and self-possessed, both sometimes restless—Grant to break through Lee's works somewhere, Lee impatient to improve any opportunity that might be offered. By mere chance both were gratified. The Forty-eighth Pennsylvania Regiment, Burnside's corps, was largely composed of Schuylkill coal miners, and its lieutenant colonel, Pleasants, had been a mining engineer. One hundred and thirty yards in front, on General Johnson's front, at the center of General Elliott's brigade, was a salient in the Confederate lines. It was a re-entrant commanded by a flank from either side; in its rear was a deep hollow. The mining men, with the instinct of their profession, conceived the idea of blowing it up. Burnside approved it, and work was commenced on June 25th. Lee knew what was going on and directed countermining, but abandoned it and threw up intrenchments at the gorge of the salient, and established 8- and 10-inch mortar batteries to give a front and cross fire on it. It was prosecuted under many difficulties. Meade, and his chief engineer, Duane, did not believe such a mine for military purposes could be excavated. The former did not think the location selected was the proper one. The part of the line containing the works to be blown up could not be assaulted with success, because it was commanded in both flanks by the fire of the Southern troops, and could be taken in reverse from their position on the Jerusalem plank road and from their works opposite the Hare House.

Pleasants deserves great credit for his perseverance. Burnside, his corps, and Potter, his division commander, of the officers of high rank, alone encouraged his efforts. On July 23d the mine was ready for the powder; for forty workmen, even with inferior implements, can move much dirt in a month. Imagine a main gallery five hundred and ten and eight tenths feet long, with lateral galleries thirty-seven and thirty-eight feet each, into which eight magazines were placed, filled with a total charge of eight thousand pounds of powder. The theodolite had accurately measured the distance; the powder was directly under the fort. To Burnside, of course, was assigned the honor of making the grand assault. He had three white divisions and one division of negro troops in his corps, and determined to charge in column of divisions on all men and guns not blown up, and directed that the negroes should lead in what was expected to be a finishing stroke to a great war, and thus give the goddess Fame the opportunity to crown the colored brow.

Burnside thought the colored division would make a better charge at that time than the white division, because the latter had been for forty days in the trenches, had few opportunities of washing, and were not in condition to make a vigorous charge. Meade and Grant objected, the former because "they were untried and could not be trusted," while the latter directed the leading column of assault to be formed of white, not black troops. The negro was a sensitive plant in the Northern greenhouses at that time; and if he had been butchered in the attack there it would have been charged by some, as Meade expressed it, that "we were shoving these people ahead to get killed because we did not care anything about them."

There was only one negro division then in the Army of the Potomac, and the fact that in over one hundred thousand men it had been selected to lead the "On-to-Petersburg!" charge would have been a striking and unique stricture upon the rest of the army. The sight of forty-three hundred howling, charging black men at the head of the column would have been a red rag to the Southern bull, and the contest would have been butcherly, bloody, and brief. A humorous picture has been drawn of these negro troops on the night they learned Burnside was going to give them the advance. They were represented sitting in circles in their company streets, intently and solemnly "studying," when all at once a heavy voice began to sing:

We-e looks li-ike me-en a-a-marching on,
We looks li-ike men-er war,

and shortly thereafter a thousand voices were upraised
to swell the refrain.   The dark men with white eyes and
teeth and red lips crouching over smoldering fires, the
rays of lanterns piercing the gloom, made a picturesque
scene.   The heroes " carved in ebony " being ruled out,
Burnside made his three white division commanders
" pull straws " to ascertain who should lead the attack
when the mine was sprung, and General Ledlie, commanding the first division, " was the unlucky victim."
At 3.30 A. M. on the morning of the 30th Ledlie was
in position, and ready to follow him were the other
divisions.

Meade had made every preparation for a general
assault, the whole army, if necessary, was to be thrust
through the broken works into the city.   Warren's Fifth
Corps, and General Ord, commanding the Eighteenth
Corps, was to support Burnside.   Hancock, who had
been moved to the north side of the James River to
threaten an attack upon Richmond to draw troops from
Lee to that side, and thus weaken his Petersburg lines,
was to move back during the night and be in position at
daylight to follow up the assaulting column, and Sheridan, with the cavalry corps, was to move on Petersburg
by the roads leading from the southward and westward.

The great mine upon whose explosion this comprehensive wholesale battle plan pivoted was to be sprung
at half-past three in the morning; but, owing to a defect
in the fuse, the wreck of matter did not begin until an
hour and a quarter afterward.   Then the earth trembled
and heaved and opened over the powder, and cannon,
caissons, sandbags, timbers, men ; smoke and fire went
up in the mass of earth to a high altitude, spread out
like an immense cloud, which " flushed to an angry crimson and floated away to meet the morning sun."   The
solid part began to fall.   The troops waiting to make
the charge thought the great descending mass was aimed
at them, and, without the word of command, broke
and scattered to the rear, and a little time, most valuable to the Confederates, was lost in reforming them.
When the order for the advance was given, more time

was consumed in climbing over their own breastworks, which broke their ranks, and in irregular order they pushed on for the crater one hundred and thirty yards distant, the *débris* having covered up the Confederate abatis and *chevaux-de-frise* in front of it.   An enormous hole in the ground here confronted them—one hundred and seventy feet long, sixty feet wide, and thirty feet deep—" filled with dust, great blocks of clay, guns, broken gun-carriages, projecting timbers, and men buried up to their necks, others to their waists, and some with only their feet and legs protruding from the earth."   Two hundred and fifty-six South Carolinians—the Eighteenth and part of the Twenty-third—and twenty-two men and officers of Pegram's Petersburg battery, were buried beneath " the jagged rocks of blackened clay."

The two advance brigades became inextricably mixed in the one great desire to look into the hole; and then, when the Confederates on either side of the crater began to take in the situation and to fire from the traverses, there was an uncontrollable and natural desire to get in the hole.   General Elliott, while forming his command on the higher ground in the rear of the crater, was severely wounded; but Colonel McMaster, who succeeded to the command, got part of his troops in the ravine in the rear, and their front fire, and the flank fire from the remainder, and Ransom's troops to the Confederate left, repulsed all attempts of the Union troops to advance. The crest of the crater was now being swept by canister, for Lieutenant-Colonel John Haskell had with great promptness brought up two light batteries, and Pegram's guns were rapidly coming up.   Wright's four guns, six hundred yards to the southern left of the salient, concealed in the woods and covered by traverses, and two guns to the right of the crater, opened a destructive fire and covered the ground between the big hole and the Union lines.   The artillery alone stood between the crater and Cemetery Hill, which, if occupied and held as had been intended, would have resulted in the fall of Petersburg.   Ledlie was in the rear ensconced in a "bomb-proof" protected angle of his own works, his division in the crater, and his orders to move forward were not obeyed.   " It was as utterly impracticable to reform brigades outside of the crater under the severe fire of front and rear as it would be to marshal bees into line after upsetting the hive, or to hold dress parade in front of a charging enemy," wrote a Federal officer.

Griffin's brigade of Potter's division was advanced, but, meeting a severe fire, fell back in the crater. Every organization melted away, as soon as it entered this hole in the ground, into a mass of human beings clinging to the almost perpendicular sides. The other brigade of Potter's division now advanced, but got no farther than the abandoned traverses and intrenchments; and then Wilcox, with the third and last division of Burnside's white troops, started forward. The crater was filled with men at this time, the thermometer above ninety degrees, and the sun beating down in the great hole caused much suffering. No more troops could get in. Wilcox was left out, and with a part of his command attempted to carry some of the works on the Confederate right of the crater, but only held them a short time. Orders were being constantly sent to push forward and occupy Cemetery Hill, but were not relished and not obeyed. It was now two hours after the explosion of the mine; Burnside determined to let loose the real dogs of war, and ordered General Edward Ferrero with his black division to advance, pass the white troops, and carry the crest of Cemetery Hill at all hazards. Ferrero did not think it advisable to move his troops in, as there were already three divisions of white troops in his front "huddled together"; but Burnside said the order was peremptory.

The colored division moved out to death or glory; its commander did not, but sought the "bomb-proof" where Ledlie was. These troops, moving by the flank, passed around the crater and attempted to advance, but a deadly fire enveloped them and they broke in disorder, some falling back to the crater, while a majority ran back to the Union defenses. General Ord's Eighteenth Corps was now ordered to go forward. He had difficulty in getting through the Ninth Corps intrenchments; the parapets and abatis were not prepared for an exit, and the covered ways were crowded with the soldiers of the Ninth Corps. Turner's, his leading division, succeeded in advancing to the Confederate works, but would not stay, and fell back to the starting point. The object now was to get the men in and around the crater back to the Union lines. The ground was so thoroughly combed with showers of shot that it was proposed to dig a covered way; but not many spades or picks were available, though it was commenced. Any advance was now hopeless, and Meade, at 1.30 P. M., gave orders for the troops to be withdrawn from the crater—a difficult undertaking. Burnside thought they should stay there until night.

In the meantime the Confederates were massing for the attack. Lee heard what had been done about 6 A. M., promptly took steps to retake the position, and sent a staff officer for troops to do it. Traveler carried him rapidly to Gee House, a commanding position five hundred yards in the rear of the crater. Beauregard was already there, and soon Mahone with two brigades—Weiseger's and Wright's—arrived, and formed in a ravine in the rear of the crater. The Virginia brigade had formed for the attack, and the Georgia troops were in the act of forming when suddenly Lieutenant-Colonel John A. Bross, of the Thirty-first United States Colored Troops, sprang upon the crater crest waving a flag and calling upon his men to follow him.

Brigadier-General Weiseger, commanding the Virginia brigade, saw him, and, thinking his position would be assailed, determined to move first, and appealed, he says, to Captain Girardy, of Mahone's staff, to give the order, for he had been directed by Mahone to wait until he or Girardy ordered him forward. The order was given, and the lines were captured by a most gallant charge. The crater remained crammed with human beings, living and dead, into which huge missiles from mortars were bursting. The Georgia brigade advanced and attempted to dislodge the Union troops in the lines south of the crater, but failed. Later the Alabama brigade came up, when a general assault by these and other troops on the lines upon either side of the crater was made, and everywhere successfully; and just then a white handkerchief on the end of a ramrod was projected above the crater, in token of the surrender of the men there.

Altogether it was a horrible affair; and what promised, Grant said, "to be the most successful assault of the campaign terminated in disaster"—a disaster in which the Federals lost four thousand men. "The operation was not successful," Meade states, "for a *coup de main* depends for success upon the utmost promptitude of movement." Fifty thousand troops were ready to support it, but proper debouches had not been prepared. The Ninth Corps had great difficulty in getting over the high works in their front, and the space was too contracted to deploy troops, preventing rapidity of execution and cordial co-operation essential to success.

From camp, July 31, 1864, General Lee wrote: "Yesterday morning the enemy sprung a mine on one of our batteries on the line and got possession of a portion of our intrenchments. It was the part defended by General Beauregard's troops. I sent General Mahone with two brigades of Hill's corps, who charged into them handsomely, recapturing the intrenchments and guns, twelve stand of colors, seventy-three officers, including General Bartlett, his staff, three colonels, and eight hundred and fifty-five enlisted men. There were upward of five hundred of his dead unburied in the trenches, among them many officers and blacks. He suffered severely. He has withdrawn his troops from the north side of the James. I do not know what he will attempt next. He is mining on other points along our line. I trust he will not succeed in bettering his last attempt." The vigilance of the Southern general was daily displayed, and his remarkable talent for promptly disregarding the feint and locating the real attack had to be incessantly exercised. If at first he was in doubt of Grant's designs, he was patient, knowing that as they developed he would fathom his purpose.

From camp, August 14, 1864, he wrote his wife: "I have been kept from church to-day by the enemy's crossing to the north side of the James River, and the necessity of moving troops to meet him. I do not know what his intentions are. He is said to be cutting a canal across the Dutch Gap—a point in the river—but

I can not as yet discover it. I was up there yesterday, and saw nothing to indicate it. We shall ascertain in a day or two. I received to-day a kind letter from the Rev. Mr. Cole, of Culpeper Court House. He is a most excellent man in all the relations of life. He says there is not a church standing in all that country within the lines formerly occupied by the enemy. All are razed to the ground, and the materials used often for the vilest purposes. Two of the churches at the Court House barely escaped destruction. The pews were all taken out to make seats for the theater. The fact was reported to the commanding officer, General Newton (from Norfolk), by their own men of the Christian Commission, but he took no steps to rebuke or arrest it. We must suffer patiently to the end, when all things will be made right."

Hancock kept Lee from attending divine services. By Grant's direction, he left City Point with the Second and Tenth Corps on steamers, at ten o'clock Saturday night, the 13th of August, to produce the impression he was going to Washington, but disembarked at the lower pontoon bridge at Deep Bottom and marched toward Richmond. Gregg's cavalry division and the artillery of the two corps went by land and across the usual pontoon bridge. The movement was made to prevent further detachments of Lee's army going to the Valley, and if possible call back those sent, and under the impression the remaining divisions of Longstreet's corps had followed Kershaw. It involved the capture of Chaffin's Bluff, one of the chief fortifications guarding the river approach to Richmond. Field's and Wilcox's divisions, re-enforced by Mahone's division of infantry, and Hampton's and W. H. F. Lee's cavalry divisions sent from the south side, interposed an effective barrier to Hancock's advance. This officer, after making one unsuccessful assault, remained quiet for four days, and then during the night withdrew to the south side with a loss of twenty-seven hundred and eighty-six men.

In a combat on the 16th between the Confederate and Gregg's Federal cavalry, General John R. Chambliss, a bold, enterprising Southern brigadier of cavalry, was killed. While Hancock was demonstrating on the north side, Warren with his Fifth Corps was withdrawn from his lines and sent to destroy, with Kautz's cavalry, the Weldon Railroad. He struck it a point four miles from Petersburg, at Globe Tavern, and was soon afterward re-enforced by three divisions of the Ninth Corps. Dearing's Confederate cavalry was there and reported to Beauregard the occupation of the railroad by infantry, who sent Heth with two brigades to attack him. A sharp encounter between Ayers's division and Heth followed, in which both sides lost heavily. On the 19th the fighting was renewed, both sides being re-enforced. Hill attacked with five brigades under Heth and Mahone, a division of cavalry, and Pegram's batteries, at the intersection of the Vaughn road with the railroad. Heth and Mahone made a fine effort, meeting with deserved success, but were later in turn repulsed. Warren lost three thousand men, and on the 20th fell back a mile and a half and intrenched. On the 21st Hill again attacked, but was unsuccessful. General Sanders, of Mahone's brigade, was killed.

Hancock was now brought up with instructions to destroy the Weldon Railroad south of Ream's Station. He was attacked by Hill on the 25th at 5 P. M. with eight infantry brigades and two divisions of cavalry under Hampton, and beaten, capturing three batteries of artillery. A disorderly rout was avoided by the personal bearing and example of General Hancock and the good behavior of a part of his first division under Miles. Gibbon's division had been so roughly handled that their commanders, said Humphreys, could not get the troops to advance; they were driven from the breastworks by Hampton's dismounted cavalry; Gregg's cavalry division was also driven back by these troopers, and during the night Hancock retreated, having lost twenty-three hundred and seventy-two men, while Hill's loss only amounted to seven hundred and twenty. Hill captured twelve stand of colors, nine guns and ten caissons, thirty-one hundred stand of small arms, and twenty-one hundred and fifty prisoners.

General Lee's labors were incessant; as soon as one attempt on his lines failed another began. His power of endurance was great, but anxiety, fatigue, and loss of rest must make inroads. Mrs. Lee, growing uneasy for fear the great strain upon him would be too heavy, remonstrated and begged him to look more to his comfort and health. From Camp Petersburg, September 18, 1864, he replies: "But what care can a man give to himself in time of war? It is from no desire of exposure or hazard that I live in a tent, but from necessity. I must be where I can speedily at all times attend to the duties of my position, and be near or accessible to the officers with whom I have to act. I have been offered rooms in the houses of our citizens, but I could not turn the dwellings of my kind hosts into a barrack, where officers, couriers, distressed women, etc., would be entering day and night."

Warren was still intrenched across the Weldon Railroad on the left of the Union lines. Ten days after Hancock and Hill had their battle, Grant next endeavored to break the Southern lines on the Richmond side. Ord and Birney, with the Tenth and Eighteenth Corps, crossed the James the night of September 28th, moved rapidly up the River and New Market roads, while Kautz's cavalry marched on the Darby road. The sixteen thousand troops sought to assail and capture the Confederate works, which were feebly garrisoned, before they could be re-enforced from the south side. Ord, nearest the river, succeeded in capturing Fort Harrison, a strong work on the Southern main line of intrenchments about a mile and a quarter from the river, with its sixteen guns and a number of prisoners, as well as two adjoining lunettes with their artillery—six guns. But Birney's attack on Fort Gilmer, three quarters of a mile north of Harrison, was repulsed with great loss to him. Grant was present urging Birney forward, but the canister and musketry fire broke his advancing lines and caused them to fall back in confusion.

Ewell was in command of the local troops on the north side, Lee joined him during the day, and at 2 P. M. on the 30th directed an assault on Fort Harrison with five brigades under Anderson, commanding Longstreet's corps; but during the night before, large working parties had made Fort Harrison an inclosed work and too strong to be carried. After this Grant's left on the south side was further extended to the Peebles farm, and co-operative movements on both Lee's flanks followed without practical results. Longstreet returned to duty on the 19th of October, and was assigned to the command of the troops on the north side and on the Bermuda Hundred front. General Weitzel was given the command of the Eighteenth Federal Corps, and General Hancock was called to Washington to organize, out of abundant material, another fresh corps to take the field in the spring.

The picture of the winter of 1864 and 1865 has a somber background. The Confederate commander had displayed "every art by which genius and courage can make good the lack of numbers and resources," but could not gather hope from coming days ; clothing, food, ammunition, and forage for animals were so scarce, suffering and distress so plentiful. The leader of a brave people must fight until the war clouds of misfortune enveloped him on so many sides he could fight no longer. "I say that, if the event had been manifest to the whole world beforehand, not even then ought Athens to have forsaken this course, if she had any regard for her glory or for her past, or for the ages to come," exclaimed Demosthenes.

Self-possessed and calm, Lee struggled to solve the huge military problem, and make the sum of smaller numbers equal to that of greater numbers. It was the old heathen picture of "man sublimely contending with Fate to the admiration of the gods, accepting the last test of endurance, and with the smile of a sublime resolution risking the last defiance of fortune." His thoughts ever turned upon the soldiers of his army—the ragged, gallant fellows around him, whose pinched cheeks told hunger was their portion, and whose shivering forms denoted the absence of proper clothing. Mrs. Lee, in her invalid chair in Richmond, with large heart and small means, assisted by friends, was busy knitting socks and sending them to him. He writes her from Petersburg, November 30, 1864: "I received yesterday your letter of the 27th, and am glad to learn your supply of socks is so large. If two or three hundred would send an equal number we should have a sufficiency. I will en-

deavor to have them distributed to the most needy."
And again on December 17, 1864: "I received day before yesterday the box with hat, gloves, and socks; also
the barrel of apples. You had better have kept the latter, as it would have been more useful to you than to
me, and I should have enjoyed its consumption by yourself and the girls more than by me." And on December
30, 1864, he tells her: "The Lyons furs and fur robe
have also arrived safely, but I can learn nothing of the
saddle of mutton. Bryan, of whom I inquired as to its
arrival, is greatly alarmed lest it has been sent to the
soldiers' dinner. If the soldiers get it I shall be content. I can do very well without it. In fact, I should
rather they would have it than I." And on January 10,
1865, after stating how the socks which Mrs. Lee had
sent had been distributed to the army, the general writes:
"Yesterday afternoon three little girls walked into my
room, each with a small basket. The eldest carried
some fresh eggs laid by her own hens; the second, some
pickles made by her mother; the third, some pop corn
which had grown in her garden. They were accompanied by a young maid with a block of soap made by her
mother. They were the daughters of a Mrs. Notting-
ham, a refugee from Northampton County, who lived
near Eastville, not far from old Arlington. The eldest
of the girls, whose age did not exceed eight years, had
a small wheel on which she spun for her mother, who
wove all the cloth for her two brothers—boys of twelve
and fourteen years. I have not had so pleasant a visit
for a long time. I fortunately was able to fill their
baskets with apples, which distressed poor Bryan [his
steward], and begged them to bring me nothing but
kisses and to keep the eggs, corn, etc., for themselves.
I pray daily, and almost hourly, to our heavenly Father
to come to the relief of you (Mrs. Lee was sick) and
our afflicted country. I know he will order all things
for our good, and we must be content."

Children always held the key which would unlock
the heart of Lee, and his description of the little girls
bringing him presents is a charming illustration of his
fondness for them.

In spite of the wonderful success attending Lee's

efforts, at every attempt Grant made to get toward Lynchburg or Southside Railroad, the Union line of contravallation continued to stretch, and it was evident, unless Lee could get more men, he would lose that line of railroad. A lodgment once effected, enormous intrenchments would follow, which could not be assailed with success; but where were men to come from when the end of conscription had been reached and exchange of prisoners stopped? Lee did not believe the white population could supply the necessities of a long war without overtaxing its capacity, and thought the time had come to enlist the negroes as soldiers, and so wrote Hon. E. Barksdale, a member of the Confederate States House of Representatives, on February 18, 1865. Six months before, he had advocated their employment as teamsters, laborers, and mechanics, in place of whites, who, being replaced, could be restored to the ranks. He thought, too, that the negroes would be used against the South as fast as the Federals got possession of them; that he could make as good soldiers of them as his enemy, who attached great importance to their assistance; that the negroes furnished more promising material than many armies mentioned in history, possessed the requisite physical qualifications, and their habits of obedience constituted a good foundation for discipline; and that those who were employed should be freed. Congress passed a bill for the purpose; but it was now too late to experiment with new measures. The Southern chief not only wanted more men, but supplies for those he already commanded. "The struggle now is," said he, "to keep the army fed and clothed. Only fifty men," he wrote, "in some regiments had shoes, and bacon is only issued once in a few days."

On January 11, 1865, he tells Mr. Seddon, the Secretary of War, that his army had only two days' supplies, the country was swept clear, and the sole reliance was on the railroads. And the next day he issued an appeal to the "farmers east of the Blue Ridge and south of the James to send food for the army, for which he would pay, or return in kind." Many months before, flour was quoted at two hundred and fifty dollars per barrel in Confederate money; meal fifty dollars, corn forty, and oats twenty-five dollars per bushel; hay twenty-five dollars per pound; beans fifty dollars, and black-eyed peas, forty-five dollars per bushel. Brown sugar, ten dollars, coffee, twelve dollars, and tea, thirty-five dollars per pound, and very scarce. Sorghum, a substitute for sugar and meat, forty dollars per gallon. In Richmond a relative offered General Lee a cup of tea, and to prevent him from knowing one cup was all she had, filled her own cup with James River water, colored by mud from recent rains, which she unconcernedly sipped with a spoon.

The capture of Fort Fisher, North Carolina, on January 15, 1865, closed the last gateway between the Southern States and the outside world. Sherman with a powerful army reached Savannah, on his march from Atlanta to the sea, on December 21, 1864, from which point he could unite with Grant by land or water. On February 1st he crossed into South Carolina, and on March 23d was at Goldsborough, N. C., one hundred and fifty miles from Petersburg.

Lee had now been made commander in chief of all the armies of the Confederacy, and assumed charge in General Orders No. 1, February 9th. He could have had practical control of military operations throughout the South before, for his suggestions would have been complied with by the constitutional commander in chief, but he always attended to his own affairs and let those of others alone. Five days after he was commissioned commander in chief he issued General Orders No. 2, exhorting Southern soldiers to respond to the call of honor and duty, pardoning deserters and those improperly absent if they returned in twenty days—except those who deserted to the enemy—and saying, " Let us oppose constancy to adversity, fortitude to suffering, and courage to danger, with the firm assurance that He who gave freedom to our fathers will bless the efforts of their children to preserve it."

The day before this order was issued " was the most inclement day of winter." Lee dispatched to Seddon, Secretary of War, that his troops "were greatly exposed in line of battle two days, had been without meat for three days, and in scant clothing took the cold hail and sleet."

The commissary general reported not a pound of meat at his disposal. "The physical strength of the men," said Lee, "if their courage survives, must fail under this treatment;" that his "cavalry had to be dispersed for want of forage; with these facts, taken in connection with paucity of numbers, you must not be surprised if calamity befalls us." General John C. Breckinridge, who had been appointed Secretary of War in Mr. Seddon's place, received and referred General Lee's letter to Mr. Davis, who indorsed upon it: "This is too sad to be patiently considered." Want of supplies, want of men, was indeed a grievous calamity. In the numerous recent combats many of his best men and officers had fallen, among the latter, General John Pegram, who was endeared to him by many personal ties. It seemed difficult to get the simplest necessaries—even soap became scarce, and, as a consequence, many of his soldiers had cutaneous diseases. "The supply from the Commissary Department is wholly inadequate," he wrote, "notwithstanding the materials for making it are found in every household and the art is familiar to all well-trained domestics." The equipments for cavalrymen were so greatly wanted that Lee issued a circular requesting the citizens to send him any saddles, revolvers, pistols, and carbines that might be in their possession. His scant battalions grew smaller and smaller, the lines to be guarded longer and longer. "Cold and hunger struck them down in the trenches, while from the desolate track of triumphant armies in their rear came the cries of starving and unprotected homes." On all sides difficulties and dangers multiplied. Beauregard had been sent South to concentrate such troops as he could in Sherman's front, and had reported that Sherman would move *via* Greensborough and Weldon to Petersburg, or unite with Schofield at Raleigh.

"Beauregard has a difficult task to perform," said Lee to Breckinridge, Secretary of War, "and one of his best officers, General Hardee, is incapacitated by sickness. I have heard his own health is indifferent; should his health give way there is no one in the department to replace him, nor have I any one to send there. General J. E. Johnston is the only officer I know who has the confidence of the army and the people, and if he were ordered to report to me I would place him there on duty." Lee had no troops to send Beauregard, and yet it was all-important to retard Sherman's march. The troops in the Valley, under General L. L. Lomax, were scattered for subsistence, and could not be concentrated. "You may expect," said Lee to Breckinridge on February 21st, "Sheridan to move up the Valley, and Stoneman from Knoxville. What, then, will become of those sections of the country? Bragg will be forced back by Schofield, I fear, and until I abandon James River nothing can be sent from the army. Grant is preparing to draw out by his left with the intent of enveloping me; he may be preparing to anticipate my withdrawal. Everything of value should be removed from Richmond. The cavalry and artillery are still scattered for want of provender, and our supply and ammunition trains, which ought to be with the army in case of a sudden movement, are absent collecting provisions and forage in West Virginia and North Carolina. You will see to what straits we are reduced."

On the same day he wrote Mrs. Lee: " After sending my note this morning I received from the express office a bag of socks. You will have to send down your offerings as soon as you can and bring your work to a close, for I think General Grant will move against us soon—within a week if nothing prevents—and no man can tell what may be the result; but, trusting to a merciful God, who does not always give the battle to the strong, I pray we may not be overwhelmed. I shall, however, endeavor to do my duty and fight to the last. Should it be necessary to abandon our position to prevent being surrounded, what will you do? Will you remain, or leave the city? You must consider the question and make up your mind. It is a fearful condition, and we must rely for guidance and protection upon a kind Providence."

General Lee determined to make one more effort by a bold stroke to break the chains forged to confine him. Grant had so extended his left that he thought he might break through his works near the Appomattox below and east of Petersburg, and hence determined to assault

Fort Stedman, two miles from the city, where the opposing lines were one hundred and fifty yards and the respective pickets fifty yards apart. General Gordon, an officer always crammed with courage and fond of enterprise, was selected to make the attack with his corps (formerly Ewell's) and parts of Longstreet's and Hill's and a detachment of cavalry. His object was to capture the fort, thrust the storming party through the gap, and seize three forts on the high ground beyond and the lines on the right and left of it, under the impression that the forts were opened at the gorge. But there were no such forts. The redoubts that had a commanding fire on Fort Stedman were on the main line in the rear, and in front were a line of intrenchments. At about half-past four on the morning of March 25th Gordon made his daring sortie, broke through the trench guards, overpowered the garrison, and captured Fort Stedman, or Hare's Hill, and two adjacent batteries; but, after a most gallant struggle, was forced to retire, losing nineteen hundred and forty-nine prisoners and one thousand killed and wounded, but bringing back five hundred and sixty prisoners and Brigadier-General McLaughlin.

On February 27th Sheridan, with two divisions of cavalry, ten thousand sabers, moved up the Valley to Staunton, pushed from his front at Waynesborough a small force under Early, and, marching *via* Charlottesville, joined Grant on March 27th. Lee now recalled Rosser's cavalry division, and his cavalry corps embraced that division, W. H. F. Lee's and Fitz Lee's old division under Munford, Fitz Lee being assigned to the command of the cavalry corps—in all, about five thousand five hundred troopers.

During the winter General Lee had given careful consideration to the question of evacuating Petersburg and Richmond. It was attended with many embarrassments. Richmond was the capital city, the machinery of the Confederate Government was in motion there, and the abandonment of a country's capital was a serious step; there, too, were the workshops, iron works, rolling mills, and foundries, which were so essential. Their loss would be a deprivation; and then, too, there

was sorrow in turning away and leaving to their fate
the noble women, children, and old men of the two
cities, whose hearths and homes he had been so long
defending. The question of withdrawal was discussed
with Mr. Davis, who consented to it, the line of retreat
was decided, and Danville, in Virginia, selected as the
point to retire upon. It was determined to collect supplies at that point, so that Lee, rapidly moving from his
lines, could form a junction with General Joseph E.
Johnston, who on February 23d had been instructed to
assume the command of the Army of the Tennessee,
and all troops in the Department of South Carolina,
Georgia, and Florida. Lee and Johnston were then to
assail Sherman before Grant could get to his relief, as
the question of supplying his enormous army, moving
from its base to the interior, would retard him after the
first few days' march.

Sherman, after his junction with Schofield at Goldsborough, had nearly ninety thousand men of the three
arms. Johnston, having only eighteen thousand seven
hundred and sixty-one, telegraphed Lee that with his
small force he could only annoy Sherman, not stop him,
adding: " You have only to decide where to meet Sherman ; I will be near him." It is possible Lee, with his
army out of the trenches, gaining strength from other
quarters as he marched to Danville, and with absentees
returning, as in that event many would, could have carried to Johnston fifty or sixty thousand fighting men—
making their combined force over seventy thousand
effectives, as against Sherman's ninety thousand. The
South would have gladly staked its fortunes upon a
battle, when Lee and Johnston rode boot to boot and
directed the tactical details. Sherman by water visited
Grant on March 27th, told him he would be ready to
move from Goldsborough by April 10th, would threat-
en Raleigh and march for Weldon, sixty miles south
of Petersburg, and to General Grant in the direction
deemed best.

Grant, apprehensive that Lee would certainly abandon his intrenchments as soon as he heard Sherman had
crossed the Roanoke, determined to take the initiative.
He could easily do it, for he had an army number-

ing* one hundred and twenty-four thousand seven hundred men for duty. The returns of February 28, 1865, gives as the strength of General Lee's army, total effective of all arms, fifty-nine thousand and ninety-three. His losses in March were great at Fort Stedman—nearly three thousand—and desertions were numerous. Colonel Taylor, on March 31st, estimates that Lee had thirty-three thousand muskets to defend a line thirty-five miles in length, or a thousand men to the mile. Lee told the writer he had at that time thirty-five thousand; but after Five Forks, and in the encounters of March 31st, April 1st and 2d, he had only twenty thousand muskets available, and of all arms not over twenty-five thousand, when he began the retreat that terminated at Appomattox Court House.

The opposing horsemen, commanded by General Wesley Merritt, were composed of three divisions, under Thomas C. Devin, Custer, and Crook and formed part of the mixed command of Sheridan. From the morning report of March 31, 1865, they numbered thirteen thousand two hundred and nine present for duty, exclusive of a division under General Ronalds Mackenzie—about two thousand effectives. The cavalry corps of the Army of the Potomac numbered over fifteen thousand men in the saddle. In other words, where Lee had one infantry or cavalry or artillery soldier Grant had three! He possessed the enormous advantage, too, of being able to hold his formidable works with a force equal to the whole of Lee's army and still manœuvre nearly one hundred thousand men outside of them, either to extend his left or for other purposes. Fully aware of his great advantage, he waited impatiently to commence the spring campaign.

He was apprehensive that Lee would quietly draw out from his front at night and, gaining a good start, appear in Sherman's front before he could reach him. Having plenty of men, why should he wait for Sherman to join him? "I have had a feeling that it is better," said

---

* Report of the Secretary of War to the Thirty-ninth Congress gives one hundred and sixty-two thousand two hundred and thirty-four.

he to Mr. Lincoln, "to let Lee's old antagonist give his army the final blow and finish up the job. If the Western armies were ever to put in an appearance against Lee's army, it might give some of our politicians a chance to stir up sectional feeling in claiming everything for the troops from their own section of the country." "I see, I see," replied Mr. Lincoln; "in fact, my anxiety has been so great that I didn't care where the help came from so the work was perfectly done." Lee, chained to his trenches by his necessities, and waiting for better roads on account of the weak condition of his artillery and transportation animals, gave General Grant the opportunity to get around his lines west of Petersburg, for which he had so long waited.

On March 28th Grant sounded the *laissez aller*, as a writer puts it, and the next day great turning columns were put in motion to swing around the flank of Lee, and get possession of his remaining lines of transportation, the Lynchburg or Southside Railroad, and the Danville Railroad at Burkesville, the junction of the two. It was calculated that Lee would largely draw troops from his lines to avert such a disaster, and in that event they could be successfully assailed by the troops on their front. On that day General Lee wrote Mrs. Lee: "I have received your note with a bag of socks. I return the bag and receipt. The count is all right this time. I have put in the bag General Scott's autobiography, which I thought you might like to read. The general, of course, stands out very prominently, and does not hide his light under a bushel, but he appears the bold, sagacious, truthful man that he is. I inclose a note for little Agnes. I shall be very glad to see her to-morrow, but can not recommend pleasure trips now."

The Southern lines south of James River stretched from the Appomattox below Petersburg along the territory south of the city, then ran in a southwest direction parallel and protecting the Lynchburg Railroad, then bending west and northwest, terminated on Hatcher's Run, a little over a mile from Sutherland Station on the railroad. From this point the White Oak road runs west to Five Forks, four miles distant, where it is crossed

by the Ford road at right angles; a road from Dinwiddie courthouse joins the intersection of the two. A
person at that point could therefore travel in five different directions—east or west, north or south, or southeast—to the courthouse, eight miles away, from which
the location probably derives its name. Five Forks, in
front of the Southern right, became a strategic point.
If Grant occupied it he could tear up the Southside
Railroad west of Sutherland Station, and, while holding
Lee in his lines, detach infantry and cavalry, and destroy
the Danville Railroad, the only connecting link with the
Southern States.

Sheridan's large cavalry corps, supported by Warren's Fifth and Humphreys's Second Corps, was directed, on the 29th, to Dinwiddie Court House, the infantry
to occupy the country between the courthouse and Federal left, the cavalry the courthouse. Parke, who had
succeeded to the command of Burnside's Ninth Corps,
Wright with his Sixth, and Ord with the Army of the
James, held the line in the order named from the Appomattox to Lee's right. Ord, in command of the Twenty-
fourth (Gibbon's) and Twenty-fifth (Weitzel's) Army
Corps, Butler's old army, had placed Weitzel in charge
of the defenses at Bermuda Hundred and on the north
side of the James.

The purpose of the Union commander to get around
his right rear and break up his railroad connections
was promptly perceived by Lee. General Anderson was
sent at once, with Bushrod Johnson's division and Wise's
brigade, to his extreme right. Pickett's division was
also transferred to that point, and Fitz Lee's division
of cavalry was brought from the north side of James
River to Five Forks, reaching there on the morning of
the 30th; this division was at once advanced toward
Dinwiddie Court House, and met, fought, and checked
the Union cavalry under Merritt, advancing from that
point to Five Forks. General W. H. Payne, whose conspicuous daring and gallant conduct on every battlefield had made him so well known to the public and the
army, was here severely wounded. At sunset Pickett,
with Corse's, Terry's, and Stuart's brigades of his own
division, and Ransom's and Wallace's of Johnson's di-

vision, arrived at Five Forks, and so did the cavalry divisions of W. H. F. Lee and Rosser. The five infantry brigades under Pickett and the three cavalry divisions of Fitz Lee moved out on the Dinwiddie Court House road on the 31st, and attacked and drove Sheridan's cavalry corps back to the courthouse. Night put an end to the contest. The Confederates fell back early on the morning of April 1st to Five Forks, to prevent Warren's Fifth Corps, which had moved during the night to Sheridan's assistance, from attacking their left rear. Sheridan followed with Warren's infantry and his cavalry; Pickett's line of battle ran along the White Oak road, Munford's cavalry division was on his left, W. H. F. Lee's on his right, and Rosser in the rear, north of Hatcher's Run, guarding the wagon trains. About 4 P. M. Sheridan, having succeeded in massing the Fifth Corps, concealed by the woods beyond Pickett's left, attacked by seizing the White Oak road between Pickett and General Lee's lines, four miles away, with Warren's infantry, which enabled him to flank Pickett's line with the Fifth Corps, while he assailed his front and right with his cavalry corps.

Pickett was connected with the main line of his army by the cavalry pickets of Roberts's brigade, and was cut off from support and badly defeated, in spite of his right making a gallant resistance, in which W. H. F. Lee, with one of his cavalry brigades, in a brilliant encounter, repulsed two brigades under Custer. The Confederates lost between three and four thousand men, thirteen colors, and six guns. Pickett's isolated position was unfortunately selected. A line behind Hatcher's Run or at Sutherland Station could not have been flanked, but might been maintained until re-enforced by troops drawn from the Southern right at the Claiborne road crossing of Hatcher's Run. The Confederate cavalry were withdrawn during the night to the Southside Railroad, and were joined there by Hunton's brigade of Pickett's division and by General Bushrod Johnson, with Wise's, Gracies's, and Fulton's brigade, all under the command of General R. H. Anderson.

The disaster at Five Forks was the beginning of the end. Two large infantry and one cavalry corps, making

a total of fifty thousand officers and men,* with a roving commission in front of Lee's extreme right, im-
periled his communications most seriously, as well as
the safety of his lines. The Southern general could not
risk another attack outside of his works, and, in order
to strengthen that portion of them sufficiently to resist
assault, had so weakened what remained that it became
vulnerable. From the Appomattox to the right center
the thin gray line was so stretched that it was not as
formidable as a well-prepared skirmish line. Though
holding with tenacity to his right, Lee must let the bars
down elsewhere. Thirty-five thousand muskets were
guarding thirty-seven miles of intrenchments.

Grant on the night of April 1st was at Dabney's
Mill, a mile or two south of Boydton plank road, which
runs from Dinwiddie Court House to Petersburg. Colonel Horace Porter, his aid-de-camp, first gave him the
news of Sheridan's success at 9 P. M. that night as he
was sitting before "a blazing camp fire with his blue
cavalry overcoat on and the ever-present cigar in his
mouth." He sent over the field-wires at once orders for
an immediate assault along the lines, but subsequently
directed the attack to be made at 4 A. M. the next day.
All during the night a bombardment was kept up on all
portions of the Confederate lines. At dawn on Sunday,
April 2d, Parke and Wright, with the Ninth and Sixth
Corps, and Ord, with the Army of the James, successfully
assaulted the attenuated lines in their front. The task
was easy, and while handfuls of brave men heroically
resisted, like shooting stars their course was brilliant
but brief. The storming pioneer parties everywhere cut
away the abatis and *chevaux-de-frise*, and through the
opening the blue masses poured into the works. There
were high parapets and high relief and deep ditches;
but the troops had been drawn away to the Southern
right, and except here and there, notably at Fort Gregg,
it was only a matter of physical agility to climb over
them. Only small garrisons were in the forts, and very
few men in the connecting lines.

Four small brigades, Wilcox's division, Hill's corps—

---

* Morning report, Army of the Potomac, March 31, 1864.

viz., Thomas's, Lane's, Davis's, and McCombs's—held
the entire line in the front of the armies of Ord and
Wright, while Gordon, with a few thousand troops, held
in front of Parke's Ninth Corps. Lee's troops were
forced back to an inner line whose flanks rested on the
river above and below Petersburg, and there resisted all
further attempts to break through them. Before 10 A. M.,
Lee knew he could only hope to cling to his trenches
until night, and that the longer defense of Richmond
and Petersburg was not possible. All his skill would be
required to extricate his army and get it out and away
from the old lines. Longstreet reached Lee from the
north side of the James about 10 A. M. on the 2d, with
Field's division. It is stated that he had not perceived
that the Federal lines in front of Richmond had been
weakened by transferring troops to the vicinity of
Petersburg, and hence did not move to Lee earlier, as
he had been instructed to do in that event. In the
midst of the turmoil, excitement, and danger, Lee was
as calm and collected as ever. When the Sixth Corps
broke over A. P. Hill's lines, that officer was at General
Lee's headquarters at the Turnbull House, and rode at
once rapidly to his front, where he was killed by some
stragglers who had crossed the Boydton road in the
direction of the railroad, whose presence in that vicinity
he did not expect. Hill in many respects was a good
officer—earnest, dashing, zealous, and prompt to execute; he had rendered marked service throughout the
whole war, and his light division had written many victories upon its proud standards.

CHAPTER XV.

EVACUATION OF RICHMOND AND THE PETERSBURG LINES.—RETREAT AND SURRENDER.

GENERAL LEE on the morning of April 2d telegraphed Breckinridge, Secretary of War, that it was necessary his position should be abandoned that night, " or run the risk of being cut off in the morning; it will be a difficult but I hope not an impracticable operation. The troops will all be directed to Amelia Court House." He advised that all preparations be made for leaving Richmond that night. The Southern President was kept informed on all subjects connected with the army, and of course knew that a crisis in its affairs was approaching, which involved the evacuation of its position; but he was not prepared for a precipitate announcement to that effect, or indeed for any change of affairs for two weeks. On April 2d he occupied his accustomed seat, about the center of the middle aisle, in St. Paul's Episcopal Church, Richmond, much interested as usual in the services conducted by his friend, the Rev. Dr. Minnigerode. There he received a dispatch. Upon reading it, he quietly rose and left the church. The telegram was from General Lee, announcing his speedy withdrawal from Petersburg. Lee's decision quickly became generally known in the two cities, and the feeling produced can readily be imagined. Women prayed, men wept, children wondered. Three exits remained only for the Army of Northern Virginia—one north of Richmond, one west, and one southwest. No object could now be achieved by marching in the first two directions, but by the remaining one Johnston might be reached, and his communications by the Danville Railroad with the South be maintained.

On the afternoon of April 2d Lee issued orders for his troops to leave their lines everywhere at 8 P. M., and take up the line of march for Amelia Court House.

This little village is on the Richmond and Danville Railroad, thirty-eight miles southwest of Richmond. At that point it was determined to concentrate, issue—wonderful to relate—abundant rations to the troops, and get them again in shape after the heavy work of the past few days and the night march. As Grant's army was stretched to the Appomattox on the south side above Petersburg, Lee must march up its north side. Longstreet's, Hill's, and Gordon's corps crossed the Appomattox that night, the two former at Battersea factory pontoon bridge, the latter at Pocahontas and Railroad bridge, and moved—*via* Bevel's and Goode's bridges on the Appomattox below where it is crossed by the Danville Railroad—to Amelia Court House. Mahone's division was directed to the same point, *via* Chesterfield Court House. Ewell, commanding the troops in front of Richmond, Kershaw's and Custis Lee's divisions, and the naval brigade, was instructed to cross to the south side of James River, cross the Appomattox at Goode's bridge, and join the army at Amelia Court House. The commands of Pickett and Bushrod Johnson and the cavalry, being west of Petersburg and of the Federal lines, moved up the south bank of the Appomattox. General Lee was not able to concentrate all his troops at Amelia Court House until midday on the 5th, Ewell being the last to arrive. The small army was now divided into four small infantry corps or commands, and a cavalry corps commanded respectively by Longstreet, Ewell, R. H. Anderson, Gordon, and Fitzhugh Lee. Mahone's division was assigned to Longstreet's corps, and the naval battalion of Commodore Tucker to General Custis Lee's division.

The troops, though suffering for food and raiment, want of sleep, and marching over roads heavy from copious rains, were buoyant in spirit, brave in heart, and of undoubted morale; nearly every one of them was a survivor of bloody battles and a veteran of years of terrible war. They were soldiers of no "ordinary mold, who had an abiding faith amounting to fanati-

cism that the God of battles would in the end send their
cause safe deliverance, and they followed Lee with an
almost childlike faith, which set no bounds to his genius
and power of achievement." Shut up so long in dismal,
dangerous trenches, the fields, running streams, trees
thick with bursting buds of spring, grass growing green
under the kisses of the sun, and new scenes, were to
them most refreshing and exhilarating.

In obedience to a law of Congress, Ewell, in command at Richmond, had made arrangements to burn
the tobacco there whenever the evacuation of the city
should render that necessary to prevent it from falling
into the hands of the enemy. After the departure of
the Southern troops, the fire got beyond local control.
Mrs. Lee's house, in the center of the square on Franklin Street between Seventh and Eighth, was at one time
in danger from the conflagration, a large church on the
opposite side having caught fire from flying sparks, and
many offers were made by persons rushing to her room
to move her elsewhere, which she resisted. In the midst
of the excitement a gentleman cried that the only way
to save the square in which she lived was to blow up
every other house, and all were so agitated that they
readily acquiesced in the remarkable suggestion, and
seemed much pleased at the ready ability of the person
who could devise at such a time a remedy; while the
poor property holder immediately began to calculate if
his dwelling would be the "every other house." Graphic
pictures have been painted in well-chosen phrase of the
exciting scenes of April 3d. On one side the retreating march of the Confederates, on the other the triumphant advance of the Federals; while between the
two, great pillars of fire rose draped in the smoke of
a burning city. The tattered, brown, weather-beaten
army is marching away through woods and over roads
with straggling trains; the faces of the soldiers are
turned from Richmond. The victorious legions, glistening with steel, with clashing music and waving banners, are pouring into the city, marching through the
streets, and stacking arms in the Public Square, where
"stood the dumb walls of the Capitol of the Confederacy." White clouds of dense smoke with the light of the

fire woven in their folds, reaching from the island-dotted river to the tall trees on the hill of the Public Square, hung in the sky above the fated city.

At the same time Grant rode into Petersburg between rows of closed houses and deserted streets, cheered here and there by a few groups of negroes, until he came to a comfortable-looking brick house with a yard in front, where he dismounted and with his staff took seats on the piazza. There Mr. Lincoln, who had been for some days at City Point, joined him. " I doubt," said an eye witness, " whether Mr. Lincoln ever experienced a happier moment in his life," as, seizing General Grant's hand, he congratulated him on his success. The Union commander then set out for Sutherland Station, above Petersburg, where he and Meade passed the night of the 3d. Mr. Lincoln afterward went to Richmond ; he was curious to see the house Mr. Davis had lived in. With a stride described as long and careless he walked its streets, and asked " Is it far to President Davis's house ? " Upon reaching the house, Captain Graves, aid-de-camp to General Weitzel, whose Twenty-fifth Corps first entered the city, states that he took a seat in a chair, remarking, " This must have been President Davis's chair," and then jumped up and said in a boyish manner, " Come, let us look at the house." Mr. Davis was then in Danville, from which place on the 5th he published a proclamation in which he tells his countrymen not to despond, " but, relying on God, meet the foe with fresh defiance and with unconquered and unconquerable hearts."

Grant gave orders for a vigorous pursuit in two columns south of Appomattox parallel to Lee's route north of it—one under Ord up the Southside or Lynchburg Railroad to Burkeville Junction, fifty-two miles from Petersburg ; the other under Sheridan, who had the cavalry corps and Second, Fifth, and Sixth Infantry Corps, on a route between Ord and Lee. These movements directly west, if properly made, would plant the Army of the Potomac across the Danville road at Burkeville, as well as at another point between there and Amelia Court House, twenty miles northeast of Burkeville. In that case Lee's withdrawal to Danville would be blocked, his junction with Johnston foiled, and the use of the Danville Railroad taken away from him. Sheridan arrived at Jetersville—on the Danville Railroad, seven miles from Amelia Court House, where Lee was that morning—on the afternoon of the 4th, with some eighteen thousand troops of all arms, and intrenched. Meade did not reach him until late in the afternoon of the 5th. The last of Lee's force, Ewell, it will be remembered, did not reach Amelia Court House until noon that day. Still, if Lee's supplies had been there as ordered, he might have moved against Sheridan at Jetersville very early on the 5th with his whole force except Ewell, over twenty thousand men, and defeated him and reached Burkeville, thirteen miles farther, before Ord, who arrived there late that night.

Had Lee once passed beyond Burkeville, the Danville road could have supplied his army, its trains transported them to Danville, and *via* Greensborough to Raleigh and Goldsborough, or wherever Johnston was, or Johnston's force could have been rapidly brought to the Army of Northern Virginia. "Not finding the supplies ordered to be placed at Amelia Court House," says Lee, "nearly twenty-four hours were lost in endeavoring to collect in the country subsistence for men and horses. The delay was fatal, and could not be retrieved." There is some mystery about these supplies. Lee ordered them to be sent there from Danville, for he has so stated; and General J. M. St. John, then commissary general, states that on April 1, 1865, there were five hundred thousand rations of bread and one million five hundred thousand rations of meat at Danville, and three hundred thousand rations of bread and meat in Richmond, and that he received no orders to send supplies to Amelia Court House either from Richmond or Danville; and Mr. Lewis Harvie, then the president of the Richmond and Danville Railroad, has testified that no orders were ever given to his officers to transport any rations to Amelia Court House. It has been stated that on that famous Sunday a train-load of supplies arrived at Amelia Court House from Danville, but the officer in charge was met there by an order to bring the train to Richmond, because the cars were needed for the transportation of the personal property of the Confederate authorities. Mr. Davis was in ignorance of any such instruction, and would be the last man to place his personal wants or desires ahead of the necessities of the soldiers, and the commissary general and the railroad president also testify that they knew nothing of any such orders.

Cut off from Danville, the Southern troops were directed on Farmville, thirty-five miles west, and broke camp on the night of the 5th. Meade had proposed to attack Lee with the Second, Fifth, and Sixth Corps and Sheridan's cavalry at Amelia Court House early on the morning of the 6th, and did not know he had moved until he had proceeded within a few miles of that village. Longstreet, in the advance, reached Rice Station, on the Lynchburg Railroad, on the morning of the 6th, and formed line of battle; he was followed by the commands of R. H. Anderson, Ewell, and Gordon, and W. H. F. Lee's cavalry division in the order named. The remainder of the cavalry, under Rosser, had been passed to the front to protect the High Bridge between Rice Station and Farmville, and were just in time, as General Ord had sent out two regiments of infantry and his headquarters cavalry to burn that bridge and the one above at Farmville.

General Theodore Read, of Ord's staff, conducted the party. A fight ensued, in which General Read and Colonel Washburn, commanding the infantry, and all the cavalry officers were killed on the Federal side, and General Dearing, commanding a brigade of Rosser's division; Colonel Boston, the Fifth Virginia Cavalry; and Major Thompson, commanding Rosser's horse artillery, were killed on the Confederate side. The Federal force surrendered. The three Southern officers killed were exceptionally fine soldiers, and their loss was greatly deplored.

Anderson's march was much interrupted by the attack of the Federal cavalry on his flank. Halting to repel them and save the trains, a gap was made between the head of his column and the rear of Longstreet's, into which, after he had crossed Sailor's Creek—a small tributary flowing north into the Appomattox—the large force of Union cavalry was thrust, and mounted and dismounted cavalry stopped him and compelled him to deploy in their front. Ewell followed Anderson across Sailor's Creek, but Gordon, guarding an immense wagon train, turned to his right down the creek before crossing it on a road running to High Bridge. The Sixth Corps getting up on Ewell's rear, made him face his two divisions about—Kershaw on the right of the road and Custis Lee on the left, the navy battalion in rear of his right. Anderson and Ewell were facing in opposite directions, and neither had any artillery. Enveloped on both flanks and front in the combat which followed, Ewell was overwhelmed, not more than three hundred men of his three thousand escaping. Anderson was simultaneously attacked on front and flank, and also defeated. Both commands lost, in killed, wounded, and prisoners nearly six thousand men. Among the prisoners were Generals Corse and Hunton, of Pickett's division, and Generals Ewell, Custis Lee, Kershaw, and Dubose, of Ewell's.

Humphreys's Second Corps in the meantime closely followed Gordon, and had a running contest with his rear for some miles, capturing thirteen flags, four guns, and some seventeen hundred prisoners. Gordon reached High Bridge that night, but lost a large part of a wagon train which had given the Confederates much trouble on the whole march and greatly delayed their progress, because drawn by weak animals over roads soft and muddy from the recent rains. Longstreet, after waiting in vain for the other commands to join him at Rice Station, under instructions marched with the divisions of Heth, Wilcox, and Field for Farmville, and that night crossed to the north side of the Appomattox. He had crossed that river twice already—once at Petersburg and once at Goode's Bridge. Fitz Lee's cavalry corps followed him, crossing the river above Farmville by a deep ford, leaving a force to burn the bridge. Gordon, to whose command Bushrod Johnson's division had been assigned, crossed at High Bridge, below Farmville, and so did Mahone with his fine division.

At Farmville the Confederates feasted. It was the first occasion since leaving Richmond that rations had been issued, and their outdoor exercise had given them

an appetite. Previous to this, organized bodies had
been marched up to the corn houses *en route*, and each
soldier given a dozen ears of corn, with a suggestion
that he parch the grains on getting into camp.   An en-
enthusiastic young Irishman from Belturbet, County of
Cavan, named Llewellyn Saunderson, reached the country in one of the last vessels running the blockade, and,
being a Southern sympathizer, reported to the War Department, asking to be commissioned and sent to the
field.   It was done, and he was ordered to report to
General Fitz Lee.   His pockets were full of gold, and
he quickly purchased a fine horse, the gray uniform of
the staff officer, and joined the staff but a short time
before the final attack.   The rear guard of cavalry from
Petersburg to Appomattox was obliged to pass over
ground gleaned by the preceding infantry and artillery.
Occasionally a trooper would secure a can of buttermilk, but corn, divided between horses and troopers,
was the "solid comfort."   Saunderson was bold, bright,
and witty of course, behaving admirably under fire, and
cheerfully under the treatment he received.   He was
paroled at Appomattox Court House, and returned to
the " Green Isle " loaded with war experience.   When
asked in Richmond what he would say to his countrymen about the Confederates, he replied, " Oh, I never
saw men fight better, but they don't ate enough."

The once great Army of Northern Virginia was now
composed of two small corps of infantry and the cavalry corps, and resumed the march toward Lynchburg
on the old stage road, but after going four miles stopped;
and was formed into line of battle in a well-chosen position to give the trains time to get ahead.   It was attacked by two divisions of Humphreys's Second Corps,
which had been long hanging on its rear, but repulsed
them, Mahone handling Miles very roughly.   Humphreys
lost five hundred and seventy-one men killed, wounded,
and missing.   Preceding this attack, Crook's cavalry division crossed the river above Farmville, and was immediately charged with great success by the Southern
cavalry and driven back.   The Federal General Gregg
and a large number of prisoners were taken.   General
Lee was talking to the commander of his cavalry when

Crook appeared, saw the combat, and expressed great pleasure at the result.

Had Lee not stopped to fight he could have reached Appomattox Station on the afternoon of the 8th, obtained rations, and moved that evening to Lynchburg. The delay allowed Sheridan—with two divisions of cavalry, followed by Ord's infantry and Fifth Corps, marching by Prince Edward Court House—to reach Appomattox Station on the evening of the 8th, where he captured trains with Lee's supplies and obstructed his march. Ord's infantry did not arrive in front of Appomattox Court House until 10 A. M. on the 9th. Having demonstrated that what was left of his proud army would rush to battle as of old, Lee on the night of the 7th continued his retreat—Gordon in advance, next Longstreet, then the cavalry—and on the evening of the 8th halted in the vicinity of Appomattox Court House. The Second and Sixth Corps resumed the direct pursuit at half-past five on the morning of the 8th, and that night went into camp three miles in the rear of Longstreet. The Confederate cavalry had marched from the rear to the front during the night, with orders to resume the march at one o'clock, on the morning of the 9th. "Fitz Lee, with the cavalry supported by Gordon," says General Lee, "was ordered to drive the enemy from his front, wheel to the left, and cover the passage of the trains, while Longstreet should close up and hold the position. During the night there were indications of a large force massing on our left and front. Fitz Lee was directed to ascertain its strength, and to suspend his advance until daylight if necessary." It was General Lee's intention to move by Campbell Court House through Pittsylvania County toward Danville. Two battalions of artillery and the ammunition wagons were directed to accompany the army, the rest of the artillery and wagons to move toward Lynchburg; but the plan could not be executed. Sheridan had been joined by Crook, and had thrown the immense cavalry corps directly across his path, between Appomattox Station and the Court House, the two places being five miles apart; and Ord, with the Army of the James and the Fifth Corps, was rapidly marching to his support, joining him at 9 or 10 A. M. on the 9th. The greater part of Gibbon's Twenty-fourth Corps, a portion of Weitzel's Twenty-fifth Corps, the Fifth Corps, and four divisions of cavalry, including Mackenzie, formed a living rampart of over forty thousand troops * to the advance of Gordon and Fitz Lee's five thousand. Directly behind Lee were the Second and Sixth Corps, over twenty-five thousand troops.†

Gracefully General Lee yielded to the inevitable. The splendid army, with whose courage and heroism a world was familiar, was reduced to a fragment of brave men, many of whom, from exposure and want of food, could not lift a musket to the shoulder. The end which Lee feared and Grant expected had come. For some days the latter had been thinking how best he could introduce the subject of surrender to Lee, to relieve him from initiating an embarrassing proposition. The Union commander arrived at Farmville a little before noon on April 7th, establishing headquarters at the village hotel. He told Ord, Gibbon, and Wright, who had called at the hotel, that he was thinking of sending a communication to General Lee "to pave the way to the stopping of further bloodshed"; he had heard, too, that Ewell, then a prisoner, had said that "it was the duty of the authorities to negotiate for peace now, and that for every man killed somebody would be responsible, and it would be little better than murder." Influenced by such reflections, he wrote the following communication:

April 7, 1865.

GENERAL : The result of the last week must convince you of the hopelessness of further resistance on the part of the Army of Northern Virginia in this struggle. I feel that it is so, and regard it as my duty to shift from myself the responsibility of any further effusion of blood, by asking of you the surrender of that portion

---

* Ord left Petersburg with twenty thousand troops all arms ; Fifth Corps, fifteen thousand nine hundred and seventy-three. (Report of March 31, 1865.) Sheridan's cavalry, thirteen thousand eight hundred and ten, to which add one thousand for the Fifth Corps artillery, makes fifty thousand seven hundred and eighty-three.

† Second Corps report, March 31, 1865: Twenty-one thousand one hundred and sixty-seven infantry, artillery, and seventy guns. Sixth: Eighteen thousand three hundred and eighty-four artillery and infantry and fifty-four guns=thirty-nine thousand five hundred and fifty-one, and one hundred and twenty-four guns.

of the Confederate States army known as the Army of Northern Virginia.   U. S. GRANT, *Lieutenant General.*
General R. E. LEE.

General Seth Williams, his adjutant general, a former intimate friend of General Lee's and his adjutant when he was superintendent at West Point, carried this communication across the river to Humphreys, who sent it at once through his lines to Lee, who was still in the position from which he had repulsed Humphreys's attack that day. Humphreys received Grant's note at 8.30 P. M., and Grant, Lee's reply after midnight, which read:

April 7, 1865.

GENERAL: I have received your note of this date. Though not entertaining the opinion you express on the hopelessness of further resistance on the part of the Army of Northern Virginia, I reciprocate your desire to avoid useless effusion of blood, and therefore, before considering your proposition, ask the terms you will offer on condition of its surrender.

R. E. LEE, *General.*
Lieutenant-General U. S. GRANT.

The next morning a reply was given to General Williams, who again went to Humphreys front to have it transmitted to Lee's. Williams overtook Humphreys on the march; his letter was sent at once through the cavalry rear guard, close to General Humphreys's front, to General Lee, whose reply was not received until dusk by Humphreys, and did not reach General Grant until after midnight, at a large, white farmhouse at Curdsville, ten miles in his rear. The two notes of that day (8th) are as follows:

April 8, 1865.

GENERAL : Your note of last evening, in reply to mine of the same date, asking the condition on which I will accept the surrender of the Army of Northern Virginia, is just received. In reply, I would say that, peace being my great desire, there is but one condition that I would insist upon—namely, that the men and officers surrendered shall be disqualified for taking up arms again against the Government of the United States until properly exchanged. I will meet you, or will designate officers to meet any officers you may name for the same purpose, at any point agreeable to you, for the purpose of arranging definitely the terms upon which the surrender of the Army of Northern Virginia will be received.   U. S. GRANT, *Lieutenant General.*
General R. E. LEE.

April 8, 1868.

GENERAL : I received at a late hour your note of to-day. In mine of yesterday I did not intend to propose the surrender of the Army of Northern Virginia, but to ask the terms of your proposition. To be frank, I do not think the emergency has arisen to call for the surrender of this army, but as the restoration of peace should be the sole object of all, I desire to know whether your proposal would lead to that end. I can not, therefore, meet you with a view to surrender the Army of Northern Virginia, but as far as your proposal may affect the Confederate States forces under my command, and tend to the restoration of peace, I should be pleased to meet you at 10 A. M. to-morrow on the old stage road to Richmond, between the picket lines of the two armies.   R. E. LEE, *General.*

Lieutenant-General U. S. GRANT.

The Federal flag of truce accompanying Williams when he bore Grant's first communication appeared in front of General Sorrel's Georgia brigade, formerly Wright's, of Mahone's division, about 9 P. M. Sorrel had been dangerously wounded at Petersburg, and the brigade was commanded by Colonel G. E. Tayloe. This officer sent Colonel Herman H. Perry, his adjutant general, to meet the flag, who advanced some distance from his lines, and met a very handsomely dressed officer, who introduced himself as General Seth Williams, of General Grant's staff. Perry's worn Confederate uniform and slouch hat did not compare favorably by moonlight with the magnificence of Williams's, but, being six feet high and a fine-looking fellow, he drew himself up proudly, as if perfectly satisfied with his personal exterior.

"After I had introduced myself," says Perry, " he felt in his side pocket for documents, as I thought, but the document was a very nice-looking silver flask, as well as I could distinguish. He remarked that he hoped I would not think it was unsoldierly if he offered me some very fine brandy. I will own up now that I wanted that drink awfully. Worn down, hungry, and dispirited, it would have been a gracious godsend if some old Confederate and I could have emptied that flask between us in that dreadful hour of misfortune. But I raised myself about an inch higher, if possible, bowed, and refused politely, trying to produce the ridiculous appearance of having feasted on champagne and pound-cake not ten minutes before, and I had not the slightest use for as plebeian a drink as 'fine brandy.'

"He was a true gentleman, begged pardon, and placed the flask in his pocket again without touching the contents in my presence. If he had taken a drink, and my Confederate olfactories had obtained a whiff of the odor of it, it is possible that I should have 'caved.' The truth is, I had not eaten two ounces in two days, and I had my coat tail then full of corn, waiting to parch it as soon as an opportunity might present itself. I did not leave it behind me, because I had nobody I could trust it with. As an excuse which I felt I ought to make for refusing his proffered courtesy, I rather haughtily said that I had been sent forward only to receive any communication that was offered, and could not properly accept or offer any courtesies. In fact, if I had offered what I could, it would have taken my corn." Grant's note to Lee being then transferred from Williams to Perry, the Confederate colonel and Federal general bowed profoundly to each other and separated.

On the morning of the 9th General Grant dispatched another note to General Lee as follows:

April 9, 1865.

GENERAL: Your note of yesterday is received. I have no authority to treat on the subject of peace; the meeting proposed for 10 A. M. to-day could lead to no good. I will state, however, General, that I am equally anxious for peace with yourself, and the whole North entertains the same feeling. The terms upon which peace can be had are well understood. By the South laying down their arms they will hasten that most desirable event, save thousands of human lives, and hundreds of millions of property not yet destroyed. Seriously hoping that all our difficulties may be settled without the loss of another life, I subscribe myself, etc.,

U. S. GRANT, *Lieutenant General.*

General R. E. LEE.

Humphreys sent it forward by Colonel Whittier, his adjutant general, who met Colonel Marshall, of Lee's staff, by whom he was conducted to the general. To this note Lee replied:

April 9, 1865.

GENERAL : I received your note of this morning on the picket line whither I had come to meet you and ascertain definitely what terms were embraced in your proposal of yesterday with refer-

ence to the surrender of the army. I now ask an interview in accordance with the offer contained in your letter of yesterday for that purpose.   R. E. LEE, *General.*
Lieutenant-General U. S. GRANT.

Grant, who received this note eight or nine miles from Appomattox, at once answered it.

April 9, 1865.

GENERAL R. E. LEE, *commanding C. S. A.:* Your note of this date is but this moment (11.50 A. M.) received. In consequence of my having passed from the Richmond and Lynchburg road to the Farmville and Lynchburg road, I am, at this writing, about four miles west of Walker's Church, and will push forward to the front for the purpose of meeting you. Notice sent to me on this road where you wish the interview to take place will meet me.
Very respectfully, your obedient servant,
U. S. GRANT, *Lieutenant General.*

The reply was sent direct to General Lee by Colonel Babcock, of his staff. Lee was obliged to confront a painful issue. His duty had been performed, but so earnest was he in trying to extricate his troops, and carry them South, that he had failed to recognize the hopelessness of further resistance, or the emergency that called for the surrender of his army. At the suggestion of some of his higher officers, General Pendleton, the commander of his reserve artillery, went to Lee on the 7th to say that their united judgment agreed that it was wrong to have more men on either side killed, and that they did not wish that he should bear the entire trial of reaching that conclusion. But Lee replied that he had too many brave men to think of laying down his arms, and that they still fought with great spirit; that if he should first intimate to Grant that he would listen to terms, an unconditional surrender might be demanded, and "sooner than that I am resolved to die." Lee had not altogether abandoned the purpose to march South, even after the notes of the 7th and 8th had been exchanged. Longstreet, Gordon, and Fitz Lee, commanding his corps, were summoned to his headquarters bivouac fires on the night of the 8th, near Appomattox Court House. The situation was explained freely, and the correspondence with Grant alluded to. It was decided that Gordon and Fitz Lee should attack Sheridan's cavalry at daylight on the 9th and open the way; but in case the cavalry was re-enforced by heavy bodies of infantry, the commanding general must be at once notified, as surrender was inevitable. The attack was made at sunrise, and the Federal cavalry driven back with the loss of two guns and a number of prisoners; the arrival at this time of two corps of Federal infantry necessitated the retirement of the Southern lines. General Ord states that he was "barely in time, for, in spite of General Sheridan's attempts, the cavalry was falling back in confusion." A white flag went out from the Southern ranks, the firing ceased; the war in Virginia was over. Colonel Babcock, the bearer of General Grant's last note, found General Lee near Appomattox Court House, lying under an apple tree upon a blanket spread on some rails, from which circumstance the widespread report originated that the surrender took place under an apple tree.

General Lee, Colonel Marshall, of his staff, Colonel Babcock, of General Grant's, and a mounted orderly rode to the village, and found Mr. Wilmer McLean, a resident, who, upon being told that General Lee wanted the use of a room in some house, conducted the party to his dwelling, a comfortable two-story brick, with a porch in front running the length of the house. General Lee was ushered into the room on the left of the hall as you enter, and about one o'clock was joined by General Grant, his staff, and Generals Sheridan and Ord. Grant sat at a marble-topped table in the center of the room, Lee at a small oval table near the front window. "The contrast between the commanders," said one who was present, "was striking." Grant, not yet forty-three years old, five feet eight inches tall, shoulders slightly stooped, hair and beard nut brown, wearing a dark-blue flannel blouse unbuttoned, showing vest beneath; ordinary top boots, trousers inside; dark-yellow thread gloves; without spurs or sword, and no marks of rank except a general's shoulder straps. Lee, fifty-eight years old, six feet tall, hair and beard silver gray; a handsome uniform of Confederate gray buttoned to the throat, with three stars on each side of the turned-down collar, fine top boots with handsome spurs, elegant gauntlets, and at his side a splendid sword.* With a magnificent physique, not a pound of superfluous flesh, ruddy cheeks bronzed by exposure, grave and dignified, he was the focus for all eyes. "His demeanor was that of a thoroughly possessed gentleman who had a disagreeable duty to perform, but was determined to get through it as well and as soon as he could" without the exhibition of temper or mortification. Generals Lee and Grant had met once, eighteen years before, when both were fighting for the same cause in Mexico—one an engineer officer on the staff of Scott, the commanding general, the other a subaltern of infantry in Garland's brigade. After a pleasant reference to that event, Lee promptly drew attention to the business before them, the terms of surrender were arranged, and at General Lee's request reduced to writing, as follows:

APPOMATTOX COURT HOUSE, VA., *April* 9, 1865.

GENERAL : In accordance with the substance of my letter to you of the 8th inst., I propose to receive the surrender of the Army of Northern Virginia on the following terms, to wit : Rolls of all the officers and men to be made in duplicate, one copy to be given to an officer to be designated by me, the other to be retained by such officer or officers as you may designate. The officers to give their individual paroles not to take up arms against the Government of the United States until properly exchanged ; and each company and regimental commander sign a like parole for the men of their commands. The arms, artillery, and public property to be parked and stacked, and turned over to the officers appointed by me to receive them. This will not embrace the side-arms of the officers nor the private horses or baggage. This done, each officer and man will be allowed to return to his home, not to be disturbed by United States authority so long as he observes his parole, and the laws in force where he may reside.

U. S. GRANT, *Lieutenant General.*

General R. E. LEE.

"Unless you have some suggestion to make, I will

---

* The handle of this sword is white, with a lion's head at the top and wrapped with gilt wire (not studded with jewels, as has been published), with gilt guard, the scabbard of blue steel with gilt trimmings. Where the rings are attached, on one side of the blade, are the words, "General Robert E. Lee, from a Marylander, 1863 "; on the other, " Aide toi et Dieu t'aidera." This sword is in the possession of General G. W. C. Lee, son of General Lee, and the President of Washington and Lee University at Lexington, Va.

have a copy of the letter made in ink and sign it," said Grant; and it gave Lee the opportunity to tell him that the cavalrymen and many of the artillerymen owned their own horses, and he wished to know whether these men would be permitted to retain their horses. The terms gave to the officers only that privilege, and so Grant stated; but seeing that Lee's face showed plainly that he would like that concession made, the former said feelingly that he supposed that most of the men in ranks were small farmers, that their horses would be useful in putting in a crop to carry themselves and families through the next winter, and that he would give instructions " to let all men who claim to own a horse or mule take the animals home with them to work their little farms." The Union commander was in touch with his President. General Weitzel, who had entered Richmond with his Twenty-fifth Corps and received its formal capitulation, asked Mr. Lincoln what he " should do in regard to the conquered people?" The latter is reported to have replied that he did not wish to give any orders on that subject, but added, " If I were in your place I'd let 'em up easy, I'd let 'em up easy." It was the fear of his men losing their horses in case of surrender that made the Confederate cavalry commander ask permission at the council the night before to extricate his cavalry in case of surrender, provided it was done before the flag of truce changed the status. To Grant's written propositions for the surrender of the Army of Northern Virginia, General Lee replied:

HEADQUARTERS ARMY OF NORTHERN VIRGINIA, *April* 9, 1865.
GENERAL: I received your letter of this date, containing the terms of the surrender of the Army of Northern Virginia as proposed by you. As they are substantially the same as those expressed in your letter of the 8th instant, they are accepted. I will proceed to designate the proper officers to carry the stipulation into effect. R. E. LEE, *General.*
Lieutenant-General U. S. GRANT.

The formalities were concluded without dramatic accessories, and then Lee's thoughts turned to his hungry veterans and to his prisoners. " I have a thousand or more of your men and officers, whom we have required to march along with us for several days," said

Lee to Grant. " I shall be glad to send them to your lines as soon as it can be arranged, for I have no provisions for them. My own men have been living for the last few days principally upon parched corn, and we are badly in need of both rations and forage." The rations sent from Lynchburg to the Southerners were captured. When Grant suggested that he should send Lee twenty-five thousand rations, the latter told him it would be ample, and assured him it would be a great relief. The Confederate commander then left, and rode away to break the sad news to the brave troops he had so long commanded.

His presence in their midst was an exhibition of the devotion of soldier to commander. The troops crowded around him, eagerly desiring to shake his hand. They had seen him when his eye calmly surveyed miles of fierce, raging conflict; had closely observed him when, tranquil, composed, undisturbed, he had heard the wild shout of victory rend the air ; now they saw their beloved chieftain a prisoner of war, and sympathy, boundless admiration, and love for him filled their brave hearts. They pressed up to him, anxious to touch his person or even his horse, and copious tears washed from strong men's cheeks the stains of powder. Slowly and painfully he turned to his soldiers, and, with voice quivering with emotion, said : " Men, we have fought through the war together ; I have done my best for you ; my heart is too full to say more." It was a simple but most affecting scene. On the next day a formal leave of his army was taken by General Lee.

HEADQUARTERS ARMY OF NORTHERN VIRGINIA, *April* 10, 1865.

After four years of arduous service, marked by unsurpassed courage and fortitude, the Army of Northern Virginia has been compelled to yield to overwhelming numbers and resources. I need not tell the survivors of so many hard-fought battles, who have remained steadfast to the last, that I have consented to this result from no distrust of them ; but feeling that valor and devotion could accomplish nothing that could compensate for the loss that would have attended the continuation of the contest, I have determined to avoid the useless sacrifice of those whose past services have endeared them to their countrymen. By the terms of agreement, officers and men can return to their homes and remain there until exchanged. You will take with you the satisfaction that proceeds from the consciousness of duty faithfully performed ; and I earnestly pray that a merciful God will extend to you his blessing and protection.   With an unceasing admiration of your constancy and devotion to your country, and a grateful remembrance of your kind and generous consideration of myself, I bid you an affectionate farewell.   R. E. LEE, *General.*

And then in silence, with lifted hat, he rode through a weeping army to his home in Richmond.   He was not present at the final act of surrender ; the details were prepared by three officers on each side, and were as follows :

APPOMATTOX COURT HOUSE, VA., *April* 10, 1865.

Agreement entered into this day in regard to the surrender of the Army of Northern Virginia to the United States authorities :

1. The troops shall march by brigades and detachments to a designated point ; stack their arms, deposit their flags, sabers, pistols, etc., and thence march to their homes, under charge of their officers, superintended by their respective division and corps commanders, officers retaining their side arms and the authorized number of private horses.

2. All public horses, and public property of all kinds, to be turned over to staff officers to be designated by the United States authorities.

3. Such transportation as may be agreed upon as necessary for the transportation of the private baggage of officers will be allowed to accompany the officers, to be turned over, at the end of the trip, to the nearest United States quartermaster, receipts being taken for the same.

4. Couriers and mounted men of the artillery and cavalry, whose horses are their own private property, will be allowed to retain them.

5. The surrender of the Army of Northern Virginia shall be construed to include all the forces operating with that army on the 8th instant, the date of the commencement of the negotiations for surrender, except such bodies of cavalry as actually made their escape previous to the surrender, and except, also, such pieces of artillery as were more than twenty miles from Appomattox Court House at the time of the surrender on the 9th instant.

(Signed)   JOHN GIBBON, *Major General Volunteers.*

CHARLES GRIFFIN,
   Brevet Major General U. S. Volunteers.

W. MERRITT, *Brevet Major General.*

J. LONGSTREET, *Lieutenant General.*

J. B. GORDON, *Major General.*

W. N. PENDLETON,
   Brigadier General and Chief of Artillery.

General Grant's behavior at Appomattox was marked by a desire to spare the feelings of his great opponent. There was no theatrical display; his troops were not paraded with bands playing and banners flying, before whose lines the Confederates must march and stack arms. He did not demand Lee's sword, as is customary, but actually apologized to him for not having his own, saying it had been left behind in the wagon; promptly stopped salutes from being fired to mark the event, and the terms granted were liberal and generous. "No man could have behaved better than General Grant did under the circumstances," said Lee to a friend in Richmond. "He did not touch my sword; the usual custom is for the sword to be received when tendered, and then handed back, but he did not touch mine." Neither did the Union chief enter the Southern lines to show himself or to parade his victory, or go to Richmond or Petersburg to exult over a fallen people, but mounted his horse and with his staff started for Washington. Washington, at Yorktown, was not as considerate and thoughtful of the feelings of Cornwallis or his men.

Charges were now withdrawn from the guns, flags furled, and the Army of the Potomac and the Army of Northern Virginia turned their backs upon each other for the first time in four long, bloody years. The Southern soldiers, wrapped in faded, tattered uniforms, shoeless and weather-beaten, but proud as when they first rushed to battle, returned to desolate fields, homes in some cases in ashes, blight, blast, and want on every side. A few days afterward General Lee rode into Richmond, accompanied by his staff, and the cheering crowds which quickly gathered told in thunder tones that a paroled prisoner of war * was still loved by his people. It was a demonstration in which men forgot their own sorrow and gave way to the glory and grati-

---

* The following parole was signed by General Lee and his staff:

We, the undersigned, prisoners of war belonging to the Army of Northern Virginia, having been this day surrendered by General R. E. Lee, commanding said army, to Lieutenant-General Grant, commanding the armies of the United States, do hereby give our solemn parole of honor that we will not hereafter serve the armies of the Confederate States, or in any military capacity whatever, against the United

tude of the past. They adored him most, not in the glare of his brilliant victories, but in the hour of his deepest humiliation.

States of America, or render aid to the enemies of the latter, until properly exchanged in such manner as shall be mutually approved by the relative authorities :

> R. E. LEE, *General.*
> W H. TAYLOR,
> > *Lieutenant Colonel and Acting Adjutant General.*
> CHARLES S. VENABLE,
> > *Lieutenant Colonel and Acting Adjutant General.*
> CHARLES MARSHALL,
> > *Lieutenant Colonel and Acting Adjutant General.*
> H. E. PEYTON, *Lieutenant Colonel and Inspector General.*
> GILES BROOKE, *Major and A. A. Surgeon General.*
> H. S. YOUNG, *Acting Adjutant General.*

Done at Appomattox Court House, Va.,
> the ninth (9th) day of April, 1865.

The parole was countersigned as follows :

The above-named officers will not be disturbed by United States authorities as long as they observe their parole and the laws in force where they may reside. GEORGE H. SHARPE,
> *General and Assistant Provost Marshal.*

CHAPTER XVI.

RETURN TO RICHMOND.—PRESIDENT OF WASHINGTON
COLLEGE.—DEATH AND BURIAL.

PERSONALLY it was a great relief to General Lee to
be transferred to domestic life and the company of his
wife and children. For forty years, including his cadet-
ship, he had been a soldier whose movements and duties
were directed by others; now he was independent of all
war departments and military orders. He was a private
citizen for the first time during his manhood, and would
not be disturbed as long as he observed his parole and
the laws in force wherever he might reside. He had
denounced the assassination of Mr. Lincoln as a crime
previously unknown to the country, and one that must
be deprecated by every American; and when President
Johnson proclaimed his policy of May 29th, in the restoration of peace, he applied on June 13th to be embraced
within its provisions, and tendered his allegiance to
the only government in existence, under whose flag he
must resume the duties of citizenship. He cited to his
friends the example of Washington, who fought against
the French in the service of the King of Great Britain,
and then with the French against the English, under the
orders of the Continental Congress. "If you intend to
reside in this country," he wrote a friend in New Orleans,
"and wish to do your part in the restoration of your
State and in the Government of the country, which I
think is the duty of every citizen to do, I know of no
objection to your taking the amnesty oath." In the
same month he was indicted by the United States grand
jury, with Mr. Davis and others, for treason. With a
clear conscience, he made up his mind, he said, "to let

the authorities take their course. I have no wish to avoid any trial the Government may order; I hope others may be unmolested."

Reverdy Johnson, the distinguished Maryland lawyer, who did not agree with General Lee's political views, hearing that he was to be prosecuted in court for the alleged crime of treason, placed the fifty years of his great study and profound experience at his command, because, as he states, "in saving him I would be saving the honor of my country." General Lee wrote General Grant to withdraw his application for amnesty under the President's proclamation, if steps were to be taken for his prosecution, as he was willing to stand the test. Grant saw the President, and protested against a procedure against General Lee, informing him that he considered his honor and the honor of the nation pledged to him, and no proceedings were taken.

General Lee's enjoyment of the society of his family and friends in Richmond was much broken into by visitors from all sections of the country. Many persons were attracted to the city because it had been the Southern capital, whose lines had for so long kept great hosts from entering her gates, and a visit to or a sight of General Lee was always on their programme. Numbers of people stood on the street and gazed at the house, hoping to catch a glimpse of its occupant. Not desiring to make a public exhibition of himself, the paroled soldier was a prisoner in his own house; and his condition produced the desire to move to more secluded quarters. Mrs. Lee's health, too, would be benefited by going out of town during the coming summer months. The house he lived in belonged to Mr. John Stewart, of Brook Hill, a fine specimen of the kind-hearted, benevolent Scotch gentleman. He had rented it to General Lee's son, General G. W. C. Lee, some time before the war closed.

The general felt that he should make post-war terms with his excellent landlord; but, before he could take any steps, Mrs. Lee received a note from Mr. Stewart which read: "I am not presuming on your good opinion when I feel that you will believe me—first, that you and yours are heartily welcome to the house as long as your convenience leads you to stay in Richmond; and, next, that you owe me nothing, but, if you insist on pay, that the payment must be in Confederate currency, for which alone it was rented to your son. You do not know how much gratification it is, and it will afford me and my whole family, during the remainder of our lives, to reflect that we have been brought into contact and to know and to appreciate you and all that are dear to you."

In looking beyond Richmond for quarters, General Lee was much in favor of purchasing a farm in Orange County, in the beautiful section near the railroad crossing of the Rapidan, with which he was so familiar; but about that time Mrs. Elizabeth Randolph Cocke, of Cumberland County, Virginia, granddaughter of Edmund Randolph, offered him the use of a dwelling house situated on a portion of her estate in Powhatan County. As it was known that he had been dispossessed of his old home at Arlington, numerous offers of money, houses, and lands almost daily reached him, as well as requests to become the president of business associations and chartered corporations. Mrs. Cocke's kind, cordial manner, for which she was proverbial, and the retired situation of the dwelling offered, induced him to put all others aside and accept her hospitable and thoughtful invitation. The spring and early summer of 1865 were spent by the great soldier in the full fruition of a well-earned and long-needed repose.

In the meantime the trustees of Washington College, at Lexington, Va., determined to reorganize the institution, pledging their personal credit to provide means to repair the ravages of war. A member of the board had accidentally heard that a daughter of General Lee had said she thought her father would like to be connected with an institution of learning, and this casual remark first directed the attention of the trustees to General Lee in connection with the presidency of their college; but, as one of them said, it was unmingled impudence to tender to General Lee the head of an institution which had nothing then, and must start at the bottom round of the collegiate educational ladder. The temerarious trustees were equal to the emergency, and boldly grappled with the subject, doubtless encouraged and inspired by the strong advice of ex-Governor John Letcher, who suggested that if the college had nothing then, its condition would instantaneously change at the moment General Lee accepted the presidency. The name of Robert E. Lee was duly proposed for the office, and the letter informing him of his unanimous election, signed by the rector, Judge John W. Brockenbrough, and the committee, was consigned to the rector, to be delivered in person rather than by mail, because its contents could be strengthened by the well-known persuasive powers of the learned judge. At this point the trustees were confronted with a fresh and apparently insurmountable obstruction. Neither the rector nor any one of them, owing to the disasters of cruel war, had raiment of sufficient texture, shape, and freshness to wear in making a trip from home, more especially when it comprised a personal interview with the great soldier upon which so much depended. After laborious search, the best-dressed citizen of that section since the war was found, whose clothes fortunately came near enough to fitting the rector to encourage him to make his appearance in them as ambassador to the county of Powhatan, where the general was then residing. The sigh of relief that this obstacle had been so successfully overcome was scarcely audible before the trustees encountered still greater trials. Neither the rector nor any one else had any finances, or possibly even financial standing. Money was as absolutely necessary, when rectors traveled so soon after the war, as it is now, and Confederate money for some time before the surrender had not been worth ten cents per yard. Finally, however, by the supreme exertion of one of the trustees, fifty dollars of "good money" was secured, and the representative of Washington College was safely started. The public and private monetary stringency was not confined at that period to Lexington.

In the letter dated August 5, 1865, carried by Judge Brockenbrough, General Lee was told that Washington College, though a great sufferer from havoc and devastation, "is still blessed with a vigorous vitality, and needs only the aid of your illustrious character and transcendent scientific attainments to reanimate her drooping for-

tunes and restore her to more than her pristine usefulness and prosperity." General Lee had already declined
the presidency of the Suwanee University of Tennessee,
and shrank from any connection with the University
of Virginia, on the ground that one was a denomina-
tional and the other a State university. He considered
this matter nineteen days, and then wrote that he feared
he would be unable to "discharge the duties to the satisfaction of the trustees or to the benefit of the country." Then, too, he was excluded from the terms of amnesty in the proclamation of the President of the United
States, he said, and "an object of censure to a portion
of the country," and he was afraid he might draw upon
the college a feeling of hostility, and therefore cause
injury to an institution which it would be his highest
desire to advance, and concluded by saying, "I think it
is the duty of every citizen, in the present condition of
the country, to do all in his power to aid in the restoration of peace and harmony, and in no way to oppose
the policy of the State or General Government directed
to that object"; and that, after what had been written,
if the board should still think his services would be advantageous to the college and country, he would yield
to their judgment and accept.

The trustees on August 31st adopted and transmitted
to General Lee resolutions that, in spite of his objections,
in their opinion, "his connection with the institution
will greatly promote its prosperity and advance the general interest of education," and solicited him to enter
upon the duties of the presidency of the college at his
earliest convenience. The "happy audacity," as one of
the professors of the Virginia Military Institute termed
it, of the trustees gave to them the victory. That General Lee should put aside the many large and lucrative
offers and accept this position at the salary then offered
—fifteen hundred dollars per annum—was but in keeping
with his great character. Washington College had de-
scended from a classical school taught in the Valley of
Virginia as early as the year 1749, known as the Augusta
Academy. On May 13, 1776, nearly two months before
the Declaration of Independence, in response to the patriotic sentiment of the times, the name was changed to

"Liberty Hall Academy." The institution was removed successively to different places, and was finally established in Lexington, Va., a town founded in 1778 as the county seat of Rockbridge County and called after Lexington, Mass., where the "embattled farmers stood and fired the shot heard round the world."

In 1784 Virginia, desiring to testify her appreciation of the services and character of her great son Washington, directed the Treasurer of the State to subscribe to one hundred shares of the par value of two hundred dollars in the stock of a company organized for the improvement of the navigation of James River, and vested the same in General Washington. The Legislature agreed to the condition upon which alone he would receive the gift—viz., that he would be permitted to present it to objects of a public nature, such as "the education of the poor, particularly the children of such as have fallen in the defense of the country." He gave this stock in 1796 to "Liberty Hall Academy" in Rockbridge County, first presided over by William Graham, an old Princeton classmate and friend of General Lee's father. "Liberty Hall" was now Washington College, that name having been adopted in 1812.

Perhaps past associations had something to do with General Lee's accepting the presidency of the college, as well as a desire to contribute his part toward laying the only true foundation upon which a republic can rest— the Christian education of its youth. His object now, as in 1861, was to render the best service he could to his native State, and to that purpose he had never been unfaithful. By the intelligent and judicious management of sums donated, principally by the patriots of the Revolution, the endowment fund, in 1861, had nearly reached one hundred thousand dollars, and the college had secured ample buildings, apparatus, and libraries, while its alumni had already richly adorned pulpit, bench, bar, medical profession, halls of legislation, seats of learning, and all the walks of life. It might have escaped war's devastation had any other Federal officer than General David Hunter marched upon its campus. This officer had no respect for colleges, or the peaceful pursuits of professors and students, or the private dwellings of citizens, though occupied by women and children only, and during his three days' occupancy of Lexington in June, 1864, the college buildings were dismantled, apparatus destroyed, and the books mutilated.

At the end of the fiscal year 1865 there was a balance in the hands of the college treasurer of two thousand four hundred and fifty-eight dollars and twenty cents in Confederate money. The assets of the college were not available, nor could the interest upon its bonds or State securities be collected. There was a balance due professors and others of nearly two thousand dollars, and the Finance Committee of the Board of Trustees recommended that the college borrow at once, to meet pressing demands, four thousand six hundred dollars. The trustees proved equal to the encounter with these discouraging difficulties, and with "happy audacity" promptly sent their rector to offer General Lee the presidency at a salary at that time not in sight of the college's treasury! General Lee's favorite war horse, Traveler, the famous gray which had borne him so faithfully amid the flying bolts of battle, now carried him to peaceful pursuits. Unheralded and unattended, having ridden from Powhatan County in four days, his simple *entrée* was made into the little mountain town of Lexington. As he drew rein in front of the village hotel, an old soldier recognized him, gave the military salute, placed one hand upon the bridle, the other upon the stirrup, and stood, waiting for him to dismount.

The general's wish for a quiet, informal inauguration was gratified, and on October 2, 1865, in the presence of the faculty, students, and board of trustees, subscribed before William White, Esq., justice of the peace, the oath * prescribed by law. During the ceremony the general, dressed in a plain but elegant suit of gray, remained standing, his arms folded, calmly and steadfastly looking into the eyes of the speaker, Judge Brockenbrough. The warrior had been transformed into a college president, who was to discharge

---

* I do swear that I will, to the best of my skill and judgment, faithfully and truly discharge the duties required of me by an act for incorporating the Rector and Trustees of Liberty Hall Academy, without favor, affection, or partiality.

his duties there as conscientiously as when his simple mandate sent thousands of men into fierce battle. "I have," said he, "a self-imposed task, which I can not forsake." The college to which he was called was broken in fortune; "the war had practically closed its doors; its buildings had been pillaged and defaced and its library scattered." He had the profoundest convictions of the importance of educational influence and the deepest sense of personal responsibility. Year by year the conception of his duty grew stronger, and year by year, as its instrument, the college grew dearer. He was no figurehead, kept in position for the attraction of his name; his energy, zeal, and administrative ability surmounted all difficulties. His great labors were directed to making Washington College the seat of science, art, and literature. Far-reaching plans laid for its success were wisely conceived.

A scholastic monument was slowly responding to his noble influence and wise administration, which would be as illustrious as his most brilliant military achievements. He mastered all details, observing the students, becoming personally acquainted with them, their aspirations and hopes; his interest followed them everywhere, and their associations, dispositions, and habits were well known to him. He never grew imperious, or tried to force a measure upon the faculty, but modestly said he had but one vote and wished to know the opinion of his colleagues, and leave the decision to be determined by the whole body. Sustained by the loftiest principles of virtue and religion, an exalted character, and a conscientious sense of duty, General Lee suffered no complaint to escape his lips during the eventful years from 1865 to 1870, though troubled by much that was taking place.

He manifested much interest in the case of Captain Wirtz, on trial for his life, accused of cruelty to the Federal prisoners of war committed to him. He knew the captain had done all that was possible with the resources at his disposal; subsistence for them had been most difficult to procure, their exchange for an equal number of Southerners had been refused, while the Federal blockade kept out medical supplies. A portion of the Northern press charged Lee with being responsible for the alleged suffering of the Union prisoners. He declined to make a public reply unless the accusation came from a responsible source, but said that he was in no way responsible for the condition of prisoners after they had been sent from his army. When the commissary general said to him, upon one occasion, that it would be necessary to reduce either the rations of the Federal prisoners or those of his men in the field, he replied, "While I have no authority in the case, my desire is that the prisoners shall have equal rations with my men." He was summoned to Washington in March, 1866, as a witness before a congressional committee which was inquiring into the condition of things in the South. His testimony was simple, direct, dignified, and elicited the admiration of all who heard or read it. It was his first appearance in any of the cities since the war, and, being at a time of public political excitement, his visit was an occasion of absorbing interest. The day after his return he proposed a walk with one of his daughters, who playfully objected to a new hat he was about to put on. "You do not like my hat?" said he; "why, there were a thousand people on Pennsylvania Avenue in Washington the other day admiring this hat!" It was his only reference to the crowds of persons who gathered around him wherever he went in the city.

General Lee was still receiving numerous letters, filled with offers of remunerative positions, to which he always replied that he preferred to continue the educational work he had undertaken; but still they came, coupled often with the condition that he should not relinquish his self-imposed task, and should not resign the college presidency. On one occasion the general said to a particular friend in his office : " My friend Mr. —— has been to see me, and offers me twenty thousand dollars per annum to take the presidency of —— Company. I would like to make some money for Mrs. Lee, as she has not much left, and he does not require me to leave the college ; what do you think of my accepting it ? " The irony of the question was appreciated, but his friend took him at his word, and expressed his opinion adversely, saying, as modestly as possible, that if he " allowed himself to be influenced by filthy lucre he would begin to gravitate." With the winsome way so characteristic of him the general replied: " I am glad to find that you agree with me. I told Mr. —— yesterday that I must decline his offer."

About this time the subject of the removal of the remains of the Southern dead from the field of Gettysburg was being considered. General Lee replied to a letter calling his attention to it:

LEXINGTON, VA., *December* 15, 1868.

MY DEAR FITZ: I have considered the subject of your letter, which has been unaccountably delayed on the journey; and though I have no desire that my views should govern in the decision of a question in which others are equally interested, I will give them for your consideration. In the first place, I have no fears that our dead will receive disrespectful treatment at the hands of the Gettysburg association. If they do so, it will then be time, as it will also furnish the occasion, for us to apply for their transfer to our care. I am not in favor of disturbing the ashes of the dead unless for a worthy object, and I know of no fitter resting-place for a soldier than the field on which he has nobly laid down his life. If our State governments could reflect the wishes of their citizens, and each State could receive its own dead, I think it would be very appropriate to return them to their native soil for final interment, if possible ; and I know it would be soothing to the feelings of their friends to have their sacred dead committed to their affectionate keeping.

The General was only induced to take the presidency of the Valley Railroad because it did not require him to leave Lexington, and because he was so interested in obtaining railroad facilities for his college. He really loved his work, in which his interest increased rather than diminished. Occasionally he would administer admonition to the students or make public his directions by circulars, which were called by them " General Orders "; for example:

WASHINGTON COLLEGE, VA., *December* 24, 1869.

Academic exercises will be suspended from the 25th to the 27th inclusive, to enable the students to join in the rites and services appropriate to the occasion ; and while enjoying these privileges with grateful hearts, all are urged to do or countenance nothing which may disturb the peace, harmony, and happiness that should pervade a Christian community.

R. E. LEE, *President.*

The labors, exposure, and responsibilities of his campaigns laid the foundation for bodily distress. Rheumatism of the heart sac and of other portions of his body was creeping by gradual approach to assault the vitals. He was reluctantly persuaded to go south in March, 1870, to look upon other scenes and enjoy the fragrant breezes in the "land of sun and flowers." In Richmond, *en route*, in response to an invitation tendering the privileges of the legislative floor, he wrote :

RICHMOND, VA., *March 26, 1870.*

Hon. J. S. MARYE, *President of the Senate of Virginia.*

SIR: It would afford me great pleasure to be able to avail myself of the privileges of the floor of the Senate extended to me by the resolution of that body to-day, but the condition of my health is such as to require me to reach a milder climate as soon as practicable. With a due sense of the honor conferred on me by the resolution of the Senate,

I have the honor to be your most obedient servant,

R. E. LEE.

His sweet daughter Agnes, who did not long survive her father, accompanied him. On the trip he embraced the opportunity to see once more his father's grave, on an island off the coast of Georgia. General Henry Lee (or "Light-Horse Harry"), in returning from the West Indies, where he had been, hoping to restore his health, was, it may be remembered, taken ill, and begged to be put ashore at General Greene's mansion, then occupied by his daughter, where he died, and where his remains now lie. From Savannah, Ga., April 18, 1870, the general wrote Mrs. Lee: "We visited Cumberland Island, and Agnes decorated my father's grave with beautiful fresh flowers. I presume it is the last time I shall be able to pay it my tribute of respect. The cemetery is unharmed and the graves are in good order, though the house of 'Dungeness' has been burned and the island devastated. I hope I am better. I know that I am stronger, but I still have the pain in my chest whenever I walk. I have felt it, too, occasionally recently, when quiescent."

He returned benefited by the trip, but the steady progress of his disease had not been checked. While absent, the college trustees appropriated money to present him with a house and settle an annuity of three thousand dollars per annum on his family, all of which he firmly declined. "I am unwilling that my family should become a tax to the college," he wrote to the board, "but desire that all its funds should be devoted to the purposes of education. I feel assured that, in case a competency should not be left to my wife, her children would never suffer her to want."

When the fall session of 1870 of the college opened, General Lee was at his post of duty, but "his step had lost something of its elasticity, the shoulders began to stoop as if under a growing burden, and the ruddy glow of health upon his countenance changed to a feverish flush." A noble life was drawing to a close. The morning of September 28, 1870, found him faithfully performing the duties of his office; the afternoon, engaged with his brother members of the vestry of Grace Episcopal Church in work congenial to the true Christian, and the autumn evening shadows fell upon a couch over which the heavenly angels were bending. The important question of rebuilding the church and increasing his faithful friend and pastor's compensation had interested him so deeply at the vestry meeting, that the cold church and the outside storm were forgotten, and it was only after a protracted session of over three hours, as he proceeded to his house, a short distance off, that weariness and weakness overtook him, and his wavering steps indicated increasing feebleness. Entering his private office as usual, he took off his hat, military cloak, and overshoes, and then proceeded to join his family, who had been waiting tea for him. Quietly he stood in his accustomed place in the dining-room, while his family with bowed heads waited to hear the well-known grace, but no sound came from his lips. Speechless the great soldier stood; an expression of despair spread over his face; and from his eyes came a dreamy, far-away look which denoted the approaching summons from his Creator.

"My husband came in," wrote Mrs. Lee, "and I asked where he had been, remarking that he had kept us waiting a long time. He did not reply, but stood up as if to say grace. No word proceeded from his lips, but with a sublime look of resignation he sat down in his

chair." With intense anxiety the family went to his assistance. A bed was brought to the dining-room, in
which he was placed, and Dr. B. L. Madison and Dr.
H. T. Barton were quickly summoned. For two weeks,

'Twixt night and morn upon the horizon's verge,
Between two worlds life hovered like a star.

Mrs. Lee tells us that his whole demeanor during his
sickness was that of one who had taken leave of earth.
He never smiled and rarely attempted to speak except
in his dreams, and then, she says, "he wandered to those
dreadful battlefields." "You must get out and ride
your faithful gray," the doctor said. He shook his head
and looked upward; and once when his daughter Agnes
urged him to take medicine, he looked at her and said,
"It is no use." Human love was powerful, human aid
powerless. Hope and Despair were twin watchers by
his bedside. At first, as his disease seemed to yield to
treatment, Hope brightened, but soon Despair alone kept
watch. During the afternoon and night of October 10th
shadowy clouds of approaching dissolution began to
gather, a creeping lethargy captured the faculties, and
the massive grandeur of form and face began to contract. During the succeeding day he rapidly grew
worse; his thoughts wandered to the fields where he
had so often led his gray battalions to victory; and like
the greatest of his captains, Stonewall Jackson, whose
expiring utterance told "A. P. Hill to prepare for
action," he too, in death's delirium, said, "Tell Hill he
must come up!" "For the last forty-eight hours he
seemed quite insensible of our presence," Mrs. Lee
states; "he breathed more heavily, and at last gently
sank to rest with one deep-drawn sigh, and oh, what a
glorious rest was in store for him!"

Robert Edward Lee died at half-past nine, on the
morning of October 12, 1870, in the sixty-fourth year of
his age. His physicians stated as the cause, "mental
and physical fatigue inducing venous congestion of the
brain, which, however, never proceeded as apoplexy or
paralysis, but gradually caused cerebral exhaustion and
death." On the 14th the casket containing the body of
the dead warrior was removed to the college chapel, and

on the 15th buried in the area of the chapel in a brick vault prepared for it. Upon the marble capping on the top of the vault, and on a level with the library floor is this simple inscription :

ROBERT EDWARD LEE,

BORN JANUARY 19, 1807,

DIED OCTOBER 12, 1870.

Tolling bells first proclaimed the sad intelligence to the citizens of Lexington, electric wires to the world. Throughout the South business was suspended, schools closed, societies and associations of all sorts assembled, where eulogistic speeches were made, and resolutions passed laudatory of General Lee's life and lamenting his death. In those adopted by the faculty of the college it was declared that "his executive ability, his enlarged views of liberal culture, his extraordinary powers in the government of men, his wonderful influence over the minds of the young, and his steady and earnest devotion to duty, made the college spring, as if by the touch of magic, from its depressions after the war to its present firm condition of permanent and widespread usefulness"; that it was "a deep satisfaction to receive his remains beneath the chapel he had built"; and that the "memory of his noble life will remain as an abiding inspiration to the young of the country as they gather at the last scene of his labors, to emulate his virtues and to follow his great example."

The board of college trustees by resolution extolled General Lee for his great military services, and for the victories won by him in the classic shades of Washington College, saying that the two most renowned names in their respective centuries were Washington and Lee, and that they "be hereafter associated indissolubly as founder and restorer of our beloved college"; that the charter be so amended as to hereafter express in fit conjunction the immortal names of Washington and Lee; that the anniversary of his birth should always be celebrated in the college; and that, with the co-operation of the faculty, measures should be taken and plans prepared for the erection within the college grounds of a suitable monument to his memory. The sorrowing students met and resolved: "We deeply mourn the loss of one who in his public career had endeared himself to us by all the virtues that adorn the character of the patriot and Christian, and who in his official and private relations with ourselves has also won our peculiar affection and confidence by his paternal sympathy and his tender regard for our interest as students." The academic board of the Virginia Military Institute, at Lexington, put on record that his life is a part of the history of the world, and that his moral excellences inspired love and admiration in the hearts of all the good.

At 12.30 P. M., October 15th, 1870, one of the most solemn, imposing, and impressive funeral processions ever assembled moved with slow tread from the late president's home, through the streets of Lexington, and thence to the college chapel. At its head, as the escort of honor, marched the old Confederate soldiers who had gathered from many quarters to pay a last tribute to their commander. In its ranks were the representatives of the Virginia Legislature, State officials, distinguished visitors, members of numerous organizations, trusteesi faculty, students, alumni, cadets of the Virginia Military Institute, and citizens. At the chapel the beaut,-ful service of the Episcopal Church was read with great solemnity by the Rev. Dr. W. N. Pendleton, the distinguished officer who had for forty-five years been the comrade and fellow-soldier of the dead chieftain. The mournful ceremonies were concluded outside the chapel in the presence of a vast throng who were unable to enter. The coffin was then removed to the vault. The large assemblage sang one of the general's favorite hymns, "How firm a foundation, ye saints of the Lord," and all that was mortal of the Christian soldier was consigned to the grave.

Traveler, who had borne in so many battles the great Confederate leader, led by two old soldiers, slowly walking, riderless, behind the hearse, covered with the sable trappings of mourning, was a tender and touching sight. He survived his master but two years.*

---

* He died in Lexington, in the summer of 1872, of lockjaw caused by a nail in one of his fore feet. He was fifteen years old.

The college pledge was sacredly kept, and a sleeping marble recumbent statue of exquisite workmanship, the production of Valentine, a Virginia sculptor, after "Rauch's figure of Louise of Prussia," is a superb monument to the memory of its president. The Washington and Lee, a great university, under the wise management of General Lee's eldest son, has linked two names which spring spontaneously to every mind. Of these two men, exemplars of a country's character, born almost a century apart, but similar in the history of their boyhood, earnest, grave, studious, alike in noble carriage and commanding dignity, it has been said that in the remarkable combination and symmetry of their intellectual qualities—all so equal, so well developed, no faculty of the mind overlapping any other—you are almost persuaded to deny them greatness, because no single attribute of the mind was projected upon itself. Well may Virginia be proud of sons who shine upon the pages of the world's history "like binary stars which open their glory and shed their splendor on the darkness of the world."

In Virginia's capital city now stand two splendid equestrian statues to George Washington and Robert E. Lee. Riding side by side in calm majesty, they are henceforth contemporaries in all the ages to come. The mother State mourned for the departed soldier, and her General Assembly passed a bill making January 19th, the birthday of General Robert E. Lee, a legal holiday in Virginia. In the universal mourning for him the sympathies of the world first flew to the smitten family. The final parting from her husband after a most happy married life was a great shock to Mrs. Lee. She had been a sufferer for years from rheumatism, unable to move without assistance, and was described at that time as having "a sad but noble countenance, her features much resembling those of her great-grandmother Martha, the wife of Washington, her expression firm, her eyes beautiful and sparkling with the uncommon intelligence which marks her conversation, her almost snowy-white, fine, soft hair, in waves and curls framing her full forehead. She sits in her widow's cap a grand and lovely picture, combining in itself much of the history and glory of the immortal past with the modern events of our history." When the South sent her sons to fight under her husband's command, she devoted every energy to the cause in which he had enlisted.

A very few extracts from communications which reached her from all sections in great numbers can be given: A cousin of the general's, Mr. Edmund I. Lee, from Shepherdstown, October 31, 1870, writes Mrs. Lee: "I can not find language to convey the distress I felt when I first read the announcement of Robert's death in the papers. The most pleasant recollections of my youth are connected with him and his mother's family. How often have I called to mind the evenings and the mornings spent in their company!—our English rabbits fed together, and our daily visits to the markets in Alexandria to procure meat and vegetables for our mothers, each carrying his own basket; his rescuing me on one occasion from the fangs of his father's mastiff, Killbuck, and the grief of his mother and sisters when your aunt—Mrs. Lewis—having procured from President Jackson a cadet warrant (which was given upon her application, as a personal favor to her), it became necessary to send him to West Point; and my proffering my own services to attend in Robert's place to his mother's business—for his gentle, affectionate manners had attached all his relations to him in early life."

From Savannah, Ga., October 15, 1870, General Joseph E. Johnston wrote her:

MY DEAR MADAM: Although you are receiving the strongest proofs that a whole people are sharing in your great sorrow, I venture to write, not merely to say how I, General Lee's earliest and most devoted friend, lament his death and how sadly the event will visit my memory while I stay on earth, but, still more, to assure you of my deep sympathy in this greatest bereavement a human being can know, and of my fervent prayers to our merciful God that he may grant his help to you and your children.

Most sincerely and truly your friend,
(Signed)   J. E. JOHNSTON.

A dear little girl wrote:

I have heard of General Lee, your husband, and of all his great and noble deeds during the war. I have also heard lately of his death. I have read in the papers that collections are being made for the Lee monument. I have asked my mother to let me send some money—not money that she gave me, but money that I earned myself. I made some of my money by keeping the door shut last winter, and the rest I made by digging up grass in the garden. I send you all I have. I wish it was more. I am nine now.   Respectfully,   MAGGIE MCINTYRE.

Rev. R. S. Stewart wrote to Mrs. Lee from Baltimore, December 29, 1872 : " Accident a few weeks ago led me to read over again after fifty years the Scottish Chiefs, and I have been so struck with the identity of character between Sir William Wallace and General Lee that I can not help mentioning it to you and asking you to read this book again, if you have not done so, since the late struggle for Southern liberty commenced. In reading it myself, I find every noble sentiment of religion, of patriotism, and of humanity expressed that we all heard from the lips or pen of your noble husband, and so similar are the natures of the two men that I could almost believe in the transmigration of souls. As a descendant of an old Scottish family I have always felt proud of Wallace and cherished his memory."

The Hon. Beresford Hope, A. B.,* wrote from Bedgebery Park, Cranbrook, England, November 25, 1872, to Mrs. Lee, thanking her for photographs of General Lee, and added, " They embody to us heroic virtue and purest patriotism, the most exalted military genius, the highest and purest domestic excellence, while the impress of your pencil and your autograph doubles their value."

From Aldenham Bridge, North Shropshire, England, a lady sent Mrs. Lee a copy of a lecture delivered by her husband, and wrote, January 24, 1866, that she did it "in order to add one to the many testimonies which

---

* Mr. Hope will be remembered as the English gentleman who principally contributed to the Jackson statue which now stands in Capitol Square, Richmond, and who had more to do with its presentation to the State of Virginia than any one else. General Lee was also presented with a magnificently illustrated Bible from Mr. Hope and his wife, Lady Mildred, a sister of the present Lord Salisbury, together with other members of the family and friends. The dedication reads thus : " General Robert E. Lee, Commanding the Confederate Army, from the Undersigned Englishmen and Englishwomen, recognizing the Genius of the General, admiring the Humanity of the Man, respecting the Virtues of the Christian. October 18, 1864."

you must have received of the sympathy and veneration which have been inspired in Europe by the illustrious career of General Lee. I have less difficulty in
presuming to do so, because the passages in which those
feelings were most strongly expressed are omitted in
this report. They were received with enthusiasm by a
Shropshire audience who believed (I know not with
what justice, though we should be proud if it were
true) that the family of the general once belonged to
this country." The Southland—plowed with graves and
reddened with blood, that can look the proudest nation
fearlessly in the face, and whose sons he led to battle—
joined in the lamentation over her distinguished son.

The Hon. Jefferson Davis, eloquently speaking at the
memorial meeting in Richmond, said that "this day we
unite our words of sorrow with those of the good and
great throughout Christendom, for his fame has gone
over the water; and when the monument we build shall
have crumbled into dust, his virtues will still live—a high
model for the imitations of generations yet unborn."
And Benjamin Hill, of Georgia, in beautiful phrase de-
claimed : " He was a foe without hate, a friend without
treachery, a soldier without cruelty, and a victim without murmuring. He was a public officer without vices,
a private citizen without wrong, a neighbor without
reproach, a Christian without hypocrisy, and a man without guilt. He was Cæsar without his ambition, Frederick without his tyranny, Napoleon without his selfish-
ness, and Washington without his reward. He was as
obedient to authority as a servant and royal in authority
as a king. He was as gentle as a woman in life, pure
and modest as a virgin in thought, watchful as a Roman
vestal, submissive to law as Socrates, and grand in battle as Achilles."

The Southern leader had no ambition except the
consciousness of duty faithfully performed. Far removed from political or civic ambition, he would have
declined the presidency of the Confederate States if his
sword had carved their independence as readily as he
did positions carrying great salaries. He once said that
the only public office he ever might be inclined to accept would be the chief magistracy of his beloved native

State; and yet when Judge Robert Ould, of Richmond, wrote him that there was a universal demand that he should become Governor of Virginia, he replied, after expressing his high appreciation of the position and the desires of the people: "I candidly confess, however, that my feelings induce me to prefer private life, which I think more suitable to my condition and age, and where I believe I can better subserve the interests of my State than in that you propose. This is no time for the indulgence of personal or political considerations in selecting individuals for supposed former services. Believing that there are many men in the State more capable than I of filling the position, and who could do more to promote the interests of the people, I most respectfully decline to be considered a candidate for the office." He thought that his election would excite hostility toward the State and injure its inhabitants in the eyes of the country, and he therefore refused to consent to become an instrument of bringing distress upon those whose prosperity and happiness were so dear to him. He adds: "If my disfranchisement and prohibition of civil rights would secure to the citizens of the State the enjoyment of civil liberty and equal rights under the Constitution, I would willingly accept them in their stead." It is perhaps well that he was not launched into public life, where all his actions would have passed in review before a hostile political party. After his sword was sheathed, the serene patience and quiet self-consecration of his latest years have filled the world with admiration.

CHAPTER XVII.

MILITARY CHARACTER.

IT is difficult to accurately compare Lee's military genius even with that of the more modern great captains of war, except in strategical science, for he believed with them that "in planning all dangers should be seen, in execution none, unless very formidable." The great improvements in firearms have changed the tactics of the battlefield. Troops are no longer brought to a halt in the polite phrase of the French, "Halt your banners, in the name of God, the king, and St. Denis," but by bugle notes. Armies are no longer unable to contest because the strings of crossbows are slackened by rain; short lances have been replaced by bayonets on revolving breech-loading rifles; arbalest, phalanx, and other former military terms are no longer heard, and wonderful transformation has taken place since the day on which the blind King of Bohemia was led on the field of Crécy that he might deal one blow of his sword in battle. Marvelous metamorphoses have taken place even since 1815. Imagine the Federal and Confederate armies in a campaign in Belgium in 1861–1865, and that the Federal commander had accepted battle on the field of Waterloo and taken up the line of defense adopted by Wellington. He would not have compressed sixty-seven thousand six hundred and sixty-one* men in battle lines within a space of two miles on the Wavre road, on a slope void of intrenchments. The château of Hougoumont and its inclosures might have been strongly occupied to add increased strength to the right of the line of battle; but it is improbable that La Haye Sainte,

---

* Number of English troops engaged at Waterloo.

three hundred yards in front of the center on the Charleroi turnpike, and the little villages of Papelotte, La Haie, and Smohain, from a quarter to a half mile in front of the left, would have been occupied except by skirmishers. The flanks of a Federal army equal in numbers to the English would have been twice as far apart, and the whole line well protected by earthworks. Lee would not have attacked as Napoleon did if the Union troops had been placed precisely as Wellington arranged his, nor would his seventy-one thousand nine hundred and forty-seven troops (number of the French) been tactically formed like the Emperor's.

The battle of Gettysburg was fought forty-eight years after that of Waterloo. A comparison of the two strikingly shows the changes in the art of war in a half-century only. There was a similarity of purpose on the part of Lee on the third day's encounter at Gettysburg and the French emperor at Waterloo. The sun rises in Belgium in June at 3.48 A. M., in Pennsylvania in July at 4.30 A. M. Napoleon, at 11.30 A. M., ordered Reille, on his left, to attack Hougoumont on the English right with his left division as a diversion, while his main intention was to attack the British center and left center by his first corps, under D'Erlon, and brought up seventy-eight cannon to fire an hour and a half, at less than a third of a mile from the crest which the English occupied; but D'Erlon was not ordered forward until half-past one. Ewell, on Lee's left, was ordered to make a demonstration on the Federal right; cannon fired for hours, and then Pickett's assaulting column attempted to pierce the center and left center of the Union lines. Count Reille managed to get nearly the whole of his corps engaged, but effected nothing. Ewell got his troops early in action, but with no results. The fighting of both had terminated before the main operations began. Napoleon's object was to seize Mont St. Jean, in rear of Wellington's center, so as to possess himself of the principal avenue of retreat open to the British— the road to Brussels. Lee's object was to get possession of the Baltimore pike and road to Westminster, Meade's chief route of retreat to his base of supplies. D'Erlon was unsuccessful; so was Pickett. Before the

former moved out, the Prussians of Blücher were seen
on the heights of St. Lambert; and the Sixth French
Corps, instead of supporting the operations of the First
Corps, as had been intended, was taken away and employed in resisting their progress. The troops ordered
to support General Pickett lay on their arms waiting
orders from a corps commander charged with the assault,
which were never given.

The formation of Count d'Erlon's corps for the
charge in 1815, and that of Pickett in 1863, is an apt
illustration of tactical mutability. D'Erlon's attack was
made in four columns in echelon, the left in advance;
the first or left column was composed of two brigades,
each brigade of four battalions, one behind the other;
each battalion was in three ranks, and the distance between the battalions five paces; the next column had
nine battalions, and the other two eight each—twenty-
nine battalions in all. Sixteen thousand men in twenty-
nine battalions would give approximately six hundred
men to the battalion; and when in three ranks a front
of two hundred men for each one of the four charging
columns. If the front of each column had been on the
same line, instead of in echelon, eight hundred men
would have been in the front rank. It was intended
that this force should break through by impact, for only
the few men in front could fire. Pickett, with nearly as
many troops,* had nine brigades in two ranks, in two
long lines—six brigades in the first and three in the
second. The front line had some ten thousand men,
which in two ranks would give a front of five thousand
men instead of eight hundred! The dense masses of
D'Erlon's corps would have been butchered by the concentrated, converging, rapid fire of modern breech-loading guns, big and small, before their banners could have
been shaken to the breeze. We say, therefore, it is not
easy to compare Lee with the great soldiers of former
ages, except as a strategist.

In strategy it is certain Lee stands in the front rank
of the great warriors of the world. He was a greater
soldier than Sir Henry Havelock, and equally as devout

---

* Exclusive of Wilcox's brigade, which was not in the charge proper.

a Christian. "There was not a heart in England," it was said, when Havelock died, thirteen years before Lee, at about the same age, "that did not feel it to be a subject for private as well as public mourning"; and so the South felt toward Lee. It is stated that it was impossible to gauge the full measure of Moltke's potentialities as a strategist and organizer, but perhaps Lee with the same opportunities would have been equally as skillful and far-seeing. The success of the former and failure of the latter does not prevent comparison. Kossuth failed in Hungary, but the close of his long life has been strewn with flowers. Scotland may never become an independent country, but Scotchmen everywhere cherish with pride the fame of Wallace and Bruce. If given an opportunity, said General Scott, who commanded the army of the United States in 1861, Lee "will prove himself the greatest captain of history." He had the swift intuition to discern the purpose of his opponent, and the power of rapid combination to oppose to it prompt resistance. The very essence of modern war was comprised in the four years' campaign, demanding a greater tax upon the mental and physical qualifications of a leader than the fifteen years of Hannibal in the remote past. Military misconceptions have been charged to him; but Marshal Turenne has said, "Show me the man who never made mistakes, and I will show you one who has never made war."

The impartial historian, in reviewing Lee's campaigns and the difficult conditions with which he was always confronted, must at least declare that no commander could have accomplished more. In his favor was, however, that ponderous force known as the spirit of the army, which counterbalanced his enemy's excess of men and guns. Important battles are sometimes lost in spite of the best-conceived plans of the general commanding. The battle of Ligny, with the fate of a great campaign trembling on the result, was not made a decisive victory because Ney, at Quatre-Bras, showed a distrust of his emperor's judgment, was unwilling to take the most obvious step, and finally disobeyed orders; and like behavior of a corps commander at Gettysburg defeated the well-devised designs of Lee.

It has been wisely said that man is under no circumstance so nearly independent as he is when the next step is for life or death; and an infinite number of such independent forces influences the course of a battle—a course which can never be foreseen, and can never coincide with that which it would take under the impulsion of a single force. There are always inevitable conditions under which a commander in chief carries on his operations. The world places Lee by the side of its greatest captains, because surrounded on all sides by conflicting anxieties, interests, and the gravity of issues involved, he only surrendered his battle-stained, bullet-riddled banners after demonstrating that all had been done that mortal could accomplish. The profession of the soldier has been honored by his renown, the cause of education by his virtues, religion by his piety.

> " The greatest gift the hero leaves his race
> Is to have been a hero."

INDEX.

THE END.

Other DA CAPO titles of interest

continued . . .

THE MORGANVILLE VAMPIRE NOVELS

Glass Houses
The Dead Girls' Dance
Midnight Alley
Feast of Fools
Lord of Misrule

LORD OF
MISRULE

THE MORGANVILLE VAMPIRES, BOOK FIVE

RACHEL CAINE

A SIGNET BOOK

SIGNET
Published by New American Library, a division of
Penguin Group (USA) Inc., 375 Hudson Street,
New York, New York 10014, USA
Penguin Group (Canada), 90 Eglinton Avenue East, Suite 700, Toronto,
Ontario M4P 2Y3, Canada (a division of Pearson Penguin Canada Inc.)
Penguin Books Ltd., 80 Strand, London WC2R 0RL, England
Penguin Ireland, 25 St. Stephen's Green, Dublin 2,
Ireland (a division of Penguin Books Ltd.)
Penguin Group (Australia), 250 Camberwell Road, Camberwell, Victoria 3124,
Australia (a division of Pearson Australia Group Pty. Ltd.)
Penguin Books India Pvt. Ltd., 11 Community Centre, Panchsheel Park,
New Delhi - 110 017, India
Penguin Group (NZ), 67 Apollo Drive, Rosedale, North Shore 0632,
New Zealand (a division of Pearson New Zealand Ltd.)
Penguin Books (South Africa) (Pty.) Ltd., 24 Sturdee Avenue,
Rosebank, Johannesburg 2196, South Africa

Penguin Books Ltd., Registered Offices:
80 Strand, London WC2R 0RL, England

Published by Signet, an imprint of New American Library, a division of Penguin
Group (USA) Inc. Previously published in an NAL Jam edition.

First Signet Printing, November 2009
10   9   8   7

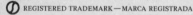

To Ter Matthies, Anna Korra'ti, and Shaz Flynn—
courageous fighters, each one.

And to Pat Flynn, who never stopped.

ACKNOWLEDGMENTS

This book wouldn't be here without the support of my husband, Cat, my friends Pat, Jackie, and Sharon, and a host of great online supporters and cheerers-on.

Special thank-you recognition to Sharon Sams, Shaz Flynn, and especially to fearless beta readers Karin and Laura for their excellent input.

Thanks always to Lucienne Diver.

THE STORY SO FAR . . .

Claire Danvers was going to Caltech. Or maybe MIT. She had her pick of great schools, but because she's only sixteen, her parents sent her to a supposedly safe place for a year to mature—Texas Prairie University, a small school in Morganville, Texas.

One problem: Morganville isn't what it seems. It's the last safe place for vampires, and that makes it not very safe at all for the humans who venture in for work or school. The vampires rule the town . . . and everyone who lives in it.

Claire's second problem is that she's gathered both human and vampire enemies. Now she lives with housemates Michael Glass (newly made a vampire), Eve Rosser (always been Goth), and Shane Collins (whose absentee dad is a wannabe vampire killer). Claire's the normal one . . . or she would be, except that she's become an employee of the town Founder, Amelie, and befriended one of the most dangerous, yet most vulnerable, vampires of them all—Myrnin, the alchemist.

Now Amelie's vampire father, Bishop, has come to Morganville and destroyed the fragile peace, turning vampires against one another and creating dangerous new alliances and factions in a town that already had too many.

Morganville's turning in on itself, and Claire and her friends have chosen to stand with the Founder, but it could mean working with their enemies . . . and fighting their friends.

1

It was all going wrong, and Morganville was burning—parts of it, anyway.

Claire stood at the windows of the Glass House and watched the flames paint the glass a dull, flickering orange. She could always see the stars out here in the Middle of Nowhere, Texas—but not tonight. Tonight, there was—

"You're thinking it's the end of the world," a cool, quiet voice said behind her.

Claire blinked out of her trance and turned to look. Amelie—the Founder, and the baddest vampire in town, to hear most of the others tell it—looked fragile and pale, even for a vampire. She'd changed out of the costume she'd worn to Bishop's masked ball—not a bad idea, since it had a stake-sized hole in the chest, and she'd bled all over it. If Claire had needed proof that Amelie was tough, she'd certainly gotten it tonight. Surviving an assassination attempt definitely gave you points.

The vampire was wearing gray—a soft gray sweater, and *pants*. Claire had to stare, because Amelie just didn't do pants. Ever. It was beneath her, or something.

Come to think of it, Claire had never seen her in the color gray, either.

Talk about the end of the world.

"I remember when Chicago burned," Amelie said.

"And London. And Rome. The world doesn't end, Claire. In the morning, the survivors start to build again. It's the way of things. The human way."

Claire didn't particularly want a pep talk. She wanted to curl up in her warm bed upstairs, pull pillows over her head, and feel Shane's arms around her.

None of that was going to happen. Her bed was currently occupied by Miranda, a freaked-out teenage psychic with dependency issues, and as for Shane . . .

Shane was about to *leave*.

"Why?" she blurted. "Why are you sending him out there? You know what could happen—"

"I know a great deal about Shane Collins that you don't," Amelie interrupted. "He's not a child, and he has survived much in his young life. He'll survive this. And he wishes to make a difference."

She was sending Shane into the predawn darkness with a few chosen fighters, both vampire and human, to take possession of the Bloodmobile: the last reliably accessible blood storage in Morganville.

And it was the last thing Shane wanted to do. It was the last thing Claire wanted for him.

"Bishop isn't going to want the Bloodmobile for himself," Claire said. "He wants it destroyed. Morganville's full of walking blood banks, as far as he's concerned. But it'll hurt *you* if you lose it, so he'll come after it. Right?"

The severe, thin line of Amelie's mouth made it clear that she didn't like being second-guessed. It definitely couldn't be called a smile. "As long as Shane has the book, Bishop will not dare destroy the vehicle for fear of destroying his great treasure along with it."

Translation: Shane was bait. Because of the *book*. Claire hated that damn book. It had brought her nothing but trouble from the time she'd first heard about it. Amelie and Oliver, the two biggest vamps in town, had both been scrambling to find it, and it had dropped into Claire's hands instead. She wished she had the courage to grab it from Shane right now, run outside, and toss it in the nearest burning house to get rid of it once and for all, because as far as she could tell, it hadn't done anybody any good, ever—including Amelie.

Claire said, "He'll kill Shane to get it."

Amelie shrugged. "I gamble that killing Shane is far more difficult than it would appear."

"Yeah, you are gambling. You're betting his life."

Amelie's ice gray eyes were steady on hers. "Be clear on this: I am, in fact, betting all our lives. So be grateful, child, and also be warned. I could concede this fight at any time. My father would allow me to walk away—only me, alone. Defeated. I stay out of duty to you and the others in this town who are loyal to me." Her eyes narrowed. "Don't make me reconsider that."

Claire hoped she didn't look as mutinous as she felt. She pasted on what was supposed to be an agreeable expression, and nodded. Amelie's eyes narrowed even more.

"Get prepared. We leave in ten minutes."

Shane wasn't the only one with a dirty job to do; they were all assigned things they didn't particularly like. Claire was going with Amelie to try to rescue another vampire—Myrnin. And while Claire liked Myrnin, and admired him in a lot of ways, she also wasn't too excited about facing down—again—the vampire holding him prisoner, the dreadful Mr. Bishop.

Eve was off to the coffee shop, Common Grounds, with the just-about-as-awful Oliver, her former boss. Michael was about to head out to the university with Richard Morrell, the mayor's son. How he was supposed to protect a few thousand clueless college students, Claire had no idea; she took a moment to marvel at the fact that the vampires really could lock down the town when they wanted. She'd have thought keeping students on campus in this situation would be impossible—kids phoning home, jumping in cars, getting the hell out of Dodge.

Except the vampires controlled the phone lines, cell phones, the Internet, the TV, and the radio, and cars either died or wrecked on the outskirts of town if the vampires didn't want you to leave. Only a few people had ever gotten out of Morganville successfully without permission. Shane had been one. And then he'd come *back*.

Claire still had no idea what kind of guts that had taken, knowing what was waiting for him.

"Hey," Claire's housemate Eve said. She paused, arms full of clothes—black and red, so they'd almost certainly come out of Eve's own Goth-heavy closet—and gave Claire a quick once-over. She'd changed to what in Eve's world were practical fighting clothes—a pair of tight black jeans, a tight black shirt with red skull patterns all over it, and stompy, thick-soled boots. And a spiked black leather collar around her throat that almost dared the vampires, *Bite that!*

"Hey," Claire said. "Is this really a good time to start laundry?"

Eve rolled her eyes. "Cute. So, some people didn't want to be caught dead in their stupid ball costumes, if you know what I mean. How about you? Ready to take that thing off?"

Claire looked down at herself. She was honestly surprised to realize that she was still wearing the tight, garish bodysuit of her Harlequin costume. "Oh, yes." She sighed. "Got anything without, you know, skulls?"

"What's wrong with skulls? And that would be a no, by the way." Eve dumped the armload of clothing on the floor and rooted through it, pulling out a plain black shirt and a pair of blue jeans. "The jeans are yours. Sorry, but I sort of raided everybody's stash. Hope you like the underwear you have on; I didn't go through your drawers."

"Afraid it might get you all turned on?" Shane asked from over her shoulder. "Please say yes." He grabbed a pair of his own jeans from the pile. "And please stay out of my closet."

Eve gave him the finger. "If you're worried about

me finding your porn stash, old news, man. Also, you have really boring taste." She grabbed a blanket from the couch and nodded toward the corner. "No privacy anywhere in this house tonight. Go on, we'll fix up a changing room."

The three of them edged past the people and vampires who packed the Glass House. It had become the unofficial campaign center for their side of the war, which meant there were plenty of people tramping around, getting in their stuff, who none of them would have let cross the threshold under normal circumstances.

Take Monica Morrell. The mayor's daughter had shed her elaborate Marie Antoinette costume and was back to the blond, slinky, pretty, slimy girl Claire knew and hated.

"Oh my God." Claire gritted her teeth. "Is she wearing my *blouse*?" It was her only good one. Silk. She'd just bought it last week. Now she'd never be able to put it on again. "Remind me to burn that later." Monica saw her staring, fingered the collar of the shirt, and gave her an evil smile. She mouthed, *Thanks.* "Remind me to burn it *twice.* And stomp on the ashes."

Eve grabbed Claire by the arm and hustled her into the empty corner of the room, where she shook out the blanket and held it at arm's length to provide a temporary shelter.

Claire peeled off her sweat-soaked Harlequin costume with a whimper of relief, and shivered as the cool air hit her flushed skin. She felt awkward and anxious, stripped to her underwear with just a blanket held up between her and a dozen strangers, some of whom probably wanted to eat her.

Shane leaned over the top. "You done?"

She squealed and threw the wadded-up costume at him. He caught it and waggled his eyebrows at her as she stepped into the jeans and quickly buttoned up the shirt.

"Done!" she called.

Eve dropped the blanket and smiled poison-sweet at Shane.

"Your turn, leather boy," she said. "Don't worry. I won't accidentally embarrass you."

No, she'd embarrass him completely on purpose, and Shane knew it, from the glare he threw her. He ducked behind the blanket. Claire wasn't tall enough to check him out over the top—not that she wasn't tempted—but when Eve lowered the blanket, bit by bit, Claire grabbed one corner and pulled it back up.

"You're no fun," Eve said.

"Don't mess with him. Not now. He's going out there alone."

Eve's face went still and tight, and for the first time, Claire realized that the shine in her eyes wasn't really humor. It was a tightly controlled kind of panic. "Yeah," she said. "I know. It's just—we're all splitting up, Claire. I wish we didn't have to do that."

On impulse, Claire hugged her. Eve smelled of powder and some kind of darkly floral perfume, with a light undertone of sweat.

"Hey!" Shane's wounded yell was enough to make them both giggle. The blanket had drooped enough to show him zipping up his pants. Fast. "Seriously, girls, *not cool.* A guy could do serious damage."

He looked more like Shane now. The leather pants had made him unsettlingly hot-model gorgeous. In jeans and his old, faded Marilyn Manson T-shirt, he was somebody down-to-earth, somebody Claire could imagine kissing.

And she did imagine, just like that. It was, as usual, heart-racingly delicious.

"Michael's going out, too," Eve said, and now the tension she'd been hiding made her voice tremble. "I have to tell him—"

"Go on," Claire said. "We're right behind you."

Eve dropped the blanket and pushed through the

crowd, heading for her boyfriend, and the unofficial head of their strange and screwed-up fraternity.

It was easy to spot Michael in any group—he was tall and blond, with a face like an angel. As he caught sight of Eve heading toward him, he smiled, and Claire thought that was maybe the most complicated smile she'd ever seen, full of relief, welcome, love, and worry.

Eve crashed straight into him, hard enough to rock him back on his heels, and their arms went around each other.

Shane held Claire back with a touch on her shoulder. "Give them a minute," he said. "They've got things to say." She turned to look at him. "And so do we."

She swallowed hard and nodded. Shane's hands were on her shoulders, and his eyes had gone still and intense.

"Don't go out there," Shane said.

It was what she'd been intending to say to *him*. She blinked, surprised.

"You stole my paranoia," she said. "*I* was going to say, *Don't go*. But you're going to, no matter what I say, aren't you?"

That threw him off just a little. "Well, yeah, of course I am, but—"

"But nothing. I'll be with Amelie; I'll be okay. You? You're going off with the cast of *WWE Raw* to fight a cage match or something. It's not the same thing."

"Since when do you ever watch wrestling?"

"Shut up. That's not the point, and you know it. Shane, *don't go*." Claire put everything she had into it.

It wasn't enough.

Shane smoothed her hair and bent down to kiss her. It was the sweetest, gentlest kiss he'd ever given her, and it melted all the tense muscles of her neck, her shoulders, and her back. It was a promise without words, and when he finally pulled back, he passed his thumb across her lips gently, to seal it all in.

"There's something I really ought to tell you," he said. "I was kind of waiting for the right time."

They were in a room full of people, Morganville was in chaos outside, and they probably didn't have a chance of surviving until sunrise, but Claire felt her heart stutter and then race faster. The whole world seemed to go silent around her. *He's going to say it.*

Shane leaned in, so close that she felt his lips brush her ear, and whispered, "My dad's coming back to town."

That *so* wasn't what she was hoping he'd say. Claire jerked back, startled, and Shane put a hand over her mouth. "Don't," he whispered. "Don't say *anything*. We can't talk about this, Claire. I just wanted you to know."

They couldn't talk about it because Shane's father was Morganville's most wanted, public enemy number one, and any conversation they had—at least here— was in danger of being overheard by unfriendly, un- dead ears.

Not that Claire was a fan of Shane's father; he was a cold, brutal man who'd used and abused Shane, and she couldn't work up a lot of dread for seeing him behind bars . . . only she knew that Amelie and Oliver wouldn't stop at putting him in jail. Shane's father was marked for death if he came back. Death by burning. And while Claire wouldn't necessarily cry any big tears over him, she didn't want to put Shane through that, either.

"We'll talk about it," she said.

Shane snorted. "You mean, you'll yell at me? Trust me, I know what you're going to say. I just wanted you to know, in case—"

In case something happened to him. Claire tried to frame her question in a way that wouldn't tip their hand to any listening ears. "When should I expect him?"

"Next few days, probably. But you know how it is. I'm out of the loop." Shane's smile had a dark, painful edge to it now. He'd defied his dad once, because of Claire, and that meant cutting the ties to his last living family in the world. Claire doubted his dad had forgotten that, or ever would.

"Why now?" she whispered. "The last thing we need is—"

"Help?"

"He's not *help.* He's chaos!"

Shane gestured at the burning town. "Take a good look, Claire. How much worse can it get?"

Lots, she thought. Shane, in some ways, still had a rose-colored view of his father. It had been a while since his dad had blown out of town, and she thought that Shane had probably convinced himself that the guy wasn't all that bad. He was probably thinking now that his dad would come sweeping in to save them.

It wasn't going to happen. Frank Collins was a fanatic, car-bomb variety, and he didn't care who got hurt.

Not even his own son.

"Let's just—" She chewed her lip for a second, staring at him. "Let's just get through the day, okay? Please? Be careful. Call me."

He had his cell phone, and he showed it to her in mute promise. Then he stepped closer, and when his arms closed around her, she felt a sweet, trembling relief.

"Better get ready," he said. "It's going to be a long day."

2

Claire wasn't sure if *get ready* meant put on her game face, brush her teeth, or pack up a lot of weapons, but she followed Shane to say good-bye to Michael first.

Michael was standing in the middle of a bunch of hard-looking types—some were vampires, and many she'd never seen before. They didn't look happy about playing defense, and they had that smelling-something-rotten expression that meant they didn't like hanging out with the human help, either.

The non-vamps with Michael were older, post-college—tough guys with lots of muscles. Even so, the humans mostly looked nervous.

Shane seemed almost small in comparison—not that he let it slow him down as he rushed the defensive line. He pushed a vampire out of his way as he headed for Michael; the vampire flashed fang at him, but Shane didn't even notice.

Michael did. He stepped in the way of the offended vamp as it made a move for Shane's back, and the two of them froze that way, predators facing off. Michael wasn't the one to look down first.

Michael had a strange intensity about him now—something that had always been there, but being a vampire had ramped it up to about eleven, Claire thought. He still looked angelic, but there were moments when his angel was more fallen than flying. But the smile was real, and completely the Michael she knew and loved when he turned it on them.

He held out his hand for a manly kind of shake. Shane batted it aside and hugged him. There were manly backslaps, and if there was a brief flash of red in Michael's eyes, Shane didn't see it.

"You be careful, man," Shane said. "Those college chicks, they're wild. Don't let them drag you into any Jell-O shot parties. Stay strong."

"You too," Michael said. "Be careful."

"Driving around in a big, black, obvious lunch wagon in a town full of starving vampires? Yeah. I'll try to keep it low profile." Shane swallowed. "Seriously—"

"I know. Same here."

They nodded at each other.

Claire and Eve watched them for a moment. The two of them shrugged. "What?" Michael asked.

"That's it? That's your big good-bye?" Eve asked.

"What was wrong with it?"

Claire looked at Eve, mystified. "I think I need guy CliffsNotes."

"Guys aren't deep enough to need CliffsNotes."

"What were you waiting for, flowery poetry?" Shane snorted. "I hugged. I'm done."

Michael's grin didn't last. He looked at Shane, then Claire, and last—and longest—at Eve. "Don't let anything happen to you," he said. "I love you guys."

"Ditto," Shane said, which was, for Shane, positively gushing.

They might have had time to say more, but one of the vampires standing around, looking pissed off and impatient, tapped Michael on the shoulder. His pale lips moved near Michael's ear.

"Time to go," Michael said. He hugged Eve hard, and had to peel her off at the end. "Don't trust Oliver."

"Yeah, like you had to tell me that," Eve said. Her voice was shaking again. "Michael—"

"I love you," he said, and kissed her, fast and hard. "I'll see you soon."

He left in a blur, taking most of the vampires with him. The mayor's son, Richard Morrell—still in his police uniform, although he was looking wrinkled and smoke stained now—led the humans at a more normal pace to follow.

Eve stood there with her kiss-smudged lips parted, looking stunned and astonished. When she regained the power of speech, she said, "Did he just say—?"

"Yes," Claire said, smiling. "Yes, he did."

"Whoa. Guess I'd better stay alive, then."

The crowd of people—fewer now than there had been just a few minutes before—parted around them, and Oliver strode through the gap. The second-most badass vampire in town had shed his costume and was dressed in plain black, with a long, black leather coat. His long graying hair was tied back in a tight knot at the back of his head, and he looked like he was ready to snap the head off anyone, vampire or human, who got in the way.

"You," he snapped at Eve. "Come."

He turned on his heel and walked away. This was not the Oliver they'd known before—certainly not the friendly proprietor of the local coffee shop. Even once he'd been revealed as a vampire, he hadn't been *this* intense.

Clearly, he was done pretending to like people.

Eve watched him go, and the look in her eyes was boiling with resentment. She finally shrugged and took a deep breath. "Yeah," she said. "This'll be *so* much fun. See ya, Claire Bear."

"See you," Claire said. They hugged one last time, just for comfort, and then Eve was leaving, back straight, head high.

She was probably crying, Claire thought. Eve cried at times like these. Claire didn't seem to be able to cry when it counted, like now. It felt like pieces of her were being pulled off, and she felt cold and empty inside. No tears.

And now it was her heart being ripped out, because Shane was being summoned impatiently by yet another hard-looking bunch of vampires and humans near the door. He nodded to them, took her hands, and looked into her eyes.

Say it, she thought.

But he didn't. He just kissed her hands, turned, and walked away, dragging her red, bleeding heart with him—metaphorically, anyway.

"I love you," she whispered. She'd said it before, but he'd hung up the phone before she'd gotten it out. Then she'd said it in the hospital, but he'd been doped up on painkillers. And he didn't hear her now, as he walked away from her.

But at least *she* had the guts to try.

He waved to her from the door, and then he was gone, and she suddenly felt very alone in the world—and very . . . young. Those who were left in the Glass House had jobs of their own, and she was in the way. She found a chair—Michael's armchair, as it turned out—and pulled her feet up under her as humans and vampires moved around, fortifying windows and doors, distributing weapons, talking in low tones.

She might have become a ghost, for all the attention they paid her.

She didn't have to wait long. In just a few minutes, Amelie came sweeping down the stairs. She had a whole scary bunch of vampires behind her, and a few humans, including two in police uniforms.

They were all armed—knives, clubs, swords. Some had stakes, including the policemen; they had them, instead of riot batons, hanging from their utility belts. *Standard-issue equipment for Morganville,* Claire thought, and had to suppress a manic giggle. *Maybe instead of pepper spray, they have garlic spray.*

Amelie handed Claire two things: a thin, silver knife, and a wooden stake. "A wooden stake in the heart will put one of us down," she said. "You must use the silver knife to kill us. No steel, unless you plan to take our heads off with it. The stake alone will not do it, unless you're very lucky or sunlight catches us helpless, and even then, we are slower to die the older we are. Do you understand?"

Claire nodded numbly. *I'm sixteen,* she wanted to say. *I'm not ready for this.*

But she kind of had to be, now.

Amelie's fierce, cold expression seemed to soften, just a touch. "I can't entrust Myrnin to anyone else. When we find him, it will be your responsibility to manage him. He may be—" Amelie paused, as if searching for the right word. "Difficult." That probably wasn't it. "I don't want you to fight, but I need you with us."

Claire lifted the stake and the knife. "Then why did you give me these?"

"Because you might need to defend yourself, or him. If you do, I don't want you to hesitate, child. Defend yourself and Myrnin at all costs. Some of those who come against us may be those you know. Don't let that stop you. We are in this to survive now."

Claire nodded numbly. She'd been pretending that all this was some kind of action/adventure video game, like the zombie-fighting one Shane enjoyed so much, but with every one of her friends leaving, she'd lost some of that distance. Now it was right here in front of her: reality. People were dying.

She might be one of them.

"I'll stay close," she said. Amelie's cold fingers touched her chin, very lightly.

"Do that." Amelie turned her attention to the others around them. "Watch for my father, but don't be drawn off to face him. It's what he wants. He will have his own reinforcements, and will be gathering more. Stay together, and watch each other closely. Protect me, and protect the child."

"Um—could you stop calling me that?" Claire asked. Amelie's icy eyes fixed on her in almost-human puzzlement. "Child, I mean? I'm not a child."

It felt like time stopped for about a hundred years while Amelie stared at her. It probably had been at *least* a hundred years since the last time anybody had dared correct Amelie like that in public.

Amelie's lips curved, very slightly. "No," she agreed. "You are not a child, and in any case, by your age, I was a bride and ruled a kingdom. I should know better."

Claire felt heat build in her face. Great, she was blushing, as everybody's attention focused on her. Amelie's smile widened.

"I stand corrected," she said to the rest of them. "Protect this *young woman.*"

She really didn't feel like that, either, but Claire wasn't going to push her luck on that one. The other vampires looked mostly annoyed with the distinction, and the humans looked nervous.

"Come," Amelie said, and turned to face the blank far wall of the living room. It shimmered like an asphalt road in the summer, and Claire felt the connection snap open.

Amelie stepped through what looked like blank wall. After a second or two of surprise, the vampires started to follow her.

"Man, I can't believe we're doing this," one of the policemen behind Claire whispered to the other.

"I can," the other whispered back. "My kids are out there. What else is there to do?"

She gripped the wooden stake tight and stepped through the portal, following Amelie.

Myrnin's lab wasn't any more of a wreck than usual. Claire was kind of surprised by that; somehow she'd expected Mr. Bishop to tear through here with torches and clubs, but so far, he'd found better targets.

Or maybe—just maybe—he hadn't been able to get in. Yet.

Claire anxiously surveyed the room, which was lit by just a few flickering lamps, both oil and electric. She'd tried cleaning it up a few times, but Myrnin had snapped at her that he liked things the way they were, so she'd left the stacks of leaning books, the piles of glassware on counters, the disordered piles of curling paper. There was a broken iron cage in the corner—broken because Myrnin had decided to escape from it once, and they'd never gotten around to having it repaired once he'd regained his senses.

The vampires were whispering to one another, in sibilant little hisses that didn't carry even a hint of meaning to Claire's ears. They were nervous, too.

Amelie, by contrast, seemed as casual and self-assured as ever. She snapped her fingers, and two of the vampires—big, strong, strapping men—stepped up, towering over her. She glanced up.

"You will guard the stairs," she said. "You two." She pointed to the uniformed policemen. "I want you here as well. Guard the interior doors. I doubt anything will come through them, but Mr. Bishop has already surprised us. I won't have him surprising us again."

That cut their forces in half. Claire swallowed hard and looked at the two vampires and one human who remained with her and Amelie—she knew the two vampires slightly. They were Amelie's personal bodyguards, and one of them, at least, had treated her kind of decently before.

The remaining human was a tough-looking African American woman with a scar across her face, from her left temple across her nose, and down her right cheek. She saw Claire watching her, and gave her a smile. "Hey," she said, and stuck out a big hand. "Hannah Moses. Moses Garage."

"Hey," Claire said, and shook hands awkwardly. The woman had muscles—not quite Shane-quality biceps, but definitely bigger than most women would have found useful. "You're a mechanic?"

"I'm an everything," Hannah said. "Mechanic included. But I used to be a marine."

"Oh." Claire blinked.

"The garage was my dad's before he passed. I just got back from a couple of tours in Afghanistan—thought I'd take up the quiet life for a while." She shrugged. "Guess trouble's in my blood. Look, if this comes to a fight, stay with me, okay? I'll watch your back."

That was so much of a relief that Claire felt weak enough to melt. "Thanks."

"No problem. You're what, about fifteen?"

"Almost seventeen." Claire thought she needed a T-shirt that said it for her; it would be a great time-saver—that, or some kind of button.

"Huh. So you're about my kid brother's age. His name's Leo. I'll have to introduce you sometime."

Hannah, Claire realized, was talking without really thinking about what she was saying; her eyes were focused on Amelie, who had made her way around piles of books to the doorway on the far wall.

Hannah didn't seem to miss anything.

"Claire," Amelie said. Claire dodged piles of books and came to her side. "Did you lock this door when you left before?"

"No. I thought I'd be coming back this way."

"Interesting. Because someone *has* locked it."

"Myrnin?"

Amelie shook her head. "Bishop has him. He has not returned this way."

Claire decided not to ask how she knew that. "Who else—" And then she knew. "Jason." Eve's brother had known about the doorways that led to different destinations in town—maybe not about how they worked (and Claire wasn't sure she did, either), but he definitely had figured out how to use them. Apart from Claire, Myrnin, and Amelie, only Oliver had the knowledge, and she knew where he'd been since her encounter with Mr. Bishop.

"Yes," Amelie agreed. "The boy is becoming a problem."

"Kind of an understatement, considering he, you know . . ." Claire mimed stabbing with the stake, but not in Amelie's direction—that would be like pointing a loaded gun at Superman. Somebody would get hurt, and it wouldn't be Superman. "Um—I meant to ask, are you—?"

Amelie looked away from her, toward the door. "Am I what?"

"Okay?" Because she'd had a stake in her chest not all that long ago, and besides that, all the vampires in Morganville had a disadvantage, whether they knew it or not: they were sick—really sick—with something Claire could only think of as vampire Alzheimer's.

And it was ultimately fatal.

Most of the town didn't have a clue about that, because Amelie was rightly afraid of what might happen if they did—vampires and humans alike. Amelie had symptoms, but so far they were mild. It took years to progress, so they were safe for a while.

At least, Claire hoped it took years.

"No, I doubt I am all right. Still, this is hardly the time to be coddling myself." Amelie focused on the door. "We will need the key to open it."

That was a problem, because the key wasn't where it was supposed to be. The key ring was gone from where Claire kept it, in a battered, sagging drawer, and the more Claire pawed through debris looking for it, the more alarmed she became. Myrnin kept the weirdest stuff. . . . Books, sure, she loved books; small, deformed dead things in alcohol, not so much. He also kept jars of dirt—at least, she hoped it was dirt. Some of it looked red and flaky, and she was really afraid it might be blood.

The keys were missing. So were a few other things—significant things.

With a sinking feeling, Claire pulled open the half-broken drawer where she'd kept the bag with all the tranquilizer stuff, and Myrnin's drug supplies.

Gone. Only a scrape in the dust to indicate where it had been.

That meant that if—*when*—Myrnin turned violent, she wouldn't have her trusty dart gun to help her. Nor would she have even her trusty injectable pen, so cool, that she'd loaded up for emergencies, because it had been in the bag with the drugs. She'd lost the other supplies she'd had with her.

But even worse, she didn't have any medicine for him, other than the couple of small vials she had with her in her pockets.

In summary: so very screwed.

"Enough," Amelie said, and turned to her bodyguard. "I know this isn't easy, but if you would?"

He gave her a polite sort of nod, stepped forward, and took the lock in his hand.

His hand *burst into flame.*

"Oh my God!" Claire blurted, and clapped her hands over her mouth, because the vampire guy wasn't letting go. His face was contorted with pain, but he held on, somehow, and jerked and twisted the silver-plated lock until, with a scream of metal, it ripped loose. The hasp came with it, right off the door.

He dropped it to the floor. His hand kept burning. Claire grabbed the first thing that came to hand—some kind of ratty old shirt Myrnin had left thrown on the floor—and patted out the fire. The smell of burned flesh made her dry heave, and so did the sight of what was left of his hand. He didn't scream. She almost did it for him.

"A trap," Amelie said. "From my father. Gérard, are you able to continue?"

He nodded as he wrapped the shirt around the ruin of his hand. He was sweating fine pink beads—blood,

Claire realized, as a trickle of it ran down his pale face. She realized that as she was standing there right in front of him, frozen in place, and his eyes flashed red.

"Move," he growled at her. "Stay behind us." And then, after a brief pause, he said, "Thank you."

Hannah took her by the arm and pulled her to the spot in the back, out of vampire-grabbing range. "He needs feeding," she said in an undertone. "Gérard's not a bad guy, but you don't want to make yourself too available for snack attacks. Remember, we're vending machines with legs."

Claire nodded. Amelie put her fingers in the hole left by the broken lock and pulled the door open . . . on darkness.

Hannah said nothing. She didn't let go of Claire's arm.

For a long moment, nothing happened, and then the darkness flickered. Shifted. Things came and went in the shadows, and Claire knew that Amelie was shuffling destinations, trying to find the one she wanted. It seemed to take a very long time, and then Amelie took a sudden step back. "Now," she said, and her two bodyguards charged forward into what looked like complete darkness and were gone. Amelie glanced back at Hannah and Claire, and her black pupils were expanding fast, covering all the gray iris of her eyes, preparing for the dark.

"Don't leave my side," she said. "This will be dangerous."

3

Amelie grabbed Claire's other arm, and before Claire could so much as grab a breath, she was being pulled through the portal. There was a brief wave of chill, and a feeling that was a little like being pushed from all sides, and then she was stumbling into utter, complete blackness. Her other senses went into overdrive. The air smelled stale and heavy, and felt cold and damp, like a cave. Amelie's icy grip on one arm was going to leave bruises, and Hannah Moses's warmer touch on the other seemed light by contrast, although Claire knew it wasn't.

Claire could hear herself and Hannah breathing, but there was no sound at all from the vampires. When Claire tried to speak, Amelie's ice-cold hand covered her mouth. She nodded convulsively, and concentrated on putting one foot in front of the other as Amelie—she hoped it was still Amelie, anyway—pulled her forward into the dark.

The smells changed from time to time—a whiff of nasty, rotten something, then something else that smelled weirdly like grapes? Her imagination conjured up a dead man surrounded by broken bottles of wine, and Claire couldn't stop it there; the dead man was moving, squirming toward her, and any second now he'd touch her and she'd scream. . . .

It's just your imagination; stop it.

She swallowed and tried to tamp down the panic. It

wasn't helping. *Shane wouldn't panic. Shane would*—whatever, Shane wouldn't be caught dead roaming around in the dark with a bunch of vampires like this, and Claire knew it.

It seemed like they went on forever, and then Amelie pulled her to a stop and let go. Losing that support felt as if she were standing on the edge of a cliff, and Claire was really, really grateful for Hannah's grip to tell her there was something else real in the world. *Don't let me fall.*

And then Hannah's hand went away. A fast tightening of her fingers, and she was gone.

Claire was floating in total darkness, disconnected, alone. Her breath sounded loud as a train in her ears, but it was buried under the thunder of her fast heartbeats. *Move,* she told herself. *Do something!*

She whispered, "Hannah?"

Cold hands slapped around her from behind, one pinning her arms to her sides, the other covering her mouth. She was lifted off the ground, and she screamed, a faint buzzing sound like a storm of bees that didn't make it through the muffling gag.

And then she went flying through the air into the darkness . . . and rolled to a stop facedown, on a cold stone floor. There was light here. Faint, but definite, painting the edges of things a pale gray, including the arched mouth of the tunnel at the end of the hall.

She had no idea where she was.

Claire got quickly to her feet and turned to look behind her. Amelie, pale as a pearl, stepped through the portal, and with her came the other two vampires. Gérard had Hannah Moses's arm gripped in his good hand.

Hannah had a bloody gash on her head, and when Gérard let go, she dropped to her knees, breathing hard. Her eyes looked blank and unfocused.

Amelie whirled, something silver in one hand, and stabbed as something came at her from the dark. It screamed, a thin sound that echoed through the tunnel, and a white hand reached out to grab Amelie's shirt.

The invisible portal slammed shut like an iris, and severed the arm just above the elbow.

Amelie plucked the still-grabbing hand from her shirt, dropped the hand to the ground, and kicked it to the side. When she turned back to the others, there was no expression on her face.

Claire felt like throwing up. She couldn't take her eyes away from that wiggling, fish-pale hand.

"It was necessary to come this way," Amelie said. "Dangerous, but necessary."

"Where are we?" Claire asked. Amelie gave her a look and ignored her as she took the lead, heading down the hall. Going through this didn't give her any right to ask questions. Of course. "Hannah? Are you okay?"

Hannah waved her hand vaguely, which really wasn't all that confidence-building. The vampire Gérard answered for her. "She's fine." Sure, he could talk, having one hand burned to the bone. He'd probably classify himself as fine, too. "Take her," Gérard ordered, and pushed Hannah toward Claire as he moved to follow Amelie. The other bodyguard—what was his name?—moved with him, as if they were an old, practiced team.

Hannah was heavy, but she pulled herself back on her own center of gravity after a breath or two. "I'm fine," she said, and gave Claire a reassuring grin. "Damn. That was not a walk in the park."

"You should meet my boyfriend," Claire said. "You two are both masters of understatement."

She thought Hannah wanted to laugh, but instead, she just nodded and patted Claire on the shoulder. "Watch the sides," she said. "We're just starting on this thing."

That was an easy job, because there was nothing to watch on the sides. They were, after all, in a tunnel. Hannah, it appeared, was the rear guard, and she seemed to take it very seriously, although it looked like Amelie had slammed the doorway behind them pretty hard, with prejudice. *I hope we don't have to go back that way,* Claire thought, and shivered at the sight of that pale severed hand behind them. It had finally stopped moving. *I really, really hope we don't have to go back there.*

At the mouth of the tunnel, Amelie seemed to pause for a moment, and then disappeared to the right, around the corner, with her two vampire bodyguards in flying formation behind her. Hannah and Claire hurried to keep up, and emerged into another hallway, this one square instead of arched, and paneled in rich, dark wood. There were paintings on the walls—old ones, Claire thought—of pale people lit by candlelight, dressed in about a thousand pounds of costume and rice white makeup and wigs.

She stopped and backed up, staring at one.

"What?" Hannah growled.

"That's her. Amelie." It definitely was, only instead of the Princess Grace–style clothes she wore now, in the picture she was wearing an elaborate sky blue satin dress, cut way low over her breasts. She was wearing a big white wig, and staring out of the canvas in an eerily familiar way.

"Art appreciation later, Claire. We need to go."

That was true, beyond any argument, but Claire kept throwing glances at the paintings as they passed. One looked like it could have been Oliver, from about four hundred years ago. One more modern one looked almost like Myrnin. *It's the vampire museum,* she realized. *It's their history.* There were glass cases lining the hall ahead, filled with books and papers and jewelry, clothing, and musical instruments. All the fine and fabulous things gathered through their long, long lives.

Ahead, the three vampires came to a sudden, motionless halt, and Hannah grabbed Claire by the arm to pull her out of the way, against the wall. "What's happening?" Claire whispered.

"Sorting credentials."

Claire didn't know what that meant, exactly, but when she risked moving out just a bit to see what was happening, she saw that there were lots of other vampires in here—about a hundred of them, some sitting down and obviously hurt. There were humans, too, mostly standing together and looking nervous, which seemed reasonable.

If these were Bishop's people, their little rescue party was in serious trouble.

Amelie exchanged some quiet words with the vampire who seemed to be in charge, and Gérard and his partner visibly relaxed. That settled the friend-or-foe question, apparently; Amelie turned and nodded to Claire, and she and Hannah edged out from behind the glass cases to join them.

Amelie made a gesture, and immediately several vampires peeled off from the group and joined her in a distant corner.

"What's going on?" Claire asked, and stared around her. Most of the vampires were still dressed in the costumes they'd worn to Bishop's welcome feast, but a few were in more military dress—black, mostly, but some in camouflage.

"It's a rally point," Hannah said. "She's talking strategy, probably. Those would be her captains. Notice there aren't any humans with her?"

Claire did. It wasn't exactly a pleasant sensation, the doubt that boiled up inside.

Whatever orders Amelie delivered, it didn't take long. One by one, the vampires nodded and peeled off from the meeting, gathered up followers—including humans this time—and departed. By the time Amelie had dispatched the last group, there were only about ten people left Claire didn't know, and they were all standing together.

Amelie came back to them, saw the group of humans and vamps, and nodded toward them.

"Claire, this is Theodosius Goldman," Amelie said. "Theo, he prefers to be called. These are his family."

Family? That was a shock, because there were so many of them. Theo seemed to be kind of middle-aged, with graying, curly hair and a face that, except for its vampiric pallor, seemed kind of . . . nice.

"May I present my wife, Patience?" he said with the kind of old manners Claire had only seen on *Masterpiece Theater.* "Our sons, Virgil and Clarence. Their wives, Ida and Minnie." There were more vampires bowing, or in the case of the one guy down on the floor, with his head held in the lap of a female vamp, waving. "And their children."

Evidently the grandkids didn't merit individual introductions. There were four of them, two boys and two girls, all pale like their relatives. They seemed younger than Claire, at least physically; she guessed the littler girl was probably about twelve, the older boy around fifteen.

The older boy and girl glared at her, as if she were personally responsible for the mess they were in, but Claire was too busy imagining how a whole family—down to grandkids—could all be made vampires like this.

Theo, evidently, could see all that in her expression, because he said, "We were made eternal a long time ago, my girl, by"—he cast a quick look at Amelie, who nodded—"by her father, Bishop. It was a joke of his, you see, that we should all be together for all time." He really did have a kind face, Claire thought, and his smile was kind of tragic. "The joke turned on him, though. We refused to let it destroy us. Amelie showed us we did not have to kill to survive, and so we were able to keep our faith as well as our lives."

"Your faith?"

"It's a very old faith," Theo said. "And today is our Sabbath."

Claire blinked. "Oh. You're Jewish?"

He nodded, eyes fixed on her. "We found a refuge here, in Morganville. A place where we could live in peace, both with our nature and our God."

Amelie said, softly, "But will you fight for it now, Theo? This place that gave you refuge?"

He held out his hand. His wife's cool white fingers closed around it. She was a delicate china doll of a woman, with masses of sleek black hair piled on top of her head. "Not today."

"I'm sure God would understand if you broke the Sabbath under these circumstances."

"I'm sure he would. God is forgiving, or we would not still be walking this world. But to be moral is not to need his divine forgiveness, I think." He shook his head again, very regretfully. "We cannot fight, Amelie. Not today. And I would prefer not to fight at all."

"If you think you can stay neutral in this, you're wrong. I will respect your wishes. My father will not."

Theo's face hardened. "If your father threatens my family again, then we *will* fight. But until he comes for us, until he shows us the sword, we will not take up arms against him."

Gérard snorted, which proved what he thought about it; Claire wasn't much surprised. He seemed like a practical sort of guy. Amelie simply nodded. "I can't force you, and I wouldn't. But be careful. I cannot spare anyone to help you. You should be safe enough here, for a time. If any others come through, send them out to guard the power station and the campus." She allowed her gaze to move beyond Theo, to touch the three humans huddled in the far corner of the room, under another painting, a big one. "Are these under your Protection?"

Theo shrugged. "They asked to join us."

"Theo."

"I will defend them if someone tries to harm them." Theo pitched his voice lower. "Also, we may need them, if we can't get supplies."

Claire went cold. For all his kind face and smile,

Theo was talking about using those people as portable blood banks.

"I don't want to do it," Theo continued, "but if things go against us, I have to think of my children. You understand."

"I do," Amelie said. Her face was back to a blank mask that gave away nothing of how she felt about it. "I have never told you what to do, and I will not now. But by the laws of this town, if you place these humans under your Protection, you owe them certain duties. You know that."

Another shrug, and Theo held out his hands to show he was helpless. "Family comes first," he said. "I have always told you so."

"Some of us," Amelie said, "are not so fortunate in our choice of families."

She turned away from Theo without waiting for his response—if he'd been intending to give one—and without so much as a pause, slammed her fist into a glass-fronted wall box labeled EMERGENCY USE ONLY three steps to the right. It shattered in a loud clatter, and Amelie shook shards of glass from her skin.

She reached into the box and took out . . . Claire blinked. "Is that a *paintball* gun?"

Amelie handed it to Hannah, who handled it like a professional. "It fires pellets loaded with silver powder," she said. "Very dangerous to us. Be careful where you aim."

"Always am," Hannah said. "Extra magazines?"

Amelie retrieved them from the case and handed them over. Claire noticed that she protected herself even from a casual touch, with a fold of fabric over her fingers. "There are ten shots per magazine," she said. "There is one already loaded, and six more here."

"Well," Hannah said, "any problem I can't solve with seventy shots is probably going to kill us, anyway."

"Claire," Amelie said, and handed over a small, sealed vial. "Silver powder, packed under pressure. It will explode on impact, so be very careful with it. If you throw it, there is a wide dispersal through the air. It can hurt your friends as much as your enemies."

There were real uses for silver powder, like coating parts in computers; Claire supposed it wasn't exactly restricted, but she was surprised the vampires were progressive enough to lay in a supply. Amelie raised pale eyebrows at her.

"You've been expecting this," Claire said.

"Not in detail. But I've learned through my life that such preparations are never wasted, in the end. Sometime, somewhere, life always comes to a fight, and peace always comes to an end."

Theo said, very quietly, "Amen."

4

They left the museum by way of a side door. It was risky to go out into the night, but since the only other way to exit the museum was to go back into the darkness, nobody argued about the choice.

"Careful," Amelie told them in a very soft voice that hardly reached past the shadows. "I have gathered my forces. My father is doing the same. There will be patrols, especially here."

The flames hadn't reached Founder's Square, which was where they came out—the heart of vamp territory. It didn't look like the calm, orderly place Claire remembered, though; the lights were all out, and the shops and restaurants that bordered it were closed and empty.

It looked afraid.

The only place she could see movement was on the marble steps of the Elders' Council building, where Bishop's welcome feast had been held. Gérard hissed a warning, and they all froze, silent and still in the dark. Hannah's grip on Claire's arm felt like an iron band.

There were three vampires standing there, scanning the area.

Lookouts.

"Go," Amelie said in a whisper so small it was like a ghost. "Move, but be careful."

They reached the edge of the shadows by the corner

of the building, but just as Claire was starting to relax a little, Amelie, Gérard, and the other vampires moved in a blur, scattering in all directions.

This left Claire flat-footed for one horrible second, before Hannah tackled her facedown on the grass. Claire gasped, got a mouthful of crunchy dirt and bitter chlorophyll, and fought to get her breath. Hannah's heavy weight held her down, and the older woman braced her elbows on Claire's back.

She's firing the pistol, Claire thought, and tried to raise her head to see where Hannah was shooting.

"Head down!" Hannah snarled, and shoved Claire down with one hand while she continued to fire with the other. From the screams in the dark, she was hitting something. "Get up! Run!"

Claire wasn't quick enough to suit either the marines or the vampires, and before she knew it, she was being half pulled, half dragged at a dead run through the night. It was all a confusing blur of shadows, dark buildings, pale faces, and the surly orange glow of flames in the distance.

"What is it?" she screamed.

"Patrols." Hannah kept on firing behind them. She wasn't firing wildly, not at all; it seemed like she took a second or two between every shot, choosing her target. Most of the shots seemed to hit, from the shouts and snarls and screams. "Amelie! We need an exit, *now!*"

Amelie looked back at them, a pale flash of face in the dark, and nodded.

They charged up the steps of another building on Founder's Square. Claire didn't have time to get more than a vague impression of it—some kind of official building, with columns in front and big stone lions snarling on the stairs—before their little party came to a halt at the top of the stairs, in front of a closed white door with no knob.

Gérard started to throw himself against it. Amelie stopped him with an outstretched hand. "It will do no good," she said. "It can't be opened by force. Let me."

The other vampire, facing away and down the steps, said, "Don't think we have time for sweet talk, ma'am. What you want us to do?" He had a drawling Texas accent, the first one Claire had heard from any vampire. She'd never heard him speak at all before.

He winked at her, which was even more of a shock. Until that moment, he hadn't even looked at her like a real person.

"A moment," Amelie murmured.

The Texan nodded behind them. "Don't think we've got one, ma'am."

There were shadows converging in the dark at the foot of the steps—the patrol that Hannah had been shooting at. There were at least twenty of them. In the lead was Ysandre, the beautiful vampire Claire hated maybe more than she hated any other vampire in the entire world. She was Bishop's girl through and through—Amelie's vampire sister, if they thought in those kinds of terms.

Claire hated Ysandre for Shane's sake. She was glad the vamp was here, and not attacking Shane's Bloodmobile—one, because she wasn't so sure Shane could resist the evil witch, and two, she wanted to stake Ysandre herself.

Personally.

"No," Hannah said, when Claire took a step out from behind her. "Are you crazy? Get back!"

Hannah fired over her shoulder. It was at the outer extreme of the paintball gun's range, but the pellet hit one of the vampires—not Ysandre, Claire was disappointed to see—right in the chest. Silver dust puffed up in a lethal mist, and the close formation scattered. Ysandre might have had a few burns, but nothing that wouldn't heal.

The vampire Hannah had shot in the chest toppled over and hit the marble stairs, smoking and flailing.

Amelie slammed her palm flat against the door and

closed her eyes, and deep inside the barrier something groaned and shifted with a scrape of metal. "Inside," Amelie murmured, still wicked controlled, and Claire spun and followed the three vampires across the threshold. Hannah backed in after, grabbed the door, and slammed it shut.

"No locks," she said.

Amelie reached over and pushed Hannah's gun hand into an at-rest position at her side. "None necessary. They won't get in." She sounded sure of it, but from the look Hannah continued to give the door—as if she wished she could weld it shut with the force of her stare—she wasn't so certain. "This way. We'll take the stairs."

It was a library, full of books. Some—on this floor—were new, or at least newish, with colorful spines and crisp titles that Claire could read even in the low light. She slowed down a little, blinking. "You guys have *vampire* stories in here?" None of the vampires answered. Amelie veered to the right, through the two-story-tall shelves, and headed for a set of sweeping marble steps at the end. The books got older, the paper more yellow. Claire caught sight of a sign that read FOLKLORE, CA. 1870–1945, ENGLISH, and then another that identified a *German* section. Then *French.* Then script that might have been Chinese.

So many books, and from what she could tell, every single one of them had to do in some way with vampires. Was it history or fiction to them?

Claire didn't really have time to work it out. They were taking the stairs, moving around the curve up to the second level. Claire's legs burned all along the calf muscles, and her breathing was getting raspy from the constant movement and adrenaline. Hannah flashed her a quick, sympathetic smile. "Yeah," she said. "Consider it basic training. Can you keep up?"

Claire gave her a gasping nod.

More books here, old and crumbling, and the air tasted like dry leather and ancient paper. Toward the

back of the room, there were things that looked like
wine racks, the fancy X-shaped kind people put in
cellars, only these held rolls of paper, each neatly tied
with ribbon. They were scrolls, probably very old ones.
Claire hoped they'd go that direction, but no, Amelie
was turning them down another book aisle, toward a
blank white wall.

No, not quite blank. It had a small painting on the
wall, in a fussy gilt frame. Some bland-looking nature
scene . . . and then, as Amelie stared at it, the painting *changed*.

It grew darker, as though clouds had come across
the meadow and the drowsy sheep in the picture.

And then it was dark, just a dark canvas, then some
pinpricks of light, like candle flames through smoke. . . .

And then Claire saw Myrnin.

He was in chains, silver-colored chains, kneeling on
the floor, and his head was down. He was still wearing
the blousy white pantaloons of his Pierrot costume,
but no shirt. The wet points of his damp hair clung to
his face and his marble-pale shoulders.

Amelie nodded sharply, and put a hand against the
wall to the left of the picture, pressing what looked
like a nail, and part of the wall swung out silently on
oiled hinges.

Hidden doors: vampires sure seemed to love them.

There was darkness on the other side. "Oh, *hell*
no," Claire heard Hannah mutter. "Not again."

Amelie sent her a glance, and there was a whisper
of amusement in the look. "It's a different darkness,"
she said. "And the dangers are very different, from
this point on. Things may change quickly. You will
have to adapt."

Then she stepped through, and the vampires followed, and it was just Claire and Hannah.

Claire held out her hand. Hannah took it, still shaking her head, and the dark closed around them like a
damp velvet curtain.

There was the hiss of a match dragging, and a flare

of light from the corner. Amelie, her face turned ivory by the licking flame, set the match to a candle and left the light burning as she flicked on a small flashlight and played it around the room. Boxes. It was some kind of storeroom, dusty and disused. "All right," she said. "Gérard, if you please."

He swung another door open a crack, nodded, and widened it enough to slip through.

Another hallway. Claire was getting tired of hallways, and they were all starting to look the same. Where were they now, anyway? It looked like some kind of hotel, with polished heavy doors marked with brass plates, only instead of numbers, each door had one of the vampire markings, like the symbol on Claire's bracelet. Each vampire had one; at least she thought they did. So these would be—what? Rooms? Vaults? Claire thought she heard something behind one of the doors—muffled sounds, thumping, scratching. They didn't stop, though—and she wasn't sure she wanted to know, really.

Amelie brought them to a halt at the T-intersection of the hall. It was deserted in every direction, and disorienting, too; Claire couldn't tell one hallway from another. *Maybe we should drop crumbs,* she thought. *Or M&M's. Or blood.*

"Myrnin is in a room on this hall," Amelie said. "It is quite obviously a trap, and quite obviously meant for me. I will stay behind and ensure your escape route. Claire." Her pale eyes fixed on Claire with merciless intensity. "Whatever else happens, you must bring Myrnin out safely. Do you understand? Do not let Bishop have him."

She meant, *Everybody else is expendable.* That made Claire feel sick, and she couldn't help but look at Hannah, and even at the two vampires. Gérard shrugged, so slightly she thought it might have been her imagination.

"We are soldiers," Gérard said. "Yes?"

Hannah smiled. "Damn straight."

"Excellent. You will follow my orders."

Hannah saluted him, with just a little trace of irony. "Yes sir, squad leader, sir."

Gérard turned his attention to Claire. "You will stay behind us. Do you understand?"

She nodded. She felt cold and hot at the same time, and a little sick, and the wooden stake in her hand didn't seem like a heck of a lot, considering. But she didn't have any time for second thoughts, because Gérard had turned and was already heading down the hall, his wing man flanking him, and Hannah was beckoning Claire to follow.

Amelie's cool fingers brushed her shoulder. "Careful."

Claire nodded and went to rescue a crazy vampire from an evil one.

The door shattered under Gérard's kick. That wasn't an exaggeration; except for the wood around the door hinges, the rest of it broke into hand-sized pieces and splinters. Before that rain of wreckage hit the floor, Gérard was inside, moving to the left while his colleague went right. Hannah stepped in and swept the room from one side to the other, holding her air pistol ready to fire, then nodded sharply to Claire.

Myrnin was just as she'd seen him in the picture—kneeling in the center of the room, anchored by tight-stretched silvery chains. The chains were double-strength, and threaded through massive steel bolts on the stone floor.

He was shaking all over, and where the chains touched him, he had welts and burns.

Gérard swore softly under his breath and fiercely kicked the eyebolts in the floor. They bent, but didn't break.

Myrnin finally raised his head, and beneath the mass of sweaty dark hair, Claire saw wild dark eyes, and a smile that made her stomach twist.

"I knew you'd come," he whispered. "You fools. Where is she? Where's Amelie?"

"Behind us," Claire said.

"Fools."

"Nice way to talk to your rescuers," Hannah said. She was nervous, Claire could see it, though the woman controlled it very well. "Gérard? I don't like this. It's too easy."

"I know." He crouched down and looked at the chains. "Silver coated. I can't break them."

"What about the bolts in the floor?" Claire asked. In answer, Gérard grabbed the edge of the metal plate and twisted. The steel bent like aluminum foil, and, with a ripping shriek, tore free of the stones. Myrnin wavered as part of his restraints fell loose, and Gérard waved his partner to work on the other two plates while he focused on the second in front.

"Too easy, too easy," Hannah kept on muttering. "What's the point of doing this if Bishop is just going to let him go?"

The eyebolts were all ripped loose, and Gérard grabbed Myrnin's arm and helped him to his feet.

Myrnin's eyes sheeted over with blazing ruby, and he shook Gérard off and went straight for Hannah.

Hannah saw him coming and put the gun between them, but before she could fire, Gérard's partner knocked her hand out of line, and the shot went wild, impacting on the stone at the other side of the room. Silver flakes drifted on the air, igniting tiny burns where they landed on the vampires' skin. The two body-guards backed off.

Myrnin grabbed Hannah by the neck.

"No!" Claire screamed, and ducked under Gérard's restraining hand. She raised her wooden stake.

Myrnin turned his head and grinned at her with wicked vampire fangs flashing. "I thought you were here to save me, Claire, not kill me," he purred, and whipped back toward his prey. Hannah was fumbling with her gun, trying to get it back into position. He stripped it away from her with contemptuous ease.

"I *am* here to save you," Claire said, and before she could think what she was doing, she buried the stake in Myrnin's back, on the left side, right where she thought his heart would be.

He made a surprised sound, like a cough, and pitched forward into Hannah. His hand slid away from her throat, clutching blindly at her clothes, and then he fell limply to the floor.

Dead, apparently.

Gérard and his partner looked at Claire as if they'd never seen her before, and then Gérard roared, "What do you think you're—"

"Pick him up," Claire said. "We can take the stake out later. He's old. He'll survive."

That sounded cold, and scary, and she hoped it was true. Amelie had survived, after all, and she knew Myrnin was as old, or maybe even older. From the look he gave her, Gérard was reassessing everything he'd thought about the cute, fragile little human he'd been nursemaiding. Too bad. Claire thought one of her strengths was that everybody always underestimated her.

She was cool on the outside, shaking on the inside, because although it *was* the only way to keep Myrnin calm right now without tranquilizers, or without letting him rip Hannah's throat out, she'd just killed her boss.

That didn't seem like a really good career move.

Amelie will help, she thought a bit desperately, and Gérard slung Myrnin over his shoulder in a fireman's carry, and then they were running, moving fast again back down the hall to where Amelie had stayed to secure their escape.

Gérard came to a fast halt, and Hannah and Claire almost skidded into him. "What?" Hannah whispered, and looked past the two vampires in the lead.

Amelie was at the corner ahead of them, but ten feet past her was Mr. Bishop.

They were standing motionless, facing each other.

Amelie looked fragile and delicate, compared to her father in his bishop's robes. He looked ancient and angry, and the fire in his eyes was like something out of the story of Joan of Arc.

Neither of them moved. There was some struggle going on, but Claire couldn't tell what it was, or what it meant.

Gérard reached out and grabbed her arm, and Hannah's, and held them in place. "No," he said sharply. "Don't go near them."

"Problem, sir, that's the way out," Hannah said. "And the dude's alone."

Gérard and the Texan sent her a wild look, almost identical in their disbelief. "You think so?" the Texan said. "Humans."

Amelie took a step backward, just a small one, but a shudder went through her body, and Claire knew—just *knew*—it was a bad sign. Really bad.

Whatever confrontation had been going on, it broke.

Amelie whirled to them and screamed, "Go!" There was fury and fear in her voice, and Gérard let go of both girls and dumped Myrnin off his shoulder, into their arms, and he and the Texan pelted not for the exit, but to Amelie's side.

They got there just in time to stop Bishop from ripping out her throat. They slammed the old man up against the wall, but then there were others coming out into the hall. Bishop's troops, Claire guessed.

There were a lot of them.

Amelie intercepted the first of Bishop's vampires to run in her direction. Claire recognized him, vaguely—one of the Morganville vamps, but he'd obviously switched sides, and he came for Amelie, fangs out.

She put him down on the floor with one twisting move, fast as a snake, and looked back at Hannah and Claire, with Myrnin's body sagging between them. "Get him *out*!" she shouted. "I'll hold the way!"

"Come on," Hannah said, and shouldered the bulk of Myrnin's limp weight. "We're leaving."

Myrnin felt cold and heavy, like the dead man he was, and Claire swallowed a surge of nausea as she struggled to support his limp weight. Claire gritted her teeth and helped Hannah half carry, half drag Myrnin's staked body down the corridor. Behind them, the sounds of fighting continued—mainly bodies hitting the floor. No screaming, no shouting.

Vampires fought in silence.

"Right," Hannah gasped. "We're on our own."

That really wasn't good news—two humans stuck God knew where, with a crazy vampire with a stake in his heart in the middle of a war zone.

"Let's get back to the door," Claire said.

"How are we going to get through it?"

"I can do it."

Hannah threw her a look. "You?"

It was no time to get annoyed; hadn't she just been thinking that being underestimated was a gift? Yeah, not so much, sometimes. "Yes, really. I can do it. But we'd better hurry." The odds weren't in Amelie's favor. She might be able to hang on and cover their retreat, but Claire didn't think she could win.

She and Hannah dragged Myrnin past the symbol-marked doorways. Hannah counted off, and nodded to the one where they'd entered.

Not too surprisingly, it was marked with the Founder's Symbol, the same one Claire wore on the bracelet on her wrist.

Hannah tried to open it. "Dammit! Locked."

Not when Claire tried the knob. It opened at a twist, and the single candle in the corner illuminated very little. Claire caught her breath and rested her trembling muscles for a few seconds as Hannah checked the room and pronounced it safe before they entered.

Claire let Myrnin slide in a heap to the floor. "I'm sorry," she whispered to him. "It was the only way. I hope it doesn't hurt too much."

She had no idea if he could hear her when he was like this. She wanted to grab the stake and pull it out, but she remembered that with Amelie, and with Sam, it had been the other vampires who'd done it. Maybe they knew things she didn't. Besides, the disease weakened them—even Myrnin.

She couldn't take the risk. And besides, having him wake up wounded and crazy would be even worse, now that they didn't have any vampires who could help control him.

Hannah returned to her side. "So," she said, as she checked the clip on her paintball gun, frowned, and exchanged it for a new one, "how do we do this? We got to go back to that museum first, right?"

Did they? Claire wasn't sure. She stepped up to the door, which currently featured nothing but darkness, and concentrated hard on Myrnin's lab, with all its clutter and debris. Light swam, flickered, shivered, and snapped into focus.

No problem at all.

"Guess it's only roundabout getting here," Claire said. "Maybe that's on purpose, to keep people out who shouldn't be here. But it makes sense that once Amelie got here, she'd want to take the express out." She turned back. "Shouldn't we wait?"

Hannah opened the door and looked out into the hall. Whatever she saw, it couldn't have been good news. She shook her head. "We bug out, right now."

With a grunt of effort, Hannah braced Myrnin's deadweight on one side and dragged him forward. Claire took his other arm.

"Did he just twitch?" Hannah asked. " 'Cause if he twitches, I'm going to shoot him."

"No! No, he didn't; he's fine," Claire said, practically tripping over the words. "Ready? One, two . . ."

And *three*, they were in Myrnin's lab. Claire twisted out from under Myrnin's cold body, slammed the door shut, and stared wildly at the broken lock. "I need to fix that," she said. But what about Amelie? No, she'd know all the exits. She didn't have to come here.

"Girl, you need to get us the hell out of here, is

what you need to do," Hannah said. "You dial up the nearest Fort Knox or something on that thing. Damn, how'd you learn this, anyway?"

"I had a good teacher." Claire didn't look at Myrnin. She couldn't. For all intents and purposes, she'd just killed him, after all. "This way."

There were two ways out of Myrnin's lab, besides the usually-secured dimensional doorway: steps leading up to street level, which were probably the absolute worst idea ever right now, and a second, an even more hidden dimensional portal in a small room off to the side. That was the one Amelie had used to get them in.

But the problem was, Claire couldn't get it to work. She had the memories clear in her head—the Glass House, the portal to the university, the hospital, even the museum they'd visited on the way here. But nothing *worked.*

It just felt . . . dead, as if the whole system had been cut off.

They were lucky to have made it this far.

Amelie's trapped, Claire realized. *Back there. With Bishop. And she's outnumbered.*

Claire double-checked the other door, too, the one she'd blocked.

Nothing. It wasn't just a malfunctioning portal; the whole network was down.

"Well?" Hannah asked.

Claire couldn't worry about Amelie right now. She had a job to do—get Myrnin to safety. And that meant getting him to the only vampire she knew offhand who could help him: Oliver. "I think we're walking," she said.

"The hell we are," Hannah said. "I'm not hauling a dead vampire through the streets of Morganville. We'll get ourselves killed by just about *everybody.*"

"We can't leave him!"

"We can't take him, either!"

Claire felt her jaw lock into stubborn position.

"Well, fine, you go ahead. Because I'm not leaving him. I can't."

She could tell that Hannah wanted to grab her by the hair and yank her out of there, but finally, the older woman nodded and stepped back. "Third option," she said. "Call in the cavalry."

5

It wasn't quite the Third Armored Division, but after about a dozen phone calls, they did manage to get a ride.

"I'm turning on the street—nobody in sight so far," Eve's voice said from the speaker of Claire's cell phone. She'd been giving Claire a turn-by-turn description of her drive, and Claire had to admit, it sounded pretty frightening. "Yeah, I can see the Day House. You're in the alley next to it?"

"We're on our way," Claire said breathlessly. She was drenched with sweat, aching all over, from the effort of helping drag Myrnin out of the lab, up the steps, and down the narrow, seemingly endless dark alley. Next door, the Founder House belonging to Katherine Day and her granddaughter—a virtual copy of the house where Claire and her friends lived—was dark and closed, but Claire saw curtains moving at the upstairs windows.

"That's my great-aunt's house, Great-Aunt Kathy," Hannah panted. "Everybody calls her Gramma, though. Always have, as far back as I can remember."

Claire could see how Hannah was related to the Days; partly her features, but her attitude for sure. That was a family full of tough, smart, get-it-done women.

Eve's big, black car was idling at the end of the alley, and the back door kicked open as the two of them—three? Did Myrnin still count?—approached. Eve took a look at Myrnin, and the stake in his back, sent Claire a you've-got-to-be-kidding-me look, and reached out to drag him inside, facedown, on the backseat. "Hurry!" she said, and slammed the back door on the way to the driver's side. "Damn, he'd better not bleed all over the place. Claire, I thought you were supposed to—"

"I know," Claire said, and climbed into the middle of the big, front bench seat. Hannah crammed in on the outside. "Don't remind me. I was supposed to keep him safe."

Eve put the car in gear and did a ponderous tank-heavy turn. "So, who staked him?"

"I did."

Eve blinked. "Okay, that's an interesting interpretation of *safe*. Weren't you with Amelie?" Eve actually did a quick check of the backseat, as if she were afraid Amelie might have magically popped in back there, seated like a barbarian queen on top of Myrnin's prone body.

"Yeah. We were," Hannah said.

"Do I have to ask? No, wait, do I *want* to ask?"

"We left her," Claire said, miserable. "Bishop set a trap. She was fighting when we had to go."

"What about the other guys? I thought you went with a whole entourage!"

"We left most of them. . . ." Her brain caught up with her, and she looked at Hannah, who looked back with the same thought in her expression. "Oh, crap. The other guys. They were in Myrnin's lab, but not when we came back. . . ."

"Gone," Hannah said. "Taken out."

"Super. So, we're winning, then." Eve's tone was wicked cynical, but her dark eyes looked scared. "I talked to Michael. He's okay. They're at the university. Things are quiet there so far."

"And Shane?" Claire realized, with a pure bolt of guilt, that she hadn't called him. If he'd called her, she wouldn't have known; she'd turned off the ringer, afraid of the noise when creeping around on a rescue mission.

But as she dug out her phone, she saw that she hadn't missed any calls after all.

"Yeah, he's okay," Eve said, and steered the car at semihigh speed around a corner. The town was dark, very dark, with a few houses lit up by lanterns or candles or flashlights. Most people were waiting in the dark, scared to death. "They had some vamps try to board the bus, probably looking for a snack, but it wasn't even a real fight. So far they're cruising without too much trouble. He's fine, Claire." She reached over and took Claire's hand to squeeze it. "You, not so much. You look awful."

"Thanks. I think I earned it."

Eve took back her hand to haul the big wheel of the car around for a turn. Headlights swept over a group on the sidewalk—unnaturally pale. Unnaturally still. "Oh, crap, we've got bogeys. Hang on, I'm going to floor it."

That was, Claire thought, a pretty fantastic idea, because the vampires on the curb were now in the street, and following. There was a kind of manic glee to how they pursued the car, but not even a vamp could keep up with Eve's driving for long; they fell back into the dark, one by one. The last one was the fastest, and he nearly caught hold of the back bumper before he stumbled and was left behind in a black cloud of exhaust.

"Damn freaks," Eve said, trying to sound tough but not quite making it. "Hey, Hannah. How's business?"

"Right now?" Hannah laughed softly. "Not so fantastic, but I'm not bothered about it. Let's see if we can make it to the morning. Then I'll worry about making ends meet at the shop."

"Oh, we'll make it," Eve said, with a confidence Claire personally didn't feel. "Look, it's already four a.m. Another couple of hours, and we're fine."

Claire didn't say, *In a couple of hours, we could all be dead*, but she was thinking it. What about Amelie? What were they going to do to rescue her?

If she's even still alive.

Claire's head hurt, her eyes felt grainy from lack of sleep, and she just wanted to curl up in a warm bed, pull the pillow over her head, and not be *so responsible*.

Fat chance.

She wasn't paying attention to where Eve was going, and anyway, it was so dark and strange outside she wasn't sure she'd recognize things, anyway. Eve pulled to a halt at the curb, in front of a row of plate glass windows lit by candles and lanterns inside.

Just like that, they were at Common Grounds.

Eve jumped out of the driver's side, opened the back door, and grabbed Myrnin under the arms, all the while muttering, "Ick, ick, ick!" Claire slid out to join her, and Hannah grabbed Myrnin's feet when they hit the pavement, and the three of them carried him into the coffee shop.

Claire found herself shoved immediately out of the way by two vampires: Oliver and some woman she didn't know. Oliver looked grim, but then, that wasn't new, either. "Put him down," Oliver said. "No, not there, idiots, over there, on the sofa. You. Off." That last was directed at the frightened humans who were seated on the indicated couch, and they scattered like quail. Eve continued her *ick* mantra as she and Hannah hauled Myrnin's deadweight over and settled him facedown on the couch cushions. He was about the color of a fluorescent lightbulb now, blue-white and cold.

Oliver crouched next to him, looking at the stake in Myrnin's back. He steepled his fingers for a moment, and then looked up at Claire. "What happened?"

She supposed he could tell, somehow, that it was *her* stake. Wonderful. "I didn't have a choice. He came after us." The *us* part might have been an exaggeration; he'd come after Hannah, really. But eventually he would have come after Claire, too; she knew that.

Oliver gave her a moment to squirm while he stared at her, and then looked back at Myrnin's still, very corpselike body. The area where the stake had gone in looked even paler than the surrounding tissue, like the edge of a whirlpool draining all the color out of him. "Do you have any of the drugs you have been giving him?" Oliver asked. Claire nodded, and fumbled in her pocket. She had some of the powder form of the drug, and some of the liquid, but she hadn't felt confident at all that she'd be able to get it into Myrnin's mouth without a fight she was bound to lose. When Myrnin was like this, you were going to lose fingers, at the very least, if you got anywhere near his mouth.

Not so much an issue now, she supposed. She handed over the vials to Oliver, who turned them over in his fingers, considering, and then handed back the powder. "The liquid absorbs into the body more quickly, I expect."

"Yes." It also had some unpredictable side effects, but this probably wasn't the time to worry about that.

"And Amelie?" Oliver continued turning the bottle over and over in his fingers.

"She's—we had to leave her. She was fighting Bishop. I don't know where she is now."

A deep silence filled the room, and Claire saw the vampires all look at one another—all except Oliver, who continued to stare down at Myrnin, no change in his expression at all. "All right, then. Helen, Karl, watch the windows and doors. I doubt Bishop's patrols will try storming the place, but they might, while I'm distracted. The rest of you"—he looked at the humans and shook his head—"try to stay out of our way."

He thumbed the top off the vial of clear liquid and

held it in his right hand. "Get ready to turn him faceup," he said to Hannah and Claire. Claire took hold of Myrnin's shoulders, and Hannah his feet.

Oliver took the stake in his left hand and, in one smooth motion, pulled it out. It clattered to the floor, and he nodded sharply. "Now."

Once Myrnin was lying on his back, Oliver motioned her away and pried open Myrnin's bloodless lips. He poured the liquid into the other vampire's mouth, shut it, and placed a hand on his high forehead.

Myrnin's dark eyes were open. Wide-open. Claire shuddered, because they looked completely dead— like windows into a dark, dark room . . . and then he blinked.

He sucked in a very deep breath, and his back arched in silent agony. Oliver held his hand steady on Myrnin's forehead. His eyes were squeezed shut in concentration, and Myrnin writhed weakly, trying without much success to twist free. He collapsed limply back on the cushions, chest rising and falling. His skin still looked like polished marble, veined with cold blue, but his eyes were alive again.

And crazy. And hungry.

He swallowed, coughed, swallowed again, and gradually, the insane pilot light in his eyes went out. He looked tired and confused and in pain.

Oliver let out a long, moaning sigh, and tried to stand up. He couldn't. He made it about halfway up, then wavered and fell to his knees, one hand braced on the arm of the couch for support. His head went down, and his shoulders heaved, almost as if he were gasping or crying. Claire couldn't imagine Oliver— *Oliver*—doing either one of those things, really.

Nobody moved. Nobody touched him, although some of the other vampires exchanged unreadable glances.

He's sick, Claire thought. It was the disease. It made it harder and harder for them to concentrate, to do the things they'd always taken for granted, like make other vampires. Or revive them. Even Oliver, who hadn't believed anything about the sickness . . . even he was starting to fail.

And he knew it.

"Help me up," Oliver finally whispered. His voice sounded faint and tattered. Claire grabbed his arm and helped him climb slowly, painfully up; he moved as if he were a thousand years old, and felt every year of it. One of the other vampires silently provided a chair, and Claire helped him into it.

Oliver braced his elbows on his thighs and hid his pale face in his hands. When she started to speak, he said, softly, "Leave me."

It didn't seem a good idea to argue. Claire backed off and returned to where Myrnin was, on the couch.

He blinked, still staring at the ceiling. He folded his hands slowly across his stomach, but didn't otherwise move.

"Myrnin?"

"Present," he said, from what seemed like a very great distance away. He chuckled very softly, then winced. "Hurts when I laugh."

"Yeah, um—I'm sorry."

"Sorry?" A very slight frown worked its way between Myrnin's eyebrows, made a slow V, and then went on its way. "Ah. Staked me."

"I . . . uh . . . yeah." She knew what Oliver's reaction would have been, if she'd done that kind of thing to him, and the outcome wouldn't have been pretty. She wasn't sure what Myrnin might do. Just to be sure, she stayed out of easy-grabbing distance.

Myrnin simply closed his eyes for a moment and nodded. He looked old now, exhausted, like Oliver. "I'm sure it was for the best," he said. "Perhaps you should have left the wood in place. Better for everyone, in the end. I would have just—faded away. It's not very painful, not comparatively."

"No!" She took a step closer, then another. He just looked so—defeated. "Myrnin, don't. We need you."

He didn't open his eyes, but there was a tiny, tired smile curving his lips. "I'm sure you think you do, but you have what you need now. I found the cure for you, Claire. Bishop's blood. It's time to let me go. It's too late for me to get better."

"I don't believe that."

This time, his great dark eyes opened and studied her with cool intensity. "I see you don't," he said. "Whether or not that assumption is reasonable, that's another question entirely. Where is she?"

He was asking about Amelie. Claire glanced at Oliver, still hunched over, clearly in pain. No help. She bent closer to Myrnin. No way she wouldn't be overheard by the other vampires, though, she knew that. "She's—I don't know. We got separated. The last I saw, she and Bishop were fighting it out."

Myrnin sat up. It wasn't the kind of smooth, controlled motion vampires usually had, as though they'd been practicing it for three or four human lifetimes; he had to pull himself up, slowly and painfully, and it hurt Claire to watch. She put her hand against his shoulder blade to brace him. His skin still felt marble-cold, but not *dead*. It was hard to figure out what the difference was—maybe it was the muscles, underneath, tensed and alive again.

"We have to find her," he said. "Bishop will stop at nothing to get her, if he hasn't already. Once you were safely away, she'd have retreated. Amelie is a guerrilla fighter. It's not like her to fight in the open, not against her father."

"We're not going anywhere," Oliver said, without taking his head out of his hands. "And neither are you, Myrnin."

"You owe her your fealty."

"I owe nothing to the dead," Oliver said. "And until I see proof of her survival, I will not sacrifice my life, or anyone else's, in a futile attempt at rescue."

Myrnin's face twisted in contempt. "You haven't changed," he said.

"Neither have you, fool," Oliver murmured. "Now shut up. My head aches."

Eve was pulling shots behind the counter, wearing a formal black apron that went below her knees. Claire slid wearily onto a barstool on the other side. "Wow," she said. "Flashback to the good times, huh?"

Eve made a sour face as she thumped a mocha down in front of her friend. "Yeah, don't remind me," she said. "Although I have to say, I missed the Monster."

"The Monster?"

Eve patted the giant, shiny espresso machine beside her affectionately. "Monster, meet Claire. Claire, meet the Monster. He's a sweetie, really, but you have to know his moods."

Claire reached out and patted the machine, too. "Nice to meet you, Monster."

"Hey." Eve caught her wrist when she tried to pull back. "Bruises? What gives?"

Amelie's grip on her really had raised a crop of faint blue smudges on her upper arm, like a primitive tattoo. "Don't freak. I don't have any bite marks or anything."

"I'll freak if I wanna. As long as Michael isn't here, I'm kind of—"

"What, my mom?" Claire snapped, and was instantly sorry. And guilty, for an entirely different reason. "I didn't mean—"

Eve waved it away. "Hey, if you can't spark a 'tude on a day like this, when can you? Your mother's okay, by the way, because I know that's your next question. So far, Bishop's freaks haven't managed to shut down the cell network, so I've been keeping in touch, since nothing's happening here except for some serious caffeine production. Landlines are dead, though. So is the Internet. Radio and TV are both off the air, too."

Claire looked at the clock. Five a.m. Two hours until

dawn, more or less—probably less. It felt like an eternity.

"What are we going to do in the morning?" she asked.

"Good question." Eve wiped down the counter. Claire sipped the sweet, chocolatey comfort of the mocha. "When you think of something, let us know, because right now, I don't think anybody's got a clue."

"You'd be wrong, thankfully," Oliver said. He seemed to come out of nowhere—*God*, didn't Claire hate that!—as he settled on the stool next to her. He seemed almost back to normal now, but very tired. There was a shadow in his eyes that Claire didn't remember seeing before. "There is a plan in place. Amelie's removal from the field of battle is a blow, but not a defeat. We continue as she would want."

"Yeah? You want to tell us?" Eve asked. That earned her a cool stare. "Yeah, I didn't think so. Vampires really aren't all about the sharing, unless it benefits them first."

"I will tell you what you need to know, when you need to know it," Oliver said. "Get me one of the bags from the walk-in refrigerator."

Eve looked down at the top of her apron. "Oh, I'm sorry, where does it say *servant* on here? Because I'm so very not."

For a second, Claire held her breath, because the expression on Oliver's face was murderous, and she saw a red light, like the embers of a banked fire, glowing in the back of his eyes.

Then he blinked and said, simply, "Please, Eve."

Eve hadn't been expecting that. She blinked, stared back at him for a second, then silently nodded and walked away, behind a curtained doorway.

"You're wondering if that hurt," Oliver said, not looking at Claire at all, but staring after Eve. "It did, most assuredly."

"Good," she said. "I hear suffering's good for the soul, or something."

"Then we shall all be right with our God by morning," Oliver swiveled on the stool to look her full in the face. "I should kill you for what you did."

"Staking Myrnin?" She sighed. "I know. I didn't think I had a choice. He'd have bitten my hand off if I'd tried to give him the medicine, and by the time it took effect, me and Hannah would have been dog food, anyway. It seemed like the quickest, quietest way to get him out."

"Even so," Oliver said, his voice low in his throat, "as an Elder, I have the power to sentence you, right now, to death, for attempted murder of a vampire. You do understand?"

Claire held up her hand and pointed to the gold bracelet on her wrist—the symbol of the Founder. Amelie's symbol. "What about this?"

"I would pay reparations," he said. "I imagine I could afford it. Amelie would be tolerably upset with me, for a while, always assuming she is still alive. We'd reach an accommodation. We always do."

Claire didn't say anything else in her defense, just waited. And after a moment, he nodded. "All right," he said. "You were right to take the action you did. You have been right about a good deal that I was unwilling to admit, including the fact that some of us are"—he cast a quick look around, and dropped his voice so low she could make out the word only from the shape his lips gave it—"unwell."

Unwell. Yeah, that was one way to put it. She resisted an urge to roll her eyes. *How about dying? Ever heard the word* pandemic?

Oliver continued without waiting for her response. "Myrnin's mind was . . . very disordered," he said. "I didn't think I could get him back. I wouldn't have, without that dose of medication."

"Does that mean you believe us now?" She meant, *about the vampire disease*, but she couldn't say that out loud. Even the roundabout way they were speaking was dangerous; too many vampire ears with too little to do, and once they knew about the sickness, there was no predicting what they might do. Run, probably. Go off to rampage through the human world, sicken, and die alone, very slowly. It'd take years, maybe decades, but eventually, they'd all fall, one by one. Oliver's case was less advanced than many of the others, but age seemed to slow down the disease's progress; he might last for a long time, losing himself slowly.

Becoming nothing more than a hungry shell.

Oliver said, "It means what it means," and he said it with an impatient edge to it, but Claire wondered if he really did know. "I am talking about Myrnin. Your drugs may not be enough to hold him for long, and that means we will need to take precautions."

Eve emerged from the curtain carrying a plastic blood bag, filled with dark cherry syrup. That was what Claire told herself, anyway. Dark cherry syrup. Eve looked shaken, and she dumped the bag on the counter in front of Oliver like a dead rat. "You've been planning this," she said. "Planning for a siege."

Oliver smiled slowly. "Have I?"

"You've got enough blood in there to feed half the vampires in town for a month, *and* enough of those heat-and-eat meals campers use to feed the rest of us even longer. Medicines, too. Pretty much anything we'd need to hold out here, including generators, batteries, bottled water. . . ."

"Let's say I am cautious," he said. "It's a trait many of us have picked up during our travels." He took the blood bag and motioned for a cup; when Eve set it in front of him, he punctured the bag with a fingernail, very neatly, and squeezed part of the contents into the cup. "Save the rest," he said, and handed it back to Eve, who looked even queasier than before. "Don't look so disgusted. Blood in bags means none taken unwillingly from your veins, after all."

Eve held it at arm's length, opened the smaller refrigerator behind the bar, and put it in an empty spot on the door rack inside. "Ugh," she said. "Why am I behind the bar again?"

"Because you put on the apron."

"Oh, you're just *loving* this, aren't you?"

"Guys," Claire said, drawing both of their stares. "Myrnin. Where are we going to put him?"

Before Oliver could answer, Myrnin pushed through the crowd in the table-and-chairs area of Common Grounds and walked toward them. He *seemed* normal again, or as normal as Myrnin ever got, anyway. He'd begged, borrowed, or outright stolen a long, black velvet coat, and under it he was still wearing the poofy white Pierrot pants from his costume, dark boots, and no shirt. Long, black, glossy hair and decadently shining eyes.

Oliver took in the outfit, and raised a brow. "You look like you escaped from a Victorian brothel," he said. "One that . . . specialized."

In answer, Myrnin skinned up the sleeves of the coat. The wound in his back might have healed—or might be healing, anyway—but the burns on his wrists and hands were still livid red, with an unhealthy silver tint to them. "Not the sort of brothel I'd normally frequent, by choice," he said, "though of course you might be more adventurous, Oliver." Their gazes locked, and Claire resisted the urge to take a step back. She thought, just for a second, that they were going to bare fangs at each other . . . and then Myrnin smiled. "I suppose I should say thank you."

"It would be customary," Oliver agreed.

Myrnin turned to Claire. "Thank you."

Somehow, she guessed that wasn't what Oliver had expected; she certainly hadn't. It was the kind of snub that got most people hurt in Morganville, but then again, she guessed Myrnin wasn't most people, even to Oliver.

Oliver didn't react. If there was a small red glow in the depths of his eyes, it could have been a reflection from the lights.

"Um—for what?" Claire asked.

"I remember what you did." Myrnin shrugged. "It was the right choice at the moment. I couldn't control myself. The pain . . . the pain was extremely difficult to contain."

She cast a nervous glance at his wrists. "How is it now?"

"Tolerable." His tone dismissed any further discussion. "We need to get to a portal and locate Amelie. The closest is at the university. We will need a car, I suppose, and a driver. Some sturdy escorts wouldn't go amiss." Myrnin sounded casual, but utterly certain that his slightest wish would be obeyed, and again, she felt that flare of tension between him and Oliver.

"Perhaps you've missed the announcement," Oliver said. "You're no longer a king, or a prince, or whatever you were before you disappeared into your filthy hole. You're Amelie's exotic pet alchemist, and you don't give me orders. Not in *my* town."

"Your town," Myrnin repeated, staring at him intently. His face had set into pleasant, rigid lines, but those eyes—not pleasant at all. Claire moved herself prudently out of the way. "What a surprise! I thought it was the Founder's town."

Oliver looked around. "Oddly, she seems unavailable, and that makes it my town, little man. So go and sit down. You're not going anywhere. If she's in trouble—which I do not yet believe—and if there's rescuing to be done, we will consider all the risks."

"And the benefits of not acting at all?" Myrnin asked. His voice was wound as tight as a clock spring. "Tell me, Old Ironsides, how you plan to win this campaign. I do hope you don't plan to reenact Drogheda."

Claire had no idea what that meant, but it meant something to Oliver, something bitter and deep, and his whole face twisted for a moment.

"We're not fighting the Irish campaigns, and whatever errors I made once, I'll not be making them again," Oliver said. "And I don't need advice from a blue-faced hedge witch."

"There's the old Puritan spirit!"

Eve slapped the bar hard. "Hey! Whatever musty old prejudices the two of you have rattling around in your heads, *stop*. We're here, twenty-first century, USA, and we've got problems that don't include your ancient history!"

Myrnin blinked, looked at Eve, and smiled. It was his seductive smile, and it came with a lowering of his thick eyelashes. "Sweet lady," he said, "could you get me one of those delicious drinks you prepared for my friend, here?" He gracefully indicated Oliver, who remembered the cup of blood still sitting in front of him, and angrily choked it down. "Perhaps warm the bag a bit in hot water first? It's a bit disgusting, cold."

"Yeah, sure," Eve sighed. "Want a shot of espresso with that?"

Myrnin seemed to be honestly considering it. Claire urgently shook her head *no*. The last thing she—any of them—needed just now was Myrnin on caffeine.

As Eve walked away to prepare Myrnin's drink, Oliver shook himself out of his anger with a physical twitch, took a deep breath, and said, "It's less than two hours to dawn. Even if something has happened to Amelie—which again, I dispute—it's too risky to launch a search just now. If Bishop has Amelie, he'll have her some place that'll hold against an assault in any case. Two hours isn't enough time, and I won't risk our people in the dawn."

Myrnin flicked a glance toward Claire. "Some of those here aren't affected by the dawn."

"Some of them are also highly vulnerable," Oliver said. "I wouldn't send a human out after Bishop. I wouldn't send a human *army* out after Bishop, unless you're planning to deduce his location from the corpses he leaves behind."

For a horrified second, Myrnin actually mulled that over, and then he shook his head. "He'd hide the bodies," he said regretfully. "A useful suggestion, though."

Claire couldn't tell if he was mocking Oliver, or if he really meant it. Oliver couldn't tell, either, from the long, considering look he gave him.

Oliver turned his attention to her. "Tell me everything."

6

In an hour, the blush of dawn was already on the horizon, bringing an eerie blue glow to the night world. Somewhere out there, vampires all over town would be getting ready for it, finding secure places to stay the day—whatever side they were fighting on.

The ones in Common Grounds seemed content to stay on, which made sense; it was kind of a secured location anyway, from what Oliver and Amelie had said before—one of the key places in town to hold if they intended to keep control of Morganville.

But Claire wasn't entirely happy with the way some of those vampires—strangers, mostly, though all from Morganville, according to Eve—seemed to be whispering in the corners. "How do we know they're on our side?" she asked Eve, in a whisper she hoped would escape vampire notice.

No such luck. "You don't," Oliver said, from several feet away. "Nor is that your concern, but I will reassure you in any case. They are all loyal to me, and through me, to Amelie. If any of them 'turn coats,' you may be assured that they'll regret it." He said it in a normal tone of voice, to carry to all parts of the room.

The vampires stopped whispering.

"All right," Oliver said to Claire and Eve. The light of dawn was creeping up like a warning outside the windows. "You understand what I want you to do?"

Eve nodded and gave him a sloppy, insolent kind of salute. "Sir, yes *sir*, General sir!"

"Eve." His patience, what little there was, was worn to the bone. "Repeat my instructions."

Eve didn't like taking orders under the best of circumstances, which these weren't. Claire quickly said, "We take these walkie-talkies to each of the Founder Houses, to the university, and to anybody else on the list. We tell them all strategic orders come through these, not through cell phone or police band."

"Be sure to give them the code," he said. Each one of the tiny little radios had a keypad, like a cell phone, but the difference was that you had to enter the code into it to access the emergency communication channel he'd established. Pretty high tech, but then, Oliver didn't really seem the type to lag much behind on the latest cool stuff. "All right. I'm sending Hannah with you as your escort. I'd send one of my own, but—"

"Dawn, yeah, I know," Eve said. She offered a high five to Hannah, who took it. "Damn, girl, love the Rambo look."

"Rambo was a Green Beret," Hannah said. "Please. We eat those army boys for breakfast."

Which was maybe not such a comfortable thing to say in a room full of maybe-hungry vampires. Claire cleared her throat. "We should—"

Hannah nodded, picked up the backpack (Claire's, now filled with handheld radios instead of books), and handed it to her. "I need both hands free," she said. "Eve's driving. You're the supply master. There's a checklist inside, so you can mark off deliveries as we go."

Myrnin was sitting off to the side, ominously quiet. His eyes still looked sane, but Claire had warned Oliver in the strongest possible terms that he couldn't trust him. Not really.

As if I would, Oliver had said with a snort. *I've known the man for many human lifetimes, and I've never trusted him yet.*

The vampires in the coffee shop had mostly retreated out of the big, front area, into the better-protected, light-proofed interior. Outside of the plate glass windows, there was little to be seen. The fires had gone out, or been extinguished. They'd seen some cars speeding about, mostly official police or fire, but the few figures they'd spotted had been quick and kept to the shadows.

"What are they doing?" Claire asked as she hitched her backpack to a more comfortable position on her shoulder. She didn't really expect Oliver to reply; he wasn't much on the sharing.

He surprised her. "They're consolidating positions," he said. "This is not a war that will be fought in daylight, Claire. Or in the open. We have our positions; they have theirs. They may send patrols of humans they've recruited, but they won't come themselves. Not after dawn."

"Recruited," Hannah repeated. "Don't you mean strong-armed? Most folks just want to be left alone."

"Not necessarily. Morganville is full of humans who don't love us, or the system under which they labor," Oliver replied. "Some will believe Bishop is the answer. Some will act out of fear, to protect their loved ones. He will know how to appeal to them, and how to pressure. He'll find his human cannon fodder."

"Like you've found yours," Hannah said.

They locked stares for a few seconds, and then Oliver inclined his head just a bit. "If you like."

"I don't," she said, "but I'm used to the front lines. You got to know, others won't be."

Claire couldn't tell anything from Oliver's expression. "Perhaps not," he said. "But for now, we can count on our enemies regrouping. We should do the same."

Hannah nodded. "I'm out first, then you, Eve. Have your keys in your hand. Don't hesitate, run like hell for the car, and get it unlocked. I'll get Claire to the passenger side."

Eve nodded, clearly jittery. She took the car keys out of her pocket and held them in her hand, sorting through until she had the right key pointing out.

"One more thing," Hannah said. "You got a flashlight?"

Eve fumbled in her other pocket and came up with a tiny little penlight. When she twisted it, it gave a surprisingly bright glow.

"Good." Hannah nodded. "Before you get in the car, you shine that in the front and backseats. Make sure you can see all the way down to the carpet. I'll cover you from the door."

The three of them moved to the exit, and Hannah put her left hand on the knob.

"Be careful," Oliver said from the back of the room, which was kind of warmly surprising. He spoiled it by continuing, "We need those radios delivered."

Should have known it wasn't personal. Claire resisted the urge to flip him off.

Eve didn't bother to resist hers.

Then Hannah was swinging open the door and stepping outside. She didn't do it like in the movies; no drama, she just stepped right out, turned in a slow half circle as she scanned the street with the paintball gun held at rest. She finally motioned for Eve. Eve darted out and headed around the hood of the big, black car. Claire saw the glow of her penlight as she checked the inside, and then Eve was in the driver's seat and the car growled to a start, and Hannah pushed her toward the passenger door.

Behind them, the Common Grounds door slammed shut and locked. When she looked back, Claire saw that they were pulling down some kind of steel shutters inside the glass.

Locking up for dawn.

Claire and Hannah made it to the car without any problems. Even so, Claire was breathing hard, her heart racing.

"You okay?" Eve asked her. Claire nodded, still gasping. "Yeah, I know. Terror Aerobics. Just wait until they get it at the gym. It'll be bigger than Pilates."

Claire choked on her fear, laughed, and felt better. "That's my girl. Locks," Eve said. "Also, seat belts, please. We may be making some sudden stops along the way. Don't want anybody saying hello to Mr. Windshield at speed."

The drive through predawn Morganville was eerie. It was very . . . quiet. They'd mapped out a route, planning to avoid the most dangerous areas, but they almost had to divert immediately, because of a couple of cars parked in the middle of the street.

The doors were hanging open, interior lights were still shining.

Eve slowed down and crawled past on the right side, two wheels up on the curb. "See anything?" she asked anxiously. "Any bodies or anything?"

The cars were completely empty. They were still running, and the keys were in the ignition. One strange thing nagged at Claire, but she couldn't think what it was. . . .

"Those are vampire cars," Hannah said. "Why would they leave them here like that?" Oh. That was the odd thing. The tinting on the windows.

"They needed to pee?" Eve asked. "When you've gotta go . . ."

Hannah said nothing. She was watching out the windows with even more focus than before.

"Yeah, that is weird," Eve said more quietly. "Maybe they went to help somebody." Or hunt somebody. Claire shivered.

They made their first radio delivery to one of the Founder Houses; Claire didn't know the people who answered the door, but Eve did, of course. She quickly explained about the radio and the code, and they were back in the car and rolling in about two minutes flat. "Outstanding," Hannah said. "You girls could give some of my buddies in the marines a run for their money."

"Hey, you know how it is, Hannah: living in Morganville really is combat training." Eve and Hannah awkwardly slapped palms—awkwardly, because Eve kept facing front, and Hannah didn't turn away from her post at the car's back window. She had the window rolled down halfway, and the paintball gun at the ready, but so far she hadn't fired a single shot.

"More cars," Claire said softly. "You see?"

It wasn't just a couple of cars, it was a bunch of them, scattered on both sides of the street now, engines running, lights on, doors open.

Empty.

They cruised past slowly, and Claire took note of the heavy tinting on the windows. They were all the same type of car, the same type Michael had been issued on his official conversion to vampire.

"What the hell is going on?" Eve asked. She sounded tense and anxious, and Claire couldn't blame her. She felt pretty tense herself. "This close to dawn, they wouldn't be doing this. They shouldn't even be outside. He said both sides would regroup, but this looks like some kind of full-on panic."

Claire had to agree, but she also had no explanation. She dug one of the radios out of her backpack, typed in the code that Oliver had given her, and pressed the TALK button. "Oliver? Come in."

After a short delay, his voice came back. "Go."

"Something strange is happening. We're seeing lots of vampire cars, but they're all abandoned. Empty. Still running." Static on the other end. "Oliver?"

"Keep me informed," he finally said. "Count the number of cars. Make a list of license numbers, if you can."

"Er—anything else? Should we come back?"

"No. Deliver the radios."

That was it. Claire tried again, but he'd shut off or he was ignoring her. She pressed the RESET button to scramble the code, and looked at Eve, who shrugged. They pulled to a halt in front of the second Founder House. "Let's just get it done," Eve said. "Let the vamps worry about the vamps."

It seemed reasonable, but Claire was afraid that somehow . . . it wasn't.

Three of the Founder Houses were piles of smoking wood and ash, and the Morganville Fire Department was still pouring water on one of them. Eve cruised by, but didn't stop. The horizon was getting lighter and lighter, and they still had a couple of stops to make.

"You okay back there?" Eve asked Hannah, as they turned another corner, heading into an area Claire actually recognized.

"Fine," Hannah said. "We going to the Day House?"

"Yeah, next on my list."

"Good. I want to talk to Cousin Lisa."

Eve pulled up outside of the big Founder House; it was lit up in every window, a stark contrast to its dark, shuttered neighboring residences. As she put the car in park, the front door opened and spilled a wedge of lemon-colored light across the immaculately kept front porch. Gramma Day's rocker was empty, nodding in the slight wind.

The person at the door was Lisa Day—tall, strong, with more than a slight resemblance to Hannah. She watched them get out of the car. Upstairs windows opened, and gun barrels came out.

"They're all right," she called, but she didn't step outside. "Claire, right? And Eve? Hey, Hannah."

"Hey." Hannah nodded. "Let's get in. I don't like this quiet out here."

As soon as they were in the front door, in a familiar-looking hallway, Lisa slammed down locks and bolts, including a recently installed iron bar that slotted into place on either side of the frame. Hannah watched this with bemused approval. "You knew this was coming?" she asked.

"I figured it'd come sooner or later," Lisa said. "Had the hardware in the basement. All we had to do was put it in. Gramma didn't like it, but I did it, anyway. She keeps yelling about me putting holes in the wood."

"Yeah, that's Gramma." Hannah grinned. "God forbid we should mess up her house while the war's going on."

"Speaking of that," Lisa said, "y'all need to stay here, if you want to stay safe."

Eve exchanged a quick glance with Claire. "Yeah, well, we can't, really. But thanks."

"You sure?" Lisa's eyes were very bright, very focused. "Because we're thinking maybe these vamps will kill each other off this time, and maybe we should all stick together. All the humans. Never mind the bracelets and the contracts."

Eve blinked. "Seriously? Just let them fight it out on their own?"

"Why not? What's it to us, anyway, who wins?" Lisa's smile was bitter and brief. "We get screwed no matter what. Maybe it's time to put a human in charge of this town, and let the vampires find someplace else to live."

Dangerous, Claire thought. Really dangerous. Hannah stared at her cousin, her expression tight and controlled, and then nodded. "Okay," she said. "You do what you want, Lisa, but you be careful, all right?"

"We're being real damn careful," Lisa said. "You'll see."

They came to the end of the hallway, where the area opened up into the big living room, and Eve and Claire both stopped cold.

"Oh, *shit*," Eve muttered.

The humans were all armed—guns, knives, stakes, blunt objects. The vampires who'd been assigned to

guard the house were all sitting tied to chairs with so
many turns of rope it reminded Claire of hangman's
loops. She supposed if you were going to restrain
vamps, it made sense, but—

"What the hell are you doing?" Eve blurted. At
least some of the vampires sitting there, tied and
gagged, were ones who'd been at Michael's house, or
who'd fought on Amelie's side at the banquet. Some
of them were struggling, but most seemed quiet.

Some looked *unconscious*.

"They're not hurt," Lisa said. "I just want 'em out
of the way, in case things go bad."

"You're making one hell of a move, Lisa," Hannah
said. "I hope you know what the hell you're about."

"I'm about protecting my own. You ought to be,
too."

Hannah nodded slowly. "Let's go," she said to
Claire and Eve.

"What about—"

"No," Hannah said. "No radio. Not here."

Lisa moved into their path, a shotgun cradled in her
arms. "Going so soon?"

Claire forgot to breathe. There was a feeling here,
a darkness in the air. The vampires, those who were
still awake, were staring at them. Expecting rescue,
maybe?

"You don't want to do this," Hannah said. "We're
not your enemies."

"You're standing with the vamps, aren't you?"

There it was, out in the open. Claire swallowed hard.
"We're trying to get everybody out of this alive," she
said. "Humans and vampires."

Lisa didn't look away from her cousin's face. "Not
going to happen," she said. "So you'd better pick a
side."

Hannah stepped right up into her face. After a cold
second, Lisa moved aside. "Already have," Hannah
said. She jerked her head at Claire and Eve. "Let's
move."

Outside in the car, they all sat in silence for a few seconds. Hannah's face was grim and closed off, not inviting any conversation.

Eve finally said, "You'd better tell Oliver. He needs to know about this."

Claire plugged in the code and tried. "Oliver, come in. Oliver, it's Claire. I have an update. Oliver!"

Static hissed. There was no response.

"Maybe he's ignoring you," Eve said. "He seemed pretty annoyed before."

"You try." Claire handed it over, but it was no use. Oliver wasn't responding. They tried calling for anyone at Common Grounds instead, and got another voice, one Claire didn't recognize.

"Hello?"

Eve squeezed her eyes shut in relief. "Excellent. Who's this?"

"Quentin Barnes."

"Tin-Tin! Hey man, how are you?"

"Ah—good, I guess." Tin-Tin, whoever he was, sounded nervous. "Oliver's kind of busy right now. He's trying to keep some people from taking off."

"Taking off?" Eve's eyes widened. "What do you mean?"

"Some of the vamps, they're just trying to leave. It's too close to dawn. He's had to lock some of them up."

Things were getting weird all over. Eve keyed the mike and said, "There's trouble at the Day House. Lisa's tied up the vamps. She's going to sit this thing out. I think—I think maybe she's working with some other people, trying to put together a third side. All humans."

"Dude," Tin-Tin sighed, "that's just what we need, getting the vampire slayers all in the mix. Okay, I'll tell Oliver. Anything else?"

"More empty vampire cars. You think they're like those guys who were trying to leave? Maybe, I don't know, getting drawn off somewhere?"

"Probably. Look, just watch yourself, okay?"

"Will do. Eve out."

Hannah stirred in the back. "Let's move out to the next location."

"I'm sorry," Claire said. "I know they're your family and all."

"Lisa always was preaching about how we could take the town if we stuck together. Maybe she's thinking it's the right time to make a move." Hannah shook her head. "She's an idiot. All she's going to do is get people killed."

Claire was no general, but she knew that fighting a war on two fronts and dividing their forces wasn't a great idea. "We have to find Amelie."

"Wherever she's gotten herself off to," Eve snorted. "If she's even still—"

"Don't," Claire whispered. She restlessly rubbed the gold bracelet on her wrist until it dug into her skin. "We need her."

More than ever, she was guessing.

By the time they'd dropped off the next to last radio, at their own home, which was currently inhabited by a bunch of freaked-out humans and a few vampires who hadn't yet felt whatever was pulling some of them off, the dawn was starting to really set in. The horizon was Caribbean blue, with touches of gold and red just flaring up like footlights at a show. Claire delivered the radio, the code, and a warning to the humans and vampires alike. "You have to watch the vamps," she pleaded. "Don't let them leave. Not in the daylight."

Monica Morrell, who was clutching the walkie-talkie in her red-taloned fingers, frowned at her. "How are we supposed to do that, freak? Give them a written warning and scold them really hard? Come on!"

"If you let them go, they may not get wherever it is they're being called before sunrise," Hannah said. She shrugged, a fluid flow that emphasized her muscles, and smiled. "Hey, no skin off my nose or anything, but we may need 'em later. And you could get blamed for not stepping up."

Monica kept on frowning, but she didn't seem inclined to argue with Hannah. Nobody did, Claire noticed. The former marine had an air about her, a confidence that somehow didn't come off at all like arrogance.

"Great," Monica finally said. "Wonderful. Like I needed another problem. By the way, Claire, your house really sucks ass. I hate it here."

It was Claire's turn to smile this time. "It probably hates you right back. I'm sure you'll figure it out," she said. "You're a natural leader, right?"

"Oh, bite it. Someday, your boyfriend won't be around to—" Monica widened her eyes. "Oh, snap! He's *isn't* around, is he? Won't be back, ever. Remind me to send flowers for the funeral."

Eve grabbed the back of Claire's shirt. "Whoa, Mini-Me, chill out. We've got to get moving. Much as I'd like to see the cage match, we're kind of on a schedule."

The hot crimson haze disappeared from Claire's eyes, and she took in a breath and nodded. Her muscles were aching. She realized she'd managed to clench just about every muscle, iron-hard, and tried to relax. Her hands twinged when she stretched them out of fists.

"See you soon," Monica said, and shut the door on them. "Wait, probably not, loser. And your clothes are pathetic, by the way!"

That last part came muffled, but clear—as clear as the sound of the locks snapping into place.

"Let's go," Hannah said, and herded them off the porch and down the walk toward the white picket fence.

Walking on the street, heading vaguely north, was a vampire. "Oh, crap," Eve said, alarmed, but the vamp didn't seem to care about them, or even know they were there. He was wearing a police uniform, and Claire remembered him; he'd been riding with Richard Morrell, from time to time. Didn't seem like a bad guy, apart from the whole vampire thing. "That's Officer O'Malley. Hey! Hey, Officer! Wait up!"

He ignored them and kept walking.

Claire looked east. The sun's golden glow was heating up the sky, fast. It wasn't over the horizon yet, but it would be in a matter of seconds, minutes at most. "We've got to get him," she said. "Get him inside somewhere."

"And do what, babysit him the rest of the day? O'Malley's not like Myrnin," Eve said. "You can't stake him. He's not that old. Seventy, eighty, something like that. He's only a little older than Sam."

"We could run him over," Hannah said. "It wouldn't kill him."

Eve sent her a wide-eyed look. "Excuse me? With my *car*?"

"You're asking for something nonlethal. That's all I've got right now. The three of us aren't any kind of match for a vampire who wants to get somewhere, if he fights us."

Claire took off running toward the vampire, ignoring their shouts. She looked back. Hannah was after her, and gaining.

She still got to Officer O'Malley first, and skidded into his path.

He paused for a second, his green eyes focusing on her, and then he reached out and moved her aside. Gently, but firmly.

And he kept on walking.

"You have to get inside!" Claire yelled, and got in front of him again. "Sir, you have to! Right now! Please!"

He moved her again, this time without as much care. He didn't say a word.

"Oh, God," Hannah said. "Too late."

The sun came up in a fiery burst, and the first rays

of sunlight hit the parked cars, Eve's standing figure, the houses . . . and Officer O'Malley's back.

"Get a blanket!" Claire screamed. She could see the smoke curling off him, like morning mist. "Do something!"

Eve ran to get something from the car. Hannah grabbed Claire and pulled her out of his way.

Officer O'Malley kept walking. The sun kept rising, brighter and brighter, and within three or four steps, the smoke rising up from him turned to flames.

In ten more steps, he fell down.

Eve ran up breathlessly, a blanket clutched in both hands. "Help me get it over him!"

They threw the fabric over Officer O'Malley, but instead of smothering the flames, it just caught fire, too.

Hannah pulled Claire back as she tried to pat out the flames. "Don't," she said. "It's too late."

Claire turned toward Hannah in a raw fury, struggling to get free. "We can still—"

"No, we can't," Hannah said. "There's not a damn thing we can do for him. He's dying, Claire. You tried your best, but he's dying. And he's not going to take our help. Look, he's still trying to crawl. He's not stopping."

She was right, but it hurt, and in the end, Claire wrapped her arms around Hannah for comfort and turned away.

When she finally looked back, Officer O'Malley was a pile of ash and smoke and burned blanket.

"Michael," Claire whispered. She looked at the sun. "We have to find Michael!"

Hannah went very still for a second, and then nodded. "Let's go."

7

The gates of the university were shut, locked, and there were paramilitary-style men posted at the gates, all in black. Armed. Eve coasted the big car slowly up to them and rolled down the window.

"Delivery for Michael Glass," she called. "Or Richard Morrell."

The guard who leaned in was huge, tough, and intimidating—until he saw Hannah in the backseat, and then he grinned like a kid with a new puppy. "Hannah Montana!"

She looked deeply pained. "Don't *ever* call me that again, Jessup, or I *will* gut you."

"Get out and make me stop, Smiley. Yeah, I heard you were back. How were the marines?"

"Better than the damn rangers."

"Don't you just wish?" He lost the smile and got serious again. "Sorry, H, orders are orders. Who sent you? Who's with you?"

"Oliver sent me. You probably know Eve Rosser—that's Claire Danvers."

"Really? Huh. Thought she'd be bigger. Hey, Eve. Sorry, didn't recognize you right off. Long time, no see." Jessup nodded to the other guard, who slung his rifle and pressed in a key code at the panel on the stone fence. The big iron gates slowly parted. "You be careful, Hannah. This town's the Af-Pak border all over again right now."

Inside, except for the guards patrolling the fence, Texas Prairie University seemed eerily normal. The birds sang to the rising sun, and there were students out—*students!*—heading to class as if there were nothing wrong at all. They were chatting, laughing, running to make the cross-campus early-morning bell.

"What the *hell*?" Eve said. Claire was glad she wasn't the only one freaked out by it. "I know they had orders to keep things low profile, but damn, this is ridiculous. Where's the dean's office?"

Claire pointed. Eve steered the car around the winding curves, past dorms and lecture halls, and pulled it to a stop on the nearly deserted lot in front of the Administration Building. There were two police cruisers there, and a bunch of black Jeeps. Not a lot of civilian cars in the lot.

As they walked up the steps to the building, Claire realized there were two more guards outside of the main door. Hannah didn't know these guys, but she repeated their names and credentials, and after a brief, impersonal search, they were allowed inside.

The last time Claire had been here she'd been adding and dropping classes, and the building had been full of grumpy bureaucrats and anxious students, all moving at a hectic pace. Now it was very quiet. A few people were at their desks, but there were no students Claire could see, and the TPU employees looked either bored or nervous. Most of the activity seemed centered down the carpeted hall, which was hung with formal portraits of the former university deans and notables.

One or two of the former deans, Claire was just now realizing, might have been vampires, from the pallor of their skins. Or maybe they were just old white guys. Hard to say.

At the end of the hallway they found not a guard, but a secretary—just as tough as any of the armed men outside, though. She sat behind an expensive-looking antique desk that had not a speck of dust on it, and nothing else except a piece of paper centered exactly in the middle, a pen at right angles to it, and a fancy, black multiline telephone. No computer that Claire could spot—no, there it was, hidden away in a roll-out credenza to the side.

The room was lushly carpeted, so much so that Claire's feet sank into the depth at least an inch; it was like walking on foam. Solid, dark wood paneling. Paintings and dim lights. The windows were covered with fancy velvet curtains, and there was music playing—classical, of course. Claire couldn't imagine anybody would ever switch the station to rock. Not here.

"I'm Ms. Nance," the woman said, and stood to offer her hand to each of them in turn; she didn't even hesitate with Eve, who intimidated most people. She was a tall, thin, gray woman dressed in a tailored gray suit with a lighter gray blouse under the jacket. Gray hair curled into exact waves. Claire couldn't see her shoes, but she bet they were fashionable, gray, and yet somehow sensible. "I'm the secretary to Dean Wallace. Do you have an appointment?"

Eve said, "I need to see Michael."

"I'm sorry? I don't think I know that person."

Eve's expression froze, and Claire could see the horrible dread in her eyes.

Hannah, seeing it too, said, "Let's cut the crap, Ms. Nance. Where's Michael Glass?"

Ms. Nance's eyes narrowed. They were pale blue, not as pale as Amelie's, but kind of faded, like jeans left in the sun. "Mr. Glass is in conference with the dean," she said. "I'm afraid you'll have to—"

The door at the far end of her office opened, and Michael came out. Claire's heart practically melted with relief. *He's okay. Michael's okay.*

Except that he closed the door and walked straight past them, a man on a mission.

He walked right past Eve, who stood there flat-footed, mouth open, fear dawning in her expression.

"Michael!" Claire yelped. He didn't even pause. "We have to stop him!"

"Great," Hannah said, and the three of them took off in pursuit.

It helped that Michael wasn't actually *running*, just moving with a purpose. Claire and Eve edged by him in the hall and blocked his path.

His blue eyes were wide-open, but he just didn't *see* them. He sensed an obstacle, at least, and paused.

"Michael," Claire said. *Dammit, why couldn't I have tranquilizers? Why?* "Michael, you can't go out there. It's already morning. You'll die."

"He's not listening," Hannah said. And she was right; he wasn't. He tried to push between them, but Eve put a hand in the center of his chest and held him back.

"Michael? It's me. You know me, don't you? Please?"

He stared at her with utterly blank eyes, and then shoved her out of his way. Hard.

Hannah sent Claire a quick, commanding look. "Get help. *Now*. I'll try to hold him."

Claire hesitated, but Hannah was without any doubt better equipped to handle a potentially hostile Michael than she was. She turned and ran, past startled desk jockeys and coffee-bearing civil servants, and slid to a stop in front of one of the black-uniformed soldiers. "Richard Morrell," she blurted. "I need him. Right *now*."

The soldier didn't hesitate. He grabbed the radio clipped to his shoulder and said, "Admin to Morrell."

"Morrell, go."

The soldier unclipped the radio and silently offered it to Claire. She took it—it was heavier than the walkie-talkies—and pressed the button to talk. "Richard? It's Claire. We have a big problem. We need to stop Michael and anybody else . . ." How could she say *vampire* without actually saying it? "Anybody else with a sun allergy from going outside."

"Why the hell would they be—"

"I don't know! They just *are*!" The image of Officer O'Malley on fire leaped into her mind, and she caught her breath on a sob. "Help us. They're going out in the sun."

"Give the radio back," he ordered. She handed it to the black-uniformed man. "I need you to go with this girl and help her. No questions."

"Yes sir." He clicked off the radio and looked down at Claire. "After you."

She led the way back toward the hallway. As they reached it, there was a crash of glass, and Hannah came flying out to land flat on her back, blinking.

Michael walked over her. Eve was hauling on his arm, trying to hold him back, but he shook her off.

"We can't let him get outside!" Claire said. She tried to grab him, but it was like grabbing a freight train. She'd forgotten how strong he was now.

"Out of the way," the soldier said, and pulled a handgun from a holster at his side.

"No, don't—"

The bureaucrats scattered, hiding under their desks, dropping their coffee to hug the carpet.

The soldier sighted on Michael's chest, and fired three times in quick succession. Instead of the loud bangs Claire had been expecting, there were soft compressed-air coughs.

And three darts feathered Michael's chest, clustered above his heart.

He *still* took three steps toward the soldier before collapsing in slow motion to his knees, and then onto his face.

"All clear," the soldier said. He took hold of Michael, turned him over, and yanked out the darts. "He'll be under for about an hour, probably no longer than that. Let's get him to the dean's office."

Hannah wiped a trickle of blood from her mouth, coughed, and rolled to her feet. She and Eve helped Claire grab Michael's shoulders and feet, and they carried him down the hallway, past paintings that were going to need some major repair and reframing, past splintered panels and broken glass, into Ms. Nance's office.

Ms. Nance took one look at them and moved smartly to the door marked with a discreet brass plaque that said DEAN WALLACE. She rapped and opened the door for them to carry Michael through.

Dean Wallace was a woman, which was kind of a surprise to Claire. She'd been expecting a pudgy, middle-aged man; *this* Dean Wallace was tall, graceful, thin, and a whole lot younger than Claire would have imagined. She had straight brown hair worn long around her shoulders, and a simple black suit that was almost the negative image of Ms. Nance's, only somehow less formal. It looked . . . lived in.

Dean Wallace's lips parted, but she didn't ask a question. She checked herself, then nodded at the leather couch on the far side of the room, across from her massive desk. "Right, put him there." She had a British accent, too. Definitely not a Texas girl. "What happened?"

"Whatever it is, it's happening all over," Hannah said as they arranged Michael's unconscious body on the sofa. "They're just taking off. It's like they don't even know or care the sun's up. Some kind of homing signal just gets switched on."

Dean Wallace thought for a second, then pressed a button on her desk. "Ms. Nance? I need a bulletin to go out through the emergency communication system. All vampires on campus should be immediately restrained or tranquilized. No exceptions. This is priority one." She frowned as she got the acknowledgment, and looked up at their little group. "Michael seemed very rational, and there was no warning this would happen. I just thought he had somewhere to go. He didn't seem odd, at least at first."

"How many other vampires on campus?" Hannah asked.

"Some professors of course, but they're mostly not here at the moment, since they teach at night. No students, obviously. Apart from the ones Michael and Richard brought in, we have perhaps five in total on the grounds. More were here earlier, but they headed for shelter before sunrise, off campus." Dean Wallace seemed calm, even in the face of all this. "You're Claire Danvers?"

"Yes ma'am," she said, and shook the hand Dean Wallace offered her.

"I had a talk with your Patron recently regarding your progress. Despite your—challenges, you have done excellent course work."

It was stupid to feel pleased about that, but Claire couldn't help it. She felt herself blush, and shook her head. "I don't think that matters very much right now."

"On the contrary, it matters a great deal, I believe."

Eve settled herself down next to the sofa, holding Michael's limp hand. She looked shattered. Hannah leaned against the wall and nodded to the soldier as he exited the office. "So," she said, "want to explain to me how you can have half the U.S. Army walking the perimeter and not have massive student panic?"

"We've told all students and their parents that the university is cooperating in a government emergency drill, and of course that all weapons are nonlethal. Which is quite true, so far as it goes. The issue of keeping students on campus is a bit trickier, but we've managed so far by linking it to the emergency drills. Can't go on for long, though. The local kids are already well informed, and it's only a matter of time before the out-of-town students begin to realize that we're having them on when they can't get word out to their friends and relatives. We're filtering all Internet and phone access, of course." Dean Wallace shook her head. "But that's my problem, not yours, and yours is much more pressing. We can't knock out every vampire in town, and we can't *keep* them knocked out in any case."

"Not enough happy juice in the world," Hannah agreed. "We need to either stop this at its source, or get the heck out of their way."

There was a soft knock on the door, and Ms. Nance stepped in. "Richard Morrell," she announced, and moved aside for him.

Claire stared. Monica's brother looked like about fifty miles of bad road—exhausted, red-eyed, pale, running on caffeine and adrenaline. Just like the rest of them, she supposed. As Ms. Nance quietly closed the door behind him, Richard strode forward, staring at Michael's limp body. "Is he out?" His voice sounded rough, too, as if he'd been yelling. A *lot.*

"Sleeping the sleep of the just," Hannah said. "Or the just drugged, anyway. Claire. Radio."

Oh. She'd forgotten about the backpack still slung over her shoulder. She quickly took out the last radio and handed it over, explaining what it was for. Richard nodded.

"I think this calls for a strategy meeting," he said, and pulled up a chair next to the couch. Hannah and Claire took seats as well, but Eve stayed where she was, by Michael, as if she didn't want to leave him even for a moment.

Dean Wallace sat behind her desk, fingers steepled, watching with interested calm.

"I put in the code, right?" He was already doing it, so Claire just nodded. A signal bleeped to show he was logged on the network. "Richard Morrell, University, checking in."

After a few seconds, a voice answered. "Check, Richard, you're the last station to report. Stand by for a bulletin."

There were a few clicks, and then another voice came over the radio.

This is Oliver. I am broadcasting to all on the network with emergency orders. Restrain every vampire allied to us that you can find, by whatever means necessary. Locked rooms, chains, tranquilizers, cells, use what you have. Until we know how and why this is happening, we must take every precaution during the day. It seems that some of us have resistance to the call, and others have immunity, but this could change at any time. Be on your guard. From this point forward, we will conduct hourly calls, and each location will report status. University station, report.

Richard clicked the TALK button. "Michael Glass and all the other vampires in our group are being restrained. We've got student containment here, but it won't last. We'll have to open the gates no later than tomorrow morning, if we can keep it together until then. Even with the phone and Internet blackout, somebody's going to get word out."

"We're following the plan," Oliver said. "We're taking the cell towers down in ten minutes, until further notice. Phone lines are already cut. The only communication from this point forward will be strategic, using the radios. What else do you need?"

"Whip and a chair? Nothing. We're fine here for now. I don't think anybody will try a daylight assault, not with as many guards as we have here." Richard hesitated, then keyed the mike again. "Oliver, I've been hearing things. I think there are some factions out there forming. Human factions. Could complicate things."

Oliver was silent for a moment, then said, "Yes, I understand. We'll deal with that as it arises."

Oliver moved on to the next station on his list, which was the Glass House. Monica reported in, which was annoying. Claire resisted the urge to grind her teeth. It was a quick summary, at least, and as more Founder Houses reported in, the situation seemed the same: some vampires were responding to the homing signal, and some weren't. At least, not yet.

Richard Morrell was staring thoughtfully into the distance, and finally, when all the reports were finished, he clicked the button again. "Oliver, it's Richard. What happens if *you* start going zombie on us?"

"I won't," Oliver said.

"If you do. Humor me. Who takes over?"

Oliver obviously didn't want to think about this, and Claire could hear the barely suppressed fury in his voice when he replied. "You do," he said. "I don't care how you organize it. If we have to hand the defense of Morganville over to mere humans, we've already lost. Oliver signing out. Next check-in, one hour from now."

The walkie-talkie clicked off.

"That went well," Dean Wallace observed. "He's named you heir apparent to the Apocalypse. Congratulations."

"Yeah, it's one hell of a field promotion." Richard stood up. "Let's find a place for Michael."

"We have some storage areas in the basement—steel doors, no windows. That's where they'll take the others."

"That'll do for now. I want to move him to the jail as soon as we can, centralize the containment."

Claire looked at Eve, and then at Michael's sleeping face, and thought about him alone in a cell—because what else could you call it? Locked away like Myrnin.

Myrnin. She wondered if he'd felt this weird pull, too, and if he had, whether or not they'd been able to stop him from taking off. Probably not, if he'd been determined to go running off. Myrnin was one of those unstoppable forces, and unless he met an immovable object . . .

She sighed and helped carry Michael down the hall, past the stunned bureaucrats, to his temporary holding cell.

Life went on, weirdly enough—human life, anyway. People began to venture out, clean up the streets, retrieve things from burned and trashed houses. The police began to establish order again.

But there were things happening. People gathering in groups on street corners. Talking. Arguing.

Claire didn't like what she saw, and she could tell that Hannah and Eve didn't, either.

Hours passed. They cruised around for a while, and passed bulletins back to Oliver on the groups they saw. The largest one was almost a hundred people, forming up in the park. Some guy Claire didn't know had a loudspeaker.

"Sal Manetti," Hannah said. "Always was a trouble-maker. I think he was one of Captain Obvious's guys for a while, but they had a falling-out. Sal wanted a lot more killing and a lot less talking."

That wasn't good. It really wasn't good how many people were out there listening to him.

Eve went back to Common Grounds to report in, and that was just when things started to go wrong.

Hannah was driving Claire back home, after drop-ping off a trunk full of blood bags from the university storage vaults, when the radio Claire had in her pocket began to chime for attention. She logged in with the code. As soon as she did, a blast of noise tumbled out of the speaker.

She thought she heard something about Oliver, but she wasn't sure. Her shouted questions weren't an-swered. It was as if someone had pressed the button by accident, in the middle of a fight, and everybody was too busy to answer.

Then the broadcast went dead.

Claire exchanged a look with Hannah. "Better—"

"Go to Common Grounds? Yeah. Copy that."

When they arrived, the first thing Claire saw was the broken glass. The shutters were up, and two front windows had been shattered out, not in; there were sprays of broken pieces all the way to the curb.

It seemed very, very quiet.

"Eve?" Claire blurted, and bailed before Hannah could tell her to stay put. She hit the front door of the coffee shop at a run, but it didn't open, and she banged into it hard enough to bruise.

Locked.

"Will you *wait*?" Hannah snapped, and grabbed her arm as she tried to duck in through one of the broken windows. "You're going to get yourself cut. Hang on."

She used the paintball gun she carried to break out some of the hanging sharp edges, and before Claire could dart ahead, she blocked the path and stepped over the low wooden sill. Claire followed. Hannah didn't try to stop her, probably because she knew better.

"Oh man," Hannah said. As Claire climbed in after her, she saw that most of the tables and chairs were overturned or shoved out of place. Broken crockery littered the floor.

And people were down, lying motionless among the wreckage. Hannah went from one to the other, quickly assessing their conditions. There were five down that Claire could see. Two of them made Hannah shake her head in regret; the other three were still alive, though wounded.

There were no vampires in the coffee bar, and there was no sign of Eve.

Claire ducked behind the curtain. More signs of a struggle. Nobody left behind, alive or dead. She sucked in a deep breath and opened up the giant commercial refrigerator.

It was full of blood bags, but no bodies.

"Anything?" Hannah asked at the curtain.

"Nobody here," Claire said. "They left the blood, though."

"Huh. Weird. You'd think they'd need that more than anything. Why attack the place if you're not taking the good stuff?" Hannah stared out into the coffee shop, her expression blank and distant. "Glass is broken out, not in. No sign anybody got in the doors, either front or back. I don't think anybody attacked from the outside, Claire."

With a black, heavy feeling gathering in her stomach, Claire swung the refrigerator door shut. "You think the vampires fought to get *out.*"

"Yeah. Yeah, I do."

"Oliver, too."

"Oliver, Myrnin, all of them. Whatever bat signal was calling them got turned up to eleven, I think."

"Then where's Eve?" Claire asked.

Hannah shook her head. "We don't know anything. It's all guesswork. Let's get some boots on the ground and figure this thing out." She continued to stare outside. "If they went out there, most of them could make it for a while in the sun, but they'd be hurt. Some couldn't make it far at all."

Some, like the policeman Claire had seen burn up in front of her, would already be gone. "You think it's Mr. Bishop?" she asked, in a very small voice.

"I hope so."

Claire blinked. "Why?"

"Because if it's not, that's got to be a whole lot worse."

8

Three hours later, they didn't know much more, except that nothing they tried to do to keep the vampires from leaving seemed to work, apart from tranquilizing them and locking them up in sturdy cells. Tracking those who did leave wasn't much good, either. Claire and Hannah ended up at the Glass House, which seemed like the best place to gather—central to most things, and close to City Hall in an emergency.

Richard Morrell arrived, along with a few others, and set up shop in the kitchen. Claire was trying to figure out what to do to feed everybody, when there was another knock at the door.

It was Gramma Day. The old woman, straight-backed and proud, leaned on her cane and stared at Claire from age-faded eyes. "I ain't staying with my daughter," she said. "I don't want any part of that."

Claire quickly moved aside to let her in, and the old lady shuffled inside. As Claire locked the door behind her, she asked, "How did you get here?"

"Walked," Gramma said. "I know how to use my feet just fine. Nobody bothered me." Nobody would dare, Claire thought. "Young Mr. Richard! Are you in here?"

"Ma'am?" Richard Morrell came out of the kitchen, looking very much younger than Claire had ever seen him. Gramma Day had that effect on people. "What are you doing here?"

"My fool daughter's off her head," Gramma said. "I'm not having any of it. Move out of the way, boy. I'm making you some lunch." And she tapped her cane right past him, into the kitchen, and clucked and fretted over the state of the kitchen while Claire stood by, caught between giggles and horror. She was just a pair of hands, getting ordered around, but at the end of it there was a plate full of sandwiches and a big jug of iced tea, and everybody was seated around the kitchen table, except for Gramma, who'd gone off into the other room to rest. Claire had hesitantly taken a chair, at Richard's nod. Detectives Joe Hess and Travis Lowe were also present, and they were gratefully scarfing down food and drink. Claire felt exhausted, but they looked a whole lot worse. Tall, thin Joe Hess had his left arm in a sling—broken, apparently, from the brace on it—and both he and his rounder, heavier partner had cuts and bruises to prove they'd been in a fight or two.

"So," Hess said, "any word on where the vampires are heading when they take off?"

"Not so far," Richard said. "Once we started tracking them, we could keep up only for a while, and then they lost us."

"Aren't they hurt by the sun?" Claire asked. "I mean—"

"They start smoking, not in the Marlboro way, and then they start crisping," Travis Lowe said around a mouthful of turkey and Swiss. "The older ones, they can handle it okay, and anyway, they're not just charging out there anymore. They're putting on hats and coats and blankets. I saw one wrapped up in a Sponge-Bob rug from some kid's bedroom, if you can believe that. It's the younger vamps that are in trouble. Some of them won't make it to the shade if they're not careful."

Claire thought about Michael, and her stomach lurched. Before she even formed the question, Richard saw her expression and shook his head. "Michael's okay," he said. "Saw to it myself. He's got himself a nice, secure jail cell, along with the other vampires we could catch before it was too late. He's not as strong as some of the others. He can't bend steel with his bare hands. Yet, anyway."

"Any word on—" Claire was wearing out the question, and Richard didn't even let her finish it.

"No sign of Eve," he said. "No word from her. I'd try to put a GPS track on her phone, but we'd have to bring the cell network up, and that's too dangerous right now. I've asked the guys on the street to keep an eye out for her, but we've got a lot of things going on, Claire."

"I know. But—" She couldn't put it into words, exactly. She just knew that somewhere, somehow, Eve was in trouble, and they needed to find her.

"So," Joe Hess said, and stood up to look at a blown-up map of Morganville taped to the wall. "This still accurate?" The map was covered in colored dots: blue for locations held by those loyal to Amelie; red for those loyal to Bishop; black for those burned or otherwise put out of commission, which accounted for three Founder Houses, the hospital, and the blood bank.

"Pretty much," Richard said. "We don't know if the vampires are leaving Bishop's locations, but we know they're digging in, just like Amelie's folks. We can verify locations only where Amelie's people were supposed to be, and they're gone from just about every location we've got up in blue."

"Where were they last seen?"

Richard consulted notes, and began to add yellow dots to the map. Claire saw the pattern almost immediately. "It's the portals," she said. "Myrnin got the portals working again, somehow. That's what they're using."

Hess and Lowe looked blank, but Richard nodded. "Yeah, I know about that. Makes sense. But where are they *going*?"

She shrugged helplessly. "Could be anywhere. I don't know all the places the portals go; maybe Myrnin and Amelie do, but I don't think anybody else does." But she felt unreasonably cheered by the idea that the vampires weren't out wandering out in the daylight, spontaneously combusting all over the place. She didn't want to see that happen to them . . . not even to Oliver.

Well, maybe to Oliver, sometimes. But not today.

The three men stared at her for a few seconds, then went back to studying the map, talking about perimeters and strategies for patrols, all kinds of things that Claire didn't figure really involved her. She finished her sandwich and walked into the living room, where tiny, wizened little Gramma Day was sitting in an overstuffed wing chair with her feet up, talking to Hannah. "Hey, little girl," Gramma Day said. "Sit yourself."

Claire perched, looking around the room. Most of the vampires were gone, either confined to cells or locked away for safety; some, they hadn't been able to stop. She couldn't seem to stop anxiously rubbing her hands together. *Shane.* Shane was supposed to be here. Richard Morrell had said that they'd arranged for the Bloodmobile to switch drivers, and that meant Shane would be coming soon for his rest period.

She needed him right now.

Gramma Day was looking at her with distant sympathy in her faded eyes. "You worried?" she asked, and smiled. "You got cause, I expect."

"I do?" Claire was surprised. Most adults tried to pretend it was all going to be okay.

"Sure thing, sugar. Morganville's been ruled by the vampires a long time, and they ain't always been the gentlest of folks. Been people hurt, people killed without reason. Builds up some resentment." Gramma nodded toward the bookcase. "Fetch me that red book right there, the one that starts with *N*."

It was an encyclopedia. Claire got it and set it in

her lap. Gramma's weathered, sinewy fingers opened it and flipped pages, then handed it back. The heading said, *New York Draft Riots, 1863*.

The pictures showed chaos—mobs, buildings on fire. And worse things. Much, much worse.

"People forget," Gramma said. "They forget what can happen, if anger builds up. Those New York folks, they were angry because their men were being drafted to fight the Civil War. Who you think they took it out on? Mostly black folks, of all things. Folks who couldn't fight back. They even burned up an orphanage, and they'd have killed every one of those children if they'd caught them." She shook her head, clicking her tongue in disgust. "Same thing happened in Tulsa in 1921. Called it the Greenwood Riot, said black folks were taking away their business and jobs. Back in France, they had a revolution where they took all those fancy aristocrat folks and cut their heads off. Maybe it was their fault, and maybe not. It's all the same thing: you get angry, you blame it on some folks, and you make them pay, guilty or not. Happens all the time."

Claire felt a chill. "What do you mean?"

"I mean, you think about France, girl. Vampires been holding us all down a long time, just like those aristocrats, or that's how people around here think of it. Now, you think about all those folks out there with generations of grudges, and nobody really in charge right now. You think it won't go bad on us?"

There weren't enough shudders in the world. Claire remembered Shane's father, the fanatical light in his eyes. He'd be one of those leading a riot, she thought. One of those pulling people out of their houses as collaborators and turncoats and hanging them up from lampposts.

Hannah patted the shotgun in her lap. She'd put the paintball gun aside—honestly, it wasn't much use now, with the vampires missing in action. "They're not getting in here, Gramma. We won't be having any Greenwood in Morganville."

"I ain't so much worried about you and me," Gramma said. "But I'd be worried for the Morrells. They're gonna be coming for them, sooner or later. That family's the poster children for the old guard."

Claire wondered if Richard knew that. She thought about Monica, too. Not that she liked Monica—God, no—but still.

She thanked Gramma Day and walked back into the kitchen, where the policemen were still talking. "Gramma Day thinks there's going to be trouble," she said. "Not the vampires. Regular people, like those people in the park. Maybe Lisa Day, too. And she thinks you ought to look after your family, Richard."

Richard nodded. "Already done," he said. "My mom and dad are at City Hall. Monica's headed there, too." He paused, thinking about it. "You're right. I should make sure she gets there all right, before she becomes another statistic." His face had tightened, and there was a look in his eyes that didn't match the way he said it. He was worried.

Given what Claire had just heard from Gramma Day, she thought he probably ought to be. Joe Hess and Travis Lowe sent each other looks, too, and she thought they were probably thinking the same thing. *She deserves it,* Claire told herself. *Whatever happens to Monica Morrell, she earned it.*

Except the pictures from Gramma Day's book kept coming back to haunt her.

The front door banged shut, and she heard Hannah's voice—not an alarm, just a welcome. She spun around and went to the door of the kitchen . . . and ran directly into Shane, who grabbed her and folded his arms around her.

"You're here," he said, and hugged her so tightly that she felt ribs creak. "Man, you don't make it easy, Claire. I've been freaking out all damn day. First I hear you're off in the middle of Vamptown; then you're running around like bait with Eve—"

"You're one to talk about bait," Claire said, and pushed back to look up into his face. "You okay?"

"Not a scratch," he said, and grinned. "Ironic, because I'm usually the one with the battle scars, right? The worst thing that happened to me was that I had to pull over and let a bunch of vampires off the bus, or they'd have ripped right through the walls. You'd be proud. I even let them off in the shade." His smile faded, but not the warmth in his eyes. "You look tired."

"Yeah, you think?" She caught herself on a yawn. "Sorry."

"We should get you home and catch some rest while we can." He looked around. "Where's Eve?"

Nobody had told him. Claire opened her mouth and found her throat clenching tight around the words. Her eyes filled with tears. *She's gone,* she wanted to say. *She's missing. Nobody knows where she is.*

But saying it out loud, saying it to Shane, that would make it real, somehow.

"Hey," he said, and smoothed her hair. "Hey, what's wrong? Where is she?"

"She was at Common Grounds," Claire finally choked out. "She—"

His hands went still, and his eyes widened.

"She's missing," Claire finally said, and a wave of utter misery broke over her. "She's out there somewhere. That's all I know."

"Her car's outside."

"We drove it here." Claire nodded at Hannah, who'd come in behind Shane and was silently watching. He acknowledged her with a glance; that was all.

"Okay," Shane said. "Michael's safe, you're safe, I'm safe. Now we're going to go find Eve."

Richard Morrell stirred. "That's not a good idea."

Shane spun on him, and the look on his face was hard enough to scare a vampire. "Want to try and stop me, *Dick*?"

Richard stared at him for a moment, then turned

back to the map. "You want to go, go. We've got things to do. There's a whole town of people out there to serve and protect. Eve's one girl."

"Yeah, well, she's our girl," Shane said. He took Claire's hand. "Let's go."

Hannah leaned against the wall. "Mind if I call shotgun?"

"Since you're carrying one? Feel free."

Outside, things were odd—quiet, but with a suppressed feeling of excitement in the air. People were still outside, talking in groups on the streets. The stores were shut down, for the most part, but Claire noticed with a stir of unease that the bars were open, and so was Morganville's gun shop.

Not good.

The gates of the university had opened, and they were issuing some kind of passes to people to leave—still sticking to the emergency drill story, Claire assumed.

"Oh, man," Shane muttered, as they turned down one of the streets that led to the heart of town, and Founder's Square—Vamptown. There were more people here, more groups. "I don't like this. There's Sal Manetti up there. He was one of my dad's drinking buddies, back in the day."

"The cops don't like it much, either," Hannah said, and pointed at the police cars ahead. They were blocking off access at the end of the street, and when Claire squinted, she could see they were out of their cruisers and arranged in a line, ready for anything. "This could turn bad, any time. All they need is somebody to strike a match out there, and we're all on fire."

Claire thought about Shane saying his father was coming to town, and she knew he was thinking about that, too. He shook his head. "We've got to figure out where Eve might be. Ideas?"

"Maybe she left us some clues," Claire said. "Back at Common Grounds. We should probably start there."

Common Grounds, however, was deserted, and the steel shutters were down. The front door was locked. They drove around back, to the alley. Nothing was there but trash cans, and—

"What the hell is that?" Shane asked. He hit the brakes and put the car in park, then jumped out and picked up something small on the ground. He got back in and showed it to Claire.

It was a small white candy in the shape of a skull. Claire blinked at it, then looked down the alley. "She left a trail of breath mints?"

"Looks like. We'll have to go on foot to follow it."

Hannah didn't seem to like that idea much, but Shane wasn't taking votes. They parked and locked Eve's car in the alley behind Common Grounds and began hunting for skull candies.

"Over here!" Hannah yelled, at the end of the alley. "Looks like she's dropping them when she makes a turn. Smart. She went this way."

After that, they went faster. The skull candies were in plain sight, easy to spot. Claire noticed that they were mostly in the shadows, which would have made sense, if Eve was with Myrnin or the other vampires. *Why didn't she stay?* Maybe she hadn't had a choice.

They ran out of candy trail after a few blocks. It led them into an area where Claire hadn't really been before—abandoned old buildings, mostly, falling to pieces under the relentless pressure of years and sun. It looked and felt deserted.

"Where now?" Claire asked, looking around. She didn't see anything obvious, but then she spotted something shiny, tucked in behind a tipped-over rusty trash can. She reached behind and came up with a black leather collar, studded with silver spikes.

The same collar Eve had been wearing. She wordlessly showed it to Shane, who turned in a slow circle, looking at the blank buildings. "Come on, Eve," he said. "Give us something. Anything." He froze. "You hear that?"

Hannah cocked her head. She was standing at the end of the alley, shotgun held in her arms in a way that was both casual and scarily competent. "What?"

"You don't hear it?"

Claire did. Somebody's phone was ringing. A cell phone, with an ultrasonic ringtone—she'd heard that older people couldn't hear those frequencies, and kids in school had used them all the time to sneak phone calls and texts in class. It was faint, but it was definitely there. "I thought the networks were down," she said, and pulled her own phone out.

Nope. The network was back up. She wondered if Richard had done it, or they'd lost control of the cell phone towers. Either one was possible.

They found the phone before the ringing stopped. It was Eve's—a red phone, with silver skull cell phone charms on it—discarded in the shadow of a broken, leaning doorway. "Who was calling?" Claire asked, and Shane paged through the menu.

"Richard," he said. "I guess he really was looking for her after all."

Claire's phone buzzed—just once. A text message. She opened it and checked.

It was from Eve, and it had been sent hours ago; the backlog of messages was just now being delivered, apparently.

It read, 911 @ GERMANS. Claire showed it to Shane. "What is this?"

"Nine one one. Emergency message. German's—" He looked over at Hannah, who pushed away from the wall and came toward them.

"German's Tire Plant," she said. "Damn, I don't like that; it's the size of a couple of football fields, at least."

"We should let Richard know," Claire said. She dialed, but the network was busy, and then the bars failed again.

"I'm not waiting," Shane said. "Let's get the car."

9

The tire plant was near the old hospital, which made Claire shudder; she remembered the deserted building way too well. It had been incredibly creepy, and then of course it had also nearly gotten her and Shane killed, too, so again, not fond.

She was mildly shocked to see the hulking old edifice still standing, as Shane turned the car down the street.

"Didn't they tear that place down?" It had been scheduled for demolition, and boy, if any place had ever needed it . . .

"I heard it was delayed," Shane said. He didn't seem any happier about it than Claire was. "Something about historic preservation. Although anybody wanting to preserve that thing has never been inside it running for their life, I'll bet."

Claire stared out the window. On her side of the car was the brooding monstrosity of a hospital. The cracked stones and tilted columns in front made it look like something straight out of one of Shane's favorite zombie-killing video games. "Don't be hiding in there," she whispered. "Please don't be hiding in there." Because if Eve and Myrnin *had* taken refuge there, she wasn't sure she'd have the courage to go charging in after them.

"There's German's," Hannah said, and nodded toward

the other side of the street. Claire hadn't really noticed it the last time she'd been out here—preoccupied with the whole not-dying issue—but there it was, a four-story square building in that faded tan color that everybody had used back in the sixties. Even the windows—those that weren't broken out—were painted over. It was plain, big, and blocky, and there was absolutely nothing special about it except its size—it covered at least three city blocks, all blind windows and blank concrete.

"You ever been inside there?" Shane asked Hannah, who was studying the building carefully.

"Not for a whole lot of years," she said. "Yeah, we used to hide up in there sometimes, when we cut class or something. I guess everybody did, once in a while. It's a mess in there, a real junkyard. Stuff everywhere, walls falling apart, ceilings none too stable, either. If you go up to the second level, you watch yourself. Make sure you don't trust the floors, and watch those iron stairs. They were shaky even back then."

"Are we going in there?" Claire asked.

"No," Shane said. "*You're* not going anywhere. You're staying here and getting Richard on the phone and telling him where we are. Me and Hannah will check it out."

There didn't seem to be much room for argument, because Shane didn't give her time; he and Hannah bailed out of the car, made lock-the-door motions, and sprinted toward a gap in the rusted, sagging fence.

Claire watched until they disappeared around the corner of the building, and realized her fingers were going numb from clutching her cell phone. She took a deep breath and flipped it open to try Richard Morrell again.

Nothing. No signal again. The network was going up and down like a yo-yo.

The walkie-talkie signal was low, but she tried it anyway. There was some kind of response, but it was swallowed by static. She gave their position, on the off chance that someone on the network would be able to hear her over the noise.

She screamed and dropped the device when the light at the car window was suddenly blocked out, and someone battered frantically on the glass.

Claire recognized the silk shirt—*her* silk shirt—before she recognized Monica Morrell, because Monica definitely didn't look like herself. She was out of breath, sweating, her hair was tangled, and what makeup she had on was smeared and running.

She'd been crying. There was a cut on her right cheek, and a forming bruise, and dirt on the silk blouse as well as bloodstains. She was holding her left arm as though it was hurt.

"Open the door!" she screamed, and pounded on the glass again. "Let me in!"

Claire looked behind the car.

There was a mob coming down the street: thirty, forty people, some running, some following at a walk. Some were waving baseball bats, boards, pipes.

They saw Monica and let out a yell. Claire gasped, because that sound didn't seem human at all—more the roar of a beast, something mindless and hungry.

Monica's expression was, for the first time, absolutely open and vulnerable. She put her palm flat against the window glass. "Please help me," she said.

But even as Claire clawed at the lock to open it, Monica flinched, turned, and ran on, limping.

Claire slid over the front seat and dropped into the driver's seat. Shane had left the keys in the ignition. She started it up and put the big car in gear, gave it too much gas, and nearly wrecked it on the curb before she straightened the wheel. She rapidly gained on Monica. She passed her, squealed to a stop, and reached over to throw open the passenger door.

"Get in!" she yelled. Monica slid inside and banged the door shut, and Claire hit the gas as something impacted loudly against the back of the car—a brick, maybe. A hail of smaller stones hit a second later. Claire swerved wildly again, then straightened the wheel and got the car moving more smoothly. Her heart pounded hard, and her hands felt sweaty on the steering wheel. "You all right?"

Monica was panting, and she threw Claire a filthy look. "No, of *course* I'm not all right!" she snapped, and tried to fix her hair with trembling hands. "Unbelievable. What a stupid question. I guess I shouldn't expect much more from someone like you, though—"

Claire stopped the car and stared at her.

Monica shut up.

"Here's how this is going to go," Claire said. "You're going to act like an actual human being for a change, or else you're on your own. Clear?"

Monica glanced behind them. "They're coming!"

"Yes, they are. So, are we clear?"

"Okay, okay, yes! Fine, whatever!" Monica cast a clearly terrified look at the approaching mob. More stones peppered the paint job, and one hit the back glass with enough force to make Claire wince. "Get me out of here! Please!"

"Hold on, I'm not a very good driver."

That was kind of an understatement. Eve's car was huge and heavy and had a mind of its own, and Claire hadn't taken the time to readjust the bench seat to make it possible for her to reach the pedals easily. The only good thing about her driving, as they pulled away from the mob and the falling bricks, was that it was approximately straight, and pretty fast.

She scraped the curb only twice.

Once the fittest of their pursuers had fallen behind, obviously discouraged, Claire finally remembered to breathe, and pulled the car around the next right turn. This section of town seemed deserted, but then, so had the other street, before Monica and her fan club had shown up. The big, imposing hulk of the tire plant glided by on the passenger side—it seemed like miles of featureless brick and blank windows.

Claire braked the car on the other side of the street, in front of a deserted, rusting warehouse complex. "Come on," she said.

"What?" Monica watched her get out of the car and take the keys with uncomprehending shock. "Where are you going? We have to get out of here! They were going to *kill* me!"

"They probably still are," Claire said. "So you should probably get out of the car now, unless you want to wait around for them."

Monica said something Claire pretended not to hear—it wasn't exactly complimentary—and limped her way out of the passenger side. Claire locked the car. She hoped it wouldn't get banged up, but that mob had looked pretty excitable, and just the fact that Monica *had* been in it might be enough to ensure its destruction.

With any luck, though, they'd assume the girls had run into the warehouse complex, which was what Claire wanted.

Claire led them in the opposite direction, to the fence around German's Tire. There was a split in the wire by one of the posts, an ancient curling gap half hidden by a tangle of tumbleweeds. She pushed through and held the steel aside for Monica. "Coming?" she asked when Monica hesitated. "Because, you know what? Don't really care all that much. Just so you know."

Monica came through without any comment. The fence snapped back into place. Unless someone was looking for an entrance, it ought to do.

The plant threw a large, black shadow on the weed-choked parking lot. There were a few rusted-out trucks still parked here and there; Claire used them for cover from the street as they approached the main building, though she didn't think the mob was close enough to really spot them at this point. Monica seemed to get the point without much in the way of instruction; Claire supposed that running for her life had humbled her a little. Maybe.

"Wait," Monica said, as Claire prepared to bolt for a broken-out bottom-floor window into the tire plant. "What are you doing?"

"Looking for my friends," she said. "They're inside."

"Well, *I'm* not going in there," Monica declared, and tried to look haughty. It would have been more effective if she hadn't been so frazzled and sweaty. "I was on my way to City Hall, but those losers got in my way. They slashed my tires. I need to get to my parents.'" She said it as though she expected Claire to salute and hop like a toad.

Claire raised her eyebrows. "Better start walking, I guess. It's kind of a long way."

"But—but—"

Claire didn't wait for the sputtering to die; she turned and ran for the building. The window opened into total darkness, as far as she could tell, but at least it was accessible. She pulled herself up on the sash and started to swing her legs inside.

"Wait!" Monica dashed across to join her. "You can't leave me here alone! You saw those jerks out there!"

"Absolutely."

"Oh, you're just loving this, aren't you?"

"Kinda." Claire hopped down inside the building, and her shoes slapped bare concrete floor. It was bare except for a layer of dirt, anyway—undisturbed for as far as the light penetrated, which wasn't very far. "Coming?"

Monica stared through the window at her, just boiling with fury; Claire smiled at her and started to walk into the dark.

Monica, cursing, climbed inside.

"I'm not a bad person," Monica was saying—whining, actually. Claire wished she could find a two-by-four to whack her with, but the tire plant, although full of wreckage and trash, didn't seem to be big on wooden planks. Some nice pipes, though. She might use one of those.

Except she really didn't want to hit anybody, deep down. Claire supposed that was a character flaw, or something.

"Yes, you really are a bad person," she told Monica, and ducked underneath a low-hanging loop of wire that looked horror-movie ready, the sort of thing that dropped around your neck and hauled you up to be dispatched by the psycho-killer villain. Speaking of which, this whole place was decorated in Early Psycho-Killer Villain, from the vast soaring darkness overhead to the lumpy, skeletal shapes of rusting equipment and abandoned junk. The spray painting—decades of it, in layered styles from Early Tagger to cutting-edge gang sign—gleamed in the random shafts of light like blood. Some particularly unpleasant spray-paint artist had done an enormous, terrifying clown face, with windows for the eyes and a giant, open doorway for a mouth. *Yeah, really not going in there,* Claire thought. Although the way these things went, she probably would have to.

"Why do you say that?"

"Say what?" Claire asked absently. She was listening for any sound of movement, but this place was enormous and confusing—just as Hannah had warned.

"Say that I'm a bad person!"

"Oh, I don't know—you tried to kill me? *And* get me raped at a party? Not to mention—"

"That was payback," Monica said. "And I didn't mean it or anything."

"Which makes it all so much better. Look, can we not bond? I'm busy. Seriously. *Shhhh.*" That last was to forestall Monica from blurting out yet another injured defense of her character. Claire squeezed past a barricade of piled-up boxes and metal, into another shaft of light that arrowed down from a high-up broken window. The clown painting felt like it was watching her, which was beyond creepy. She tried not to look too closely at what was on the floor. Some of it was animal carcasses, birds, and things that had gotten inside and died over the years. Some of it was old cans, plastic wrappers, all kinds of junk left behind by adventurous kids looking for a hideout. She didn't imagine any of them stayed for long.

This place just felt . . . haunted.

Monica's hand grabbed her arm, just on the bruise that Amelie's grip had given her earlier. Claire winced.

"Did you hear that?" Monica's whisper was fierce and hushed. She needed mouthwash, and she smelled like sweat more than powder and perfume. "Oh my *God*. Something's in here with us!"

"Could be a vampire," Claire said. Monica sniffed.

"Not afraid of those," she said, and dangled her fancy, silver Protection bracelet in front of Claire's face. "Nobody's going to cross Oliver."

"You want to tell that to the mob of people chasing you back there? I don't think they got the memo or something."

"I mean, no vampire would. I'm Protected." Monica said it like there was simply no possibility anything else could be true. The earth was round, the sun was hot, and a vampire would never hurt her because she'd sold herself to Oliver, body and soul.

Yeah, right.

"News flash," Claire whispered. "Oliver's missing in action from Common Grounds. Amelie's disappeared. In fact, most of the vampires all over town have dropped out of sight, which makes these bracelets cute fashion accessories, but not exactly bulletproof vests or anything."

Monica started to speak, but Claire frowned angrily at her and pointed off into the darkness, where she'd heard the noise. It had sounded odd—kind of a sigh, echoing from the steel and concrete, bouncing and amplifying.

It sounded as if it had come out of the clown's dark mouth.

Of course.

Claire reached into her pocket. She still had the vial of silver powder that Amelie had given her, but she was well aware that it might not do her any good. If her friend-vampires were mixed in with enemy-vamps, she was out of luck. Likewise, if what was waiting for her out there was trouble of a human variety, instead of bloodsuckers . . .

Shane and Hannah were in here. Somewhere. And so—hopefully—was Eve.

Claire eased around a tattered sofa that smelled like old cats and mold, and sidestepped a truly impressive rat that didn't bother to move out of her way. It sat there watching her with weird, alert eyes.

Monica looked down, saw it, and shrieked, stumbling backward. She fell into a stack of ancient cartons that collapsed on her, raining down random junk. Claire grabbed her and pulled her to her feet, but Monica kept on whimpering and squirming, slapping at her hair and upper body.

"Oh my *God*, are they on me? Spiders? Are there spiders?"

If there were, Claire hoped they bit her. "No," she said shortly. Well, there were, but they were little ones. She brushed them off Monica's back. "Shut *up* already!"

"Are you kidding me? Did you see that rat? It was the size of freaking Godzilla!"

That was it, Claire decided. Monica could just wander around on her own, screaming about rats and spiders, until someone came and ate her. What. *Ever*.

She got only about ten feet away when Monica's very small whisper stopped her dead in her tracks.

"Please don't leave me." That didn't sound like Monica, not at all. It sounded scared, and very young. "Claire, please."

It was probably too late for being quiet, anyway,

and if there were vampires hiding in German's Tire Plant, they all knew exactly where they were, and for that matter, could tell what blood type they were. So stealth didn't seem a priority.

Claire cupped her hands over her mouth and yelled, very loudly, "Shane! Eve! Hannah! Anybody!"

The echoes woke invisible birds or bats high overhead, which flapped madly around; her voice rang from every flat surface, mocking Claire with her own ghost.

In the whispering silence afterward, Monica murmured, "Wow, I thought we were being subtle or something. My mistake."

Claire was about to hiss something really unpleasant at her, but froze as another voice came bouncing through the vast room—Shane's voice. "Claire?"

"Here!"

"Stay there! And shut up!"

He sounded frantic enough to make Claire wish she'd stuck with the whole quiet-time policy, and then Monica stopped breathing and went very, very still next to her. Her hands closed around Claire's arm, squeezing bruises again.

Claire froze, too, because something was coming out of the mouth of that painted clown—something white, ghostly, drifting like smoke. . . .

It had a face. Several faces, because it was a group of what looked like vampires, all very pale, all very quiet, all heading their way.

Staying put was not such a great plan, Claire decided. She was going to go with *run away.*

Which, grabbing Monica's wrist, she did.

The vampires did make sounds then, as their quarry started to flee—little whispering laughs, strange hisses, all kinds of creepy noises that made the skin on the back of Claire's neck tighten up. She held the glass vial in one hand, running faster, leaping over junk when she could see it coming and stumbling across it when she couldn't. Monica kept up, somehow, although

Claire could hear the tortured, steady moaning of her breath. Whatever she'd done to her right leg must have hurt pretty badly.

Something pale landed ahead of her, with a silent leap like a spider pouncing. Claire had a wild impression of a white face, red eyes, a wide-open mouth, and gleaming fangs. She drew back to throw the vial . . . and realized it was Myrnin facing her.

The hesitation cost her. Something hit her from the back, sending her stumbling forward across a fallen iron beam. She dropped the vial as she fell, trying to catch herself, and heard the glass break on the edge of the girder. Silver dust puffed out. Monica shrieked, a wild cry that made the birds panic again high up in heaven; Claire saw her stumble away, trying to put distance between herself and Myrnin.

Myrnin was just outside of the range of the drifting silver powder, but it wasn't Myrnin who was the problem. The other vampires, the ones who'd come out of the clown's mouth, leaped over stacks of trash, running for the smell of fresh, flowing blood.

They were coming up behind them, fast.

Claire raked her hand across the ground and came up with a palm full of silver powder and glass shards as she rolled up to her knees. She turned and threw the powder into the air between her, Monica, and the rest of the vampires. It dispersed into a fine, glittering mist, and when the vampires hit it, every tiny grain of silver caught fire.

It was beautiful, and horrible, and Claire flinched at the sound of their cries. There was so much silver, and it clung to their skin, eating in. Claire didn't know if it would kill them, but it definitely stopped them cold.

She grabbed Monica's arm and pulled her close.

Myrnin was still in front of them, crouched on top of a stack of wooden pallets. He didn't look at all human, not at *all*.

And then he blinked, and the red light went out in

his eyes. His fangs folded neatly backward, and he ran his tongue over pale lips before he said, puzzled, "Claire?"

She felt a sense of relief so strong it was like falling. "Yeah, it's me."

"Oh." He slithered down off the stacked wood, and she realized he was still dressed the way she'd seen him back at Common Grounds—a long, black velvet coat, no shirt, white pantaloons left over from his costume. He should have looked ridiculous, but somehow, he looked . . . right. "You shouldn't be here, Claire. It's very dangerous."

"I know—"

Something cold brushed the back of her neck, and she heard Monica make a muffled sound like a choked cry. Claire whirled and found herself face-to-face with a red-eyed, angry vampire with part of his skin still smoking from the silver she'd thrown.

Myrnin let out a roar that ripped the air, full of menace and fury, and the vampire stumbled backward, clearly shocked.

Then the five who'd chased them silently withdrew into the darkness.

Claire turned to face Myrnin. He was staring thoughtfully at the departing vamps.

"Thanks," she said. He shrugged.

"I was raised to believe in the concept of noblesse oblige," he said. "And I do owe you, you know. Do you have any more of my medication?"

She handed him her last dose of the drug that kept him sane—mostly sane, anyway. It was the older version, red crystals rather than clear liquid, and he poured out a dollop into his palm and licked the crystals up, then sighed in deep satisfaction.

"Much better," he said, and pocketed the rest of the bottle. "Now. Why are you here?"

Claire licked her lips. She could hear Shane—or someone—coming toward them through the darkness, and she saw someone in the shadows behind Myrnin.

Not vampires, she thought, so it was probably Hannah, flanking Shane. "We're looking for my friend Eve. You remember her, right?"

"Eve," Myrnin repeated, and slowly smiled. "Ah. The girl who followed me. Yes, of course."

Claire felt a flush of excitement, quickly damped by dread. "What happened to her?"

"Nothing. She's asleep," he said. "It was too dangerous out here for her. I put her in a safe place, for now."

Shane pushed through the last of the barriers and stepped into a shaft of light about fifty feet away. He paused at the sight of Myrnin, but he didn't look alarmed.

"This is your friend as well," Myrnin said, glancing back at Shane. "The one you care so much for." She'd never discussed Shane with Myrnin—not in detail, anyway. The question must have shown in her face, because his smile broadened. "You carry his scent on your clothes," he said. "And he carries yours."

"Ewww," Monica sighed.

Myrnin's eyes focused in on her like laser sights. "And who is this lovely child?"

Claire almost rolled her eyes. "Monica. The mayor's daughter."

"Monica Morrell." She offered her hand, which Myrnin accepted and bent over in an old-fashioned way. Claire assumed he was also inspecting the bracelet on her wrist.

"Oliver's," he said, straightening. "I see. I am charmed, my dear, simply charmed." He hadn't let go of her hand. "I don't suppose you would be willing to donate a pint for a poor, starving stranger?"

Monica's smile froze in place. "I—well, I—"

He pulled her into his arms with one quick jerk. Monica yelped and tried to pull away, but for all his relatively small size, Myrnin had strength to burn.

Claire pulled in a deep breath. "Myrnin. Please."

He looked annoyed. "Please *what*?"

"She's not free range or anything. You can't just munch her. Let go." He didn't look convinced. "Seriously. *Let go.*"

"Fine." He opened his arms, and Monica retreated as she clapped both hands around her neck. She sat down on a nearby girder, breathing hard. "You know, in my youth, women lined up to grant me their favors. I believe I'm a bit offended."

"It's a strange day for everybody," Claire said. "Shane, Hannah, this is Myrnin. He's sort of my boss."

Shane moved closer, but his expression stayed cool and distant. "Yeah? This the guy who took you to the ball? The one who dumped you and left you to die?"

"Well . . . uh . . . yes."

"Thought so."

Shane punched him right in the face. Myrnin, surprised, stumbled back against the tower of crates, and snarled; Shane took a stake from his back pocket and held it at the ready.

"No!" Claire jumped between them, waving her hands. "No, honest, it's not like that. Calm down, everybody, please."

"Yes," Myrnin said. "I've been staked quite enough today, thank you. I respect your need to avenge her, boy, but Claire remains quite capable of defending her own honor."

"Couldn't have said it better myself," she said. "Please, Shane. Don't. We need him."

"Yeah? Why?"

"Because he may know what's going on with the vampires."

"Oh, that," Myrnin said, in a tone that implied they were all idiots for not knowing already. "They're being called. It's a signal that draws all vampires who have sworn allegiance to you with a blood exchange— it's the way wars were fought, once upon a time. It's how you gather your army."

"Oh," Claire said. "So . . . why not you? Or the rest of the vampires here?"

"It seems as though your serum offers me some portion of immunity against it. Oh, I feel the draw, most certainly, but in an entirely academic way. Rather curious. I remember how it felt before, like an overwhelming panic. As for those others, well. They're not of the blood."

"They're not?"

"No. Lesser creatures. Failed experiments, if you will." He looked away, and Claire had a horrible suspicion.

"Are they *people*? I mean, regular humans?"

"A failed experiment," he repeated. "You're a scientist, Claire. Not all experiments work the way they're intended."

Myrnin had done this to them, in his search for the cure to the vampire disease. He had turned them into something that wasn't vampire, wasn't human, wasn't—well, wasn't anything, exactly. They didn't fit in either society.

No wonder they were hiding here.

"Don't look at me that way," Myrnin said. "It's not my fault the process was imperfect, you know. I'm not a monster."

Claire shook her head.

"Sometimes, you really are."

Eve was fine—tired, shaking, and tear streaked, but okay. "He didn't, you know," she said, and made two-finger pointy motions toward her throat. "He's kind of sweet, actually, once you get past all the crazy. Although there's a lot of the crazy."

There was, as Claire well knew, no way of getting past the crazy. Not really. But she had to admit that at least Myrnin had behaved more like a gentleman than expected.

Noblesse oblige. Maybe he'd felt obligated.

The place he'd kept Eve had once been some kind of storage locker within the plant, all solid walls and a single door that he'd locked off with a bent pipe. Shane hadn't been all that happy about it. "What if something had happened to you?" he'd asked, as Myrnin untwisted the metal as though it were solder instead of iron. "She'd have been locked in there, all alone, no way out. She'd have starved."

"Actually," Myrnin had answered, "that's not very likely. Thirst would have killed her within four days, I imagine. She'd never have had a chance to starve." Claire stared at him. He raised his eyebrows. "What?"

She just shook her head. "I think you missed the point."

Monica tagged along with Claire, which was annoying; she kept casting Shane nervous glances, and she was now outright terrified of Myrnin, which was probably how it should have been, really. At the very least, she'd shut up, and even the sight of another rat, this one big and kind of albino, hadn't set off her screams this time.

Eve, however, was less than thrilled to see Monica. "You're kidding," she said flatly, staring first at her, then at Shane. "You're okay with this?"

"Okay would be a stretch. Resigned, that's closer," Shane said. Hannah, standing next to him with her shotgun at port arms, snorted out a laugh. "As long as she doesn't talk, I can pretend she isn't here."

"Yeah? Well *I* can't," Eve said. She glared at Monica, who glared right back. "Claire, you have to stop picking up strays. You don't know where they've been."

"You're one to talk about diseases," Monica shot back, "seeing as how you're one big, walking social one."

"That's not pot, kettle—that's more like cauldron, kettle. Witch."

"Whore!"

"You want to go play with your new friends back there?" Shane snapped. "The really pale ones with the taste for plasma? Because believe me, I'll drop your skanky butt right in their nest if you don't shut up, Monica."

"You don't scare me, Collins!"

Hannah rolled her eyes and racked her shotgun. "How about me?"

That ended the entire argument.

Myrnin, leaning against the wall with his arms folded over his chest, watched the proceedings with great interest. "Your friends," he said to Claire. "They're quite . . . colorful. So full of energy."

"Hands off my friends." Not that that statement exactly included Monica, but whatever.

"Oh, absolutely. I would never." Hand to his heart, Myrnin managed to look angelic, which was a bit of a trick considering his Lord-Byron-on-a-bender outfit. "I've just been away from normal human society for so long. Tell me, is it usually this . . . spirited?"

"Not usually," she sighed. "Monica's special." Yeah, in the short-bus sense, because Monica was a head case. Not that Claire had time or inclination to explain all the dynamics of the Monica-Shane-Eve relationship to Myrnin right now. "When you said that someone was calling the vampires together for some kind of fight—was that Bishop?"

"Bishop?" Myrnin looked startled. "No, of course not. It's Amelie. Amelie is sending the call. She's consolidating her forces, putting up lines of defense. Things are rapidly moving toward a confrontation, I believe."

That was exactly what Claire was afraid he was going to say. "Do you know who answered?"

"Anyone in Morganville with a blood tie to her," he said. "Except me, of course. But that would include almost every vampire in town, save those who were sworn through Oliver. Even then, Oliver's tie would bind them in some sense, because he swore fealty to her when he came to live here. They might feel the pull less strongly, but they would still feel it."

"Then how is Bishop getting an army? Isn't everybody in town, you know, Amelie's?"

"He bit those he wished to keep on his side." Myrnin shrugged. "Claimed them from her, in a sense. Some of them went willingly, some not, but all owe him allegiance now. All those he was able to turn, which is a considerable number, I believe." He looked sharply at her. "The call continued in the daytime. Michael?"

"Michael's fine. They put him in a cell."

"And Sam?"

Claire shook her head in response. Next to Michael, his grandfather Sam was the youngest vampire in town, and Claire hadn't seen him at all, not since he'd left the Glass House, well before any of the other vamps. He'd gone off on some mission for Amelie; she trusted him more than most of the others, even those she'd known for hundreds of years. That was, Claire thought, because Amelie knew how Sam felt about her. It was the storybook kind of love, the kind that ignored things like practicality and danger, and never changed or died.

She found herself looking at Shane. He turned his head and smiled back.

The storybook kind of love.

She was probably too young to have that, but this felt so strong, so real. . . .

And Shane wouldn't even man up and tell her he loved her.

She took a deep breath and forced her mind off that. "What do we do now?" Claire asked. "Myrnin?"

He was silent for a long moment, then moved to one of the painted-over first-floor windows and pulled it open. The sun was setting again. It would be down completely soon.

"You should get home," he said. "The humans are

in charge for now, at least, but there are factions out there. There will be power struggles tonight, and not just between the two vampire sides."

Shane glanced at Monica—whose bruises were living proof that trouble was already under way—and then back at Myrnin. "What are you going to do?"

"Stay here," Myrnin said. "With my friends."

"*Friends?* Who, the—uh—failed experiments?"

"Exactly so." Myrnin shrugged. "They look upon me as a kind of father figure. Besides, their blood is as good as anyone else's, in a pinch."

"So much more than I wanted to know," Shane said, and nodded to Hannah. "Let's go."

"Got your back, Shane."

"Watch Claire's and Eve's. I'll take the lead."

"What about me?" Monica whined.

"Do you really want to know?" Shane gave her a glare that should have scorched her hair off. "Be grateful I'm not leaving you as an after-dinner mint on his pillow."

Myrnin leaned close to Claire's ear and said, "I think I like your young man." When she reacted in pure confusion, he held up his hands, smiling. "Not in that way, my dear. He just seems quite trustworthy."

She swallowed and put all that aside. "Are you going to be okay here? Really?"

"Really?" He locked gazes with her. "For now, yes. But we have work to do, Claire. Much work, and very little time. I can't hide for long. You do realize that stress accelerates the disease, and this is a great deal of stress for us all. More will fall ill, become confused. It's vital we begin work on the serum as quickly as possible."

"I'll try to get you back to the lab tomorrow."

They left him standing in a fading shaft of sunlight, next to a giant rusting crane that lifted its head three stories into the dark, with pale birds flitting and diving overhead.

And wounded, angry failed experiments lurking in

the shadows, maybe waiting to attack their vampire creator.

Claire felt sorry for them, if they did.

The mobs were gone, but they'd given Eve's car a good battering while they were at it. She choked when she saw the dents and cracked glass, but at least it was still on all four tires, and the damage was cosmetic. The engine started right up.

"Poor baby," Eve said, and patted the big steering wheel affectionately as she settled into the driver's seat. "We'll get you all fixed up. Right, Hannah?"

"And here I was wondering what I was going to do tomorrow," Hannah said, taking—of course—the shotgun seat. "Guess now I know. I'll be hammering dents out of the Queen Mary and putting in new safety glass."

In the backseat, Claire was the human equivalent of Switzerland between the warring nations of Shane and Monica, who sat next to the windows. It was tense, but nobody spoke.

The sun was going down in a blaze of glory in the west, which normally would have made Morganville a vampire-friendly place. Not so much tonight, as became evident when Eve left the dilapidated warehouse district and cruised closer to Vamptown.

There were people out on the streets, *at sunset*.

And they were angry, too.

"Shouty," Eve said, as they passed a big group clustered around a guy standing on a wooden box, yelling at the crowd. He had a pile of wooden stakes, and people were picking them up. "Okay, this is looking less than great."

"You think?" Monica slumped down in her seat, trying not to be noticed. "They tried to kill me! And I'm not even a vampire!"

"Yeah, but you're you, so there's that explained." Eve slowed down. "Traffic."

Traffic? In Morganville? Claire leaned forward and

saw that there were about six cars in the street ahead. The first one was turned sideways, blocking the second—a big van, which was trying to back up but was handicapped by the third car.

The trapped passenger van was vampire-dark. The two cars blocking it in were old, battered sedans, the kind humans drove.

"That's Lex Perry's car, the one turned sideways," Hannah said. "I think that's the Nunally brothers in the third one. They're drinking buddies with Sal Manetti."

"Sal, as in, the guy out there rabble-rousing?"

"You got it."

And now people were closing in around the van, pushing against it, rocking it on its tires.

Nobody in their car spoke a word.

The van rocked harder. The tires spun, trying to pull away, but it tipped and slammed over on its side, helpless. With a roar, the crowd climbed on top of it and started battering the windows.

"We should do something," Claire finally said.

"Yeah?" Hannah's voice was very soft. "What, exactly?"

"Call the police?" Only the police were already here. There were two cars of them, and they couldn't stop what was happening. In fact, they didn't even look inclined to try.

"Let's go," Shane said quietly. "There's nothing we can do here."

Eve silently put the car in reverse and burned rubber backing up.

Claire broke out of her trance. "What are you doing? We can't just leave—"

"Take a good look," Eve said grimly. "If anybody out there sees Princess Morrell in this car, we've all had it. We're all collaborators if we're protecting her, and *you're* wearing the Founder bracelet. We can't risk it."

Claire sank back in her seat as Eve shifted gears

again and turned the wheel. They took a different street, this one unblocked so far.

"What's happening?" Monica asked. "What's happening to our town?"

"France," Claire said, thinking about Gramma Day. "Welcome to the revolution."

Eve drove through a maze of streets. Lights were flickering on in houses, and the few streetlamps were coming on as well. Cars—and there were a lot of them out now—turned on their headlights and honked, as if the local high school had just won a big football game.

As if it were one big, loud party.

"I want to go home," Monica said. Her voice sounded muffled. "Please."

Eve looked at her in the rearview mirror, and finally nodded.

But when they turned down the street where the Morrell family home was located, Eve slammed on the brakes and put the car into reverse, instantly.

The Morrell home looked like the site of another of Monica's infamous, unsupervised parties . . . only this one really was unsupervised, and those uninvited guests, they weren't just there for the free booze.

"What are they doing?" Monica asked, and let out a strangled yell as a couple of guys carried a big plasma television out the front door. "They're stealing it! They're stealing our stuff!"

Pretty much everything was being looted—mattresses, furniture, art. Claire even saw people upstairs tossing linens and clothing out the windows to people waiting on the ground.

And then, somebody ran up with a bottle full of liquid, stuffed with a burning rag, and threw it into the front window.

The flames flickered, caught, and gained strength.

"No!" Monica panted and clawed at the door handle, but Eve had locked it up. Claire grabbed Monica's arms and held them down.

"Get us out of here!" she yelled.

"My parents could be in there!"

"No, they're not. Richard told me they're at City Hall."

Monica kept fighting, even as Eve steered the car away from the burning house, and then suddenly just . . . stopped.

Claire heard her crying. She wanted to think, *Good, you deserve it,* but somehow she just couldn't force herself to be that cold.

Shane, however, could. "Hey, look on the bright side," he said. "At least your little sister isn't inside."

Monica caught her breath, then kept crying.

By the time they'd turned on Lot Street, Monica seemed to be pulling herself together, wiping her face with trembling hands and asking for a tissue, which Eve provided out of the glove box in the front.

"What do you think?" Eve asked Shane. Their street seemed quiet. Most of the houses had lights on, including the Glass House, and although there were some folks outside, talking, it didn't look like mobs were forming. Not here, anyway.

"Looks good. Let's get inside."

They agreed that Monica needed to go in the middle, covered by Hannah. Eve went first, racing up the walk to the front door and using her keys to open it up.

They made it in without attracting too much attention or anybody pointing fingers at Monica—but then, Claire thought, Monica definitely didn't look much like herself right now. More like a bad Monica impersonator. Maybe even one who was a guy.

Shane would laugh himself sick over that if she mentioned it. After seeing the puffy redness around Monica's eyes, and the shattered expression, Claire kept it to herself.

As Shane slammed, locked, and dead bolted the front door, Claire felt the house come alive around them, almost tingling with warmth and welcome. She heard people in the living room exclaim at the same time, so it wasn't just her; the house really had reacted, and reacted strongly, to three out of four of its residents coming home.

Claire stretched out against the wall and kissed it. "Glad to see you, too," she whispered, and pressed her cheek against the smooth surface.

It almost felt like it hugged her back.

"Dude, it's a *house*," Shane said from behind her. "Hug somebody who cares."

She did, throwing herself into his arms. It felt like he'd never let her go, not even for a second, and he lifted her completely off the ground and rested his head on her shoulder for a long, precious moment before setting her gently back on her feet.

"Better see who's here," he said, and kissed her very lightly. "Down payment for later, okay?"

Claire let go, but held his hand as they walked down the hallway and into the living room of the Glass House, which was filled with people.

Not vampires.

Just people.

Some of them were familiar, at least by sight— people from town: the owner of the music store where Michael worked; a couple of nurses she'd seen at the hospital, who still wore brightly colored medical scrubs and comfortable shoes. The rest, Claire barely knew at all, but they had one thing in common—they were all scared.

An older, hard-looking woman grabbed Claire by the shoulders. "Thank God you're home," she said, and hugged her. Claire, rigid with surprise, cast Shane a what-the-hell look, and he shrugged helplessly. "This damn house won't do *anything* for us. The lights keep going out, the doors won't open, food goes bad in the fridge—it's as if it doesn't want us here!"

And it probably didn't. The house could have ejected them at any time, but obviously it had been a bit uncertain about exactly what its residents might want, so it had just made life uncomfortable for the intruders instead.

Claire could now feel the air-conditioning switching on to cool the overheated air, hear doors swinging open upstairs, see lights coming on in darkened areas.

"Hey, Celia," Shane said, as the woman let go of Claire at last. "So, what brings you here? I figured the Barfly would be doing good business tonight."

"Well, it would be, except that some jerks came in and said that because I was wearing a bracelet I had to serve them for free, on account of being some kind of sympathizer. What kind of sympathizer, I said, and one of them tried to hit me."

Shane lifted his eyebrows. Celia wasn't a young woman. "What did you do?"

"Used the Regulator." Celia lifted a baseball bat propped against the wall. It was old hardwood, lovingly polished. "Got myself a couple of home runs, too. But I decided maybe I wouldn't stay for the extra innings, if you know what I mean. I figure they're drinking me dry over there right now. Makes me want to rip my bracelet off, I'll tell ya. Where are the damn vampires when you need them, after all that?"

"You didn't take your bracelet off? Even when they gave you the chance?" Shane seemed surprised. Celia gave him a glare.

"No, I didn't. I ain't breaking my word, not unless I have to. Right now, I don't have to."

"If you take it off now, you may never need to put it on again."

Celia leveled a wrinkled finger at him. "Look, Collins, I know all about you and your dad. I don't hold with any of that. Morganville's an all-right place. You follow the rules and stay out of trouble—about like anyplace, I guess. You people wanted chaos. Well, this is what it looks like—people getting beaten, shops looted, houses burned. Sure, it'll settle down sometime, but into what? Maybe no place I'd want to live."

She turned away from him, shouldered her baseball

bat, and marched away to talk with a group of adults her own age.

Shane caught Claire looking at him, and shrugged. "Yeah," he sighed. "I know. She's got a point. But how do we know it won't be better if the vamps just—"

"Just what, Shane? *Die?* What about Michael, have you thought about him? Or Sam?" She stomped off.

"Where are you going?"

"To get a Coke!"

"Would you—"

"No!"

She twisted the cap off the Coke she'd retrieved from the fridge—which was stocked up again, although she knew it hadn't been when they'd left. Another favor from the house, she guessed, although how it went shopping on its own she had no idea.

The cold syrupy goodness hit her like a brick wall, but instead of energizing her, it made her feel weak and a little sick. Claire sank down in a chair at the kitchen table and put her head in her hands, suddenly overwhelmed.

It was all falling apart.

Amelie was calling the vampires, probably going to fight Bishop to the death. Morganville was ripping itself in pieces. And there was nothing she could *do*.

Well, there was one thing.

She retrieved and opened four more bottles of Coke, and delivered them to Hannah, Eve, Shane, and—because it felt mean to leave her out at a time like this—Monica.

Monica stared at the sweating bottle as if she suspected Claire had put rat poison in it. "What's this?"

"What does it look like? Take or don't, I don't really care." Claire put it down on the table next to where Monica sat, and went to curl up on the couch next to Shane. She checked her cell phone. The network was back up again, at least for the moment, and she had a ton of voice mails. Most were from Shane,

so she saved them to listen to later; two more were
from Eve, which she deleted, since they were instructions on where to find her.

The last one was from her mother. Claire caught
her breath, tears pricking in her eyes at the sound of
Mom's voice. Her mother sounded calm, at least—
mostly, anyway.

> *Claire, sweetie, I know I shouldn't be worrying
> but I am. Honey, call us. I've been hearing some
> terrible things about what's happening out there.
> Some of the people with us here are talking about
> fights and looting. If I don't hear from you
> soon—well, I don't know what we'll do, but your
> father's going crazy. So please, call us. We love
> you, honey. Bye.*

Claire got her breathing back under control, mainly
by sternly telling herself that she needed to sound together and completely in control to keep her parents
from charging out there into the craziness. She had it
more or less managed by the time the phone rang on
the other end, and when her mother picked it up, she
was able to say, "Hi, Mom," without making it sound
like she was about to burst into tears. "I got your
message. Is everything okay there?"

"Here? Claire, don't you be worrying about us!
We're just fine! Oh, honey, are you okay? Really?"

"Honestly, yes, I'm okay. Everything's—" She
couldn't say that everything was okay, because of
course it wasn't. It was, at best, kind of temporarily
stable. "It's quiet here. Shane's here, and Eve." Claire
remembered that Mom had liked Monica Morrell, and
rolled her eyes. Anything to calm her fears. "That girl
from the dorm, Monica, she's here, too."

"Oh, yes, Monica. I liked her." It really did seem to
help, which was not exactly an endorsement of Mom's

character-judging ability. "Her brother came by here to check on us about an hour ago. He's a nice boy."

Claire couldn't quite imagine referring to Richard Morrell as a *boy*, but she let it go. "He's kind of in charge of the town right now," she said. "You have the radio, right? The one we dropped off earlier?"

"Yes. We've been doing everything they say, of course. But honey, I'd really like it if you could come here. We want to have you home, with us."

"I know. I know, Mom. But I think I'd better stay here. It's important. I'll try to come by tomorrow, okay?"

They talked a little more, about nothing much, just chatter to make life seem kind of normal for a change. Mom was holding it together, but only barely; Claire could hear the manic quaver in her voice, could almost see the bright tears in her eyes. She was going on about how they'd had to move most of the boxes into the basement to make room for all the company— *company?*—and how she was afraid that Claire's stuff would get damp, and then she talked about all the toys in the boxes and how much Claire had enjoyed them when she was younger.

Normal Mom stuff.

Claire didn't interrupt, except to make soothing noises and acknowledgments when Mom paused. It helped, hearing Mom's voice, and she knew it was helping her to talk. But finally, when her mother ran down like a spring-wound clock, Claire agreed to all the parental requirements to be careful and watch out and wear warm clothes.

Good-bye seemed very final, and once Claire hung up, she sat in silence for a few minutes, staring at the screen of her cell phone.

On impulse, she tried to call Amelie. It rang and rang. No voice mail.

In the living room, Shane was organizing some kind of sentry duty. A lot of people had already crashed out in piles of pillows, blankets, sometimes just on a

spare rug. Claire edged around the prone bodies and
motioned to Shane that she was going upstairs. He
nodded and kept talking to the two guys he was with,
but his gaze followed her all the way.

Eve was in her bedroom, and there was a note on
the door that said DO NOT KNOCK OR I WILL KILL YOU.
THIS MEANS YOU, SHANE. Claire considered knocking,
but she was too tired to run away.

Her bedroom was dark. When she'd left in the
morning, Eve's kind-of-friend Miranda had been sleeping here, but she was gone, and the bed was neatly
made again. Claire sat down on the edge, staring out
the windows, and then pulled out clean underwear and
her last pair of blue jeans from the closet, plus a tight
black shirt Eve had lent her last week.

The shower felt like heaven. There was even
enough hot water for a change. Claire dried off,
fussed with her hair a bit, and got dressed. When she
came out, she listened at the stairs, but didn't hear
Shane talking anymore. Either he was being quiet, or
he'd gone to bed. She paused next to his door, wishing
she had the guts to knock, but she went on to her own
room instead.

Shane was inside, sitting on her bed. He looked up
when she opened the door, and his lips parted, but he
was silent for a long few seconds.

"I should go," he finally said, but he didn't get up.

Claire settled in next to him. It was all perfectly
correct, the two of them sitting fully dressed like this,
but somehow she felt like they were on the edge of a
cliff, both in danger of falling off.

It was exciting, and terrifying, and all kinds of
wrong.

"So what happened to you today?" she asked. "In
the Bloodmobile, I mean?"

"Nothing really. We drove to the edge of town and
parked outside the border, where we'd be able to see
anybody coming. A couple of vamps showed, trying
to make a withdrawal, but we sent them packing.

Bishop never made an appearance. Once we lost contact with the vampires, we figured we'd cruise around and see what was going on. We nearly got boxed in by a bunch of drunk idiots in pickup trucks, and then the vampires in the Bloodmobile went nuts—that call thing going off, I guess. I dropped them at the grain elevator—that was the biggest, darkest place I could find, and it casts a lot of shadows. I handed off the driving to Cesar Mercado. He's supposed to drive it all the way to Midland tonight, provided the barriers are down. Best we can do."

"What about the book? Did you leave it on board?"

In answer, Shane reached into his waistband and pulled out the small leather-bound volume. Amelie had added a lock on it, like a diary lock. Claire tried pressing the small, metal catch. It didn't open, of course.

"You think you should be fooling with that thing?" Shane asked.

"Probably not." She tried prying a couple of pages apart to peek at the script. All she could tell was that it was handwritten, and the paper looked relatively old. Oddly, when she sniffed it, the paper smelled like chemicals.

"What are you doing?" Shane looked like he couldn't decide whether to be repulsed or fascinated.

"I think somebody restored the paper," she said. "Like they do with really expensive old books and stuff. Comics, sometimes. They put chemicals on the paper to slow down the aging process, make the paper whiter again."

"Fascinating," Shane lied. "Gimme." He plucked the book from her hands and put it aside, on the other side of the bed. When she grabbed for it, he got in her way; they tangled, and somehow, he was lying prone on the bed and she was stretched awkwardly on top of him. His hands steadied her when she started to slide off.

"Oh," she murmured. "We shouldn't—"

"Definitely not."

"Then you should—"

"Yeah, I should."

But he didn't move, and neither did she. They just looked at each other, and then, very slowly, she lowered her lips to his.

It was a warm, sweet, wonderful kiss, and it seemed to go on forever. It also felt like it didn't last nearly long enough. Shane's hands skimmed up her sides, up her back, and cupped her damp hair as he kissed her more deeply. There were promises in that kiss.

"Okay, red flag," he said. He hadn't let her go, but there was about a half an inch of air between their lips. Claire's whole body felt alive and tingling, pulse pounding in her wrists and temples, warmth pooling like light in the center of her body.

"It's okay," she said. "I swear. Trust me."

"Hey, isn't that my line?"

"Not now."

Kissing Shane was the reward for surviving a long, hard, terrifying day. Being enfolded in his warmth felt like going to heaven on moonbeams. She kicked off her shoes, and, still fully dressed, crawled under the blankets. Shane hesitated.

"Trust me," she said again. "And you can keep your clothes on if you don't."

They'd done this before, but somehow it hadn't felt so . . . intimate. Claire pressed against him, back to front under the covers, and his arms went around her. Instant heat.

She swallowed and tried to remember all those good intentions she'd had as she felt Shane's breath whisper on the back of her neck, and then his lips brushed her skin. "So wrong," he murmured. "You're killing me, you know."

"Am not."

"On this, you'll have to trust *me*." His sigh made her shiver all the way to her bones. "I can't believe you brought Monica back here."

"Oh, come on. You wouldn't have left her out there, all alone. I know you better than that, Shane. Even as bad as she is—"

"The satanic incarnation of evil?"

"Maybe so, but I can't see you letting them get her and . . . hurt her." Claire turned around to face him, a squirming motion that made them wrestle for the covers. "What's going to happen? Do you know?"

"What am I, Miranda the teen screwed-up psychic? No, I don't know. All I know is that when we get up tomorrow, either the vampires will be back, or they won't. And then we'll have to make a choice about how we're going to go forward."

"Maybe we don't go forward. Maybe we wait."

"One thing I do know, Claire: you can't stay in the same place, not even for a day. You keep on moving. Maybe it's the right direction, maybe not, but you still move. Every second things change, like it or not."

She studied his face intently. "Is your dad here? Now?"

He grimaced. "Truthfully? No idea. I wouldn't be surprised. He'd know that it was time to move in and take command, if he could. And Manetti's a running buddy from way back. This kind of feels like Dad's behind it."

"But if he does take over, what happens to Michael? To Myrnin? To any other vampire out there?"

"Do you really need me to tell you?"

Claire shook her head. "He'll tell people they have to kill all the vampires, and then, he'll come after the Morrells, and anybody else he thinks is responsible for what happened to your family. Right?"

"Probably," Shane sighed.

"And you're going to let all that happen."

"I didn't say that."

"You didn't say you weren't, either. Don't tell me it's complicated, because it isn't. Either you stand up for something, or you lie down for it. You said that to me one time, and you were right." Claire burrowed closer into his arms. "Shane, you were *right* then. Be right now."

He touched her face. His fingers traced down her cheek, across her lips, and his eyes—she'd never seen that look in his eyes. In anyone's, really.

"In this whole screwed-up town, you're the only thing that's always been right to me," he whispered. "I love you, Claire." She saw something that might have been just a flash of panic go across his expression, but then he steadied again. "I can't believe I'm saying this, but I do. I love you."

He said something else, but the world had narrowed around her. Shane's lips kept moving, but all she heard were the same words echoing over and over inside her head like the tolling of a giant brass bell: *I love you.*

He sounded like it had taken him completely by surprise—not in a bad way, but more as if he hadn't really understood what he was feeling until that instant.

She blinked. It was as if she'd never really seen him before, and he was *beautiful.* More beautiful than any man she'd ever seen in her entire life, ever.

Whatever he was saying, she stopped it by kissing him. A lot. And for a very long time. When he finally backed up, he didn't go far, and this look in his eyes, this intense and overwhelming *need*—that was new, too.

And she liked it.

"I love you," he said, and kissed her so hard he took her breath away. There was more to it than before—more passion, more urgency, more . . . everything. It was as if she were caught in a tide, carried away, and she thought that if she never touched the shore again, it would be good to drown like this, just swim forever in all this richness.

Red flag, some part of her screamed, *come on, red flag. What are you doing?*

She wished it would just shut up.

"I love you, too," she whispered to him. Her voice

was shaking, and so were her hands where they rested on his chest. Under the soft T-shirt, his muscles were tensed, and she could feel every deep breath he took. "I'd do anything for you."

She meant it to be an invitation, but that was the thing that shocked sense back into him. He blinked. "Anything," he repeated, and squeezed his eyes shut. "Yeah. I'm getting that. Bad idea, Claire. Very, very bad."

"Today?" She laughed a little wildly. "Everything's crazy today. Why can't we be? Just once?"

"Because I made promises," he said. He wrapped his arms around her and pulled her close, and she felt a groan shake his whole body. "To your parents, to myself, to Michael. To you, Claire. I can't break my word. It's pretty much all I've got these days."

"But . . . what if—"

"Don't," he whispered in her ear. "Please don't. This is tough enough already."

He kissed her again, long and sweetly, and somehow, it tasted like tears this time. Like some kind of good-bye.

"I really do love you," he said, and smoothed away the damp streaks on her cheeks. "But I can't do this. Not now."

Before she could stop him, he slid out of bed, put on his shoes, and walked quickly to the door. She sat up, holding the covers close as if she were naked underneath, instead of fully clothed, and he hesitated there, one hand gripping the doorknob.

"Please stay," she said. "Shane—"

He shook his head. "If I stay, things are going to happen. You know it, and I know it, and we just can't do this. I know things are falling apart, but—" He hitched in a deep, painful breath. "No."

The sound of the door softly closing behind him went through her like a knife.

Claire rolled over, wretchedly hugging the pillow that smelled of his hair, sharing the warm place in the bed where his body had been, and thought about crying herself to sleep.

And then she thought of the dawning wonder in his eyes when he'd said, *I love you.*

No. It was no time to be crying.

When she did finally sleep, she felt safe.

10

The next day, there was no sign of the vampires, none at all. Claire checked the portal networks, but as far as she could tell, they were down. With nothing concrete to do, she helped around the house—cleaning, straightening, running errands. Richard Morrell came around to check on them. He looked a little better for having slept, which didn't mean he looked good, exactly.

When Eve wandered down, she looked almost as bad. She hadn't bothered with her Goth makeup, and her black hair was down in a lank, uncombed mess. She poured Richard some coffee from the ever-brewing pot, handed it over, and said, "How's Michael?"

Richard blew on the hot surface in the cup without looking at her. "He's at City Hall. We moved all the vampires we still had into the jail, for safekeeping."

Eve's face crumpled in anguish. Shane put a hand on her shoulder, and she pulled in a damp breath and got control of herself.

"Right," she said. "That's probably for the best, you're right." She sipped from her own battered coffee mug. "What's it like out there?" *Out there* meant beyond Lot Street, which remained eerily quiet.

"Not so good," Richard said. His voice sounded hoarse and dull, as if he'd yelled all the edges off it. "About half the stores are shut down, and some of those are burned or looted. We don't have enough police and volunteers to be everywhere. Some of the store owners armed up and are guarding their own places—I don't like it, but it's probably the best option until everybody settles down and sobers up. The problem isn't everybody, but it's a good portion of the town who's been down and angry a long time. You heard they raided the Barfly?"

"Yeah, we heard," Shane said.

"Well, that was just the beginning. Dolores Thompson's place got broken into, and then they went to the warehouses and found the bonded liquor storage. Those who were inclined to deal with all this by getting drunk and mean have had a real holiday."

"We saw the mobs," Eve said, and glanced at Claire. "Um, about your sister—"

"Yeah, thanks for taking care of her. Trust my idiot sister to go running around in her red convertible during a riot. She's damn lucky they didn't kill her."

They would have, Claire was certain of that. "I guess you're taking her with you . . . ?"

Richard gave her a thin smile. "Not the greatest houseguest?"

Actually, Monica had been very quiet. Claire had found her curled up on the couch, wrapped in a blanket, sound asleep. She'd looked pale and tired and bruised, and much younger than Claire had ever seen her. "She's been okay." She shrugged. "But I'll bet she'd rather be with her family."

"Her *family's* under protective custody downtown. My dad nearly got dragged off by a bunch of yahoos yelling about taxes or something. My mom—" Richard shook his head, as if he wanted to drive the pictures right out of his mind. "Anyway. Unless she likes four walls and a locked door, I don't think she's going to be very happy. And you know Monica: if she's not happy—"

"Nobody is," Shane finished for him. "Well, I want her out of our house. Sorry, man, but we did our duty and all. Past this point, she'd have to be a friend to keep crashing here. Which, you know, she isn't. Ever."

"Then I'll take her off your hands." Richard set the cup down and stood. "Thanks for the coffee. Seems like that's all that's keeping me going right now."

"Richard . . ." Eve rose, too. "Seriously, what's it like out there? What's going to happen?"

"With any luck, the drunks will sober up or pass out, and those who've been running around looking for people to punish will get sore feet and aching muscles and go home to get some sleep."

"Not like we've had a lot of luck so far, though," Shane said.

"No," Richard agreed. "That we haven't. But I have to say, we can't keep things locked down. People have to work, the schools have to open, and for that, we need something like normal life around here. So we're working on that. Power and water's on, phone lines are back up. TV and radio are broadcasting. I'm hoping that calms people down. We've got police patrols overlapping all through town, and we can be anywhere in under two minutes. One thing, though: we're getting word that there's bad weather in the forecast. Some kind of real big front heading toward us tonight. I'm not too happy about that, but maybe it'll keep the crazies off the streets for a while. Even riots don't like rain."

"What about the university?" Claire asked. "Are they open?"

"Open and classes are running, believe it or not. We passed off some of the disturbances as role-playing in the disaster drill, and said that the looting and burning was part of the exercise. Some of them believed us."

"But . . . no word about the vampires?"

Richard was silent for a moment, and then he said, "No. Not exactly."

"Then what?"

"We found some bodies, before dawn," he said.

"All vamps. All killed with silver or decapitation. Some of them—I knew some of them. Thing is, I don't think they were killed by Bishop. From the looks of things, they were caught by a mob."

Claire caught her breath. Eve covered her mouth. "Who—?"

"Bernard Temple, Sally Christien, Tien Ma, and Charles Effords."

Eve lowered her hand to say, "Charles Effords? Like, Miranda's Charles? Her Protector?"

"Yeah. From the state of the bodies, I'd guess he was the primary target. Nobody loves a pedophile."

"Nobody except Miranda," Eve said. "She's going to be really scared now."

"Yeah, about that . . ." Richard hesitated, then plunged forward. "Miranda's gone."

"Gone?"

"Disappeared. We've been looking for her. Her parents reported her missing early last night. I'm hoping she wasn't with Charles when the mob caught up to him. You see her, you call me, okay?"

Eve's lips shaped the agreement, but no sound came out.

Richard checked his watch. "Got to go," he said. "Usual drill: lock the doors, check IDs on anybody you're not expecting who shows up. If you hear from any vampire, or hear anything *about* the vampires, you call immediately. Use the coded radios, not the phone lines. And be careful."

Eve swallowed hard, and nodded. "Can I see Michael?"

He paused, as if that hadn't occurred to him, then shrugged. "Come on."

"We're all going," Shane said.

It was an uncomfortable ride to City Hall, where the jail was located, mainly because although the police cruiser was large, it wasn't big enough to have Richard, Monica, Eve, Shane, and Claire all sharing

the ride. Monica had taken the front seat, sliding close
to her brother, and Claire had squeezed in with her
friends in the back.

They didn't talk, not even when they cruised past
burned-out, broken hulks of homes and stores. There
weren't any fires today, or any mobs that Claire spotted. It all seemed quiet.

Richard drove past a police barricade around City
Hall and parked in the underground garage. "I'm taking Monica to my parents'," he said. "You guys go
on down to the cells. I'll be there in a minute."

It took a lot more than a minute for them to gain
access to Michael; the vampires—all five of those the
humans still had in custody—were housed in a special
section, away from daylight and in reinforced cells.
It reminded Claire, with an unpleasant lurch, of the
vampires in the cells where Myrnin was usually locked
up, for his own protection. Had anyone fed them? Had
anyone even tried?

She didn't know three of the vampires, but she
knew the last two. "Sam!" she blurted, and rushed to
the bars. Michael's grandfather was lying on the bunk,
one pale hand over his eyes, but he sat up when she
called his name. Claire could definitely see the resemblance between Michael and Sam—the same basic bone
structure, only Michael's hair was a bright gold, and
Sam's was red.

"Get me out," Sam said, and lunged for the door.
He rattled the cage with unexpected violence. Claire
fell back, openmouthed. "Open the door and get me
out, Claire! *Now!*"

"Don't listen to him," Michael said. He was standing at the bars of his own cell, leaning against them,
and he looked tired. "Hey, guys. Did you bring me a
lockpick in a cupcake or something?"

"I had the cupcake, but I ate it. Hard times, man."
Shane extended his hand. Michael reached through
the bars and took it, shook solemnly, and then Eve
threw herself against the metal to try to hug him. It

was awkward, but Claire saw the relief spread over Michael, no matter how odd it was with the bars between the two of them. He kissed Eve, and Claire had to look away from that, because it seemed like such a private kind of moment.

Sam rattled his cage again. "Claire, open the door! I need to get to Amelie!"

The policeman who'd escorted them down to the cells pushed off from the wall and said, "Calm down, Mr. Glass. You're not going anywhere; you know that." He shifted his attention to Shane and Claire. "He's been like that since the beginning. We had to trank him twice; he was hurting himself trying to get out. He's worse than all the others. They seem to have calmed down. Not him."

No, Sam definitely hadn't calmed down. As Claire watched, he tensed his muscles and tried to force the lock, but subsided in panting frustration and stumbled back to his bunk. "I have to go," he muttered. "Please, I need to go. She needs me. Amelie—"

Claire looked at Michael, who didn't seem to be nearly as distressed. "Um . . . sorry to ask, but . . . are you feeling like that? Like Sam?"

"No," Michael said. His eyes were still closed. "For a while there was this . . . call, but it stopped about three hours ago."

"Then why is Sam—"

"It's not the call," Michael said. "It's Sam. It's killing him, knowing she's out there in trouble and he can't help her."

Sam put his head in his hands, the picture of misery. Claire exchanged a look with Shane. "Sam," she said. "What's happening? Do you know?"

"People are dying, that's what's happening," he said. "Amelie's in trouble. I need to go to her. I can't just sit here!"

He threw himself at the bars again, kicking hard enough to make the metal ring like a bell.

"Well, that's where you're going to stay," the policeman said, not exactly unsympathetically. "The way you're acting, you'd go running out into the sunlight, and that wouldn't do her or you a bit of good, now, would it?"

"I could have gone hours ago before sunrise," Sam snapped. *"Hours ago."*

"And now you have to wait for dark."

That earned the policeman a full-out vicious snarl, and Sam's eyes flared into bright crimson. Everybody stayed back, and when Sam subsided this time, it seemed to be for good. He withdrew to his bunk, lay down, and turned his back to them.

"Man," Shane breathed softly. "He's a little intense, huh?"

From what the policeman told them—and Richard, when he rejoined them—all the captured vampires had been at about the same level of violence, at first. Now it was just Sam, and as Michael said, it didn't seem to be Amelie's summons that was driving him. . . . It was fear for Amelie herself.

It was love.

"Step back, please," the policeman said to Eve. She looked over her shoulder at him, then at Michael. He kissed her, and let go.

She did take a step back, but it was a tiny one. "So—are you okay? Really?"

"Sure. It's not exactly the Ritz, but it's not bad. They're not keeping us here to hurt us, I know that." Michael stretched out a finger and touched her lips. "I'll be back soon."

"Better be," Eve said. She mock-bit at his finger. "I could totally date somebody else, you know."

"And I could rent out your room."

"And I could put your game console on eBay."

"Hey," Shane protested. "Now you're just being mean."

"See what I mean? You need to come home, or it's

total chaos. Dogs and cats, living together." Eve's voice dropped, but not quite to a whisper. "And I miss you. I miss seeing you. I miss you all the time."

"I miss you, too," Michael murmured, then blinked and looked at Claire and Shane. "I mean, I miss all of you."

"Sure you do," Shane agreed. "But not in that way, I hope."

"Shut up, dude. Don't make me come out there."

Shane turned to the policeman. "See? He's fine."

"I was more worried about you guys," Michael confessed. "Everything okay at the house?"

"I have to burn a blouse Monica borrowed," Claire said. "Otherwise, we're good."

They tried to talk a while longer, but somehow, Sam's silent, rigid back turned toward them made conversation seem more desperate than fun. He was really hurting, and Claire didn't know—short of letting him go for a jog in the noontime sun—how to make it any better. She didn't know where Amelie was, and with the portals shut, she doubted she could even know where to start looking.

Amelie had gathered up an army—whatever Bishop hadn't grabbed first—but what she was doing with it was anybody's guess. Claire didn't have a clue.

So in the end, she hugged Michael and told Sam it would all be okay, and they left.

"If they stay calm through the day, I'll let them out tonight," Richard said. "But I'm worried about letting them roam around on their own. What happened to Charles and the others could keep on happening. Captain Obvious used to be our biggest threat, but now we don't know who's out there, or what they're planning. And we can't count on the vampires to be able to protect themselves right now."

"My dad would say that it's about time the tables turned," Shane said.

Richard fixed him with a long stare. "Is that what you say, too?"

Shane looked at Michael, and at Sam. "No," he said. "Not anymore."

The day went on quietly. Claire got out her books and spent part of the day trying to study, but she couldn't get her brain to stop spinning. Every few minutes, she checked her e-mail and her phone, hoping for something, anything, from Amelie. *You can't just leave us like this. We don't know what to do.*

Except keep moving forward. Like Shane had said, they couldn't stay still. The world kept on turning.

Eve drove Claire to her parents' house in the afternoon, where she had cake and iced tea and listened to her mother's frantic flow of good cheer. Her dad looked sallow and unwell, and she worried about his heart, as always. But he seemed okay when he told her he loved her, and that he worried, and that he wanted her to move back home.

Just when she thought they'd gotten past that . . .

Claire exchanged a quick look with Eve. "Maybe we should talk about that when things get back to normal?" As if they ever were normal in Morganville. "Next week?"

Dad nodded. "Fine, but I'm not going to change my mind, Claire. You're better off here, at home." Whatever spell Mr. Bishop had cast over her father, it was still working great; he was single-minded about wanting her out of the Glass House. And maybe it hadn't been a spell at all; maybe it was just normal parental instinct.

Claire crammed her mouth with cake and pretended not to hear, and asked her mom about the new curtains. That filled another twenty minutes, and then Eve was able to make excuses about needing to get home, and then they were in the car.

"Wow," Eve said, and started the engine. "So. Are you going to do it? Move in with them?"

Claire shrugged helplessly. "I don't know. I don't know if we're going to get through the day! It's kind of hard to make plans." She wasn't going to say anything, truly, she wasn't, but the words had been boiling and bubbling inside her all day, and as Eve put the car in drive, Claire said, "Shane said he loved me."

Eve hit the brakes, hard enough to make their seat belts click in place. "Shane *what*? Said *what*?"

"Shane said he loved me."

"Okay, first impressions—fantastic, good, that's what I was hoping you'd said." Eve took a deep breath and let up on the brake, steering out into the deserted street. "Second impressions, well, I hope that you two . . . um . . . how can I put this? Watch yourselves?"

"You mean, don't have sex? We won't." Claire said it with a little bit of an edge. "Even if we wanted to. I mean, he promised, and he's not going to break that promise, not even if I say it's okay."

"Oh. *Oh.*" Eve stared at her, wide-eyed, for way too long for road safety. "You're kidding! Wait, you're not. He said he loved you, and then he said—"

"No," Claire said. "He said no."

"Oh." Funny, how many meanings that word could have. This time it was full of sympathy. "You know, that makes him—"

"Great? Superbly awesome? Yeah, I know. I just—" Claire threw up her hands. "I just *want* him, okay?"

"He'll still be there in a couple of months, Claire. At seventeen, you're not a kid, at least in Texas."

"You've put some thought into this."

"Not me," Eve said, and gave her an apologetic look.

"*Shane?* You mean—you mean you talked about this? With Shane?"

"He needed some girl guidance. I mean, he's taking this really seriously—a lot more seriously than I expected. He wants to do the right thing. That's cool, right? I think that's cool. Most guys, it's just, whatever."

Claire clenched her jaw so hard she felt her teeth grinding. "I can't believe he talked to you about it!"

"Well, you're talking to me about it."

"He's a guy!"

"Guys occasionally talk, believe it or not. Something more than *pass the beer* or *where's the porn?*" Eve turned the corner, and they cruised past a couple of slow blocks of houses, some people out walking, an elementary school with a TEMPORARILY CLOSED sign out front. "You didn't exactly ask for advice, but I'm going to give it: don't rush this. You may think you're good to go, but give it some time. It's not like you have a sell-by date or anything."

Despite her annoyance, Claire had to laugh. "Feels like it right now."

"Well, duh. Hormones!"

"So how old were you when—"

"Too young. I speak from experience, grasshopper." Eve's expression went distant for a second. "I wish I'd waited for Michael."

That was, for some reason, kind of a shock, and Claire blinked. She remembered some things, and felt deeply uncomfortable. "Uh . . . did Brandon . . . ?" Because Brandon had been her family's Protector vampire, and he'd been a complete creep. She couldn't imagine much worse than having Brandon be your first.

"No. Not that he didn't want to, but no, it wasn't Brandon."

"Who?"

"Sorry. Off-limits."

Claire blinked. There wasn't much Eve considered off-limits. "Really?"

"Really." Eve pulled the car up to the curb. "Bottom line? If Shane says he loves you, he does, full stop. He wouldn't say it if he didn't mean it, all the way. He's not the kind of guy to tell you what you want to hear. That makes you really, really lucky. You should remember that."

Claire was trying, really, but from time to time that moment came back to her, that blinding, searing moment when he'd looked into her face and said those words, and she'd seen that amazing light in his eyes. She'd wanted to see it again, over and over. Instead, she'd seen him walk away.

It felt romantic. It also felt frustrating, on some level she didn't even remember feeling before. And now there was something new: doubt. *Maybe that was my fault. Maybe I was supposed to do something I didn't do. Some signal I didn't give him.*

Eve read her expression just fine. "You'll be okay," she said, and laughed just a little. "Give the guy a break. He's the second actual gentleman I've ever met. It doesn't mean he doesn't want to throw you on the bed and go. Just means he won't, right now. Which you have to admit: kinda hot."

Put in those terms, it kind of was.

As it got closer to nightfall, Richard called to say he was letting Michael go. For the second time, the three of them piled into the car and went racing to City Hall. The barricades had mostly come down. According to the radio and television, it had been a very quiet day, with no reports of violence. Store owners—the human ones, anyway—were planning on reopening in the morning. Schools would be in session.

Life was going on, and Mayor Morrell was expected to come out with some kind of a speech. Not that anybody would listen.

"Are they letting Sam out, too?" Claire asked, as Eve parked in the underground lot.

"Apparently. Richard doesn't think he can really keep anybody much longer. Some kind of town ordinance, which means law and order really is back in fashion. Plus, I think he's really afraid Sam's going to hurt himself if this goes on. And also, maybe he thinks he can follow Sam to find Amelie." Eve scanned the dark structure—there were a few dark-tinted cars in the lot, but then, there always were. The rest of the vehicles looked like they were human owned. "You guys see anything?"

"Like what? A big sign saying This Is a Trap?" Shane opened his door and got out, taking Claire's hand to help her. He didn't drop it once she was standing beside him. "Not that I wouldn't put it past some of our finer citizens. But no, I don't see anything."

Michael was being let out of his cell when they arrived, and there were hugs and handshakes. The other vampires didn't have anyone to help them, and looked a little confused about what they were supposed to do.

Not Sam.

"Sam, wait!" Michael grabbed his arm on the way past, dragging his grandfather to a stop. Looking at them standing together, Claire was struck again by how alike they were. And always would be, she supposed, given that neither one of them was going to age any more. "You can't go charging off by yourself. You don't even know where she is. Running around town on your white horse will get you really, truly killed."

"Doing nothing will get *her* killed. I can't have that, Michael. None of this means anything to me if she dies." Sam shook Michael's hand away. "I'm not asking you to come with me. I'm just telling you not to get in my way."

"Grandpa—"

"Exactly. Do as you're told." Sam could move vampire-quick when he wanted to, and he was gone almost before the words hit Claire's ears—a blur, heading for the exit.

"So much for trying to figure out where she is from where he goes," Shane said. "Unless you've got light speed under the hood of that car, Eve."

Michael looked after him with a strange expression on his face—anger, regret, sorrow. Then he hugged Eve closer and kissed the top of her head.

"Well, I guess my family's no more screwed up than anybody else's," he said.

Eve nodded. "Let's recap. My dad was an abusive jerk—"

"Mine, too." Shane raised his hand.

"Thank you. My brother's a psycho backstabber—"

Shane said, "You don't even want to talk about my dad."

"Point. So, in short, Michael, your family is *awesome* by comparison. Bloodsucking, maybe. But kind of awesome."

Michael sighed. "Doesn't really feel like it at the moment."

"It will." Eve was suddenly very serious. "But Shane and I don't have that to look forward to, you know. You're our only real family now."

"I know," Michael said. "Let's go home."

11

Home was theirs again. The refugees were all out now, leaving a house that badly needed picking up and cleaning—not that anybody had gone out of their way to trash the place, but with that many people coming and going, things happened. Claire grabbed a trash bag and began clearing away paper plates, old Styrofoam cups half full of stale coffee, crumpled wrappers, and papers. Shane fired up the video game, apparently back in the mood to kill zombies. Michael took his guitar out of its case and tuned it, but he kept getting up to stare out the windows, restless and worried.

"What?" Eve asked. She'd heated up leftover spaghetti out of the refrigerator, and tried to hand Michael a plate first. "Do you see something?"

"Nothing," he said, and gave her a quick, strained smile as he waved away the food. "Not really hungry, though. Sorry."

"More for me," Shane said, and grabbed the plate. He propped it on his lap and forked spaghetti into his mouth. "Seriously. You all right? Because you never turn down food."

Michael didn't answer. He stared out into the dark.

"You're worried," Eve said. "About Sam?"

"Sam and everybody else. This is nuts. What's going on here—" Michael checked the locks on the window, but as a kind of automatic motion, as though his mind wasn't really on it. "Why hasn't Bishop taken over?

What's he *doing* out there? Why aren't we seeing the fight?"

"Maybe Amelie's kicking his ass out there in the shadows somewhere." Shane shoveled in more spaghetti.

"No. She's not. I can feel that. I think—I think she's in hiding. With the rest of her followers, the vampires, anyway."

Shane stopped chewing. "You know where they are?"

"Not really. I just feel—" Michael shook his head. "It's gone. Sorry. But I feel like things are changing. Coming to a head."

Claire had just taken a plate of warm pasta when they all heard the thump of footsteps overhead. They looked up, and then at each other, in silence. Michael pointed to himself and the stairs, and they all nodded. Eve opened a drawer in the end table and took out three sharpened stakes; she tossed one to Shane, one to Claire, and kept one in a white-knuckled grip.

Michael ascended the stairs without a sound, and disappeared.

He didn't come back down. Instead, there was a swirl of black coat and stained white balloon pants tucked into black boots; then Myrnin leaned over the railing to say, "Upstairs, all of you. I need you."

"Um . . ." Eve looked at Shane. Shane looked at Claire.

Claire followed Myrnin. "Trust me," she said. "It won't do any good to say no."

Michael was waiting in the hallway, next to the open, secret door. He led the way up.

Whatever Claire had been expecting to see, it wasn't a *crowd*, but that was what was waiting upstairs in the hidden room on the third floor. She stared in confusion at the room full of people, then moved out of the way for Shane and Eve to join her and Michael.

Myrnin came last. "Claire, I believe you know Theo Goldman and his family."

The faces came into focus. She *had* met them—in that museum thing, when they'd been on the way to rescue Myrnin. Theo Goldman had spoken to Amelie. He'd said they wouldn't fight.

But it looked to Claire like they'd been in a fight anyway. Vampires didn't bruise, exactly, but she could see torn clothes and smears of blood, and they all looked exhausted and somehow—hollow. Theo was worst of all. His kind face seemed made of nothing but lines and wrinkles now, as if he'd aged a hundred years in a couple of days.

"I'm sorry," he said, "but we had no other place to go. Amelie—I hoped that she was here, that she would give us refuge. We've been everywhere else."

Claire remembered there being more of them, somehow—yes, there were at least two people missing. One human, one vampire. "What happened? I thought you were safe where you were!"

"We were," Theo said. "Then we weren't. That's what wars are like. The safe places don't stay safe. Someone knew where we were, or suspected. Around dawn yesterday, a mob broke in the doors looking for us. Jochen—" He looked at his wife, and she bowed her head. "Our son Jochen, he gave his life to delay them. So did our human friend William. We've been hiding, moving from place to place, trying not to be driven out in the sun."

"How did you get here?" Michael asked. He seemed wary. Claire didn't blame him.

"I brought them," Myrnin said. "I've been trying to find those who are left." He crouched down next to one of the young vampire girls and stroked her hair. She smiled at him, but it was a fragile, frightened smile. "They can stay here for now. This room isn't common knowledge. I've left open the portal in the attic in case they have to flee, but it's one way only, leading out. It's a last resort."

"Are there others? Out there?" Claire asked.

"Very few on their own. Most are either with

Bishop, with Amelie, or"—Myrnin spread his hands—
"gone."

"What are they doing? Amelie and Bishop?"

"Moving their forces. They're trying to find an advantage, pick the most favorable ground. It won't last."
Myrnin shrugged. "Sooner or later, sometime tonight,
they'll clash, and then they'll fight. Someone will win,
and someone will lose. And in the morning, Morganville will know its fate."

That was creepy. *Really* creepy. Claire shivered and
looked at the others, but nobody seemed to have anything to say.

"Claire. Attend me," Myrnin said, and walked with
her to one corner of the room. "Have you spoken
with your doctor friend?"

"I tried. I couldn't get through to him. Myrnin, are
you . . . okay?"

"Not for much longer," he said, in that clinical way
he had right before the drugs wore off. "I won't be
safe to be around without another dose of some sort.
Can you get it for me?"

"There's none in your lab—"

"I've been there. Bishop got there first. I shall need
a good bit of glassware, and a completely new library." He said it lightly, but Claire could see the
tension in his face and the shadow in his dark, gleaming eyes. "He tried to destroy the portals, cut off
Amelie's movements. I managed to patch things together, but I shall need to instruct you in how it's
done. Soon. In case—"

He didn't need to finish. Claire nodded slowly.
"You should go," she said. "Is the prison safe? The
one where you keep the sickest ones?"

"Bishop finds nothing to interest him there, so yes.
He will ignore it awhile longer. I'll lock myself in for
a while, until you come with the drug." Myrnin bent
over her, suddenly very focused and very intent. "We
must refine the serum, Claire. We *must* distribute it.

The stress, the fighting—it's accelerating the disease. I've seen signs of it in Theo, even in Sam. If we don't act soon, I'm afraid we may begin to lose more to confusion and fear. They won't even be able to defend themselves."

Claire swallowed. "I'll get on it."

He took her hand and kissed it lightly. His lips felt dry as dust, but it still left a tingle in her fingers. "I know you will, my girl. Now, let's rejoin your friends."

"How long do they need to be here?" Eve asked, as they moved closer. She asked not unkindly, but she seemed nervous, too. There were, Claire thought, an awful lot of near-stranger vampire guests. "I mean, we don't have a lot of blood in the house. . . ."

Theo smiled. Claire remembered, with a sharp feeling of alarm, what he'd said to Amelie back at the museum, and she didn't like that smile at all, not even when he said, "We won't require much. We can provide for ourselves."

"He means, they can munch on their human friends, like takeout," Claire said. "No. Not in our house."

Myrnin frowned. "This is hardly the time to be—"

"This is *exactly* the time, and you know it. Did anybody ask *them* if they wanted to be snack packs?" The two remaining humans, both women, looked horrified. "I didn't think so."

Theo's expression didn't change. "What we do is our own affair. We won't hurt them, you know."

"Unless you're getting your plasma by osmosis, I don't really know how you can promise that."

Theo's eyes flared with banked fire. "What do you want us to do? Starve? Even the youngest of us?"

Eve cleared her throat. "Actually, I know where there's a big supply of blood. If somebody will go with me to get it."

"Oh, hell no," Shane said. "Not out in the dark. Besides, the place is locked up."

Eve reached in her pocket and took out her key

ring. She flipped until she found one key in particular, and held it up. "I never turned in my key," she said. "I used to open and close, you know."

Myrnin gazed at her thoughtfully. "There's no portal to Common Grounds. It's off the network. That means any vampire in it will be trapped in daylight."

"No. There's underground access to the tunnels; I've seen it. Oliver sent some people out using it while I was there." Eve gave him a bright, brittle smile. "I say we move your friends there. Also, there's coffee. You guys like coffee, right? Everybody likes coffee."

Theo ignored her, and looked to Myrnin for an answer. "Is it better?"

"It's more defensible," Myrnin said. "Steel shutters. If there's underground access—yes. It would make a good base of operations." He turned to Eve. "We'll require your services to drive."

He said it as if Eve were the help, and Claire felt her face flame hot. "Excuse me? How about a *please* in there somewhere, since you're asking for a favor?"

Myrnin's eyes turned dark and very cold. "You seem to have forgotten that I employ you, Claire. That I *own* you, in some sense. I am not required to say please and thank you to you, your friends, or *any* human walking the streets." He blinked, and was back to the Myrnin she normally saw. "However, I do take your point. Yes. *Please* drive us to Common Grounds, dear lady. I would be extravagantly, embarrassingly grateful."

He did all but kiss her hand. Eve, not surprisingly, could say nothing but yes.

Claire settled for an eye roll big enough to make her head hurt. "You can't all fit," she pointed out. "In Eve's car, I mean."

"And she's not taking you alone, anyway," Michael said. "My car's in the garage. I can take the rest of you. Shane, Claire—"

"Staying here, since you'll need the space," Shane said. "Sounds like a plan. Look, if there are people looking for them, you ought to get them moving. I'll call Richard. He can assign a couple of cops to guard Common Grounds."

"No," Myrnin said. "No police. We can't trust them."

"We can't?"

"Some of them have been working with Bishop, and with the human mobs. I have proof of that. We can't take the risk."

"But Richard—," Claire said, and subsided when she got Myrnin's glare. "Right. Okay. On your own, got it."

Eve didn't want to be dragged into it, but she went without much of a protest—the number of fangs in the room might have had something to do with it. As the Goldmans and Myrnin, Eve and Michael walked downstairs, Shane held Claire back to say, "We've got to figure out how to lock this place up. In case."

"You mean, against—" She gestured vaguely at the vampires. He nodded. "But if Michael lives here, and we live here, the house can't just bar a whole group of people from entry. It has to be done one at a time—at least that's what I understood. And no, before you ask me, I don't know how it works. Or how to fool it. I think only Amelie has the keys to that."

He looked disappointed. "How about closing off these weird doors Myrnin and Amelie are popping through?"

"I can work them. That doesn't mean I can turn them on and off."

"Great." He looked around the room, then took a seat on the old Victorian couch. "So we're like Undead Grand Central Station. Not really loving that so much. Can Bishop come through?"

It was a question that Claire had been thinking about, and it creeped her out to have to say, "I don't know. Maybe. But from what Myrnin said, he set the doorway to exit-only. So maybe we just . . . wait."

Robbed of doing anything heroic, or for that matter even useful, she warmed up the spaghetti again, and she and Shane ate it and watched some mindless TV show while jumping at every noise and creak, with weapons handy. When the kitchen door banged open nearly an hour later, Claire almost needed a heart transplant—until she heard Eve yell, "We're home! Ooooh, spaghetti. I'm starved." Eve came in holding a plate and shoveling pasta into her mouth as she walked. Michael was right behind her.

"No problems?" Shane asked. Eve shook her head, chewing a mouthful of spaghetti.

"They should be fine there. Nobody saw us get them inside, and until Oliver turns up, nobody is going to need to get in there for a while."

"What about Myrnin?"

Eve swallowed, almost choked, and Michael patted her kindly on the back. She beamed at him. "Myrnin? Oh yeah. He did a Batman and took off into the night. What is *with* that guy, Claire? If he was a superhero, he'd be Bipolar Man."

The drugs were the problem. Claire needed to get more, and she needed to work on that cure Myrnin had found. That was just as important as anything else . . . providing there were any vampires left, anyway.

They had dinner, and at least it was the four of them again, sitting around the table, talking as if the world were normal, even if all of them knew it wasn't. Shane seemed especially jumpy, which wasn't like him at all.

For her part, Claire was just tired to the bone of being scared, and when she went upstairs, she was asleep the minute she crawled between the covers.

But sleep didn't mean it was restful, or peaceful.

She dreamed that somewhere, Amelie was playing chess, moving her pieces at lightning speed across a black-and-white board. Bishop sat across from her, grinning with too many teeth, and when he took her rook, it turned into a miniature version of Claire, and suddenly both the vampires were huge and she was so small, so small, stranded out in the open.

Bishop picked her up and squeezed her in his white

hand, and blood drops fell onto the white squares of the chessboard.

Amelie frowned, watching Bishop squeeze her, and put out a delicate fingertip to touch the drops of blood. Claire struggled and screamed.

Amelie tasted her blood, and smiled.

Claire woke up with a convulsive shudder, huddled in her blankets. It was still dark outside the windows, though the sky was getting lighter, and the house was very, very quiet.

Her phone was buzzing in vibrate mode on the bedside table. She picked it up and found a text message from the university's alert system.

CLASSES RETURN TO NORMAL SCHEDULE EFFECTIVE 7 A.M. TODAY.

School seemed like a million miles away, another world that didn't mean anything to her anymore, but it would get her on campus, and there were things she needed there. Claire scrolled down her phone list and found Dr. Robert Mills, but there was no immediate answer on his cell. She checked the clock, winced at the early hour, but slid out of bed and began grabbing things out of drawers. That didn't take a lot of time. She was down to the last of everything. Laundry was starting to be a genuine priority.

She dialed his phone again after she'd dressed.

"Hello?" Dr. Mills sounded as if she'd dragged him out of a deep, probably happy sleep. *He* probably hadn't been dreaming about being squeezed dry by Mr. Bishop.

"It's Claire," she said. "I'm sorry to call so early—"

"Is it early? Oh. Been up all night, just fell asleep." He yawned. "Glad you're all right, Claire."

"Are you at the hospital?"

"No. The hospital's going to need a lot of work before it's even halfway ready for the kind of work I need to do." Another jaw-cracking yawn. "Sorry. I'm on campus, in the Life Sciences Building. Lab Seventeen. We have some roll-away beds here."

"We?"

"My wife and kids are with me. I didn't want to leave them on their own out there."

Claire didn't blame him. "I've got something for you to do, and I need some of the drug," she said. "It could be really important. I'll be at school in about twenty minutes, okay?"

"Okay. Don't come here. My kids are asleep right now. Let's meet somewhere else."

"The on-campus coffee bar," she said. "It's in the University Center."

"Trust me, I know where it is. Twenty minutes."

She was already heading for the door.

With no sounds coming from any of the other rooms, Claire figured her housemates were all crashed out, exhausted. She didn't know why she wasn't, except for a suppressed, vibrating fear inside her that if she slept any more, something bad was going to happen.

Showered, dressed in her last not-very-good clothes, she grabbed up her backpack and repacked it. Her dart gun was out of darts anyway, so she left it behind. The samples Myrnin had prepared of Bishop's blood went into a sturdy padded box, and on impulse, she added a couple of stakes and the silver knife Amelie had given her.

And books.

It was the first time Claire had been on foot in Morganville since the rioting had started, and it was eerie. The town was quiet again, but stores had broken windows, some boarded over; there were some buildings reduced to burned-out hulks, with blind, open doorways. Broken bottles were on the sidewalks and spots of what looked like blood on the concrete—and, in places, dark splashes.

Claire hurried past it all, even past Common Grounds, where the steel shutters were down inside the windows. There was no sign of anyone within. She imagined Theo Goldman standing there watching her from cover, and waved a little, just a waggle of fingers.

She didn't really expect a response.

The gates of the university were open, and the guards were gone. Claire jogged along the sidewalk, going up the hill and around the curve, and began to see students up and moving, even so early in the morning. As she got closer to the central cluster of buildings, the foot traffic intensified, and here and there she saw alert campus police walking in pairs, watching for trouble.

The students didn't seem to notice anything at all. Not for the first time, Claire wondered if Amelie's semipsychic network that cut Morganville off from the world also kept people on campus clueless.

She didn't like to think they were just naturally that stupid. Then again, she'd been to some of the parties.

The University Center had opened its doors only a few minutes before, and the coffee barista was just taking the chairs down from the tables. Usually it would have been Eve on duty, but instead, it was one of the university staffers, on loan from the food service most likely. He didn't exactly look happy to be there. Claire tried to be nice, and finally got a smile from him as he handed her a mocha and took her cash.

"I wouldn't be here," he confessed, "except that they're paying us triple to be here the rest of the week."

"Really? Wow. I'll tell Eve. She could use the money."

"Yeah, get her in here. I'm not good at this coffee stuff. Give me the plain stuff. Water, beans—can't really screw that up. This espresso is hard."

Claire decided, after tasting the mocha, that he was right. He really wasn't cut out for it. She sipped it anyway, and took a seat where she could watch the majority of the UC entrances for Dr. Mills.

She almost didn't recognize him. He'd shed his white

doctor's coat, of course, but somehow she'd never expected to see someone like him wearing a zip-up hoodie, sweatpants, and sneakers. He was more the suit-and-tie type. He ordered plain coffee—good choice—and came to join her at the table.

Dr. Mills was medium everything, and he blended in at the university just as easily as he had at the hospital. He'd have made a good spy, Claire thought. He had one of those faces—young from one angle, older from another, with nothing you could really remember later about it.

But he had a nice, comforting smile. She supposed that would be a real asset in a doctor.

"Morning," he said, and gulped coffee. His eyes were bloodshot and red rimmed. "I'm going back to the hospital later today. Damage assessments, and we've already reopened the trauma units and CCU. I'm going to catch some sleep as soon as we're done, in case any crash cases come in. Nothing worse than an exhausted trauma surgeon."

She felt even more guilty about waking him up. "I'll make this quick," she promised. Claire opened her backpack, took out the padded box, and slid it across the table to him. "Blood samples, from Myrnin."

Mills frowned. "I've already got a hundred blood samples from Myrnin. Why—"

"These are different," Claire said. "Trust me. There's one labeled *B* that's important."

"Important, how?"

"I don't want to say. I'd rather you took a look first." In science, Claire knew, it was better to come to an analysis cold, without too many expectations. Dr. Mills knew that, too, and he nodded as he took possession of the samples. "Um—if you want to sleep, maybe you shouldn't drink that stuff."

Dr. Mills smiled and threw back the rest of his coffee. "You get to be a doctor by developing immunity to all kinds of things, including caffeine," he said.

"Trust me. The second my head touches the pillow, I'm asleep, even if I've got a coffee IV drip."

"I know people who'd pay good money for that. The IV drip, I mean."

He shook his head, grinning, but then got serious. "You seem okay. I was worried about you. You're just so . . . young, to be involved in all this stuff."

"I'm all right. And I'm really—"

"Not that young. Yes, I know. But still. Let an old man fret a little. I've got two daughters." He tossed his coffee cup at the trash—two points—and stood. "Here's all I could get together of the drug. Sorry, it's not a lot, but I've got a new batch in the works. It'll take a couple of days to finish."

He handed her a bag that clinked with small glass bottles. She peeked inside. "This should be plenty." Unless, of course, she had to start dosing all over Morganville, in which case, they were done, anyway.

"Sorry to make this a gulp-and-run, but . . ."

"You should go," Claire agreed. "Thanks, Dr. Mills." She offered her hand. He shook it gravely.

Around his wrist, there was a silver bracelet, with Amelie's symbol on it. He looked down at it, then at her gold one, and shrugged.

"I don't think it's time to take it off," he said. "Not yet."

At least yours does come off, Claire thought, but didn't say. Dr. Mills had signed agreements, contracts, and those things were binding in Morganville, but the contract she'd signed had made her Amelie's property, body and soul. And her bracelet didn't have a catch on it, which made it more like a slave collar.

From time to time, that still creeped her out.

It was getting close to time for her first class, and as Claire hefted her backpack, she wondered how many people would show up. Lots, probably. Knowing most of the professors, they'd think today was a good day for a quiz.

She wasn't disappointed. She also wasn't panicked, unlike some of her classmates during her first class, and her third. Claire didn't panic on tests, not unless it was in a dream where she also had to clog dance and twirl batons to get a good grade. And the quizzes weren't so hard anyway, not even the physics tests.

One thing she noticed, more and more, as she went around campus: fewer people had on bracelets. Morganville natives got used to wearing them twenty-four/seven, so she could clearly see the tan lines where the bracelets had been . . . and weren't anymore. It was almost like a reverse tattoo.

Around noon, she saw Monica Morrell, Gina, and Jennifer.

The three girls were walking fast, heads down, books in their arms. There was a whole lot different about them; Claire was used to seeing those three stalking the campus like tigers, confident and cruel. They'd stare down anyone, and whether you liked them or not, they were wicked fashion queens, always showing themselves off to best advantage.

Not today.

Monica, who usually was the centerpiece, looked awful. Her shiny, flirty hair was dull and fuzzy, as if she had barely bothered to brush it, much less condition or curl. What little Claire could see of her face looked makeup free. She was wearing a shapeless sweater in an unflatteringly ugly pattern, and sloppy blue jeans, the kind Claire imagined she might keep around to clean house in, if Monica ever did that kind of thing.

Gina and Jennifer didn't look much better, and they all looked defeated.

Claire still felt a little, tiny, unworthy tingle of satisfaction . . . until she saw the looks they were getting. Morganville natives who'd taken off their bracelets were outright glaring at Monica and her entourage, and a few of them did worse than just give them dirty looks. As Claire watched, a big, tough jock wearing a TPU jacket bumped into Jennifer and sent her books flying. She didn't look at him. She just bent over to pick them up.

"Hey, you clumsy whore, what the hell?" He shoved her onto her butt as she tried to get up, but she wasn't his real target; she was just standing between him and Monica. "Hey. Morrell. How's your daddy?"

"Fine," Monica said, and looked him in the eyes. "I'd ask about yours, but since you don't know who he was—"

The jock stepped very close to her. She didn't flinch, but Claire could tell that she wanted to. There were tight lines around her eyes and mouth, and her knuckles were white where she gripped her books.

"You've been Princess Queen Bitch your whole life," he said. "You remember Annie? Annie McFarlane? You used to call her a fat cow. You laughed at her in school. You took pictures of her in the bathroom and posted them on the Internet. Remember?"

Monica didn't answer.

The jock smiled. "Yeah, you remember Annie. She was a good kid, and I liked her."

"You didn't like her enough to stand up for her," Monica said. "Right, Clark? You wanted to get in my pants more than you wanted me to be kind to your little fat friend. Not my fault she ended up wrecking that stupid car at the town border. Maybe it's your fault, though. Maybe she couldn't stand being in town with you anymore after you dumped her."

Clark knocked the books out of her hand and shoved her up against a nearby tree trunk. Hard.

"I've got something for you, bitch." He dug in his pocket and came up with something square, about four inches across. It was a sticky label like a name tag, only with a picture on it of an awkward but sweet-looking teenage girl trying bravely to smile for the camera.

Clark slapped it on Monica's chest and rubbed it so it stuck to the sweater.

"You wear that," he said. "You wear Annie's picture. If I see you take it off today, I swear, what you did to Annie back in high school's going to seem like a Cancún vacation."

Under Annie's picture were the words KILLED BY MONICA MORRELL.

Monica looked down at it, swallowed, and turned bright red, then pale. She jerked her chin up again, sharply, and stared at Clark. "Are you done?"

"So far. Remember, you take it off—"

"Yeah, Clark, you weren't exactly subtle. I get it. You think I care?"

Clark's grin widened. "No, you don't. Not yet. Have a nice day, Queenie."

He walked away and did a high five with two other guys.

As Monica stared down at the label on her chest in utter disgust, another girl approached—another Morganville native who'd taken off the bracelet. Monica didn't notice her until the girl was right in her face.

This one didn't talk. She just ripped the backing off another label and stuck it on Monica's chest next to Annie McFarlane's photo.

This one just said KILLER in big red letters.

She kept on walking.

Monica started to rip it off, but Clark was watching her.

"Suits you," he said, and pointed to his eyes, then to her. "We'll be watching you all day. There are a lot more labels coming."

Clark was right. It was going to be a really long, bad day to be Monica Morrell. Even Gina and Jennifer were fading back now, heading out in a different direction and leaving her to face the music.

Monica's gaze fell on Claire. There was a flash of fear in her eyes, and shame, and genuine pain.

And then she armored up and snapped, "What are you looking at, freak?"

Claire shrugged. "Justice, I guess." She frowned. "How come you didn't stay with your parents?"

"None of your business." Monica's fierce stare wavered. "Dad wanted us all to go back to normal. So people could see we're not afraid."

"How's that going?"

Monica took a step toward her, then hugged her books to her chest to cover up most of the labels, and hurried on.

She hadn't gotten ten feet before a stranger ran up and slapped a label across her back that had a picture of a slender young girl and an older boy of maybe fifteen on it. The words beneath said KILLER OF ALYSSA.

With a shock, Claire realized that the boy in that picture was *Shane*. And that was his sister, Alyssa, the one who'd died in the fire that Monica had set.

"Justice," Claire repeated softly. She felt a little sick, actually. Justice wasn't the same thing as mercy.

Her phone rang as she was trying to decide what to do. "Better come home," Michael Glass said. "We've got an emergency signal from Richard at City Hall."

12

The signal had come over the coded strategy network, which Claire had just assumed was dead, considering that Oliver had been the one running it. But Richard had found a use for it, and as she burst in the front door, breathless, she heard Michael and Eve talking in the living room. Claire closed and locked the door, dumped her backpack, and hurried to join them.

"What did I miss?"

"Shhh," they both said. Michael, Eve, and Shane were all seated at the table, staring intently at the small walkie-talkie sitting upright in the middle. Michael pulled out a chair for Claire, and she sat, trying to be as quiet as possible.

Richard was talking.

—No telling whether or not this storm will hit us full on, but right now, the Weather Service shows the radar track going right over the top of us. It'll be here in the next few hours, probably right around dark. It's late in the year for tornado activity, but they're telling us there's a strong possibility of some real trouble. On top of all the other things we have going on, this isn't good news. I'm putting all emergency services and citizen patrols on full alert. If we get a tornado, get to your designated shelters.

Designated shelters? Claire mouthed to Michael, who shrugged.

If you're closer to City Hall, come here; we've got a shelter in the basement. Those of you who are Civil Defense wardens, go door-to-door in your area, tell people we've got a storm coming and what to do. We're putting it on TV and radio, and the university's going to get ready as well.

"Richard, this is Hector," said a new voice. "Miller House. You got any news about this takeover people are talking about?"

"We've got rumors, but nothing concrete," Richard said. "We hear there's a lot of talk going around town about taking back City Hall, but we've got no specific word about when these people are meeting, or where, or even who they are. All I can tell you is that we've fortified the building, and the barricades remain up around Founder's Square, for all the good that does. I need everybody in a security-designated location to be on the alert today and tonight. Report in if you see any sign of an attack, any sign at all. We'll try to get to you in support."

Michael exchanged a look with the rest of them, and then picked up the radio. He pressed the button. "Michael Glass. You think Bishop's behind this?"

"I think Bishop's willing to let humans do his dirty work for him, and then sweep in to make himself lord and master on the ashes," Richard said. "Seems like his style. Put Shane on."

Michael held out the radio. Shane looked at it like it might bite, then took it and pressed TALK. "Yeah, this is Shane."

"I have two unconfirmed sightings of your father in town. I know this isn't easy for you, but I need to know: is Frank Collins back in Morganville?"

Shane looked into Claire's eyes and said, "If he is, he hasn't talked to me about it."

He *lied.* Claire's lips parted, and she almost blurted something out, but she just couldn't think what to say. "Shane," she whispered. He shook his head.

"Tell you what, Richard, you catch my dad, you've got my personal endorsement for tossing him in the deepest pit you've got around here," Shane said. "If he's in Morganville, he's got a plan, but he won't be working for or with the vamps. Not that he knows, anyway."

"Fair enough. You hear from him—"

"You're on speed dial. Got it." Shane set the radio back in the center of the table. Claire kept staring at him, willing him to speak, to say *something*, but he didn't.

"Don't do this," she said. "Don't put me in the middle."

"I'm not," Shane said. "Nothing I said was a lie. My dad told me he was coming, not that he's here. I haven't seen him, and I don't want to. I meant what I said. If he's here, Dick and his brownshirts are welcome to him. I've got nothing to do with him, not anymore."

Claire wasn't sure she believed that, but she didn't think he was intentionally lying now. He probably did mean it. She just thought that no matter how much he thought he was done with his dad, all it would take would be a snap of Frank Collins's fingers to bring him running.

Not good.

Richard was answering questions from others on the radio, but Michael was no longer listening. He was fixed on Shane. "You knew? You knew he was coming back here, and you didn't warn me?"

Shane stirred uneasily. "Look—"

"No, *you* look. I'm the one who got knifed and decapitated and buried in the *backyard*, among other things! Good thing I was a ghost!"

Shane looked down. "Who was I supposed to tell? The vamps? Come on."

"You could have told me!"

"You're a vamp," Shane said. "In case you haven't checked the mirror lately."

Michael stood up. His chair slid about two feet across the floor and skidded to an uneven stop; he leaned his hands on the table and loomed over Shane. "Oh, I do," he said. "I check it every day. How about you? You taken a good look recently, Shane? Because I'm not so sure I know you anymore."

Shane looked up at that, and there was a flash of pain in his face. "I didn't mean—"

"I could be just about the last vampire around here," Michael interrupted. "Maybe the others are dead. Maybe they will be soon. Between the mobs out there willing to rip our heads off and Bishop waiting to take over, having your dad stalking me is all I need."

"He wouldn't—"

"He killed me once, or tried to. He'd do it again in a second, and he wouldn't blink, and you know that, Shane. You know it! He thinks I'm some kind of a traitor to the human race. He'll come after me in particular."

Shane didn't say anything this time. Michael retrieved the radio from the table and clipped it to the pocket of his jeans. He shone, all blazing gold and hard, white angles, and Shane couldn't meet his stare.

"You decide you want to help your dad kill some vampires, Shane, you know where to find me."

Michael went upstairs. It was as if the room had lost all its air, and Claire found herself breathing very hard, trying not to tremble.

Eve's dark eyes were very wide, and fixed on Shane as well. She slowly got up from the table.

"Eve—" he said, and reached out toward her. She stepped out of reach.

"I can't believe you," she said. "You see me running over to suck up to my mom? No. And she's not even a murderer."

"Morganville needs to change."

"Wake up, Shane, it *has*! It started months ago. It's been changing right in front of you! Vampires and humans working together. Trusting one another. They're *trying*. Sure, it's hard, but they've got reason to be afraid of us, good reason. And now you want to throw all that away and help your dad set up a guillotine in Founder's Square or something?" Eve's eyes turned bitter black. "Screw you."

"I didn't—"

She clomped away toward the stairs, leaving Shane and Claire together.

Shane swallowed, then tried to make it a joke. "That could have gone better." Claire slipped out of her chair. "Claire? Oh, come on, not you, too. Don't go. Please."

"You should have told him. I can't believe you didn't. He's your friend, or at least I thought he was."

"Where are you going?"

She pulled in a deep breath. "I'm packing. I've decided to move in with my parents."

She didn't pack, though. She went upstairs, closed the door to her room, and pulled out her pitifully few possessions. Most of it was dirty laundry. She sat there on the bed, staring at it, feeling lost and alone and a little sick, and wondered if she was making a point or just running like a little girl. She felt pretty stupid now that she had everything piled on the floor.

It looked utterly pathetic.

When the knock came on her door, she didn't immediately answer it. She knew it was Shane, even though he didn't speak. *Go away,* she thought at him, but he still wasn't much of a mind reader. He knocked again.

"It's not locked," she said.

"It's also not open," Shane said quietly, through the wood. "I'm not a complete ass."

"Yes, you are."

"Okay, sometimes I am." He hesitated, and she heard the floor creak as he shifted his weight. "Claire."

"Come in."

He froze when he saw the stuff piled in front of her, waiting to be put in bags and her one suitcase. "You're serious."

"Yes."

"You're just going to pick up and leave."

"You know my parents want me to come home."

He didn't say anything for a long moment, then reached into his back pocket and took out a black case, about the size of his hand. "Here, then. I was going to give it to you later, but I guess I'd better do it now, before you take off on us."

His voice sounded offhand and normal, but his fingers felt cold when she touched them in taking the case, and there was an expression on his face she didn't know—fear, maybe; bracing himself for something painful.

It was a hard, leather-wrapped case, on spring hinges. She hesitated for a breath, then pried up one end. It snapped open.

Oh.

The cross was beautiful—delicate silver, traceries of leaves wrapped around it. It was on a silver chain so thin it looked like a breath would melt it. When Claire picked up the necklace, it felt like air in her hand.

"I—" She had no idea what to say, what to feel. Her whole body seemed to have gone into shock. "It's beautiful."

"I know it doesn't work against the vamps," Shane said. "Okay, well, I didn't know that when I got it for you. But it's still silver, and silver works, so I hope that's okay."

This wasn't a small present. Shane didn't have a lot

of money; he picked up odd jobs here and there, and spent very little. This wasn't some cheap costume jewelry; it was real silver, and really beautiful.

"I can't—it's too expensive." Claire's heart was pounding again, and she wished she could *think*. She wished she knew what she was supposed to feel, supposed to do. On impulse, she put the necklace back in the box and snapped it shut, and held it out to him. "Shane, I can't."

He gave her a broken sort of smile. "It's not a ring or anything. Keep it. Besides, it doesn't match my eyes."

He stuck his hands in his pockets, rounded his shoulders, and walked out of the room.

Claire clutched the leather box in one sweaty hand, eyes wide, and then opened it again. The cross gleamed on black velvet, clean and beautiful and shining, and it blurred as her eyes filled with tears.

Now she felt something, something big and overwhelming and far too much to fit inside her small, fragile body.

"Oh," she whispered. "Oh *God*." This hadn't been just any gift. He'd put a lot of time and effort into getting it. There was love in it, real love.

She took the cross, put it around her neck, and fastened the clasp with shaking fingers. It took her two tries. Then she went down the hall and, without knocking, opened Shane's door. He was standing at the window, staring outside. He looked different to her. Older. Sadder.

He turned toward her, and his gaze fixed on the silver cross in the hollow of her throat.

"You're an idiot," Claire said.

Shane considered that, and nodded. "I really am, mostly."

"And then you have to go and do these awesome things—"

"I know. I did say I was *mostly* an idiot."

"You kind of have your good moments."

He didn't quite smile. "So you like it?"

She put her hand up to stroke the cross's warm silver lines. "I'm wearing it, aren't I?"

"Not that it means we're—"

"You said you loved me," Claire said. "You did say that."

He shut his mouth and studied her, then nodded. There was a flush building high in his cheeks.

"Well, I love you, too, and you're still an idiot. Mostly."

"No argument." He folded his arms across his chest, and she tried not to notice the way his muscles tensed, or the vulnerable light in his eyes. "So, you moving out?"

"I should," she said softly. "The other night—"

"Claire. Please be straight with me. Are you moving out?"

She was holding the cross now, cradling it, and it felt warm as the sun against her fingers. "I can't," she said. "I have to do laundry first, and that might take a month. You saw the pile."

He laughed, and it was as if all the strength went out of him. He sat down on his unmade bed, hard, and after a moment, she walked around the end and sat next to him. He put his arm around her.

"Life is a work in progress," Shane said. "My mom used to say that. I'm kind of a fixer-upper. I know that."

Claire sighed and allowed herself to relax against his warmth. "Good thing I like high-maintenance guys."

He was about to kiss her—finally—when they both heard a sound from overhead.

Only there was nothing overhead. Nothing but the attic.

"Did you hear that?" Shane asked.

"Yeah. It sounded like footsteps."

"Oh, well, that's fantastic. I thought it was supposed to be exit-only or something." Shane reached under his bed and came up with a stake. "Go get Michael and Eve. Here." He handed her another stake. This one had a silver tip. "It's the Cadillac of vampire killers. Don't dent it."

"You are so weird." But she took it, and then dashed to her room to grab the thin silver knife Amelie had given her. No place to put it, but she poked a hole in the pocket of her jeans just big enough for the blade. The jeans were tight enough to keep the blade in place against her leg, but not so much it looked obvious, and besides, it was pretty flexible.

She hurried down the hall, listening for any other movement. Eve's room was empty, but when she knocked on Michael's door, she heard a startled yelp that sounded very Eve-like. "What?" Michael asked.

"Trouble," Claire said. "Um, maybe? Attic. Now."

Michael didn't sound any happier about it than Shane had been. "Great. Be there in a second."

Muffled conversation, and the sound of fabric moving. Claire wondered if he was getting dressed, and quickly tried to reject that image, not because it wasn't awesomely hot, but because, well, it was *Michael*, and besides, there were other things to think about.

Such as what was upstairs in the attic.

Or who.

The door banged open, and Eve rushed out, flushed and mussed and still buttoning her shirt. "It's not what you think," she said. "It was just—oh, okay, whatever, it was exactly what you think. Now, *what*?"

Something dropped and rolled across the attic floor directly above their heads. Claire silently pointed up, and Eve followed the motion, staring as if she could see through the wood and plaster. She jumped when Michael, who'd thrown on an unbuttoned shirt, put a hand on her shoulder. He put a finger to his lips.

Shane stepped out of his room, holding a stake in either hand. He pitched one underhand to Michael.

Where's mine? Eve mouthed.

Get your own, Shane mouthed back. Eve rolled her eyes and dashed into her own room, coming back with a black bag slung across her chest, bandolier-style. It was, Claire assumed, full of weapons. Eve fished around in it and came up with a stake of her very own. It even had her initials carved in it.

"Shop class," she whispered. "See? I *did* learn something in school."

Michael pressed the button to release the hidden door, and it opened without a sound. There were no lights upstairs that Claire could see. The stairs were pitch-black.

Michael, by common consent, went first, vampire eyes, and all. Shane followed, then Eve; Claire brought up the rear, and tried to move as silently as possible, although not really all that silently, because the stairs creaked beneath the weight of four people. At the top, Claire ran into Eve's back, and whispered, "What?"

Eve, in answer, reached back to grip her hand. "Michael smells blood," she whispered. "Hush."

Michael flicked on a light at the other end of the small, silent room. There was nothing unusual, just the furniture that was always here. There were no signs anybody had been here since the Goldmans and Myrnin had departed.

"How do we get into the attic?" Shane asked. Michael pressed hidden studs, and another door, barely visible at that end of the room, clicked open. Claire remembered it well; Myrnin had shown it to her, when they'd been getting stuff together to go to Bishop's welcome feast.

"Stay here," Michael said, and stepped through into the dim, open space.

"Yeah, sure," Shane said, and followed. He popped his head back in to say, "No, not you two. Stay here."

"Does he just not get how unfair and sexist that is?" Eve asked. "Men."

"You really want to go first?"

"Of course not. But I'd like the chance to *refuse* to go first."

They waited tensely, listening for any sign of trouble. Claire heard Shane's footsteps moving through the attic, but nothing else for a long time.

Then she heard him say, "Michael. Oh man . . . over here." There was tension in his voice, but it didn't sound like he was about to jump into hand-to-hand combat.

Eve and Claire exchanged looks, and Eve said, "Oh, screw it," and dived into the attic after them.

Claire followed, gripping the Cadillac of stakes and hoping she wasn't going to be forced to try to use it.

Shane was crouched down behind some stacked, dusty suitcases, and Michael was there, too. Eve pulled in a sharp breath when she saw what it was they were bending over, and put out a hand to stop Claire in her tracks.

Not that Claire stopped, until she saw who was lying on the wooden floor. She hardly recognized him, really. If it hadn't been for the gray ponytail and the leather coat . . .

"It's Oliver," she whispered. Eve was biting her lip until it was almost white, staring at her former boss. "What *happened*?"

"Silver," Michael said. "Lots of it. It eats vampire skin like acid, but he shouldn't be this bad. Not unless—" He stopped as the pale, burned eyelids fluttered. "He's still alive."

"Vampires are hard to kill," Oliver whispered. His voice was barely a creak of sound, and it broke at the end on what sounded almost like a sob. "*Jesu*. Hurts."

Michael exchanged a look with Shane, then said, "Let's get him downstairs. Claire. Go get some blood from the fridge. There should be some."

"No," Oliver grated, and sat up. There was blood leaking through his white shirt, as if all his skin were gone underneath. "No time. Attack on City Hall, coming tonight—Bishop. Using it as a—diversion—to—" His eyes opened wider, and went blank, then rolled up into his head.

He collapsed. Michael caught him under the shoulders.

He and Shane carried Oliver out to the couch, while Eve anxiously followed along, making little shooing motions.

Claire started to follow, then heard something scrape across the wood behind her, in the shadows.

Oliver hadn't come here alone.

A black shadow lunged out, grabbed her, and something hard hit her head.

She must have made some sound, knocked something over, because she heard Shane call her name sharply, and saw his shadow in the doorway before darkness took all of it away.

Then she was falling away.

Then she was gone.

13

Claire came awake feeling sick, wretched, and cold. Someone was pounding on the back of her head with a croquet mallet, or at least that was how it felt, and when she tried to move, the whole world spun around.

"Shut up and stop moaning," somebody said from a few feet away. "Don't you dare throw up or I'll make you eat it."

It sounded like Jason Rosser, Eve's crazy brother. Claire swallowed hard and squinted, trying to make out the shadow next to her. Yeah, it looked like Jason—skanky, greasy, and insane. She tried to squirm away from him, but ran into a wall at her back. It felt like wood, but she didn't think it was the Glass House attic.

He'd taken her somewhere, probably using the portal. And now none of her friends could follow, because none of them knew how.

Her hands and feet were tied. Claire blinked, trying to clear her head. That was a little unfortunate, because with clarity came the awareness of just how bad this was. Jason Rosser really *was* crazy. He'd stalked Eve. He'd—at least allegedly—killed girls in town. He'd definitely stabbed Shane, and he'd staked Amelie at the feast when she'd tried to help him.

And none of her friends back at the Glass House

would know how to find her. To their eyes, she would have just . . . vanished.

"What do you want?" she asked. Her voice sounded rusty and scared. Jason reached out and moved hair back from her face, which creeped her out. She didn't like him touching her.

"Relax, shortcake, you're not my type," he said. "I do what I'm told, that's all. You were wanted. So I brought you."

"Wanted?"

A low, silky laugh floated on the silence, dark as smoke, and Jason looked over his shoulder as the hidden observer rose and stepped into what little light there was.

Ysandre, Bishop's pale little girlfriend. Beautiful, sure. Delicate as jasmine flowers, with big, liquid eyes and a sweetly rounded face.

She was poison in a pretty bottle.

"Well," she said, and crouched down next to Claire. "Look at what the cat dragged in. Meeow." Her sharp nail dragged over Claire's cheek, and judging from the sting, it drew blood. "Where's your pretty boyfriend, Miss Claire? I really wasn't done with him, you know. I hadn't even properly *started*."

Claire felt an ugly lurch of anger mix with the fear already churning her stomach. "He's probably not done with you, either," she said, and managed to smile. She hoped it was a cold kind of smile, the sort that Amelie used—or Oliver. "Maybe you should go looking. I'll bet he'd be *so* happy to see you."

"I'll show that boy a real good time, when we do meet up again," Ysandre purred, and put her face very close to Claire's. "Now, then, let's talk, just us girls. Won't that be fun?"

Not. Claire was struggling against the ropes, but Jason had done his job pretty well; she was hurting herself more than accomplishing anything else. Ysandre grabbed Claire's shoulder and wrenched her up-

right against the wooden wall, hard enough to bang
Claire's injured head. For a dazed second, it looked
like Ysandre's ripe, red smile floated in midair, like
some undead Cheshire cat.

"Now," Ysandre said, "ain't this nice, sweetie? It's
too bad we couldn't get Mr. Shane to join us, but my
little helper here, he's a bit worried about tackling
Shane. Bad blood and all." She laughed softly. "Well,
we'll make do. Amelie likes you, I hear, and you've
got on that pretty little gold bracelet. So you'll do
just fine."

"For what?"

"I ain't telling you, sweetie." Ysandre's smile was
truly scary. "This town's going to have a wild night,
though. Real wild. And you're going to get to see the
whole thing, up close. You must be all atingle."

Eve would have had a quip at the ready. Claire just
glared, and wished her head would stop aching and
spinning. What had he hit her with? It felt like the
front end of a bus. She hadn't thought Jason could hit
that hard, truthfully.

Don't try to find me, Shane. Don't. The last thing
she wanted was Shane racing to the rescue and taking
on a guy who'd stabbed him, and a vampire who'd led
him around by a leash.

No, she had to find her own way out of this.

Step one: figure out where she was. Claire let Ysandre ramble on, describing all kinds of lurid things that
Claire thought it was better not to imagine, considering they were things Ysandre was thinking of doing
to *her*. Instead, she tried to identify her surroundings.
It didn't look familiar, but that was no help; she was
still relatively new to Morganville. Plenty of places she'd
never been.

Wait.

Claire focused on the crate that Jason was sitting
on. There was stenciling on it. It was hard to make it
out in the dim light, but she thought it said BRICKS

BULK COFFEE. And now that she thought about it, it smelled like coffee in here, too. A warm, morning kind of smell, floating over dust and damp wood.

And she remembered Eve laughing about how Oliver bought his coffee from a place called Bricks. *As in, tastes like ground-up bricks,* Eve had said. *If you order flavored, they add in the mortar.*

There were only two coffee shops in town: Oliver's place, and the University Center coffee bar. This didn't look like the UC, which wasn't that old and was mostly built of concrete, not wood.

That meant . . . she was at Common Grounds? But Common Grounds didn't make any sense; there wasn't any kind of portal leading to it.

Maybe Oliver has a warehouse. That sounded right, because the vampires seemed to own a lot of the warehouse district that bordered Founder's Square. Brandon, Oliver's second-in-vampire-command, had been found dead in a warehouse.

Maybe she was close to Founder's Square.

Ysandre's cold fingers closed around Claire's chin and jerked it up. "Are you listening, honey?"

"Truthfully, no," Claire said. "You're kind of boring."

Jason actually laughed, and turned it into a fake cough. "I'm going outside," he said. "Since this is going to get all personal now." Claire wanted to yell to him not to go, but she bit her tongue and turned it into a subsonic whine in the back of her throat as she watched him walk away. His footsteps receded into the dark, and then finally a small square of light opened a long way off.

It was a door, too far for her to reach—way too far.

"I thought he'd never leave," Ysandre said, and put her cold, cold lips on Claire's neck, then yelled in shock and pulled away, covering her mouth with one pale hand. "You *bitch*!"

Ysandre hadn't seen the silver chain Claire was

wearing in the dim light, as whisper-thin as it was. Now there were welts forming on the vampire's full lips—forming, breaking, and bleeding.

Fury sparked in Ysandre's eyes. Playtime was over.

As Claire squirmed away, the vampire followed at a lazy stroll. She wiped her burned lips and looked at the thin, leaking blood in distaste. "Tastes like silver. Disgusting. You've just ruined my good mood, little girl."

As she rolled, Claire felt something sharp dig into her leg. *The knife.* They'd found the stake, but she guessed their search hadn't exactly been thorough; Jason was too crazy, and Ysandre too careless and arrogant.

But the knife wasn't going to do her any good at all where it was, unless . . .

Ysandre lunged for her, a blur of white in the darkness, and Claire twisted and jammed her hip down at an awkward angle.

The knife slipped and tore through the fabric of her jeans—not much of it, just a couple of inches, but enough to slice open Ysandre's hand and arm as it reached for her, all the way to the bone.

Ysandre shrieked in real pain, and spun away. She didn't look so pretty now, and when she turned toward Claire again, from a respectful distance this time, she hissed at her with full cobra fangs extended. Her eyes were wild and bloodred, glowing like rubies.

Claire twisted, nearly yanking her elbow out of its joint, and managed to get the ropes around her wrist against the knife. She didn't have long; the shock wouldn't keep Ysandre at bay for more than a few seconds.

But getting a silver knife to cut through synthetic rope? That was going to take a while—a while she didn't have.

Claire sawed desperately, and got a little bit of give on the bonds—enough to *almost* get her hand into her pocket.

But not.

Ysandre grabbed her by the hair. "I'm going to destroy you for that."

The pain in her head was blinding. It felt like her scalp was being ripped off, and on top of that, the massive headache roared back to a new, sickening pulse.

Claire loosened the rope enough to plunge her aching hand into her pocket and grab the handle of the knife. She yanked it out of the tangle of fabric and held it at a trembling, handicapped *en garde*—still tied up, but whatever, she wasn't going to stop fighting, not *ever*.

Ysandre shrieked and let her go, which made no sense to Claire's confused, pain-shocked mind. *I didn't stab her yet. Did I?* Not that she wanted to stab anybody, even Ysandre. She just wanted—

What was going on?

Ysandre's body slammed down hard on the wooden floor, and Claire gasped and flinched away . . . but the vampire had fallen facedown, limp, and weirdly broken.

A small woman dressed in gray, her pale hair falling wild around her shoulders, dropped silently from overhead and put one impeccably lovely gray pump in the center of Ysandre's back, holding her down as she tried to move.

"Claire?" The woman's face turned toward her, and Claire blinked twice before she realized whom she was looking at.

Amelie. But not Amelie. Not the cool, remote Founder—this woman had a wild, furious energy to her that Claire had never seen before. And she looked *young.*

"I'm okay," she said faintly, and tried to decide whether this version of Amelie was really here, or a function of her smacked-around brain. She decided it would be a good idea to get her hands and feet untied before figuring anything else out.

That took long minutes, during which Amelie

(really?) dragged Ysandre, whimpering, into the corner and fastened her wrists to a massive crossbeam with chains. The chains, Claire registered, had been there all along. Lovely. This was some kind of vamp playpen/storage locker—probably Oliver's. And she felt sick again, thinking about it. Claire sawed grimly at the ropes binding her and finally parted one complete twist around her hands. As she struggled out of the loops of rope, she saw deep white imprints in her skin, and realized that her hands were red and swollen. She could still feel them, at least, and the burn of circulation returning felt as if she were holding them over an open flame.

She focused on slicing the increasingly dulled knife through the rope on her feet, but it was no use.

"Here," Amelie said, and bent down to snap the rope with one twist of her fingers. It was *so* frustrating, after all that hard work, to see just how easy it was for her. Claire stripped the ties away and sat for a moment breathing hard, starting to feel every cut, bump, and bruise on her body.

Amelie's cool fingers cupped Claire's chin and forced her head up, and the vampire's gray eyes searched hers. "You have a head injury," Amelie said. "I don't think it's too serious. A headache and some dizziness, perhaps." She let go. "I expected to find you. I did not expect to find you *here*, I confess."

Amelie looked *fine*. Not a prisoner. Not a scratch on her, in fact. Claire had lots more damage, and she hadn't been dragged off as Bishop's prisoner. . . .

Wait. "You—we thought Bishop might have gotten you. But he didn't, did he?"

Amelie cocked an eyebrow at her. "Apparently not."

"Then where did you go?" Claire felt a completely useless urge to lash out at her, crack that extreme cool. "Why did you *do* this? You left us alone! And you called the vampires out of hiding—" Her voice failed her for a second as she thought about Officer

O'Malley, and the others she'd heard about. "You got some of them killed."

Amelie didn't respond to that. She simply stared back, as calm as an ice sculpture—calmer, because she wasn't melting.

"Tell me why," Claire said. "Tell me why you did that."

"Because plans change," Amelie replied. "As Bishop changes his moves, I must change mine. The stakes are too high now, Claire. I've lost half the vampires of Morganville to him. He's taking away my advantage, and I needed to draw them to me, for their own safety."

"You got *vampires* killed, not just humans. I know humans don't mean anything to you. But I thought the whole point of this was to save *your* people!"

"And so it is," Amelie said. "As many as can be saved. As for the call, there is a thing in chess known as a blitz attack, you see—a distraction, to cover the movement of more important pieces. You retrieved Myrnin and set him in play again; this was most important. I need my most powerful pieces on the board."

"Like Oliver?" Claire rubbed her hands together, trying to get the annoying tingle out of them. "He's hurt, you know. Maybe dying."

"He's served his purpose." Amelie turned her attention toward Ysandre, who was starting to stir. "It's time to take Bishop's rook, I believe."

Claire clutched the silver knife hard in her fist. "Is that all I am, too? Some kind of sacrifice pawn?"

That got Amelie's attention again. "No," she said in surprise. "Not entirely. I do care, Claire. But in war, you can't care too much. It paralyzes your ability to act." Those luminous eyes turned toward Ysandre again. "It's time for you to go, because I doubt you would enjoy seeing this. You won't be able to return here. I'm closing down nodes on the network. When I'm finished, there will be only two destinations: to me, or to Bishop."

"Where is he?"

"You don't know?" Amelie raised her eyebrows again. "He is where it is most secure, of course. At City Hall. And at nightfall, I will come against him. That's why I came looking for you, Claire. I need you to tell Richard. Tell him to get all those who can't fight for me out of the building."

"But—he *can't*. It's a storm shelter. There are supposed to be tornadoes coming."

"Claire," Amelie said. "Listen to me. If innocents take refuge in that building, they will be killed, because I can't protect them anymore. We're at endgame now. There's no room for mercy." She looked again at Ysandre, who had gone very still, listening.

"Y'all wouldn't be saying this in front of me if I was going to walk out of here, would you?" Ysandre asked. She sounded calm now. Very still.

"No," Amelie said. "Very perceptive. I wouldn't." She took Claire by the arm and helped her to her feet. "I am relying on you, Claire. Go now. Tell Richard these are my orders."

Before Claire could utter another word, she felt the air shimmer in front of her, in the middle of the big warehouse room, and she fell . . . out over the dusty trunk in the Glass House attic, where Oliver had been. She sprawled ungracefully on top of it, then rolled off and got to her feet with a thump.

When she waved her hand through the air, looking for that strange heat shimmer of an open portal, she felt nothing at all.

I'm closing the portals, Amelie had said.

She'd closed this one, for sure.

"Claire?" Shane's voice came from the far end of the attic. He shoved aside boxes and jumped over jumbled furniture to reach her. "What happened to you? Where did you go?"

"I'll tell you later," she said, and realized she was still holding the bloody silver knife. She carefully put it back in her pocket, in the makeshift holster against her leg. It was so dull she didn't think it would cut anything again, but it made her feel better. "Oliver?"

"Bad." Shane put his hands around her head and tilted it up, looking her over. "Is everything okay?"

"Define *everything*. No, define *okay*." She shook her head in frustration. "I need to get the radio. I have to talk to Richard."

Richard wasn't on the radio. "He's meeting with the mayor," said the man who answered. Sullivan, Claire thought his name was, but she hadn't really paid attention. "You got a problem there?"

"No, Officer, you've got a problem *there*," she said. "I need to talk to Richard. It's really important!"

"Everybody needs to talk to Richard," Sullivan said. "He'll get back to you. He's busy right now. If it's not an emergency response—"

"Yes, okay! It's an emergency!"

"Then I'll send units out to you. Glass House, right?"

"No, it's not—" Claire wanted to slam the radio down in frustration. "It's not an emergency *here*. Look, just tell Richard that he needs to clear everybody out of City Hall, as soon as possible."

"Can't do that," Sullivan said. "It's our center of operations. It's the main storm shelter, and we've got one heck of a storm coming tonight. You're going to have to give me a reason, miss."

"All right, it's because—"

Michael took the radio away from her and shut it off. Claire gaped, stuttered, and finally demanded, "Why?"

"Because if Amelie says Bishop's got himself installed in City Hall, somebody there has to know. We don't know who's on his team," Michael said. "I don't know Sullivan that well, but I know he never was happy with the way things ran in town. I wouldn't put it past him to be buying Bishop's crap about giving the city back to the people, home rule, all that stuff.

Same goes for anybody else there, except maybe Joe Hess and Travis Lowe. We have to know who we're talking to before we say anything else."

Shane nodded. "I'm thinking that Sullivan's keeping Richard out of the loop for a reason."

They were downstairs, the four of them. Eve, Shane, and Claire were at the kitchen table, and Michael was pacing the floor and casting looks at the couch, where Oliver was. The older vampire was asleep, Claire guessed, or unconscious; they'd done what they could, washed him off and wrapped him in clean blankets. He was healing, according to Michael, but he wasn't doing it very fast.

When he'd woken up, he'd seemed distant. Confused.

Afraid.

Claire had given him one of the doses she'd gotten from Dr. Mills, and so far, it seemed to be helping, but if Oliver was sick, Myrnin's fears were becoming real.

Soon, it'd be Amelie, too. And then where would they be?

"So what do we do?" Claire asked. "Amelie said we have to tell Richard. We have to get noncombatants out of City Hall, as soon as possible."

"Problem is, you heard him giving instructions to the Civil Defense guys earlier—they're out telling everybody in town to *go* to City Hall if they can't make it to another shelter. Radio and TV, too. Hell, half the town is probably there already."

"Maybe she won't do it," Eve said. "I mean, she wouldn't kill *everybody* in there, would she? Not even if she thinks they're working for Bishop."

"I think it's gone past that," Claire said. "I don't know if she has any choice."

"There's always a choice."

"Not in chess," Claire replied. "Unless your choice is to lie down and die."

*   *   *

In the end, the only way to be sure they got to the right person was to get in the car and drive there. Claire was a little shocked at the color of the sky outside—a solid gray, with clouds moving so fast it was like time-lapse on the Weather Channel. The edges looked faintly green, and in this part of the country, that was never a good sign.

The only good thing about it was that Michael didn't have to worry about getting scorched by sunlight. He brought a hoodie and a blanket to throw over his head, just in case, but it was dark outside, and getting darker fast. Premature sunset.

Drops of rain were smacking the sidewalk, the size of half-dollars. Where they hit Claire's skin, they felt like paintball pellets. As she looked up at the clouds, a horizontal flash of lightning peeled the sky in half, and thunder rumbled so loudly she felt it through the soles of her shoes.

"Come on!" Eve yelled, and started the car. Claire ran to open the backseat door and piled in beside Shane. Eve was already accelerating before she could fasten her seat belt. "Michael, get the radio."

He turned it on. Static. As he scanned stations, they got ghosts of signals from other towns, but nothing came through clearly in Morganville—probably because the vampires jammed it.

Then one came in, loud and clear, broadcasting on a loop.

Attention Morganville residents: this is an urgent public service announcement. The National Weather Service has identified an extremely dangerous storm tracking toward Morganville, which will reach our borders at six twenty-seven this evening at its present speed. This storm has already been responsible for devastation in several areas in its path, and there has been significant loss of life due to tornadic activity. Morganville and the surrounding areas are on tornado watch through ten p.m. this evening. If you hear an alert siren, go immediately to a designated Safe Shelter location, or to the safest area of your home if you cannot reach a Safe Shelter. Attention Morganville residents—

Michael clicked it off. There was no point in listening to the repeat; it wasn't going to get any better.

"How many Safe Shelters are there?" Shane asked. "University dorms have them, the UC—"

"Founder's Square has two," Michael said, "but nobody can get to them right now. They're locked up."

"Library."

"And the church. Father Joe would open up the basements, so that'll fit a couple of hundred people."

Everybody else would head to City Hall, if they didn't stay in their houses.

The rain started to fall in earnest, slapping the windshield at first, and then pounding it in fierce waves. The ancient windshield wipers really weren't up to it, even at high speed. Claire was glad she wasn't trying to drive. Even in clear visibility she wasn't very good, and she had no idea how Eve was seeing a thing.

If she was, of course. Maybe this was faith-based driving.

Other cars were on the road, and most of them were heading the same way they were. Claire looked at the clock on her cell phone.

Five thirty p.m.

The storm was less than an hour away.

"Uh-oh," Eve said, and braked as they turned the last corner. It was a sea of red taillights. Over the roll of thunder and pounding rain, Claire heard horns honking. Traffic moved, but slowly, one car at a time inching forward. "They're checking cars at the barricade. I can't believe—"

Something happened up there, and the brake lights began flicking off in steady rows. Cars moved. Eve fell

into line, and the big, black sedan rolled past two police cars still flashing their lights. In the red/blue/red
glow, Claire saw that they'd moved the barricades aside
and were just waving everyone through.

"This is crazy," she said. "We can't get people out.
Not fast enough! We'd have to stop everybody from
coming in first, and then give them somewhere to
go. . . ."

"I'm getting out of the car here," Michael said. "I
can run faster than you can drive in this. I'll get to
Richard. They won't dare stop me."

That was probably true, but Eve still said, "Michael,
don't—"

Not that it stopped him from bailing out into the
rain. A flash of lightning streaked by overhead and
showed him splashing through thick puddles, weaving
around cars.

He was right; he was faster.

Eve muttered something about "Stupid, stubborn,
bloodsucking boyfriends," and followed the traffic toward
City Hall.

Out of nowhere, a truck pulled out in front of them
from a side street and stopped directly in their path.
Eve yelled and hit the brakes, but they were mushy
and wet, and not great at the best of times, and Claire
felt the car slip and then slide, gathering speed as
it went.

Glad I put on my seat belt, she thought, which was
a weird thing to think, as Eve's car hydroplaned right
into the truck. Shane stretched out his arm to hold
her in place, anyway—instinct, Claire guessed—and
then they all got thrown forward hard as physics took
over.

Physics hurt.

Claire rested her aching head against the cool
window—it was cracked, but still intact—and tried to
shake it off. Shane was unhooking himself from the
seat belt and asking her if she was okay. She made

some kind of gesture and mumbled something, which she hoped would be good enough. She wasn't up to real reassurances at the moment.

Eve's door opened, and she got dragged out of the car.

"Hey!" Shane yelled, and threw himself out his own door. Claire fumbled at the latch, but hers seemed stuck; she navigated the push button on her seat belt and opted for Shane's side of the car instead.

As she stumbled out into the shockingly warm rain, she knew they were really in trouble now, because the man holding a knife to Eve's throat was Frank Collins, Shane's father and all-around badass, crazy vampire hater. He looked exactly like she remembered—tough, biker-hard, dressed in leather and tattoos.

He was yelling something at Eve, something Claire couldn't hear over the crash of thunder. Shane threw himself into a slide over the trunk of the car and grabbed at his dad's knife hand.

Dad elbowed him in the face and sent him staggering. Claire grabbed for the silver knife in her jeans, but it was gone—she'd dropped it somewhere. Before she could look for it, Shane was back in the fight, struggling with his dad. He moved the knife enough that Eve slid free and ran to grab on to Claire.

Frank shoved his son down on the hood of the car and raised the knife. He froze there, with rain pouring from his chin like a thin silver beard, and off the point of the knife.

"No!" Claire screamed, "No, don't hurt him!"

"Where's the vampire?" Frank yelled back. "Where is Michael Glass?"

"Gone," Shane said. He coughed away pounding rain. "Dad, he's gone. He's not here. *Dad.*"

Frank seemed to focus on his son for the first time. "Shane?"

"Yeah, Dad, it's me. Let me up, okay?" Shane was careful to keep his hands up, palms out in surrender. "Peace."

It worked. Frank stepped back and lowered the knife. "Good," he said. "I've been looking for you, boy." And then he hugged him. Shane still had his hands up, and froze in place without touching his father. Claire shivered at the look on his face.

"Yeah, good to see you, too," he said. "Back off, man. We're not close, in case you forgot."

"You're still my son. Blood is blood." Frank pushed him toward the truck, only lightly crushed where Eve's car had smacked it. "Get in."

"Why?"

"Because I said so!" Frank shouted. Shane just looked at him. "Dammit, boy, for once in your life, do what I tell you!"

"I spent most of my life doing what you told me," Shane said. "Including selling out my friends. Not happening anymore."

Frank's lips parted, temporarily amazed. He laughed. "Done drunk the suicide cola, didn't you?" When he shook his head, drops flew in all directions, and were immediately lost in the silver downpour. "Just get in. I'm trying to save your life. You don't want to be where you're trying to go."

Strangely enough, Frank Collins was making sense. Probably for all the wrong reasons, though.

"We have to get through," Claire shouted over the pounding rain. She was shivering, soaked through every layer of clothing. "It's important. People could die if we don't!"

"People are going to die," Collins agreed. "Omelets and eggs. You know the old saying."

Or chess, Claire thought. Though she didn't know whose side Frank Collins was playing on, or even if he knew he was being manipulated at all.

"There's a plan," Frank was saying to his son. "In all this crap, nobody's checking faces. Metal detectors are off. We seize control of the building and make things right. We shuffle these bastards off, once and for all. We can *do it!*"

"Dad," Shane said, "everybody in that building to-night is going to be killed. We have to get people *out*, not get them *in*. If you care anything about those idi-ots who buy your revolutionary crap, you'll call this off."

"Call it off?" Frank repeated, as uncomprehending as if Shane were speaking another language. "When we're this close? When we can *win*? Dammit, Shane, you used to believe in this. You used to—"

"Yeah. Used to. Look it up!" Shane shoved his fa-ther away from him, and walked over to Eve and Claire. "I've warned you, Dad. Don't do this. Not today. I won't turn you in, but I'm telling you, if you don't back off, you're dead."

"I don't take threats," Frank said. "Not from you."

"You're an idiot," Shane said. "And I tried."

He got back in the car, on the passenger-side front seat where Michael had been. Eve scrambled behind the wheel, and Claire in the back.

Eve reversed.

Frank stepped out into the road ahead of them, a scary-looking man in black leather with his straggling hair plastered around his face. Add in the big hunting knife, and cue the scary music.

Eve let up on the gas. "No," Shane said, and moved his left foot over to jam it on top of hers. "Go. He wants you to stop."

"Don't! I can't miss him, no—"

But it was too late. Frank was staring into the head-lights, squarely in the center of the hood, and he was getting closer and closer.

Frank Collins threw himself out of the way at the last possible second, Eve swerved wildly in the oppo-site direction to miss him, and somehow, they didn't kill Shane's dad.

"What the hell are you *doing*?" Eve yelled at Shane. She was shaking all over. So was Shane. "You want to run him over, do it on your own time! *God!*"

"Look behind you," Shane whispered.

There were people coming after them. A *lot* of people. They'd been hiding in the alley, Claire guessed. They had guns, and now they opened fire. The car shuddered, and the back window exploded into cracks, then fell with a crash all over Claire's neck.

"Get up here!" Shane said, and grabbed her hands to haul her into the front seat. "Keep your head down!"

Eve had sunk down on the driver's side, barely keeping her eyes above the dashboard. She was panting hoarsely, panicked, and more gunshots were rattling the back of the car. Something hit the front window, too, adding more cracks and a round, backward splash of a hole.

"Faster!" Shane yelled. Eve hit the gas hard, and whipped around a slower-moving van. The firing ceased, at least for now. "You see why I didn't want you to stop?"

"Okay, your father is officially *off my Christmas list*!" Eve yelled. "Oh my God, look at my car!"

Shane barked out a laugh. "Yeah," he agreed. "That's what's important."

"It's better than thinking about what would have happened," Eve said. "If Michael had been with us—"

Claire thought about the mobs Richard had talked about, and the dead vampires, and felt sick. "They'd have dragged him off," she said. "They'd have killed him."

Michael had been right about Shane's dad, but then, Claire had never really doubted it. Neither had Shane, from the sick certainty on his face. He wiped his eyes with his forearm, which really didn't help much; they were all dripping wet, from head to toe.

"Let's just get to the building," Shane said. "We can't do much until we find Richard."

Only it wasn't that simple, even getting in. The underground parking was crammed full of cars, parked haphazardly at every angle. As Eve inched through the shadows, looking for any place to go, she shook her head. "If we do manage to get people to leave, they won't be able to take their cars. Everybody's blocked in," she said. "This is massively screwed up." Claire, for her part, thought some of it seemed deliberate, not just panic. "Okay, I'm going to pull it against the wall and hope we can get out if we need to."

The elevator was already locked down, the doors open but the lights off and buttons unresponsive. They took the stairs at a run.

The first-floor door seemed to be locked, until Shane pushed on it harder, and then it creaked open against a flood of protests.

The vestibule was full of people.

Morganville's City Hall wasn't all that large, at least not here in the lobby area. There was a big, sweeping staircase leading up, all grand marble and polished wood, and glass display cases taking up part of one wall. The License Bureau was off to the right: six old-time bank windows, with bars, all closed. Next to each window was a brass plaque that read what the windows were supposed to deliver: RESIDENTIAL LICENSING, CAR REGISTRATION, ZONING CHANGE REQUESTS, SPECIAL PERMITS, TRAFFIC VIOLATIONS, FINE PAYMENTS, TAXES, CITY SERVICES.

But not today.

The lobby was jammed with people. Families, mostly—mothers and fathers with kids, some as young as infants. Claire didn't see a single vampire in the crowd, not even Michael. At the far end, a yellow Civil Defense sign indicated that the door led to a Safe Shelter, with a tornado graphic next to it. A policeman with a bullhorn was yelling for order, not that he was getting any; people were pushing, shoving, and shouting at one another. "The shelter is now at maximum capacity! Please be calm!"

"Not good," Shane said. There was no sign of Richard, although there were at least ten uniformed police officers trying to manage the crowd. "Upstairs?"

"Upstairs," Eve agreed, and they squeezed back into the fire stairs and ran up to the next level. The sign in the stairwell said that this floor contained the mayor's office, sheriff's office, city council chambers, and something called, vaguely, Records.

The door was locked. Shane rattled it and banged for entrance, but nobody came to the rescue.

"Guess we go up," he said.

The third floor had no signs in the stairwell at all, but there was a symbol—the Founder's glyph, like the one on Claire's bracelet. Shane turned the knob, but again, the door didn't open. "I didn't think they could do that to fire stairs," Eve said.

"Yeah, call a cop." Shane looked up the steps. "One more floor, and then it's just the roof, and I'm thinking that's not a good idea, the roof."

"Wait." Claire studied the Founder's glyph for a few seconds, then shrugged and reached out to turn the knob.

Something clicked, and it turned. The door opened.

"How did you . . . ?"

Claire held up her wrist, and the gold bracelet. "It was worth a shot. I thought, maybe with a gold bracelet—"

"Genius. Go on, get inside," Shane said, and hustled them in. The door clicked shut behind them, and locked with a snap of metal. The hallway seemed dark, after the fluorescent lights in the stairs, and that was because the lights were dimmed way down, the carpet was dark, and so was the wood paneling.

It reminded Claire eerily of the hallway where they'd rescued Myrnin, only there weren't as many doors opening off it. Shane took the lead—of course—but the doors they could open were just simple offices, nothing fancy about them at all.

And then there was a door at the end of the hall with the Founder's Symbol etched on the polished brass doorknob. Shane tried it, shook his head, and motioned for Claire.

It opened easily at her touch.

Inside were—apartments. Chambers? Claire didn't know what else to call them; there was an entire complex of rooms leading from one central area.

It was like stepping into a whole different world, and Claire could tell that it had once been beautiful: a fairytale room, of rich satin on the walls, Persian rugs, delicate white and gold furniture.

"Michael? Mayor Morrell? Richard?"

It was a queen's room, and somebody had completely wrecked it. Most of the furniture was overturned, some kicked to pieces. Mirrors smashed. Fabrics ripped.

Claire froze.

Lying on the remaining long, delicate sofa was François, Bishop's other loyal vampire buddy, who'd come to Morganville along with Ysandre as his entourage. The vampire looked completely at ease—legs crossed at the ankles, head propped on a plump satin pillow. A big crystal glass of something in dark red rested on his chest.

He giggled and saluted them with the blood. "Hello, little friends," he said. "We weren't expecting you, but you'll do. We're almost out of refreshments."

"Out," Shane said, and shoved Eve toward the door.

It slammed shut before she could reach it, and there stood Mr. Bishop, still dressed in his long purple cassock from the feast. It was still torn on the side, where Myrnin had slashed at him with the knife.

There was something so ancient about him, so completely uncaring, that Claire felt her mouth go dry. "Where is she?" Bishop asked. "I know you've seen my daughter. I can smell her on you."

"Ewww," Eve said, very faintly. "So much more than I needed to know."

Bishop didn't look away from Claire's face, just pointed at Eve. "Silence, or be silenced. When I want to know your opinion, I'll consult your entrails."

Eve shut up. François swung his legs over the edge

of the sofa and sat up in one smooth motion. He downed the rest of his glass of blood and let the glass fall, shedding crimson drops all over the pale carpet. He'd gotten some on his fingers. He licked them, then smeared the rest all over the satin wall.

"Please," he said, and batted his long-lashed eyes at Eve. "Please, say something. I love entrails."

She shrank back against the wall. Even Shane stayed quiet, though Claire could tell he was itching to pull her to safety. *You can't protect me,* she thought fiercely. *Don't try.*

"You don't know where Amelie is?" Claire asked Bishop directly. "How's that master plan going, then?"

"Oh, it's going just fine," Bishop said. "Oliver is dead by now. Myrnin—well, we both know that Myrnin is insane, at best, and homicidal at his even better. I'm rather hoping he'll come charging to your rescue and forget who you are once he arrives. That would be amusing, and very typical of him, I'm afraid." Bishop's eyes bored into hers, and Claire felt the net closing around her. "Where is Amelie?"

"Where you'll never find her."

"Fine. Let her lurk in the shadows with her creations, until hunger or the humans destroy them. This doesn't have to be a battle, you know. It can be a war of attrition just as easily. I have the high ground." He gestured around the ruined apartment with one lazy hand. "And of course, I have everyone here, whether they know it or not."

She didn't hear him move, but flinched as François trailed cold fingers across the back of her neck, then gripped her tightly.

"Just like that," Bishop said. "Just precisely like that." He nodded to François. "If you want her, take her. I'm no longer interested in Amelie's pets. Take these others, too, unless you wish to save them for later."

Claire heard Shane whisper, "No," and heard the complete despair in his voice just as Bishop's follower wrenched her head over to the side, baring her neck.

She felt his lips touch her skin. They burned like ice.

"Ah!" François jerked his head back. "You little peasant." He used a fold of her shirt to take hold of the silver chain around her neck, and broke it with a sharp twist.

Claire caught the cross in her hand as it fell.

"May it comfort you," Bishop said, and smiled. "My child."

And then François bit her.

"Claire?" Somewhere, a long way off, Eve was crying. "Oh my God, Claire? Can you hear me? Come on, please, *please* come back. Are you sure she's got a pulse?"

"Yes, she's got a pulse." Claire knew that voice. Richard Morrell. But why was he here? Who called the police? She remembered the accident with the truck—no, that was before.

Bishop.

Claire slowly opened her eyes. The world felt very far away, and safely muffled for the moment. She heard Eve let out a gasp and a flood of words, but Claire didn't try to identify the meaning.

I have a pulse.

That seemed important.

My neck hurts.

Because a vampire had bitten her.

Claire raised her left hand slowly to touch her neck, and found a huge wad of what felt like somebody's shirt pressed against her neck.

"No," Richard said, and forced her hand back down. "Don't touch it. It's still closing up. You shouldn't move for another hour or so. Let the wounds close."

"Bit," Claire murmured. "He bit me." That came in a blinding flash, like a red knife cutting through the fog. "Don't let me turn into one."

"You won't," Eve said. She was upside down—no,

Claire's head was in her lap, and Eve was leaning over her. Claire felt the warm drip of Eve's tears on her face. "Oh, sweetie. You're going to be okay. Right?" Even upside down, Eve's look was panicked as she appealed to Richard, who sat on her right.

"You'll be all right," he said. He didn't look much better than Claire felt. "I have to see to my father. Here." He moved out of the way, and someone else sat in his place.

Shane. His warm fingers closed over hers, and she shivered when she realized how cold she felt. Eve tucked an expensive velvet blanket over and around her, fussing nervously.

Shane didn't say anything. He was so *quiet*.

"My cross," Claire said. It had been in her hand. She didn't know where it was now. "He broke the chain. I'm sorry—"

Shane opened her fingers and tipped the cross and chain into her hand. "I picked it up," he said. "Figured you might want it." There was something he wasn't saying. Claire looked at Eve to find out what it was, but she wasn't talking, for a change. "Anyway, you're going to be okay. We're lucky this time. François wasn't that hungry." He closed her fingers around the cross and held on.

His hands were shaking. "Shane?"

"I'm sorry," he whispered. "I couldn't move. I just *stood there*."

"No, he didn't," Eve said. "He knocked Franny clear across the room and he would have staked him with a chair leg, except Bishop stepped in."

That sounded like Shane. "You're not hurt?" Claire asked.

"Not much."

Eve frowned. "Well—"

"Not much," Shane repeated. "I'm okay, Claire."

She kind of had to take that at face value, at least right now. "What time—"

"Six fifteen," Richard said, from the far corner of

the small room. This, Claire guessed, had been some
kind of dressing area for Amelie. She saw a long closet
to the side. Most of the clothes were shredded and
scattered in piles on the floor. The dressing table was
a ruin, and every mirror was broken.

François had had his fun in here, too.

"The storm's heading for us," Eve said. "Michael
never got to Richard, but he got to Joe Hess, apparently. They evacuated the shelters. Bishop was pretty
mad about that. He wanted a lot of hostages between
him and Amelie."

"So all that's left is us?"

"Us. And Bishop's people, who didn't leave. And
Fabulous Frank Collins and his Wild Bunch, who
rolled into the lobby and now think they've won some
kind of battle or something." Eve rolled her eyes, and
for an instant was back to her old self. "Just us and
the bad guys."

Did that make Richard—no. Claire couldn't believe
that. If anyone in Morganville had honestly tried to
do the right thing, it was Richard Morrell.

Eve followed Claire's look. "Oh. Yeah, his dad got
hurt trying to stop Bishop from taking over downstairs. Richard's been trying to take care of him, and
his mom. We were right about Sullivan, by the way.
Total backstabber. Yay for premonitions. Wish I had
one right now that could help get us out of this."

"No way out," Claire said.

"Not even a window," Eve said. "We're locked in
here. No idea where Bishop and his little sock monkey
got off to. Looking for Amelie, I guess. I wish they'd
just kill each other already."

Eve didn't mean it, not really, but Claire understood
how she felt. Distantly. In a detached, shocked kind
of way.

"What's happening outside?"

"Not a clue. No radios in here. They took our cell
phones. We're"—the lights blinked and failed, putting the room into pitch darkness—"screwed," Eve

finished. "Oh man, I should not have said that, should I?"

"Power's gone out to the building, I think," Richard said. "It's probably the storm."

Or the vampires screwing with them, just because they could. Claire didn't say it out loud, but she thought it pretty hard.

Shane's hand kept holding hers. "Shane?"

"Right here," he said. "Stay still."

"I'm sorry. I'm really, really sorry."

"What for?"

"I shouldn't have gotten angry with you, before, about your dad. . . ."

"Not important," he said very softly. "It's okay, Claire. Just rest."

Rest? She couldn't rest. Reality was pushing back in, reminding her of pain, of fear, and most important, of time.

There was an eerie, ghostly sound now, wailing, and getting louder.

"What is that?" Eve asked, and then, before anybody could answer, did so herself. "Tornado sirens. There's one on the roof."

The rising, falling wail got louder, but with it came something else—a sound like water rushing, or—

"We need to get to cover," Richard said. A flashlight snapped on, and played over Eve's pallid face, then Shane's and Claire's. "You guys, get her over here. This is the strongest interior corner. That side faces out toward the street."

Claire tried to get up, but Shane scooped her in his arms and carried her. He set her down with her back against a wall, then got under the blanket next to her with Eve on his other side. The flashlight turned away from them, and in its sweep, Claire caught sight of Mayor Morrell. He was a fat man, with a politician's smooth face and smile, but he didn't look anything like she remembered now. He seemed older, shrunken inside his suit, and very ill.

"What's wrong with him?" Claire whispered.

Shane's answer stirred the damp hair around her face. "Heart attack," he said. "At least, that's Richard's best guess. Looks bad."

It really did. The mayor was propped against the wall a few feet from them, and he was gasping for breath as his wife (Claire had never seen her before, except in pictures) patted his arm and murmured in his ear. His face was ash gray, his lips turning blue, and there was real panic in his eyes.

Richard returned, dragging another thick blanket and some pillows. "Everybody cover up," he said. "Keep your heads down." He covered his mother and father and crouched next to them as he wrapped himself in another blanket.

The wind outside was building to a howl. Claire could hear things hitting the walls—dull thudding sounds, like baseballs. It got louder. "Debris," Richard said. He focused the light on the carpet between their small group. "Maybe hail. Could be anything."

The siren cut off abruptly, but that didn't mean the noise subsided; if anything, it got louder, ratcheting up from a howl to a scream—and then it took on a deeper tone.

"Sounds like a train," Eve said shakily. "Damn, I was really hoping that wasn't true, the train thing—"

"Heads down!" Richard yelled, as the whole building started to shake. Claire could feel the boards vibrating underneath her. She could see the walls bending, and cracks forming in the bricks.

And then the noise rose to a constant, deafening scream, and the whole outside wall sagged, dissolved into bricks and broken wood, and disappeared. The ripped, torn fabric around the room took flight like startled birds, whipping wildly through the air and getting shredded into ever-smaller sections by the wind and debris.

The storm was screaming as if it had gone insane.

Broken furniture and shards of mirrors flew around, smashing into the walls, hitting the blankets.

Claire heard a heavy groan even over the shrieking wind, and looked up to see the roof sagging overhead. Dust and plaster cascaded down, and she grabbed Shane hard.

The roof came down on top of them.

Claire didn't know how long it lasted. It seemed like forever, really—the screaming, the shaking, the pressure of things on top of her.

And then, very gradually, it stopped, and the rain began to hammer down again, drenching the pile of dust and wood. Some of it trickled down to drip on her cheek, which was how she knew.

Shane's hand moved on her shoulder, more of a twitch than a conscious motion, and then he let go of Claire to heave up with both hands. Debris slid and rattled. They'd been lucky, Claire realized—a heavy wooden beam had collapsed in over their heads at a slant, and it had held the worst of the stuff off them.

"Eve?" Claire reached across Shane and grabbed her friend's hands. Eve's eyes were closed, and there was blood trickling down one side of her face. Her face was even whiter than usual—plaster dust, Claire realized.

Eve coughed, and her eyelids fluttered up. "Mom?" The uncertainty in her voice made Claire want to cry. "Oh God, what happened? Claire?"

"We're alive," Shane said. He sounded kind of surprised. He brushed fallen chunks of wood and plaster off Claire's head, and she coughed, too. The rain pounded in at an angle, soaking the blanket that covered them. "Richard?"

"Over here," Richard said. "Dad? Dad—"

The flashlight was gone, rolled off or buried or just plain taken away by the wind. Lightning flashed, bright as day, and Claire saw the tornado that had hit them still moving through Morganville, crashing through buildings, spraying debris a hundred feet into the air.

It didn't even look *real*.

Shane helped move a beam off Eve's legs—thankfully, they were just bruised, not broken—and crawled across the slipping wreckage toward Richard, who was lifting things off his mother. She looked okay, but she was crying and dazed.

His father, though . . .

"No," Richard said, and dragged his father flat. He started administering CPR. There were bloody cuts on his face, but he didn't seem to care about his own problems at all. "Shane! Breathe for him!"

After a hesitation, Shane tilted the mayor's head back. "Like this?"

"Let me," Eve said. "I've had CPR training." She crawled over and took in a deep breath, bent, and blew it into the mayor's mouth, watching for his chest to rise. It seemed to take a lot of effort. So did what Richard was doing, pumping on his dad's chest, over and over. Eve counted slowly, then breathed again—and again.

"I'll get help," Claire said. She wasn't sure there *was* any help, really, but she had to do something. When she stood up, though, she felt dizzy and weak, and remembered what Richard had said—she had holes in her neck, and she'd lost a lot of blood. "I'll go slow."

"I'll go with you," Shane said, but Richard grabbed him and pulled him down.

"No! I need you to take over here." He showed Shane how to place his hands, and got him started. He pulled the walkie-talkie from his belt and tossed it to Claire. "Go. We need paramedics."

And then Richard collapsed, and Claire realized that he had a huge piece of metal in his side. She stood there, frozen in horror, and then punched in the code for the walkie-talkie. "Hello? Hello, is anybody there?"

Static. If there was anybody, she couldn't hear it over the interference and the roaring rain.

"I have to go!" she shouted at Shane. He looked up.

"No!" But he couldn't stop her, not without letting the mayor die, and after one helpless, furious look at her, he went back to work.

Claire slid over the pile of debris and scrambled out the broken door, into the main apartment.

There was no sign of François or Bishop. If the place had been wrecked before, it was unrecognizable now. Most of this part of the building was gone, just— gone. She felt the floor groan underneath her, and moved fast, heading for the apartment's front door. It was still on its hinges, but as she pulled on it, part of the frame came out of the wall.

Outside, the hallway seemed eerily unmarked, ex- cept that the roof overhead—and, Claire presumed, all of the next floor above—was missing. It was a hall- way open to the storm. She hurried along it, glad now for the flashes of lightning that lit her way.

The fire stairs at the end seemed intact. She passed some people huddled there, clearly terrified. "We need help!" she said. "There are people hurt upstairs— somebody?"

And then the screaming started, somewhere about a floor down, lots of people screaming at the same time. Those who were sitting on the stairs jumped to their feet and ran up, toward Claire. "No!" she yelled. "No, you can't!"

But she was shoved out of the way, and about fifty people trampled past her, heading up. She had no idea where they'd go.

Worse, she was afraid their combined weight would collapse that part of the building, including the place where Eve, Shane, and the Morrells were.

"Claire?" Michael. He came out of the first-floor

door, and leaped two flights of stairs in about two jumps to reach her. Before she could protest, he'd grabbed her in his arms like an invalid. "Come on. I have to get you out of here."

"No! No, go up. Shane, they need help. Go up; leave me here!"

"I can't." He looked down, and so did she.

Vampires poured into the stairwell below. Some of them were fighting, ripping at one another. Any human who got between them went down screaming.

"Right. Up it is," he said, and she felt them leave the ground in one powerful leap, hitting the third-floor landing with catlike grace.

"What's happening?" Claire twisted to try to look down, but it didn't make any sense to her. It was just a mob, fighting one another. No telling who was on which side, or even why they were fighting so furiously.

"Amelie's down there," Michael said. "Bishop's trying to get to her, but he's losing followers fast. She took him by surprise, during the storm."

"What about the people—I mean, the humans? Shane's dad, and the ones who wanted to take over?"

Michael kicked open the door to the third-floor roofless hallway. The people who'd run past Claire were milling around in it, frightened and babbling. Michael brought down his fangs and snarled at them, and they scattered into whatever shelter they could reach—interior offices, mostly, that had sustained little damage except for rain.

He shoved past those who had nowhere to go, and down to the end of the hall. "In here?" He let Claire slide down to her feet, and his gaze focused on her neck. "Someone bit you."

"It's not so bad." Claire put her hand over the wound, trying to cover it up. The wound's edges felt ragged, and they were still leaking blood, she thought, although that could have just been the rain. "I'm okay."

"No, you're not."

A gust of wind blew his collar back, and she saw the white outlines of marks on his own neck. "Michael! Did you get bitten, too?"

"Like you said, it's nothing. Look, we can talk about that later. Let's get to our friends. First aid later."

Claire opened the door and stepped through . . . and the floor collapsed underneath her.

She must have screamed, but all she heard was the tremendous cracking sound of more of the building falling apart underneath and around her. She turned toward Michael, who was frozen in the doorway, illuminated in stark white by a nearby lightning strike.

He reached out and grabbed her arm as she flung it toward him, and then she was suspended in midair, wind and dust rushing up around her, as the floor underneath fell away. Michael pulled, and she almost flew, weightless, into his arms.

"Oh," she whispered faintly. "Thanks."

He held on to her for a minute without speaking, then said, "Is there another way in?"

"I don't know."

They backed up and found the next office to the left, which had suspicious-looking cracks in its walls. Claire thought the floor felt a little unsteady. Michael pushed her back behind him and said, "Cover your eyes."

Then he began ripping away the wall between the office and Amelie's apartments. When he hit solid red brick, he punched it, breaking it into dust.

"This isn't helping keep things together!" Claire yelled.

"I know, but we need to get them out!"

He ripped a hole in the wall big enough to step through, and braced himself in it as the whole building seemed to shudder, as if shifting its weight. "The floor's all right here," he said. "You stay. I'll go."

"Through that door, to the left!" Claire called. Michael disappeared, moving fast and gracefully.

She wondered, all of a sudden, why he wasn't downstairs. Why he wasn't fighting, like all the others of Amelie's blood.

A couple of tense minutes passed, as she stared through the hole; nothing seemed to be happening. She couldn't hear Michael, or Shane, or anything else.

And then she heard screaming behind her, in the hall. *Vampires,* she thought, and quickly opened the door to look.

Someone fell against the wood, knocking her backward. It was François. Claire tried to shut the door, but a bloodstained white hand wormed through the opening and grabbed the edge, shoving it wider.

François didn't look even remotely human anymore, but he did look absolutely desperate, willing to do anything to survive, and very, very angry.

Claire backed up, slowly, until she was standing with her back against the far wall. There wasn't much in here to help her—a desk, some pens and pencils in a cup.

François laughed, and then he growled. "You think you're winning," he said. "You're not."

"I think you're the one who has to worry," Michael said from the hole in the wall. He stepped through, carrying Mayor Morrell in his arms. Shane and Eve were with him, supporting Richard's sagging body between them. Mrs. Morrell brought up the rear. "Back off. I won't come after you if you run."

François' eyes turned ruby, and he threw himself at Michael, who was burdened with the mayor.

Claire grabbed a pencil from the cup and plunged it into François' back.

He whirled, looking stunned . . . and then he slowly collapsed to the carpet.

"That won't kill him," Michael said.

"I don't care," Eve said. "Because that was *fierce.*"

Claire grabbed the vampire's arms and dragged him out of the way, careful not to dislodge the pencil; she wasn't really sure how deep it had gone, and if it slipped out of his heart, they were all in big trouble. Michael edged around him and opened the door to check the corridor. "Clear," he said. "For the moment. Come on."

Their little refugee group hurried into the rainy hall, squishing through soggy carpet. There were people hiding in the offices, or just pressed against the walls and hoping not to be noticed. "Come on," Eve said to them. "Get up. We're getting out of here before this whole thing comes down!"

The fighting in the stairwell was still going on—snarling, screams, bangs, and thuds. Claire didn't dare look over the railing. Michael led them down to the locked second-floor entrance. He pulled hard on it, and the knob popped off—but the door stayed locked.

"Hey, Mike?" Shane had edged to the end of the landing to look over the railing. "Can't go that way."

"I know!"

"Also, time is—"

"I know, Shane!" Michael started kicking the door, but it was reinforced, stronger than the other doors Claire had seen. It bent, but didn't open.

And then it did open . . . from the inside.

There, in his fancy but battered black velvet, stood Myrnin.

"In," he said. "This way. Hurry."

The falling sensation warned Claire that the door was a portal, but she didn't have time to tell anybody else, so when they stepped through into Myrnin's lab, it was probably kind of a shock. Michael didn't pause; he pushed a bunch of broken glassware from a lab table and put Mr. Morrell down on it, then touched pale fingers to the man's throat. When he found nothing, he started CPR again. Eve hurried over to breathe for him.

Myrnin didn't move as the refugees streamed in past

him. He was standing with his arms folded, a frown grooved between his brows. "Who are all these people?" he asked. "I am not an innkeeper, you know."

"Shut up," Claire said. She didn't have any patience with Myrnin right now. "Is he okay?" She was talking to Shane, who was easing Richard onto a threadbare rug near the far wall.

"You mean, except for the big piece of metal in him? Look, I don't know. He's breathing, at least."

The rest of the refugees clustered together, filtering slowly through the portal. Most of them had no idea what had just happened, which was good. If they'd been part of Frank's group, intending to take over Morganville, that ambition was long gone. Now they were just people, and they were just scared.

"Up the stairs," Claire told them. "You can get out that way."

Most of them rushed for the exit. She hoped they'd make it home, or at least to some kind of safe place.

She hoped they had homes to go back to.

Myrnin glared at her. "You do realize that this was a *secret* laboratory, don't you? And now half of Morganville knows where it is?"

"Hey, I didn't open the door; you did." She reached over and put her hand on his arm, looking up into his face. "Thank you. You saved our lives."

He blinked slowly. "Did I?"

"I know why you weren't fighting," Claire said. "The drugs kept you from having to. But . . . Michael?"

Myrnin followed her gaze to where Eve and Michael remained bent over the mayor's still form. "Amelie let him go," he said. "For now. She could claim him again at any time, but I think she knew you needed help." He uncrossed his arms and walked over to Michael to touch his shoulder. "It's no use," he said. "I can smell death on him. So can you, if you try. You won't bring him back."

"No!" Mrs. Morrell screamed, and threw herself over her husband's body. "No, you have to try!"

"They did," Myrnin said, and retreated to lean against a convenient wall. "Which is more than I would have." He nodded toward Richard. "He might live, but to remove that metal will require a chirurgeon."

"You mean, a doctor?" Claire asked.

"Yes, of course, a doctor," Myrnin snapped, and his eyes flared red. "I know you want me to feel some sympathy for them, but that is not who I am. I care only about those I know, and even then, not all that deeply. Strangers get nothing from me." He was slipping, and the anger was coming back. Next it would be confusion. Claire silently dug in her pockets. She'd put a single glass vial in, and miraculously, it was still unbroken.

He slapped it out of her hand impatiently. "I don't need it!"

Claire watched it clatter to the floor, heart in her mouth, and said, "You do. You know you do. Please, Myrnin. I don't need your crap right now. Just *take your medicine.*"

She didn't think he would, not at first, but then he snorted, bent down, and picked up the vial. He broke the cap off and dumped the liquid into his mouth. "There," he said. "Satisfied?" He shattered the glass in his fingers, and the red glow in his eyes intensified. "Are you, little Claire? Do you enjoy giving me orders?"

"Myrnin."

His hand went around her throat, choking off whatever she was going to say.

She didn't move.

His hand didn't tighten.

The red glow slowly faded away, replaced by a look of shame. He let go of her and backed away a full step, head down.

"I don't know where to get a doctor," Claire said, as if nothing had happened. "The hospital, maybe, or—"

"No," Myrnin murmured. "I will bring help. Don't let anyone go through my things. And watch Michael, in case."

She nodded. Myrnin opened the portal doorway in the wall and stepped through it, heading—where? She had no idea. Amelie had, Claire thought, shut down all the nodes. But if that was true, how had they gotten here?

Myrnin could open and close them at will. But he was probably the only one who could.

Michael and Eve moved away from Mayor Morrell's body, as his wife stood over him and cried.

"What can we do?" Shane asked. He sounded miserable. In all the confusion, he'd missed her confrontation with Myrnin. She was dimly glad about that.

"Nothing," Michael said. "Nothing but wait."

When the portal opened again, Myrnin stepped through, then helped someone else over the step.

It was Theo Goldman, carrying an antique doctor's bag. He looked around the lab, nodding to Claire in particular, and then moved to where Richard was lying on the carpet, with his head in his mother's lap. "Move back, please," he told her, and knelt down to open his bag. "Myrnin. Take her in the other room. A mother shouldn't see this."

He was setting out instruments, unrolling them in a clean white towel. As Claire watched, Myrnin led Mrs. Morrell away and seated her in a chair in the corner, where he normally sat to read. She seemed dazed now, probably in shock. The chair was intact. It was just about the only thing in the lab that was—the scientific instruments were smashed, lab tables overturned, candles and lamps broken.

Books were piled in the corners and burned, reduced to scraps of leather and curling black ash. The whole place smelled sharply of chemicals and fire.

"What can we do?" Michael asked, crouching down on Richard's other side. Theo took out several pairs of latex gloves and passed one set to Michael. He donned one himself.

"You can act as my nurse, my friend," he said. "I would have brought my wife—she has many years of training in this—but I don't want to leave my children on their own. They're already very frightened."

"But they're safe?" Eve asked. "Nobody's bothered you?"

"No one has so much as knocked on the door," he said. "It's a very good hiding place. Thank you."

"I think you're paying us back," Eve said. "Please. Can you save him?"

"It's in God's hands, not mine." Still, Theo's eyes were bright as he looked at the twisted metal plate embedded in Richard's side. "It's good that he's unconscious, but he might wake during the procedure. There is chloroform in the bag. It's Michael, yes? Michael, please put some on a cloth and be ready when I tell you to cover his mouth and nose."

Claire's nerve failed around the time that Theo took hold of the piece of steel, and she turned away. Eve already had, to take a blanket to Mrs. Morrell and put it around her shoulders.

"Where's my daughter?" the mayor's wife asked. "Monica should be here. I don't want her out there alone."

Eve raised her eyebrows at Claire, clearly wondering where Monica was.

"The last time I saw her, she was at school," Claire said. "But that was before I got the call to come home, so I don't know. Maybe she's in shelter in the dorm?" She checked her cell phone. No bars. Reception was usually spotty down here in the lab, but she could usually see something, even if it was only a flicker. "I think the cell towers are down."

"Yeah, likely," Eve agreed. She reached over to tuck the blanket around Mrs. Morrell, who leaned her head back and closed her eyes, as if the strength was just leaking right out of her. "You think this is the right thing to do? I mean, do we even know this guy or anything?"

Claire didn't, really, but she still wanted to like Theo, in much the same way as she liked Myrnin—against her better sense. "I think he's okay. And it's not like anybody's making house calls right now."

The operation—and it was an operation, with suturing and everything—took a couple of hours before Theo sat back, stripped off the gloves, and sighed in quiet satisfaction. "There," he said. Claire and Eve got up to walk over as Michael rose to his feet. Shane had been hanging on the edges, watching in what Claire thought looked like queasy fascination. "His pulse is steady. He's lost some blood, but I believe he will be all right, provided no infection sets in. Still, this century has those wonderful antibiotics, yes? So that is not so bad." Theo was almost beaming. "I must say, I haven't used my surgical skills in years. It's very exciting. Although it makes me hungry."

Claire was pretty sure Richard wouldn't want to know that. She knew she wouldn't have, in his place.

"Thank you," Mrs. Morrell said. She got up from the chair, folded the blanket and put it aside, then walked over to shake Theo's hand with simple, dignified gratitude. "I'll see that my husband compensates you for your kindness."

They all exchanged looks. Michael started to speak, but Theo shook his head. "That's quite all right, dear lady. I am delighted to help. I recently lost a son myself. I know the weight of grief."

"Oh," Mrs. Morrell said, "I'm so sorry for your loss, sir." She said it as if she didn't know her husband was lying across the room, dead.

Tears sparkled in his eyes, Claire saw, but then he blinked them away and smiled. He patted her hand gently. "You are very generous to an old man," he said. "We have always liked living in Morganville, you know. The people are so kind."

Shane said, "Some of those same people killed your son."

Theo looked at him with calm, unflinching eyes. "And without forgiveness, there is never any peace. I tell you this from the distance of many centuries. My son gave his life. I won't reply to his gift with anger, not even for those who took him from me. Those same poor, sad people will wake up tomorrow grieving their own losses, I think, if they survive at all. How can hating them heal me?"

Myrnin, who hadn't spoken at all, murmured, "You shame me, Theo."

"I don't mean to do so," he said, and shrugged. "Well. I should get back to my family now. I wish you all well."

Myrnin got up from his chair and walked with Theo to the portal. They all watched him go. Mrs. Morrell was staring after him with a bright, odd look in her eyes.

"How very strange," she said. "I wish Mr. Morrell had been available to meet him."

She spoke as if he were in a meeting downtown instead of under a sheet on the other side of the room. Claire shuddered.

"Come on, let's go see Richard," Eve said, and led her away.

Shane let out his breath in a slow hiss. "I wish it were as simple as Theo thinks it is, to stop hating." He swallowed, watching Mrs. Morrell. "I wish I could, I really do."

"At least you want to," Michael said. "It's a start."

They stayed the night in the lab, mainly because the storm continued outside until the wee hours of the morning—rain, mostly, with some hail. There didn't seem to be much point running out in it. Claire kept checking her phone, Eve found a portable radio buried in piles of junk at the back of the room, and they checked for news at regular intervals.

Around three a.m. they got some. It was on the radio's emergency alert frequency.

All Morganville residents and surrounding areas: we remain under severe thunderstorm warnings, with high winds and possible flooding, until seven a.m. today. Rescue efforts are under way at City Hall, which was partially destroyed by a tornado that also leveled several warehouses and abandoned buildings, as well as one building in Founder's Square. There are numerous reports of injuries coming in. Please remain calm. Emergency teams are working their way through town now, looking for anyone who may be in need of assistance. Stay where you are. Please do not attempt to go out into the streets at this time.

It started to repeat. Eve frowned and looked up at Myrnin, who had listened as well. "What aren't they saying?" she asked.

"If I had to guess, their urgent desire that people stay within shelter would tell me there are other things to worry about." His dark eyes grew distant for a moment, then snapped back into focus. "Ibid nothing."

"What?" Eve seemed to think she'd misheard.

"Ibid nothing carlo. I don't justice."

Myrnin was making word salad again—a precursor to the drugs wearing off—more quickly than Claire had expected, actually, and that was worrying.

Eve sent Claire a look of alarm. "Okay, I didn't really understand that at all—"

Claire put a hand on her arm to silence her. "Why don't you go see Mrs. Morrell? You too, Shane."

He didn't like it, but he went. As he did, he jerked his head at Michael, who rose from where he was sitting with Richard and strolled over.

Casually.

"Myrnin," Claire said. "You need to listen to me, okay? I think your drugs are wearing off again."

"I'm fine." His excitement level was rising; she could see it—a very light flush in his face, his eyes starting to glitter. "You worry over notebook."

There was no point in trying to explain the signs; he never could identify them. "We should check on the prison," she said. "See if everything's still okay there."

Myrnin smiled. "You're trying to trick me." His eyes were getting darker, endlessly dark, and that smile had edges to it. "Oh, little girl, you don't know. You don't know what it's like, having all these guests here, and all this"—he breathed in deeply—"all this blood." His eyes focused on her throat, with its ragged bite mark hidden under a bandage Theo had given her. "I know it's there. Your mark. Tell me, did François—"

"Stop. Stop it." Claire dug her fingers into her palms. Myrnin took a step toward her, and she forced herself not to flinch. She knew him, knew what he was trying to do. "You won't hurt me. You need me."

"Do I?" He breathed deeply again. "Yes, I do. Bright, so bright. I can feel your energy. I know how it will feel when I . . ." He blinked, and horror sheeted across his face, fast as lightning. "What was I saying? Claire? What did I just say?"

She couldn't repeat it. "Nothing. Don't worry. But I think we'd better get you to the cell, okay? Please?"

He looked devastated. This was the worst part of it, she thought, the mood swings. He'd tried so hard, and he'd helped, he really had—but he wasn't going to be able to hold together much longer. She was seeing him fall apart in slow motion.

Again.

Michael steered him toward the portal. "Let's go," he said. "Claire, can you do this?"

"If he doesn't fight me," she said nervously. She remembered one afternoon when his paranoia had taken over, and every time she'd tried to establish the portal, he'd snapped the connection, sure something was waiting on the other side to destroy him. "I wish we had a tranquilizer."

"Well, you don't," Myrnin said. "And I don't like being stuck with your needles, you know that. I'll behave myself." He laughed softly. "Mostly."

Claire opened the door, but instead of the connection snapping clear to the prison, she felt it shift, pulled out of focus. "Myrnin, stop it!"

He spread his hands theatrically. "I didn't do anything."

She tried again. The connection bent, and before she could bring it back where she wanted it, an alternate destination came into focus.

Theo Goldman fell out of the door.

"Theo!" Myrnin caught him, surprised out of his petulance, at least for the moment. He eased the other vampire down to a sitting position against the wall. "Are you injured?"

"No, no, no—" Theo was gasping, though Claire knew he didn't need air, not the way humans did. This was emotion, not exertion. "Please, you have to help, I beg you. Help us, help my family, please—"

Myrnin crouched down to put their eyes on a level. "What's happened?"

Theo's eyes filled with tears that flowed over his lined, kind face. "Bishop," he said. "Bishop has my family. He says he wants Amelie and the book, or he will kill them all."

14

Theo hadn't come straight from Common Grounds, of course; he'd been taken to one of the open portals—he didn't know where—and forced through by Bishop. "No," he said, and stopped Michael as he tried to come closer. "No, not you. He only wants Amelie, and the book, and I want no more innocent blood shed, not yours or mine. Please. Myrnin, I know you can find her. You have the blood tie and I don't. Please find her and bring her. This is not our fight. It's family; it's father and daughter. They should end this, face-to-face."

Myrnin stared at him for a long, long moment, and then cocked his head to one side. "You want me to betray her," he said. "Deliver her to her father."

"No, no, I wouldn't ask for that. Only to—to let her know what price there will be. Amelie will come. I know she will."

"She won't," Myrnin said. "I won't let her."

Theo cried out in misery, and Claire bit her lip. "Can't you help him?" she said. "There's got to be a way!"

"Oh, there is," Myrnin said. "There is. But you won't like it, my little Claire. It isn't neat, and it isn't easy. And it will require considerable courage from you, yet again."

"I'll do it!"

"No, you won't," Shane and Michael said, at virtu-

ally the same time. Shane continued. "You're barely
on your feet, Claire. You don't go anywhere, not without me."

"And me," Michael said.

"Hell," Eve sighed. "I guess that means I have to
go, too. Which I may not ever forgive you for, even
if I don't die horribly."

Myrnin stared at each of them in turn. "You'd go.
All of you." His lips stretched into a crazy, rubber-
doll smile. "You are the best toys, you know. I can't
imagine how much *fun* it will be to play with you."

Silence, and then Eve said, "Okay, that was extra
creepy, with whipped creepy topping. And this is me,
changing my mind."

The glee faded from Myrnin's eyes, replaced with a
kind of lost desperation that Claire recognized all too
well. "It's coming. Claire, it's coming, I'm afraid. I
don't know what to do. I can feel it."

She reached out and took his hand. "I know. Please,
try. We need you right now. Can you hold on?"

He nodded, but it was more a convulsive response
than confirmation. "In the drawer by the skulls," he
said. "One last dose. I hid it. I forgot."

He did that; he hid things and remembered them at
odd moments—or never. Claire dashed off to the far
end of the room, near where Richard slept, and opened
drawer after drawer under the row of skulls he'd
nailed to the wall. He'd promised that they were all
clinical specimens, not one of them victims of violence.
She still didn't altogether believe him.

In the last drawer, shoved behind ancient rolls of
parchment and the mounted skeleton of a bat, were
two vials, both in brown glass. One, when she pried
up the stopper, proved to be red crystals.

The other was silver powder.

She put the vial with silver powder in her pants
pocket—careful to use the pocket without a hole in
it—and brought the red crystals back to Myrnin. He

nodded and slipped the vial into his vest pocket, inside the coat.

"Aren't you going to take them?"

"Not quite yet," he said, which scared the hell out of her, frankly. "I can stay focused a bit longer. I promise."

"So," Michael said, "what's the plan?"

"This."

Claire felt the portal snap into place behind her, clear as a lightning strike, and Myrnin grabbed the front of her shirt, swung her around, and threw her violently through the doorway.

She seemed to fall a really, really long time, but she hit the ground and rolled.

She opened her eyes on pitch darkness, smelling rot and old wine.

No.

She knew this place.

She was trying to get up when something else hit her from behind—Shane, from the sound of his angry cursing. She writhed around and slapped a hand over his mouth, which made him stop in midcurse. "Shhhh," she hissed, as softly as she could. Not that their rolling around on the floor hadn't rung the dinner bell loud and clear, of course.

Damn you, Myrnin.

A cold hand encircled her wrist and pulled her away from Shane, and when she hit out at it, she felt a velvet sleeve.

Myrnin. Shane was scrambling to his feet, too.

"Michael, can you see?" Myrnin's voice sounded completely calm.

"Yes." Michael's didn't. At *all.*

"Then *run*, damn you! I've got them!"

Myrnin followed his own advice, and Claire's arm was almost yanked from its socket as he dragged her with him. She heard Shane panting on his other side. Her foot came down on something springy, like a body, and she yelped. The sound echoed, and from the darkness on all sides, she heard what sounded like fingers tapping, sliding, coming closer.

Something grabbed her ankle, and this time Claire screamed. It felt like a wire loop, but when she tried to bat at it, she felt fingers, a thin, bony forearm, and nails like talons.

Myrnin skidded to a halt, turned, and stomped. Her ankle came free, and something in the darkness screamed in rage.

"Go!" He roared—not to them, but to Michael, Claire guessed. She saw a flash of something up ahead that wasn't quite light—the portal? That looked like the kind of shimmer it made when it was being activated.

Myrnin let go of her wrist, and shoved her forward.

Once again, she fell. This time, she landed on top of Michael.

Shane fell on top of her, and she gasped for air as all the breath was driven out of her. They squirmed around and separated. Michael pulled Eve to her feet.

"I know this place," Claire said. "This is where Myrnin—"

Myrnin stepped through the portal and slammed it shut, just as Amelie had done not so long ago. "We won't come back here," he said. "Out. Hurry. We don't have much time."

He led the way, long black coat flapping, and Claire had to dig deep to keep up, even with Shane helping her. When he slowed down and started to pick her up, she swatted at him breathlessly. "No, I'll make it!"

He didn't look so sure.

At the end of the stone hallway, they took a left, heading down the dark, paneled hall that Claire remembered, but they passed up the door she remembered as Myrnin's cell, where he'd been chained.

He didn't even slow down.

"Where are we going?" Eve gasped. "Man, I wish I'd worn different shoes—"

She cut herself off as Myrnin stopped at the end of the hallway. There was a massive wooden door there, medieval style with thick, hand-hammered iron bands, and the Founder's Symbol etched into the old wood.

He hadn't even broken a sweat. Of course. Claire windmilled her arms as she stumbled to a halt, and braced herself against the wall, chest heaving.

"Shouldn't we be armed?" Eve asked. "I mean, for a rescue mission, generally people go armed. I'm just pointing that out."

"I don't like this," Shane said.

Myrnin didn't move his gaze away from Claire. He reached out and took her hand in his. "Do you trust me?" he asked.

"I will if you take your meds," she said.

He shook his head. "I can't. I have my reasons, little one. Please. I must have your word."

Shane was shaking his head. Michael wasn't seeming any too confident about this, either, and Eve—Eve looked like she would gladly have run back the other way, if she'd known there was any other choice than going back into that darkness.

"Yes," Claire said.

Myrnin smiled. It was a tired, thin sort of smile, and it had a hint of sadness in it. "Then I should apologize now," he said. "Because I'm about to break that trust most grievously."

He dropped Claire's hand, grabbed Shane by the shirt, and kicked open the door.

He dragged Shane through with him, and the door slammed behind him before any of them could react— even Michael, who hit the wood just an instant later, battering at it. It was built to hold out vampires, Claire realized. And it would hold out Michael for a long, long time.

"Shane!" She screamed his name and threw herself against the wood, slamming her hand over and over into the Founder's Symbol. "Shane, *no*! Myrnin, bring him back. Please, don't do this. Bring him *back*. . . ."

Michael whirled around, facing the other direction. "Stay behind me," he said to Eve and Claire. Claire looked over her shoulder to see doors opening, up and down the hall, as if somebody had pressed a button.

Vampires and humans alike came out, filling the hallway between the three of them, and any possible way out.

Every single one of them had fang marks in their necks, just like the ones in Claire's neck.

Just like the ones in *Michael's* neck.

There was something about the way he was standing there, so still, so quiet. . . .

And then he walked away, heading for the other vampires.

"Michael!" Eve started to lunge after him, but Claire stopped her.

When Michael reached the first vampire, Claire expected to see some kind of a fight—*something*—but instead, they just looked at each other, and then the man nodded.

"Welcome," he said, "Brother Michael."

"Welcome," another vampire murmured, and then a human.

When Michael turned around, his eyes had shifted colors, going from sky blue to dark crimson.

"Oh *hell*," Eve whispered. "This isn't happening. It can't be."

The door opened behind them. On the other side was a big stone hall, something straight out of a castle, and the wooden throne that Claire remembered from the welcome feast was here, sitting up on a stage. It was draped in red velvet.

Sitting on the throne was Mr. Bishop.

"Join us," Bishop said. Claire and Eve looked at each other. Shane was lying on the stone floor, with Myrnin's hand holding him facedown. "Come in, children. There's no point anymore. I've won the night."

Claire felt like she'd stepped off the edge of the

world, and everything was just . . . gone. Myrnin wouldn't look at her. He had his head bowed to Bishop.

Eve, after that first look, returned her attention to Michael, who was walking toward them.

It was not the Michael they knew—not at all.

"Let Shane go," Claire said. Her voice trembled, but it came out clearly enough. Bishop raised one finger, and Michael lunged forward, grabbed Eve by the throat, and pulled her close to him with his fangs bared. "No!"

"Don't give me orders, child," Bishop said. "You should be dead by now. I'm almost impressed. Now, rephrase your request. Something with a *please*."

Claire licked her lips and tasted sweat. "Please," she said. "Please let Shane go. Please don't hurt Eve."

Bishop considered, then nodded. "I don't need the girl," he said. He nodded to Michael, who let Eve go. She backed away, staring at him in disbelief, hands over her throat. "I have what I want. Don't I, Myrnin?"

Myrnin pulled up Shane's shirt. There, stuffed in his waistband at the back, was the book.

No.

Myrnin pulled it free, let Shane up, and walked to Bishop. *I'm about to break that trust most grievously,* he'd said to Claire. She hadn't believed him until this moment.

"Wait," Myrnin said, as Bishop reached for it. "The bargain was for Theo Goldman's family."

"Who? Oh, yes." He smiled. "They'll be quite safe."

"And unharmed," Myrnin said.

"Are you putting conditions on our little agreement?" Bishop asked. "Very well. They go free, and unharmed. Let all witness that Theo Goldman and his family will take no harm from me or mine, but they are not welcome in Morganville. I will not have them here."

Myrnin inclined his head. He lowered himself to one knee in front of the throne, and lifted the book in both hands over his head, offering it up.

Bishop's fingers closed on it, and he let out a long, rattling sigh. "At last," he said. "At last."

Myrnin rested his forearms across his knee, but didn't try to rise. "You said you also required Amelie. May I suggest an alternative?"

"You may, as I'm in good humor with you at the moment."

"The girl wears Amelie's sigil," he said. "She's the only one in town who wears it in the old way, by the old laws. That makes her no less than a part of Amelie herself, blood for blood."

Claire stopped breathing. It seemed as if every head turned toward her, every pair of eyes stared. Shane started to come toward her.

He never made it.

Michael darted forward and slammed his friend down on the stones, snarling. He held him there. Myrnin rose and came to Claire, offering her his hand in an antique, courtly gesture.

His eyes were still dark, still mostly sane.

And that was why she knew she could never really forgive him, ever again. This wasn't the disease talking.

It was just Myrnin.

"Come," he said. "Trust me, Claire. Please."

She avoided him and walked on her own to the foot of Bishop's throne, staring up at him.

"Well?" she asked. "What are you waiting for? Kill me."

"Kill you?" he repeated, mystified. "Why on earth would I do such a foolish thing? Myrnin is quite right. There's no point in killing you, none at all. I need you to run the machines of Morganville for me. I have already declared that Richard Morrell will oversee the humans. I will allow Myrnin the honor of ruling those vampires who choose to stay in my kingdom and swear fealty to me."

Myrnin bowed slightly, from the waist. "I am, of course, deeply grateful for your favor, my lord."

"One thing," Bishop said. "I'll need Oliver's head."

This time, Myrnin smiled. "I know just where to find it, my lord."

"Then be about your work."

Myrnin gave a bow, flourished with elaborate arm movements, and to Claire's eyes, it was almost mocking.

Almost.

While he was bowing, she heard him whisper, "Do as he says."

And then he was gone, walking away, as if none of it meant anything to him at all.

Eve tried to kick him, but he laughed and avoided her, wagging a finger at her as he did.

They watched him skip away down the hall.

Shane said, "Let me up, Michael, or fang me. One or the other."

"No," Bishop said, and snapped his fingers to call Michael off when he snarled. "I may need the boy to control his father. Put them in a cage together."

Shane was hauled up and marched off, but not before he said, "Claire, I'll find you."

"I'll find you first," she said.

Bishop broke the lock on the book that Myrnin had given him, and opened it to flip the pages, as if looking for something in particular. He ripped out a page and pressed the two ends together to make a circle of paper, thickly filled with minute, dark writing. "Put this on your arm," he said, and tossed it to Claire. She hesitated, and he sighed. "Put it on, or one of the many hostages to your good behavior will suffer. Do you understand? Mother, father, friends, acquaintances, complete strangers. You are not Myrnin. Don't try to play his games."

Claire slipped the paper sleeve over her arm, feeling stupid, but she didn't see any alternatives.

The paper felt odd against her skin, and then it sucked in and clung to her like something alive. She panicked and tried to pull it off, but she couldn't get a grip on it, so closely was it sticking to her arm.

After a moment of searing pain, it loosened and slipped off on its own.

As it fluttered to the floor, she saw that the page was blank. Nothing on it at all. The dense writing that had been on it stayed on her arm—no, *under the skin*, as if she'd been tattooed with it.

And the symbols were *moving*. It made her ill to watch. She had no idea what it meant, but she could feel something happening inside, something . . .

Her fear faded away. So did her anger.

"Swear loyalty to me," Bishop said. "In the old tongue."

Claire got on her knees and swore, in a language she didn't even know, and not for one moment did she doubt it was the right thing to do. In fact, it made her happy. Glowingly happy. Some part of her was screaming, *He's making you do this!* but the other parts really didn't care.

"What shall I do with your friends?" he asked her.

"I don't care." She didn't even care that Eve was crying.

"You will, someday. I'll grant you this much: your friend Eve may go. I have absolutely no use for her. I will show I am merciful."

Claire shrugged. "I don't care."

She did, she knew she did, but she couldn't make herself feel it.

"Go," Bishop said, and smiled chillingly at Eve. "Run away. Find Amelie and tell her this: I have taken her town away, and all that she values. Tell her I have the book. If she wants it back, she'll have to come for it herself."

Eve angrily wiped tears from her face, glaring at him. "She'll come. And I'll come with her. You don't own jack. This is *our* town, and we're going to kick you out if it's the last thing we do."

The assembled vampires all laughed. Bishop said, "Then come. We'll be waiting. Won't we, Claire?"

"Yes," she said, and went to sit down on the steps by his feet. "We'll be waiting."

He snapped his fingers. "Then let's begin our celebration, and in the morning, we'll talk about how Morganville will be run from now on. According to *my* wishes."

Author's Note

I had an especially great track list to help me through this book, and I thought you might enjoy listening along. Don't forget: musicians need love and money, too, so buy the CDs or pay for tracks.

"On and On" .... Nikka Costa
"Everybody Got Their Something" .... Nikka Costa
"Above the Clouds" .... Delirium & Shelly Harland
"2 Wicky" .... Hooverphonic
"Is You Is or Is You Ain't My Baby" ....
.... Rae & Christian Remix, Dinah Washington
"Enjoy the Ride" .... Morcheeba
"Hate to Say I Told You So" .... The Hives
"See You Again" .... Miley Cyrus
"Fever" .... Sarah Vaughn, Verve Remix
"Peter Gunn" .... Max Sedgley Remix, Sarah Vaughn
"Blade"..
.... Spacekid & Maxim Yul Remix, Warp Brothers
"Aly, Walk with Me" .... The Raveonettes
"Hunting for Witches" .... Bloc Party
"Cuts You Up".. Peter Murphy
"Hurt"... Christina Aguilera
"Run" .... Gnarls Barkley
"Electrofog".. Le Charme
"Where I Stood" .... Missy Higgins
"Children (Dream Version)" .... Robert Miles
"Grace".. Miss Kittin
"Walkie Talkie Man" .... Steriogram
"Living Dead Girl" .... Rob Zombie

"Saw Something"... Dave Gahan
"Boy with a Coin" .... Iron & Wine
"Fever".. Stereo MC's
"Kaybettik".. Candan Ercetin
"Playing with Uranium"........................... Duran Duran
"Staring at the Sun" .... TV on the Radio
"The Moment I Said It"......................... Imogen Heap
"This Is the Sound" .... The Last Goodnight
"Juicy".. Better Than Ezra
"One Week of Danger".............................. The Virgins
"Wolf Like Me" .... TV on the Radio
"Poison Kiss" .... The Last Goodnight
"Beat It" .... Fall Out Boy
"Old Enough" .... The Raconteurs
"I Will Possess Your Heart"..... Death Cab for Cutie

Read on for an exciting excerpt
from Rachel Caine's
Morganville Vampires novel

CARPE CORPUS

Available from Signet

"Claire," Bishop said. He didn't sound pleased. "Did I summon you?"

Claire's heart jumped as if he'd used a cattle prod. She willed herself not to flinch. "No sir," she said, and kept her voice low and respectful. "I came to ask a favor."

Bishop—who was wearing a plain black suit today, with a white shirt that had seen brighter days—picked a piece of lint from his sleeve. "The answer is no. Anything else?"

Claire wet her lips and tried again. "I wanted to see Shane, sir. Just for a few—"

"I said *no*," Bishop snapped, and she felt his anger crackle through the room. Michael and a strange vamp both looked up at her, eyes luminously threatening. Myrnin—dressed in some ratty assortment of Goodwill reject pants and a frock coat from a costume shop, plus several layers of Mardi Gras beads—just seemed bored. He yawned, showing lethally sharp fangs.

"Oh, don't be so harsh," Myrnin said, and rolled his eyes. "Let the girl have her moment. It'll hurt her more in the end. Parting is such sweet sorrow, according to the bards. I wouldn't know, myself."

Claire forgot to breathe. She hadn't expected Myrnin, of all of them, to take up her cause—not that he had, really. But he'd given Bishop pause, and she kept very still, letting him think it over.

Bishop finally crossed his arms, and Michael and the other vampire relaxed in their seats, like puppets with their strings loosened. "This will need supervision," he said. "Myrnin, it's your pet. Clean up after it."

Myrnin gave Bishop a lazy salute. "As my master commands." He stood with that unconscious vampire grace that made Claire feel heavy, stupid, and slow, and his bright black eyes locked with hers for a long moment. If he was trying to tell her something, she had no idea what it was. "Out, girl. Master Bishop has work to do here."

Before she could even start to back away, Myrnin crossed the room and closed ice-cold fingers around her arm. She pulled in a breath for a gasp, but he didn't give her time to react; she was yanked along with him down the hall, moving at a stumbling run.

Myrnin stopped only when there were two closed doors, and about a mile of hallway, between them and Mr. Bishop.

"Let go!" Claire spat, and tried to yank free. Myrnin looked down at her arm, where his pale fingers were still wrapped around it, and raised his eyebrows as if he couldn't quite figure out what his hand was doing. Claire yanked again. "Myrnin, *let go!*"

He did, and stepped back. She thought he looked disappointed for a flicker of a second, and then his loony smile returned. "Will you be a good little girl?"

She glared at him.

"Ah. Probably not. All right, then, on your head be it, little Claire. Come. I'll take you to the boy."

He turned, and the skirts of his frock coat flared. He was wearing flip-flops again, and his feet were dirty, though he didn't smell bad in general. Layers of cheap metallic beads clicked and rattled as he walked, and the slap of his flip-flops made him just about the noisiest vampire Claire had ever heard.

"Are you taking your medicine?" she asked. Myrnin sent her a glance over his shoulder, and once again she didn't know what his look meant at all. "Is that a no?"

"I thought you hated me," he said. "If you do, you really shouldn't care, should you?"

He had a point. Claire shut up and hurried along as he walked down a long, curved hallway to a big wooden door. There was a vampire guard at the door, a tall man who'd probably been Asian in his regular life but was now the color of old ivory. He wore his hair long, braided in the back, and he wasn't much taller than Claire.

Myrnin exchanged some Chinese words with the other vampire—who, like Michael, sported Bishop's fang marks on his neck—and the vampire unlocked the door and swung it open.

This was as far as Claire had ever been able to get. She felt a wave of heat race through her, and then she shivered. Now that she was here, actually walking through the door, she felt faintly sick with anticipation. *If they've hurt him . . .*

Another locked door, another guard, and then they were inside a plain stone hallway with barred cells on the left side. No windows. No light except for blazing fluorescent fixtures far overhead. The first cell was empty. The second held two humans, but neither was Shane. Claire tried not to look too closely. She was afraid she might know them.

The third cell had two small cots, one on each side of the tiny room, and a toilet and sink in the middle. Nothing else. There was an old man with straggly gray hair asleep on one of the beds, and it took Claire a few seconds to realize that he was Frank Collins, Shane's dad. She was used to seeing him awake, and it surprised her to see him so . . . fragile.

Shane was sitting on the other bed.

He looked up from the book he was reading and jerked his head to get the hair out of his eyes. The guarded, closed-in look on his face reminded Claire of his father, but it shattered when Shane saw her.

He dropped the book, surged to his feet, and was at the bars in a little under two seconds. His hands curled around the iron, and his eyes glittered wildly until he squeezed them shut.

When he opened them again, he'd gotten himself under control. Mostly.

"Hey," Shane said, as if they'd just run into each other in the hallway. As if months hadn't gone by since they'd parted. "So . . . happy birthday."

Claire felt tears burn in her eyes, but she blinked them back and put on a brave smile. "Thanks," she said. "What'd you get me?"

"Um . . ." Shane looked around and shrugged. "Must have left it at the club. You know how it is, out all night partying, you get baked and forget where you parked the car."

She stepped forward and wrapped her hands around his. She felt tremors race through him, and Shane sighed, closed his eyes, and rested his forehead against the bars. "Yeah," he whispered. "Shutting up now."

She pressed her forehead against his, and then her lips, and it was hot and sweet and desperate, and the feelings that exploded inside her made her shake in reaction. Shane let go of the bars and reached through to run his fingers through her soft, short hair, and the kiss deepened, darkened, took on a touch of yearning that made Claire's heart pound.

When their lips finally parted, they didn't pull away from each other. Claire threaded her arms through the bars and around his neck, and his hands moved down to her waist.

"I'm really sick of kissing you through bars," Shane said. "I'm all for restraint, but self-restraint is so much more fun."

Claire had almost forgotten that Myrnin was still there, so his soft chuckle made her flinch. "There speaks a young man with little experience," he said, yawned, and draped himself over a bench on the far side of the wall. He propped his chin up on the heel of one hand. "Enjoy that ignorance while you can."

Shane held on to her, and his dark eyes stared into hers. *Ignore him,* they seemed to say. *Stay with me.*

She did.

"I'm trying to get you out," she whispered. "I can't stand knowing you're in here with *him.*"

Shane's eyebrows rose just a little. "Dad? Yeah, well . . . He's okay."

And that, Claire realized, was what she was afraid of—that Shane had forgiven his father for all his crazy stunts. That the Collins boys were together again, united in their hatred of Morganville.

Shane read it in her face. "Not like that," he said, and shook his head. "We had to either get along in here, or kill each other. We decided to get along, that's all."

"Yeah," said a deep, scratchy voice from the other bunk. "It's been one big, sloppy bucket of joy, getting to know my son."

"Shut up, Frank," Shane said.

"That any way to talk to your old man?"

"This is the two of you getting along?" Claire whispered.

"You see any bruises?"

"Good point." This was not how she'd imagined this moment to go, except for the kissing. Then again, the kissing was better than her imagination. "Shane—"

"Shh." He kissed her forehead. "How's Michael?" She didn't want to talk about Michael, so she just shook her head. Shane swallowed hard. "He's not . . . dead?"

"Define *dead* around here," Claire muttered. "No, he's okay. He's just, you know."

"Bishop's, yeah." He knew. "What about Eve?"

"She's working. I haven't seen her in a couple of weeks." Eve, like everyone else in Morganville, treated Claire like the enemy these days, and Claire honestly couldn't blame her. Not that she was about to load Shane up with that knowledge, though. "She's busted up about Michael."

"No doubt," Shane said softly. He seemed to hesitate for a heartbeat. "Have you heard anything about us? What Bishop has planned?"

Claire shook her head. Even if she knew—and she didn't, in detail—she wouldn't have told him. "Let's not talk about it. Shane, I've missed you so much."

He kissed her again, and the world melted into a wonderful spinning blend of heat and bells, and it was only when she finally, regretfully pulled back that she heard Myrnin's mocking, steady clapping.

"Love conquers all," he said. "How quaint."

Claire turned on him, feeling fury erupt like a volcano in her guts. "*Shut up*, Myrnin!"

He didn't even bother to glance at her, just leaned back against the wall and smiled. "You want to know what he's got planned for you, Shane? Do you really?"

"Myrnin, don't!"

Shane reached through the bars and grabbed Claire's shoulders, turning her back to face him. "It doesn't matter," he said. "*This* matters, right now. Claire, we're going to get out of this. We're going to live through it. Both of us."

"Both of us," she repeated. "We're going to live."

Myrnin's cold hand closed around her wrist, and he dragged her away from the bars. The last thing she let go of was Shane's hand.

"Hey!" Shane yelled as Claire fought, lost, and was pulled through the door. "Claire! We're going to live!"

Myrnin slammed the door, rolled his eyes, and said, "Theatrical, isn't he? Come on, girl. We have work to do."

"I'm not going anywhere with you!"

Myrnin didn't give her a choice; he half dragged, half marched her away from the first vampire guard, then the second, and then pulled her into an empty, quiet room off the long hallway. He shut the door with a wicked boom and whirled to face her.

Claire grabbed the first thing she saw—it happened to be a heavy candlestick—and swung it at his head. He ducked, rushed in, and effortlessly took it away from her. "Girl. *Claire!*" He shook her into stillness. His eyes were wide and very dark. Not at all crazy. "If you want the boy to live, you'll stop fighting me. It's not productive."

"Why should I help Bishop?" she said, and twisted to throw him off. It was like trying to throw off a granite statue.

"Who says you would be?" Myrnin asked, very reasonably. "Who says I work for him?"

She wouldn't have believed him, not for a second, except that a section of the wall opened, there was a flash of white-hot light, and a woman stepped through, followed by a long line of people.

Amelie, though she didn't look anything like the perfect white queen whom Claire had always seen. Amelie had on black pants, a black zip-up hoodie, and *running shoes.*

And behind her was the frickin' vampire army. Led by Oliver, all in black, looking scarier than Claire could remember having ever seen him—he usually at least tried to look nondangerous, but today he obviously didn't care.

He crossed his arms and looked at Myrnin and Claire as if they were something slimy on his coffee-shop floor.

"Myrnin," Amelie said, and nodded graciously. He nodded back, as though they were passing on the street. As if it were a normal day. "What's the girl done?"

Myrnin looked at Claire, grinned, and let go of her.

"Oh, she's been quite difficult," he said, "which helped convince Bishop that I am, indeed, his creature. But I think it's best if you leave us behind now. We have more work to do here, work that can't be done in hiding."

Claire opened her mouth, and then closed it without having thought of a single coherent question to ask. Oliver dismissed both of them with a shake of his head and signaled for his vampire shock troops to fan out around the room on either side of the door to the hallway.

"Can you protect her, Myrnin?" Amelie asked, and her pale gray eyes bored into his, colder than marble. "I will hold you to your answer."

"With my last breath," he promised, and clasped his hand dramatically to his ragged frock coat. "Oh, wait. That doesn't mean much, does it? Sorry. I mean, yes. Of course. With what's left of my life."

"I'm not joking, jester."

"And I'm not laughing, my lady."

Claire's head was spinning. She looked from Myrnin to Amelie to Oliver, and finally thought of a decent question to ask. "Why are you here?"

"They're here to rescue your boyfriend," Myrnin said. "Happy birthday, my dear."

ABOUT THE AUTHOR

In addition to the Morganville Vampires series, **Rachel Caine** is the author of the popular Weather Warden series, which includes *Ill Wind*, *Heat Stroke*, *Chill Factor*, *Windfall*, *Firestorm*, *Thin Air*, and *Gale Force*. Rachel and her husband, fantasy artist R. Cat Conrad, live in Texas with their iguanas, Popeye and Darwin; a *mali uromastyx* named (appropriately) O'Malley; and a leopard tortoise named Shelley (for the poet, of course).

Please visit her Web site at www.rachelcaine.com and her MySpace, www.myspace.com/rachelcaine.

Welcome to Morganville, Texas.
Just don't stay out after dark.

The *New York Times* bestselling Morganville Vampires series

by Rachel Caine

College freshman Claire Danvers has her share of challenges—like being a genius in a school that favors beauty over brains, battling homicidal girls in her dorm, and finding out that her college town is overrun with the living dead.

Glass Houses
The Dead Girls' Dance
Midnight Alley
Feast of Fools
Lord of Misrule
Carpe Corpus
Fade Out
Kiss of Death
Ghost Town

rachelcaine.com